GENDERED WORLDS

Gendered Worlds

JUDY ROOT AULETTE

UNIVERSITY OF NORTH CAROLINA–CHARLOTTE

JUDITH WITTNER

LOYOLA UNIVERSITY CHICAGO

KRISTIN BLAKELY

LOYOLA UNIVERSITY CHICAGO

New York   Oxford

OXFORD UNIVERSITY PRESS

2009

Oxford University Press, Inc., publishes works that further Oxford University's
objective of excellence in research, scholarship, and education.

Oxford   New York
Auckland   Cape Town   Dar es Salaam   Hong Kong   Karachi
Kuala Lumpur   Madrid   Melbourne   Mexico City   Nairobi
New Delhi   Shanghai   Taipei   Toronto

With offices in
Argentina   Austria   Brazil   Chile   Czech Republic   France   Greece
Guatemala   Hungary   Italy   Japan   Poland   Portugal   Singapore
South Korea   Switzerland   Thailand   Turkey   Ukraine   Vietnam

Published by Oxford University Press, Inc.
198 Madison Avenue, New York, New York 10016
http://www.oup.com

Oxford is a registered trademark of Oxford University Press

Library of Congress Cataloging-in-Publication Data
Aulette Root, Judy.
  Gendered worlds / Judy Root Aulette, Judith Wittner, Kristin Blakely.
    p.   cm.
  Includes bibliographical references and index.
  ISBN 978-0-19-537111-6 (alk. paper)
  1. Sex role.   2. Women–Social conditions.   3. Feminist theory.
  I. Wittner, Judith G.   II. Blakely, Kristin.   III. Title.
  HQ1075.A95 2009
  305.42—dc22   2008032409

Printing number: 9 8 7 6 5 4 3 2 1

Printed in the United States of America
on acid-free paper.

CONTENTS

PREFACE

In four decades, feminism has become a global movement, and its goals of creating a more egalitarian and democratic future continue to drive the movement forward. Scholarship about gender, perhaps more than in most other disciplines, has grown from this activism and in turn has contributed to it. Forty years of studying gender has produced an array of empirical findings, bold concepts, and transformative theories that feminist scholars could not have imagined when we first began our inquiries. Because of its successes, it is becoming increasingly difficult to grasp the field of feminist gender studies in its entirety, and it is particularly hard for students to comprehend its breadth and complexity.

Sound bites about feminism and women, platitudes about gendered work and violence, and ideologies about sex and gender make up the sum and substance of most popular understandings. Widely circulated in the popular media and among our students are such notions as "feminism is racist," "militant feminists ('feminazis') want to subjugate men," and "the differences between men and women are genetically programmed," alongside assertions that "I'm not a feminist, but," and "this generation has pretty much eliminated gender inequality." To make a world in which gender and other inequalities do not prevail, it is important to introduce students to the reorganized and reconstituted knowledge that has emerged from feminist work.

This book is our attempt to bring together the multiple strands of gender and associated research reaching from local and everyday manifestations of masculinity and femininity to the gendered global forces that lie beneath today's political and social crises. To do so, each chapter builds on four principles.

First, we weave together theory and empirical data, rather than segregate theories of gender into a separate chapter. The book gathers together much of the empirical scholarship—mainly sociological, but also interdisciplinary—that has accumulated around a long list of substantive areas. Students will learn here about the mass of research on violence, families, media, sports, politics, sexuality, religion, education, health, and bodies that ground knowledge about gender relations and structures of gender. Theories that have grown up alongside this research and help to interpret its meanings are woven into each chapter so that students are able to understand how theory emerges from and helps to explain the research presented here, and how theories relate to students' own everyday experiences and observations of their worlds.

Second, we connect local events with large-scale organizations, institutions, and global phenomena to show how power operates at the narrowest and the broadest levels of society and how the two levels are connected. We offer both social constructionist and social structural approaches to explain the production of inequality in face-to-face interaction within constraining institutional structures. We ask how the gendered features of our everyday lives are given life and shape by the larger institutional and organizational structures that contain them and how, in turn, we act back on those forces, shaping new forms of gendered relationships, remaking gendered worlds, and perhaps even eliminating gendered differences.

Third, this is a book about gender and gendered relationships *between* men and women. We recognize that men's lives are influenced by gender relations as much as women's lives, but many people still see gender as synonymous with women. We have taken special care to make sure that readers are provided with evidence and ways to understand how gender touches everyone's life. We also recognize that the categories of "men" and "women" are binary constructs that conceal and constrain the existence of other sexualities and other genders. Constructionists argue that gendered identities are accomplishments, not fixed states of being. Moreover, if men are privileged as men, they might nevertheless be subordinated along racial ethnic, national, sexual, and class lines. In each chapter we explore these advantages and disadvantages, as well as women's and men's complicity with and resistance to them.

Finally, this book takes seriously the understanding that there are important differences among women and among men. The "intersectionality" that differentially locates individuals and groups in what black feminist theorist Patricia Hill Collins (2000) called a "matrix of domination" is a core feature of each chapter. There is no way to understand gender inequality as a thing in itself, as a phenomenon that can be separated from the multiple cross-cutting inequalities of class, race, sexuality, and nation. Third-world feminists have decisively shown how multiple structures of inequality intersect and how intersecting oppressions and privileges shape identities. The theory of intersectionality and the matrix of domination are concepts that help to show how race ethnicity, class, sexuality, and national identity shape gender identities and experiences and how gender differences contribute to differences in the impact of racial, ethnic, sexual, class, and national experience.

This book originated in a project first conceived by Judy Aulette and later joined by Judith Wittner and Kristin Blakely in the fall of 2003. Aulette and Wittner were among the first generation of scholar/teachers who helped to introduce sociology of gender courses in their respective universities. Aulette was an activist in the Women's Liberation Movement in Detroit in the 1960s and took her first women's studies course and one of the earliest university courses on gender, "Sex Roles," in 1969 at Wayne State University. She continued her work as a scholar activist finishing a PhD at Michigan State University in sociology with a specialization in gender inequality while working with peace, environmental, labor, and poverty political organizations, all with a focus on gender and especially women's experience. Her work has persisted on these two fronts, scholarship and activism, teaching courses in the United States, Poland, Scotland, and South Africa; conducting research on women; and working with feminist political activists, most recently in the peace movement in the United States and around HIV and poverty issues in the United States and South Africa.

Wittner came to sociology as an activist in the women's liberation movement of the late 1960s and 1970s and as an opponent of the war in Vietnam. The movements sparked her interest in learning everything she could about women's place in history and in contemporary society, a project that in those days seemed possible to accomplish. In study groups with other young women, she and they began to chart the enterprise first known as women's studies. In 1971, in Chicago, she taught two of the earliest courses on women to be offered at a university. Around the country were similar stories of local origins that would ultimately lead to one of the most transformative intellectual movements of our time. Like many activists of her generation Wittner returned to school to earn a PhD from Northwestern University in sociology and now teaches sociology and women's studies at Loyola University in Chicago. She was among the group of faculty who founded the Loyola Women's Studies Program in 1979 (now Women's and Gender Studies) and directed the program from 1987 to 1991. Like Judy Aulette, she has actively supported peace, justice, antiracist, labor, and women's movements throughout her life.

Blakely brings to this book a younger generation's experience and perspective. She was a doctoral student in sociology at Loyola University Chicago when she was invited by Wittner to join the project. After combined degrees in sociology and women's studies at York University in Toronto, Canada, Blakely moved to Chicago to complete a PhD. Blakely has taught courses in the sociology of gender, women, and sexualities at Loyola University Chicago and Wilfrid Laurier University in Waterloo, Ontario. She is active in the Canadian women's movement, serving as a National Board Member for YWCA Canada and Vice-President of the Board for YWCA Toronto.

WORK CITED

Collins, Patricia Hill. 2000. *Black Feminist Thought: Knowledge, Consciousness, and the Politics of Empowerment (Revised 10th Anniv 2nd Edition)* New York: Routledge.

ACKNOWLEDGMENTS

Writing a book such as this one requires the authors to learn new areas of research about which they may initially have known little. Judy Aulette thanks Anna Aulette-Root, Elizabeth Aulette-Root, and Albert Aulette for their careful reading and essential feedback on many drafts of chapters, especially regarding issues related to gender and religion and gender and the media. In addition, she thanks them for living with this project for so many years. She also thanks Claude Teweles and Phong Ho for inviting her to consider the project for Roxbury Press and for patiently waiting for the project to be completed. Most important, she thanks her co-authors for their knowledge, creativity, and tenacity.

For teaching her more than she once knew about gender and health, Judith Wittner thanks Anne Figert and Diane Horwitz. For patient tutoring in biology, she thanks Kathryn Scarbrough. For encouraging her to keep going, she thanks the members of her writing group, Susan Stall and Martha Thompson. Thanks to Judy Aulette for hand-holding and great patience and to Kristin Blakely for the intelligence and energy she brought to our project. For bringing fun and joy into her life during the long years of writing, she thanks her grandchildren, Nathaniel and Alex Pinheiro and Mollie, Mario, and Lily Pepper.

Kristin Blakely thanks Judy Aulette and Judith Wittner for their incredible mentorship and the opportunity to be a part of this project. She has learned infinitely more than she could have imagined. She is most grateful for the feedback from Judy, Judith, and the reviewers. She extends a special thank you to David, her partner in life, for his love and encouragement, and to her parents and sisters for their support.

We all thank Sherith Pankratz from Oxford University Press for choosing to continue the project from Roxbury and Whitney Laemmli and Brian Black for assistance in the final stages. We also are grateful to the several anonymous reviewers who provided vital and supportive suggestions for making this text something of which we are all very proud.

1

INTRODUCTION

A FEW MORE INCONVENIENT TRUTHS

Climate change and the environmental disasters that accompany it would seem to be one issue that touches all humans in the same way. But in 2004, when a tsunami in Indonesia killed more than a quarter of a million people, 75 percent of them were women (Oxfam 2005). This scenario is not unusual. Women typically far outnumber men in mortalities resulting from environmental disasters. This effect is strongest in countries with very low social and economic rights for women (Neumayer and Pluemper 2007).

Physical differences between men and women are unlikely to explain the higher mortality rate for women. For example, women are often at an advantage in famines because they can cope better with food shortages due to their lower nutritional requirements and higher levels of body fat (Neumayer and Pluemper 2007). In the case of the tsunami, some people may have survived because of greater physical strength that allowed them to hang on to trees or to stay afloat. However, social factors were far most significant, especially the social factor of gender (Oxfam 2005; Doocy et al. 2007). Reports on the tsunami identify a number of social factors that contributed to the fact that women were so much more likely to have died:

- Swimming and tree climbing are taught mainly to boys. These skills, of course, were essential to survival when the waves of the tsunami hit.
- Women stayed indoors whereas men were more likely to be outside working, shopping, and socializing; therefore, information warning residents to leave the area reached the women later than it did men who were out in public.
- Responsibilities for others, especially children, prevented women from moving fast enough to escape the floods. In Aceh, for example, many women were found dead with babies still clutched in their arms. Some personal accounts from survivors tell of mothers pushing their children to safety on buildings or trees that withstood the tsunami, but being swept away themselves.

- The clothing women wore, long dresses, inhibited their ability to run or swim to save themselves from the floods. In addition, some who were in their homes but casually dressed when the first wave struck ran to put on "acceptable" outdoor clothes before seeking safety, and as a result were drowned or barely escaped.
- A division of labor that placed men in fishing boats at sea (a tsunami wave is not as dangerous at sea as when it crashes to shore), farming in agricultural areas away from the beach, or serving as soldiers in conflict areas away from those affected by the tsunami, making them less likely to be affected.

Are you surprised that gender played such an important role in determining whether people lived or died in this environmental disaster? Do the differences in gender seem relatively insignificant if they are taken out of context? For example, would you have thought that gender differences in clothing or play activities like swimming and tree climbing could be so important?

This scenario emphasizes gender differences, but you are probably familiar with images of Hurricane Katrina flooding and the importance of race ethnicity, and social class in that disaster. How does gender add to or interact with the variation in our experience by race ethnicity and social class?

The researchers argue that biology had little to do with differences in survival. What do you think of this argument in general? Is gender mostly a function of biology? Or are social factors most important?

What exactly is gender? Is gender only a problem for women? Or does gender cause problems for men, too? Some researchers have noted that in some environmental disasters such as Hurricane Mitch in Central America, men were more likely to die because of the expectation that they take more risks trying to save others from the mudslides and floods.

This scenario describes a situation in Asia. How does gender vary around the globe? How are gender expectations being challenged locally and globally? How is gender changing?

These are the kinds of questions we will be asking in this text. Our goal is to explore the ways that gender appears in every corner of our lives and of our globe. Before the tsunami, very few scholars had ever considered the connections among gender, environmental disasters, and mortality (Enarson and Morrow 1998). Every day, researchers are "discovering" new places where gender plays a role. We will be trying to keep up with them as we travel around the world looking for gender and seeking ways to understand how it works, what its effects are, and the ways we might address the problems it causes.

SOME GROUND RULES FOR STUDYING GENDER

Trying to determine a place to begin answering questions about gender is difficult. How to consider the subject, what to focus on, and what to ignore are all challenging issues. In this book we approach the subjects with a few important assumptions: Social life is socially based and politically structured, gender is part of a network of social inequalities, and scholarship is political.

Social Life Is Socially Based and Politically Structured

Like many features of social life, gender is a factor that has been seen and felt by all of us and in some ways that experience makes us all "experts" about it. Our familiarity with the topic, however, may make us prone to look only at the surface or to accept the conventional wisdom of the time and therefore, to have distorted or superficial views of issues. One especially important aspect of conventional wisdom about gender, as well as two other key issues in this text, race ethnicity and sexuality, is the belief that these are bedrock biological certainties. Conventional wisdom tells us that every individual can be placed into one of a few categories by gender, race, and sexuality and that these categories are inborn, natural, unchanging givens. This book challenges this idea by emphasizing the social character of gender, race ethnicity, and sexuality.

In addition, we propose that race, gender, and sexuality are among the fictions that support relations of power. "There is no race—just colors—before it is socially constructed," writes Zillah Eisenstein (2004, 45). We add, there is no gender or sexuality—just bodies—before they are socially constructed. This book is dedicated to showing you how and with what consequences gender, race ethnicity, and sexuality are social constructions, not biological truths. In addition, we explain how these constructions are part of the "ruling relations" of society helping to maintain the status quo in power systems.

Gender Is Part of a Network of Social Inequalities

This book explores inequalities of gender, their consequences, and the movements challenging them. However, gender analysis alone will not help us to understand the ways that this particular inequality shapes our lives and the lives of people around the globe. We live in a world built atop gendered difference, but also built by race and class-based systems of power: patriarchal privileges, the racist repercussions of colonization and slavery, and the dynamic of global capitalism that feeds the growing gap between the rich and powerful few and the excluded many.

Sometimes scholars use the word *lenses* to talk about the complexity of social life. If you were to put on a pair of glasses that allowed you to see only objects that were green and another pair blocked everything but blue or red, and so on, each time you took off one pair of glasses and put on another you would only see a piece of the total view and never be able to see the whole picture. Similarly, if we investigate this world using only one lens, whether the lens of gender or of race ethnicity or of class, nation, or sexuality, we have a distorted view of history as well as the present. In this book we put on our "rainbow glasses" and try to see the whole picture with all of its variations and intersections.

Scholarship Is Political

Sociologists have long debated whether the study of humans can be based on a model that demands distanced objectivity from the scholar observer and promotes the idea that only the experts can tell us all we need to know about social life. More than three decades of feminist activism and research has developed the idea that researchers cannot and should not claim to be neutral outside observers and that knowledge is best produced collaboratively among scholars and others, including the people being observed. In particular, our knowledge should be grounded in the experience of people at the bottom of the power systems of gender, race ethnicity, sexuality, and class. To build knowledge that begins from the perceptions and lives of the marginalized and least powerful members of society produces knowledge *for*—in contrast with knowledge *about*—people (Smith 1999). It is this knowledge *for* rather than *about* people that brings us closest to seeing the broadest and most valid view of social life.

This book is written in the tradition of those scholars who take this political view of scholarship. We seek to replace the "view from above" with the "view from below" by exploring the lives of people who have often been invisible, ignored, censored, or oppressed (Mies 1986). The topics we examine and the perspective we take attempt to see the world from the point of view of those who are marginalized by gender, as well as race ethnicity, sexuality, social class, and nation. In addition, our exploration seeks not only to describe and explain the social world, but to discover ways to transform it by making groups and individuals marginalized by race ethnicity, gender, sexuality, and citizenship central to producing knowledge of the social world.

OVERARCHING THEORY OF INTERSECTIONALITY

In our explorations in this text, we look at a wide range of gendered practices and institutions, assembling knowledge that shows the distribution of inequality, its consequences, and the ways people organize to challenge it. Throughout the book we present the most current research, bringing in data from qualitative and quantitative studies. In addition to describing the issues and providing empirical data, we also offer an analysis to explain the issues. In each chapter we look at the cross-cutting inequalities that complicate gendered differences, a method that is called *intersectional analysis*.

Try this on yourself: How would you describe yourself? Probably your first response would be to identify yourself as belonging to one of two genders. If you are a person of color or have recently immigrated to this country you are likely to name your membership in a racial or ethnic group. If you are white, perhaps you neglect to note your race because you are not accustomed to thinking of yourself as having a race. Of course whiteness is racial, but it is the default category, the unmarked dominant status in North America, and often invisible as such. Did you call yourself middle class or working class, rich or poor? Does your sexuality have anything to do with who you are? Do you think of yourself as gay or lesbian, bisexual, transgendered, or heterosexual? Do you identify yourself as a person of Greek descent or from Mexico or the horn of Africa? Of course you have many other identities: You are a student, a lover, a part-time worker, a daughter or son, a sister or brother, a musician, a dreamer, a political activist. Maybe others have labeled you with identities that are not so honorable (at least to the labelers): stoner, gossip, cheater. These and other multiple identities locate you in a web of cross-cutting and interacting communities and relationships. Today in most places in the world, though, the categories of gender, race ethnicity, class, sexuality, and nation are the central categories of intersectional analysis (Collins 2000).

Intersectional analyses focus on the attributes assigned to members of oppressed communities of gender, race, class, sexuality, and nation. The gender order is hierarchical: Overall, men dominate women in terms of wealth, power, and social position, but not all men dominate all women. The racial ethnic order is a hierarchy in which whites have power over people of color. It cross-cuts gender so that, for example, some white women are richer, more powerful, and more privileged than many men who are not white. The sexual order makes heterosexuality supreme and puts gay men, lesbians, transgendered people, and members of other sexual communities at a decided disadvantage. Through its wealth and power, rich nations of the Global North (nations and regions of the world that are mostly at the top of the globe such as the United States and Europe) still dominate those in the Global South (poorer, less powerful nations and regions such as Africa, Latin America, and India, which are in the south).

The lesson of intersectional analysis is this: Gender arrangements create relationships of inequality between women and men but gender disadvantages both women and men. Most important, all women do not suffer oppression in the same way, nor do all men always benefit from patriarchal privilege simply because they are men. Being a white, well-born man opens doors, offers privileges, and produces rewards. Being a poor black woman increases the difficulties and barriers a woman faces in her life. However, no person is completely oppressed or completely privileged, because oppressions and privileges shift with the social context. A working-class man may be privileged in the context of his family, where he dominates his wife and children by virtue of his paycheck and patriarchal privilege. In the workplace, however, he in turn may be dominated by his boss and relatively powerless to change the terms of his employment. Intersectionality, then, focuses attention on the ways that multiple and sometimes conflicting sources of oppression and power are intertwined.

HEGEMONIC MASCULINITIES AND EMPHASIZED FEMININITIES

The insights of intersectional analyses help us to see that there cannot be only one, universally valid way to be a man or a woman, but there are certainly images of the "right" way to be a man or a woman that dominate our thinking and our experience. Australian sociologist Robert Connell (1987) first introduced the idea of hegemonic masculinity—idealized, culturally ascendant masculinity—into feminist men's studies scholarship. The word *hegemony* means dominance and Connell uses the term *hegemonic masculinity* to refer to the culturally exalted form of masculinity that is linked to institutional power, such as that displayed at the top levels of the military, business, and government. This form of masculinity regularly appears in the media or as a component of our image of political leaders. Think of the film persona of John Wayne, "Indian" fighter and tough soldier in America's wars or "Rambo," Sylvester Stallone, who won the on-screen Vietnam war for the United States. Is the patriotic, violent, tough, uncompromising hero still hegemonic or are there other ideals of manhood competing with it? If so, what is their message (Connell and Messerschmidt 2005)?

In the real world, dominant men are usually white; from elite schools; with professional, managerial, or political careers; citizens of nations in the Global North; and heterosexual. Hegemonic men are the powerful members of national and increasingly global orders. Some men are hegemonic within local or specific orders. The coach and the drill sergeant are usually working-class men with authority over their men or their team and fans. Connell also identifies "subordinated" masculinities, among which he includes sexually marginalized gay men, "sissies," "mother's boys," and "wimps." The intersections of class and race produce other forms of subordinated or marginalized masculinity, men rendered socially invisible or outside the gender order.

There are different sorts of femininity as well. What Connell named *emphasized femininity* is the media version of womanhood that is "organized, financed, and supervised by men" (Connell 1987, 188). Women in TV-land are young, thin, conventionally beautiful, heterosexual, and often nurturant. Other forms of femininity resist and remake femininity, hidden in the experiences of women on the margins, "spinsters, lesbians, unionists, prostitutes, madwomen, rebels and maiden aunts, manual workers, midwives and witches" (Connell 1987, 188). The recovery of these marginalized forms of masculinity and femininity has been the work of feminism. Throughout the text, we look at the hegemonic forms of masculinity and emphasized femininity as well as the way masculinities and femininities vary and are challenged.

MAKING HISTORY

At the core of sociology is the idea that although individuals make choices about their destinies, they make them within the limits of the society in which they live. We are all constrained by the ideas and social institutions that surround us. The laws that protect equality (or not), the media messages we are sent about what are acceptable ways for women and men to behave, the technology available for health care or warfare, and the pay scales and the jobs available in our economic system, for example, all shape, limit, and sometimes even determine the "choices" we make as we interact with one another.

It is unlikely that we can successfully challenge these constraints as long as the systems are in place. We cannot live "outside" society and therefore have to live at least to some extent within the rules. We can, however, change the systems. C. Wright Mills was one sociologist who explained that the laws, ideas, technology, social institutions, and ways of doing things did not drop from the sky or emerge as a fact of nature, but were invented and implemented by humans and are constantly being reinvented and re-created. Mills wrote, "By the fact of his living he [each individual within a society] contributes, however minutely, to the shaping of this society and to the course of its history, even as he is made by society and by its historical push and shove" (Mills 1959, 11).

This quote has two important implications. First it means that our experience of gender and our gendered relationships with one another are subjects of constant debate and struggle among all of the people who are seeking to maintain or change the status quo. Second, it means that we have the opportunity to shape the course of history—our own and our society's—by entering into these disputes and the social movements that have surrounded them. Sociologists use the term *agency* to describe the ways that people seek to change their social circumstances, to dismantle existing ways of thinking and acting, and to create new ideas and new social institutions. Throughout the text, we call your attention to the ways organizations, small and large, local and global, are challenging systems of gender inequality as they intersect with other systems of inequality. In regard to the issue challenging systems of gender, feminists have been at the forefront of revisioning and reinvention.

FEMINIST SCHOLARS SEEKING ANSWERS

Feminists, however, are not a monolithic group. There are many different feminisms, and enormously diverse women's movements throughout the world. One version of feminism that has dominated popular awareness is liberal white American feminism. This particular form of feminism has played an important historical role as it has "discovered" gender inequality and sought to challenge it on many fronts.

Three Waves

When speaking about liberal white American feminism, it is customary to refer to three waves of the women's movement. The first wave refers to the feminist movement that focused on the fight for women's suffrage in the United States and grew out of abolitionism (the struggle to abolish slavery in the United States). That wave ended in 1920, with the passage of the Nineteenth Amendment granting women the right to vote.

The second wave refers to the re-emergence of feminism in the 1960s and 1970s, ending what many claimed was forty years of quiescence in the movement. During the second wave, activists and scholars broadened the scope of feminist concerns beyond voting rights to include women's health, women's work, and women's contributions to knowledge, and moved from an exclusive concern with women to a focus on the relationships of gender.

The third wave refers to the work of a new generation of feminists who emerged in the 1990s. Rebecca Walker, the daughter of African American novelist Alice Walker, first used the term "third wave" in an article in *MS. Magazine* in 1992. She argued that the third wave movement embraced women from all backgrounds and identities, young women who had entered a variety of occupations and activities, who took for granted the privileges won by their mothers' generation, embraced racial ethnic, and global differences among women, and lived feminism in their everyday lives.

Periodicizing American feminist activism in this manner is useful in some ways because it provides a quick sketch of what different feminists sought in different historical periods and how their perception of gender, gender inequality, and the need for change varied over time. Most important, it tells us that gender was not a settled subject and that people fought hard to change the social context so that their lives were not constrained in inhumane ways by gender expectations and the social institutions that sustained those expectations.

PROBLEMS WITH THE THREE WAVES

Despite these contributions to our thinking, however, the idea of three waves is also flawed. First, it is inaccurate. Some activities are ignored. For example, the wave model asserts that the first wave crashed to shore with the passage of the Nineteenth Amendment and ebbed for many years until it reemerged in the 1960s with the women's liberation movement and the second wave. Historians, however, have found that activism continued during the years between the three defined waves in periods referred to as the doldrums (Rupp and Taylor

1987; Barnett, 1995). The women's movement did not just die after women got the vote in the United States. Many organizations continued in their pursuit for women's equality albeit in less visible ways—ways that mainstream history often overlooks.

Second, the historical accuracy of the waves in terms of the ordering and naming of the periods is challengeable. As feminist activist and scholar Jo Freeman (1999, ix–x) explains:

> Those of us who started the women's liberation movement in the 1960s thought we were the second wave of female political activism because we knew very little about our own history. We were vaguely aware of the Suffrage Movement and mistakenly thought that was all our foremothers had done. One of our magazines was even named *The Second Wave*. Now that we know more, it is time to drop it. If anything, what began in the 1960s was the third wave of women's activism in the US, and maybe even the fourth.

In addition to questioning the historical correctness of the waves, Freeman's comment reveals a third problem with the concept of waves, which describes the women's movement from the perspectives of a few white women engaged in struggles from within mainstream politics. As a result, it overlooks the activism of American women of color and working-class women both within and outside of mainstream feminist resistance in the United States (Cott, 1987). Furthermore it ignores feminists around the world who had a very different story to tell. For example, there is an altogether different history of feminist activism from the point of view of women in Africa.

WAVES OF AFRICAN FEMINISM

African women's activism has also been divided into waves, but the turning points and the focal issues are quite different from the three waves identified with the American women's movement. Freeman reminds us that we Americans often know little about our history. We are frequently even more ignorant of the long history of women's contributions to their societies around the world, to the invention of democratic institutions, and to ways of life that build on and celebrate the strengths of women that precede the colonization of the third world (Eisenstein 2004). A global history of women's movements would grow from such knowledge.

Using the model of the waves, scholars of African history have proposed a postcolonial time line of African women's activism running from 1950 to 1970. During this period, the focus was on development issues such as "integrating women into development, promoting women's cooperatives, developing small-scale industries, training rural women to take on leadership positions, and establishing national mechanisms for integrating women in development projects" (Adams 2006, 189).

A second wave of regional activism in Africa began in 1980 and continues today. This period is marked by global debt, structural adjustment, and economic crisis. The globalized economy introduced problems to the people of Africa, but it also facilitated international communication and organization that helped African women, such as the growth of nongovernmental organizations (NGOs) committed to solving women's problems and providing alternatives to the official views and activities of governments. Peace and the elimination of poverty have dominated the agendas of these NGOs.

At the beginning of the twenty-first century, another turning point emerged suggesting that perhaps a third wave is developing. In 2002, the launching of the African Union (AU) gave impetus to the struggle for gender justice. The AU is modeled after the European Union and "seeks to promote unity among African countries and peoples, political and economic integration, peace and respect for democracy and human rights" (Adams 2006, 196). A centerpiece of the AU is its commitment to gender equity. Women make up fully half of the executive body of the organization. In 2003, it passed the Protocol on the Rights of Women in Africa, which explicitly endorsed quotas to increase women's representation in decision-making bodies, prohibition of female genital cutting, setting of the minimum age of marriage at 18, and guarantee of a woman's right to terminate a pregnancy in the case of rape, incest, or to save the mother's life (Adams 2006).

Africa's waves of feminist activism show different turning points and different activities and organizations than those of women in the United States. It also shows a different trajectory as the gains made by African women seem to be occurring at the same time American women are losing ground, for example, on the issue of abortion.

A number of explanations have been given for why the United States in particular has fallen from its leadership role (Tripp 2006):

- A growing complacency among Americans about defending gender equality.
- The demise of the labor movement, which has been the seedbed of much of American reform.
- A general increase in the position of conservative political forces.
- Few feminists in public office.
- Poor media coverage resulting in a lack of awareness of international initiatives and of how far the United States has fallen behind.

Throughout this text, we look at the organized activism of people seeking to change the gendered context of their lives. We explore the historical roots and may refer to the three waves in our discussion of the United States. We need to be careful, however, to remember that one size does not fit all and the experience of gender in other regions and nations, or even within a nation by race ethnicity or social class, might be quite different. This comparison of waves also reminds us of another important issue in this text: the tendency of people from the Global North to think about themselves as providing a model while the rest of the world needs only to "catch up." Activism by women in Africa and other places today tells us that we will find models of equality all over the world and that the United States may sometimes be a leader but may also often be a nation that could benefit by looking at solutions that have developed in other areas of the world.

PLAN OF THE BOOK

Now that we have introduced the point of view of this text and some of the important assumptions and tools we use to proceed with our exploration, let us now take a look at the topics we will be covering.

Agree or disagree: No matter how much gender relations have changed and are changing, biological sex—the underlying differences between human males and females—are important natural facts. If you agree with this statement, chapter 2 will try to convince you that you are mistaken. Even at the most basic level of genes and hormones, not everyone fits into one of the two standard and supposedly exclusive sex categories of male or female. Historically, the conventional idea of "opposite" sexes turns out to be a relatively recent invention, and cross-culturally, different societies employ different and sometimes more numerous sex categories. The chapter concludes with a section on a gender-bending movement of intersexual people, a movement that underscores the political nature of biological categories. Overall, this chapter makes the case for biological sex as a continuum, not a dichotomy of male or female, and suggests that by relinquishing our faith that male and female bodies are naturally and forever different in consequential ways, we make space for the "playful exploration" of the many possibilities of embodiment (Fausto-Sterling 2000).

If biology is not the basis of gender difference, racial variation, or alternative sexualities, then what is? Chapter 3 reviews three answers to that question. Regarding gender, one answer is we learn appropriate ways of being gendered from our parents, teachers, and friends. We see examples of gendered behavior on television and in books. From our first days we are schooled in gender roles and most of us are good students. A second answer to the question of how gender differences arise draws on the idea that interacting together we actively produce the worlds in which we live. Instead of "being" a gender, we "do" gender (and more generally, "do" difference) in social encounters. A third answer points to the ways organizations and institutions build gender and other inequalities into the ways they function. As you read this chapter, test these theories against your own experiences and observations of the ways you have become gendered, raced, sexualized, and turned into a member of your class. Have you ever resisted some of these identities? How, and in what contexts?

Chapter 4 explores sexuality through intersecting dimensions of gender, race, and citizenship (nation). Normatively, men and women are expected to be sexually attracted to and engage in sexual activity only with each other. In fact, actual sex practices offer much more complicated and interesting examples of the ways racial ethnic and gender identities enter into and produce sexuality and sexual identity and of the impacts of globalization on sexualities. The 1992 film, *The Crying Game*, treats these complexities against the political backdrop of the Irish Troubles, the thirty years of violent struggle between Catholic Nationalists and Protestant Unionists. Feminist and antiracist studies of sexuality have exposed the very political character of constructions of sexuality that the film suggests. The chapter moves from discussing the construction of conventional sexualities by means of sexual scripts and gendered double standards to describing the global sexual politics of sex tourism and sex trafficking, and exploring the queer movement's resistances and challenges to normative sexualities mounted by queers and others demanding sexual human rights.

What does water have to do with education? In chapter 5 you'll read about how lack of access to water and sanitation in poor countries directly affects girls' ability to enter and remain in school. In the West, girls' education has increasingly become more equal to that of boys in terms of attendance, graduation, and choice of studies, and in some ways girls have surpassed boys. Globally, however, the story is quite different. In the poorest countries of Haiti, Colombia, Malawi, Madagascar, Surinam, Tanzania, and Lesotho, boys are less likely than girls to go to school, but school is a luxury many children cannot afford, boys and girls alike. Overall, girls around the world are less likely to be in school (Human Rights Watch 2006). Two thirds of children not attending schools in the world are girls and on a global scale, 60 percent of illiterate young people are girls. Illiteracy, low education, and poverty mean higher mortality rates, decreased income, hunger, and even death. Clearly, the intersections of gender, race, and nation can be deadly.

You've been students now for at least fourteen or fifteen years, and perhaps longer. Can you recall the ways that you and your teachers relied on gender in your classrooms? Most studies show that for many years, teachers often consciously and unconsciously built on the dichotomy between boys and girls for purposes of teaching and to exercise control over their students. Did you make separate girls' and boys' lines at lunchtime? Did girls and boys play separate games in the schoolyard during recess? Did boys and girls compete at spelling and geography in class? Did the teacher listen more attentively to boys' answers or give more time to unruly boys than well-behaved girls in class? These were common practices in American classrooms of the past and perhaps in some classrooms today. This chapter shows how assuming the difference between boys and girls in the classroom becomes a self-fulfilling prophecy, another piece of the puzzle helping to explain how gender differences are created. Racial ethnic differences also matter in classrooms, and the cross-cutting dimensions of race ethnicity and gender construct hierarchies of educational success. This chapter makes clear that gendering in education is not a simple story. Gendering creates problems for boys, too, exemplified by the greater proportion of boys who are diagnosed and treated for hyperactivity. Racism and poverty contribute to the diminished educations that many children receive. Overall, chapter 5 shows how gender, class position, and race ethnicity intertwine to play central roles from kindergarten through graduate school and professional education, and the price we pay for these inequalities.

Chapter 6 turns the lenses of gender, race ethnicity, class, and nation on local and global economies and on the gendered and raced character of work. For example, the relationship between paid and unpaid work is also a relationship between men and women in the gendered division of labor. Much of domestic labor—cleaning, cooking, shopping, and caring for children and other dependents—was for a long time and, to a certain extent, still is invisible. Only work men did, for pay outside families, appeared to be "real" work. Was such invisible work invisible because it was the work of women? Was it invisible because it was not paid?

The gender perspective has contributed many useful concepts to the study of working lives, concepts that you will learn about in this chapter. The *glass ceiling* is a term for the invisible obstacles facing women who try to make it up the ladders that professional men have been climbing for generations. The *glass escalator* signifies the seemingly effortless ways men rise to top positions in women's professions such as elementary school teaching or nursing. *Emotional labor* captures some of the invisible work required of workers—being nice and absorbing abuse from customers in the service economy; being tough and instilling fear in the work of bill collecting and policing. The former is work more likely to be required of workers in jobs assigned to women; the latter in men's jobs. The *pay gap* and the *feminization of poverty* describe the consequences of gender, class, and racial inequalities in the labor force, and *comparable worth* is a policy invented by activists to remedy such inequalities. In recent decades, the global economy has come into view as a reality directly connecting the fates of workers around the world. Despite the better situation of some women in the West, globally women have less status, power, and wealth than men. Free trade agreements have meant the loss of jobs in the United States to countries in which labor is vastly cheaper. It has also meant that workers in those nations with cheap labor are working for wages that cannot sustain life. It has also meant the impoverishment of millions of third-world farmers, who cannot compete with subsidized American goods from corporate farms that undersell their products and drive local growers out of business.

The family has been a loaded political issue in the United States for the past thirty years, as conservatives hold its so-called decline responsible for the ills of contemporary life. In chapter 7 you will have a chance to draw your own conclusions about family life today. Does marriage prevent poverty, as those who promote marriage by welfare recipients believe? Is marriage between a man and a woman essential to preserving the institution of marriage? Sometimes the same people who think marriage is a solution to poverty oppose gay marriage. The dream of love has propelled marriage choice for middle-class heterosexuals in the West for generations. On the other hand, marriage promotion for the poor and marriage prohibition for gays and lesbians dispenses with love as the basis of marriage. Likewise, middle-class women have been and still are exhorted to be good mothers by staying home with their children, even as mothers on welfare are required to enter the labor force.

The chapter demonstrates that the massive entry of women into the labor force is producing serious conflicts between the needs of families and the requirements of jobs. Among other things, these conflicts have produced a serious child care crisis in the United States. Mothering and caretaking are examples of invisible and unpaid labor, absolutely vital to the well-being of families and absolutely necessary to sustain the labor force. Comparative data from other industrial countries shows that the United States provides the least family and parental support for child care and gender equity. With such comparative data at hand, women and men are making headway in demanding greater public support for families.

Chapter 8 shows that gender is a central feature of the continuum of violence that stretches from our most intimate lives to the ongoing global tragedies wrought by militarism and war. Street harassment, rape, domestic violence, gendered violence in prisons, militarist masculinity, wartime rape, the enslavement of women by militias, sex trafficking, and growing civilian casualties in wartime of women, children, and elderly—what do you think can explain such relentless and pervasive gendered violence? Why is most violence the violence of men against women and other men? And there is a related question: Are these different kinds of violence related in any way? Some observers have attempted to naturalize violence as evolutionarily or psychologically necessary. Some feminists evoked biology as an explanation for violence by characterizing it as men's violence against women. Feminist antiracist research has broadened and complicated this simplistic naturalized picture of gendered violence. Some women—poor, working class, of color—are at greater risk of sexual and gendered violence than others. Likewise, inequalities of race ethnicity, class, gender, and sexuality shape men's relationship to violence, both as victims and perpetrators. These new understandings of the ways gendered violence enters into the life of individuals, communities, and nation states suggest pioneering remedies and courses of action that we explore in the chapter.

Chapter 9 recounts the many ways that illness and health are gendered around the globe. Everything you have read until this chapter helps to structure the distribution of health and illness: the sexual division of paid and unpaid labor, race ethnicity, the political economies and ruling orders of the nations in which people live, membership in particular sexual communities, and so forth. After reading this material, you will understand why health is a collective good requiring collective action to secure it for all people. This chapter also describes feminist and antiracist social movements around reproductive rights that have grown from local actions into transnational movements linking reproductive and general health to a wide range of rights: housing, education, employment, freedom from violence, and health services that take priority over market forces.

Is changing the gender of officeholders sufficient to make positive political change? According to the studies reported in chapter 10, the evidence is mixed. Some studies show that with education, men become more conservative and women more liberal (Carpini and Keeter 2000). Women's greater liberalism may be a function of their lower income, lesser power, and diminished status relative to men. As people on the outside, they are more critical of existing political realities. Sometimes, when women achieve insider status, it is hard to see any difference between them and men. The iconic example is Margaret Thatcher, who was British Prime Minister from 1979 to 1990. Thatcher was a neo-conservative whose free-market economic ideology and policies, like that of her contemporary, U.S. President Ronald Reagan, favored big business through deregulation and privatization of state-owned industries and utilities. She advocated reform of the trade unions, lowered taxes, and reduced social expenditures.

The question of women's impact on politics remains open because men dominate all channels of contemporary politics around the world: electoral politics, the news media, and the metaphors of political discourse, war and sports. Despite the prevalent belief of Americans that they are leaders in and teachers of democracy and equal participation, the participation of U.S. women in legislative and executive positions is close to that of women in Chad or Morocco. It is Rwanda and Costa Rica that have the largest proportion of women in government.

Politics is not just about elections and offices. There is a gender politics of women in prisons, girls in gangs, the war on drugs, and women in combat. Some suggest that politics is even broader, including all activities in which people engage to link public and private concerns and to develop power that brings about change in people's everyday lives. Given the broader definition, think about the ways your activities and those of your friends and family could be seen as political.

You are the media generation. Your daily lives are saturated with media. Try this test: Keep a diary of all the media-connected contacts you have from the time you wake up in the morning until the time you go to bed. Note when and how long you listen to the radio or watch television. Don't forget to list the advertisements you encounter, including those that come to you in the mail, on bulletin boards at school and work, on billboards along the roads you travel, and on the Internet. Remember to add the papers and books you pick up today to your list. The thousands of images and messages we receive in these ways exhort us overtly or subtly to view, experience, and act on the world in certain ways. Chapter 11 explores the gendering of these messages. Women are still missing as subjects of media stories and behind the scenes as reporters and writers. Stereotypes of women and men abound. The ads show some differences in different countries. Women outnumber men in Japanese and Turkish ads, although men are, unsurprisingly, the primary characters in automobile, financial services, and food and drink advertisements. One consistent image is that women are nearly always young. Middle-aged and older women have been "annihilated" globally in such ads. In the United States, the images are of powerful white men, white women as sex objects, aggressive black men, and inconsequential black women. Men and women who are Latino, Asian American, and First Nations people are nearly nonexistent in the ads.

Similar stereotypes and absences can be found in movies, magazines, video games, sexist lyrics, and televised sports. Where there is power, there is resistance, according to Foucault. The media are also the medium of resistance. For example, music videos are among the most blatantly sexist and racist forms of entertainment, but they are also a forum for black women's resistance.

Chapter 11 also discusses a media-related area of entertainment, sports. Sports are tied to media, to ads, and to gender in many ways. For women, athletics have been a place of exclusion, expressing the idea that femininity does not include athletic ability and experience. Learning to be athletes and learning to be masculine are closely related. Critics of organized sports cite violence, disrespect for human bodies, and excessive competitiveness that damages athletes. Athleticism for women is different. One student of women in sports claims that women's athletics creates new images and new ways of being women that challenge men's dominance (Messner 1992). Ironically, sports is a way men prove they are masculine, but participation in sports often forces women to prove they are feminine. Studying gender and sports forces comparisons between highly organized and competitive fan-supported sports that have become big business today and participation sports, comprised of more loosely defined and organized activities, the former the sport of spectacle, the latter its democratic and participatory alternative.

In chapter 12 we focus on gender and religion, one of the most loaded topics of debate today as the rise of religious fundamentalism has put the roles of women in the spotlight. Although fundamentalist religions restrict women, it might surprise you to learn that more women than men are fundamentalists. Women's support of these religions makes sense when we realize that religious communities, regardless of doctrine, can be places where women find collective support and the social space for expression, arenas of freedom in otherwise restrictive societies. Not all forms of spirituality and religious organization constrain women. Women often resist the constraints imposed on them religiously. For example, some Catholic women are calling for an end to the ban on women priests. Also, religion has played important positive roles in movements for social justice. The black church in the South, with its high level of women members, played a pivotal role in the civil rights movement. The peace and antiwar movements of the past century attracted many religious activists who were women. Finally, ancient and indigenous societies created forms of worship that were egalitarian and that revered women's bodies for their life-giving abilities. In this chapter we ask if these partnership forms of worship could provide the models of more humane and socially constructive forms of religion.

Our world is filled with injustice, inequality, and pain. It is also filled with the hope and promise that grows from the many who contribute to resisting injustices, promoting equality, and creating a world of that promotes our potentials and our pleasures. We dedicate this book to furthering those ends.

REFERENCES

Adams, Melinda. 2006. Regional women's activism: African women's networks and the African Union. 187–218 in Myra Marx Ferree and Aili Mari Tripp eds. *Global Feminism: Transnational women's activism, organizing, and human rights*. New York: New York University Press.

Barnett, Bernice McNair. 1995. Black women's collectivist movement organizations: Their struggle during the doldrums. In Feminist organizations: Harvest of the new women's movement, 199–219. edited by Myra Marx Ferree and Patricia Yancey Martin.Philadelphia: Temple University Press.

Collins, Patricia Hill. 2000. *Black Feminist Thought: Knowledge, Consciousness, and the Politics of Emmpowerment*. Second edition. New York: Routledge.

Connell, Robert W. 1987. *Gender and Power*. Stanford, CA: Stanford University Press.

Connell, Robert W. and James Messerschmidt. 2005. Hegemonic masculinity: Rethinking the concept. Gender & Society 19(6). 829–859.

Cott, Nancy F., *The grounding of modern feminism*, New Haven, Conn.: Yale University Press, 1987.

Doocy, Shannon, Abdur Rofi, Gilbert Burnham, and Courtland Robinson. 2007. Tsunami mortality in Aceh Province, Indonesia. *Bulletin of the World Health Organization* 85 (4): 245–324.

Eisenstein, Zillah. 2004. *Against empire: Feminisms, racism, and the West*. London: Zed Books.

Enarson, Elaine, and Betty Hearn Morrow, eds. 1998. *The gendered terrain of disaster: Through women's eyes*. Westport, CT: Greenwood.

Fausto-Sterling, Anne. 2000. *Sexing the body: Gender politics and the construction of sexuality*. New York: Basic Books.

Freeman, Jo and Victoria Johnson, eds. 1999. Waves of protest: Social movements since the sixties. Preface ix–x. Lanham, MD: Rowman and Littlefield.

Human Rights Watch. 2006. Children's rights: Education. http://www.hrw.org/children/education.htm Accessed June 26, 2008.

Messner, Michael. 1992. *Power at play: Sports and the problem of masculinity*. Boston: Beacon Press.

Mies, Maria. 1986. *Patriarchy and accumulation on a world scale: women in the international division of labour*. London: Zed Books.

Mills, C. Wright. 1959. *The sociological imagination*. New York: Oxford University Press.

Neumayer, Eric, and Thomas Pluemper. 2007. The gendered nature of natural disasters. *Social Science Research Network*. http://ssrn.com/abstract=874965.

Oxfam. 2005. *Gender and the tsunami*. Oxfam briefing note.

March 30. London: Oxfam. http://www.oxfamamerica.org/newsandpublications/publications/briefing_papers/briefing_note.2005–03–30.6547801151/bn_tsunami_gender033005.pdf.

Rupp, Leila and Verta J. Taylor. 1987. *Survival in the doldrums: the American women's rights movement, 1945 to the 1960s*. New York : Oxford University Press.

Smith, Dorothy E. 1999. Contradictions for feminist social scientists. *Writing the social: Critique, theory, and investigations*. 15–28. Toronto: University of Toronto Press.

Tripp, Aili Mari. 2006. The evolution of transnational feminisms: Consensus, conflict and new dynamics. 51–78 in *Global Feminism: Transnational women's activism, organizaing, and human rights*. Myra Marx Ferree and Aili Mari Tripp, eds. New York: New York University Press.

2

BODIES AND GENDERS

Becoming a person who is comfortable standing up in public, literally on television and saying, "No matter what you think of how I look or how I speak, no matter what I've done to fit into this world, I am not male and I am not female. And probably neither are you." (Preves 2005, 137)

THE STANDARD STORY

In the not-too-distant past, many of us believed that there were clear connections among sex, sexuality, and gender. An infant with a female body would grow up to be a woman who is sexually attracted to men. An infant with a male body would become a man who is sexually attracted to women. There was no in-between or "other" status, such as that claimed by the speaker in the preceding epigraph. This was once the story most of us learned about sex, what philosopher Judith Butler (1990) has named the *heterosexual matrix*, or what we might call the *standard story line*. The epigraph that begins this chapter suggests that new stories about sex are emerging.

Many tacit assumptions support the old story:

- *Biology is destiny*. Underlying social behavior (gender) and sexual choice (normatively, heterosexuality) is the substratum of nature. One's biological sex determines one's sexual and social identity, one's needs and desires, and one's sexual potentials.
- *There are only two sexes, male and female*. Male infants will become boys and men; female infants will become girls and women. This is the "normal" and "natural" course of development dictated by our genes, hormones, and gonads (testes or ovaries). A person with a penis and testes is a man; a person with a vagina and ovaries is a woman.

16

- *The two-sex order is universal, a fact of nature*. Deviations from this natural order are mistakes of nature or of culture. They require intervention to restore this order, lest we "subvert nature's plan" (Oyama, Griffiths, and Gray 2001).

This chapter explores these assumptions and the challenges to them. We begin by critically examining the claim, recently disputed by feminist and queer theorists, that our chromosomes, hormones, and genitalia work together to create "purely" female or "purely" male bodies. In some quarters even now, nonconforming bodies—those that do not easily fit the categories male or female—are seen as "mistakes of nature" that require correction. However, increasingly activists, scholars, physicians, and even ordinary people argue that multiple sex statuses and sexed bodies are arrayed along a continuum, with fully male and fully female at the extreme ends of that range containing three, four, five, or more mixed "sexes" (Fausto-Sterling 2000b). Here we describe this emergent view.

Next, the chapter reviews the historical and anthropological evidence that shows how in other times and other places, people perceived sexed bodies differently and treated them differently from the way they are seen and treated today. In fact, the once seemingly immutable ways of seeing and understanding the sexes, outlined earlier, developed as recently as the nineteenth century, alongside new divisions of labor, new forms of production, and new patterns of social relations. In contrast, many ancient and medieval naturalists and physicians compared male and female anatomy to prove there was one sex, not two. Likewise, many anthropologists describe cultures in which life is built around the existence of three or more sexes. To the people of these other worlds, the shape and functions of sexed bodies seemed just as obvious as our two-sex system appears to us.

Third, the chapter examines dualist and biological explanations of sexuality and bodies and compares these to current research that claims sexuality and desire have histories, and that they are constructed socially out of bodily potentials. Finally, the chapter examines the public emergence of intersexuals and their increasingly influential impact on thinking about sex.

Intersexuals are (1) individuals born with ambiguous genitalia such as penises that look small enough to be clitorises or clitorises that look large enough to be penises; (2) people whose bodies develop sexually along unexpected paths, such as infants with "5-alpha reductase deficiency" who may be mistakenly categorized as girls at birth, but who at puberty develop beards, lower voices, and larger penises; and (3) people who reject their assigned sex category and feel they are in the "wrong" body. Intersexual advocates and activists argue that the excluded middle categories, neither fully male nor fully female, show that sex is not sharply dichotomous. Humans, they argue, are more androgynous than our sexually polarized world allows. This is not to claim that sexed bodies have changed in some objective or material way over time. Rather, the claim is that our ways of seeing sex are changing. Instead of considering ambiguously sexed bodies as mistakes of nature that modern medical science can correct, intersexuals and others have begun to challenge beliefs that "sex categories are binary, that is there are only males and females, and that anything not clearly one or the other is abnormal" (Dreger 1998, 8). As these sexual stories reach wider audiences, and as the previously shared assumptions about sex differences are increasingly questioned, a *paradigm shift* (Kuhn 1996) regarding how we understand bodily sex may be in the offing.

THE INTERPLAY OF SEX, GENDER, AND SEXUALITY

At one time, scholars agreed that binary sex differences were the sum and substance of embodied sex, asking only if nature or culture was responsible for turning sex (the biological substratum) into gender (the social arrangements built on sex differences). Now growing numbers of scholars are trying to disentangle the complex interplay of sex, gender, and sexuality. For example, Edward Stein suggests using the term *sex-gender* to reflect the fact that some things we attribute to biological sex might turn out to be the outcome of social gender. For him, the boundary between what is sex (nature) and gender (society and culture) is dissolving. His category sex-gender "includes all the characteristics (biological, psychological, cultural, and social) that are supposed to distinguish males/men from females/women" (Stein 1999, 33).

Sociologists Suzanne Kessler and Wendy McKenna (1978) go even further than Stein. They treat sex as an *aspect* of gender, where even genes, chromosomes, and hormones are socially constructed. They begin from the ethnomethodological premise that in our everyday lives we proceed on the basis of a *natural attitude*, a belief in the objectivity and rationality of the world as we apprehend it. In other words, reality is what we see and experience directly. In the natural attitude, gender (and we could add, race) is a biological, universal, and unchanging reality in which, unerringly, men are men and women are women.

Kessler and McKenna assert that most scientific approaches to sex have failed to question the premise that there are two and only two sexes. Instead scientists use the "everyday attribution process" that nonscientists use in daily interaction. They mean that scientists, like the rest of us, assign individuals to one or the other sex category based on their observations of a person's demeanor, clothing, mannerisms, name, and so forth. Scientists, like the rest of us, adopt the *natural attitude* that there are, objectively, only two sexes.

Kessler and McKenna, however argue that the natural attitude assumes what scientists should question. They offer an example of how that assumption produces circular reasoning about the reality of sex difference. To know if women and men differ in brain structures, we would need to get a group of [deceased] women and a group of [deceased] men, label their brains according to the donor's gender, and then examine the brains for differences. But if this group of dead men and women is assembled by asking the morgue to supply brains from male and female corpses, the research will be tainted. As you will learn shortly, a person who looks female might have undescended testicles and an XY genetic makeup; a person who looks male could have ovaries and an enlarged clitoris. If scientists base their tests of brain structure simply on corpses that *look* female or male, they are likely to have contaminated the categories of analysis and their conclusions would be meaningless (Kessler and McKenna 1978, 75).

Judith Lorber (1994) suggests that women and men are fairly alike biologically and that social and cultural selection processes produce individuals we see as men or women. Gendered people, she writes, "do not emerge from physiology or hormones but from the exigencies of the social order." Quoting philosopher Judith Butler, she continues:

There is no core or bedrock human nature below these endlessly looping processes of the social production of sex and gender, self and other, identity and psyche, each of which is a "complex cultural construction" (Butler 1990, 36). The paradox of "human nature" is that it is always a manifestation of cultural meanings, social relationships, arid power politics—[quoting Butler again] "not biology, but culture, becomes destiny." (Lorber 1994, 568)

Sex, gender, sexuality—these are terms that can confuse us now because what they refer to in the real world is becoming blurred. Following Lorber (2005, 9), we use the terms in the following ways.

- Sex is "a complex interplay of genes, hormones, environment, and behavior with loopback effects between bodies and society." We use the adjectives *male, female,* and *intersexed* when referring to apparent biological—chromosomal, gonadal, or genital (phenotype of one's genitalia)—features of sex.
- Sexuality involves "lustful desire, emotional involvement, and fantasy." We use the terms *homosexuality, heterosexuality, bisexuality, omnisexuality,* and *asexuality* when referring to sexuality. Just as studies of embodied sex suggest that it is a continuum, not a dichotomy, studies of sexual orientation suggest that there are no hard and fast divides among individuals in the objects of their sexual desires. An individual's feelings of homosexuality, heterosexuality, and bisexuality need not be "fixed for life" nor mutually exclusive. These ideas will be explored further in chapter 4.
- Gender is "a social status, a legal designation, and a personal identity." Gender divisions and their accompanying norms and expectations are part of major social institutions. We use the terms *woman* and *man* when referring to gender.

CHROMOSOMES, HORMONES, AND GENES

What **sex** are you? How do you know? As you will discover later in this chapter, these questions are not as silly as they may seem now. We can categorize you in terms of chromosomes, and indeed that was how the International Olympic Committee (IOC) policed the sex status of female competitors in the Olympic games, starting in 1968, to make sure no "men" would compete in women's events. As Anne Fausto-Sterling (2000a) writes in her introduction to *Sexing the Body,* only female athletes, defined as people with XX chromosomal makeup, were allowed to compete in the women's events. One athlete, Maria Patino, was removed from competition when a DNA test revealed she had a Y chromosome and hidden testes. According to the test, she was not a woman. The IOC based its action on the idea that a person is either a man or a woman, an XX or an XY. However, the biology of sex is more complicated than this single either–or test suggests. Indeed, the decision to rule that Patino was not a woman was based on cultural beliefs about gender, not scientific facts. As Fausto-Sterling describes her, Patino had breasts, a narrow waist, and broad hips. She had the strength of a woman, was raised as a woman, and felt herself to be a woman. Despite her Y chromosome, she had grown up female.

How would you decide whether Patino was eligible to compete in the Olympics? By the time you finish reading this chapter, your answer may change. Biological sex is complicated and chromosomal makeup is only one part of it. Usually human beings have twenty-three pairs of chromosomes, one pair of which are called sex chromosomes. In most instances, the egg contributes only X chromosomes to the embryo, and the sperm contributes either an X or a Y chromosome. The resulting individual, then, is chromosomally either an XX (a female) or an XY (a male). However, that is not the end of the story. In a number of instances a person will inherit only one chromosome, an X; in others she or he will have an extra X or Y chromosome (notice that language forces us to accept the male–female dichotomy). The result is that there are a range of solely X chromosome people (XO, XX, XXX), as well as XYs and XYYs and XXYs. Chromosomally, then, we could say that there are five sexes, not two, which is the point Fausto-Sterling made, tongue in cheek, in her famous article, "The Five Sexes" (Fausto-Sterling 1993).

Not all reasons for variations in biological sex are chromosomal. Congenital adrenal hyperplasia (CAH), a condition related to steroid hormone production, masculinizes XX individuals. Androgen insensitivity syndrome (AIS), the condition that made Patino feminine despite her Y chromosome, causes XY children to develop female genitalia. Hermaphroditism and gonadal dysgenesis—abnormal gonadal development—refers to various conditions in which individual anatomies include gonads or secondary sex characteristics of both sexes.

Embryonically, we all develop our sex from a shared, unsexed body. In the first six weeks of gestation, an embryo has undifferentiated external genitalia that will usually develop either into a penis, testicles, and scrotum or a clitoris, labia, and vagina. Some individuals are born with the genitalia of both sexes, or their genital makeup does not match their chromosomal category, as with Patino. There are people who are born with both ovarian and testicular tissue, and others who have the external genitalia of one sex and the internal gonads (ovaries or testes) of the other. Until recently in the United States, many of these individuals did not survive intact to adulthood. Instead they were surgically and hormonally altered at birth to appear more "normal," or fully and unambiguously male or female. Fausto-Sterling has attempted to estimate the frequencies of such births (see Table 2-1), but with difficulty due to the shame and secrecy that has surrounded them. Nonetheless, it is clear that such births

TABLE 2–1 Frequencies of Various Causes of Ambiguous, Nonnormal, or Unclear Sexual Development (Fausto-Sterling 2000, 53)

Cause	Estimated Frequency/100 Live Births
Non-XX or non-XY (except Turner's or Klinefelter's)	0.0639
Turner Syndrome	0.0369
Klinefelter Syndrome	0.0922
Androgen Insensitivity Syndrome	0.0076
Partial Androgen Insensitivity Syndrome	0.00076
Classic congenital adrenal hyperplasia (omitting very high-frequency population)	0.00779
Late-onset congenital adrenal hyperplasia	1.5
Vaginal agenesis	0.0169
True hermaphrodites	0.0012
Ideopathic	0.0009
Total	1.728

are more common than most people believe. In the last analysis, the epigraph to this chapter becomes more intelligible: In more than a few instances, biological makeup is far from clear, far from either simply male or female.

The binaries of sex and gender may seem eternal to you. But science shows that behind what we "see" is another reality. Moreover, historians show that our "eternal" categories originated relatively recently, as the next section of this chapter demonstrates.

SEXED BODIES IN OTHER TIMES AND OTHER PLACES

How do we get beyond the natural attitude, the conviction that everyone is either a male or a female? One way to make visible our unexamined commonsense beliefs is to compare social worlds in other times and places. Are the sexes "opposite?" Not in medieval Europe, where naturalists and physicians demonstrated that women were like men, although biologically inferior. How many sexes are there? In some societies there can be more than two sex *statuses* that are socially relevant if not biologically "real" categories. Such examples show that what we "see" and "know" is rooted in our specific histories, contexts, and practices. Different times and places have their own common sense and their own ways of seeing. Freud reputedly claimed that "biology is destiny." Thanks to the examples presented in this section, readers might counter with Judith Butler's (1990) claim that it is not biology, but culture and history that are destiny.

Whether or not biology is fixed and immutable, the way we understand the biology of sex is not. Historian Thomas Laqueur shows that how we view, understand, and use bodies is enmeshed in social and cultural ways of seeing, and not simply in some nonsocial biological core. Today the conventional understanding is that there are two sexes and that sex is the underpinning of gender. Laqueur reverses this conventional understanding. In his view, our gender relations and ideologies shape observed sex and sexuality. Our ways of seeing, our tacit understandings of reality, our suppositions about men and women, indeed the very idea that men and women exist, affect how bodies appear to laypeople and scientists alike. To demonstrate this truth, his book shows that many doctors, naturalists, and anatomists from ancient times until the dawn of the modern scientific era in the late eighteenth century believed in a one-sex world, not the seemingly self-evident two-sex world with which we are so familiar. This difference in perspective is linked to a society's more general understandings of social reality.

Laqueur shows that how people saw (and continue to see) biology and sexuality mirrored the social order. Medieval scientists and doctors saw bodies as miniature societies that corresponded to the society's gendered hierarchies of power. Bodily structures reflected and legitimized men's social dominance.

> In a public world that was overwhelmingly male, the one-sex model displayed what was already massively evident in culture more generally: man is the measure of all things, and woman does not exist as a...distinct category. Not all males are masculine, potent, honorable, or hold power, and some women exceed some men in each of these categories. But the standard of the human body and its representations is the male body. (Laqueur 1990, 62)

FIGURE 2–1 The vagina as penis.

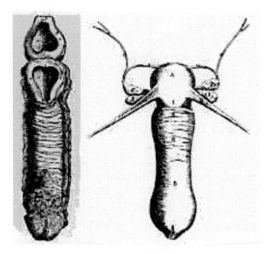

(Left) Vagina as penis, from Vesalius, *Fabrica*, sixteenth century. (Right) The vagina and uterus from Vidus Vidius, *De anatome corporis humani*(1611). From Thomas Laqueur *Making Sex*, 82.

Within the bodily and social hierarchy there was only one sex: the male sex. Women were like men, but lesser and less perfect. Naturalists and physicians of the time offered "proof" of this assumption in female reproductive anatomy and wrote many treatises proving the likenesses between men and women. For example, Aristotle believed the vagina and cervix looked like an internal penis. Five centuries after Aristotle, Galen, the second-century Roman physician and philosopher whose studies of anatomy remained influential into the nineteenth century, wrote that women's reproductive organs were like men's "turned outside in."

Similarly, bodily fluids—semen, menstrual blood, and milk-were seen as male and female versions of the same substance, but hierarchically ordered according to their power. Again, the female versions of these fluids were not essentially different, but instead were lesser, weaker, and corrupted versions of male secretions. Orgasm, also, was common to both men and women, although male orgasm was believed to be more intense and more violent than female orgasm. Renaissance anatomical illustrators—Vesalius, Berengario, and even the great artist, Leonardo—represented the vagina as an internal penis (see Figure 2-1). Such beliefs about the hierarchy of the sexes helped to determine how people saw actual bodily organs. Ideologies about sex guided how people interpreted the evidence presented by actual male and female bodies.

To summarize, Laqueur's study of premodern views of sexed bodies showed how ideas and beliefs about men and women shaped the ways people understood sexual anatomy and its functions, *how believing is seeing* (Lorber 1994). A belief in male perfection and dominance contributed to a vision of sexed bodies that reflected and supported those beliefs. Men were the standard against which women's bodies were compared, women's bodies the metaphorical "rib" springing from men.

Metaphors About Bodies in the New World

The male–female polarity came into being in a very different social world from the world of the premodern naturalists. As industrial capitalism grew, it brought with it a new division of labor between women and men. In the precapitalist agricultural economies of the American colonies, prior to this great transformation, women partnered with men in producing the family's subsistence, as had been true of peasants in premodern Europe. In the new world, like the old, a hierarchical, "one-sex" view seemed to prevail. Historian Mary Ryan claimed that members of colonial society viewed differences between men and women as differences of degree, not kind, just as medieval naturalists had viewed them.

> Colonial men and women were held to a single standard of good behavior and equipped with a will free to perfect the temporal manifestations of their character. Therefore, unlike their progeny, early Americans rarely wrote or spoke of the "nature of woman" as opposed to the "nature of man." The concepts of masculinity and femininity remained ill-defined in agrarian America.... The agrarian frontier economy kept the sexual division of labor simple and primitive, while the household system of social organization precluded the isolation of women in a private and undervalued sphere. (Ryan 1975, 63–64)

By the end of the eighteenth century, a different understanding of sexual natures was emerging, as the scientific and capitalist revolutions began to change how Westerners perceived the world and themselves. Commercial capitalism–production for the market, not for subsistence—began to undermine rural, family-based production. The new system instituted novel divisions of labor that segregated the domestic productive work of women from the productive work of men outside their homes and families. The development of scientific medicine contributed to the doctrine of separate spheres the idea that women's bodily differences from men made them unfit for public life and civic responsibilities. Healing had been women's sphere before physicians laid claim to it and usurped women's position. New economic relations separated men from women and the new sciences of the body uncovered what appeared to be fundamental biological differences between the sexes that made these social arrangements mandatory.

Contemporary medicine still shows the traces of these early modern views of sex. Emily Martin explored how women's biological differences from men are presented in medical science as pathologies. For example, medical models of menstruation, pregnancy, and menopause implied "failed production, waste, decay, and breakdown." A 1984 medical text described menstruation as follows:

> [M]uch of the endometrial tissue dies and sloughs into the uterine cavity. Then, small amounts of blood ooze from the denuded endometrial wall, causing a blood loss of about 50 ml during the next few days. The sloughed endometrial tissue plus the blood and much serous exudates from the denuded uterine surface, all together called the menstrum, is gradually expelled by intermittent contractions of the uterine muscle for about 3 to 5 days. (Martin 1992, 47)

Box 2–1 GLORIA STEINEM, "IF MEN COULD MENSTRUATE" (*MS MAGAZINE*, OCTOBER, 1978)

A white minority of the world has spent centuries conning us into thinking that a white skin makes people superior—even though the only thing it really does is make them more subject to ultraviolet rays and to wrinkles. Male human beings have built whole cultures around the idea that penis envy is "natural" to women—though having such an unprotected organ might be said to make men vulnerable, and the power to give birth makes womb envy at least as logical. In short, the characteristics of the powerful, whatever they may be, are thought to be better than the characteristics of the powerless—and logic has nothing to do with it.

What would happen, for instance, if suddenly, magically, men could menstruate and women could not? The answer is clear—menstruation would become an enviable, boast-worthy, masculine event: Men would brag about how long and how much. Boys would mark the onset of menses, that longed-for proof of manhood, with religious ritual and stag parties. Congress would fund a National Institute of Dysmenorrhea to help stamp out monthly discomforts. Sanitary supplies would be federally funded and free. (Of course, some men would still pay for the prestige of commercial brands such as John Wayne Tampons, Muhammad Ali's Rope-a-dope Pads, Joe Namath Jock Shields—"For Those Light Bachelor Days," and Robert "Baretta" Blake Maxi-Pads.) Military men, right-wing politicians, and religious fundamentalists would cite menstruation ("men-struation") as proof that only men could serve in the Army ("you have to give blood to take blood"), occupy political office ("can women be aggressive without that steadfast cycle governed by the planet Mars?"), be priests and ministers ("how could a woman give her blood for our sins?") or rabbis ("without the monthly loss of impurities, women remain unclean"). Male radicals, left-wing politicians, mystics, however, would insist that women are equal, just different, and that any woman could enter their ranks if she were willing to self-inflict a major wound every month ("you MUST give blood for the revolution"), recognize the preeminence of menstrual issues, or subordinate her selfness to all men in their Cycle of Enlightenment. Street guys would brag ("I'm a

Perhaps you think that this description of the biology of menstruation sounds accurate and objective. Not according to Martin, who contrasts it with accounts of the shedding of the lining of the stomach, a more neutral bodily location shared by women and men. When it comes to stomachs, medical texts represent the process of shedding as a process of renewal, not of degeneration. Couldn't menstruation be represented just as legitimately in this way, too? The case is even stronger when Martin compares descriptions of menstruation with passages describing male sexual processes. Such passages are celebratory, gushing (pardon the pun) over the wonder of ejaculation. But there is no reason, except for the ideology of male bodily supremacy, that female bleeding should appear as degenerative whereas male three pad man") or answer praise from a buddy ("Man, you lookin' good!") by giving high fives and saying, "Yeah, man, I'm on the rag!" TV shows would treat the subject at length. ("Happy Days": Richie and Potsie try to convince Fonzie that he is still "The Fonz," though he has missed two periods in a row.) So would newspapers. (SHARK SCARE THREATENS MENSTRUATING MEN. JUDGE CITES MONTHLY STRESS IN PARDONING RAPIST.) And movies. (Newman and Redford in "Blood Brothers"!) Men would convince women that intercourse was more pleasurable at "that time of the month." Lesbians would be said to fear blood and therefore life itself—though probably only because they needed a good menstruating man. Of course, male intellectuals would offer the most moral and logical arguments. How could a woman master any discipline that demanded a sense of time, space, mathematics, or measurement, for instance, without that in-built gift for measuring the cycles of the moon and planets—and thus for measuring anything at all? In the rarefied fields of philosophy and religion, could women compensate for missing the rhythm of the universe? Or for their lack of symbolic death-and-resurrection every month? Liberal males in every field would try to be kind: the fact that "these people" have no gift for measuring life or connecting to the universe, the liberals would explain, should be punishment enough. And how would women be trained to react? One can imagine traditional women agreeing to all arguments with a staunch and smiling masochism. ("The ERA would force housewives to wound themselves every month": Phyllis Schlafly. "Your husband's blood is as sacred as that of Jesus—and so sexy, too!": Marabel Morgan.) Reformers and Queen Bees would try to imitate men, and pretend to have a monthly cycle. All feminists would explain endlessly that men, too, needed to be liberated from the false idea of Martian aggressiveness, just as women needed to escape the bonds of menses envy. Radical feminist would add that the oppression of the nonmenstrual was the pattern for all other oppressions ("Vampires were our first freedom fighters!") Cultural feminists would develop a bloodless imagery in art and literature. Socialist feminists would insist that only under capitalism would men be able to monopolize menstrual blood. . . . In fact, if men could menstruate, the power justifications could probably go on forever. If we let them.

ejaculate seems glorious. The truth is that a large proportion of male ejaculate is shredded cellular material (Martin 1992, 51). Martin quotes a medical explanation of spermatogenesis, which makes the point quite well.

> The mechanisms which guide the *remarkable* cellular transformation from spermatid to mature sperm remain uncertain. . . . Perhaps the most *amazing* characteristic of spermatogenesis is its *sheer magnitude:* the normal human male may manufacture several hundred million sperm per day. (Martin 1992, 48, emphasis in original)

In another article, Martin appraises the imagery of eggs and sperm. She writes that where once the gendered metaphors were of passive eggs invaded by active sperm, by the 1980s, scientific and medical texts were offering a more interactive view, but one that nevertheless preserved the idea of the sperm as the active party, the one that penetrates and fertilizes. In the more contemporary version, however, the egg is not passive matter waiting to be chosen by the active sperm, but a "female aggressor who 'captures and tethers' the sperm...rather like a spider lying in wait in her web" (Martin 1997, 1992). This image resonates with the backlash against feminist politics that emerged in the 1980s (see Box 2–1).

Martin concludes that we must pay attention to such hidden metaphors and biased attitudes in matters that claim to be objective and scientific. If we fail to become aware of the cultural imagery that shapes the scientific discourses about bodies, such discourses retain the power to make our social conventions about gender seem natural. If we become aware of these metaphors and their implications, we rob them of their power (Martin 1992, 1997).

HOW MANY GENDERS ARE THERE? THE EVIDENCE FROM OTHER CULTURES

Recall Lorber's distinction between sex and gender (2005). Sex is "a complex interplay of genes, hormones, environment, and behavior with loopback effects between bodies and society," whereas gender is "a social status, a legal designation, and a personal identity." We have seen how in everyday life, sex is not as straightforward and as clearly distinct from gender as it has been made out to be. Ancient and medieval naturalists and physicians looked at male and female bodies and saw them as a hierarchy of more and less perfect expressions of the same (male) anatomy. Modern observers looked on the same male and female bodies and saw that there were fundamental differences between them. This is not to deny the materiality of bodies. Sexed bodies are not simply what we *think* they are. Certainly, medieval bodies were not actually different from modern bodies. But to explain, we invoke a somewhat different proposition from sociology.

In the 1920s, Chicago School sociologist W. I. Thomas wrote what came to be known as the "Thomas theorem": If men [and women] believe things to be real, they are real in their consequences (Thomas 1928, 571–72). Using the Thomas theorem to explain the science of sex we might say, "If we believe men and women are biologically different, then we build social institutions and practices that embed and honor this belief." The consequences are that such institutions and practices create a world organized around gendered differences. In this way, embodied sex grows from our beliefs about masculinity and femininity. History shows that maleness and femaleness, the bodily expressions of gender, are socially malleable. Part of what we see grows from our expectations about what exists, and part of what we see is the consequence of acting on those expectations, acting as *if* gender differences were real. As socially competent members of our own society, we see bodies through the cultural lenses of sex and gender, and we shape actual bodies to our expectations (Connell 1999).

Just as the historical record demonstrates the socially malleable character of sex and gender, so too does the cross-cultural evidence. Many cultures recognize multiple gender categories that are different from those of modern Western culture. One alternative to our two-gender system is the third genders or "women-men" of some First Nation societies.

Named *berdaches* by the anthropologists who first studied them, or "two-spirit" peoples in some of their own languages, such "third genders" often were socially distinct from their fully male and fully female kin.

In many First Nation societies, two-spirit women-men took up occupations designated as women's, dressed as women, and had sexual relations with men. A possible fourth category was that of "men-women," biological females who lived as men, hunted, took up men's work, fought in wars with the men of the tribe, and married women (Lang 1998; Roughgarden 2004). As young girls they showed an interest in learning boys' roles and avoided girls' tasks. In our society we might label these children "tomboys" and perhaps guide them to take up more feminine pursuits. In some First Nation societies, adults accepted their children's choice and taught such girls the skills boys learned. In some cases, a family with no sons might select one of their daughters and encourage her to be "like a man." As adults, cross-gender females hunted, trapped, cultivated crops, and fought in wars.

In these societies, native gender categories did not equate gender with biological sex or sexual identity. A woman who married a cross-gendered woman was not considered homosexual or cross-gender herself. If the relationship ended in divorce, the ex-wife could enter into any number of possible arrangements, including heterosexual marriage (Blackwood 1984, 30).

Blackwood connects the possibilities for third-sex and fourth-sex status to the political and economic context within which these genders appeared. For example, prior to contact with Europeans, several First Nation people in western North America, were egalitarian subsistence societies. In these communities, there was no accumulation of wealth or private wealth-holding. The sexual division of labor was not highly developed, and all members of the group contributed to production. Both men's and women's tasks were valued by the wider community and men and women often worked at the same or similar tasks. Note, by the way, how this minimal gender division of labor is similar to that of peasant-based European societies and rural colonial American societies before the advent of capitalism.

Contact with the westward-moving European Americans brought catastrophic changes to many First Nation societies. By introducing guns, horses, and the fur trade to the First Nation tribes, the European settlers disrupted First Nation society. By the early nineteenth century, some First Nation men were able to accumulate wealth through trade in hides. Such trade required that they acquire additional wives who could handle the tanning and preparation of the hides for trade. As women lost control over production and men gained authority over women's labor, women's status declined, and their autonomy was limited. In addition, First Nation men were killed in significant numbers due to the constant state of war with whites. Under these circumstances, the First Nation communities were less tolerant of losing women's reproductive abilities to cross-gendering. Finally, Western sexual ideologies of female inferiority and heterosexuality replaced First Nation beliefs. Cross-gender women were harassed, accused of not being *real* men, and not equipped to satisfy a wife. In these later developments, gender roles and sexuality were associated with an ideology and a practice of male dominance (Blackwood 1984).

Many other cultures have institutionalized alternative genders. One well-known example is that of the hijras of India, studied by Serena Nanda. The common view in India is that hijras are neither men nor women, nor are they seen as homosexuals. The key defining characteristic of this group is the absence of male external genitalia (often a result of elective surgery) or "imperfect genitals" (ambiguous genitalia at birth). Culturally hijras are "not-men" and view themselves as "man minus maleness" (Nanda 1990). Hijras also claim an identity as "man plus woman." They dress as women when they perform on ritual occasions such as weddings, or beg, engage in prostitution, and visit the temple of their goddess Bahuchara. They wear their hair long, pluck out their facial hair, and adopt what they claim is "female" behavior.

Some hijras work as electricians or on construction—men's jobs—but they are more likely to take jobs that are held by both men and women, as household servants and cooks. They take feminine names and sometimes demand to be counted as women in the census (Nanda 1990, 16–17). Despite their naming practices and their occasional demand to be counted as women, hijras see themselves and are seen by others as "not-women," as well as "not-men." Their performances as women are over-the-top parodies of femininity, outrageous practices that no ordinary woman would dare to enact. Hijras swear and threaten others, expose their genitals, smoke, and dance in public. No "decent" Hindu woman would behave in these ways.

In contrast to the West, where intersexed children are often subjected to "normalizing" surgeries, intersex children in India may be categorized as "born hijras." However, many if not most hijras are chromosomal and gonadal males who have elected as adults to be surgically emasculated. These surgically altered individuals are known as "made hijras."

As discussed in the final section of this chapter, many Westerners are uncomfortable with such in-between sexual and gender categories, and try to resolve such ambiguities. However, Indian culture has a long tradition of accommodating alternative sexes and genders. For example, the Hindu deity Shiva combines both male and female characteristics, and Vishnu and Krishna are deities who are sexually ambiguous. Telling the story of her childhood, Salima, a "real" hijra, treats her status matter-of-factly and as a real third sex (Nanda 1990, 99):

> My parents felt sad about my birth, but they realized it was their fate to have me born to them. They were looking forward to my birth—I was the eldest child—and they were sad that I was born "neither here nor there." From my birth, my organ was very small. My mother felt, as I grew up, naturally it will grow also. But it didn't, so she tried taking me to doctors and all that. But the doctors said, "No, it won't grow, your child is not a man and not a woman, this is God's gift." I am a real hijra, not like those converts—those men who have the operation.

Other examples of alternative sexes and genders can be found around the world. In Islamic Oman on the Saudi Arabian peninsula, there is a group of cross-gender behaving "not-men," known as Xanith. Xanith retain the rights of men—for example, they have the right to worship in the mosque with men and to move about outside freely during the day (but not at night)—but they do women's work and are judged according to feminine standards of beauty. Xanith eat and socialize with women. Only they, but not other men, may view brides on their wedding nights.

In Omani society, manliness rests on men's active, penetrating role in sexual intercourse. Xanith, like women in that society, are passive receivers. However, there are ways in which Xanith are neither women nor men. Their clothing is a mixture of men's and women's styles. Unlike most Muslim women in Oman, they are often prostitutes. Xanith are not men, but they are not women either. They have some of the privileges of men, some of the restrictions of women, and their own particular place in society (Nanda 1990, 130–31).

The historical and cross-cultural research shows that sex and gender are not static. Our own fixed and universalistic sex categories are challenged by this evidence of the fluidity of sex and gender. Today the cultural and ideological conviction that sex is an unchanging bedrock of bodily constitution linked to gender in determinate ways is being shaken by new claims and new evidence.

SEXUALITY AND SEXUAL ORIENTATION: GENDERING DESIRE

The contrasts in the belief that gender is rooted in biological sex (essentialism) and the belief that gender is a product of social relationships (social constructionism) also shapes debates about the foundations of sexuality. Among those on the side of biology are sociobiologists and evolutionary psychologists who directly connect Darwinian processes of natural selection—a process favoring those organisms that adapt to assure species survival—with specific sexual and gendered practices. For example, some evolutionary psychologists and sociobiologists have argued that rape may be a male adaptation assuring that humans will reproduce successfully (see chapter 4). They contend that particular gendered arrangements between the sexes (male dominance, female passivity) and particular gendered sexualities (heterosexual desire, male competitiveness for women) are naturally selected, genetically programmed adaptive survival mechanisms benefiting the human race. Feminists, as well as most biologists, disagree with this conflation of gender power relations with Darwin's theory of natural selection, but some feminists have also used biologically-based logic to make their own case, as when they proclaim men naturally aggressive and women naturally peaceful. On the other side are those who claim new and newly valued identities that are beginning to cross the once seemingly impermeable biological divide between male and female sex and sexuality.

At first inspired by the civil rights movement of the 1960s, gays, lesbians, transsexuals, intersexuals, and queers have "come out" publicly to question long-standing beliefs in the determinate male–female sexual story and in the forms of properly sexual bodies. Their questions are challenges to the power relations underpinning these beliefs (Lancaster 2003). Chapter 4 explores the many issues surrounding gender and sexuality. Here we focus on some of the ways that scholars have advanced the claim that sexuality is structured socially, not by nature.

Of course the genetic, hormonal, and physiological makeup of bodies is a material reality that cannot be willed away. What then does it mean to claim that sexuality—the array of bodily responses that seem to originate in the deepest, nonconscious part of ourselves and are experienced as "coming from within"(Simon 1996,138)—are, in some measure, social constructions? How do social scientists reconcile the physicality of sexuality with its social forms? One line of thinking tries to marry biology and society. A second uses the metaphor of scripting to explain gendered sexuality. A third tries to show how sexed bodies are socially produced. A fourth explores the changing histories of sexuality.

The Basis of Sexuality Is Not "Either–Or" But "Both–And"

Dualist thinking demands that you are either male or female and that traits are either biologically given or culturally constructed. But some social scientists encourage "both–and" ways of thought. To anthropologist Clifford Geertz, humans are "incomplete or unfinished animals who complete or finish ourselves through culture" (quoted in Lancaster 2003, 204). Geertz means that sexuality is part of the animal world and we are certainly members of that world. But we take the raw material of animal sexuality and craft it into something uniquely human through our various cultures. Sociologists Pepper Schwartz and Virginia Rutter (1998, 22) make a similar point. They write, "Although people tend to think of sex as primarily a biological function—tab B goes into slot A—biology is only one part of the context of desire. Such sociological factors as family relationships and social structure also influence sex. A complex mix of anatomy, hormones, and the brain provides the basic outline for the range of acts and desires possible, but biology is neither where sexuality begins nor where it ends."

Schwartz and Rutter (1998) describe several experimental studies that show how social and biological processes together produce sexual desire. In one experiment men were connected to a phony heartbeat monitor and told that the heartbeat "surges" they heard when viewing photos of women models would indicate their preference for one photograph over the others. In fact, the fake heartbeats they heard were randomly produced by the experimenters. Nonetheless, the men chose the woman based on hearing what they believed was their own speeding heartbeat. In a second experiment, men were asked to cross either a stable or unstable bridge where an attractive researcher on the other side spoke with the men and gave them her phone number. In this experiment the men confounded their anxiety on crossing an unstable bridge with the sexual arousal caused by meeting a desirable person, measured by the numbers of men who phoned the woman later. In this experiment, anxiety—the physiological response—was interpreted as sexual desire.

A third study found that testosterone levels among a group of homosexual men and a group of military men were similarly low. What common situation influenced testosterone levels among men traditionally reputed to be lower and higher on indexes of "masculinity"? The researchers suggested the common denominator was stress and anxiety—the impact on a gay man of life in a straight world, on a military man of constant direction from superiors—that depressed hormone levels. A stressful social situation produced a biological response. Geertz, Schwartz and Rutter, and the researchers who conceived of the experimental research believe biology is implicated in the bodily sensations that we call "desire." However they also believe that the social context in which we feel desire organizes and gives meaning to these sensations (Schwartz and Rutter 1998, 25).

Sexuality Is Socially Scripted

In 1973, sociologists John Gagnon and William Simon proposed that sexuality was governed by sexual "scripts" derived from socially learned gender roles. This idea was at odds with the popular notion that sexuality was innate, inborn, and unsocial. It also contradicted the Freudian concept of the *id*, the source of libido or sexual energy. According to Freud, the id—the primitive, irrational, and ungovernable part of the mind—functioned on the basis of the "pleasure principle" and in opposition to the "reality principle," which he believed was the basis of society and civilization. Becoming a member of society in Freud's view entailed reigning in and repressing sexuality. Gagnon and Simon did not treat sexuality as a drive that needed containment and repression. Quite the contrary, they envisioned sexuality as the outcome of learning a sexual "vocabulary of motives" in adolescence, when young people are socially defined as potential sexual actors. Hormonal changes may be taking place at the time, but newly sexualized actors must learn the meaning of their feelings and internal states, the specifically sexual acts they must deploy, the situations in which sexuality is expected and appropriate, the limits and boundaries of sexual responses, and the like.

> Without the proper elements of a script that defines the situation, names the actors and plots the behavior, nothing sexual is likely to happen…[C]ombining such elements as desire, privacy and physically attractive person of the appropriate sex, the probability of something happening will, under normal circumstances, remain exceedingly small until either one or both actors organize these behaviours into an appropriate script. (Gagnon and Simon 1973, quoted in Jackson and Stevi 1996, 71)

Gagnon and Simon believed that we must learn to recognize sexual feelings and desires and learn how to translate them into socially validated actions. To whom are we supposed to be attracted? What sexual cues must we learn and interpret? Where and when are we supposed to have sex? When they developed their theory of sexual scripts several decades ago, boys and girls were perhaps learning to be sexual differently from what and how they learn to be sexual today. Then, girls' scripts centered on romantic love; boys' scripts on sexual interest and getting over on girls. The sexual scripts Simon and Gagnon encountered have probably changed since that time. Do girls still learn to be romantic about sex? Do boys still learn that men are expected to be sexually predatory? What are today's ruling sexual scripts?

Bodies Are Produced Within Society

A third way of thinking about the social production of sexuality holds that specific bodies are produced through what sociologist Robert Connell calls "body-reflexive practices." In Connell's view, the physical body is enmeshed in a social world of practices and activities that have physical outcomes regarding reproduction, sexuality, and masculinity or femininity. He views bodies as the *sites* or *arenas* of social practice, in which "bodies are brought into social processes" (Connell 2002, 10), rather than, as the "both–and" theorists see it, the biological starting points or underpinning of that practice. Bodies are materially transformed through social practices.

Think about the ways that class transforms bodies. Working-class men have higher accident rates and fatal injuries; working-class women have higher rates of repetitive strain injuries. Race ethnicity transforms bodies. African American men and women have increased incidence of high blood pressure, a condition linked by medical research to the effects on black people of living in a racist society (see chapter 9). Gender also transforms bodies. Sexually, steroids and diet pills shape bodies. Genital surgeries and cosmetic surgeries shape bodies. Some of us sit like men, taking up the space around us; others sit like women, with arms folded and legs crossed. We informally learn gestures and nonverbal forms of communication—the hip-swaying walk, the swagger—that become our sometimes unconscious repertoires of gendered and sexualized bodily practice. Formal learning also marks our bodies, as we learn to build or to knit, to play some sports and not others, to do math or to type, even to engage in sex. In regard to the last item, scan the magazine racks while you are waiting on line in the grocery store and note the many articles on how to "please your man" or enjoy "the best sex ever."

Box 2–2 ANDREA DWORKIN, "BIOLOGICAL SUPERIORITY: THE
WORLD'S MOST DANGEROUS AND DEADLY IDEA"

Hisses. Women shouting at me: slut, bisexual, she fucks men. And before I had spoken, I had been trembling, more afraid to speak than I had ever been. And, in a room of 200 sister lesbians, as angry as I have ever been. "Are you a bisexual?" some woman screamed over the pandemonium, the hisses and shouts merging into a raging noise. "I'm a Jew," I answered; then, a pause, "and a lesbian and a woman." And a coward. Jew was enough. In that room, Jew was what mattered . . .

The event was a panel on "Lesbianism as a Personal Politic" that took place in New York City, Lesbian Pride Week, 1977. A self-proclaimed lesbian separatist had spoken. Amidst the generally accurate description of male crimes against women came this ideological rot, articulated of late with increasing frequency in feminist circles: women and men are distinct species or races (the words are used interchangeably); men are biologically inferior to women; male violence is a biological inevitability; to eliminate it, one must eliminate the species/race itself (means stated on this particular evening developing parthenogenesis as a viable reproductive reality); in eliminating the bio-logically inferior species/race Man, the new *Ubermensch* Woman . . . will have the earthly dominion that is her true biological destiny . . .

In the audience I saw women I like or love, women not strangers to me, women who are good not because of biology but because they care about being good, swept along in a sea of affirmation. I spoke out because those women had applauded. I spoke out too because I am a Jew who has studied Nazi Germany, and I know that many Germans who followed Hitler also cared about being good, but found it easier to be good by biological definition than by act. . . . So I spoke, afraid. I said that I would not be associated with a movement that advocated the most pernicious ideology on the face of the earth. It was this very ideology of biological determinism that had licensed the slaughter and/or enslavement of virtually any group one could name, including women by men. ("Use

Sexuality is learned. Sexual arousal and sexual "turn-offs" are bodily responses mediated by social relationships. Our sexed bodies are produced in society and often announce to society our gendered identities and our sexual selves (Connell 2000, 27).

Connell's biography of the iron man athlete, Steve, illustrates the interplay between bodies and social processes. In childhood and adolescence Steve was physically big and did well in sports. By the age of 13, he began to specialize in swimming. In adulthood, Steve's day centered on maintaining his body to compete. The irony of Steve's life, writes Connell, is that because "the business of winning has consumed his life," he cannot live the kind of ideally masculine life of a young, handsome bachelor. His training regimen requires that he go to bed early, exercise daily, avoid drink, and even avoid sex. Because of his athletic career, he has become socially isolated, uninvolved in the wider world, unable to maintain relation-ships with women, and without inner direction. Connell writes that "hegemonic masculinity their own poison against them," one woman screamed.) Anywhere one looked it was this philosophy that justified atrocity...

The newest variations on this distressingly ancient theme centre on hormones and DNA: men are biologically aggressive; their fetal brains are awash in androgen and their DNA, in order to perpetuate itself, hurls them into murder and rape; in women, pacifism is hormonal and addiction to birth is molecular...

Recently, more and more feminists have been advocating social, spiritual, and mythological models that are female-supremacist and/or matriarchal. To me, this advocacy signifies a basic conformity to the tenets of biological determinism that underpin the male social system. Pulled toward an ideology based on the moral and social significance of a distinct female biology because of its emotional and philosophical familiarity, drawn to the spiritual dignity inherent in a "female principle" (essentially as defined by men), of course unable to abandon by will or impulse a lifelong and centuries-old commitment to childbearing as the female creative act, women have increasingly tried to transform the very ideology that has enslaved us into a dynamic, religious, psychologically compelling celebration of female biological potential. This attempted transformation may have survival value—that is, the worship of our procreative capacity as power may temporarily stay the male-supremacist hand that cradles the test tube. But the price we pay is that we become carriers of the disease we must cure. It is no accident that some female supremacists now believe men to be a distinct and inferior species or race. Wherever power is accessible or bodily integrity honored on the basis of biological attribute, systematized cruelty permeates the society and murder and mutilation will contaminate it. We will not be different.

[G]enocide begins, however improbably, in the conviction that classes of biological distinction indisputably sanction social and political discrimination. We, who have been devastated by the concrete consequences of this idea, still want to put our faith in it. Nothing offers more proof—sad, irrefutable proof—that we are more like men than either they or we care to believe.

[the dominant and idealized form of masculinity in contemporary Western culture] appropriates Steve's body and gives it a social definition" (Connell 2000, 69–85). In other words, Steve's bodily practices, propelled by parents, coaches, fans, and his own ambitions, have created a person who looks the part of the handsome, virile, charismatic athlete, but whose life has been stolen by these very practices.

Erotic Relations Are Historical Relations

The fact that sexuality has changed and evolved historically—that it is not universal and fixed—removes bodies from the biological realm and places them firmly in the social realm. Would it surprise you to know that heterosexuality and homosexuality and the identities "heterosexual" and "homosexual" were invented in the late nineteenth century by doctors and scientists who created the science of sexology? Before that time people engaged in heterosexual and homosexual acts, but their acts did not adhere to them as identities. Sometime in the late nineteenth century, however, a new group of people was identified, people interested in sex only for pleasure. These people were first called heterosexuals to distinguish them from that generation's "normals," people who reputedly only used sex for procreation. Only later did heterosexuality become the "natural" norm, to contrast with (equally newly invented) homosexual identities. John D'Emilio (1983) situates this sexual history within the wider political economy of industrializing America. According to D'Emilio, capitalist industrialization created the conditions that allowed some men and women to leave their families and to organize their personal lives around erotic or emotional attractions, whether in relation to the other sex or to their own sex. As the rural economy declined and wage labor spread in nineteenth-century America, production brought people together around factories and offices, where family oversight and family ties were less controlling. Ideologically, heterosexual and homosexual expression came to be understood as a way to pursue intimacy, promote happiness, and experience pleasure, contributing to the release of sexuality from the imperative to procreate. In these ways the growth of cities as the locations of industry made possible transformations of sexuality, its emergence as a central feature of individual identity, the formation of urban communities of lesbians and gays, and a politics based on sexual identity (D'Emilio 1983, 104). In other words, the socioeconomic organization of society—not genes, not brains—created the conditions for living heterosexual and gay or lesbian lives.

Sexuality Is Racialized, Race Is Sexualized

Think about this: Racial boundaries are sexual boundaries; race and sex are integrally bound together. As more fully discussed in chapter 4, sexual stereotypes, sexual fears, and sexual identities are central components of race relations. Racial ethnic differences serve to heighten or dampen sexual desire, to place some groups off limits sexually, or to fuel secret longings and underground connections for others (Nagel 2003). Colonialism and slavery were the contexts within which the bodies of subjugated peoples were controlled, exploited, and dominated. The racial past of colonialism and slavery has contributed to sexual images of black women as promiscuous and black men as dangerous (Davis 1983). In fact most sexual danger comes from white men's violence against black women or the long history of lynching and violence against black men for presumed interest in white women.

Constructing social worlds on the idea of essential differences between groups is dangerous business. We remain unaware of the intersecting inequalities and divisions that together construct our commonsense understandings and everyday practices at our peril, as Andrea Dworkin points out (see Box 2–2).

INTERSEX

Each year about seventeen ambiguously sexed infants are born for every 1,000 births (see Table 2-1). What is the social place of intersexed individuals in a two-sex world? In recent years, a growing number of intersexed adults have "come out" to speak about their experience. What has been the lived experience of intersexuality in the century since the condition was named? In the past decade, many intersex adults and their supporters have joined with other activists to challenge the two-sex model of sexuality. What accounts for the new politics of intersex and what does that politics suggest about the future?

Embodiment and Intersexuality

The National Institutes of Health divides intersex into four categories (U.S. National Library of Health and National Institutes of Health 2006):

- *XX intersex* (formerly female pseudo-hermaphroditism). A person with the chromosomes and ovaries of a woman, but with external genitals that appear male, usually resulting from exposure of a female fetus to excess male hormones before birth or from CAH as noted earlier. The person has a normal uterus and Fallopian tubes, but the labia fuse and the clitoris is large and penis-like.
- *XY intersex* (formerly male pseudo-hermaphroditism). A person with XY chromosomes, but with ambiguous, or clearly female external genitals. Internally, testes may be normal, malformed, or absent. In one type of the condition 5-alpha-reductase deficiency, more widely known because of the best-selling novel *Middlesex* (Eugenides 2002), infants *appear* female until puberty, when their bodies are virilized. Androgen insensitivity syndrome (AIS) or testicular feminization is a condition in which a person has XY chromosomes, but the receptors to male hormones do not function and the genitals of these individuals appear female.
- *True gonadal intersex*. A person has both ovarian and testicular tissue in one or both gonads. In most people with true gonadal intersex, the underlying cause is unknown, although in some animal studies it has been linked to exposure to common agricultural pesticides. Dreger (1998) suggests that environmental pollutants that mimic estrogen are driving an increase in intersex births. Another suspected cause of rising rates of intersex births is in vitro fertilization in which an XX and XY embryo merge (Dreger 1998).
- *Complex or undetermined intersex.* Many chromosome configurations other than simple XX or XY can result in ambiguous sex development. These include XO (only one X chromosome), and XXY, XXX—both cases have an extra sex chromosome, either an X or a Y.

What is the social relevance of these physical states? Recall Geertz's statement that we are "incomplete or unfinished animals who complete or finish ourselves through culture." The physical condition of most infants born intersexed is not life-threatening, or even unhealthy. But the intersexed infant will be completed—that is, turned into an "intersexual"—in society. In this sense, the categories just described are not in any meaningful sense descriptions of intersex conditions. They are the raw material from which society constructs the meanings and practices surrounding people identified as intersexed.

In contemporary Western societies, our bodies have become cultural projects and extensions of our selves. We act on our bodies to remake our selves through cosmetic surgery, dieting, nutrition, transplants, workouts, and a host of other practices. In many respects the project to transform ambiguously sexed infants and children into members of one or the other "natural" sex, described later, is no different from these other cultural projects of embodiment. The project to remake intersexed children into "real" girls and boys has both social and historical dimensions comparable to the ways we complete ourselves by dieting, working out, and other transformative projects. Like these other projects, it is a product of historically specific, socially constructed, and institutionalized networks and practices around binary sex difference. There is, however, one important difference between other projects of the self and the project to remake ambiguously sexed infants' and children's bodies into acceptably sexed bodies. The project to eliminate intersex is almost always chosen *for* intersexed individuals, not *by* them. That vital difference raises issues that bring these bodies clearly into the realms of politics and ethics.

We begin with a look at how obstetricians are counseled by their professional association to cope with an intersex birth. The American Academy of Pediatrics (2000) calls the birth of a child with ambiguous genitals a "social emergency" and recommends that doctors immediately and carefully explain to parents that the condition is correctible and their children can become boys or girls, "as appropriate."

> Because words spoken in the delivery room may have a lasting impact on parents and their relationship with their infant, it is important that no attempt be made to suggest a diagnosis or offer a gender assignment.
>
> The infant should be referred to as "your baby" or "your child"—not "it," "he," or "she." It is helpful to examine the child in the presence of the parents to demonstrate the precise abnormalities of genital development, emphasizing that the genitalia of both sexes develop from the same primordial fetal structures, that both incomplete development or overdevelopment of the external genitalia can occur, and that *the abnormal appearance can be corrected and the child raised as a boy or a girl as appropriate*. (American Academy of Pediatrics 2000,138 emphasis added)

Although today it is less routine for intersex infants to undergo surgical and hormonal sex reassignment, there are still many physicians and parents who are moved to act out of the fear that intersexed children are so psychologically at risk and so sexually grotesque that anything that helps to normalize them is worth the cost. This attitude has justified what Dreger (1998) has called "monster ethics," which accepts treatment of intersex in ways that would be considered unethical under any other circumstances: lying to patients, performing risky procedures without follow-up, and failing to obtain informed consent.

The medicalized management of intersexuality rests on cultural beliefs that living within the normative sex and gender categories is the best life strategy. Many, if not most surgeries and hormonal treatments of intersex infants have been performed for cosmetic purposes rather than to correct life- or health-threatening medical conditions. How genitals and secondary sex characteristics will look to others takes primacy over assuring the potential of genitalia for pleasure or even for reproduction (Kessler 1990).

For many years—and to some extent still today—if a baby is born with a "micro-penis" (less than 1.5 centimeters long and 0.7 centimeters wide) it is a candidate for sex reassignment surgery. Doctors have reasoned that such a penis is too small to allow the child to urinate standing up (a condition they believe could lead to psychologically damaging ridicule once the child is in school) and too short to penetrate a vagina during sexual intercourse. Similarly, babies born with large clitorises have also been surgically altered to make their sex organs look right, a treatment that Westerners severely criticize when it is named female genital mutilation (FGM) and occurs in third-world countries. Wherever it is done, excision of the clitoris severely limits a woman's ability to experience orgasm. Remaking a boy's penis into a vagina does away with that child's ability to have children. Critics call these surgeries "social surgeries," akin to facelifts and nose jobs. Will the girl look right to others? Will the boy perform adequately during sexual intercourse?

A Brief History of Intersex

The physical facts of intersexed bodies do not translate directly into the identity of intersexual. The concept of ambiguously sexed bodies can only exist if there is a companion concept of normally sexed bodies. When, where, and how did the *social* category, intersexual, emerge? Around the turn of the last century, as this chapter has shown, bodies came under the scrutiny of men of science and medicine, who helped to create sex as a new object of study and to identify sexuality (homo or hetero) as a fundamental personal identity. Experts' strong belief in a two-sex system brought intersexuality into view as a problem that called for medical intervention. Before this time, most intersexuals lived average lives, generally free from public attention, medical intervention, or state oversight. By the late nineteenth century, however, gynecological medicine and state-mandated medical supervision of soldiers and prostitutes in wartime revealed that there were many nonstandard sexual anatomies. How was it possible to categorize people who did not fit comfortably into the categories of male or female? Doctors named the variations they discovered hermaphroditism (after the Greek god Hermaphroditus) and pseudo-hermaphroditism, and designated these as pathological abnormalities. (Contemporary nomenclature to some extent continues the pathological designation by referring to these conditions as "*disorders* of sex development.") The discovery of intersexual bodies did not prompt experts to rethink the two-sex system. Instead they sought to uphold it by remaking individuals with healthy but nonconforming bodies into 100 percent men and women.

By the 1920s, experts were beginning to use surgery to bring bodies into line with their beliefs in a two-sex system. Their project was delayed during the years of depression and war, but was resurrected in the 1950s at Johns Hopkins University, where an interdisciplinary team of surgeons, endocrinologists, and psychologists developed an "optimum gender of rearing model" to eliminate intersexuality. Their goal was to work with a child's body, mind, and upbringing to create a standard, heterosexual gender identity.

Why heterosexual? In the 1950s many feared the consequences of living outside normative sexual boundaries. Vice squads regularly raided gay and lesbian bars and hangouts. Senator Joseph McCarthy paired his crusade against Communists in the government and in Hollywood with the persecution of gays. He charged that there was a "homosexual underground" that was "abetting the Communist conspiracy," and the national media regularly supported his charges with stories on the "pervert peril." As a consequence, businessmen and heads of government agencies, afraid of being accused of protecting "subversives," began to dismiss homosexuals from their jobs (Reeves 1997). However, more than political fear drove the project to eliminate intersex. Doctors working with intersex infants believed that such babies were doomed to a life of misery if they did not have surgery. In this postwar world in which nuclear families were the norm and the ideal, it is no wonder that an intersex baby would precipitate a crisis.

Harvard-trained psychologist John Money provided theoretical support for the project. Money believed that when it came to sex and sexuality, society trumped biology. He was certain of the infinite malleability of infants' sexed bodies and minds. The case that supported his ideas, but ultimately produced serious challenges to his project, was the famous case of John/Joan. In 1965, at the age of eight months, John (who came forward in the 1990s as David Reimer) was the victim of a botched circumcision that destroyed his penis. Money advised David's parents to make him a girl through surgery and hormonal treatments, a course of action Money had been advising for children born intersexed. Money continued to see David each year, and claimed that the boy, now called Brenda, had developed a successful feminine gender identity. Word of Money's success was broadcast widely among sex researchers. The case of John/Joan became the "hallmark case" for legitimizing sex reassignment for newborns with ambiguous genitalia around the globe (Colapinto 1997). However, as you will learn here, David Reimer later revealed that his childhood had been miserable and that the primary architect of his misery was John Money. As a teen, Reimer underwent surgery to restore his penis, later married, and adopted children. In his thirties he committed suicide.

Intersex as Lived Reality

The ways that intersexuality was a social invention should now be clear. Rather than a physiological problem demanding active intervention as, for example, an infant born with a serious heart defect would require, intersex was *constructed* as a medical and social problem by a particular group of medical experts at a particular historical moment and in a particular socio-historical context. What has been the impact of the medicalization of intersex on the generation of children born in the second half of the twentieth century and raised in the shadow of Money's optimum gender of rearing model? Based on her interviews with thirty-seven intersexed adults between 1997 and 1998, Sharon Preves (2005, 9) summarized what they told her of their childhood struggles.

> Interview after interview, participants shared stories of feeling scrutinized and sexualized by medical professionals, of being treated as oddities and freaks, of lacking control over their own bodies, and of the resulting shame and secrecy of such experiences. They also spoke of arduous battles to gain accurate information about their bodies and attempts to find other intersexuals—aiming to piece together a puzzle whose solution was sure to hold the key to identity.

The stories Preves heard also show that a confluence of events and opportunities helped intersex adults reinterpret their biographies, make contact with others like themselves, and build networks, support groups, and political associations that have become the basis of the intersex rights movement. In the process, participants in the movement have joined feminists, queers, and transsexuals in posing compelling challenges to the two-sex system.

Preves's study chronicles the "careers" as intersexuals of the study's participants. Their collective story is the story of their advance from being "objects" of other people's design and practice to becoming autonomous individuals and collective actors determined to challenge and change the social conditions that once entrapped them.

Study participants begin their stories with accounts that describe their "prehistory," a name we might give to the time in their lives when they were more acted on than actors, a period when others determined their fates. During this time, doctors regularly lied to patients about their condition, their surgeries, and their ongoing treatment and withheld vital information from their parents and guardians. Doctors' intentions were good—to save patients from the shame and pain that they believed would be the fate of their patients if they were not "fixed." However, normalizing surgeries and body-changing hormone treatments created, rather than alleviated, the children's feelings of difference and of their own freakishness. Despite the treatments—many say because of them—participants felt isolated, shamed, stigmatized, and abused, but also powerless to bring the treatment to an end. They looked back on childhoods filled with visits to doctors, group medical exams, hospitalizations, and surgeries as invasions of their bodies, over which they had no control. Here is how Gaby remembers her regular checkups:

> I was the local dog and pony show. "Come here. You wanna see something interesting?" Yeah, definitely medical traumatization. I probably went about once every three months up 'til a certain age. Then I went twice a year. The worst thing [about] being in a clinic is the dog and pony show. The worst thing is being put in a prone position, half-naked, [and] told to spread your legs while five or six other people look in your crotch and probe. (Preves 2005, 67)

Making these treatments more traumatizing, no one—not parents, not doctors—told the children what was happening to them and why. At the age of nineteen, Carol went to the hospital for what she thought was a checkup and overheard staff discussing her surgery:

> [I said to the doctor] as he was leaving, "Excuse me, the nurse said I'm having surgery." And he said, "Yes, it'll be first thing in the morning." And I said, "For what?" And he said, "Don't worry, everything will be fine." And I said, "Why? Fine from what? Why am I having surgery?" And he said, "Well your condition has gonads that could have abnormal cell growth and we must remove them before it gets out of hand." And I said, "I have cancer, don't I?" And he said, "Oh, don't worry about it. Don't worry about it, you're just fine. No, no, no don't be silly. No, you don't have cancer. Don't worry." I said, "Well, then why do I have...?" "Don't worry about it, you're just fine." And I thought, "He's lying; I have cancer." Cause that was the best diagnosis I'd come up with yet. (Preves 2005, 68)

Lies and evasions by doctors about the reasons for this intense medical scrutiny were, ironically, carried out in the interest of "normalizing" intersex patients. Quite the contrary, this treatment sent the unmistakable message to the children that they were so horrifically different and so freakish, that no one, not even they, could know the cause. Childhood mysteries did not end when the children grew up. At the age of twenty-four, Flora's genetic counselor refused to tell her about her condition.

> [The geneticist] said, "I'm obliged to tell you that certain details of your condition have not been divulged to you, but I cannot tell you what they are because they would upset you too much." So she's telling us we don't know everything, but she can't tell us what it is because it's too horrible (Preves 2005, 75).

Imagine how you might respond to hearing such news.

The stories of intersexuals reveal a tragic history of people being subjected to all manner of medical and social abuse because their bodies do not fit the conventional images of our

Box 2–3 THE SUCCESSES OF ISNA

Since 1993, due to increased public education, tens of millions of people have learned about intersex. Thanks to the Internet, thousands of people with intersex have met others like them, in spite of having been told by their doctors they would never be able to do that; their conditions were supposedly so rare.

ISNA members have gone from picket lines to having a seat at the table in medical conferences. We give grand rounds presentations, help with medical school curricular development, and receive e-mails from physicians asking for our advice on how to handle intersex cases. Our website is recognized as *the* definitive source for all things intersex, and for being a life-saving porthole for thousands of people desperate for answers and directions to "their tribe." We have convinced hospitals around the world to examine their practices, to find out what has happened to former patients, and to be accountable for the sometimes-poor effects of good intentions.

Over a decade into the work of ISNA, medical professionals are less inclined to lie to patients and parents in intersex cases, are less likely to make openly homophobic or sexist remarks, and are more likely to admit uncertainty about the right course of action. A number of teams are engaged in active outcomes research, though opinions still differ about what outcomes should be sought; some think stable gender identity and heterosexuality are the objective; others suggest it should be lack of depression. What type of care an individual or family will receive now varies dramatically; what happens to a child with intersex today appears to depend not only on where she or he is born, but who happens to be on call when she or he is born.

ideas of what humans are supposed to be like. Real human bodies are variable. Our ideas about human bodies, however, demand that we all fit the model of belonging to one of two opposite sexes. It would seem that the obvious solution to finding that many people do not fit into one of the two "proper" slots is to question the slots themselves. Instead, as we have seen in these accounts about intersexuals, real people are forced to alter their physical bodies and their lives so that they fit into an idea about what it means to be human. Should we continue to surgically reconstruct real people? Or should we change our ideas about sex? Intersex activists have answered this last question with a resounding "yes." They are challenging dominant ideas about sex and demanding that we quit surgically altering intersexuals.

Intersex Activism Takes Off

The convergence of several factors set off the growing resistance to medical interventions for the purpose of maintaining gender polarity. The outcome has been to interpret gender polarity—not intersexuality itself—as pathological. In the 1990s, increasing publicity about sex reassignment surgeries that turned out to be failures accounted for growing public concern. The pivotal case was that of David Reimer. Despite Money's claim that the sex reassignment of Reimer had been successful, that claim was far from the truth. Reimer's childhood

But we're not done.

Even today, the goal of many leading teams treating intersex is still to make intersex disappear. Pediatric endocrinologist Maria New recommends Dexamethasone to women who may be carrying an XX child with CAH; these treatments do not alleviate CAH, it only makes the child's clitoris appear smaller (and, clinicians hope, makes the child less likely to grow up lesbian). Abortion is routinely offered to women who are likely pregnant with children with intersex conditions, including Klinefelter's Syndrome. Many surgeons maintain the paternalistic attitude that they should remove healthy testes from babies with AIS to "spare them the trauma later," thereby denying these girls the opportunity to have a natural puberty and to come to know themselves, in a sexual way, free from surgical scars. Many endocrinologists press unnecessary—sometimes devastating—"normalizing" hormone treatments on patients who are otherwise healthy. Finally, doctors continue constructing vaginas in infants and young children, despite arguments by many medical professionals that early vaginoplasties fail too often and are unnecessary to begin with.

By contrast, as in the women's rights movement, the civil rights movement, and the LGBT rights movements, the goal of intersex advocacy groups is to have people understand intersex conditions as human rights issues. ISNA maintains as its fundamental principle the principle also fundamental to the women's health movement and the LBGT rights movements: that one's genitals are primarily for one's own use, not for the comfort of others.

Source: Website of the Intersex Society of North America. http://www.isna.org/faq/history (accessed May 29, 2007).

was harsh, troubled, and lonely because of his sex reassignment, and when he learned at the age of fourteen what had been done to him, he reclaimed his identity as a boy. In the 1990s, Reimer gave up his anonymity to tell his story, first to Milton Diamond, Professor of Anatomy at the University of Hawaii, who published a paper based on the interviews in the *Archives of Adolescent and Pediatric Medicine* (Diamond 1997). A more widely read journalist's account appeared in *Rolling Stone* that same year (Colapinto 1997) and was later issued as a book (Colapinto 2000). The story produced widespread coverage in the media, ending forty years of silence on intersexuality. In that year alone, periodicals such as *Newsweek*, *Time*, and *Mademoiselle* featured stories about sex reassignment, and television news featured Reimer, leaders of intersex groups, Milton Diamond, and biologist Anne Fausto-Sterling as guests.

In 1993, Anne Fausto-Sterling published "The Five Sexes," in which she argued that the two-sex system was too narrow to encompass the many varieties of human sexuality. Several years later, Fausto-Sterling recalled the reaction to her article (Fausto-Sterling 2000b, 19).

I had intended to be provocative, but I had also written with tongue firmly in cheek. So I was surprised by the extent of the controversy the article unleashed. Right-wing Christians were outraged....At the same time, the article delighted others who felt constrained by the current sex and gender system. Clearly, I had struck a nerve. *The*

Box 2–4 THE INTERNATIONAL BILL OF GENDER RIGHTS

Adopted June 17, 1995 Houston, Texas, U.S.A.

- "The International Bill of Gender Rights (IBGR) strives to express human and civil rights from a gender perspective. However, the ten rights enunciated below are not to be viewed as special rights applicable to a particular interest group. Nor are these rights limited in application to persons for whom gender identity and gender role issues are of paramount concern. All ten sections of the IBGR are universal rights which can be claimed and exercised by every human being."

  The IBGR was first drafted in committee and adopted by the International Conference on Transgender Law and Employment Policy (ICTLEP) at that organization's second annual meeting, held in Houston, Texas, August 26–29, 1993.

  The IBGR has been reviewed and amended in committee and adopted with revisions at subsequent annual meetings of ICTLEP in 1994 and 1995. The IBGR is a theoretical construction which has no force of law absent its adoption by legislative bodies and recognition of its principles by courts of law, administrative agencies and international bodies such as the United Nations. However, individuals are free to adopt the truths and principles expressed in the IBGR, and to lead their lives accordingly. In this fashion, the truths expressed in the IBGR will liberate and empower humankind in ways and to an extent beyond the reach of legislators, judges, officials and diplomats.

  When the truths expressed in the IBGR are embraced and given expression by humankind, the acts of legislatures and pronouncements of courts and other governing structures will necessarily follow. Thus, the paths of free expression trodden by millions of human beings, all seeking to define themselves and give meaning to their lives, will ultimately determine the course of governing bodies. The IBGR is a transformative and revolutionary document but it is grounded in the bedrock of individual liberty and free expression. As our lives unfold these kernels of truth are here for all who would claim and exercise them.

  This document, though copyrighted, may be reproduced by any means and freely distributed by anyone supporting the principles and statements contained in the International Bill of Gender Rights.

- The Right To Define Gender Identity. All human beings carry within themselves an ever-unfolding idea of who they are and what they are capable of achieving. The individual's sense of self is not determined by chromosomal sex, genitalia, assigned birth sex, or initial gender role. Thus, the individual's identity and capabilities cannot be circumscribed by what society deems to be masculine or feminine behavior. It is fundamental that individuals have the right to define, and to redefine as their lives unfold, their own gender identities, without regard to chromosomal sex, genitalia, assigned birth sex, or initial gender role. Therefore, all human beings have the right to define their own gender identity regardless of chromosomal sex, genitalia, assigned birth sex, or initial gender role; and further, no individual shall be denied Human or Civil Rights by virtue of a self-defined gender identity which is not in accord with chromosomal sex, genitalia, assigned birth sex, or initial gender role.

- The Right To Free Expression Of Gender Identity. Given the right to define one's own gender identity, all human beings have the corresponding right to free expression of their self-defined gender identity. Therefore, all human beings have the right to free expression of their self-defined gender identity; and further, no individual shall be denied Human or Civil Rights by virtue of the expression of a self-defined gender identity.

- The Right To Secure And Retain Employment And To Receive Just Compensation. Given the economic structure of modern society, all human beings have the right to train for and to pursue an occupation or profession as a means of providing shelter, sustenance, and the necessities and bounty of life, for themselves and for those dependent upon them, to secure and retain employment, and to receive just compensation for their labor regardless of gender identity, chromosomal sex, genitalia, assigned birth sex, or initial gender role. Therefore, individuals shall not be denied the right to train for and to pursue an occupation or profession, nor be denied the right to secure and retain employment, nor be denied just compensation for their labor, by virtue of their chromosomal sex, genitalia, assigned birth sex, or initial gender role, or on the basis of a self-defined gender identity or the expression thereof.

- The Right Of Access To Gendered Space And Participation In Gendered Activity. Given the right to define one's own gender identity and the corresponding right to free expression of a self-defined gender identity, no individual should be denied access to a space or denied participation in an activity by virtue of a self-defined gender identity which is not in accord with chromosomal sex, genitalia, assigned birth sex, or initial gender role. Therefore, no individual shall be denied access to a space or denied participation in an activity by virtue of a self-defined gender identity which is not in accord with chromosomal sex, genitalia, assigned birth sex, or initial gender role.

- The Right To Control And Change One's Own Body. All human beings have the right to control their bodies, which includes the right to change their bodies cosmetically, chemically, or surgically, so as to express a self-defined gender identity. Therefore, individuals shall not be denied the right to change their bodies as a means of expressing a self-defined gender identity; and further, individuals shall not be denied Human or Civil Rights on the basis that they have changed their bodies cosmetically, chemically, or surgically, or desire to do so as a means of expressing a self-defined gender identity.

- The Right To Competent Medical And Professional Care. Given the individual's right to define one's own gender identity, and the right to change one's own body as a means of expressing a self-defined gender identity, no individual should be denied access to competent medical or other professional care on the basis of the individual's chromosomal sex, genitalia, assigned birth sex, or initial gender role. Therefore, individuals shall not be denied the right to competent medical or other professional care when changing their bodies cosmetically, chemically, or surgically, on the basis of chromosomal sex, genitalia, assigned birth sex, or initial gender role.

- The Right To Freedom From Psychiatric Diagnosis Or Treatment. Given the right to define one's own gender identity, individuals should not be subject to psychiatric diagnosis or treatment solely on the basis of their gender identity or role. Therefore, individuals shall not be subject to psychiatric diagnosis or treatment as mentally disordered or diseased solely on the basis of a self-defined gender identity or the expression thereof.

- The Right To Sexual Expression. Given the right to a self-defined gender identity, every consenting adult has a corresponding right to free sexual expression. Therefore, no individual's Human or Civil Rights shall be denied on the basis of sexual orientation; and further, no individual shall be denied Human or Civil Rights for expression of a self-defined gender identity through sexual acts between consenting adults.

- The Right To Form Committed, Loving Relationships And Enter Into Marital Contracts. Given that all human beings have the right to free expression of self-defined gender identities, and the right to sexual expression as a form of gender expression, all human beings have a corresponding right to form committed, loving relationships with one another, and to enter into marital contracts, regardless of their own or their partner's chromosomal sex, genitalia, assigned birth sex, or initial gender role. Therefore, individuals shall not be denied the right to form committed, loving relationships with one another or to enter into marital contracts by virtue of their own or their partner's chromosomal sex, genitalia, assigned birth sex, or initial gender role, or on the basis of their expression of a self-defined gender identity.

- The Right To Conceive, Bear, Or Adopt Children; The Right To Nurture And Have Custody Of Children And To Exercise Parental Capacity. Given the right to form a committed, loving relationship with another, and to enter into marital contracts, together with the right to express a self-defined gender identity and the right to sexual expression, individuals have a corresponding right to conceive and bear children, to adopt children, to nurture children, to have custody of children, and to exercise parental capacity with respect to children, natural or adopted, without regard to chromosomal sex, genitalia, assigned birth sex, or initial gender role, or by virtue of a self-defined gender identity or the expression thereof. Therefore, individuals shall not be denied the right to conceive, bear, or adopt children, nor to nurture and have custody of children, nor to exercise parental capacity with respect to children, natural or adopted, on the basis of their own, their partner's, or their children's chromosomal sex, genitalia, assigned birth sex, initial gender role, or by virtue of a self-defined gender identity or the expression thereof.

*fact that so many people could get riled up by my proposal to revamp our sex and gen-
der system suggested that change—as well as resistance to it—might be in the offing.*
(emphasis added)

Moved by Fausto-Sterling's article, Cheryl Chase, who had suffered under the medical
regime for intersexuals as a child, announced the formation of the Intersex Society of North
America (ISNA). Born with an enlarged clitoris, Chase had been raised as a boy until the
age of eighteen months, when doctors performed a cliterodectomy on her. After the operation, her parents changed her name and began to raise her as a girl. It was not until she was
twenty-three that she learned she had been diagnosed as a "true hermaphrodite" and surgically altered to be female (Fausto-Sterling 2000a, 80–81). In a few short years, Chase and the
organization she founded have gone from picketing outside medical conventions in which
physicians discussed intersexuality to being invited to address such conventions and participate in task forces trying to establish ethical treatments and courses of action (Dreger 1998).
Today, ISNA has become the most important advocate for the human rights of intersexuals
(see Box 2–3). Readers of this book are encouraged to visit ISNA at http://www.isna.org.

Starting in the late 1980s, and continuing today with the help of Internet technology,
intersexuals and their families formed networks of support. These networks brought together
similarly affected people from around the globe, challenging medical secrecy, eroding the
isolation that made intersexuals vulnerable to accepting conventional medical assessments,
and establishing the conditions that allowed intersexuals and their families to challenge conventional wisdom around treatment. (For addresses and contact information for intersex support and advocacy resources in North America, see Preves 2005, 93.)

Alice Dreger (1998, 170–73) identifies a host of other factors, which she calls "post-
modernism," that helped to give voice to the growing community of intersexuals and their
families. These factors include the rising regard for the testimonies of ordinary people, non-
experts, and the disempowered, who are encouraged to speak out about their experience;
the recognition that there are many stories about intersex, in addition to the dominant medical story featuring nature's mistakes and bodily pathologies; challenges to the imbalance of
power between doctors and patients; patients' demands for active roles in their own health
care; and an awareness among intersex patients of the ways their problems with medical
experts recapitulate the problems experienced by gays and lesbians and by women who were
once also labeled as "fundamentally unacceptable or flawed."

Intersex as a Human Rights Issue

The intersex rights movement of the twenty-first century has joined the gay, lesbian, bisexual,
and transgender rights movements that emerged in the late twentieth century to compel
many of us to rethink our basic cultural assumptions about sex and gender, maleness and
femaleness, femininity and masculinity. Instead of hiding in shame and isolation, which
once was their fate, many intersexuals are publicly challenging the domination of a two-sex-
only view. Their challenge suggests that we may be moving from a system based on sexual
dimorphism—male–female difference—to one that includes a continuum based on many
sexualities and multiple genders. Social scientists have described gender and sexual diversity in the non-Western world and are giving these sex and gender variations in our own

society more attention and respect today, undoubtedly because gay, lesbian, bisexual, and transgendered movements have given voice to their members and power to such analyses.

The idea that men are men and women are women, a modern conception of sex, gender, and sexuality, is no longer as safely part of our definition of reality as it once was. Here we have tried to capture recent sociological thinking about the role of the social in the creation of our embodied selves. Under the guidance of sex and gender-bending movements, we are more than ever able to relinquish the biological straightjackets of the past. As gender variations become normalized, they become arenas "for playful exploration" of our possibilities (Fausto-Sterling 2000b), and we are made freer.

CONCLUDING THOUGHTS

People come in a wide array of sexual identities and they practice social selection by inventing an exploding array of gendered and sexual possibilities. This practice may ultimately put an end to sex and gender as relevant categories of existence. Nevertheless, the attempt to free ourselves from older normative sexual and gender identities can be dangerous. This danger is the reason why, according to Fausto-Sterling, legal protection is necessary in the transition to a more gender-diverse world. The International Bill of Gender Rights shown in Box 2–4 speaks to these needs.

REFERENCES

American Academy of Pediatrics. Committee on Genetics. 2000. Evaluation of the newborn with developmental anomalies of the external genitalia. *Pediatrics* 106 (1 Pt. 1): 138–42.

Blackwood, Evelyn. 1984. Sexuality and gender in certain Native American tribes: The case of cross-gender females. *Signs* 10 (1): 27–42.

Butler, Judith. 1990. *Gender trouble*. New York: Routledge.

Colapinto, John. 1997. The true story of John/Joan. *Rolling Stone*, December 11: 54–97.

——. 2000. *As nature made him: The boy who was raised as a girl*. New York: HarperCollins.

Connell, R. W. 1999. Making gendered people: Bodies, identities, sexualities. In *Revisioning gender*, ed. Myra Marx Ferree, Judith Lorber, and Beth Hess, 449–71. Thousand Oaks, CA: Sage.

——. 2000. *The men and the boys*. Berkeley: University of California Press.

——. 2002. *Gender*. Cambridge, UK: Polity Press

Davis, Angela. 1983. *The myth of the black rapist: Women, race, and class*. New York: Vintage.

D'Emilio, John. 1983. Capitalism and gay identity. In *Powers of desire: The politics of sexuality*, ed. Ann Snitow, Christine Stansell, and Sharon Thompson, 100–116. New York: Monthly Review Press.

Diamond, Milton and H.K. Sigmundson. 1997. Sex reassignment at birth: Long term review and clinical implications. *Archives of Pediatrics and Adolescent Medicine* 151. March, 298–304.

Dreger, Alice Domurat. 1998. *Hermaphrodites and the medical invention of sex*. Cambridge, MA: Harvard University Press.

Eugenides, Jeffery. 2002. *Middlesex: A novel*. New York: Picador.

Fausto-Sterling, Anne. 1985. *Myths of gender: Biological theories about women and men*. New York: Basic Books.

——. 1993. The five sexes: Why male and female are not enough. *The Sciences* March/April: 20–24.

———. 2000a. *Sexing the body: Gender politics and the construction of sexuality.* New York: Basic Books.

———. 2000b. The five sexes, revisited. *The Sciences* 40 (4):19–23.

Gagnon, John, and William Simon. 1973. *Sexual conduct: The social sources of human sexuality.* Chicago: Aldine.

Herdt, Gilbert. 1997. *Same sex, different cultures: Gays and lesbians across cultures.* Boulder, CO: Westview.

Jackson, Stevi, and Sue Scott, eds. 1996. *Feminism and sexuality: A reader.* New York: Columbia University Press.

Kessler, Suzanne, and Wendy McKenna. 1978. *Gender: An ethnomethodological approach.* New York: Wiley.

Kuhn, Thomas S. 1996. *The structure of scientific revolutions.* 3 edition. Chicago: University of Chicago Press.

Lancaster, Roger. 2003. *The trouble with nature: Sex in science and popular culture.* Berkeley: University of California Press.

Lang, Sabine. 1998. *Men as women, women as men: Changing gender in Native American cultures.* Austin: University of Texas Press.

Laqueur, Thomas. 1990. *Making sex: Body and gender from the Greeks to Freud.* Cambridge, MA: Harvard University Press.

Lorber, Judith. 1994. *Paradoxes of gender.* New Haven: Yale University Press.

———. 2005. *Gender inequality: Feminist theories and politics.* 3rd ed. Los Angeles: Roxbury.

Martin, Emily. 1992. *The woman in the body: A cultural analysis of reproduction.* Boston: Beacon Press.

———. 1997. The egg and the sperm: How science has constructed a romance based on stereotypical male-female roles. In *Situated lives: Gender and culture in everyday life,* ed. Louise Lamphere, Helena Rogone, and Patricia Zavella, 85–98. New York: Routledge.

Nagel, Joane. 2003. *Race, ethnicity, and sexuality: Intimate intersections, forbidden frontiers.* New York: Oxford University Press.

Nanda, Serena. 1990. *Neither man nor woman: The hijras of India.* Belmont, CA: Wadsworth.

Oyama, Susan, Paul E. Griffiths, and Russell D. Gray, eds. 2001. *Cycles of contingency: Developmental systems and evolution.* Cambridge, MA: MIT Press.

Preves, Sharon. 2005. *Intersex and identity: The contested self.* New Brunswick, NJ: Rutgers University Press.

Reeves, Thomas. 1997. *The life and times of Joe McCarthy: A biography.* New York: Madison Books.

Roughgarden, Joan. 2004. *Evolution's rainbow: Diversity, gender, and sexuality.* Berkeley: University of California Press.

Ryan, Mary P. 1975. *Womanhood in America: From colonial times to the present.* New York: New Viewpoints.

Schwartz, Pepper, and Virginia Rutter. 1998. *The gender of sexuality.* Thousand Oaks, CA: Pine Forge Press.

Simon, William. 1996. *Postmodern sexualities.* London and New York: Routledge.

Stein, Edward. 1999. *The mismeasure of desire: The science, theory, and ethics of sexual orientation.* New York: Oxford University Press.

Thomas, W. I. 1928. *The child in America: Behavior problems and programs.* New York: Knopf.

U.S. National Library of Health and National Institutes of Health. 2006. Intersex. http://www.nlm.nih.gov/medlineplus/ency/article/001669.htm.

3

SOCIALIZATION AND THE SOCIAL CONSTRUCTION OF GENDER

Recently a university professor in Indiana asked more than 1,200 college students to participate in a study (Blakemore and Centers 2005). The students were shown pictures of a large number of common American toys and told to label each toy according to how feminine or masculine they believed it to be. They sorted the toys into these categories:

- Strongly masculine (for example, GI Joe, footballs, Matchbox cars, miniature weapons, and toolboxes).
- Moderately masculine (for example, Wheel, basketball hoop, Lincoln Logs, and microscope).
- Neutral (for example, wagon, Play Doh, doctor kit, trampoline).
- Moderately feminine (for example, toy kitchen, Ken doll, costume, horses).
- Strongly feminine (for example, Easy Bake Oven, Barbie doll, ballerina costume, vanity set).

In a second part of the study another group of more than 700 students were asked to describe the characteristics of the toys. The students came up with descriptors such as violent, competitive, exciting, and somewhat dangerous for the masculine toys. They described the feminine toys as associated with physical attractiveness, nurturance, and domestic skill. The toys rated as most likely to be educational and to develop children's physical, cognitive, artistic, and other skills were typically rated as neutral or moderately masculine.

This study illustrates an important area of study for scholars who have been interested in the question of what the social sources of gender are. In the last chapter we argued that biology does not seem to provide a valid explanation for where gender comes from. We asserted that gender is socially structured, but what does that mean?

How does the way we socialize our children help to create and perpetuate gender? How do toys, for example, teach children about what is expected of them as "properly" gendered people? Is social learning the only social source of gender? Is gender also something we create and perpetuate as we interact with others? Adults do not usually play with children's toys but we do express gender, perpetuating it as we interact with one another.

What about social structure? What role does it play? If children were all given the same toys and socialized in the same way, would they still face gendered social institutions and social structures that would demand that they "choose" a gender and play the role?

How do all of these social factors—social learning, social interaction, and social structure—fit together to create our gendered experience?

This chapter seeks to answer these questions by describing how social psychologists and sociologists have attempted to explain the emergence and persistence of gender differences. We explore these approaches to gender at three levels: (1) at the individual level of social learning and psychological sex differences; (2) at the interactional level of social relations in everyday life; and (3) at the level of structural and institutional forces that constrain and shape action. We conclude by comparing these approaches and suggesting how an integration of the three perspectives can help us explain how gender differences and similarities are produced and how they may be transformed.

THE GENDER LENSES OF ANDROCENTRISM, GENDER POLARIZATION, AND ESSENTIALISM

The women's movement that arose in the 1960s challenged a number of tacit assumptions about sex and gender, assumptions that shaped both individual perceptions and social institutions. In her book, _The Lenses of Gender_, Sandra Bem (1993) likened these assumptions to gender lenses that filter what we see and color how we see it. In particular, Bem identified three such lenses. The lens of _androcentrism_, or male-centeredness, makes everything male appear the neutral norm, the universally human. Viewed against this standard, women appear deviant, less than human, and "other" or alien. One of many possible examples of androcentrism we could cite is the use of the generic "he" to refer to men _and_ women, or "mankind" to refer to all human beings.

A second lens, the lens of _gender polarization_, refers to the ways that diverse aspects of human experience are culturally linked to sex differences. Cultural items, emotions, social positions, and needs are _either_ male or female. For example, it has been a North American cultural mandate that only women wear pink. A gender-polarized view holds that men are authoritative, rational, and unemotional, whereas women are submissive, irrational, and highly emotional. Men and women supposedly have different inborn capacities that fit them for different kinds of work. Engineering is properly men's work, just as child care is appropriately women's work. Women need romance; men need to "score." As discussed in chapter 2, gender scholars argue that these polarities or binaries in men's and women's emotions, needs, abilities, and desires are socially constructed, not biologically determined.

A third lens, _essentialism_, is the view that gender is a fixed biological or social trait that "That is just how men + women are" does not vary among individuals or over time. Essentialist thinking has also been used to argue that racial ethnic capacities and traits are inborn and immutable. In fact it may be easier for many people to understand how essentialism in matters of race supports racist thinking than to understand the sexism implicit in gender essentialism. In both cases, a human-made or socially constructed but powerful fiction about race or gender is treated as if it were an indisputable biological reality. It is always helpful to remember the Thomas theorem: "If men [sic] believe things are real, they are real in their consequences." Based in reality or not, beliefs about gender and race have tremendous consequences for individual life chances.

As a claim based on biology, essentialism is problematic. First, as we saw in the previous chapter, not all individuals can be categorized as either male or female. What would be the *essential* sex or gender characteristics of people who are born with ambiguously sexed bodies or those with the bodies of one sex who envision themselves as members of the other ("opposite") sex?

Second, essentialist thinking is akin to stereotyping, which categorizes and judges groups of individuals according to a few shared characteristics such as sex, skin tone, or age. An early form of what is now discredited essentialism is the claim that all women are emotional and all men are rational due to their biological or psychological makeup. Feminist research has by now undermined this broad generalization. The work of Arlie Hochschild (1983) on the sociology of emotions explored masculine emotionality in feelings of anger and fear. Feminist studies of militarism and war-making exposed how the narrow rationality of military tactics and strategies exists within an irrational context of gendered violence and threat (Cohn 1987). In the wake of such studies, it is no longer possible to explain gender as an inborn and universal quality dividing male from female, masculinity from femininity, and men from women.

If gender difference isn't biologically based, where does it come from? In this chapter we explore the ways sociologists have attempted to explain the construction of differences between men and women. We know from chapter 2 that ideas about gender have evolved historically. The feminist movements of the nineteenth and twentieth centuries have made important contributions to that evolution of thinking about gender. In the earlier movements in the United States (the first wave), women's demands for the vote, property, and access to education and the professions challenged prevailing beliefs that women were men's natural inferiors. Such challenges raised questions about the origins of the sexual division of labor and laid the groundwork for a social science of gender (Connell 1987, 25).

Later in the century, feminist activists (the second and third waves) again contested academic and popular representations of women's place and initiated studies of hidden assumptions, shifting categories, and processes of gender production, hoping to make visible how gender is organized as the first step toward dismantling it (see Lorber 1994).

INDIVIDUAL-LEVEL THEORIES: SOCIAL ROLES AND SOCIAL LEARNING

Role theory flourished in the mid-twentieth century when the functionalist paradigm was predominant in sociology. Functionalists described society as a system of interdependent parts—the family, the economy, the political system, the educational system—that worked together to meet the system's functional needs and keep it stable. Individuals socialized into roles that fulfilled societal needs were the key to maintaining the social system. Their socialization involved internalizing social norms as expectations about how to feel, think, and behave in the social roles they inhabited as parents and children, husbands and wives, employers and workers, teachers and students.

In middle-class American families fifty years ago, it was normative, valued, and expected that a single male breadwinner would support his family and equally normative, valued, and expected that a wife and mother would care exclusively for her children and make a home for her husband. To fail to live up to the requirements of these roles, scholars and ordinary people believed, would undermine the social system itself. For example, if women were to abandon their roles as full-time wives and mothers, men would not be freed to fulfill their functions in the public sphere as breadwinners. In many ways, functional theory supported the status quo as the best, and perhaps the only, way to organize an ongoing, stable society.

Until the second wave of the women's movement, there had been few challenges to the idea that complementary sex roles in families and in society were socially required. In keeping with the perception that women's lives in the private sphere were less important than men's public roles, the little research on women focused primarily on women's family responsibilities. If there were people who did not live according to the functionalist view of a socially harmonious and socially necessary division of labor, they were labeled deviant.

One exception to this consensus was the research of sociologist Mirra Komarovsky, who found that educated women were greatly dissatisfied with their allotted roles. In a 1946 study she showed that college women were torn between the injunction to commit their lives exclusively to marriage and motherhood and their interests in successful academic and professional careers. In another study published fully ten years prior to Betty Friedan's *Feminine Mystique*, Komarovsky (1953) noted how full-time mothers were wondering "what is wrong with me that home and family are not enough?"(127).

Komarovsky was almost alone in the study of the conflicts and dilemmas of conventional sex roles until the 1970s, when the women's movement stimulated an explosion of research questioning the desirability and social utility of complementary sex roles. Although not yet departing from the focus on individual learning of sex roles, feminist scholars argued that sex roles were unequal and oppressive. Many of their studies showed how girls were socialized to concentrate on marriage and motherhood by parents, schools, and the media and attributed women's lesser status to such learning. As women moved into the labor force, it was becoming increasingly apparent that there were serious conflicts between women's family and work roles, between being adequate wives and mothers on the one hand, and pursuing satisfying public careers on the other. Something would have to change.

In its feminist version, sex-role research remained focused on the level of individuals. Like the functionalists before them, feminist scholars argued that sex roles were rooted in individuals' social positions or statuses and the expectations that accompanied such positions (West and Fenstermaker 1995, 17). They explained that children were socialized into roles by families, textbooks, teachers, and the media. Sex-role learning, they argued, produced girls and women who were nurturant, child-centered, dependent, and family-oriented, and boys and men who were work-oriented, competitive, aggressive, and ambitious. Their focus was on the differences between boys and girls, men and women.

The new research, however, tended to concentrate narrowly on white and middle-class women pioneering in men's professions (see, for example, Epstein 1970; Lorber 1975). Almost no one studied the lives and work of African American women, whose generations-long involvement in paid labor seriously challenged the conventional wisdom that most women were exclusively housewives, that employment for women was something new, and that the breadwinner–housewife family was the norm (Cole 1971; Hochschild 1973). Some social scientists called nonnormative lone-parent families or those without single male bread-winners pathological, disorganized, and out of step with mainstream society (Hill 2005, 63). In particular some social scientists blamed strong black mothers, whom they called "matri-archs," for emasculating black men and failing to provide black boys the authority figures that would allow them to learn appropriate masculine roles (Coontz 1992).

In later years, revisionist family scholars (those who rewrote the stories of African American families) rejected this view of black families, noting their strengths, their rich, extended kin and family life, and the adaptive strategies they devised to relieve the impact on black people of racist social policies supporting housing, educational, and job discrimination.

The explosion of feminist and antiracist research starting in the latter years of the twen-tieth century addressed the intersecting issues of race and gender. For example, feminists of color argued that it was misguided to build theory solely from the opposition between women and men. Instead, they argued, we must attend to the cross-cutting dimensions of race and class inequalities that complicate that story. As we discussed in chapter 1, many sociologists are now engaged in studies of the ways interactions between race ethnicity, class, citizenship, and sexuality affect sexism and gendered behavior.

Patricia Hill Collins (2000, 66), one of the most important theorists of intersectionality, suggests that it is important to understand how intersecting oppressions of class and gender differentially position black women nationally and globally.

> Large numbers of U.S. Black women in the working poor are employed as cooks, laundry workers, nursing home aides, and child-care workers. These women serve not only U.S. Whites, but more affluent U.S. Blacks, other people of color, and recent immigrants. Dependent on public services of all sorts—public schools for their children, health-care clinics for their checkups, buses and other public trans-portation to get them to work, and social welfare bureaucracies to fill in the gap between paychecks and monthly bills—these women can encounter Black middle-class teachers, nurses, bus drivers, and social workers who are as troublesome to them as White ones.

These experiences challenge simplistic hierarchies of domination and resistance and models of binary thinking. All of us are in some ways privileged and in other ways oppressed, writes Collins. Privilege and oppression are context-dependent. In some settings white women may be oppressed by their gender, but privileged by their race. In developing countries and international settings U.S. black women may be privileged by their citizenship, but oppressed racially. In some settings men may be oppressed by their racial ethnic and class position, although privileged by their gender (Collins 2000, 245–46).

Issues of power are front and center in more recent research on sex roles. Glick and Fiske (1999) suggest sex-categorization, a form of stereotyping of occupants of social roles, is resilient because it functions as a "cognitive labor-saving device" and is "the most automatic, pervasive, and earliest learned way we classify others on first encounter" (368–71). Knowing a person's role—mother, secretary, wife—tells us what to expect from that person. However, according to the authors, this knowledge is not "innocent," because power is embedded in these sex-role relationships, based as they are on a sexual division of labor in which men monopolize high-status positions that sustain their dominance in interpersonal interactions. Bringing power into the research on role relationships is important, because it offers a more accurate portrait of how such relationships work. At the same time, recent research also considers how women's subordinate positions may position them to resist men's control even in the most conservative patriarchal societies.

Individual-level research on gender and race ethnicity helps us to explore the ways we and others shape and are shaped by our identities in everyday life. However, this research cannot answer many questions. Where do sex roles come from? How do they persist and change? Interactionist theory provides some of the answers.

THE INTERACTIONIST THEORY OF GENDER: GENDER AS A COURSE OF ACTION

Rather than focus on childhood socialization and the internalization of roles and rules, social constructionists attempt to understand the impact on individuals of the contexts of social action. To constructionists, gender is *situational* and *contextual*. That is, the situations we find ourselves in draw from us particular ways of acting and particular identities. When you are with your family, you act as a daughter or a son. When you are with your friends, you act as a friend, or if not, you may sacrifice the friendships you have. When you are in class, you act as a student. Of course we improvise within the broad channels marking what is expected, and sometimes we move beyond these. History, past practice, and the communities within which we act, interact, and shape our worlds create boundaries outside of which our actions may shock, confuse, and anger the audiences for whom we perform.

Social constructionism is very different from essentialist and individualist thinking. Constructionists hold that gender differences are created socially and historically, rather than on account of an individual's biology or psychology. In their view, collective life is not simply the sum of individual lives. Rather, the social organization of families, workplaces, sports teams, and other sets of social relationships must be understood as wholes or systems that provide individuals with ways of acting and interacting, statuses, honors, and sanctions. These are the factors that shape and condition who we are and what we do.

In *Gender Blending*, a book about women who are often mistaken in public for men, a woman explains to author Holly Devor why she decided to emphasize her masculine appearance.

> The first time that I realized that I could pass was when I was living…in a rooming house near the university. And it was pretty much the first I'd been off for any length of time where no one would know if I ever disappeared. So I was a bit concerned about walking around on the streets at night…
>
> I had a jacket that could've looked like a leather jacket, and I had short hair. And I put the jacket on and I sort of greased my hair back and put my hands in my pockets and I really startled myself because I looked like such a young punk… I really looked like a guy.…It worked. Nobody hassled me.…I thought it was a great joke. I was really chuckling away to myself. And also I thought I felt a lot of freedom. This was great. I could pass. I didn't have to worry about it.
>
> I used it to my benefit…I would take longer steps and hunch my shoulders up.…Once I decided that it would work I put on this "I'm not afraid" business and

took big steps. You know there's a posture that you use to show that you're casual in the situation, and that's what I did. (Devor 1989, 111)

This woman and others Devor interviewed for her book could not take their gender identity for granted. On the contrary, they were often forced to consider consciously a matter that normally goes without saying. They had to think strategically about their appearance and negotiate with their audiences about who they "really" were. In public restrooms, for example, other women often challenged these women's right to be there. Sometimes they called the police to remove them.

Because most people assume there are only two sexes, if a person is not clearly female, she must be male (and vice versa). If actors display and perform gender with skill, using dress and demeanor to present themselves to others as men or women, audiences generally take their displays and performances as evidence of an underlying, appropriate biology. Devor's informants took advantage of the widespread belief that gender is biological, permanent, and transparent. The woman quoted earlier remade her gender identity through clothing, body language, and hairstyle. She designed this strategy to make herself safer on the streets. In the language of interactionist sociology, this young woman was consciously *doing gender*.

Some women might choose to do gender by adopting the manner and dress that signals male identity. The performance, of course, can also go in the other direction. Harold Garfinkel (1967) provides a famous example of doing gender in his description of Agnes, who was born and raised as a boy "with normal appearing male genitals." Although Agnes believed that her femininity was ascribed by nature, and that her genitals and other bodily signs of masculinity were mistakes to be surgically corrected, she was forced by her situation to *achieve* the status of "natural normal female" (157). Agnes's claims to female status required her to manage the impressions of others about her. To do so meant that she had to present herself as a woman in everyday interaction, to display and perform femininity in a conscious and purposeful manner. To learn what her past life as a male had failed to teach her, Agnes actively set out to study how to act feminine by imitating and apprenticing to others who had the appropriate social skills. From her boyfriend's mother she learned how to cook, what clothes to wear, and how to manage a household. From her boyfriend she learned not to "display" herself in front of other men; not to insist on her own way; to be sweet, innocent, and uncomplaining; and to serve rather than to demand service. Not only did Agnes have to *act* like a woman, the external manifestation of her sexual status, she had to manage her internal emotional states to *feel* like a woman as well, a kind of method acting. For example, from her roommates and girlfriends she learned both to accept instructions passively and to value "passive acceptance as a desirable feminine character trait" (Garfinkel 1967, 147). Agnes had to accomplish consciously what most adult women and men know how to do without thinking about it. Because we are tutored in femininity and masculinity from infancy, and because gendered actions are supported or required in many social contexts, our performances feel instinctive and natural. Agnes did not possess the commonsense knowledge that generally resides below conscious awareness and shapes feminine (and masculine) behavior and interaction. To appear feminine, Agnes had to pay close attention to the ways "natural" women acted. On the basis of what she observed, Agnes monitored her appearance and calculated her actions. She was attentive to subtle cues and clues about what others expected from her and what they understood to be "normal" female behavior. Garfinkel (1967) called Agnes a *practical methodologist.* By that he meant that Agnes turned a sociological eye on the "trivial but necessary social tasks" that women enacted to appear "normally" female (180). Agnes made conscious what most of us do as a matter of course: She "[made gender] happen." Garfinkel explains:

> The scrutiny she paid to appearances; her concerns for adequate motivation, relevance, evidence, and demonstration; her sensitivity to devices of talk; her skill in detecting and managing "tests" were attained as part of her mastery of *trivial but necessary social tasks,* to secure ordinary rights to live. Agnes was self-consciously equipped to teach normals *how normals make [gender] happen in commonplace settings* as an obvious, familiar, recognizable, natural, and serious matter of fact. Her specialty consisted of treating the "natural facts of life" of socially recognized, socially managed sexuality as a managed production. . . . in short, so as unavoidably in concert with others to be making these facts of life visible and reportable—*accountable*—for all practical purposes. (Garfinkel 1967, 180, emphasis added)

The studies by Devor and Garfinkel report on how people on the margins of society actively construct the appearance of masculinity or femininity. However, as is often the case, extraordinary lives can tell us about ourselves and about the processes that hold our own worlds together. Garfinkel called attention to two essential aspects of Agnes's performance. First, representing herself as female required Agnes to master the trivia of everyday life. That Agnes adopted a willingness to serve exposed how this trait was a subtle but important dimension of femininity in public. Devor's informant mastered the walk and hunched shoulders that signaled the "young punk" form of masculinity. Probably most of us could understand the meaning of the walk, part of our own everyday knowledge about the types of people we see on the streets. Devor and Garfinkel show how gendered identities rest on a foundation of mundane and trivial acts, noticeable only, perhaps, in their absence.

Second, Garfinkel showed that Agnes was *accountable* to her audience (as were Devor's women, and other female and male "impersonators" and the rest of us). If she was to be accepted as the woman she claimed to be, she had to perform femininity in expected, adequate, and recognized ways. By successfully achieving femininity on the basis of acting and feeling appropriately, as defined by her audiences, Agnes reinforced the femininity she sought to embody. For Agnes and for the women Devor studied, gender was an *achieved* status, an accomplishment, rather than something affixed to us at birth by virtue of our chromosomes or genitals. In a sense, Agnes and the women who passed for men were making false, albeit successful, claims. What do these accounts suggest about our own gendered selves? Do we also display and perform our gender? The concept of doing gender suggests that we do, that all of us, in a sense, are in drag.

Doing Gender

The mannerisms, speech, dress, and demeanor of the women who passed for men and of Agnes, the biological male who passed for a woman, were performances that broadcast to their audiences the essential gendered natures of these individuals. These actors achieved or earned their gendered status by learning how to be and to act feminine or masculine. They did not receive their gendered status as women or men as a birthright, nor did they adopt it as

Box 3–1 TRANSGENDERED COMMUNITY REMEMBERS DEATH THAT SPARKED A MOVEMENT

—Ten years ago, a handsome, brown-haired 21-year-old named Brandon Teena was raped and later murdered by two men after they discovered he wasn't born a man. The New Year's Eve tragedy in rural southeastern Nebraska inspired the award-winning 1999 film, *Boys Don't Cry*. It also touched off a movement in the transgendered community.

In the days after Teena was killed, a new generation of activists banded together to demand greater civil rights protections. Ten years later, 65 municipalities and states have hate crime laws that specifically include transgendered people, according to the Transgender Law Policy Institute. California became the fourth state to adopt such a law earlier this year. Big corporations, such as Hewlett-Packard and Nike, have adopted similar rules. And 145 members of Congress have banned such discrimination from their offices, said Riki Wilchins, executive director of the Washington-based Gender Public Advocacy Coalition. "How many times do you get to see a giant sea change like this in people's perceptions? But you look at Congress, corporate America, and cities and states...and you see this enormous change in how people are looking at gender as a civil rights issue," Wilchins said.

Nebraska passed a hate-crime law in 1997, but it did not refer specifically to trans-gendered people. It was found unconstitutional after a 2000 U.S. Supreme Court ruling in another case involving sentencing provisions. One problem for the transgendered community—which encompasses a range of identities including cross-dressers and transsexuals—is that allies have been hard to come by. Although they were at the fore-front of New York City's 1969 Stonewall Riots, which led to the gay rights movement, the relationship between the transgendered and gay communities hasn't always been easy. "For a long time, the gay movement was like, 'Well, that's an interesting problem, but it's not our problem. You folks are too weird. We don't want to talk to you.'" said Paisley Currah, executive director of the Center for Lesbian and Gay Studies at Brooklyn College in New York.

The national attention given to Teena's murder also helped introduce the idea of being transgendered to mainstream America, said Shannon Minter, a board member of

a role and status laid out for them to fill as they matured. Their dress and demeanor signaled that the unseen body parts signifying male or female status were actually there, although they in fact were not.

The studies reviewed in this chapter and the previous one show that (1) our biological sex, (2) our status as males or females, and (3) the ways we live our lives as sexed beings, with all the appropriate demeanor, emotions, understandings, and practices such living entails, need not coincide. Candace West and Don Zimmerman (1987) published a highly influen-tial article in which they distinguished among these three analytically distinct but overlapping the Transgender Law and Policy Institute in New York. "People are just much less freaked out about the concept, and see us more as human beings with partners, families, children," said Minter, who is transgendered. Many activists say Teena's murder attracted so much attention because of its brutality and the failure of law enforcement to protect Teena. John Lotter and Marvin Nissen were convicted of murdering Teena, who had dated a female friend of the two men. They also killed Lisa Lambert, 24, and Philip DeVine, 22, who had witnessed Teena's death in a farmhouse. A week before the killing, Teena had told the local sheriff the men had raped him, but the sheriff took no action.

In a scathing court opinion in 2001, Nebraska Supreme Court Chief Justice John Hendry said former Richardson County Sheriff Charles Laux showed indifference by referring to Teena as "it" and not immediately arresting the suspects. Laux, reached by telephone at his home, decline to comment. A judge initially awarded Teena's mother, Joann Brandon, $17,360 in damages, saying that Teena's own lifestyle was partly responsible for his death. The state Supreme Court ordered him to reconsider, and he later awarded Brandon $98,223. Brandon's lawyer, Herb Friedman, said she no longer wanted to talk about case. Lotter is now on Nebraska's death row. Nissen was sentenced to life in prison.

Though much has improved for the transgendered community in the last 10 years, there is still a long way to go, Minter said. In the past year alone, Remembering Our Dead, an online memorial that tracks bias killing of transgendered people around the world, recorded 17 deaths in the United States. The few people in Falls City willing to talk about the case voiced a desire to move on and frustration at its cost to the county. "Every town's got some weird people," said resident Mary Symonds.

About 25 miles from Falls City in the tiny town of Humboldt, the small farmhouse where Teena, Lambert and DeVine were killed attracts a regular stream of sightseers. "They just drive and stare and I guess get a thrill out of that," said Dagmar Jansen, who moved into the house about two years ago with her family. "It's horrible. It probably comes from prejudice and people not being open-minded," Jansen said. "I think by the year 2003 people should be able to live for who they are and not for what people think they should be."

Source: Associated Press, December 28, 2003. http://www.cnn.com/2003/US/Central/12/28/brandon.death.transgender.ap/

categories. These categories are slightly different from the ones presented in chapter 2. As in that chapter, the category *sex* refers to a person's biology—whether a person has a penis and testicles or a vagina and clitoris. *Sex* may be a biological category, but in practice it depends on social cues. As argued in chapter 2, the fact that we "know" that there are two and only two sexes is based on our belief that this is the case. Our "moral certainty" leads us to deduce sex from what we see before us. We do not ask people to disrobe in front of us to ascertain their biological sex. In everyday life we take their appearance at face value. A person wearing a suit and tie probably has a penis; a person in a dress or lipstick probably has a vagina. Of course these categories are becoming less distinct as clothing, hairstyles, and body language become more "unisexualized."

Sex category refers to the status of male or female that most persons inhabit unambiguously. However, some people with a penis are able to claim the status of woman. Their clothing, their demeanor, and their claims to womanhood help their audiences to locate them in the category of female. If people around these individuals had known that they possessed penises, that knowledge would have discredited their claims, no matter how skilled their performance. *Gender* refers to the performance itself, the ways people accomplish being a man or a woman, a boy or a girl. Agnes's gender problem, according to West and Zimmerman, was to learn to behave and think like a "normal" woman, as defined by her audiences. Agnes had to act in the presence of "normals" and interact with them in ways that validated her claim to female status. If men and women do not act in gender-appropriate ways, they risk being found socially incompetent or, worse, fraudulent. In this way, people are accountable for their performances. The sanctions imposed on people who act "inappropriately" in the opinion of their audience have ranged from ridicule and ostracism to imprisonment and even death, as the story in Box 3–1 of Brandon Teena's murder illustrates.

Viewing gender in this manner directs attention to the interactional contexts of social life and away from the biological and psychological states of individuals. From this perspective, gender is a property of and emerges in social situations. Doing gender involves acting appropriately in specific contexts and for specific audiences. For example, recall that Agnes was counseled not to insist on having her way. A woman who insists on her way is, in some circles, unfeminine. Agnes did gender during a time when feminist ideas were less powerful. Certainly today there are contexts in which it would not be "unfeminine" to insist on one's way. Doing gender involves managing one's emotions and desires, as well as one's actions. Agnes's teachers also coached her to value passive acceptance, to embrace emotionally their understanding that this was an appropriately feminine way of living.

How have you been held accountable for your gendered behavior? Think about a time when you refrained from acting because you worried that observers might think you were being unfeminine or not manly enough. In these cases, you were being held or were holding yourself accountable for your actions. You can be held accountable for doing gender almost anywhere. Try to imagine situations where your performance as a man or woman would never be relevant. It's not easy! In fact, Garfinkel's work with Agnes led him to claim that gender is "omnirelevant" (relevant in every situation) and that doing gender is unavoidable.

The concept of doing gender was a major advance in sociological thinking about gender. It showed how we create gender differences between men and women, boys and girls in social interaction. It demonstrated how gender is a social category. Genitalia, hormones, and genes cannot tell us what is sociologically interesting about gender differences. The real news about gender can be found in the ways local contexts and social institutions shape gender identities and relations in systematic ways.

Props and Resources for Doing Gender

People enact gender by drawing on the "resources" that are features of local settings and that guide actions that produce and reproduce gender difference. For example, public bathrooms differentiate men from women although, as Erving Goffman explains, there is no biological reason for doing so. In fact, he suggests that these arrangements produce the difference they are meant to respect.

> The *functioning* of sex-differentiated organs is involved, but there is nothing in this functioning that biologically recommends segregation; *that* arrangement is a totally cultural matter...toilet segregation is presented as a natural consequence of the difference between the sex-classes when in fact it is a means of honoring, if not producing, this difference. (Goffman 1977, 316, quoted in West and Zimmerman 1987, 137)

Other resources for doing gender cited by Goffman (1977) are organized sports and "assortative mating practices." This phrase refers to the practices that produce, in couples, older, taller, and stronger boys and men, and younger, smaller, and weaker girls and women. Note the heterosexual couples you encounter in your daily life who do or do not conform to this expectation. Any situation can be an occasion for doing gender. A flat tire can become such an occasion. How many women have you passed on the highway fixing their flat tires? How many women do you see mowing their lawns? When men and women are together in an automobile, who drives? When parents are walking with their babies, who is pushing the stroller or holding a child's hand? Be alert to these interesting measures of changing (or not) gender practices.

What maintains gender differences? For interactionists, interaction is the process through which we create and maintain ourselves and our society. Accountability explains why gender is a central and persistent feature of everyday life. Think about a time when you worried about how others might respond to something you did or planned to do. In these cases, you were being held accountable for your actions by others in your social world. Accountability is one of the mechanisms that holds gender differences and gender relationships in place. Moreover, interactionists believe that in everyday life, sex category is almost always relevant. Often what we do is designed with an eye to how it will look to others—a concern that Agnes took to necessary extremes—or it is done so as not to attract attention, such as passing as a man or a woman. There is virtually no activity for which you could not be held accountable for performance as a woman or man. That means that doing gender is unavoidable. At stake is the management of our most valued identities.

Doing gender reinforces the illusion that there are essential differences between women and men when, in fact, the *doing* is what creates these very differences. Gender is a fundamental category for the allocation of resources and power in many contexts, from interpersonal interaction and the household division of labor to global political and economic relations. So even as we do gender at the local, interactional level of social life, that activity supports, reinforces, and re-creates broader structural and institutional processes. It is those processes, with their seeming natural ways of organizing work, family, love, war, and all the other dimensions of our collective lives that support, reinforce, and re-create our production of gender in the interactional sphere. In other words, we interactionally create the social worlds we are part of, but we are, in turn, constrained and pressed into certain courses of action as our creations take on a life of their own. Let's take Agnes's experience as an example. Some women and men believed it was unfeminine for a woman to insist on having her own way. This belief and practice arose in a definite historical period and among certain people—the middle classes of North America in the nineteenth century—but it has persisted into our own time. By the time Agnes appeared on the scene, it was institutionalized as part of feminine behavior. Agnes could flout that practice at her peril.

GENDER STRUCTURES: ROSABETH MOSS KANTER

There is much evidence—including evidence from our own daily lives—to support interactionist theories that locate the production of gender in everyday social conduct. But what accounts for the strength and persistence of gendered inequality in interaction, its occurrence across social situations and contexts, and its reproduction over time? Some sociologists focus on the way that gender inequalities are produced and maintained at the level of institutions and social structures. Where interactionists concern themselves with the everyday world and the social meanings of actors in it, structuralists maintain that the rules and resources that frame local action should have primacy of place in social theories about gender.

The concept of "social structures" is notoriously slippery. A common mistake is to be too literal in conceptualizing social structure and to imagine it as a sort of permanent edifice that determines our thoughts and acts. Social theorist Anthony Giddens (1984) focuses on the social processes that create and change structures. Structures to Giddens are both the result and the medium of acting subjects. We interact with one another to produce gender, for example, and the gendered social relations we produce over and over again (or, reproduce) push us to act in gendered ways. In other words, we are the product of structures that we ourselves create. In *The Eighteenth Brumaire of Louis Napoleon*, Karl Marx (1972, 10) put it this way: "Men [sic] make their own history, but they do no make it just as they please; they do not make it under circumstances chosen by themselves, but under circumstances directly encountered, given and transmitted from the past." Marx meant that we make the worlds we share, but we cannot just create anything that comes to mind (in fact, what will come to mind is limited by what we know and how we think about that). What Marx called the "dead weight of history" limits us and shapes what is possible. Understanding that we are the producers of that which limits our social action is vitally important. For example, we have invented war as a way to resolve conflict. If war is a human creation and not a fact of nature, and if we can imagine an end to war, then we may be capable of actually putting an end to it. Likewise, once we understand how gendered action creates structures of femininity and masculinity, those structures may themselves become the objects of our practice to change or eliminate them (see Connell 1987).

Sociologists often use the concept of *structure* to refer to the constraints built into social organizations and relationships. Think about how you have acceded to the rules and demands of the education system in your lifetime as a student. As a youngster you had to follow rules that may have seemed arbitrary, but about which you could do little. You had to wake up at a certain time to get to school on time and you had to forgo playing in the park on school days. As a college student you must accumulate credit hours by writing papers, taking exams, and reading what your instructors tell you to read if you want your education to count for future employment or graduate school. Historically, structured racial ethnic and gender inequalities in education have meant that schooling has not provided a level playing field to girls and boys, young men and women. Gendered inequalities have also been a part of your education. These often take the form of "microinequities" (Sandler 1986), the small and not so small ways we are treated differently because of our race ethnicity, gender, age, or sexuality. Sandler identified more than 50 ways that women and men are treated differently in the classroom. For example, teachers call on men more often, ask them more questions, nod and gesture when men speak, and look elsewhere when women talk.

Not surprisingly, race ethnicity enters into these microinequities. White men get the most questions, then minority men, then white women, with black women receiving the least attention in classrooms. Such classroom structures limit and restrict your education, whether you are a man or a woman. Another way structure restricts us is that it shapes our choices and interests. Maybe you are a man interested in nursing, but you consider it too feminine, too low status, or too low paying to be a reasonable career choice. The gender-segregated structure of occupations in the United States means that women's pay is on the average lower than men's by about 30 percent. Working conditions differ for women and men as well. Women's jobs and professions such as nursing have lower mobility structures. On the other hand, although men are also disadvantaged in terms of pay, prestige, and working conditions when they enter women's occupations, they also retain certain advantages as men, often riding the glass escalator to the top echelons of management in these occupations (Williams 1995).

The gender division of labor is a structural concept. It refers to how women and men are sorted into jobs and occupations in the labor force, as well as who is responsible for unpaid work. In the early days of the second wave of the women's movement, feminists focused on the gender division of labor and the exclusion of women from better paid and more interesting men's jobs. Rosabeth Moss Kanter studied a large industrial supply firm to learn how "organizational structure forms people's sense of themselves and of their possibilities" (Kanter 1977, 3). Her project was to show that gender differences in organizational behavior were the result of structures rather than of personality differences between men and women. She identified three structural features of the corporation that explained the differences she observed between women and men in their workplace performance, relations on the job, and attitudes toward work. The three structural features were (1) the structure of opportunity offered by the organization, (2) the structure or distribution of power, and (3) the relative numbers of men and women employed, especially as managers, professionals, and executives.

Opportunity Structures

The principle measure of success in the corporation was upward mobility through promotion. Why weren't more women in top-level managerial positions? Most women, it appeared, did not have the aspirations, commitment, and dependability that would have earned them promotions. They cared more about relationships with others on the job and less about occupational success. Most observers attributed these differences to deficiencies women brought with them to the job. Note that this is an individual-level explanation of women's failure to rise in the corporate hierarchy.

Kanter suggested a different reason for women's immobility at work. She argued that opportunity is not a result of behavior on the job. Quite the opposite: Opportunity structures produce gendered behavior.

> When women seem to be less motivated or committed, it is probably because their
> jobs carry less opportunity. There is evidence that in general the jobs held by most

Box 3–2 THE SECRETARY'S DESK

Secretaries added a personal touch to Industrial Supply Corporation workplaces. Professional and managerial offices tended to be austere: generally uniform in size and coloring, and unadorned except for a few family snapshots or discrete artworks. ("Welcome to my beige box," a rising young executive was fond of saying to visitors.) But secretaries' desks were surrounded by splashes of color, displays of special events, signs of the individuality and taste of the residents: postcards from friends' or bosses' travels pasted on walls, newspaper cartoons, large posters with funny captions, huge computer printouts that formed the names of the secretaries in gothic letters. It was secretaries who remembered birthdays and whose birthdays were celebrated, lending a legitimate air of occasional festivity to otherwise task-oriented days. Secretaries could engage in conversations about the latest movies, and managers often stopped by their desks to join momentarily in a discussion that was a break from the more serious business at hand. It was secretaries who were expected to look out for the personal things, to see to the comfort and welfare of guests, to show them around and make sure that they had what they needed. And it was around secretaries that people at higher levels in the corporation could stop to remember the personal things about themselves and each other (appearance, dress, daily mood), could trade the small compliments and acknowledgments that differentiated them from the mass of others and from their formal role. In many ways—visually, socially, and organizationally—the presence of secretaries represented a reserve of the human inside the bureaucratic.

women workers tend to have shorter chains of opportunity associated with them and contain fewer advancement prospects. (Kanter 1977, 159)

Kanter cited studies that contradict the picture of women as less committed to work than men (remember, this study was done in the 1970s, when stereotypes and beliefs about women as workers were somewhat different from what they are today). She showed that when men's opportunity structures were also limited, their behavior resembled women's.

Women can also be more committed than men at upper levels when they have had to work harder to overcome barriers; effort helps build commitment. At the same time, *men with low opportunity look more like the stereotype of women in their orientations toward work*, as research on blue-collar men has shown; they limit their aspirations, seek satisfaction in activities outside of work, dream of escape, interrupt their careers, emphasize leisure and consumption and create sociable peer groups in which interpersonal relationships take precedence over other aspects of work. (Kanter 1977, 160–61, emphasis in original)

Kanter's point is that people with little opportunity behave in one way and people with a great deal of opportunity behave in another way. Low-opportunity people do not aspire to

Nowhere were the contradictions and unresolved dilemmas of modern bureaucratic life more apparent than in the secretarial function. The job, made necessary by the growth of modern organizations, lay at the very core of bureaucratic administration, yet it often was the least bureaucratized segment of corporate life. The product of the rationalization of work and the vast amount of paperwork that entailed, it still remained resistant to its own rationalization. At Indsco, secretarial positions were unique in a number of ways: for one thing, they were the only jobs in the company ranked merely by the status of the manager, and attempts to change this arrangement were resisted. The secretarial job involved the most routine of tasks in the white-collar world, yet the most personal of relationships. The greatest time was spent on the routine, but the greatest reward was garnered for the personal.

Understanding the nature of this bureaucratic anomaly sheds light on several features of life in the corporation: the functions served by pockets of the personal inside the bureaucratic, but the tradeoffs for people who become trapped as an underclass in those pockets; the sources of both the intensity and the awkwardness that can emerge in relationships between bosses and secretaries; and the origin, in job conditions, of those work orientations that tend to be adopted by secretaries. Secretaries' characteristic ways of managing their organizational situation—their strategies for attaining recognition and control—as well as the behaviors and attitudes they develop, can all be seen as a response to the role relations surrounding the secretarial function. Here also are found the sources of resistance to change in the secretarial function: by the organization at large, by managers, and by secretaries themselves. From awareness of the resistances can come better designs for change. (Kanter 1977)

more exalted positions at work, have low self-esteem, and are resigned to staying where they are. People with substantial opportunity have high aspirations, have high self-esteem, are more interested in work, and are more competitive. It is the structure of opportunity, not the gender of workers, that makes the difference.

Power Structures

Power—"the ability to get things done, to mobilize resources, to get and whatever it is that a person needs for the goals he or she is attempting to meet"—is also the result of structural position rather than gender (Kanter 1977, 167). People with fewer resources available to them, a function of position in networks, have little power. If women or men in supervisory positions are excluded by others from the knowledge and means to do their jobs, their responses are likely to include closely supervising workers under them and jealously guarding their domain—features of the stereotypic woman boss. People who can mobilize resources to get the job done are less rigid and authoritarian, better liked, seen as helpful, more cooperative, and exercise fewer strong controls. Again, what looks like gender differences at work are actually produced by differential abilities to get the job done, a structural problem.

Relative Numbers

Relative numbers also contribute to outcomes that look like—but do not originate in—gendered social relations at the individual level. When Kanter was studying the Industrial Supply Corporation, pioneer women were fighting for the right to be police officers, firefighters, mechanics, doctors, attorneys, and corporate leaders. These pioneers faced a phenomenon that Kanter labeled *tokenism*, the social relations that grow from belonging to a tiny minority amidst a large majority. At the upper levels of corporate management, token women were highly visible and their work—especially their perceived missteps and mistakes—were subject to public scrutiny. They were treated as symbols, representing all women. They were under pressure to perform well, and also under the conflicting pressure not to make the dominant group look bad by performing too well. Their presence stimulated the men of the company to magnify their own group solidarity against such intruders. Here is what Kanter observed:

> Around token women…men sometimes exaggerated displays of aggression and potency: instances of sexual innuendos, aggressive sexual teasing, and prowess-oriented "war stories." When a woman or two were present, the men's behavior involved "showing off," telling stories in which "masculine prowess" accounted for personal, sexual, or business success. They highlighted what they could do, as men, in contrast to the women. (Kanter 1977, 223)

Men interrupted women, reminded them of their difference ("Can we still swear?"), kept them out of informal meetings, and subjected them to other forms of "boundary heightening" behavior. Women were stereotyped, treated as mothers, temptresses, pets, or iron maidens. Kanter's observations about token women also seem to apply to racial and ethnic, religious, and other minorities within larger, homogeneous groups. For example, in some majority white colleges where students of color are "tokens," they may be called on in class to represent all members of their group or held accountable for stereotypes of the group's supposed cultural behaviors.

Kanter saw the corporation as a gender-neutral setting. Anyone in the same low-status position would be likely to behave and be treated similarly, regardless of their sex. However, studies of men who are tokens in majority female occupations suggest otherwise. Whereas the work of men in low-status positions in hierarchical organizations may be "feminized," white men who are token workers in women's occupations (nursing and elementary education, for example) are likely to be evaluated positively and to move rapidly into positions of authority. Such findings suggest that gendering is not an accident of structure, but integral to its existence. In the excerpt from *Men and Women of the Corporation*, "The Secretary's Desk" (Box 3–2), we see how secretaries accumulate resources for doing gender as the structures of work at INDSCO push them into wife-like relationships with their bosses.

GENDERED ORGANIZATIONS: JOAN ACKER

To Kanter, organizational structures were gender neutral. If there were differences in women's and men's jobs, opportunities, or experiences, Kanter believed those differences were just as likely to be produced between any two differently situated and unequal groups in the organization: blue collar versus managerial employees, majority versus token workers. She recognized that the male culture at Industrial Supply Corporation was incited to resist the entry of a few women into managerial positions. She acknowledged that men in general were overwhelmingly dominant in corporate positions of power and prestige, that men's work was valued (and paid) more highly than women's work, and that token women faced many forms of gender harassment on the job, from sexist joking and stereotyping to overt hostility. Nonetheless, she reasoned that gender inequality grew out of more generic hierarchical rules and practices. Gender was not intrinsic to organizational structure.

For many scholars, however, gendered inequalities were too pervasive to be explained away as the random effects of neutral structures and impartial organizational practices. Everywhere one looked one saw differences between women and men that made a difference: the gender segregation of work and the boundary between paid and unpaid labor; the income and status inequality between men and women; and the male dominance and masculine culture of many large, hierarchical organizations. After reviewing the research of Kanter, Joan Acker (1990) wrote, "Gender is not an addition to ongoing processes, conceived as gender neutral. Rather, it is an integral part of those processes, which cannot be properly understood without an analysis of gender" (146).

What does it mean to say that organizational structures are gendered? Acker identified several ways that gender difference creates and sustains inequalities in organizations.

- Organizational processes create gendered divisions—of labor, of space, of behavior, of power. One spatial difference that has come into view recently is the ladies room as the corporate space for nursing infants.
- Organizational processes construct symbols and images that support gender differences in organizations—the masterful business leader, the difficult female boss.
- Organizations promote gendered components of individual identity—appropriate (gendered) clothing, workplace demeanor, language.
- There is a gendered logic discernable in the work rules, labor contracts, and other documents that are part of organizational discourses.

An example of the gendered logic implicit in organizations is the category of the job, the basic unit of work. On its face, a job is a neutral thing, a set of tasks and responsibilities that has no particularly gendered aspect to it (except for a few jobs such as wet nurse—the woman who takes on the task of nursing another woman's baby—or surrogate mother). However, Acker asks us to consider the fact that we all understand that jobs are separate from family life. The job itself presupposes the existence of a split between unpaid domestic labor and child care (the so-called private sphere) and social labor, which takes place in a separate location, away from families and communities. That split, of course, is built on a gendered division of labor that assigns women to the domestic sphere even when they are also employed. In other words the category, job, although apparently neutral, implicitly rests on the gendered division of labor in society. Acker argues that although the category "worker" also appears neutral, in fact "ideal" workers are gendered. Who are the ideal workers? Individuals who are committed to work, who have no outside responsibilities that distract them from the tasks at hand, and who need not concern themselves with caring for sick members of their households, delivering the children to and from day care, and shopping for and cooking the family's daily meals. Ideal workers have no obligations outside the job. Ideal workers "exist only for [their] work" (Acker 1990, 149). Who, then, are the ideal workers? Men with stay-at-home wives.

Another indicator that jobs depend on the sexual division of labor and assume that workers are male is the fact that women's bodily needs and rhythms are excluded from the ideal workplace. Emotions, reproduction, and women's bodies disrupt the efficient ordering of the work day, whereas men's bodies fit organizational demands and symbols.

> [I]t is the man's body, its sexuality, minimal responsibility in procreation, and conventional control of emotions that pervades work and organizational processes. Women's bodies—female sexuality, their ability to procreate and their pregnancy, breast-feeding, and child care, menstruation, and mythic "emotionality"—are suspect, stigmatized, and used as grounds for control and exclusion.... While women's bodies are ruled out of order, or sexualized and objectified, in work organizations, men's bodies are not. Indeed, male sexual imagery pervades organizational metaphors and language, helping to give form to work activities. For example, the military and male worlds of sports are considered valuable training for organizational success and provide images for teamwork, campaigns, and tough competition. The symbolic expression of male sexuality may be used as a means of control over male workers, too, allowed or even encouraged within the bounds of the work situation to create cohesion or alleviate stress. Management approval of pornographic pictures in the locker room or support for all-male work and play groups where casual talk is about sexual exploits or sports are examples. (Acker 1990, 153)

Acker makes a strong case for the inherent gendering of organizational structures and for understanding the ideal worker as male. As more women enter the workforce, these gendered underpinnings of jobs and workers create crises of care and a time crunch for women workers and their families. The abstract, deceptively gender-neutral classifications and systems of work conceal a gender substructure that controls women workers and women's work. Through Acker's theory we can see how gender is a product of large-scale organizations and organizational processes.

GENDERED INSTITUTIONS

The term *social institution* refers to a persistent constellation of practices, power relations, norms, interactional dynamics, and ideologies surrounding social phenomena. Some sociologists identify particular substantive areas as institutions. They study the institutions of family, education, work, religion, or media. Others conceptualize institutions as processes. Interacting human beings create social institutions and these in turn create us. Using this view of institutions, some scholars argue that gender is an institution. As processes, institutions entail recurring and predictable social practices, ways to distribute scarce resources, ways to care for those who cannot care for themselves, ways of identifying and legitimating leaders and so forth. Gender is the process by which we accomplish these tasks.

Institutions are not "out there," but are inside and around us. Through the recurring practices and ever-present pressures of institutional processes we live out the constraints and possibilities that they make thinkable and possible. We feel these constraints and potentials as parts of our selves, as emotions, desires, and goals. As we act on these feelings, we reproduce the very institutions that have made us. As the early twentieth-century American sociologist Charles Horton Cooley (1962, 5)_wrote, "self and society are twin born". We give birth to our world and our world gives birth to us. These births are ongoing, not one-time events. Neither selves nor societies are static. C. Wright Mills (1967, 6) called the individual and social forms of existence "biography" and "history." Biography, the history of an individual life, is always in a state of transformation or "becoming." History is the story of groups, peoples, and national entities that are constantly evolving and changing. As we produce and reproduce the institutions that shape us and our worlds, we change them and ourselves, sometimes consciously, more often subtly and without conscious intent. Through our collective actions, then, we maintain, but also resist, and change institutions.

The vignette, "Tom, Betsy, and the Telephone" (Box 3–3) shows the unconscious operation of gender in a workplace and demonstrates (1) how gender is a part of our psychological makeup, (2) how we act to reproduce the institution that shapes us, and (3) how resistance emerges and leads to changes in the institution of gender.

Studying institutions involves understanding their history and the power relations that constitute them. Gender relations have changed radically over time—gender has a history. Institutions involve power, and the institution of gender is suffused with power relations. For example, the claim that gender is natural is a political claim that suppresses gender's history and dismisses the possibility of gender equality. Gender history is about changes in gender relations produced by our collective and individual actions in the world. We do not simply react to the world, we actively make it. That is what sociologists mean by agency. Institutions are social creations that constrain their creators, but their creators also have agency and can change institutions.

"Gender is done from birth, constantly and by everyone" and "one of the major ways people organize their lives; where there is gender difference there is inequality and stratification" (Lorber 1994, 14–15). This is true, to a greater or lesser extent, in every known society. The more power, prestige, and wealth at stake, the more gender difference is the case. Within contemporary class societies, gender inequality is more pronounced among the wealthy than among the poor. Lorber (1994, 34) summarizes a variety of studies of inequality and stratification as follows:

> The more economic resources, such as education and job opportunities, are available to a group, the more they tend to be monopolized by men. In poorer groups that have few resources (such as working-class African Americans in the United States), women and men are more nearly equal, and the women may even outstrip the men in education and occupational status.

In the gender stratification system of the United States, wealthy businessmen and corporate executives control more resources, and are more likely to be in political and economic leadership positions. In 2004, only 14 percent of the U.S. Congress was female. In 2002, there were six women chief executive officers among the Fortune 500 (1.2 percent). Race complicates this picture of stratification. In 2004, African American women were 1.1 percent

Box 3–3 TOM, BETSY, AND THE TELEPHONE: AN ORGANIZATIONAL STORY

Tom and Betsy, both vice-presidents in a Fortune 100 company, stood talking in a hallway after a meeting. Along the hallway were offices but none was theirs. A phone started to ring in one office and after three or so rings, Tom said to Betsy, "Why don't you get that?" Betsy was surprised by Tom's request but answered the phone anyway and Tom returned to his office. Afterwards, Betsy found Tom to ask if he realized what he had done. She Told him: "I'm a vice-president too, Tom, and you treated me like a secretary. What were you thinking?" Betsy's reaction surprised Tom. He did not mean anything by his action, he said, commenting: "I did not even think about it." Tom apologized to Betsy. She told Tom his behavior was "typical of how men in High Tech Corporation [a pseudonym] treat women. You're patronizing and [you] don't treat us as equals." Tom was again surprised and decided to ask other women if they agreed with Betsy.

Tom discussed this event with 18 women from the organization, who told him "about the hurtfulness of their experiences" at High Tech. Tom was inspired to start a group of 18 men and 18 women to discuss gender issues in the corporation. Martin comments:

> According to everyone who knew this story . . . Betsy became angry with Tom for asking and with herself for answering the telephone. Tom and Betsy were both familiar with and skilled in gender practices; thus they simply "hopped into the [gender] river and swam." . . . They did not reflect. They did not analyze the situation; they were "practiced" in gender; they practiced gender. The gender institution holds women accountable to pleasing men; it tells men/boys they have a (gender) right to be assisted by women/girls; Tom and Betsy knew this. Tom's request and Betsy's behavior are thus unsurprising. Without stopping to reflect, Tom practiced a kind of masculinity that the gender institution makes available to him, which is to request practical help from women; Betsy responded in kind by complying with his request.

> Martin explains that such requests (and there are others, such as "cook my food," "raise my kids," and "wash my clothes") are usually not articulated, but rather built into the language of institutionalized positions, such as secretary, "that are gendered over time and across situations." Notice that Betsy did not object to the assumptions about secretaries ("like a subordinate" and "like a woman"). "In Judith Butler's terms, Tom's and Betsy's actions were citational of the gender order. They showed awareness and skill in reinstituting the gender institution within which they live—as man, as woman." Nevertheless, Betsy's subsequent complaints shifted the gender order in that workplace.

SOURCE: Patricia Yancey Martin, 2003, Gender & Society (17): 342–66.

of corporate officers in Fortune 500 companies, a mere 106 individuals out of a group of 10,092 (Brown 2004). Gender stratification is evident even at the highest levels of business. In 2001, women held the highest number of Fortune 1000 board seats in toys and sporting goods (25%), in soaps and cosmetics (22%), in publishing and printing (18%), and in computers and office equipment (18%). They held the lowest number of Fortune 1000 board seats in oilfield services (0%), transportation (0%), and automotive retailing and services (3%; Business and Professional Women 2003).

In a gender-structured and gender-stratified society, what certain men do is more highly valued than what women and lower class, lower status men do. Women everywhere are systematically worse off than men, although women from the professional and managerial middle classes and from the upper class are better off in terms of security, wealth, and opportunity than, for example, working-class and poor men of color. If money is the measure of value in our capitalist society, then women are of lesser value as workers. Are men's jobs more vital, more central to the economy? Try this thought experiment. Think for a minute about one of the least valued and most dishonored forms of work: domestic labor. Think now about a world in which no one did that work. Make a list of what would not get done if there were not a group of people, unpaid or underpaid, who do housework. Think now about child care and the care of old people. Imagine that there was not a group—again, unpaid or severely underpaid—who do the work of caring. What would happen to the wealthy and powerful members of society if there were no such group?

We have come a long way from the idea of gender as a function of individual psychology. Far from a necessity external to the social order, rooted perhaps in our biological or psychological makeup, gender is a construction within and of society. The implication of this perspective is radical. It forces us to ask, what is the point of distinguishing men from women? Lorber suggests that the point is to create a class of subordinates.

> Gender inequality—the devaluation of "women" and the social domination of "men"—has social functions and a social history. It is not the result of sex, procreation, physiology, anatomy, hormones, or genetic predispositions. It is produced and maintained by identifiable social processes and built into the general social structure and individual identities deliberately and purposefully. The social order as we know it in Western societies is organized around racial, ethnic, class, and gender inequality. I contend, therefore, that the continuing purpose of gender as a modern social institution is to construct women as a group to be the subordinates of men as a group. (Lorber 1994, 35)

At this juncture we must consider whether gender is a relationship with a future. Holly Devor imagines a future in which gender is "obsolete and meaningless." If sex and gender were to become as meaningless as eye color, she writes,

> the social entities we now call women and men would become archaic and the basis for gender as a meaningful concept would become irreparably eroded. Were people to become no longer distinguishable on the basis of sex, were all gender choices open to all people, were there to cease to be a cognitive system which measured the world in gendered units, the material basis for sexism would cease to exist. (Devor 1989, 154)

This chapter has presented three stories about gender difference. Stories based on social roles and social learning tell us about the ways individuals learn gender norms and behave in gendered ways. Interactionist stories move beyond the individual level of explanation to focus on the relationships among individuals and within groups in daily life. Stories at the structural and institutional levels inform us about the gendered distribution of material and social resources and the gendered ideologies and discourses that support these gender inequalities. Do we need to decide which one is the "best" story? Perhaps not. Each story tells us something we need to know and each story is linked to the others in important ways. One way to think about these linkages is to imagine that (1) gender roles internalized and adopted by individuals through gender socialization; (2) sustained by social expectations, gender categorization, and accountability (doing gender) at the interactional level; and (3) shaped by constraints and possibilities at the structural and institutional levels are three interconnected chapters in the story about gender differences and gendered inequalities. Each chapter of this story adds a dimension to our understanding of the whole and no chapter tells us all of what we need to know. Tying these chapters together is the process Anthony Giddens called "structuration."

Giddens (1984) developed this term to refer to the relationship between human agency and social structure, between the individual level of action, in which we exercise choice, and the structural or institutional level of tradition, moral codes, institutions, and established ways of doing things, which constrains our choices. In Giddens's theory, human agency and social structure are two sides of the same coin, or to use Mead's metaphor, "twin-born." Structures shape individuals and individuals shape structures. Human action reproduces structure but also creates new conditions of action. Sociologist Barbara Risman puts it this way:

> Gender is deeply embedded as a basis for stratification not just in our personalities, our cultural rules, or institutions but in all these, and in complicated ways. The gender structure differentiates opportunities and constraints based on sex category and thus has consequences on three dimensions: (1) At the individual level, for the development of gendered selves; (2) during interaction as men and women face different cultural expectations even when they fill the identical structural positions; and (3) in institutional domains where explicit regulations regarding resource distribution and material goods are gender specific. (Risman 2004, 433)

When sociologists argue that gender is a social construction, they are referring to this complex, multilevel process. At the individual level, we grow up with gender expectations, gender rules, and gendered practices that we may or may not come to question. Where do such expectations come from? Studies of social learning have shown how adults socialize children into existing gender arrangements. Our own recollections remind us of that strong influence families have on most of us when we are very young. Sometimes parents and others select toys or clothing for children that mark gender differences (or, as likely, are persuaded to do so by their own children): baby dolls and pretend make-up for small girls; militarized and muscled "dolls" for boys. Perhaps the kids on the block or in the schoolyard create gendered forms of play and interaction. However, that answer only pushes the question back a notch, for we must then ask where do our parents or our friends get their ideas? When they were very young, they learned a lot from their own parents and other caretakers, as you learned from yours. Times change, though, and with them social contexts and gendered expectations, as well as the problems we confront and solutions to them we devise collectively.

Box 3–4 IMAGINING A DIFFERENT FUTURE

Twenty years ago, when the second wave of feminism was just beginning, we were preoccupied with countering biological arguments that had long been used to justify gender divisions and inequalities. Now many of us are concerned less about biology than about the hold of existing arrangements on our imaginations and desires. How do we become invested in particular forms of femininity and masculinity, in oppositional gender, in arrangements based on domination? What are sources of resistance, of opposition, of alternative arrangements based on equality and mutuality? How can we imagine, and realize, other possibilities?

When I grasp for a concrete image to hold an abstraction like gender equality and mutuality, I sometimes think about Hansel and Gretel, extracted, if they can be, from the adults of the story—the wicked stepmother, the witch, the irresponsible father. Gretel and Hansel (I exchange the order of their names to animate the image of equality) provide mutual support as they go through the dangers of the forest. They each take the lead, Hansel in gathering and scattering the pebbles and, later, the bread crumbs to mark their path, and Gretel in tricking the witch. They confront the vicissitudes of life as brother and sister, as caring friends.

In fact, in our culture the model of sisters and brothers offers one of the few powerful images of relatively equal relationships between girls and boys, and between adult men and women. It is not by chance that relationships between brothers and sisters begin in childhood, a period in which gender relations are relatively egalitarian. Boys of elementary school age lack major sources of adult male privilege, such as access to greater income and material resources, control of political and other forms of public power, and the legal and labor entitlements of husbands compared with wives. The "protected" status of children (which, from another vantage point, constitutes a pattern of legal, economic, and political subordination) cuts across gender and mutes male privilege. The dominance of boys over girls may, as a result, be more anxious, but it also has a weaker material and legal base than the dominance of men over women.

The painfully sparse language that kids have for relationships between girls and boys—"like" charged with romantic connotations, "hate" as a quick nullification—underscores the need for more images of, and more experience with, cross-gender relationships based on friendship and collegiality. The culture of heterosexual romance needs fundamental reconstruction so that it no longer overshadows other possibilities for intimacy and sexuality. Friendship and equality are a much better basis for intimate relationships than mistrust and a sense of being strangers.

As adults we can help kids, as well as ourselves, imagine and realize different futures, alter institutions, craft new life stories. A more complex understanding of the dynamics of gender, of tensions and contradictions, and of the hopeful moments that lie within present arrangements, can help broaden our sense of the possible. (Thorne 1997***)

In *Gender Play,* her ethnographic study of the ways schoolchildren construct and overcome gendered boundaries, Barrie Thorne (1997) shows how an individual-level framework that explains gender as a system learned through socialization pushes us to see gender differentiation, but makes invisible the nongendered social activity in children's play. Good researchers know that the questions one asks determine the answers one gets. If researchers believe that there are differences between boys and girls, and devise tests to capture those differences, they will not notice all the moments when boys and girls are similar. Just as public restrooms create the differences they exist to honor, as Goffman pointed out, studies based on the assumption of difference will probably find the difference they assume exists. In her study of children's play, Thorne asks and answers a different question, one that does not assume difference: How do children together create gender structures and gendered meanings and how do they also challenge these structures and meanings? She writes:

> In shifting the focus from individual to social relations, I move away from the question, Are girls and boys different? which centers most of the research on children and gender. Instead I ask: How do children actively come together to help create, and sometimes challenge, gender structures and meanings? (Thorne 1997, 4)

Such questions can help us to see the dimension of socially constructed differences in the wider context of our similarities and common interests.

Imagine a world without gender! (See Box 3–4.)

REFERENCES

Acker, Joan. 1990. Hierarchies, jobs, bodies: A theory of gendered organizations. *Gender & Society* 4 (2): 139–58.

Bem, Sandra. 1993. *The lenses of gender: Transforming the debate on sexual inequality.* New Haven, CT: Yale University Press.

Blakemore, Judith, and Renee Centers. 2005. Characteristics of boys' and girls' toys. *Sex Roles* 53 (9/10): 619–33.

Business and Professional Women. 2003. *Women in the Fortune 500.* http://www.bpwusa.org/content/PressRoom/101Facts/101_Fortune500.htm.

Brown, Carolyn. 2004. Advancing African American women in the workplace: new study finds challenges remain despite push for diversity. *Black Enterprise.* June. http://findarticles.com/p/articles/mi_m1365/is_11_34/ai_n6168973 Accessed June 20, 2008.

Cohn, Carol. 1987. Sex and death in the rational world of defense intellectuals. *Signs: Journal of Women in Contemporary Society* 12 (4): 687–718.

Cole, Johnneta. 1971. Black women in America: An annotated bibliography. *The Black Scholar* (December): 42–53.

Collins, Patricia Hill. 2000. *Black feminist thought: Knowledge, consciousness, and the politics of empowerment.* 2nd ed. New York: Routledge.

Connell, R. W. 1987. *Gender and power.* Stanford, CA: Stanford University Press.

Cooley, Charles Horton. 1962. *Social Organization.* NY: Schocken.

Coontz, Stephanie. 1992. *The way we never were: American families and the nostalgia trap.* New York: Basic Books.

Devor, Holly. 1989. *Gender blending: Confronting the limits of duality.* Bloomington: University of Indiana Press.

Epstein, Cynthia. 1970. *Women's place: Options and limits in professional careers.* Berkeley: University of California Press.

Garfinkel, Harold. 1967. *Studies in ethnomethodology.* New York: Prentice-Hall.

Giddens, Anthony. 1984. *The Constitution of Society: Outline of the Theory of Structuration.* Berkeley, University of California Press.

Glick, Peter, and Susan T. Fiske. 1999. Gender, power dynamics, and social interaction. In *Revisioning gender,* ed. Myra Marx Ferree, Judith Lorber, and Beth Hess, 365–98. Thousand Oaks, CA: Sage.

Goffman, Erving. 1977. The arrangement between the sexes. *Theory and Society* 4(3). Autumn. 301–331.

Hill, Shirley. 2005. *Black intimacies: A gender perspective on families and relationships.* Walnut Creek, CA: Altamira Press.

Hochschild, Arlie. 1973. A review of sex role research. *American Journal of Sociology* 78 (4): 1011–29.

——— . 1983. *The managed heart: Commercialization of human feeling.* Berkeley: University of California Press.

Kanter, Rosabeth Moss. 1977. *Men and women of the corporation.* New York: Basic Books.

Komarovksy, Mirra. 1953. *Women in the modern world: Their education and their dilemmas.* Boston: Little Brown and Company.

Lorber, Judith. 1975. Women and medical sociology: Invisible professionals and ubiquitous patients. In *Another voice: Feminist perspectives on social life and social science,* ed. Marcia Millman and Rosabeth Moss Kanter, 75–105. New York: Anchor.

——— . 1994. *Paradoxes of gender.* New Haven, CT: Yale University Press.

Martin, Patricia Yancey. 2003. 'Said and Done' vs. 'Saying and Doing': Gendering practices, practicing gender at work. *Gender and Society* 17: 342–66.

Marx, Karl. 1972. *The eighteenth brumaire of Louis Bonaparte.* Moscow: Progress Publishers.

Mills, C. Wright. 1967. *The sociological imagination.* New York: Oxford University Press.

Risman, Barbara. 2004. Gender as social structure. *Gender & Society* 18 (4): 429–50.

Sandler, Bernice. 1986. The Campus Climate Revisited: Chilly for Women Faculty, Administrators, and Graduate Students. Project on the Status and Education of Women of the Association of American Colleges, Washington DC.

Thorne, Barrie. 1997. *Gender play: Girls and boys in school.* New Brunswick, NJ: Rutgers University Press.

West, Candace, and Don H. Zimmerman. 1987. Doing gender. *Gender & Society* 1 (2): 125–51.

West, Candace, and Sarah Fenstermaker. 1995. Doing difference. *Gender and Society* 9 (1): 8–37.

Williams, Christine. 1995. *Still a man's world: Men who do women's work.* Berkeley: University of California Press.

4

SEXUALITIES

SEX AND THE CITY

MIRANDA: We should start a brothel where the men are cute and the sheets are 500-count Egyptian cotton. Samantha can be the Madam.
SAMANTHA: At least something exciting would be happening in this town.
CARRIE: We could have one in every neighborhood, like Starbucks.

SAMANTHA: I never leave underwear at a guy's place because I never see it again.
CHARLOTTE: What happens to it?
SAMANTHA: Nothing; I just never go back.
CARRIE: Doesn't that get a little expensive, disposing of lingerie every time you sleep with a guy?
SAMANTHA: That's why I stopped wearing underwear on dates.
MIRANDA: And that's why I'm never borrowing a dress from you again.

CARRIE: Are we simply romantically challenged, or are we sluts?
CARRIE: Men who have had a lot of sexual partners are not called sluts. They're called very good kissers, a few are even called romantics.

CHARLOTTE: I just don't understand. How could you forget someone you slept with?
CARRIE: Toto, I don't think we're in single digits anymore.

MIRANDA: Everybody masturbates.
SAMANTHA: Mmm, I did it this morning.
CARRIE: Well, that explains why I got your voice mail.

CARRIE: I'm not going to replace a man with some battery-operated device.
MIRANDA: You haven't met "The Rabbit."
SAMANTHA: Oh come on, if you're going to get a vibrator, at least get one called "The Horse."

MIRANDA: I'm trying to change my bed karma. I figure if I can make my bed a place
I really want to be, others will feel the same.
CARRIE: Aah, the Field of Dreams.
MIRANDA: Exactly. If you build it, he will come.

SAMANTHA: I'm a trisexual. I'll try anything once.

CHARLOTTE: After the wedding, I finally get to sleep with Trey.
CARRIE: Excuse me?
MIRANDA: You haven't slept with him yet?
SAMANTHA: Honey, before you buy the car you take it for a test drive!

CARRIE: There are 1.3 million single men in New York, 1.8 million single women, and
of these more than 3 million people, about 12 think they're having enough sex.

These are all quotes from the scripts of the television show *Sex and the City*, which centers
around Carrie Bradshaw, a journalist, and her three best friends: Charlotte, an art dealer;
Miranda, a lawyer; and Samantha, a publicist and business woman. These four single women
live in New York City and meet frequently to talk about men, relationships, and sex. Carrie's
character is based on Candace Bushnell (1997), a real journalist who wrote a sex column for
the *New York Observer* and a novel derived from the letters she received and the responses
she wrote for her column. The HBO series was nominated for fifty Emmy Awards and has a
huge following of fans.

Even though *Sex and the City* no longer is producing new episodes, its popularity continues through syndication, with DVD sales, websites, and fan clubs, as well as a feature film
based on the show released in 2008. The series has been claimed both as a sign of the sexual
liberation U.S. women have achieved and the sexual oppression of women that remains. The
characters relish their sexual freedom and pleasures, but they also constantly talk about their
clothing, their hair, their weight, and their age. They also frequently fall into discussions of
what they might be missing as single women.

Carrie and her friends are supposed to depict a range of experiences, with Samantha the
most daring and Charlotte the most conservative. However, the four are remarkably similar:
All are glamorous, wealthy, living in New York, dressed in designer clothes, eating at fashion-
able restaurants, and attending operas, plays, and concerts. The four women are all heterosexual, although Samantha had a brief fling with another woman, and all are white. This is
especially odd in New York, one of the most cosmopolitan places in the world.

- Are Carrie and her friends sexually liberated? What does it mean to be sexually
  liberated for both men and women? Is the double standard a thing of the past?
- Do Carrie and her friends represent the new woman in the United States? In
  the world? Who is left out of the picture? Do their problems represent the issues
  women around the world face regarding sex? What might their stories be like?
- We described Samantha as a heterosexual even though she had an affair with another
  woman. How would you describe Samantha's sexuality? What is sexuality?
- Carrie and her friends are obsessed consumers. Their stories often blend themes
  of closets full of expensive shoes and purses with sexual encounters. What is the
  connection between sex and money or shopping?

This chapter tries to answer these questions. As we will see, many of our attitudes and beliefs about gender are reflected in our opinions and ideas about sexuality. In other words, sexuality is gendered in our thinking and in practice. Different standards, expectations, and experiences exist about sex for women and men. We begin this chapter by looking at some statistics and comparing the United States to other nations.

COMPARING SEXUAL ATTITUDES AND BEHAVIORS AROUND THE GLOBE

Ideas about sex vary across many social lines such as age and nation. One study of ideas about sexual issues among more than 33,000 people in twenty-four nations found they clustered into categories depending on their attitudes about sexual behavior (Widmer, Treas, and Newcomb 1998). The questions asked whether they believed that teen sex (under age sixteen), premarital sex, extramarital sex, and homosexual sex were always wrong, almost always wrong, only sometimes wrong, or not wrong at all. The researchers determined the average for all of the participants and then looked at how the clusters differed from the average.

The first cluster included Australia, Great Britain, Hungary, Italy, Bulgaria, Russia, New Zealand, and Israel. Respondents from these nations believed that extramarital sex and teen sex were always or almost always wrong. Sex before marriage was only sometimes or not at all wrong and respondents were somewhat evenly divided on whether homosexual sex was wrong or not.

A second cluster included people from Germany, Austria, Sweden, and Slovenia. People in these nations had the most liberal attitudes about teens under sixteen having sex, premarital sex, and extramarital sex, but their opinion of homosexual sex was more divided. A third category included the United States, Ireland, and Poland. This was the most conservative group, with high proportions believing that sex outside of marriage, teen sex, and homosexual sex were always or almost always wrong. A fourth group included people from the Netherlands, Norway, the Czech Republic, Canada, and Spain. They believed that extramarital sex was wrong and were about evenly divided about teen sex. They were the most likely to say that premarital sex and homosexual sex were not wrong at all (Widmer, Treas, and Newcomb 1998).

In addition to variation in ideas about sex, sexual behavior also varies by nation and sometimes seems to contradict opinions. For example, by age thirty, 93 percent of both women and men in the United States have had premarital sex. Despite the more conservative opinions of sex, young Americans have sex at the same age or earlier than Europeans, and have more sexual partners and higher rates of teen pregnancy, abortion, and sexually transmitted diseases (STDs), including HIV (Finer 2007). In other words, American teens may enjoy sex as frequently as European teens, but they pay a high price for it. The dangers of sexuality in the United States have been linked to the absence of adequate government policies, little openness about teen sexuality, little or no access to information about sex, and restricted availability of services. Ironically, in European nations where young people have access to information and services and where tolerance for teen nonmarital sex is high, rates of adolescent sexual activity are lower than in the United States (Feijoo 2001).

Young people, however, are not the only ones who have sex. Edward Laumann and his colleagues (2006) studied the sexual activities of more than 27,000 adults over age forty in twenty-nine nations to see what their experience was and how it varied by nation and gender. The researchers asked people, "In the past twelve months how physically pleasurable did you find your relationship

TABLE 4-1 Sexual Satisfaction, Gender, and Nation Among Adults over 40

Region	Satisfying sexual relations	Satisfied with sexual ability	Sex is very or extremely important
Western			
Men	67	80	50
Women	67	80	33
Middle Eastern			
Men	50	70	60
Women	38	70	37
East Asia			
Men	25	67	28
Women	25	50	12
N = 27,500.			

SOURCE: Laumann et al. (2006).

with your partner to be?" They found that the average responses for each nation could be organized into categories centered around regions in the world: West (Austria, Belgium, France, Germany, Spain, Sweden, United Kingdom, Mexico, Australia, Canada, New Zealand, South Africa, and the United States), Middle East (Algeria, Egypt, Israel, Italy, Morocco, Korea, Turkey, Malaysia, and the Philippines), and East Asia (China, India, Japan, Taiwan, and Thailand).

Table 4–1 shows how the responses differed for women and men in these three categories for three issues: satisfaction with sexual relations, satisfaction with their own sexual ability, and how important sex was for them. The Table 4–1 shows that relationships among region, gender, and sexual issues are complex, with differences between women and men for most questions in most of the regions, and differences from one region to the next on all three questions.

Laumann and his colleagues (2006) argue that the differences from one nation to another are related to ideas about gender equality. In nations in the West where women have relatively more equality with men, sexual satisfaction is relatively high for both women and men. In nations where women have less equality with men, in the Middle East and East Asia, men and especially women have less sexual satisfaction. In East Asia sexual satisfaction is particularly low, A=as is the proportion who says that sex is important to them. These numbers are intriguing and it will take much theoretical analysis to sort out how gender is both a cause and effect of sexual satisfaction and how and why this relationship varies from one culture, nation, or region to another.

CHANGING ATTITUDES TOWARD SEXUALITY IN THE UNITED STATES

Although Americans are more conservative than people from other nations regarding ideas about sex, national survey data reveals that they are much more liberal than they were forty or fifty years ago. In 1937 and 1959, 22 percent of adult Americans approved of either or both parties to a marriage having had previous sexual experience. Gallup poll numbers indicate a minimal decline in 1969 to 21.4 percent. By 1973, 43 percent of Americans surveyed felt that premarital sex was not wrong and by 1985, this proportion had reached 52 percent (Smith, 1994). Today 61 percent of people in the United States say they believe premarital sex is okay (ABC News 2004).

Americans' attitudes toward premarital sex have become increasingly liberal since the "sexual revolution" of the 1960s and 1970s. The slogan "Make love, not war" captured the essence of this time of great political and moral change. Young people were protesting not only against the war in Vietnam, but also against dominant values in post–World War II America. The cracks in the moral terrain of post–World War II America that developed into the free love era of the 1960s and 1970s appeared in the 1950s during the "Playboy Revolution" of the 1950s (Ehrenreich 1984).

Playboy, an iconic men's magazine that began publication in 1953, depicted a lifestyle of carefree sex and fun devoid of consequences. For many middle-class men in the 1950s, becoming an adult meant marrying and settling down. *Playboy* presented the alternative life of the bachelor playboy surrounded by beautiful women who were willing sex partners. Playboy assured us that men could be "real" men—adults, successful in their careers, heterosexual—without being married. For women, the introduction of the oral contraceptive pill in the early 1960s played a role in this sexual sea change, reflecting and contributing to transformed sexual practices and ideas about sex without marriage and sex for pleasure (Rosen 2000).

Feminists were at the forefront of challenging ideas about sex, campaigning for women's rights to control their own bodies and for sexual expression in the new forms of public testimony they invented during the early days of the women's movement. Coming together in "rap" groups to discuss their place as women in a society torn by political debates over war and over the constraints on women's private and public lives, they shared their private troubles and turned them into public issues. They discussed everything from sharing housework and child care with husbands to participating as equals in antiwar struggles and community organizing campaigns run by men. Among the most riveting and instructive discussions carried on by women in these consciousness-raising groups was the talk about sexuality.

In these groups women discovered that their private troubles were shared. They learned that the "experts" on sex did not know much about female sexuality, but were in fact experts on men's sexuality, imposed on women. Women's actual experiences were very different from the experts' discourse. In rap groups women learned to explore their worlds from their own experiences by coming together in small groups to tell their stories about sexuality and domestic life. For the first time, they spoke with others about the disappointments of their sex lives with husbands and boyfriends, about faked orgasms and their fears of being "frigid," about the need to please one's man or any man, and about sex on men's terms. Ruth Rosen (2000) explains:

> In the future, people may wonder why the "faked orgasm" became such an important topic in women's liberation groups. Many young movement men, products of the fifties, had only the vaguest ideas about female sexuality. And daughters of the fifties often knew even less. Initially, sexual experimentation seemed exhilarating,

but it didn't take long for young women to realize that more sex did not necessarily result in better sex. Ignorant of their own bodies, embarrassed to discuss sexual matters, many young women faked orgasm for fear of being labeled with that terrifying accusatory term of the fifties, "frigid." (148)

Although rap groups no longer exist and the orgasm gap may be closing, gender differences in sexual pleasure persist. A recent survey of women and men in the United States found that 75 percent of sexually active men report they always have an orgasm, whereas only 30 percent of women say they always have an orgasm. An additional 45 percent of the women, however, say they have an orgasm "most of the time" (ABC News 2004).

Orgasm and Sexual Politics

In the early days of the women's liberation movement, the discussion about sex was centered on heterosexuality and women's relationships with men. A central focus was on penetrative sex and on the vaginal orgasm. Freud, whose ideas were a powerful force in the middle of the twentieth century, held that mature female sexuality entailed relinquishing clitoral for vaginal orgasms. Based on listening to one another and learning from their own experience, feminists challenged the claim that "mature" orgasms were exclusively located in the vagina, asserting that this idea came out of a focus on men's sexual needs and on vaginal sexual intercourse with men as the only "right" way for women to have sex.

Anne Koedt's (1996) 1970 paper, "The Myth of the Vaginal Orgasm," criticized this point of view, and was widely circulated among rap groups around the country. Koedt wrote: "Women have been defined sexually in terms of what pleases men; our own biology has not been properly analysed. Instead, we are fed the myth of the liberated woman and her vaginal orgasm—an orgasm that in fact does not exist" (Koedt 1996,115). Koedt argued that the Freudian distinction between clitoral (or "immature") and vaginal ("mature") orgasms privileged men's pleasure and questioned the supposed "naturalness" or inevitably of heterosexuality. "It would thus open up the whole question of *human* sexual relationships beyond the confines of the present male-female role system" (Koedt 1996, 116).

At the same time feminists were criticizing male-centered heterosexuality, critical discussion of the institution of heterosexuality itself was part of the growing lesbian movement of the day. For lesbian feminists, lesbianism was a political statement, a rejection of the patriarchal institutions of heterosexuality and marriage, and an expression of women's sexual liberation. Adrienne Rich (1996) contributed the concept of "compulsory heterosexuality," to the discussion, arguing that social institutions and popular culture assume heterosexuality and that heterosexuality maintained women's subordination. Rich was one of the first scholars to question the existence of the sexual binaries of heterosexuality and homosexuality. She placed women on a "lesbian continuum." One pole of this continuum included women's friendships and loving connections to other women and active lesbian sexuality was at the other pole. Rich maintained that the alliances of women throughout the continuum were a key factor in overturning patriarchy.

The politics of sexuality was a central aspect of women's struggles for gender equality in the emerging feminism of the 1970s. To be truly free and equal women needed to be sexually liberated. Sexual liberation included (1) access to birth control and safe, legal abortions;

(2) free sexuality, including the right to pleasure; (3) the right to say no to sex; and (4) the sexual option of lesbianism.

Sex Talk

Despite changes in ideology, reproductive technology, laws, and even sexual behaviors, the double standard of sexuality for men and women persists. In the *Sex and the City* quotes at the beginning of the chapter, Carrie asks, "Are we simply romantically challenged, or are we sluts? Men who have had a lot of sexual partners are not called sluts. They're called very good kissers, a few are even called romantics." The rules about what is sexually appropriate vary by gender.

The double standard is reflected in the language we use to talk about sex. "Dick," "dong," "pecker," "woody," "tool," "snake," "skin flute," and "third leg" are a sampling of colloquial penis pseudonyms. Try to make a list of ten or even fifteen more penis names. You probably can. Now, try to do the same for vaginas. You will probably find that constructing a list of vagina pseudonyms is more challenging. This is a part of the sexual double standard.

Now ask five close men and five close women friends if they have named their genitals or if during sex play their partners use names for their genitals. Don't be surprised to see a gender difference here as well. Talking about women's genitals is restricted because we do not have the language. Our lack of words makes women's sexuality less visible. At the same time, the focus on men's genitals makes the penis seem like the only source of men's sexual identity.

As the "penis talk" activity shows, there is a sexual double standard both in how we talk about genitals and how much talk there is about them. These gender differences are also embedded in the language of sex that is the words, expressions, and ways we talk about sex. Robert Baker (2000) looked at the words used to describe heterosexual intercourse and found that the American cultural conception of sex between a man and a woman reflects traditional gender relations, specifically that of man as aggressor and initiator and woman as passive receptor. When we speak of heterosexual intercourse, the man is usually the grammatical subject and the woman is the grammatical object. For example, we say "Dick screwed Jane." The man subject plays an active role, and Jane, the woman subject, plays a passive role. She is having these actions done to her. Thus, our linguistic choices reflect stereotyped and unequal gender relations. Although this study is more than thirty years old, the language used to describe heterosexual intercourse persists.

So how do we explain the positioning of Dick as the active subject and Jane as the passive object? It could be argued that the language of sex reflects anatomical differences. The penis does the inserting and the vagina is inserted into. As such, one might argue that sentences like "Jane screwed Dick," "Jane fucked Dick," or "Jane had Dick" simply do not make sense given the natural biological asymmetry between the sexes.

Baker (2000) disagrees. He argues that the way we talk about sex is shaped by social forces, not biology. Political relationships between women and men determine the language we use to describe sexual relationships between women and men. The way we talk about sex reinforces the political relationships in which men tend to dominate. He writes:

> Anatomical differences do not determine how we are to conceptualize the relation
> between penis and vagina during intercourse. Thus one can easily imagine a society

in which the female normally played the active role during intercourse, where female subjects required active constructions with verbs indicating copulation, and where the standard metaphors were terms like "engulfing"—that is, instead of saying "he screwed her," one would say "she engulfed him." It follows that the use of passive constructions for female subjects of verbs indicating copulation does not reflect differences determined by human anatomy but rather reflects those generated by human customs. (Baker 2000, 279)

Masturbation

Norms about masturbation provide another example of the double standard. Masturbation for men is less stigmatized, reflecting the rule that holds that men's sexual expression is expected and encouraged. Men must masturbate to be masculine. Masturbation for men is unavoidable, a rite of passage during puberty, and socially tolerated as part of a traditional view of sexuality that places entitlement and pleasure at the center of men's sexuality.

For women, masturbation is discouraged as shameful and unfeminine. In the scenario at the beginning of the chapter, Carrie and her friend tease each other about masturbation. On the one hand the discussion of women masturbating on a popular television show like *Sex and the City* shows that perhaps this area of sexuality is opening up for women. On the other hand, however, Carrie and her friends represent ultraliberal women in TV land so their discussion makes masturbation appear to be an activity of only the most radical women.

Why is masturbation so taboo for women? Some scholars argue that like lesbianism, masturbation provides evidence that women do not need a man to achieve orgasm. Masturbation demonstrates a form of sexual agency and autonomy that threatens the status quo (Rich 1996). In the script from *Sex and the City*, Carrie says, "I'm not going to replace a man with some battery-operated device." But her friends tell her that vibrators are useful tools. Their discussion illustrates the way masturbation can remove men from the picture. Cultural messages like "Nice girls don't touch themselves" maintain gendered sexual relations because they assert that women cannot "replace men" but must seek men out for satisfying sex.

The Racial Subtext of the Sexual Double Standard

The sexual double standard is racialized as well as gendered in the United States. For African Americans, the sexual double standard means that black men are subject to sexual surveillance and restriction and are severely punished if they do not follow the rules or if they are falsely accused of breaking the norms. Black women are subjected to sexual exploitation and violence by white men (Nagel 2003).

Until the 1960s, antimiscegenation laws in the Southern United States were enacted to prevent interracial marriages and sexual encounters. White men, however, were not obligated to follow the laws and white men raped black women at will, often impregnating them. Box 4–1 describes a sexual relationship between Thomas Jefferson and one of his adolescent slaves illustrating the impunity of white men. From 1865 well into the twentieth century, no Southern white man was convicted of raping a black woman (White 1985).

Powerful myths about black sexuality served as justifications for racial oppression and to this day act as controlling images "designed to make racism, sexism, poverty, and other forms of social injustice appear to be natural, normal, and inevitable parts of everyday life" (Collins 2000,69). The controlling images either depict black men and women (images of Bigger Thomas and Jezebel) as sexually powerful and threatening or as harmless, desexed subordinates of white society(Uncle Tom and Aunt Jemima) (West 1993; Collins 2000).

The Bigger Thomas image of black men's sexuality is particularly important because of its connection to sexual violence and to the myth of the Black rapist (Davis 1990). In fact, accusations of rape were common and used to justify lynchings in the United States well into the twentieth century. It is estimated that between 1882 and 1968, 539 African Americans were lynched in Mississippi alone (Payne 1994, 7).

The death of Emmett Till in 1955 was a brutal demonstration of a modern-day lynching. While visiting family in Mississippi from Chicago during his summer vacation, fourteen-year-old Emmett Till went into a grocery store to buy some candy. As he left, Emmett reportedly whistled at Carolyn Bryant, the white clerk and wife of the store's owner. A few days later, Carolyn's husband Roy Bryant, along with his half-brother, John W. Milam, kidnapped and murdered Emmett Till. His mutilated body was recovered from the Tallahatchie River. A 75-pound electric fan was tethered to his neck with barbed wire, his nose was crushed, his right eye was hanging down the middle of his face, and there was a bullet hole through his head (Hudson-Weems 1994). Bryant and Milam were charged with the murder of Emmett Till and were acquitted by a jury of twelve white men. They confessed to the murder in a magazine article published in 1956 but were never brought up on any additional charges. Milam died in 1980 and Bryant in 1990. They lived out the rest of their natural lives in Mississippi. Emmett Till is an important figure in the Civil Rights Movement as his death ignited Black communities across the South that were outraged not only by the savagery of this modern-day lynching but by the failure of the legal system to provide justice. Till's murder is regarded by some historians as the catalyst for the Civil Rights Movement (Hudson-Weems 1994).

Today, the myth of the black rapist continues. Davis (1990) argues that white women in the United States are socialized to fear black men even though they are statistically more likely to be raped by men of their own race. Approximately 90 percent of all rapes in the United States are intraracial (Greenfield 1997). The frequent portrayal of black men in movies and on television as brutish and aggressive whether as rapists, pimps, gangsters, drug dealers, or wife abusers, however, perpetuates this fear (Entman and Rojecki 2001).

The myth of the black rapist, however, is not just an image on television. Differential treatment of black and white men in the criminal justice system also reflects and perpetuates a racialized sexual double standard. Angela Davis (1990) points out that in the United States, rape laws were framed to protect the daughters and wives of upper class men. Few of these men have been prosecuted for the considerable sexual violence they inflicted on working-class women, particularly black women. Indeed the few rapists brought to justice have been overwhelmingly African American, and of these, many have been proved innocent. Of the 455 men executed between 1930 and 1967 on the basis of rape convictions, 405 of them were black. The history of lynching shows that what Davis calls the "frameup rape charge," or "the myth of the Black rapist," has incited and justified racist aggression against black men while erasing the sexual violence that white men have inflicted on black women (Davis 1983).

Box 4–1 SALLY HEMINGS AND THOMAS JEFFERSON

For a long time, historians have been debating whether President Thomas Jefferson had sexual relations with his slaves that produced slave children. During his presidency, a journalist named James Callender was the first to publicly make such charges. Many others have debated the issue since then. Recently, biologists have provided empirical evidence of these relationships through DNA tests. The tests conclude that at least one of Sally Hemings's seven children was fathered by Jefferson (Lander & Ellis 1998).

Sally Hemings was a slave who was owned by Jefferson. She was the half sister of his wife because Mrs. Jefferson's father had sexual relations with Hemings's mother, who was also a slave. When Jefferson first engaged in sex with Hemings, she was only about fourteen years old, thirty years younger than he was. Their sexual relationship lasted for a long time, and at least one of the children she bore was his. Jefferson never freed Hemings or his children who were born to her (Burstein, Isenberg, and Gordon-Reed 1999).

Some scholars have portrayed the relationship between Hemings and Jefferson as a love affair. Others have questioned whether a teenage slave who had no right to refuse her master's sexual advances could enter into a relationship of love or even consent. What do you think of this debate? Were slave women who were subjected to sex with their owners sometimes their lovers? Or were these encounters always a form of rape because the women could not voice their own feelings and, regardless of their feelings, they did not have the right to refuse the slave owner (Aulette 2007)?

Racialized Images of Women's Sexuality

The sexual stereotypes of women of color reflect two extremes of sexual expression. Black women are either Aunt Jemimas or Jezebels. Latinas are Madonnas or whores (Espín 1986; Almquist 1994; Cofer 1993). First Nations women are often labeled as Pocahontas—the Indian princess who assists white men—or squaw, an untamed, sexual being. The 1995 Disney movie *Pocahontas* tells the apocryphal story of Pocahontas, daughter of Chief Powhatan, who convinced her father to spare the life of the colonist John Smith (Green 1975).

The legend of Pocahontas, as told in the movie, is based on the relationship between a young, Native American princess and a Virginia colonist, Captain John Smith. Pocahontas is said to have had his life spared by her father, Chief Powhatan and to have warned whites of First Nations attacks. At the other end of the spectrum from the "helper" image, Native American women are also stereotyped as the "savage squaw." The term *squaw* is an Algonquin word that literally means "woman." It is used derogatorily, often on its own to mean female genitalia or as a negative term in general for First Nations women. The "savage squaw" is the untamed, highly sexual whore who lacks Pocahontas's beauty and civility.

Asian women are also stereotyped as sexually threatening dragon ladies, cunning femme fatales who seduce white men, or geishas, who exist to please white men sexually and domestically (Tajima 1989; Espiritu 1997). This image of gentleness and submission has helped fuel the demand for Asian mail-order brides, which we discuss in chapter 7. In addition, governments in Thailand, Vietnam, and the Philippines have built sex tourism on this image of exotic Asian female sexuality to bring foreign exchange into their countries.

Sex Tourism

The sex tourism industry is based on sexual and racial ethnic stereotypes. Sex tourism typically involves men from the Global North traveling to countries and regions in the Global South such as Thailand, the Philippines, Central and South America, and the Caribbean for the purpose of engaging in sexual acts with local sex workers, many of whom are illegally trafficked or are children. In her fieldwork in Cuba, Julia O'Connell Davidson (1996) found that the sex tourists were predominately white British, Canadian, Italian, and Spanish men, "Mr. Averages" in their own countries who perceive Cuban culture as sexually permissive and Cuban women, especially black Cuban women, as sexually available.

> Cuban girls are "racialised" Others who are "hot for it" (so hot, they'll go with you for a bar of soap; so hot, even the 14-year-olds are begging for it; so hot, they don't care how old or obese or unappealing the man is). (46)

For between twenty and forty dollars plus the cost of meals, these men can have full sexual access to a Cuban woman for an entire day, hence the motto "Find them, feed them, fuck them, forget them." Seabrook's (1996) research reveals how Western men who are drawn to Thailand's sex industry claim sex workers in their home countries are less considerate and tender in comparison to Thai women.

Very little research has been done on sex tourism for women seeking men. A growing population of single women tourists, however, appears to be increasing the numbers of white Western women trading money for sex, intimacy, and romance with black men in the Caribbean, for example in Costa Rica. These exchanges are more ambiguous than sex tourism for heterosexual men. Negotiations between white women tourists and local black men place more emphasis, at least for the women tourists, on intimacy compared to encounters between men tourists and local women. Exchanges between women tourists and local men are also more ambiguous in regard to the money to be paid in the interactions (Frohlick 2007).

WHAT IS YOUR SEXUALITY?

The "ideal" heterosexual fantasizes, feels attracted to, and engages in sexual behavior only with members of the other sex. The "ideal" homosexual fantasizes, feels attracted to, and engages in sexual behavior only with members of the same sex (Jay 1996). Who is to say that there is such a thing as a pure heterosexual or homosexual, man or woman? Fausto-Sterling (1993) argues that there are no universal categories of sex, gender, and sexuality that hold up over time and cross-culturally. You should recall from our discussion in chapter 2 on sex and gender that it is impossible to slot everyone into the two-sex model of man or woman. Similarly, not everyone is either gay or straight. Sex and gender do not fit together into an inevitable package and sexuality and sex or sexuality and gender do not always fit together the same way. The range of real people and their actual sexual experiences challenge the conventional categories. Intersexed, transgendered, third gender, bisexual, omnisexual, asexual, and transsexual are all part of the landscape of sexuality.

The terms *sexual identity* or *sexual orientation* refer to how people identify or classify themselves sexually. In the United States, we tend to assume that sexual behaviors and desires are consistent with orientation. We often believe that if we identify as heterosexual we will not fantasize about or engage in sex with people of the same sex. All cultures do not see this link between identity and practice in the same way, however. For example, in his ethnographic research on the sexual rituals of the Sambia in Papua New Guinea, Gilbert Herdt (1997) found that the way Sambia people define their sexual orientation does not directly correspond to the types of sexual behavior in which they engage. Young Sambian boys are initiated into manhood through the daily fellating of older boys and men. However, neither the boys nor the men think of themselves or their behavior as homosexual.

> The sexual culture of the Sambia men instills definite and customary lifeways that involves a formula for the life course. Once initiated (before age ten), boys undergo ordeals to have their "female" traces (left over from birth and from living with their mothers) removed; these ordeals involve painful rites, such as nosebleedings, that are intended to promote masculinity and aggression. The boys are then in a ritually "clean" state that enables the treatment of their bodies and minds in new ways. These boys are regarded as "pure" sexual virgins, which is important for their insemination. The men believe that the boys are unspoiled because they have not been exposed to the sexual pollution of women, which the men greatly fear. It is thus through oral intercourse that the men receive a special kind of pleasure, unfettered by pollution, and the boys are thought to acquire semen for growth, becoming strong and fertile. All the younger males are thus inseminated by older bachelors, who were once themselves semen recipients. (Herdt 1997, 117)

Don Kulick (1997) studied transgendered prostitutes called *travestis* in Salvador, Brazil. *Travestis* are gay male prostitutes who enjoy anal penetration and go to great lengths to look like women. They take female hormones and inject industrial (not surgical) silicone purchased illegally into their buttocks, hips, knees, and inner thighs. They have boyfriends (*maridos*) who are men who dress like men and self-identify as heterosexual. *Travestis*, on the other hand, regard themselves as gay but not as men. This is because in Salvador, gender identity is thought to be determined by one's sexual behavior. In other words, it is not what your genitals are, nor with whom you have sex, but what you do that counts. As Kulick (1997) explains:

> One of the defining attributes of being a *homen* (man) in the gender system that the *travestis* draw on and invoke is that a man will not be interested in another male's penis. A man, in this interpretative framework, will happily penetrate another male's anus. But he will not touch or express any desire for another male's penis. For him to do would be tantamount to relinquishing his status as a man. (577)

"Culturally speaking," writes Kulick, "*travestis*, because they enjoy being penetrated, are structurally equivalent to, even if they are not biologically identical to, women" (581).

In the United States and Canada, people's sexual behavior also does not necessarily correspond with their sexual identity. Most people in North America identify as either straight, gay, lesbian, bisexual, or queer. Although these labels or categories have cultural currency—that

TABLE 4–2 Sexuality in the United States, 2002

	Women	Men
Identify as gay or lesbian	2.3%	2.3%
Identify as bisexual	1.8	1.8
Identify as heterosexual	90.0	90.0
Had homosexual or lesbian experience	11.1	6.0
Had sex with same-sex partner in last year	4.0	3.0
Had sex with same-sex partner and opposite sex in last year	3.0	1.0
Sexually attracted to opposite sex only	86	92
*Find the fantasy of homosexual or lesbian experience appealing	5.5	6.0

SOURCE: * Laumann et al. (1994); all others Mosher, Chandra, and Jones (2005).

is, we all understand their meanings—peoples' behaviors are not always consistent with their sexual identity. Table 4–2 shows the data from a recent study of sexuality in the United States. Table 4–2 shows that the numbers of people who identify as gay, lesbian, or bisexual are lower than the proportion that have had sex with someone of the same sex or who are attracted to those of the same sex (Mosher, Chandra, and Jones 2005). These contrasts have caused researchers to rethink categories and develop concepts that capture such behavior and identity differences, such as "Men who have sex with men" and "lesbian and bisexual chic" (King 2004).

Studies in New Guinea, Brazil, and the United States show three different ways of understanding the links between sexual identity and behavior. Americans say they believe that sexual identity is tightly tied to behavior but the real behavior of Americans frequently does not reflect this link, as people claim a sexual identity but behave in ways that are inconsistent with their identity. In New Guinea, men and boys claim a sexual identity of heterosexual but engage in homosexual activities and in fact maintain that those homosexual activities are the path to being heterosexual and masculine men. In Brazil the specific sexual behavior rather than who one's partner is determines one's sexual identity. Two men engaging in sexual intercourse are not both perceived as homosexual. The man who is inserting his penis is considered heterosexual and the other man is considered gay.

Lesbian or Bisexual Chic

The recent phenomenon in the United States and Canada referred to as "lesbian or bisexual chic" illustrates a mismatch between sexual behavior and sexual identity. Paula Rust (2002, 5) defines the phenomenon as "same-sex behavior engaged in by essentially heterosexual individuals under certain extenuating circumstances, in keeping with the cultural belief that there are only two true forms of sexuality." (Rust 2002, 2) She argues that the behavior is most likely found "in a cultural milieu favoring sexual experimentation." This includes teenage and college parties, bars, and nightclubs. Such "girl-on-girl" action has been popularized by the "Girls Gone Wild" franchise, Hollywood publicity of stars such as the Madonna–Britney Spears kiss at the MTV Video Music Awards in 2003, and radio shock jocks such as Howard Stern.

In a popular advice book, *The Straight Girl's Guide to Sleeping with Chicks,* Jen Sincero (2005) argues that getting physical with a woman does not imply what it used to—lesbianism. Sincero reports more than 100 interviews with women who still think of themselves as straight even though they have kissed or engaged in other sexual behaviors with women.

Some critics have suggested that the increasing cultural acceptance of "girl on girl" sexual relations is not necessarily progressive. They maintain the images are marketed for audiences of heterosexual men, and are focused on using women to please men (Luscombe 2004). Others are concerned its popularization might perpetuate the myth that bisexuality is a phase and not a real sexual identity. On the other hand, it can be seen as subversive in its challenge to heterosexist social norms and patriarchal restrictions of "compulsory heterosexuality."

Bisexuality also creates challenges within gay and lesbian communities. According to a survey of 835 self-identified bisexual men and women, 35 percent had considered themselves gay or lesbian earlier in their lives (Fox 1995). Theories of lesbian and gay development have typically regarded bisexuality as a transitional phase on the way to establishing a lesbian or gay identity. Fox (1995) argues that bisexuality can be an endpoint stage itself, however. It is society's polarizing categories of homosexual versus heterosexual that reinforce the idea that bisexuals are confused and that there cannot be any "in between" categories of sexual identity.

Ochs and Deihl (1992) refer to the fear of the space between categories as *biphobia*. They argue that bisexuals are relegated to a "netherwold by heterosexuals and homosexuals alike," ostracized by the heterosexual community as well as the lesbian and gay communities. Rust (1995) suggests that bisexuality poses a personal and political threat to lesbians because it undermines the political identity of the lesbian community as an oppressed sexual minority struggling for their civil rights. Rust's study of 470 lesbian and bisexual women found that the majority of lesbian participants were reluctant to engage politically and socially with bisexual women. This unwillingness stems from a distrust of heterosexuals and heterosexist politics. As Rust explains, "To people who feel threatened, trust is a very important issue; in a heterosexual world, lesbians are threatened, and they do not trust bisexual women because bisexual women appear to be connected to that world" (101).

Ostracism of bisexuals within the gay and lesbian community is ironic because "the gay and lesbian liberation movement in the United States is united around the right to love whomever we please, and to have our relationships validated and recognized, even when they do not conform to society's norms. Bisexuals are often pushed into a closet within a closet" (Deihl and Ochs 2004, 183–84).

Competing Perspectives on Gendered Sexuality

A central theme in research on sexualities has been on understanding gender differences in sexual behaviors and attitudes. Scholars have taken several positions on this question including: a biological framework; a sexual script framework; or a queer theorist framework.

The biological focus is represented by William Masters, a gynecologist, and Virginia Johnson, a psychologist, who were pioneers in sexuality research and founded the field we know today as sex therapy. They focused exclusively on physical sexuality to understand bodily differences in sexual arousal of men and women. Their research involved extensive laboratory observations of more than 10,000 sexual encounters from a sample of 382 women and 312 men (Masters and Johnson 1966). Photographs and measurement instruments recorded muscular and vascular changes in vaginas and penises revealing that the key difference in patterns of arousal is in the timing of the excitement. The male cycle of arousal from excitement to plateau to orgasm is much quicker than the female cycle. However, the male refractory period (or the time needed before sexual excitement and erection can be resumed) is much slower in comparison. This led Masters and Johnson to highlight women's capacity for multiple orgasms and to take note of their sexual stamina. These differences in arousal cycles formed the basis of their theory for the mismatch of mating styles. They advocated sexual counseling that would enable men and women to become more synchronized with each other sexually. In other words, they advocated teaching men to slow down.

Masters and Johnson were not concerned with the social environment and external factors that affect sexuality. Instead, their exploration of male and female sexual response focused on biological factors. Other biologists have looked at differences in sexuality in regard to choice of partners. For example, Simon LeVay (1991), a neurobiologist, examined the brain tissues of forty-one deceased people in his research on homosexuality. He found that the anterior hypothalamus was twice the size in the men believed to be heterosexual than in the men who identified as homosexual and bisexual. The anterior hypothalamuses of the homosexual and bisexual men were the same size as those of the six deceased women in the sample. From these findings, LeVay (1991) deduced that there is a biological basis to sexual orientation.

LeVay's work has been strongly criticized because nearly half of his sample had died of AIDS, including all of the gay men in the study. HIV is known to reduce testosterone and affect the brain. This means that LeVay might only have been measuring the dual effect of HIV infection and high-strength formaldehyde solution (in which the brains of gay men were preserved out of fear of HIV transmission) and not differences in brain structure for heterosexuals and homosexuals (Kimmel 2004).

Claims that there is a "gay gene" or that homosexuals show androgen deficiencies have been put forward to show that sexual orientation has its basis in biology. None of these scientific studies search for the "straight gene" or hormonal imbalances among heterosexuals. Because heterosexuality is posited as the norm, the hormones, brain structures, and genetic composition of straight people become the standard from which all other sexualities are measured and judged. This "othering" of sexual minorities is part of "heterosexism," which privileges the position of heterosexuals.

Sexual Scripts

A second framework has been developed by scholars who take a social constructionist view of the issues. They argue that the categories that we often take for granted and accept as real are in fact, socially constructed; that is, people and groups interact within particular sociohistorical contexts.

An example is Gagnon and Simon's (1973) theory of sexual scripts holding that sexual relations are scripted interactions based on prevailing gender ideologies. Gagnon and Simon's theory of sexual scripts grows from Erving Goffman's (1959) dramaturgic sociology. Goffman argued that in their everyday lives people are like actors performing on a stage, playing roles to an audience. In the dramaturgical tradition, Gagnon and Simon (1973) apply the notion of the script to show how sexual interactions follow a script-like sequence. Take the following script as an example:

Stage: A bedroom
Lighting: Dim to Dark
Props: Television and remote control
Actors: Louisa (dressed in nightgown) and Peter (dressed in pajamas)

Scene opens with Peter lying on the bed, channel surfing with the remote control.

Louisa enters and lies down beside Peter.

Dialogue:

Louisa (L): "Oh am I tired." [yawn] "It's been a long day."
Peter (P): "How tired are you? Not too tired…I hope?"
L: "Oh, Peter" (laughs)
P: "C'mon Louisa, I am totally in the mood."
L: "I guess that means Letterman's ended"

[audience laughs]

Lights dim and Peter and Louisa get under the covers. Actors start rolling around, simulating the beginning of sex. Peter, while on top of Louisa, turns his head around to the audience and flashes a big smile.

Scene ends.

So what do you make of this fictitious scene? Most likely, it will seem familiar you. Why is that? This scene follows a predictable sequence of events that has been popularized in our culture where men like Peter are supposed to be the dominant, sexual initiators and women are supposed to be sexually shy and submissive but also the sexual gatekeepers (deciding if and how far the sexual encounter will go).

As discussed in chapter 2, sexual scripts are shared cultural instructions for "normal" sexual behaviors. These behaviors are different for men and women. In our scene, Peter had adopted a dominant role in the sexual encounter both as the verbal initiator and even in their sexual position (Steedman 1987). Peter appears more "into" the sex, or at least vocalized it more than Louisa. According to sexual script theorists, in Western culture sex means love and intimacy for women and orgasm and physical pleasure for men. The actors' roles in a traditionally scripted sexual encounter are thus extensions of a society's expectations of gender. Women initiating sex and embracing sexual pleasure, men who wait for women to initiate, and gay men and lesbians are all deviants from their "proper roles."

Violent scripts. Feminists have used the concept of sexual scripts to explain gendered patterns of violence. The emphasis on men's initiation and pleasure in traditional sexual scripts is thought to be linked to men's sexual aggression. Men are supposed to be demanding sex and women are supposed to be the sexual gatekeeper as well as the passive recipient "on the bottom," making men more likely to feel they must aggressively seek sexual encounters and making it more difficult for women to refuse unwanted sex (Tolman and Higgins 1996, 209).

These sexual scripts create barriers to egalitarian heterosexual relationships and there is some evidence that they play a part in rape and sexual violence. For example, in rape trials before the feminist reforms of the 1980s, women's actions, dress, and words could become implicated in the rape. Often the rape victim herself was on trial, as rapists' excuses and justifications—"she asked for it" or "no *really* means yes"–blamed the victim for the crime (Smart 1989).

Traditional sexual scripts are also associated with decreased condom usage and thus increased risk of HIV. Research shows that most women want men to use condoms but because men control the sexual activity, they also control condom use. And, because men are supposed to be risk takers and desperate for sex, they do not want anything to create a barrier to their pleasure. In this way, stereotyped versions of masculinity and femininity inhibit the use of condoms.

RESISTANCE SCRIPTS AND *THE VAGINA MONOLOGUES*. Sexual scripts can represent and perpetuate power relations in sexual encounters that privilege dominant groups such as heterosexuals and men, but scripts can also challenge those discourses. In the 1990s, Eve Ensler wrote the *Vagina Monologues* as an attempt to explicitly expose the dominant discourse and offer an alternative.

The Vagina Monologues is a one-woman play based on Ensler's interviews with more than 200 women from diverse backgrounds about their sexualities. The play is a series of first-person vignettes or monologues that address such topics as pubic hair, thong underwear, pap smears, tampons, and the more serious subjects of rape and childhood experiences of sexual violence. *The Monologues* first debuted off-Broadway in New York City in 1996. There are now more than 1,000 productions of the play performed each year with half of them at universities and colleges (Marklein 2004).

The Vagina Monologues is often a source of campus controversy. The play has been cancelled at more than fifteen Catholic universities in the United States and banned altogether in Uganda. In February 2004, a prayer vigil was held outside of the production at Loyola Marymount University in Los Angeles by a small group of students, parents, and alumni whose objections to *The Monologues* were based on their moral and religious convictions (Marklein 2004). Protests, boycotts, heated debates, and strongly worded editorials in student, local, and national newspapers on the play have become a part of *The Vagina Monologues* phenomenon. Why?

For starters, there is the title, which at the very least gets one's attention. It also makes many people uncomfortable. The word *vagina* is not often spoken in public outside of a medical or health setting. Recall that there are relatively few words for women's genitals compared to those for men. Women are not given many words to talk about their genitals and they are not supposed to talk about their vaginas, unless of course it is to their gynecologist. The opening sequence of the play is all about breaking the silence about vaginas. Here's an excerpt:

> I bet you're worried. I was worried. That's why I began this piece. I was worried about vaginas. I was worried about what we think about vaginas, and even more worried that we don't think about them. I was worried about my own vagina. It needed a context of other vaginas—a community, a culture of vaginas. There's so much darkness and secrecy surrounding them—like the Bermuda Triangle. Nobody ever reports back from there. Let's just start with the word "vagina." It sounds like an

infection at best, maybe a medical instrument: "Hurry, Nurse, bring me the vagina." "Vagina." "Vagina." Doesn't matter how many times you say it, it never sounds like a word you want to say. It's a totally ridiculous, completely unsexy word. If you use it during sex, trying to be politically correct-"Darling, could you stroke my vagina?"-you kill the act right there. (Ensler 2001, 3–5)

In 2002, a woman appeared on a local San Francisco television morning news show to promote an upcoming production of *The Vagina Monologues* for a V-Day fundraiser. V-Day benefit events raise both awareness and funds for stopping violence against women. Ironically, she was instructed by the news director not to use the word *vagina* on the air even though it is frequently used on television, as is the word *penis*. His reasoning: "In the morning, we recognize that a lot of parents are watching the show with their kids," the director explained. "As a parent, I'm not sure I'd be comfortable hearing that word in front of my kids. I think a lot of people would find it objectionable. Children might ask what it means" (Ryan 2002). The discomfort around *The Vagina Monologues*, or even speaking of women's vaginas, reveals a discomfort around women's sexuality. Gender expectations and gender norms for women tell us that women's sexuality should be kept under wraps.

Who do *The Vagina Monologues* speak for? Although *The Vagina Monologues* has been an important vehicle for bringing women's sexuality into the open as a legitimate and important subject, feminists in nations outside the United States have wished to localize the play by changing it in ways that make it more appropriate to their particular community (Cheng 2004). To protect Ensler's intellectual property rights, however, strict rules are in place for anyone who uses the script. There can be no changes in the dialogue and if someone wishes to present it in a language other than English, they must use the "official translation" provided by the publishers. This has ironically meant that the play, which was written to represent a broad spectrum of women's experiences, in fact, is imposing on the rest of the world a universal model of a set of very American experiences and a very American point of view.

One artist in Hong Kong, Sea Ling Cheng (2004), has conducted her own much smaller set of interviews of Chinese women to try to create a Hong Kong version that she has entitled *Little Sister*. Hong Kong women frequently refer to their vaginas as "little sister." Her research has resulted in another version of *The Vagina Monologues* that includes changes such as "Labia Dance" because of her finding that Hong Kong women had never seen a vagina, including their own. In the dance she positions her body, head, and arms to depict a vagina. In addition, Cheng eliminated stories about motherhood because she felt that this aspect of vaginas was overemphasized in Hong Kong culture. Cheng was also critical of the inclusion of female genital mutilation (FGM) in the original *Monologues* because she felt that Americans discussing FGM created a perception that cruel misogyny was something other cultures did. Instead, Cheng included stories of cruelty and control of Hong Kong women's sexuality and bodies that came from their own culture.

QUEER THEORY

"As far as I'm concerned, being any gender is a drag" (musician Patti Smith, quoted in Levine 1998). The third framework for exploring the connections between genders and sexualities is called queer theory. The term *queer* was once used as an insult against gay men and lesbians but it has been appropriated as a source of pride and reclaimed to unify all sexual minorities, not just gay men and lesbians. This includes other marginalized sexual identities such as bisexuality, transsexualism, and transgenderism, as well as discredited sexual communities such as S&M and other fetish communities. Queerness is subversive because it criticizes sexual norms—what might be called the "regime of normalization"—from the position of outsiders (Epstein 1994). The "regime of normalization," refers to the domination of the "shoulds" and "musts" and sanctions that hold society and its members in place. In this way, queer theory serves an important political function, as well as an important theoretical function, helping us to understand ties among genders and sexualities.

Queer theorists, like social constructionists, assert that sexualities are created through social interaction. Queer theorists go further, however, rejecting traditional categories of sexual orientation like homosexuality, heterosexuality, or any fixed identity. Kinsey and his colleagues were among the first to try to capture queer theorists' insights about the dynamic and diverse character of sexuality. Before queer theory became a theoretical perspective, more than fifty years ago, Kinsey (Kinsey, Pomeroy, and Martin 1948; Kinsey et al. 1953) proposed a continuum that recognized the fluidity of sexuality and more accurately described peoples' sexual experiences.

Building on the work of Kinsey and Michael Foucault (1978), one of the original theorists to explore the social construction of sexuality and gender, contemporary queer theorist Judith Butler (1990) challenges the naturalness of sexuality. Like other theorists who use the idea of sexual script, Butler sees gender and sexuality as an act or a performance, a form of "drag" where people play the role of a man or a woman, and sometimes a "sexy" man or woman. If we see a male wearing a wig and makeup and a tight, low-cut, pink satin gown we understand it as a performance of gender and sexuality and many people would laugh because it seems inconsistent with the man's true gender. But how is his costume any different from a female wearing the same costume? Isn't she performing sexual femininity also?

Butler goes further with this concept, noting how the roles are scripted in ways that create and maintain structures of power and inequality. In addition to privileging men over women, the performance privileges heterosexuality by making it appear natural. The male in the pink gown appears to be gay and feminine and therefore laughable. The woman in the pink gown appears to be feminine and heterosexual and therefore attractive. Butler's ideas recall Rich's concept of "compulsory heterosexuality." Butler challenges the gay and lesbian claim that homosexuality is as "natural" as heterosexuality. She claims that all of it, heterosexual and homosexual, is "un-natural." They are performances, not essences.

In her book *Gender Trouble*, Butler (1990) writes, "There is no gender identity behind the expressions of gender; . . . identity is performatively constituted by the very 'expressions' that are said to be its results" (25). In other words, we produce the illusion of gendered essences in performing them. The essences are no more "real" than the performance. Gender is nothing but the performance of gender. Queer theory totally severs biological sex, social gender, and desire. Therefore, according to Butler, we cannot be slotted into a few categories. Rather our sexuality—identity, feelings, opinions, fantasies, and behavior—creates complex variations of many types. Furthermore, these feelings, identities, fantasies, and behaviors are socially constructed, acted, and reenacted as we relate with one another.

Homophobia

Most people know that Jewish people were forced to wear arm bands with the symbol of a yellow star in Germany during the Nazi regime; fewer know about the arm bands with pink triangles. These were assigned to homosexual men and those suspected of being homosexual. It is estimated that 100,000 gay men were arrested, 50,000 were imprisoned, and as many as 15,000 sent to concentration camps, where many were killed. Heinrich Himmler, head of the Nazi police and security forces, was strongly homophobic. He created a special division of the Gestapo (secret state police) called the "Reich Central Office for the Combating of Homosexuality and Abortion." Himmler's homophobia was connected to his sexism (Plant 1986). Himmler believed that homosexuals were "like women" who were weak and inferior to men. To Himmler, homosexuals were a disgrace to the state and their presence, like that of Jewish and Roma peoples, would contaminate and demoralize the pure Aryan race. These were Himmler's justifications for annihilating homosexuals during the Nazi regime.

George Weinberg (1972) coined the term *homophobia* to describe the hatred Himmler expressed toward gay men and lesbians. Weinberg used this term because he thought it captured the "fear of contagion" he observed in clinical psychological situations where patients expressed fear of being tainted with the stigma of homosexuality and fear of being "gay by association" due to contact with homosexuals (Koch 2007).

Homophobia is intimately connected to sexism and the devaluation of that which is feminine. Gay men are stereotyped as effeminate in our culture and lesbians are stereotyped as masculine "butches." When a girl who likes sports is called a "tomboy" and accused of being a "dyke" or a boy who does not like sports is called a "sissy" and accused of being a "faggot," it demonstrates the interplay between homophobia and sexism.

Suzanne Pharr (1988) expands on these links among heterosexuality, patriarchal power, and homophobia arguing that homophobia is a weapon of sexism. To Pharr, hatred of gay men is based on fears that men who fail to uphold hegemonic masculinity will "bring down the entire system of male dominance and compulsory heterosexuality." (p.18) Lesbian baiting is a way to control women who are independent, who struggle for women's human rights, and who "resist male dominance and control."

Heterosexism

As scholars and activists have developed their understanding of homophobia, they have come feel that the concept is no longer sufficient. First, the term homophobia literally means "fear of homosexuals." Although fear may be a feature of what we see as homophobic behavior, hatred, anger, and aggression are stronger components (Logan 1996; Herek 2004). Some scholars have argued that the continued use of the term homophobia may not only be a mislabel, it may even help to excuse hostile behavior as the (understandable) result of inescapable fear (Logan 1996).

Homophobia also refers to individual beliefs and behaviors, not institutionalized discrimination. Heterosexism is a concept that directs us to consider antihomosexual beliefs and practices embedded in social institutions. A list of examples of heterosexism are given in Box 4–2.

Box 4–2 EXAMPLES OF HETEROSEXISM

- Assuming that everyone that you meet is heterosexual.
- Assuming that everyone has or is interested in having an opposite-sex partner.
- Assuming that all mothers and fathers are heterosexual.
- Assuming all sexually active women use birth control.
- Assuming that all unmarried people are "single" while in reality they may have a same-sex partner.
- Assuming all children live in families with a man–woman couple as parental roles.
- Using language that presumes heterosexuality in others, such as husband or wife, instead of gender-neutral language such as partner. Using official forms that allow only for designation as married or single.
- Denying equal employment benefits to people with same-sex partners such as spousal insurance.
- Omitting any discussion of LGBTQ persons as part of educational curricula.

Source: http://outwilmington.com/ForAllies%20heterosexism.htm

It helps to understand heterosexism by comparing it to "white privilege." White privilege is to racism as heterosexual privilege is to heterosexism. Peggy McIntosh (1988) uses the metaphor of an "invisible knapsack" to illustrate how white privilege functions.

> I have come to see white privilege as an invisible package of unearned assets that I can count on cashing in each day, but about which I was "meant" to remain oblivious. White privilege is like an invisible weightless knapsack of special provisions, assurances, tools, maps, guides, codebooks, passports, visas, clothes, compass, emergency gear, and blank checks. (95)

McIntosh argues that white people are not taught to see how racism puts them in a position of privilege but rather come to view it only as something that puts racial ethnic minorities at a disadvantage. Take the issue of routine police stops that have been labeled "driving while black." According to the Bureau of Justice, African Americans are more likely to be pulled over by the police than whites. During a traffic stop, police are about three times more likely to carry out some type of search on an African American (10.2 percent) or Latino motorist (11.4 percent) than a white motorist (3.5 percent). Searches of whites in traffic stops are four times more likely to find criminal evidence (14.5 percent) than their African American counterparts (3.3 percent) and slightly more than their Latino counterparts (13 percent; Bureau of Justice Statistics 2005).

The racial discrepancy is often explained as an illustration of racism in policing. An overlooked aspect of this form of racial discrimination is the advantage to white people who are pulled over and searched less frequently. This is white privilege. Similarly, we might label

---

Box 4–3 EXAMPLES OF HETEROSEXUAL PRIVILEGE

- Ability to talk openly, comfortably, and without fear of judgment about one's friends, social activities, and personal relationships.
- Never having one's normalcy questioned.
- Ability to show affection in public with one's partner without fear of negative reactions or hostility.
- Ability to have children without any questions of one's fitness to do so.
- Right to legally marry.
- Right to purchase insurance benefits for a partner, such as health care.
- Right to job security and freedom from sanctioned discrimination.
- Right to take family or medical leave for a partner.
- Ability to purchase family memberships in health clubs or other recreational activities.
- Validation of one's human dignity by one's chosen religion.

SOURCE: http://outwilmington.com/ForAllies%20heterosexism.htm

---

a hospital policy that explicitly prevents gay men and lesbians from visiting their same-sex partners as a form of heterosexism. That heterosexuals can visit their spouses in the hospital without the worry that they might be kicked out because of their sexual orientation or forced to pose as their loved one's relative is heterosexual privilege. Box 4–3 lists examples of heterosexual privilege.

SEX FOR SALE

Sex sells. Advertising products such as cars or beer in a commercial with a thin, attractive, big-breasted model has become a cliché in American culture—sex, itself really does sell. The business of sex or how sex is bought and sold like a commodity in the marketplace is an important dimension of gendered sexuality. In the global marketplace, sex work is one of the largest and fastest growing industries. Although men and women are involved in both the provision and consumption of sex through prostitution, pornography, stripping and exotic dancing, and for-profit telephone and cyber sex, men comprise the majority of consumers and women are the majority of workers. Take pornography as an example.

Pornography

In the United States alone, the pornography industry totals $13.3 billion in sales each year, which is more than the profits of the NBA, the NFL, and Major League Baseball combined. Worldwide, the pornography industry is worth close to $60 billion (Ropelato 2007). The

TABLE 4–3 Pornography Industry Revenue in the United States for 2006 (in Billions)

Video sales and rental	$ 3.62
Internet	$ 2.84
Cable/pay-per-view/in-room/mobile/phone sex	$ 2.19
Exotic dance clubs	$ 2.00
Novelties	$ 1.73
Magazines	$ 0.95
Total	$13.33

SOURCE: http://internet-filter-review.toptenreviews.com/internet-pornography-statistics.html.

sheer volume of videos, websites, and magazines produced each year is staggering. In the Los Angeles area—the center of U.S. porn production—10,000 hard-core pornographic movies are produced annually. Hollywood, in comparison, produces an average of 400 major movies each year (F. Rich 2001).

Pornographic websites now make up 12 percent of all sites on the Web (or 4.2 million) and 8 percent of all e-mail is porn-related. Video pornography is the most popular and profitable sector of the industry with an average of 700 million pornographic videos rented each year (F. Rich 2001). Table 4–3 shows the breakdown in terms of revenue of the industry as a whole.

Because the sources are industry insiders like *Adult Video News*, an industry trade magazine, some skepticism about these statistics may be warranted. According to David Klatell, associate Dean of the Columbia Graduate School of Journalism, "[pornography] is an industry where they exaggerate the size of everything" (quoted in Ackman 2001). Nevertheless, pornography is a huge pervasive industry all over the world.

GENDERED PORN. Most pornography, but certainly not all, is targeted to heterosexual men. Naked or partially naked women are presented in sexual poses or engaging in sex acts catering to the men's sexual fantasies. Seventy-two percent of visitors to pornographic websites are men (Ropelato 2007) and men, on average, consume more (both in terms of volume and duration) pornographic materials than women. The number of adult films, magazines, websites, and clubs targeted for heterosexual women, however, has risen in recent years as has the entire gay and lesbian porn industry. The latter is one of the fastest growing sectors of the entire industry. Pornography not explicitly geared toward women and gay men and lesbians does not mean, however, that it is not consumed by them. For instance, *Playboy*—the epitome of heterosexual men's magazines—estimates that 17 percent of the magazine's readers are women (Frontline 2002).

Heterosexual video pornography is the largest genre of pornography and is comprised of two types of films: features that mimic a Hollywood film in terms of a script, set, and characters and often in their titles such as *Pulp Friction*, *Saving Ryan's Privates*, and *There's*

Something In and Out of Mary; as well as gonzos, which are amateur films of recorded sex with no storylines. Three main themes dominate in heterosexually focused pornographic film (Dines and Jensen 2004):

1. All women want sex from men.
2. Women like all the sexual acts that men perform or demand.
3. Any woman who does not at first realize her desire for sex can be easily persuaded with a little force. Such force is rarely necessary, however, for most of the women in pornography are "nymphomaniacs", always on the lookout for sexual encounters and hyperorgasmic sex.

Heterosexual video pornography perpetuates traditional sexual scripts with men as the subjects in control of the sexual situation and women as objects whose role is to fulfill men's desires (Dines and Jensen 2004). The focus in this genre is on vaginal, oral, and anal penetration, women performing fellatio on men and other women, and ejaculations onto women—the cum, or money shot—as indicators of men's heterosexual fantasies in the films. Common sexual positions in this genre such as the "reverse cowgirl" with the woman on top and facing away from the man, and "double penetration" in which two men simultaneously enter the woman (vaginally and anally) maximize the visibility of women's bodies and facilitate getting close-ups of women's genitals. Men's bodies, on the other hand, are not scrutinized in the same way. Their penises are only focused on at the point of ejaculation and men often remain clothed in the films up until the sex requires them to undress.

"The objectification of women in pornography is a foundation of the genre, and the gender hierarchy that pervades the wider culture is, if anything, more intense in the pornographic world" (Dines and Jensen 2004, 370). This view is shared by a number of antipornography scholars, most notably radical feminists. However, not all feminists agree. Pornography is a divisive issue among feminists (Segal 1993). At the heart of the debate is whether or not pornography is oppressive and contributes to violence against women. Also at issue is the extent to which pornography should be controlled by the government or censored.

THE FEMINIST CENSORSHIP DEBATE. There are three positions held by feminists in the debate over pornography. Antiporn feminists hold that pornography is an expression of men's sexual dominance that commodifies, objectifies, and exploits women. They assert that sexuality is the source of women's subordination in society and claim that pornography is an instrument of power that reinforces women's oppression. Catherine MacKinnon (1987), a major spokesperson for this point of view writes that pornography is "sexual terrorism" that eroticizes rape and sexual abuse and promotes violence against women. She and radical feminist Andrea Dworkin (1981) advocate banning pornography altogether. They claim that free speech protection for pornography impedes women's struggle for equality. Ironically, antiporn feminists have aligned with the religious right on the subject of pornography.

A second point of view is held by liberal feminists who argue that pornography, although it may be personally offensive or morally reprehensible to some (including many liberal feminists themselves), in the name of free speech and civil liberties it should not be regulated. They argue that feminists have a lot to lose by supporting censorship. These feminists are anticensorship but not pro-pornography.

The least understood and perhaps, least heard position in the pornography debate is that of the third position, pro-sex feminists. Pro-sex feminists, like liberal feminists, are against censorship because they view it as an attack on free speech and civil rights. Pro-sex feminists argue further that pornography has benefits for women (McElroy 1995; Strossen 1995). Judith Kegan Gardiner (1993) argues that pornography has many positive aspects for women. She writes,

> For some women, pornography may actually de-objectify women because they can use it to validate their own desires and pleasures. They can also reinterpret or take control of the fantasy. For example, they may point out that a particular pictured position is not fun, but awkward and uncomfortable. Furthermore, women too can make comparisons between their lovers and the performers, for instance to the male stars' larger organs or more sustained erections, and they can use the pornography to encourage or instruct their partners how to please them. (331)

McElroy (1995) suggests that pornography politically benefits women in ways similar to feminism.

> Pornography is one of the windows through which women glimpse the sexual possibilities that are open to them. It is nothing more or less than freedom of speech applied to the sexual realm. Feminism is freedom of speech applied to women's sexual rights.
>
> Both pornography and feminism rock the conventional view of sex. They snap the traditional ties between sex and marriage, sex and motherhood. They both threaten family values and flout the status quo. (128)

Instead of viewing women as degraded and exploited in pornography as radical feminists and liberal feminists do, pro-sex feminists claim that women are sexual agents, subjects and not objects, who make choices and decisions about their bodies and sexualities. The questions over whether women are victims or agents in controversial sexual practices is also part of the debate over another important feminist issue—prostitution.

Prostitution

Many people think of "hookers" or "streetwalkers" when they think of prostitution, young, scantily clad women walking a downtown street in search of a "trick" or a "date." But most prostitution is off the street, in saunas and spas, brothels, massage parlors, and through escort services and exotic dancing venues. Most people also think of women when they think of prostitutes, but not all prostitutes are women although most are. In the United States, 67.2 percent of all people arrested for prostitution are women (Department of Justice 2006).

Clients of prostitutes are almost exclusively men, and that holds true for both men and women prostitutes. It is estimated that 16 percent of adult men in the United States have paid for sex (Laumann et al. 1994). Nevada, where prostitution is legal in ten counties, is home to thirty-five licensed brothels. The clientele consists of men construction workers, military personnel, truckers, and tourists. Aside from the occasional heterosexual couple who come to one of the brothels, the industry is geared toward the man customer. The Chicken

Ranch, a brothel in Pahrump, Nevada, also known as "The Best Little Whorehouse in the West," offers special promotions for "birthday boys." The Bunny Ranch offered free sex to the first fifty soldiers to arrive at the ranch who had served in Iraq. This unique patriotic gesture amounted to $50,000 in sexual services (BBC 2003).

LEGAL PROSTITUTION. There are around 300 legally registered prostitutes in Nevada. All are women. Plans are underway at the time of this writing, for the opening of Stud Farm in Nye County, Nevada—a brothel with men as prostitutes to be owned and operated by legendary Hollywood madam Heidi Fleiss (Frey 2005). Women prostitutes in Nevada are legal, and they are tested weekly for STDs and monthly for HIV; and they must use condoms. Brothels typically take half of the prostitutes' earnings and enforce health and safety laws. Since the mid- to late 1980s when the mandatory health testing and condom laws took effect, not a single licensed brothel prostitute in Nevada has ever tested positive for HIV (Albert 2001). In the remaining counties of Nevada and all other states in the United States, prostitution is against the law and classified as a misdemeanor.

In many countries however, such as Australia, Canada, Israel, Mexico, Singapore, Brazil, Venezuela, New Zealand, and most of Europe, prostitution is legal. It is often heavily regulated with restrictions on advertising and soliciting. In Canada, buying and selling sex is not illegal, but soliciting and running a brothel is. In Denmark, prostitution is not illegal so long as it is not a woman's sole means of income. The Netherlands restricts prostitution to brothels. In the famous Red Light District of Amsterdam, several hundred one-room shops are rented out by prostitutes who typically sit in the windows to attract passersby. Prostitutes are treated as self-employed tradespersons in the Netherlands. They are unionized, pay taxes, and have full access to health and social services.

THE FEMINIST PROSTITUTION DEBATE. Are prostitutes victims or agents? Some feminists argue that prostitutes are victims of sexual and economic exploitation, whereas others claim that prostitutes have agency and are in control of their lives. They are neither better nor worse off than most women workers. One organization, COYOTE (Call Off Your Old Tired Ethics) is a prostitutes' rights group that claims that prostitutes have the "right to engage in sex work." They advocate that prostitution be decriminalized in the United States because it would give prostitutes more control over their bodies. COYOTE opposes legalization because it implies regulation, that is, licensing or registration, zoning of street prostitution, legal brothels, mandatory medical exams, and special business taxes. COYOTE activists argue that these regulations would allow the state to control what a woman does with her body (Weitzer 2000).

WHISPER (Women Hurt in Systems of Prostitution Engaged in Revolt) is a leading organization in the antiprostitution campaign in the United States. Unlike the pro-sex work stance taken by COYOTE, WHISPER holds that prostitution is never freely chosen by women. They believe prostitution is inherently traumatizing to the prostitute and is not a valid career that should be organized or regulated by the state (Weitzer 2000). Some critics even label prostitution an act of violence against women and a form of female sexual slavery (Barry 1979; MacKinnon 1993).

Instead of seeing prostitutes either as victims or agents, Carpenter (2000) recommends embracing the contradictions by recognizing the ways that prostitutes are both victims and agents. There can be violence, exploitation, and substance abuse in prostitutes' lives as well as autonomy, free will, and job satisfaction, depending on who the prostitute is, where she works, and how much control she has over her work.

Although WHISPER and COYOTE disagree on many points, they do agree that the current conditions under which prostitutes work must be improved. A study of 475 prostitutes (which included men, women, and transgendered persons) in five countries (South Africa, Thailand, Turkey, the United States, and Zambia) found that violence marked the lives of the majority of prostitutes (Farley et al. 1998), including those who are trafficked and forced into prostitution and those under the control of pimps and brothel owners. Here are some of the highlights from the study:

- Seventy-three percent of prostitutes reported being physically assaulted in prostitution and 68 percent reported being threatened with a weapon.
- Sixty-two percent reported being raped since entering prostitution and of those who were raped, 46 percent were raped more than five times.
- Fifty-four percent of prostitutes reported being physically abused as children and 58 percent reported being sexually abused as children by an average of four perpetrators.
- Seventy-two percent reported current or past homelessness.
- Sixty-one percent reported current physical health problems.
- Fifty-two percent reported a problem with alcohol addiction and 45 percent with drug addiction.
- Ninety-two percent stated wanting to leave prostitution.
- Twenty-four percent supported the legalization of prostitution.

SEX TRAFFICKING. Globalization has created a global labor force in every industry, including sex work. It also has created systems of communication and transportation that move workers, including sex workers, around the world. Some people choose to be sex workers but their choices are seriously constrained by the poverty and desperation they find in countries with few economic opportunities. Furthermore, many of them are trafficked in order to be exploited against their will.

About 4 million women and girls are trafficked every year around the world. One quarter of them are forced to work in the sex industry. With profits of $7 billion to $12 billion a year, sex trafficking has become the third most profitable illegal industry behind drugs ($150–400 billion in profits) and arms smuggling ($56 billion in profits) (Farr 2005).

Most of the sex trafficked women and girls come from Thailand, Bangladesh, the former Soviet Union, and Brazil (Farr 2005). Many are kidnapped or sold to brokers who move them to another country. The highest prices are paid for girls from ten to twelve years old. A typical situation is where a young woman hears of a job in a wealthy nation working in a restaurant, or as a nanny or dancer in a newspaper or from a friend. When she arrives, she finds she is part of a debt bondage system that requires her to pay back the expenses of her transportation and help with passports and arrangements and her room and board when she arrives. The job turns out to be sex work and she is held captive until she pays off her debt. She is never told how much she owes, how much she makes, and what her expenses are so she never gets

Box 4–4 DECLARATION OF SEXUAL RIGHTS

1. The right to sexual freedom. Sexual freedom encompasses the possibility for individuals to express their full sexual potential. However, this excludes all forms of sexual coercion, exploitation, and abuse at any time and situations in life.
2. The right to sexual autonomy, sexual integrity, and safety of the sexual body. This right involves the ability to make autonomous decisions about one's sexual life within a context of one's own personal and social ethics. It also encompasses control and enjoyment of our own bodies free from torture, mutilation, and violence of any sort.
3. The right to sexual privacy. This involves the right for individual decisions and behaviors about intimacy as long as they do not intrude on the sexual rights of others.
4. The right to sexual equity. This refers to freedom from all forms of discrimination regardless of sex, gender, sexual orientation, age, race, social class, religion, or physical and emotional disability.
5. The right to sexual pleasure. Sexual pleasure, including autoeroticism, is a source of physical, psychological, intellectual, and spiritual well-being.
6. The right to emotional sexual expression. Sexual expression is more than erotic pleasure or sexual acts. Individuals have a right to express their sexuality through communication, touch, emotional expression, and love.
7. The right to sexually associate freely. This means the possibility to marry or not, to divorce, and to establish other types of responsible sexual associations.
8. The right to make free and responsible reproductive choices. This encompasses the right to decide whether or not to have children, the number and spacing of children, and the right to full access to the means of fertility regulation.
9. The right to sexual information based upon scientific inquiry. This right implies that sexual information should be generated through the process of unencumbered and yet scientifically ethical inquiry, and disseminated in appropriate ways at all societal levels.
10. The right to comprehensive sexuality education. This is a lifelong process from birth throughout the life cycle and should involve all social institutions.
11. The right to sexual health care. Sexual health care should be available for prevention and treatment of all sexual concerns, problems, and disorders.

Sexual Rights are Fundamental and Universal Human Rights
Adopted in Hong Kong at the 14th World Congress of Sexology, August 26, 1999

SOURCE: http://www.worldsexology.org/about_sexualrights.asp

out of bondage. Her work is to service twelve to thirty men a night. She is fined and beaten if she breaks house rules such as turning down a customer, trying to escape, gaining weight, or failing to get customers to buy drinks (Farr 2005).

Sexual Rights

There is a new concern in international human rights forums that "marks a historic achievement that feminist, and gay and lesbian, movements should proudly claim" (Petchesky 2000, 100). This concept is sexual rights. Discussions of sexual and reproductive rights have a short history on the international political stage. In fact, there is no mention of sexuality in any human rights document prior to 1993. Rosalind Petchesky (2000) sees this as related to the dualistic nature of sexual rights as victim and the right to sexual agency. She asks:

> Why is it so much easier to assert sexual freedom in a negative than in an affirmative, emancipatory sense; to gain consensus for the right not to be abused, exploited, raped, trafficked, or mutilated in one's body, but not the right to fully enjoy one's body? (82)

At the 14th World Conference of Sexology in 1999, Petchesky's question was answered when a Declaration of Sexual Rights, shown in Box 4–4, was adopted.

REFERENCES

ABC News. 2004. American Sex survey. October 21. ABCNews.go.com/images/politics/959a1AmericanSexSurvey.pdf.

Ackman, Dan. 2001. How big is porn? *Forbes.com*. May 25. http://www.forbes.com/2001/05/25/0524porn.html.

Albert, Alexa. 2001. *Brothel: Mustang Ranch and its women*. New York: Random House.

Almquist, E. 1994. The experience of minority women in the United States. Pp.573–606 In *Women: A feminist perspective*, 5th ed., ed. J. Freeman. Mountain View, CA: Mayfield.

Baker, Robert. 2000. The language of sex: Our conception of sexual intercourse. Pp.277–280 In *Gender basics: Feminist perspectives on women and men*, 2nd ed., ed. Anne Minas. Belmont, CA: Wadsworth.

Barry, Kathleen. 1979. *Female sexual slavery*. New York: Avon Books.

BBC News. 2003. Free sex offer for US troops. *BBC News World Edition*. June 4. http://news.bbc.co.uk/2/hi/americas/2961288.stm.

Bureau of Justice Statistics. 2005. Contacts between the police and the public: Findings from the 2002 national survey. http://www.ojp.usdoj.gov/bjs/abstract/cpp02.htm.

Burstein, Andrew, Nancy Isenberg, and Annette Gordon-Reed. 1999. Three perspectives on America's Jefferson fixation. *The Nation*, January 16.

Bushnell, Candace. 1997. *Sex and the city*. New York: Warner Books.

Butler, Judith. 1990. *Gender trouble: Feminism and the subversion of identity*. New York: Routledge.

Carpenter, Belinda J. 2000. *Re-thinking prostitution: Feminism, sex, and the self*. New York: Peter Lang.

Cheng, Sea-Ling. 2004. Vagina Monologues. *International Feminist Journal of Politics* 6 (2): 326–34.

Cofer, Judith Ortiz. 1993. The myth of the Latin woman: I just met a girl named María. Pp. 148–154 In *The Latin deli: Prose and poetry*. J.Cofer (ed.) Athens, GA: University of Georgia Press.

Collins, Patricia Hill. 2000. *Black feminist thought: Knowledge, consciousness, and the politics of empowerment*. New York: Routledge.

Davidson, Julia O'Connell. 1996. Sex tourism in Cuba. *Race and Class* 38 (1): 39–48.

Davis, Angela. 1983. *Women, race and class*. New York: Random House.

———. 1990. *Women, culture, politics*. New York: Vintage Books.

Deihl, Marcia, and Robyn Ochs. 2000. Biphobia. pp. 267–275 in *Readings for Diversity and Social Justice: An Anthology on Racism, Antisemitism, Sexism, Heterosexism, Ableism, and Classism* Maurianne Adams, Warren J. Blumenfeld, Rosie Castañeda, Heather W. Hackman, Madeline L. Peters, and Ximena Zúñiga (eds.)New York: Routledge.

Department of Justice (DOJ)—Federal Bureau of Investigation. 2006. Table 48—Crime in the United States 2005. http://www.fbi.gov/ucr/05cius/data/table_48.html.

Dines, Gail, and Robert Jensen. 2004. Pornography and media: Toward a more critical analysis. Pp.369–379 In *Sexualities: Identities, behaviors, and society*, ed. Michael Kimmel and Rebecca F. Plante. New York: Oxford University Press.

Dworkin, Andrea. 1981. *Pornography: Men possessing women*. New York: Perigee.

Ehrenreich, Barbara. 1984. *The hearts of men: American dreams and the flight from commitment*. New York: Doubleday.

Ensler, Eve. 2001. *The vagina monologues: The V-day edition*. New York: Villard.

Entman, Robert, and Andrew Rojecki. 2001. *The black image in the white mind: Media and race in America*. Chicago: University of Chicago Press.

Epstein, Steven. 1994. A queer encounter: Sociology and the study of sexuality. *Sociological Theory* 12 (2): 188–202.

Espín, O. M. 1986. Cultural and historical influences on sexuality in Hispanic/Latina women. Pp. 272–284 In *All American women*, ed. J. Cole. New York: Free Press.

Espiritu, Yen E. 1997. *Asian American women and men*. Thousand Oaks, CA: Sage.

Farley, Melissa, Isin Baral, Merab Kiremire, and Ufuk Sezgin. 1998. Prostitution in five countries: Violence and post-traumatic stress disorder. *Feminism and Psychology* 8 (4): 405–26.

Farr, Kathryn. 2005. *Sex trafficking: The global market in women and children*. New York: Worth.

Fausto-Sterling, Anne. 1993. The five sexes: Why male and female are not enough. *The Sciences* (March/April): 20–24.

Feijoo, Ammie N. 2001. *Adolescent sexual health in Europe and the U.S.—Why the difference?* 2nd ed. Advocates for Youth. http://www.advocatesforyouth.org/publications/factsheet/fsest.htm.

Finer, Lawrence. 2007. Trends in premarital sex in the U.S. *Public Health Reports* 122(1) :73–78.

Foucault, Michel. 1978. *An introduction*. Vol. I of *The history of sexuality*. Trans. Robert Hurley. New York: Pantheon.

Fox, Ron C. 1995. Bisexual identities. Pp. 48–86 In *Lesbian, gay and bisexual identities across the lifespan*, ed. A. R. D'Augelli and C. J. Patterson. New York: Oxford University Press.

Frey, Hillary. 2005. Finally, women can pay for sex too! *Salon.com*. November 17. http://www.salon.com/mwt/broadsheet/2005/11/17/fleiss/index.html.

Frohlick, Susan. 2007. Fluid exchanges. *City and Society* 19 (1): 139–68.

Frontline. 2002. Playboy magazine demographics. http://www.pbs.org/wgbh/pages/frontline/shows/porn/business/havedemos.html.

Gagnon, John, and William Simon. 1973. *Sexual conduct: The social sources of human sexuality*. Chicago: Aldine.

Gardiner, Judith Kegan. 1993. What I didn't get to say on TV about pornography, masculinity, and representation. *New York Law School Law Review* 38:319–33.

Goffman, Erving. 1959. *The presentation of self in everyday life*. Garden City, NY: Doubleday.

Green, Rayna. 1975. The Pocahontas perplex: The image of Indian women in American culture. *The Massachusetts Review* 16 (4): 698–714.

Greenfield, Lawrence A. 1997. *Sex offenses and offenders: An analysis of data on rape and sexual assault.* Washington, DC: Bureau of Justice Statistics, U.S. Department of Justice. http://www.ojp.usdoj. gov/bjs/pub/pdf/soo.pdf.

Herdt, Gilbert. 1997. *Same sex, different cultures: Gays and lesbians across cultures.* New York: Westview.

Herek, Gregory. 2004. Beyond "homophobia": Thinking about sexual prejudice and stigma in the twenty-first century. *Sexuality Research and Social Policy* 1: 6–24.

Jay, Paul. 1996. Bisexuality. In *The lives of lesbians, gays and bisexuals*, ed. R. Savin-Williams and K. Cohen, 436–61. New York: Harcourt Brace.

Kimmel, Michael. 2004. *The gendered society.* 2nd ed. New York: Oxford University Press.

King, J. L. 2004. *On the down low: A journey into the lives of "straight" black men who sleep with men.* New York: Broadway Books.

Kinsey, Alfred C., Wardell B. Pomeroy, and Clyde E. Martin. 1948. *Sexual behavior in the human male.* Philadelphia: Saunders.

Kinsey, Alfred C., Wardell B. Pomeroy, Clyde E. Martin, and Paul H. Gebhard. 1953. *Sexual behavior in the human female.* Philadelphia: Saunders.

Koch, Stephanie. 2007. Is she heterosexual, bisexual or lesbian? MA thesis, University of North Carolina, Charlotte.

Koedt, Anne. 1996[1970]. The myth of the vaginal orgasm.pp. 111–116 in S. Jacson and S. Scott (eds.) Feminist Sexualities: A Reader. New York: Columbia University Press.

Kulick, Don. 1997. The gender of Brazilian transgendered prostitutes. *American Anthropologist* 99 (3): 574–85.

Lander, Eric, and Joseph Ellis. 1998. Founding father. *Nature* 396:13–14.

Laumann, Edward O., John H. Gagnon, Robert T. Michael, and Stuart Michaels. 1994. *The social organization of sexuality: Sexual practices in the United States.* Chicago: The University of Chicago Press.

Laumann, Edward, Anthony Paik, Dale Glasser, Jeong-Han Kang, Tianfu Wng, Bernard Levinson, Edson Moreira, Alfredo Nicolosi, and Clive Gingell. 2006. Cross national study of subjective well-being among older women and men. *Archives of Sexual Behavior* 35(2): 143–159

LeVay, Simon. 1991. A difference in hypothalamic structure between heterosexual and homosexual men. *Science* 253:1034–37.

Levine, Martin. 1998. *Gay macho.* New York: New York University Press.

Logan, Colleen. 1996. Homophobia? Homoprejudice. *Journal of Homosexuality* 31:31–53.

Luscombe, Richard. 2004. US girls embrace gay passion fashion. *The Observer.* January 4. http://www .guardian.co.uk/gayrights/story/0,12592,1115656,00.html.

MacKinnon, Catherine. 1987. *Feminism unmodified: Discourses on life and law.* Cambridge, MA: Harvard University Press.

——. 1993. Prostitution and civil rights. *Michigan Journal of Gender and Law* 1:13–31.

Marklein, Mary Beth. 2004. "Vagina Monologues" becoming college phenomenon. *USA Today.* March 1. http://www.usatoday.com/life/theater/2004–03–01-monologues-usat_x.htm.

Masters, William, and Virgina Johnson. 1966. *Human sexual response.* London: Churchill.

McElroy, Wendy. 1995. *A woman's right to pornography.* New York: St. Martin's.

McIntosh, Peggy. 1988. White privilege and male privilege: A personal account of coming to see correspondences through work in women's studies. Pp.70–81 In *Race, class, and gender: An anthology.* 4th ed., ed. Margaret L. Andersen and Patricia Hill Collins. Belmont, CA: Wadsworth.

Mills, C. Wright. 1959. *The sociological imagination.* New York: Oxford University Press.

Mosher, William, Chandra Anjani, and Jo Jones. 2005. Sexual behavior and selected health measures: Men and women 15–44 years of age, U.S. 2002. Advance data from Vital and Health Statistics No. 362 (September 15). Atlanta, GA: CDC. http://www.cdc.gov/nchs/products/pubs/pubd/ad/ 361–370/ad362.htm.

Nagel, Joanne. 2003. *Race, ethnicity, and sexuality: Intimate intersections, forbidden frontiers*. New York: Oxford University Press.

National Organization for Women (NOW) (2004) "Why You Should March." http://march.now.org/whywemarch.html

Ochs, R., and M. Deihl. 1992. Moving beyond binary thinking. Pp. 67–78 In *Homophobia: How we all pay the price*, ed. W. Blumenfeld. Boston: Beacon.

Payne, Charles. 1994. *I've got the light of freedom: The organizing tradition and the Mississippi freedom struggle*. Berkeley: University of California Press.

Petchesky, Rosalind P. 2000. Sexual rights: Inventing a concept, mapping an international practice. Pp. 81–103 In *Framing the sexual subject: The politics of gender, sexuality, and power*, ed. Richard Parker, Regina Maria Barbosa, and Peter Aggleton. Berkeley: University of California Press.

Pharr, Suzanne. 1988. *Homophobia: A weapon of sexism*. Inverness, CA: Chardon.

Plant, Richard. 1986. *The pink triangle: The Nazi war against homosexuals*. New York.

Rich, Adrienne. 1996. Compulsory heterosexuality and lesbian existence. Pp. 130–143 In *Feminism and sexuality—A reader*, ed. Stevi Jackson and Sue Scott. New York: Columbia University Press.

Rich, Frank. 2001. Naked capitalists: There's no business like porn business. *New York Times Magazine*. May 20. http://www.nytimes.com/2001/05/20/magazine/20PORN.html?ex=1168232400&en=6d1d58426e373abd&ei=5070.

Ropelato, Jerry. 2007. Internet pornography statistics. *TopTenReviews*. http://internet-filter-review.toptenreviews.com/internet-pornography-statistics.html.

Rosen, Ruth. 2000. *The world split open: How the modern womens' movement changed America*. New York: Penguin.

Rust, Paula C. 1995. *Bisexuality and the challenge to lesbian politics: Sex, loyalty, and revolution*. New York: New York University Press.

——. 2002. "Bisexuality: The state of the union" *Annual Review of Sex Research* 6:1–57.

Ryan, Joan. 2002. A 6-letter, 4-letter word. *San Francisco Chronicle*. February 19. http://www.sfgate.com/cgi-bin/article.cgi?f=/chronicle/archive/2002/02/19/ED62608.DTL.

Seabrook, Jeremy. 1996. *Travels in the skin trade: Tourism and the sex industry*. Chicago: Pluto Press.

Segal, Lynne. 1993. Introduction. Pp. 1–14 In *Sex exposed: Sexuality and the pornography debate*, ed. Lynn Segal and Mary McIntosh. London: Virago.

Sincero, Jen. 2005. *The straight girl's guide to sleeping with chicks*. New York: Fireside.

Smart, Carol. 1989. *Feminism and the power of the law*. New York: Routledge.

Smith, Tom W. 1994. Attitudes toward sexual permissiveness: Trends, correlates, and behavioral connections. Pp. 63–98 In *Sexuality across the life course*, ed. Alice S. Rossi. Chicago: University of Chicago Press.

Steedman, Mercedes. 1987. Who's on top? Heterosexual practices and male dominance during the sex act. pp. 83–111 In *Who's on top? The politics of heterosexuality*, ed. Varda Burstyn, H. Buchbinder, Dinah Forbes, and Mercedes Steedman. Toronto: Garamond Press.

Strossen, Nadine. 1995. *Defending pornography: Free speech, sex, and the fight for women's rights*. New York: Scribner.

Tajima, Renee E. 1989. Lotus blossoms don't bleed: Images of Asian women. Pp. 308–317 In *Making waves: An anthology of writings by and about Asian American women*, ed. Asian Women United of California. Boston: Beacon Press.

Tolman, Deborah L., and Tracy E. Higgins. 1996. How being a good girl can be bad. In *Bad girls/Good girls: Women, sex, and power in the nineties*, ed. Nan Bauer Maglin and Donna Perry. New Brunswick, NJ: Rutgers University Press.

Weinberg, George. 1972. *Society and the healthy homosexual*. New York: St. Martin's.

Weitzer, Ronald. 2000. The politics of prostitution in America. Pp. 159–180 In *Sex for sale: Prostitution, pornography, and the sex industry*, ed. Ronald Weitzer. New York: Routledge.

West, Cornel. 1993. Black sexuality: The taboo subject. Pp. 299–303 In *Gender basics: Feminist perspectives on women and men*, ed. Anne Minas. Belmont, CA: Wadsworth.

White, Deborah Gray. 1985. *Ar'n't I a woman? Female slaves in the plantation South*. New York: Norton.

Widmer, Eric D., Judith Treas, and Robert Newcomb. 1998. Attitudes toward nonmarital sex in 24 countries. *Journal of Sex Research* 25 (4): 349–58.

5

EDUCATION

ELEMENTARY SCHOOL SNAPSHOTS

- Snapshot 1: Keisha and Jessica sit with hands raised while Andrew blurts out the answer to a question.
- Snapshot 2: the teacher reprimands Ernesto, telling him to stay in his seat.
- Snapshot 3: Brittany answers a question. The teacher responds with a nod and moves on.
- Snapshot 4: The teacher praises Marcus for skill in reading.
- Snapshot 5: The teacher helps Sam with a spelling mistake, telling him to sound out the word.
- Snapshot 6: The teacher compliments Annalisa on her new shoes.
- Snapshot 7: Students are in lines to go to lunch. Boys are one side of the room, girls on the other (M. Sadker and Sadker 1994).
- Snapshot 8: Mr. Chang goes to visit his daughter's "graduation" from kindergarten. He notices the boys are given awards for "Very Best Thinker" and "Most Eager Learner" while the girls are awarded "Sweetest Personality" and "Best Helper." (Deveny 1994)

School takes up much time in children's lives and most of us attend school for many years. Not surprisingly, our experience in education is an important force in shaping our personalities, skills, and interactions in the rest of our lives. These snapshots show that gender is an important part of the lessons we learn in school, although they may be unintentional and largely "hidden agendas" in the school curriculum (M. Sadker and Sadker 1994).

This chapter reviews the ways in which gender shows up in schools, from our first day in kindergarten to the moment we receive our PhD and even after if we choose to become teachers ourselves. Although gender inequity remains in schools, education is an area where great strides have been made in the United States in regard to equality. Especially in higher education, women have caught up and surpassed men in many ways.

This chapter explores gender in the classroom through the different levels from primary to secondary to higher education in regard to the ways students are treated, the courses they take, the materials used, and the ways teachers are evaluated. The chapter then looks at the theoretical idea of the correspondence principle as a way of understanding why our schools are so hierarchical and gendered. The final section examines policies to address inequity, including Title IX.

GENDER IN THE K–12 CLASSROOM

About the same number of girls and boys attend school at all levels from preschool through high school. In terms of attendance, girls and boys seem to be equal in their participation in education in the United States. Does that mean gender equity has been achieved? Researchers have entered public school classrooms to find out what is happening with gender equity in the classroom (Orenstein 1994; American Association of University Women [AAUW] 1999). As the opening scenario revealed, their studies find that teachers treat boys and girls differently in the classroom. Children are automatically and with little thought segregated by gender.

You will see in this chapter that thinking and treating students as two distinct and very different categories by gender is so pervasive in schools that it is difficult to write about education and gender without repeating this kind of dichotomous thinking. As you read, think about how schools create the dichotomy of boys and girls rather than how they reflect some "natural" distinction among children.

Children are not only segregated into two groups, but the two categories are treated differently. Teachers respond to boys more frequently and when they do call on girls, they wait less time to allow girls to respond before interrupting them with an answer or moving on to another topic or student. Girls, however, are often less assertive and like to think about their answers. The boys beat them to the punch and the teacher ends up interacting with the boys as the girls sit in silence (M. Sadker and Sadker 1994). The end result is that teachers pay more attention to boys, allowing them to speak out of turn, praising and helping them more often, and calling on them more. Sometimes the teachers respond positively and sometimes negatively, but boys successfully demand their time more often, whereas girls more often sit quietly, wait patiently, and become fringe elements in the classroom action.

The amount of attention paid to students also varies by race ethnicity. White boys receive the most attention, followed by minority boys, then white girls. Minority girls are least likely to gain the teachers' attention.

The type of interaction teachers have with children also differs by the gender of the student. Teachers engage in fewer complex interactions with girls. When boys speak out in class, teachers comment on their observations. They encourage boys to correct a wrong answer or expand a correct one. With girls, teachers more often respond with nod or a brief "okay," and then move on to the next topic (M. Sadker and Sadker 1994).

Another difference in interactions with students occurs when students ask for help. When a girl asks for help, teachers show her how to do things by doing it themselves. A teacher might take the pencil and write on the girl's paper to show her how to solve a math problem, for example. In contrast, when a boy asks for help, teachers give elaborate instructions to the student as he does the work (M. Sadker and Sadker 1994).

Teachers are also more apt to comment on the appearance and clothing of girls. This kind of attention is probably intended to be complimentary and supportive. Focus on appearances, however, may be an important source of the feelings of self-consciousness that girls experience and that interfere with their self-confidence and academic performance.

These kinds of gender biases vary from one course to another, with math and science classes showing the most bias against girls. Chemistry classes, in particular, have boys dominating the discussion and teachers favoring boys and humiliating girls (Lee, Marks, and Byrd 1994). However, most of these discrepancies occur without the teacher or the students being aware of them. Teachers are not consciously creating discrimination and are usually stunned to see the differences when they view themselves on videotape (M. Sadker and Sadker 1994; Ridgeway and Healy 1997).

In addition to this kind of discrimination against girls by teachers, girls are also often subjected to sexual harassment by some boy classmates, who tease them about their bodies and do things such as surround girls and simulate sexual intercourse when their teacher leaves the room (Orenstein 1994). Although most schools have written policy against such kind of harassment, social pressures keep girls from reporting the incidents.

What Difference Does Differential Treatment in Schools Make?

These differences are strongly felt by girls in schools. The decline in self-confidence among girls during their school years, especially during adolescence, is remarkable (AAUW 1995). Researchers maintain that a drop in positive feelings about themselves and their achievements is a critical aspect of nearly all children's school career. When self-esteem is measured in students in elementary, middle, and high school, the scores decline for both boys and girls, but the slide is greater for girls. In addition, girls are much lower at all three levels. On a self-esteem index where higher scores indicate stronger self-esteem, the numbers go from 4 to about 2.8 for girls as they move from elementary school to high school. The scores for boys go from 5 to about 4.8.

This change in self-esteem varies by race ethnicity as well as gender. African American girls see a decline, but it is not as sharp as that for white girls. African American girls, for example, are twice as likely as other girls to say they are "happy with the way I am" and "pretty good at a lot of things." Latina girls' self-esteem falls further than that of either white or African American girls (Orenstein 2002).

How is self-esteem measured in these kinds of surveys? Boys are more likely than girls to say they are pretty good at a lot of things and twice as likely to name their talents as the thing they like best about themselves. Girls name aspects of their appearance as what they like about themselves. Teenage girls are much more likely than boys to also say that they are "not smart enough" or "not good enough" to achieve their dreams (Orenstein 2002).

Taming Warriors in the Kindergarten Classroom

Schools seem to be a place where girls are harmed by gender inequality. However, boys also find difficulties negotiating gender. Little boys enter kindergarten already well versed in masculine activities involving guns, fighting, and fast cars. The boys bring with them behaviors that reflect an ideology that violence is legitimate and even honorable as long as it occurs in a struggle between good and evil and they are on the proper side. Schools, however, are places where children are supposed to learn the ideals of rationality, responsibility, and decorum. What happens when the boys enter kindergarten and find their favorite activities are not in line with school discipline?

Researchers in Australia tried to answer this question by sitting in on kindergarten classes to observe boys and the transition they made as they progressed through the program (Jordan & Cowan 2004). They found that boys actively participated in what the researcher called warrior narratives. The stories in their play-acting centered around fighting, destroying, and identifying "good guys" and "bad guys" even in the most unlikely of places, turning teddy bears into the enemy, plastic cutlery from tea sets into swords, and cupboards in the play kitchen into jails. The toys and activities offered by the teacher were designed to encourage them to develop skills in cooperation and positive productivity by playing house, farm, and shop, or using tools and toys to construct roads and cities. The boys, however, transformed the available objects into symbolic ones that they could use for their warrior activities. This process of transforming objects and putting something together from whatever happens to be available is called brico-lage. In this case, bricolage occurs when Mac creates a car/weapon from a baby carriage:

> Mac threw a doll into the largest pram in the Doll Corner. He walked the pram [baby carriage] out past a group of his friends who were playing "crashes" on the Car Mat. Three of the five boys turned and watched him wheeling the pram toward the classroom door. Mac performed a sharp three-point turn; raced his pram past the Car Mat group, striking one boy on the head with the pram wheel. (Field notes quoted in Jordan and Cowan 2004,107)

The teacher responded by gently but persistently attempting to control the boys' behavior and showing them the "proper" use of the objects. She argued that the rules of "no shout-ing," "no running," and "no using classroom materials inappropriately" were rational ways of preventing the toys from being damaged and the children from being hurt. Because their behavior directly contradicts these ideas, their warrior narratives became part of a "'deviant' masculine subculture" (Jordan and Cowan 2004, 110).

At the same time, the girls' feminine games "of nurturing and self-display—mothers, nurse, brides, princesses—were accommodated easily within the classroom" (Jordan & Cowan 2004, 110). Their favorite activities and their ways of expressing themselves were in line with the rules of rationality, responsibility, and decorum the school wanted to establish.

Sometimes the school is able to drive the boys' warrior narratives underground or trans-fer it to the sports fields. Sometimes, the boy's behavior is diagnosed as Attention Deficit/ Hyperactivity Disorder (ADHD) and they are medicated.

Medicalizing and Medicating Boys in Schools

Ritalin, a medication used to treat ADHD, is one of the top-selling drugs today. Diagnosis for ADHD increased by 700 percent in the 1990s and Ritalin is now the drug most often dispensed in school to students in the United States (Rafalovich 2005). Of all the Ritalin prescriptions in the world, 90 percent are written for Americans (Leo 2002). It is mostly boys who are diagnosed with the disorder and prescribed the drugs. Boys are from three to ten times more likely to be identified with ADHD (Biederman et al. 2002).

ADHD is a cluster of problems that include hyperactivity and difficulty concentrating. Children who are diagnosed have symptoms such as inability to sit and focus on their school-work or to get along in a classroom setting that demands that they wait their turn, raise their hand, and stay in their seats.

A brochure for teachers about identifying ADHD describes a typical case:

> John, a third grade student, is often noncompliant and does not begin tasks when asked. During a two week observation period, he exhibited the following behaviors on a routine basis: John sharpened his pencil three times before beginning work. John fell out of his chair when given an assignment with 50 problems. He pretended to be the class clown. The class laughed. After leaving his reading group on the way back to his seat for independent work, John tripped Sally. He was sent to the corner of the room. (Leo 2002)

Some psychologists argue that ADHD is a serious problem and that Ritalin has saved children like John from failure and helped them to be happier and more successful in every area of their lives, especially school. They argue that, if anything, we should be concerned with the underdiagnosis of girls. They assert that a particular type of the disorder, the "inattentive type," is more prevalent in girls and may be overlooked by teachers because it is marked less by disruptive, impulsive behavior and more by disorganized, unfocused performance (Hinshaw 2002). The disorder may be equally destructive to the girl's life but it is not as disruptive to the classroom and, therefore, is ignored and goes untreated.

Others, however, worry that ADHD is an excuse for medicating children's, especially boys' behavior that is in the normal range or caused by social factors rather than neurological ones (Goldman et al. 1998; Timimi 2002). The critics point out that Ritalin and other ADHD drugs are given to children at two to three times the rate one might normally expect. Although ADHD is estimated to affect 3 percent to 5 percent of school-age children, some 8 percent to 10 percent of children have been diagnosed with ADHD and are taking drugs for it (Shaw 2002). Others have noted the geographic disparity of prescription rates, suggesting that children, at least in some states (the highest rates are North Carolina and Louisiana; the lowest in California, Nevada, and Colorado) are being overprescribed (Cox et al. 2003).

Geographic variation and the gap between what the numbers of those who randomly might be expected to exhibit the disorder and the numbers that are being treated suggest that factors in the social context may be incorrectly labeling and treating children as disabled (Diller 1996). Critics argue that the social structure of schools constrains children for long periods of time and leaves little room for individual variation. They also assert that our culture gives a double message to boys in particular, who are supposed to be active, assertive, and outspoken—boisterous—but who are made to set aside these boyish traits when they go to school (Hart, Grant, and Riley 2006).

Teaching Materials

Reading materials in schools are another critical feature of the gendered terrain. Books and other resources that are used for instruction, compared to other sources of information, are especially powerful because they are presented to students as authoritative and students are asked to see them uncritically (Stewart et al. 2003).

> Students are less free to disregard or be critical of educational materials than they are of the media. In fact, they are frequently required to absorb and assimilate the material in minute detail. Second, people attach a great deal of credibility and authority to educational and reference material and are, therefore, probably much more attentive to the messages they convey and susceptible to the sway of their influence. (Smith 1985, 37)

In the 1970s, a number of studies were done on the books children read and remarkable gender differences were found (Weitzman & Rizzo 1975). Three times as many men and boys were characters in reading books, six times as many men and boys were subjects of autobiographies, and pictures showed fifteen times more boys and men in them (Milner 1977). In collections of essays and stories for English class, six times as many men authors were included (Arlow & Froschel 1976).

These studies were replicated in the 1990s and the ratio of men and boys to women and girls had improved, but men and boy characters were still more visible and more likely to be active and involved in important areas of social life. Boys and men were portrayed as more adventurous, participating in a wider range of occupations, and often shown as rescuing girls and women. Pictures in high school chemistry books still showed three times as many boys and men in the 1990s (Bazler and Simonis 1991). Literature anthologies also continued to show a preponderance of men authors (Stewart et al. 2003).

These problems persist into higher education. A review of introductory sociology texts for college students showed a similar invisibility of women in the photos (Ferree & Hall 1990). Of the pictures, 44 percent included only men and only 19% included only women. Pictures of women also were likely to occur in chapters on family, sexuality, education, and gender inequality; they were underrepresented in chapters on politics (Spade 2001).

One result of the invisibility of women in students' reading material is ignorance about the contribution women have made to our ideas, social institutions, and history. Research on elementary school children finds that they do not know much about what women have contributed to society. In one study, children were asked to name famous women in history. Most could only name a few and some could not name any famous women. In 1992, a survey of their history books pointed to a probable explanation when it found that only eleven feminine names were even mentioned in the text and no adult American women were mentioned.

Another study explored the effect of the invisible woman in textbooks by asking fifth- to eighth-graders to illustrate passages from a history book. The boys drew all men—mostly warriors. The girls drew families with women in them but they also always included at least one man. The children's view of history reflected the words and illustrations they had seen in the text and that view sometimes showed women as participants in history but men were always there (Fournier and Wineburg 1997).

HIGH SCHOOL

Most people in the United States finish high school. The numbers of students who did not complete high school declined from about 27.2 percent in 1960 to 9 percent in 2005, but

TABLE 5–1 High School Drop Out Rates by Gender and Race Ethnicity, 1998

	Men	Women
White	8.6%	6.9%
Black	15.5%	12.2%
Hispanic	33.5%	25.0%

Source: Blair and Northway (2001, 63).

TABLE 5–2 Participation in High School Extracurricular Activities by Gender, 2001

	Girls	Boys
Newspaper/yearbook	13%	6%
Music and performing arts	31	9
Athletic teams	32	45
Academic clubs	19	12
Student government	13	8
Other activities	44	26

Source: Freeman (2004).

these numbers vary by gender and race ethnicity. Boys (11%) in the United States drop out of school more often than do girls (8%), but race ethnicity make an even bigger difference than gender (US Bureau of the Census 2005). Table 5–1 shows the dropout rate for boys and girls of different racial ethnic groups. Hispanic people, in particular, are likely to drop out of high school. Latinas are a little more likely to graduate than Latinos but both are much less likely to graduate than white or black students and the racial ethnic gap is growing (Perreira, Harris and Dohoon 2006; King 2006).

Not only are girls more likely to complete high school, they also seem to be more involved in school activities. Table 5–2 shows that compared to boys, girls are more often involved in all extracurricular activities except for sports in high school and we will see in chapter 11 on media and sports that girls are making gains in athletics as well.

Math and Science and Gender

Math and science are areas of particular concern because so many jobs are attached to success in these disciplines. Girls now outnumber boys in college preparatory courses. About 2 percent of girls and boys were in these courses in the early 1980s but today 33 percent of girls are and 29 percent of boys are. Table 5–3 shows that high school girls have caught up and now surpass boys in the proportion enrolled in geometry, algebra II, biology, and chemistry courses. They are only slightly behind boys in calculus and physics.

TABLE 5–3 Percentage of Students Enrolled in High School Math and Science Classes by Gender, 2000

	Geometry	Algebra II	Calculus	Biology	Chemistry	Physics
Girls	81	71	11	93	66	29
Boys	75	65	12	83	58	34

SOURCE: Freeman (2004).

College women are also catching up with men in their participation in math and science in almost every field. Women are nearly half of the graduates in physical sciences (41 percent), agriculture and natural resources (45 percent), math (48 percent), and business (39 percent), and they are the majority in biology (60 percent). Only in engineering are women (20 percent) still significantly less likely to earn a degree and even there, the numbers have increased 2,000 percent since 1969 (see Box 5–1).

Although women are equalling men and in some cases surpassing them in obtaining degrees in math and science, ideas about gender still identify these fields as masculine. One of the important results of the identification of math and science as masculine is that women may be less likely to recognize their abilities in these fields.

Shelley Correll (2001) examined this question by looking at the math scores and grades in math courses of eighth-grade students in the United States. She then looked at how the students assessed their skill by asking true–false questions such as, "Mathematics is one of my best subjects," "I have always done well in math," and "I get good marks in math." In addition, she looked at students' scores and grades in English and their answers to the same questions about their success in English courses.

She found that when she compared boys and girls with similar scores and grades in math courses, the boys were more likely to perceive themselves as good at math. The boys did not, however, assess themselves as better than girls with similar scores and grades in English. In other words, the boys did not think they were better at everything; they just thought they were better at math.

Box 5–1 MARS MISSION

When the second robotic rover, *Opportunity*, landed on Mars, it represented an important landmark for women scientists. Only a century ago women were not allowed to look into a telescope and a half-century ago, women were not hired at observatories because there were no women's bathrooms. But 20 percent of the 154-member team of scientists and 10 percent of the engineers who put *Opportunity* on Mars are women. The numbers are still small but they are growing and women are now in every category at the National Aeronautics and Space Administration (NASA). Even more important, in the younger ranks, women are equal to or even surpassing men in their numbers. Fifty-seven percent of astronomers under age twenty-three and the majority of graduate assistants and research fellows are women (Ginty 2004).

TABLE 5-4 Gender Segregation in Vocational and Technical Courses, 2002

	Men Enrolled	Women Enrolled
Cosmetology	4%	96%
Child care	13	87
Health aide	14	86
Drafting	77	23
Automotive	92	8
Carpentry	93	7
Welding	93	7
Electrician	94	6
Plumbing	94	6

SOURCE: Washington Post (2002, A8).

Correll (2001) argues that our feelings about our competence may have a powerful effect on our future choices. She writes, "Boys do not pursue mathematical activities at a higher rate than girls do because they are better at mathematics. They do so, at least partially, because they think they are better.(P.1728)" The association of math and math-related skills with masculinities may allow boys to assess themselves as more competent and may therefore lead them to pursue further education and career paths in these fields. The association of math with masculinity at the same time may be holding back equally or more competent girls.

Vocational Education

Girls have made impressive strides in education, but vocational education programs continue to reflect patterns that existed twenty years ago. Surveys show that young women are still clustered in a few programs and those vocations have median hourly wages of about $9 an hour. Young men, in contrast, are likely to be training in skilled trades with median hourly wages of about $30 an hour (*Washington Post* 2002, A8). Table 5–4 shows the proportion of men and women in the different areas of study in vocational education programs in twelve regions.

Title IX, No Child Left Behind, and Single-Sex Schools

Civil rights laws passed in the 1960s began to protect women from discrimination at work, but the protection did not extend to education. Title IX, which we examine more fully in chapter 11 on media and sports, was passed in 1972 to try to address gender inequity in schools from kindergarten through graduate school. Title IX made it illegal for schools that received any federal assistance, including universities that received federally funded scholarships or research grants, to discriminate against girls and women. Title IX was a turning point in gender in education in the United States. Before 1972, public universities restricted the entrance of women through quotas and higher standards. For example, women who applied to study at some colleges needed to present scores thirty to forty points higher on achievement tests than men who applied. Even in fields dominated by women, women students were restricted. For example, nursing schools often did not permit married women to be students (General Accounting Office 2001).

Title IX outlaws treating boys and girls differently in school in the United States. It currently permits select single-sex classes—in physical education for example—but it does not allow schools to segregate students arbitrarily. This is because when groups have been segregated in the past, the least-valued group has ended up with fewer resources and fewer opportunities. In looking at the problems for girls and boys in K–12 classrooms, some educators are now suggesting that we should establish more same-sex schools. Single-sex schools are unusual in the United States but they have been established to try to create gender equity in Australia, England, Ireland, and Jamaica (Steitmatter 1999). The No Child Left Behind Act may increase same-sex schools in the United States because it encourages schools to try same-sex classrooms.

No Child Left Behind is the name of the education policy established by the Bush administration in 2002. Title IX and No Child Left Behind appear to conflict and which one will supersede the other will be decided in the courts. In the meantime, about 250 schools in the United States only accept one sex or have some same-sex classrooms. This number has increased from three classrooms in 1996. In 2006, the federal government began to actively promote same-sex classrooms. The government predicts that about 10 percent of the nation's 90,000 public schools will become same-sex schools (Toppo 2006).

Those who support girls-only classrooms assert that girls feel like outsiders in coeducational classrooms, their voices are silenced, and their confidence is diminished (Steitmatter 1999). They maintain that coeducation only appears to be equal. Girls may sit side by side with boys but they are not fully integrated and they do not have the same educational experience as boys do.

Some research on all-girls schools provides support for this point of view. The research shows that students in all-girls schools speak out in class and participate more. In physics classes, the girls in the all-girls classes understand the material better, work together more often, and are not afraid to ask questions. When physics classes are coed, the boys tend to dominate and create a climate of competition (Blair and Northway 2001).

Studies have also shown a shift in participation of women and men as the proportion of men in a class increases. The more men there are in a class, the less women enter into sustained discussion, and men became more active as their numbers increased (Canada and Pringle 1995). In addition, single-sex classrooms report less gender stereotyping and fewer explicit sexual harassment incidents such as drawing unflattering pictures of the girls (Lee, Marks, and Byrd 1994).

Not all researchers agree, however. Some studies have found little difference in achievement between single-sex schools and coeducational schools (Carpenter & Hayden 1987; Bell 1989). One large study concluded that all-girls schools are detrimental to girls. It found that in contrast to all-boys schools and coeducational schools, teachers in all-girls schools talked down to the students, encouraged students in hard work rather than correct work, and created dependency (Lee, Marks, and Byrd 1994).

What accounts for these disagreements in the research? One study comparing single-sex education for girls in a physics class suggests that the variable of whether there are boys in the class or not is not the only significant one (Illinois Mathematics and Science Academy (IMSA) 1995). This study showed the all-girls classes to be a success. Students in all-girls classes compared to girls in coeducational classes scored higher on physics tests, improved their problem-solving and analytical skills, and decided to take more physics and math classes in subsequent semesters. Girls who attended these schools also spoke more freely in class, and more often majored in math and science and attended college and graduate school.

Are these benefits the result of single-sex classrooms or is it something else? The study also reported that the more successful classes were not just all girls. They also created a girl culture in which the classroom dynamics were altered. Students in all-girls classes had more influence over classroom dynamics and a special rapport developed in which students took greater responsibility for their own learning as well as that of their classmates. Furthermore, single-sex classrooms that report higher levels of learning are also of higher quality in other ways. For example they have smaller class size, more engaged parents, better trained teachers, and stronger academic emphasis (D. Sadker and Zittleman 2004).

Even though all-girls classes have been shown in some instances to be more effective in teaching girls, this solution may still be a dangerous one. Civil rights advocates are concerned that recent changes in federal policy that allow schools to set up same-sex schools and classrooms might mean that school districts will begin segregating girls and boys based on "outdated and dangerous stereotypes" (Toppo 2006, 1). Barrie Thorne (1993) also warns that the underlying assumption of much of this research—if girls are left alone they will create a different kind of classroom atmosphere that reflects girl culture with more turn taking and supportive learning groups—may not be valid. Her research shows that the picture is more complex. Many or maybe even most boys are not really part of "boy culture" because they, too, are dominated by more aggressive boys. And, all girls do not participate in the cooperative classrooms that make up the picture of girl culture.

Kimmel (2000) asserts that the promotion of single-sex schools is a sign that we have abandoned the goal of transforming our social institutions as safe equal places for both women and men. If we believe that the only way for girls and women to be safe and enjoy access to social benefits like education is to establish single-sex "safe havens," we have given up critical goals for a more human-friendly society. He cites John Dewey (1911), who scoffed at single-sex schools, asking do we have "'female botany,' 'female algebra' and for all I know 'female multiplication tables'?" Dewey argued that "co-educated girls become more self-reliant and more willing to gain approval for their work rather than their ability to [manipulate] work others." In addition he maintained that boys learn gentleness, unselfishness, courteousness, and more helpful channels for expression than "'lawless boisterousness.'" (p.59).

Kimmel (2000) agrees with Dewey, arguing that single-sex schools may challenge men's domination of our educational institutions but they also perpetuate and reproduce that masculine dominance. Single-sex schools imply that women must have special schools because they cannot do well without special treatment and they imply that men cannot change. Single-sex schools insult both women and men.

SAT Scores

As all American college students know, SATs are an important gateway to higher education. SAT I assesses students' potential for learning about a subject. SAT II is an achievement test

TABLE 5–5 National SAT Scores by Gender, 2006

	Reading	*Writing*	*Mathematics*
Girls	502	502	502
Boys	505	491	536

SOURCE: College Board (2006).

that measures what students have learned in a particular subject area. SAT I is the test we normally think of when we say SAT and it is the test that large numbers of students take as a requirement for entrance into college.

These standardized tests are usually a key feature in each student's college application and decisions about who will be admitted are frequently determined by scores. Besides surpassing men in the proportion who enter college, women are now the majority of those students who take SATs (55 percent). Men, however, score higher on average on the test.

Table 5–5 shows recent scores of boys and girls on SAT I tests in reading, writing, and mathematics. The scores show that they are nearly identical on reading, girls outscore boys a little in writing, and boys outscore girls quite a bit in math. These numbers have not varied much in the past few decades. Overall boys earned 1,532 points and girls 1,504 on all three tests. Why do men receive higher numbers on SATs?

One explanation is that women do not do as well because more women take the test, which means that a more select group of men take SATs. However, men have scored higher than women for a long time, even before women were the majority of test takers.

Some people believe that the test is gender biased although the College Board, which designs the questions, claims to make every effort to eliminate gender and racial ethnic bias. Gender bias in the questions may, however, be an issue. In 1998, after persistent complaints about gender bias in the test, the College Board changed the exam and the gender gap narrowed. Gender bias appears in the questions, for example, when activities with which boys might be more familiar, such as sports or auto racing, are used in word problems in the math section. Girls do better on questions that relate to relationships, aesthetics, and the humanities (Rosser 1989).

The history of the SAT is interesting in this regard. When the test was first developed and given to high school students, boys did better than girls on the math section, whereas girls outperformed boys on the verbal section. The test makers went back to readjust the questions to close the gap on the verbal sections. The company that designed the test, ETS, believed that the verbal score gap was biased against boys, so they added more questions pertaining to politics, business, and sports, topics in which boys tended to do better. They did not adjust the math test, perhaps believing that when girls are superior, balancing is required but when boys are superior no adjustment is necessary (Dwyer 1996).

Another explanation for the gap is the format of the test, which coincides with a masculine style of test taking. Boys tend to do better on multiple-choice exams, whereas girls are better at short-answer, essay, and constructed response questions. The math and reading sections of the SAT I are multiple choice.

The SAT also rewards "guessing." Boys are more likely to take the risk and guess rather than leave a question blank. The ACT does not have a guessing penalty and the gender gap on that test is much smaller (Fairtest 2002).

Furthermore, SATs are timed tests rewarding speed. Research shows that boys and girls approach problem solving differently. Girls are more likely to work a problem out completely, to consider more than one possible correct answer, and to check their answers. These are probably good study skills, but they are not useful for achieving high SAT scores. Studies show that when the time constraint is removed girls do much better, whereas boys' scores remain about the same (Fairtest 2002).

The most important explanation for why boys have higher scores in math on the SAT I is that boys are better prepared in high school for taking SATs because of the kinds of courses they take. As students move through middle school and high school, girls used to be less likely to take math classes and often took only the minimum requirement. When boys and girls with identical backgrounds in math take standardized tests, their scores on math tests are more similar (Entwisle, Alexander, and Olson 1994). As girls catch up with boys in the courses they take in math and science they are also catching up on the standardized tests in these areas.

Not only is the gap diminishing, but the distribution of SAT I math scores for boys and girls is becoming more similar. Scores for boys are more variable, with more boys at the extremes with very high scorers and very low scorers, whereas girls tend to have scores in the middle. This difference, however, is also changing. In the 1980s, thirteen times more boys than girls scored 700 or more out of a possible 800 in math on the SAT. Today boys are about three times more likely than girls to score in this high range. Although girls have not caught up with boys, the number of girl "junior math wizards" has soared in the last two decades. This improvement has corresponded with a change in educational opportunities for girls whereby special programs and mentoring have increasingly encouraged girls to take higher level math and science courses (Halpern et al. 2007). Girls are now nearly identical to boys in the high school math and science courses and their math scores on SATs are similar although still not identical.

These tests, however, remain important gatekeepers and because women still do not score quite as well, women may be prevented from entering the most prestigious institutions or receiving scholarships. However, are they valid criteria for making these kinds of decisions about prospective students? The purpose of SATs is to try to predict which students will be successful in college. Because girls score lower then boys on the tests, we might expect that girls would not do as well in college and would receive lower grades or fail to complete their degrees. Women, in fact, get better grades in college courses on average and are more likely to finish their degrees. SAT scores for boys are on average thirty-three points higher than the scores of girls who receive the same grade in the same college courses (Wainer and Steinberg 1992). The SATs, therefore, appear to be measuring something other than skills required for success in college, or at least they are measuring them differently for women and men. The best predictor of success in the college classroom is high school grade point average, followed by SAT II. SAT I is not a good predictor.

International Comparisons on Standardized Tests

Since 1995, forty-one countries representing 14 percent of the world's population have reported education data by gender for eighth-graders. The data from these reports show that in eleven countries there are no gender gaps in math or science: the United States, Singapore, Russia, Thailand, Australia, Ireland, Romania, Flemish Belgium, Cyprus, Colombia, and South Africa.

You might be thinking that these data seem to contradict the SAT I score report for the United States cited in the previous section. The reason the SAT I shows a gender gap in math and the international reports do not show a gender gap in math (or science) is because the SAT I assesses the potential for someone to do well in a course. The international scores are of tests of achievement assessing how much a student knows having taken a course in math. Given the same background in course work, therefore, it appears that boys and girls in many nations score about the same when given exams on that course work.

There are also important differences by gender in language skills. For example, in literacy scores of girls and boys in fourth grade, girls scored above boys in all sixty-eight nations reporting. The largest gaps were in Kuwait, Iran, New Zealand, and Belize. Remember, of course, that these tests were only given to children attending school.

The international educational reports, however, point to many other inequities besides gender. The biggest gaps are not between boys and girls within a country but the gap from one country to the next. For example, the very highest scores from students in the United States in math are about equal to the average score of students in the top-scoring nations such as Singapore, Korea, Japan, the Czech Republic, and Hungary.

HIGHER EDUCATION AND GENDER

Higher education is one place where women in many places in the world have made remarkable gains in the past few decades. In Algeria, for example, 70 percent of lawyers and 60 percent of judges are women, and women dominate in medicine as well. These changes have been spurred by increasing numbers of women in higher education. Sixty percent of college students in Algeria are women (Slackman 2007).

The United States now has the highest proportion of women attending college of any nation in the world. In the 1800s, however, education experts in the United States claimed that women should not become too educated because it diverted energy to their brains from their uteruses and made them too feeble to bear healthy children. The first university to integrate by gender in the United States was Oberlin College in 1833. Oberlin officials originally decided to allow women in because they believed that coeducation would enhance the education of men. University officials argued that as part of a solid education, men students needed a "more wholesome and realistic view of women" that could be accomplished by permitting them to be educated along with women (Stock 1978, 190).

In 1870, the first survey of college graduates in the United States showed that about 85 percent of the 9,400 BAs were awarded to men. During the twentieth century, women began to catch up with men and are now pulling ahead in admissions to college and finishing bachelor's and master's degrees. The gap between women and men is expected to continue to grow with women in the lead as they pass men in their pursuit of higher education. Men are still more likely to obtain doctoral degrees but even that gap is diminishing. Table 5–6 shows the way these numbers changed and are projected to continue to change. Table 5-6 shows that the degrees earned by women have not diminished the numbers of those earned by men. Men's graduation rates appear to have remained constant as women's have risen.

TABLE 5-6 BA, MA, and PhD Degrees Earned by Gender, 1985–2008

	Bachelor's		Master's		Doctorate's	
	Women	Men	Women	Men	Women	Men
1965–1966	220,228	299,287	47,521	93,081	2,116	16,121
1974–1975	418,092	504,841	130,880	161,570	7,266	26,817
1999–2000	659,000	502,000	227,000	187,000	19,000	27,400
2007–2008 (projected)	739,000	503,000	243,000	203,000	22,900	26,600

SOURCE: Blair and Northway (2001, 62).

TABLE 5-7 Percentage of BA Degrees, by Discipline, Awarded to Women, 1969 and 2001

	1969	2001
Total	43%	57%
Engineering	1	20
Information technology	13	28
Physical sciences	14	41
Agriculture and natural resources	4	45
Math	37	48
Business	9	49
Social sciences and history	36	52
Biology	30	60
Accounting	9	61
Education	75	77
Psychology	43	78
Health professions	69	84

SOURCE: Freeman (2004).

In addition to women catching up and surpassing men in the total number of degrees obtained, the gender balance in many fields of university study has also become more equal as women enter fields once thought to be for men only. For example, in 1971 only about 1 percent of dentistry degrees went to women, but in 1997, 37 percent of the graduates of dental schools were women. In business degrees women have almost caught up with men. In 1971, 10 percent of business degrees went to women and in 1997, 49 percent went to women. Women students have surpassed the numbers of men in law school. Women have made some headway in engineering, computer sciences, and physical sciences, although the numbers of women receiving degrees in these fields remains low. At the same time between 1971 and 1996, men became more likely to earn degrees in fields dominated by women like nursing (from 3 percent to 11 percent), elementary education (from 9 percent to 12 percent),

TABLE 5–8 Undergraduates by Age, Race Ethnicity and Gender, 2004

	UNDER 24			OVER 25		
	Total%	Men	Women	Total%	Men	Women
White	63	29	34	37	15	22
African American	50	20	30	50	16	34
Hispanic	61	26	35	39	15	24
Asian American	65	32	33	35	14	21
American Indian	49	21	28	51	16	35
All	61	28	34	39	15	24

SOURCE: U.S. Department of Education (2004).

and home economics (from 4 percent to 12 percent). Table 5–7 shows the contrast in several disciplines in degrees awarded in 1969 and 2001.

Important differences within fields, however, remain. For example, the number of degrees awarded in social sciences is about the same for women and men, but women are more likely to receive a degree in sociology or anthropology, whereas men receive them in economics and geography. Business management is also nearly equal, but women are concentrated in the specialty of human resource management and men in finance. Law is gender stratified with women in family law and men in taxes; physicians divide themselves into women in family practice and men in anesthesiology specialties (Sapiro 2003).

The gender gap in enrollment and graduation in higher education is most pronounced in the historically black colleges where women comprise 70 percent of the student body despite efforts to recruit men. However, the trend exists in universities across the board and some institutions are concerned. In 1990, the University of Georgia became so disturbed that women were the majority of graduates (55 percent) they began giving an edge to men applicants who were admitted with lower scores on SATs and high school grades. The practice was discontinued when they were threatened with a federal lawsuit (Fletcher 2002). Other colleges and universities, especially private ones, are still using different criteria for choosing men and women for admission into their institutions.

Race ethnicity is not the only variable that intersects with gender, however. Age is also important. Table 5–8 shows the proportion of undergraduate degrees by gender, race ethnicity, and age. Read the rows across to see that nontraditional students (over twenty-five years old), who make up a growing proportion of college students, are much more likely to be women. African American and Native American women undergraduates particularly fall into this over twenty-five category.

Social class also intersects with gender to create different rates of college attendance. In Table 5–9, the data are divided by race ethnicity and by income level. A quartile refers to one-fourth of the population. The lowest quartile indicates the poorest 25 percent of the population and the highest quartile the richest. Table 5-9 then allows us to look at the different racial

TABLE 5-9 Percentage of Dependent Undergraduates Who Are Men by Race Ethnicity and Income, 2003–2004

	Lowest Quartile	Middle Quartile	Highest Quartile
White	44	47	51
African American	42	44	54
Hispanic	43	46	51
Asian American	48	52	54

SOURCE: U.S. Department of Education (2004).

and ethnic groups in each of three of four quartiles. The number is the proportion of college students who are men in a specific quartile and racial ethnic group. For example, the number on the right side of the first line tells us that if we look at the category of white students in the highest income bracket, 51 percent of them are men. Women are not the majority in this socioeconomic group. Table 5-9 tells us that women have made the greatest strides in catching up and surpassing men in college attendance in the poorest households.

In the United States, both men and women are increasingly likely to enter and complete college. In 1940 about one-quarter of Americans finished high school and 5 percent received a bachelor's degree. In 1999, 83 percent completed high school and 25 percent received a bachelor's degree. Both women and men have increased their participation in postsecondary education, but women have increased their participation much more rapidly than men have and no one knows why. Several possible reasons have been suggested: Women's learning styles may fit better into the typical college classroom; men may be more enticed by the popular culture to avoid further education and enter the labor market; and men may have more pressure on them, especially in low-income families, to choose a paid job rather than college (Fletcher 2002).

Others have suggested that women are just more serious about education in the transition from high school to college. Girls more likely to enter college right after high school (almost 70 percent of high school grads in 2003) compared to boys (a little over 60 percent). Entering college immediately after high school is strongly associated with staying in college and graduating (King 2006). In addition, the annual survey of U.S. college freshmen finds that boys often spend large amounts of time watching television, partying, and exercising during their senior year of high school. High school girls spend more time studying and doing homework, talking with teachers outside of school, and participating in volunteer work. And as we saw in Table 5–2, girls participate in more extracurricular activities. In addition, girls more often take honors courses and college prep courses and have higher academic aspirations (Fletcher 2002).

What About the Boys?

The discussion of higher education in the United States shows that women have caught up with and surpassed men in many ways in higher education. This has caused some people to question whether we have gone too far. They are concerned that focusing on the problems in education for girls detracts from our commitment to educate boys. They ask "What about the boys?" and fear that as women and girls gain access to education, boys will be left out. Are schools designed to support girls and women more than boys and men? Has the pendulum swung in the United States from schools that ignored and discriminated against girls and women to ones that are now privileging them and mistreating boys and men?

As we have noted, some universities and colleges have created affirmative action programs for men and are now even accepting men into their programs with weaker records than the women they are refusing admission to try to "balance" out the proportion of women and men in the institution.

Recently, critics within the educational system and those in the popular press have sounded an alarm asking whether strides made by girls and women in schools are accompanied by a drag or even a decline in boys' and men's educational attainment. Observations of the suppression of the "warrior narratives" of boys in the schools have caused some to claim that elementary schools are bad for boys. They argue that normal boyish behaviors have been pathologized. The demands that children sit still, raise their hands, and take naps are argued to be ways to discourage boys from liking school and from doing well there. Similarly, the statistics that show women moving ahead of men in finishing high school and enrolling in and completing university degrees have been met with assertions that ever since feminists have called attention to inequity for girls and women in schools, boys and men have been ignored and they have slipped further and further behind.

Michael Kimmel (2004) argues this social movement is really a counterfeminist one. Feminists are being blamed for the success of girls as well as the problems boys face. But are boys' problems caused by feminism or girls? Kimmel says that neither feminism nor girls are the problem; the real underlying issues are race ethnicity and social class. If the statistics on high school and college graduation are examined carefully, they show that not all men are falling behind. Lower income men, especially African American and Hispanic men, are rapidly dropping out of education. Racial ethnic inequality and social class differences play a major role. Look back at Table 5–8 to see that among the wealthiest households, men are more likely to attend college than are women. Focusing on gender in isolation obscures our ability to see racism and class inequities in schools.

Kimmel says that posing the debate as feminists versus boys and men is deceptive. First it creates a false opposition between the needs of boys and girls and women and men. In fact, improvements in education that help girls also help boys. When schools are made girl-friendly they become boy-friendly as well because what they really become is child-friendly. For example, schools that are "girl-friendly" provide flexible scheduling to allow children to continue work and family commitments as well as education. They also are closer to their homes and provide children with toilets and running water. Schools that are made safer to protect girls from bullying and sexual harassment and assault are safer for boys who are also victims of school bullying (United Nations 2004).

Second, blaming feminists causes us to ignore major issues related to education such as cuts in spending on education that hurt both genders. Children, regardless of gender, do not have sufficient materials or services for special needs. Scholarships, work-study opportunities, fellowships, and assistantships for men and women college students have been drastically cut or almost eliminated in recent years.

GLOBAL RATES OF ILLITERACY

Although problems remain, girls in the United States have made significant gains in school in regard to equality in attendance and graduation. In many ways today, girls are doing better than boys. The picture at the global level, however, is quite different. In some countries boys are less likely to attend school. Colombia, Haiti, Lesotho, Madagascar, Malawi, Surinam, and Tanzania are all countries where boys are less likely to go to school than girls. Taken as a whole, however, girls around the world are less likely to be in school (United Nations 2004). Two-thirds of children not attending schools in the world are girls, and of the 140 million illiterate young people in the world, 86 million are girls. Frequently this gap in education is not by choice but because of discrimination against girls by governments, families, and schools that exclude girls from educational institutions (Pizozzi 1998; Otis 2003). Research on this question shows that girls have not yet caught up with boys at the global level (United Nations 2000).

Illiteracy among women is intertwined with other factors resulting in serious consequences. Low education levels among women are associated with higher fertility, lower paid jobs, decreased income, greater poverty, and higher mortality rates. Sometimes the connections among all of these factors are critical, although not necessarily obvious. One study in sub-Saharan Africa, for example, found that the 30 percent of children whose mothers had no formal schooling were immunized compared to 70 percent of children whose mothers had a secondary education. Other research has shown that educating women increased the crop production of women farmers and reduced malnutrition of their families (*Economist* 2002).

Unexpected Connections Between Water and Education

We do not usually think about literacy being connected to water and sewage systems, but in fact one of the major barriers to education for girls in poor countries is the lack of access to water and sanitation. In the Global South, 1.1 billion people lack access to clean water. Because carrying water is considered women's work in many of these countries, women and girls bear the brunt of that burden. Walking to water sources, waiting in line, and carrying water back home can take up to four hours a day in many places.

This job cuts into the time available for girls to attend school, so access to water is directly related to education. In Senegal, Mozambique, Uganda, and Tanzania, research has shown that school attendance is 12 percent higher for girls who live within fifteen minutes of a water source compared to those girls who live further away.

One ten-year-old Bolivian girl explained as she waited to fill her container with water from the community well, "Of course I wish I were in school. I want to learn to read and write—and I want to be there with my friends. But how can I? My mother needs me to get water and the pipe is only open from 10 to 12. You have to get in line early because so many people come here." (United Nations 2006a, 18)

Access to sanitation is also important. If schools do not have toilets, boys are sent into the fields to relieve themselves but girls must wait all day until they can return to their home or community to find a toilet. One half of the dropouts of girls from school are because of lack of access to water or sanitation. In the Global South, 60 percent of the population does not have access to safe sewage systems (United Nations 2006b).

GENDER AND TEACHERS

Gender bias in academic settings is called "the chilly climate." Not just students, but teachers and even the organization of schools are affected by the chilly climate (Blakemore et al. 1997). Jobs in education are gendered with men at the top. Table 5–10 shows the proportion of women at different levels within the school system from preschool to higher education. In public schools, about 7 percent of superintendents are women, 24 percent of assistant superintendents are women, and 34 percent of principals are women. Even those women who do become principals tend to be relegated to less prestigious positions, as women are 37 percent of grade school principals, 23 percent of middle-school principals, and only 8 percent of high school principals (Spade 2001).

In higher education, researchers (Spade 2001) have found a range of economic equity issues. Women are clustered in the lowest ranks of the faculty. Seventeen percent of full professors are women and 30 percent of associate professors are women, but 50 percent of the lowest ranks of instructors and lecturers with lowest pay, fewest benefits, and least voice on the faculty are women (National Coalition for Women and Girls in Education 1997). Within each of these ranks, women receive lower salaries on average. Women are also more likely to be in part-time or temporary positions and advance in rank or are tenured more slowly.

Women also express concern about social factors on the job. From their colleagues, women professors feel less supported in their social interactions on campus because of sexist jokes, sexual harassment, and exclusion from social networks. In addition, women faculty

TABLE 5–10 Percentage of Women Teachers and Administrators at Varying Levels of Education

	% Women
Teachers aides, elementary school teachers	91
Pre-K and kindergarten teachers	98
Elementary school teachers	83
Secondary school teachers	58
Principals	34
College and university instructors	51
Assistant professors	45
Associate professors	30
Professors	17
College and university administrators	20

Source: U.S. Department of Education (2001); Spade (2001).

TABLE 5–11 Proportion of Women in Faculty in Higher Education by Discipline

36% of the law faculty
31% of the business faculty
20% of the computer science faculty
17% of the political science faculty
12% of the physical sciences faculty

SOURCE: General Accounting Office (2001).

find their students are more demanding and give them lower evaluations, especially if they violate gender norms.

Although women have made great strides, they still are outnumbered by men in most fields. Women in full-time academic positions make up 24 percent of the total faculty (General Accounting Office 2001). Table 5–11 shows that women still are the minority in many faculties, especially those that have historically been associated with men's professions.

Evaluating Professors

If you have been around a university for even a short time, you have heard teachers talking about annual reviews and evaluations for tenure and promotion. One important piece of evidence used to justify raises, promotions, and granting or denying tenure is student evaluations of teaching. Comparisons of the scores students give professors for their teaching do not find much difference between those given to men and those given to women (Basow 1998; Kardia & Wright 2004). Diana Kardia and Mary Wright (2004), however, argue that the similar numbers hide a dissimilar experience in teaching and teaching evaluations. They assert that students hold women teachers to different standards and evaluate them more harshly. The similar scores, therefore, indicate that women professors try harder and perform better in the classroom—they are better teachers than men.

Rather than asking students what score they give to teachers when they evaluate them, Kardia and Wright (2004) asked students how they arrived at the scores. Students readily admitted they had higher expectations of women faculty. One man student explained:

> I think that stereotypes play a big role. I mean if you're looking at a male teacher and he's overbearing, you might just excuse it and say "Yeah, well, you know, he's a professor. He's just doing his job." But if you look at it as a woman professor you'd be like, "Women are supposed to be a lot nicer, and, you know, a lot more friendlier and she's acting like such a bitch." (Kardia and Wright 2004, 8)

Another student said that he would not only judge the woman professor more harshly, he would respond differently in the classroom. He described his response to a bad teacher:

> I don't think highly of this guy to begin with and I think if he was a woman I would think less of him...I hate to admit it but...he's very disorganized and he doesn't

articulate his thoughts well. . . . If he was a woman, I would just probably have no tolerance for that. . . . You sit there and you really try to figure out what he's trying to say. You're very attentive, trying to get into it. But if he was a woman, I think I would just sit back and be like, "This is ridiculous." (Kardia and Wright 2004, 8)

Professors are not only evaluated by students; their work is evaluated by other scholars for publication and promotion. Christine Wenneras and Agnes Wold (1997) studied decisions about scholars in Sweden. When they did their study, Sweden had recently been named the leading country in the world in regard to equal opportunities for women and men. Wenneras and Wold studied how the Swedish Medical Research Council rated women and men on scientific competence, quality of proposed methodology, and relevance of research proposal. They found the Council rated all of the women below the least competent men. On other measures of productivity such as publishing, being cited, and quality of publications, however, women rated equal to the men. In other words, the peer-review system of the Swedish Medical Research Council rated women scholars much more critically than men. When other kinds of measures were used to determine the caliber of the women's scholarship, their peer reviews did not correspond to the real quality and impact of the women's research. The reviewers consistently gave women applicants lower scores than equally productive men. For example, in some cases, Wenneras and Wold (1997) found that women applicants for funding from the Swedish Medical Research Council needed to publish three extra papers in prestigious journals or twenty extra papers in less prestigious journals, to be ranked the same as men applicants (Halpern et al. 2007).

THE CORRESPONDENCE PRINCIPLE

Why are schools organized as they are? Samuel Bowles and Herbert Gintis (1978) have tried to explain this through an idea known as the correspondence principle. They argue that much of what we learn at school is preparation for our future roles as workers in a capitalist society. Capitalists need a docile, obedient, motivated workforce and schools prepare us for this. What happens at school corresponds to what happens at work.

Schools teach us these lessons, however, in a "hidden agenda." The teachers do not explicitly tell us how to be good cogs in the wheels of the economic system, but the unwritten lessons are built into the organization of the school and the behaviors that are rewarded or discouraged (Illich 1983).

The first lesson is to follow the rules of the social institution, first at school and then in the workplace. Business owners need a subservient workforce with employees who come to work prepared to do what the managers tell them to do to make the business run efficiently, productively, and competitively. Schools teach children that they will be successful in the classroom if they are compliant and dependable and that they will not succeed if they are aggressive and independent.

The second lesson is to accept the hierarchy of authority. We learn that some people are in charge and that those whom they supervise need to accept that authority. At school the teacher controls what the students do and how they will do it. Teachers are also part of a hierarchy and they will be seen with principals or classroom evaluators listening to what they must do and how they must do it. At work, the boss is much like a teacher and the whole system of managers and managed are parallel to the organization of the school and the school system.

The third lesson is that the most important goals of a student are external rewards. Students learn that mastering information or sharing ideas are secondary to the more important issues of exam scores, course grades, and credentials such as passing into the next grade or a diploma or degree. These are all external rewards. An internal reward might be the delight of learning something new or exchanging ideas about issues of importance with others. At work we will find that our work often is largely focused on the external reward of a paycheck rather than the intrinsic value of the activities we engage in on the job.

Bowles and Gintis's (1978) theory does not really speak to the issue of gender in schools, but we can see from the information in this chapter that part of the "hidden agenda" is the lesson of gender. Gender differentiation is built into schools where boys and girls are frequently separated and treated differently. Many of the differences are not conscious. Teachers usually do not plan to treat their students differently. As we have seen, however, the research suggests that they interact quite differently with boys and girls. Schools become a kind of gender factory.

The school hierarchy's levels of authority are also gendered. Teachers are often women, especially in lower grades, whereas those in charge (e.g., principals) are more often men. These kinds of differentiation in experience and authority are parallel to what we find in the workforce. Gender in the schools corresponds with gender in the workplace.

A second gender issue that we can link to Bowles and Gintis's (1978) theory is the way that masculinity seems to conflict to a greater extent than does femininity with the hidden agenda—the rules of schools. In the discussion of the kindergarten warrior, we witnessed the introduction of boys to the contradictory lessons of being a masculine boy and being a successful student. This conflict corresponds to a conflict in the workplace. Aggression in the workplace is strongly associated with lower wages. Every 1 percent change in aggression is associated with an 8 percent decrease in wages (Andrisanni 1978; Duncan and Dunifon 1998).

Women and men in high-status occupations, however, have a somewhat different experience. Women in high-status jobs face significantly larger wage penalties for being aggressive, whereas men in these kinds of jobs are penalized for being withdrawn. The workplace has a hierarchy that places some men in charge of everyone else. Businesses need some men who learn a different set of rules. Although most workers, both women and men, should ideally learn to submit to authority, some workers, mostly men, must learn to be the authorities.

The third issue that correspondence theory cites that can be related to gender is the issue of extrinsic rewards. Here the experience in schools may be more consistent with expectations for men than for women at work, or at least the connection is more complex. Both boys and girls as students learn to value the extrinsic reward. When they enter the workplace they are supposed to focus on the paycheck as the key element in their employment. Of course, both women and men work because they earn a paycheck. For women, however, gender "interferes" with their valuing only the extrinsic reward. As we will see in chapter 6 on work, women do a lot of unpaid work. In addition many of the paid jobs women have are not paid as well, but may provide greater intrinsic rewards. Working as a teacher or a nurse does not usually result in a big paycheck, but it may feel good to be contributing to the community and the lives of others.

A fourth issue that links Bowles and Gintis's (1978) theory to gender has to do with a critique of their ideas. Bowles and Gintis's discussion did not leave much room for change or even for resistance to the structure of the social institutions of schools and businesses by students or employees. Scholars who have criticized Bowles and Gintis have noted that no social institution is without critics and that social institutions change as a result of the resistance of those whose lives are constrained by them. The change over time in the treatment of girls and women in primary, secondary, and higher education shows remarkable improvement in the success of girl and women students in the past few decades in the United States and other nations around the world. In many areas, women's and girls' opportunities and successes have met and even surpassed those of boys and men. This progress illustrates the vulnerability of social institutions to conscious change. The women's movement undoubtedly has played an important role in exposing gender inequities and developing policies, such as Title IX in the United States and the Beijing recommendations for nations all over the globe, to create a more equal system. Correspondence theory, however, is still valid because women have simultaneously entered the labor market in greater numbers and employers need women who have been properly trained in job skills as well as the lessons of the hidden agenda.

REFERENCES

American Association for University Women (AAUW).
——. 1999. *Gender gap: Where schools still fail our children*. New York: Marlowe.
——. 2001. *Beyond the "gender wars": A conversation about girls, boys, and education*. Washington, DC: AAUW.
Andrisanni, Paul, ed. 1978. *Work attitudes and labor market experience*. New York: Praeger.
Arlow, P., and M. Froschel. 1976. Women in the high school curriculum. In *High school feminist studies*, ed. C. Ahlum, J. Fralley, and F. Howe, xi–xxviiiiii. Old Westbury, NY: Feminist Press.
Basow, Susan. 1998. Student evaluations. In *Career strategies for women in academe*, ed. L. Collins, J. Chrisler, and K. Quina, 135–56. Thousand Oaks, CA: Sage.
Bazler, J., & D. Simonis. 1991. Are high school chemistry books gender free? *Journal of Research in Science Teaching* 28:353–62.
Bell, J. 1989. A comparison of science performance and uptake by fifteen year old girls in coeducational and single sex schools. *Educational Studies* 25:193–203.
Biederman, Joseph, Eric Mick, Stephen V. Faraone, Ellen Braaten, Alysa Doyle, Thomas Spencer, Timothy E. Wilens, Elizabeth Frazier, and Mary Ann Johnson. 2002. Influence of gender on Attention Deficit Hyperactivity Disorder in children referred to a psychiatric clinic. *American Journal of Psychiatry* 159 (January): 36–42.
Blair, Cornelia, and Helene Northway. 2001. *Women: New roles in society*. New York: Gale Group.
Blakemore, Judith, Jo Young Switzer, Judith DiIorio, and David Fairchild. 1997. "Exploring the Campus Climate for Women Faculty." Pp. 54–71 in N. Benokraitis (Ed), *Subtle Sexism*. Thousand Oaks, CA: Sage.
Bowles, Samuel, and Herbert Gintis. 1978. *Schooling in capitalist America*. New York: Basic Books.
Canada, Katherine, and Richard Pringle. 1995. The role of gender in college classroom interactions: A social context approach. *Sociology of Education* 68 (3): 161–86.
Carpenter, P., and M. Hayden. 1987. Girls academic achievements: Single sex versus coeducational schools in Australia. *Sociology of Education* 60 (July): 156–167.

College Board. 2006. *2006 college bound seniors*. http://www.collegeboard.com/prod_downloads/about/news_info/cbsenior/yr2006/national-report.pdf.

Correll, Shelley. 2001. Gender and the career choice process. *American Journal of Sociology* 106 (6): 1691–730.

Cox, Emily R., Brenda R. Motheral, Rochelle R. Henderson, and Doug Mager. 2003. Geographic variation in the prevalence of stimulant medication use among children 5 to 14 years old: Results from a commercially insured US sample. *Pediatrics* 111 (2): 237–43.

Deveny, K. 1994. Chart of kindergarten awards. *Wall Street Journal*, December 4.

Dewey, John. 1911. Is co-education injurious to girls? *Ladies Home Journal*, June 11.

Diller, Lawrence. 1996. The run on Ritalin. *Hastings Center Report* 26 (2): 12.

Duncan, Rachel, and Greg Dunifon. 1998. Long run effects of motivation on labor market success. *Social Psychology Quarterly* 61:33–48.

Dwyer, Carol. 1996. Fighting the gender gap: Standardized tests are poor indicators of ability in physics. *APS News-Online* 5(July). http://www.aps.org/publications/apsnews/199607/gender.cfm Accessed June 2008.

Economist. 2002. The female poverty trap. July 3.

Entwisle, D. R., K. Alexander, and L. Olson. 1994. The gender gap in math. *American Sociological Review* 59:822–38.

Fairtest. 2002. *Gender bias in college admissions tests: The SAT I.* Cambridge, MA: Fairtest.

Ferree, Myra Marx, and Elaine Hall. 1990. Visual images of American society: Gender and race in introductory sociology textbooks. *American Sociological Review* 61:929–50.

Fletcher, Michael. 2002. Degrees of separation: Gender gap among college graduates has educators wondering where the men are. *Washington Post*, June 25.

Fournier, Janice, and Samuel S. Wineburg. 1997. Picturing the past: Gender differences in the depiction of historical figures. *American Journal of Education* 105 (2): 160–85.

Freeman, Catherine. 2004. Trends in educational equity of girls and women. *Washington, DC: IES National Center for Educational Statistics. http://nces.ed.gov/pubsearch/pubsinfo.asp?pubid=2005016.*

General Accounting Office (GAO). 2001. *Gender equity: Men's and women's participation in higher education*. Report to the ranking minority member subcommittee on criminal justice, drug policy and human resources, committee on government reform, House of Representatives. www.gao.gov.

Ginty, Molly. 2004. Mars mission a landmark for female astronomer. *WENews*, February 1.

Goldman, L. S., Genel, M., Bezman, R. J., and Slanetz, P. J., for the Council on Scientific Affairs, American Medical Association. 1998. Diagnosis and treatment of attention-deficit/hyperactivity disorder in children and adolescents. *Journal of the American Medical Association* 279:1100–07.

Halpern, Diane, Camilla Benbow, David Geary, Ruben Geir, Janet Hyde, and Morton Gernsbacker. 2007. Sex, math and scientific achievement. *Scientific American*, November 28.

Hart, Nicky, Noah Grant, and Kevin Riley. 2006. Making the grade. In *Medicalized masculinities*, ed. D. Rosenfeld and C. Faircloth, 132–37. Philadelphia: Temple University Press.

Hinshaw, S. P. 2002. Preadolescent girls with attention-deficit/hyperactivity disorder: I. Background characteristics, comorbidity, cognitive and social functioning, and parenting practices. *Journal of Consulting and Clinical Psychology* 70:1086–98.

Illich, Ivan. 1983. *Deschooling society*. New York: Harper & Row.

Illinois Math and Science Academy (IMSA). 1995. *Statement: 1993–1994 calculus based physics and mechanics study*. Aurora: Illinois Mathematics Academy.

Jordan, Ellen, and Angela Cowan. 2004. Warrior narratives in the kindergarten classroom: Renegotiating the social contract? In *Men's lives*, 6th ed., ed. M. Kimmel and M. Messner, 103–15. Boston: Allyn & Bacon.

Kardia, Diana, and Mary Wright. 2004. Instructor identity: The impact of gender and race on faculty experiences with teaching. CRLT Occasional Papers No. 19. Ann Arbor, MI: CLRT.

Kimmel, Michael. 2000. "Saving the Males" Gender & Society 14(4):494–516.

King, Jacqueline. 2006. *Gender equity in higher education*. Washington, DC: American Council on Education.

Lee, Valerie, Helen Marks, and Tina Byrd. 1994. Sexism in single sex and coeducational independent secondary school classrooms. *Sociology of Education* 67:92–120.

Leo, Johnathan. 2002. American preschoolers on Ritalin. *Society* 39(2):52–61.

Milner, J. 1977. *Sex stereotypes in mathematics and science textbooks*. New York: National Organization for Women.

National Coalition for Women and Girls in Education. 1997. *Title IX at 25: Report card on gender equity*. Washington, DC: National Coalition for Women and Girls in Education.

Orenstein, Peggy, in association with American Association of University Women. 1994. *School girls: Young women, self-esteem and the confidence gap*. New York: Doubleday.

Orenstein, Peggy. 2002. Shortchanging girls. In *Workplace/Women's place*, ed. P. Dubeck and D. Dunn, 38–46. Los Angeles: Roxbury.

Otis, Ginger. 2003. Women gain in clout, lag in school. *WeNews*, May 30.

Perreira, Krista M.; Harris, Kathleen Mullan; Lee, Dohoon. 2006. "Making It in America: High School Completion by Immigrant and Native Youth" Demography 43(3):511–536.

Pigozzi, Mary Joy. 1999. Educating the girl children: Best foot forward. *UN Chronicle* 36(2)_: 39–41.

Rafalovich, Adam. 2005. Exploring clinician uncertainty in the diagnosis and treatment of ADHD. *Sociology of Health and Illness* 27 (3): 305–23.

Ridgeway, Carolyn, and Christopher Healy. 1997. Evaluation of empowerment in a high school geometry class. *Mathematics Teachers* 90 (December): 738–41.

Rosser, Phyllis. 1989. *The SAT gender gap: Identifying causes*. Washington, DC: Center for Women Policy Studies.

Sadker, David, and Karen Zittleman. 2004. Single-sex schools: A good idea gone wrong? *Christian Science Monitor*, April 8.

Sadker, Myra, and David Sadker. 1994. The miseducation of boys: Changing the script. In *Failing at fairness: How America's schools cheat girls*, ed. D. Sadker, 42–76. New York: Scribner.

Sapiro, Virginia. 2003. *Women in American society*. 5th ed. New York: McGraw-Hill.

Shaw, Gina. 2002. The Ritalin controversy. *Washington Diplomat*, March.

Slackman, Michael. 2007. A quiet revolution in Algeria. *New York Times*, May 26.

Smith, P. M. 1985. *Language, the sexes and society*. Oxford, UK: Basil Blackwell.

Spade, Joan. 2001. Gender and education in the United States. In *Gender mosaics*, ed. D. Vannoy, 85–93. Los Angeles: Roxbury.

Steitmatter, Janice. 1999. *For girls only: Making a case for single-sex schooling*. Albany: State University of New York Press.

Stewart, Lea, Pamela Cooper, Alan Stewart, and Sheryl Friedley. 2003. *Communication and gender*. 4th ed. Boston: Allyn and Bacon.

Stock, P. 1978. *Better than rubies: A history of women's education*. New York: Putnam's.

Thorne, Barrie. 1993. *Gender play: Girls and boys at school*. New Brunswick, NJ: Rutgers University Press.

Timimi, Sami. 2002. *Pathological child psychiatry and the medicalization of childhood*. Hove, UK: Brunner-Routledge.

Toppo, Greg. 2006. U.S. eases limits on single-sex schools. *USA Today*, October 25.

United Nations. 2000. *Gender equality and equity*. New York: UNESCO. http://unesdoc.unesco.org/images/0012/001211/121145e.pdf.

—— . 2004. *State of the world's children*. New York: United Nations.

—— . 2006a. *Human Development Report 2006: Water rights and wrongs*. New York: United Nations.

—— . 2006b. *Human development report 2006: Beyond scarcity—Power, poverty and the global water crises*. New York: United Nations.

U.S. Census Bureau. *2005 School enrollment–social and economic characteristics of students: October 2005: Detailed Tables*. Washington, DC: U.S. Government Printing Office.http://www .census.gov/population/www/socdemo/school/cps2005.html

U.S. Department of Education, National Center for Education Statistics. 2001. *Digest of education statistics 2000*. Washington, DC: U.S. Government Printing Office.

—— . 2004. *National postsecondary student aid studies, 2003–2004*. Washington, DC: U.S. Government Printing Office.

Wainer, Howard, and Linda Steinberg. 1992. Sex differences in performance on the mathematics section of the Scholastic Aptitude Test: A bidirectional validity study. *Harvard Educational Review* 62 (3): 323–36.

Washington Post. 2002. Sex bias cited in vocational ed: Girls clustered in training for lower-paying jobs, study says. June 2.

Weitzman, Lenore, and D. Rizzo 1975. Sex bias in textbooks. *Today's Education* 64 (1): 49–52.

Wenneras, Christine, and Wold, Agnes. 1997. Nepotism and sexism in peer review. *Nature* 307 (6631): 341.

6

WORK

WAL-MART

If you look at a list of the wealthiest people in the world, you will see that five of the top twenty-one come from one family, the Waltons. They are the widow and four children who inherited Sam Walton's hugely profitable Wal-Mart company. Together they are worth $78.7 billion, more than the wealthiest man in the world, Bill Gates, who is worth $50 billion (Kroll and Fass 2006). Measured by revenue, Wal-Mart is the largest private employer in the world and the largest corporation in history (Featherstone 2005).

Nearly everyone in the United States and increasingly people all over the world have a Wal-Mart in their neighborhood, a big-box department store stacked high from floor to ceiling with just about anything you can think of, open long hours and bustling with customers and workers. If you glance around you will notice that most of the hourly employees are women (65 percent). Most of the supervisors are men (67 percent). If you were to meet the top managers of each store, you would find that 90 percent of them are men. If you happen to get a look at the paychecks of Wal-Mart employees you would find that the company has two pay scales, one for women and one for men. Women in hourly positions earn thirty-seven cents an hour less than do men on average. The pay gap widens as you move up the ladder. Men management trainees make an average of $23,175 a year, compared with $22,371 for women trainees. The four women at the very top earn an average of $279,772 compared to the hundreds of men in senior vice president positions who average $419,435 a year (Featherstone 2005).

In 2001, women who are current or former employees at Wal-Mart filed a massive nation-wide sex discrimination lawsuit in U.S. District Court against Wal-Mart Stores, Inc. (Case No. C 01–2252 MJJ). In 2003, the suit became the largest class-action lawsuit ever—with well over 1 million participants. The suit charged that Wal-Mart discriminates against its women employees in promotions, compensation, and job assignments. Women who work at

Wal-Mart are assigned to the lowest paying positions and are systematically denied advancement opportunities. Six years later, the case was slowly moving forward because, as you might imagine, taking Wal-Mart to court is no easy task (Cornwell 2007). However, the women who have charged Wal-Mart are not taking no for an answer (Joyce 2005).

The Wal-Mart case shows gender inequality in jobs, pay, and promotion, but the grievances of the women at Wal-Mart are not unique. Women today have joined men in the paid labor force, but men are often paid better, promoted faster, and employed in different work altogether.

This chapter looks at gender in the workplace. The chapter is divided into two main sections: paid work and unpaid work, or housework. We begin with a comparison of women and men in the paid labor force and then explore some of the explanations for those differences and the kinds of changes that have been recommended for addressing the inequities. Our focus then shifts to the global economy as the economic context of work and the ways globalization influences our work lives. In the second section we examine unpaid domestic work as it shapes and reflects gender.

As of 2011, walmart won the case...

PAID WORK
Who Is in the Paid Workplace?

The entry of women into the paid labor force is one of the key events of the twentieth century. With every decade more women began to go to work for wages. In 1900, about 20 percent of women were in the labor force in the United States. In the early decades of the twentieth century, African American women were much more likely to be in the paid labor force and single women and women without children were more likely to be employed. As the years passed, women of all racial ethnic groups, married women, and mothers increasingly began to work for pay. By the end of the century most women were in paid employment and 90 percent of them would be in the paid workforce sometime during their lifetime (Bianchi and Dye 2001).

Around the world, these numbers vary from one nation to another. Countries in northern Africa and the Middle East and west Asia have the lowest proportion of women in the labor force. For example, only 12 percent of women are employed in Saudi Arabia. In nations outside of these regions, however, at least one-third of women are working for wages and these numbers are rising. When it comes to working for wages, women's lives are more and more similar to men's.

Table 6–1 displays labor force participation rates for women and men in the United States. Table 6–1 shows that women have almost caught up with men in regard to working for wages, although there are important differences among different racial ethnic groups. Hispanic men are most likely to be in the paid labor force and Hispanic women are least likely. In terms of the proportion of women and men who are engaged in paid work, equality is nearly here. Women now comprise about half (47 percent) of paid laborers in the United States.

As women have entered the labor force, attitudes about working women have changed. Table 6–2 shows the change in the opinions of women and men about women in the labor

TABLE 6-1 U.S. Labor Force Participation Rates for All Adults over Age Twenty by Race Ethnicity, and Gender, 2006

	All	Whites	Blacks	Hispanics	Asians
Men	75.9%	76.2%	71.1%	85.6%	78.3%
Women	59.7%	59.9%	64.2%	55.6%	60.4%

SOURCE: U.S.Bureau of Labor Statistics 2006a, 2006b.

TABLE 6-2 Changes in Attitudes About Employed Women by Gender, 1977 and 1994

	1977		1994	
Attitude	Men	Women	Men	Women
Disapprove of married woman working if her husband can support her	32%	35%	19%	19%
Agree that it is more important for a wife to help her husband's career than to have one herself	53	61	22	21
Agree that it is better for everyone if a man achieves outside the home and women take care of home and family	69	63	38	33
Believe preschool child is likely to suffer if mother works	73	63	51	37
Believe a working mother cannot have as warm and secure a relationship with a child as a nonworking mother	58	45	39	24

SOURCE: Bianchi and Dye 2001.

force in the United States between 1977 and 1994. Compared to the 1970s, both women and men have become more supportive of women and mothers joining the paid labor force. They also are more likely to believe that employed women can make good mothers. However, a gap remains in the opinions of women and men. On the first three questions about whether women have a right to be in the paid labor force, the differences in opinion are small. The last two questions, though, show that many people, especially men, still are not convinced that employed mothers can take proper care of their children. In the next chapter on families, we take up this question of balancing work and family.

Equal Pay?

The image of men at work and women in the home is no longer the experience of almost all people in the United States and large numbers all over the world. We have nearly achieved equality in the proportion of women and men in the paid labor force. But has equality been achieved in the workplace in terms of how much pay women and men are receiving for their work? The women at Wal-Mart entered the twenty-first century working for a company that still had two pay scales based on gender. Wal-Mart may lag behind most other companies

TABLE 6–3 Median Annual Earnings for Full-Time, Year-Round Wage and Salary Workers by Gender, Race Ethnicity, and Education, 2003

	High School	Bachelor's	Master's	PhD
Men				
All	$ 33,815	$ 57,403	$ 74,286	$ 91,140
White	36,731	60,420	75,207	93,290
Black	29,947	46,437	60,865	Base too small to report
Hispanic	26,685	45,145	61,522	Base too small to report
Asian	27,368	52,295	76,805	85,221
Women				
All	$ 26,154	41,481	51,326	70,526
White	27,274	41,852	51,482	70,635
Black	23,716	38,842	49,232	Base too small to report
Hispanic	21,887	45,615	51,007	Base too small to report
Asian	21,887	38,178	51,164	Base too small to report

SOURCE: U.S. Census Bureau 2005.

in moving toward gender equality in pay, but the gap remains throughout the labor market. Overall in the United States, the gap has become smaller in the last few decades but wage inequality remains. After significant improvement in the 1970s and 1980s, progress seems to have stalled in the past two decades.

Every year in April a date is declared Equal Pay Day. Although this special date is not well known, it is important. What is Equal Pay Day? The average woman in a full-time job would have to work until Equal Pay Day of the next year to catch up with the wages of the average man from the year before. In 2007 it was April 24. Every year, of course, the average individual woman falls further and further behind (Steinberg 2001).

Look at Table 6–3 to see the pay differences for men and women of different racial ethnic groups and different levels of education. White men stand out as significantly better paid than men in all the other racial ethnic categories and all women. Men in each racial ethnic group make more than women in that category. Education improves everyone's paycheck but increased levels of education are not enough to allow women to catch up with men or African Americans and Latinos and Latinas to catch up with whites.

Besides race ethnicity and gender, age also plays a role in the income gap between women and men. Women and men are very close in median earnings from age sixteen until about thirty. They both see their wages rise at about the same rate until they are thirty, when women's wages seem to stagnate. Men's wages continue to rise until they are in their early fifties and then they level off and fall (Regensburger 2001).

Notice the amounts of the differences in Table 6–3. If we compare the category all men to all women, men make $7,661 more than women. This is enough to pay for a year in college or to buy at least a used car. What about over a decade or over a lifetime of work? The numbers are huge and could make a significant difference in a person's life. For example,

TABLE 6-4 Earnings Ratios for Women and Men in Nonagricultural Work in Japan, South Korea, the United States and Europe, 1993–1994

Australia	.90	United States	.76
Sweden	.90	Belgium	.75
Norway	.87	Germany	.74
Denmark	.83	Ireland	.71
Iceland	.82	Luxembourg	.71
France	.81	United Kingdom	.71
New Zealand	.81	Portugal	.68
Greece	.80	Switzerland	.67
Netherlands	.79	South Korea	.57
Finland	.78	Japan	.51

Source: Lips and Andrews 2005.

over a forty-year career, the gap would amount to about $306,440 in a comparison of all men and all women.

Although the wage gap is still large and cuts across education and race ethnicity, it has closed in recent years. For example, in the United States in the 1970s, women earned only fifty-nine cents on the dollar compared to men. Today they earn about seventy-five cents for every dollar a man earns. Part of this improvement, however, is a result of men's falling wages rather than women's gains (Amott 1999).

Now look at the kind of data that are in the tables. These are wages for year-round, full-time workers over the age of twenty-five. These are people who have the most secure and generally best-paid jobs. Women (27 percent) tend to be more likely than men (11 percent) to have part-time or temporary jobs, but men and women in these less well-paid positions are not included in the table (Mishel, Bernstein, and Allegretto 2005). That means that Table 6-3 is showing data that provide the best case scenario for a small gap. Furthermore, median rather than mean wages are reported in the table. The median is the halfway point in contrast to the mean, which is the average. The median diminishes the affect of people at the very lowest and the very highest ends of the scale, which shrinks the gap as well.

Additional research has shown that the 25 percent gap between women and men is an underestimate of the real picture (Rose and Hartmann 2004). Because women are more likely to work part time, less likely to work year-round, and more likely to have entire years out of the labor force, often to care for children or other family members, the gap is actually twice as big. If women's part-time, intermittent lifetime employment is taken into consideration, women make only about 38 percent, not 75 percent, of what men earn. Across the fifteen years of a study of women's and men's pay and work histories, the average prime-age working woman earned only $273,592 whereas the average working man earned $722,693 (in 1999 dollars). This amounts to almost half a million dollars just in the fifteen-year period (Rose and Hartmann 2004).

All over the world women are paid less than men, but there are differences from one nation to another. Table 6–4 shows the gap in a few countries, indicating that the pay gap ranges from Australia and Sweden where women earn about 90 percent of what men do to Japan where women earn about 51 percent of men's pay on average.

The Glass Ceiling

Besides having different pay, women and men have different ranks in workplaces. Most companies are like Wal-Mart: The higher you go, the fewer women and minorities you will see. Research on a number of corporate headquarters in the United States finds that of all the high-level employees, 37.2 percent are women and 15.5 percent are minorities. Only 16.9 percent of the management are women and 6 percent are minorities. At the highest level of management, the numbers fall even more: 6.6 percent of managers at the vice president level or higher are women and 2.6 percent are minorities. Of Fortune 500 CEOs, only 1.8 percent are women (Catalyst 2007). Government jobs are a little better, but women and minorities are still underrepresented at the top. Women hold 43.5 percent of government jobs, but only 31.3 percent of higher level positions. African American women comprise 9.8 percent of government workers but only 5.1 percent of the top jobs (Lorber 2000).

Although women are strikingly underrepresented in corporate leadership, the United States has a higher proportion of women in the top ranks than all but two other nations (Norway and Sweden). Only 5 percent of the top executives in France are women and no woman has ever headed a large British company (*Economist* 2005). Although women seem to be increasing their numbers in the higher rungs of the corporate ladder all over the world, at the current rate of progress, it would take women 475 years to reach equal representation as senior managers (Peterson and Runyon 1999; International Labour Office 2007).

This is called the glass ceiling: Women and minorities seem to be able to only go so far in their jobs because some invisible force is holding them back. Later in this chapter we explore what these invisible forces might be. The U.S. Department of Labor defines the glass ceiling as "artificial barriers based on attitudinal or organizational bias that prevent qualified individuals from advancing upward in their organization into management level positions" (Martin 1991, 1).

THE GLASS ESCALATOR. What happens when men enter women-dominated professions? Does a glass ceiling prevent them from rising to positions of leadership? Christine Williams (2000) has looked at these questions in four occupations: nurses, elementary school teachers, social workers, and librarians. Before the Civil War, these jobs were more likely to be held by men than women, but today they are dominated by women.

It seems reasonable that men in women-dominated professions would face similar barriers to those that women face in men-dominated occupations. Williams (2000), however, discovered that instead of barriers, men find themselves welcome and even given preferential treatment when they are tokens. When asked whether he encountered any problems when he applied for positions as a pediatric nurse, for example, one man explained "No, no, none....I've heard this from managers and supervisory-type people with men in pediatrics: 'It's nice to have a man because it's such a female-dominated position.'" (p.12)

Some men, however, said they had been tracked away from the most woman-dominated specialties, such as obstetrics and gynecology wards. The effect of the tracking, however, was to kick the men upstairs. The specialties that are considered most appropriate for men in the field are the most prestigious and best paid. Instead of being held back, men face invisible pressures to move up in their professions. Williams (2000) calls this the glass escalator. Whether they want to ride or not, men are expected to move up and out of the most "feminine" low-prestige and low-paying jobs.

Men's experience in women-dominated jobs also differs from women in men-dominated work settings because both are likely to have men supervisors. The men to whom Williams spoke said that they became very friendly with their supervisor, which provided them with a mentor. One man who was a special education teacher explained: "Occasionally I've had a principal who would regard me as 'the other man on the campus' and 'it's us against them,' you know? I mean nothing really that extreme except that some male principals feel like there's nobody there to talk to except the other man. So I've been in that position" (Williams 2000, 301).

Openly gay men did not necessarily meet with this kind of support. One nurse said that one of the physicians he worked with preferred to staff the operating room with exclusively men nurses, as long as they were not gay. Although this example results from a prejudiced colleague, heterosexism was especially likely to come from the clients being served. Men who were in the "women's profession" of elementary school teachers, for example, were sometimes accused of being pedophiles. A kindergarten teacher described his problems with stereotypes from parents who had met with his principal:

> [The principal] indicated to me that parents had come to him and indicated to him that they had a problem with the fact that I was a male....I recall almost exactly what he said. There were three specific concerns that the parents had: One parent said, "how can he love my child; he's a man." The second that I recall, he said the parent said, "He has a beard." And the third thing was "Aren't you concerned about homosexuality?" (Williams 2000, 301)

EMOTIONAL LABOR. Another way that women's and men's work differs is the amount and kind of emotional labor involved in their jobs. Emotional labor, a special kind of work that is invisible, is associated with many occupations. This kind of work involves face-to-face or voice-to-voice contact between workers and customers. The employee is supposed to display certain feelings like attentiveness and caring and suppress others like boredom or irritation. Approximately one-third of people in the United States are employed in jobs like flight attendant, waitstaff, secretary, teacher, sales clerk, and health care worker (Hochschild 1983). These all require this kind of emotion work of smiling, nodding, greeting, paying attention, and thanking (Bellas 2001).

A handbook for supermarket checkout clerks provides a prescription for proper emotion work by telling the employees:

YOU are the company's most effective representative. Your customers judge the entire company by your actions. A cheerful "Good Morning" and "Good Evening" followed by courteous attentive treatment and a sincere "Thank you, please come again" will send them away with a friendly feeling and a desire to return. A friendly smile is a must. (Bellas 2001, 271)

Women are more likely than men to be required to do emotion work in their jobs (Bellas 2001). About one-fourth of men's jobs require emotion work, whereas more than half of the jobs women do require emotion work (Hochschild 1983).

Men's emotion work also often contrasts with women's by the type of emotions that are supposed to be expressed. For example, both nursing and police work demand much emotional labor, and some of the work is similar. Both nurses and police officers are supposed to listen empathetically, to express understanding, and motivate others to comply. However, nurses are supposed to show the emotions of caring and nurturance, whereas police officers are supposed to exhibit strength and toughness. Both of these professions are supposed to be emotionally expressive and sometimes they are supposed to express emotions that are generally similar but often they must be framed in gendered forms (Steinberg and Figart 1999).

Men and women in the same job may have different expectations about the emotion work they should do. Customers, employers, and coworkers may expect women to be nicer and friendlier and especially to smile more. Women college professors, for example, are evaluated more highly if they are friendly, although men professors are not judged by this criterion (Kierstead, D'Agostino, and Dill 1988; Statham, Richardson, and Cook 1991; Bellas 1999). In a job interview or in salary decisions, women and men may be judged differently depending on whether they express the proper emotion.

In one study, participants viewed a video of someone in a job interview. The person in the interview was asked about his or her experience when a coworker arrived late and subsequently lost an important account. In one version of the video, the job seeker expressed sadness and in the other he or she expressed anger. After seeing the video, the participants were asked to assign the person a salary. Angry men were offered the highest salary ($38,000), followed by sad women and sad men. Angry women were offered the lowest salary ($23,000) (Belkin 2007).

Emotional labor adds to the other tasks of a job. It makes work harder. Requiring that employees do emotional work can also cause psychological problems for them. Performing in ways that are not consistent with their true feelings and constantly having to suppress their own emotions can cause burnout. Some workers, however, resist by refusing to do the emotional work or at least reducing it (Bellas 2001). For example, in this exchange a flight attendant confronts a customer on her flight by refusing to do the expected emotional work: "A young businessman said to a flight attendant, 'Why aren't you smiling?' She put her tray back on the food cart, looked him in the eye, and said, 'I'll tell you what. You smile first, then I'll smile.' The businessman smiled at her. 'Good,' she replied. 'Now freeze, and hold that for fifteen hours'" (Hochschild 1983, 127, quoted in Bellas 2001, 275).

Working as a trial lawyer is an occupation that is mostly held by men (88 percent are men) and requires much emotion work. It also requires emotional expression and emotional manipulation that are identified with hypermasculinity, the Rambo litigator (Pierce 2001). Courtroom attorneys must manipulate defendants, witnesses, jurists, and opposing counsel through intimidation, persuasion, and aggression. Lawyers also use "strategic friendliness" (Pierce 2001). Unlike the previous example of "feminine" emotion work by the flight attendant, lawyers are not required to use friendliness to emotionally support their clients or show deference. Lawyers must use a range of emotions to win over, dominate, and control.

A law school text (Berg 1987) advises lawyers to "stride to the podium...exude confidence...take command of the courtroom" (quoted in Pierce 2001, 227). Trial attorneys are also taught to intimidate witnesses in cross-examination, "to control the witness by never asking a question which he does not already know the answer and to regard the impeachment of the witness as a highly confrontational act" (Menkel-Meadow 1985, 54).

While role playing in courses on courtroom behavior, students in law school are criticized for not being forceful enough or for being too nice (Pierce 2001). They are applauded for looking angry, aggressive, and dominating. Lawyers and flight attendants both do emotion work but they use different emotions to deal with their clients or customers. Those differences fall along lines of gender, with flight attendants, a feminine occupation performing one kind of emotion work, and lawyers, a masculine occupation, another.

Why Is There a Wage Gap Between Women and Men?

Three explanations have been offered for the gap that exists between women and men in pay:

- Discrimination
- Human capital
- Organization of jobs

DISCRIMINATION. Those scholars who argue that the pay gap is a result of discrimination are called bias theorists. They argue that decisions about who will be hired, promoted, or fired and what an employee will be paid are made in ways that discriminate against women. Sometimes discrimination occurs in obvious ways (see Box 6–1). Women are explicitly barred from jobs or promotions. The FBI, for example, openly refused to hire women until J. Edgar Hoover died in 1972. This kind of discrimination was prevalent before the 1970s but has become much less common over the past few decades. In 1963 the Equal Pay Act was passed, making it illegal to pay workers differently solely on the basis of gender. The Equal Employment Opportunity Commission (EEOC) filed just 393 lawsuits on sex discrimination grounds in 2003 and this number has been fairly stable in the last decade (see Box 6–2). In a country of 146 million workers, this number is quite small (Ackman 2004). The Wal-Mart case, however, reminds us that overt explicit discrimination is not entirely a thing of the past. Wal-Mart has been accused of having two pay scales and two tracks for promotion based on gender. Discrimination also occurs more subtly, however.

Subtle Tactics. Nijole Benokraitis and Joe Feagin (1986) suggest that men can use a number of tactics to subtly undercut women with whom they work (Lorber 2000; see Box 6–3). Many

---

Box 6–1 MARKING GENDER IN THE WORKPLACE

Darlene Jesperson worked for Harrah's Resort as a bartender for twenty years when her employers decided to fire her because she refused to abide by the new dress code in 2006. The dress codes require women employees to style their hair and wear full makeup, including foundation, blush, mascara, lipstick, and nail polish. Men are required to cut their hair above their collar and to have a clean face and clean fingernails.

Jesperson took her case to court to get her job back but lost the case when judges decided that Harrah's had the right to require their employees to abide by the rules. The decision was made by a panel of judges, however, and all of them did not agree with the ruling. One judge who dissented with it said the decision "implies that women's faces compare unfavorably to men's [and that] women's faces are incomplete, unattractive or unprofessional without full make-up" (*Hospitality Industry Quarterly* 2005).

This case shows a surprising level of differential treatment of men and women workers in the twenty-first century. It also, as the judge says, implies that women should not only be treated differently in the workplace but that there is something wrong with women's appearance that needs to be remedied with cosmetics if they are to be acceptable coworkers and employees.

---

of these have positive features and appear to be attempts to help women in some way, but they ultimately work to prevent women from contending and winning in workplace competition. Their subtlety makes these tactics difficult to address or even acknowledge.

Backhanded tactics include the following (Benokraitis 1997):

- Condescending chivalry: A supervisor withholding useful criticism of a woman employee to "protect" her.
- Supportive discouragement: Discouraging a woman from competing for a challenging opportunity because she might not make it.
- Friendly harassment: Kidding a woman in public for being pregnant or some other aspect of her appearance.
- Subjective objectification: Believing all women fit some particular stereotype.
- Radiant devaluation: Exaggerated praise for accomplishments that should be expected as routine.
- Liberated sexism: Inviting a woman for a drink after work as one of the boys but refusing to let her pay for a round of drinks.
- Benevolent exploitation: Giving a woman a chance to work on a project to learn the job, but taking full credit for the final product.
- Considerate domination: Making decisions for women about what they can handle, for example, as new mothers, rather than allowing them to decide how best to divide their time.
- Collegial exclusion: Scheduling networking meetings at times when parents (often mothers) have family responsibilities that may conflict.

Box 6–2 BRINGING A DISCRIMINATION CASE AGAINST AN EMPLOYER

In bringing a case of discrimination against an employer, three types of proof can be used. The first is intent to discriminate. A company document that shows discrimination or an employer stating in front of witnesses that they will treat women (or other groups) differently in hiring, promotion, or pay are examples of this type of proof (Conway, Ahern, and Steuernagel 1999). This kind of evidence is probably rare today, but companies used to have openly separate pay scales for women and men workers. Until the 1970s, newspapers listed job opportunities under separate headings for "men wanted" and "women wanted."

A second type is proof of disparate treatment. In these cases a person in a protected category (by race, color, religion, sex, or national origin) of Title VII of the Civil Rights Act of 1964, which protects people from discrimination at work, is denied a job even though he or she is qualified. Someone from another category is given the job and the employer claims that the decision was made for some legitimate nondiscriminatory reason. The person denied the job must prove that the reason given is not valid. The prospective employee must show that she or he is as well qualified or that the criteria used for making the choice were discriminatory. For example, employers in a security guard business might argue that they must hire only men because customers feel better protected with men guards. Customer preference is not a valid reason for discrimination.

A third type is proof of disparate effects. An employer argues that she or he used neutral criteria to choose which applicant to hire. The person who wasn't hired has to show that the criteria may appear neutral but operate in a discriminatory manner. For example, fire departments formerly had height requirements that discriminated against women and members of racial ethnic groups who tend to be shorter on average than white men. The height requirements were not necessary to the job and although they appeared to be neutral, they ended up discriminating (Conway, Ahern, and Steuernagel 1999).

Why are men colleagues and managers so hesitant to allow women in? Competition is one explanation, but other men are competitors, too. Why are women so likely to be excluded? Perhaps men fear that if a profession becomes too feminized it will be devalued. Men may be afraid that if too many women enter their ranks, their profession will become "women's work" and those in the occupation, including men, will lose prestige, income, and control over resources (Lorber 2000).

HUMAN CAPITAL THEORY. A second explanation for the gap in pay between women and men is put forth by human capital theorists, who argue that people invest in their own human

Box 6–3 SEXUAL HARASSMENT AS DISCRIMINATION

Fifty percent of women can expect to experience behaviors at the workplace that legally constitute sexual harassment. Between 30 percent and 66 percent of women students will experience sexual harassment at school. Most of this, however, will go unreported. The cost to businesses remains high in the form of sick leave, job turnover, and lost productivity. Private industries have estimated the cost as $6,719,593 annually for each Fortune 500 company (Rondblud 2001). The cost to individual women is significant as well. Sexual harassment can result in feelings of helplessness, confusion, depression, and lower self-esteem and even physical problems like headaches, sleep disturbances, tiredness, and nausea (Paludi 1997).

Harassment can be seen as a continuum from "gender harassment which is inappropriately calling attention to women or men's bodies, sexuality or marital status, to sexual harassment which is turning a professional, work or student-teacher relationship into a sexual relationship *that is not wanted by one of the people involved and that is coercive because the initiator has some power over the other person*" (Lorber 2000, 291).

The three key words for sexual harassment are inappropriate, unwanted, and power.

Behavior is inappropriate if it is not gender-neutral in a situation that should be gender-neutral. Gender-neutral does not mean cold or hostile. It means cordial and friendly but not in a sexual manner (Lorber 2000).

Unwanted means that one person does not want to engage in the interaction. This means that the "test" of sexual harassment is at least partly subjective; it can only be determined by the person who does not want the attention. Sometimes this causes problems because men and women may have different reactions to similar behavior. One researcher (Gutek 1985) found that 67.2 percent of men said they would be flattered if a woman coworker asked them to have sex. Of women, however, (62.8 percent) said they would be insulted by a sexual invitation from a man with whom they worked (Lorber 2000).

Power is the final important factor. One effective reaction to harassment is to leave the situation, but power means that a person who feels sexually harassed may not be able to immediately leave. The person who is being harassed may be in a situation in which he or she will have to pay a price for leaving—a good job or a useful educational opportunity.

Catherine MacKinnon (1979) was the first to define sexual harassment in the l970s. Her definition became part of EEOC guidelines in l980 and was upheld in the courts in the late l980s (Lorber 2000).

abilities, including the skills that allow them to move up the ladder at work and receive raises. Human capital refers to the talents that we have to do our jobs. They include our attitudes, education, and experience (Wharton 2005). Human capital theorists believe that: (1) women do not have as much commitment to paid work; (2) men invest more in themselves than women do; and (3) men obtain more education or job training.

Research has shown that women have similar commitment to their careers as men do. The first human capital claim, therefore, is not correct (Wharton 2005). The other two claims are partially correct, but women may lag behind men in their education and experience not because they choose to invest less in their human capital. Women may be prevented from investing in themselves because of gender barriers in schools and workplaces. Girls and women have made great strides in education, but they still remain somewhat behind in some professions. Even when women have similar or even better education, however, their paychecks do not reflect their educational achievement.

Women also are less likely to receive on-the-job training. However, restricted opportunities for developing their skills are undoubtedly the explanation, rather than making the wrong choices. For example, an increasingly global economy is making international experience a prerequisite for executive positions but men are much more likely to receive international assignments than are women (Antal and Izraeli 1993). As recently as 1988, 36 percent of U.S. companies that posted employees in other nations did not send women at all to these assignments (Moran, Stahl, and Boyer 1988).

Human capital theory is probably the most prevalent social theory among the general population in the United States because it rests on an important tenet of the American belief system, individualism. Individualism asserts that "There are abundant economic opportunities. Individuals must be industrious and competitive. Rewards in the form of education, jobs, income and status are, and should be, the result of individual talent and efforts. Therefore, the distribution of rewards is generally fair and equitable" (Rothman 2002, 55).

This ideology is strongly held by the majority of Americans. A recent poll asked people to answer whether they thought success was mostly a result of hard work or mostly a result of luck or the help of others. Among respondents, 69 percent said that it was the result of hard work and 11 percent said it was the result of luck or the help of others. Another 19 percent said it was a combination of these factors (Mitchell 1996).

SOCIAL STRUCTURAL EXPLANATIONS OF PAY GAP. The third and most powerful explanation for the gender pay gap is a social structural one. Social structural explanations point to the ways the workplace and the labor market are organized. One feature of workplace organization that can quietly exclude women and minorities is homosociality (Kanter 1977). Managers, who are often men, may feel more comfortable around people they feel are like themselves. They may feel safer if they are working with people who are likely to make the same decisions as they would. Managers seek colleagues who are of the same gender, race ethnicity, social class, religion, and even those who are from the same colleges or clubs and enjoy the same hobbies (Reskin and Padavic 2001). Women and people who are different in other ways from the established management are intimidating because they might see things differently or they might challenge the status quo.

People who work together are organized into three concentric circles: inner circles, friendly colleagues, and isolated loners. Power is concentrated in the inner circle. People in

TABLE 6-5 Top Ten Jobs for Women, 2004

Occupation	% of Workers in Job Who Are Women
Secretary	97%
Elementary and middle school teacher	97
Registered nurses	92
Nurse's aide, home health aide	88
Cashiers	75
Office managers	70
Retail sales managers	44
Customer service reps	70
Bookkeeper, auditor	92
Accountant	61

Source: U.S. Department of Labor 2004.

the inner circle are similar to one another and in jobs dominated by men, women are not likely to be a part of the center. If women are allowed in, they become tokens and must show they can overcome their difference and be just like those in the inner circle—"one of the boys" (Lorber 2000).

Kanter (1977) predicted in the 1970s that as the numbers of women grew in an occupation, they would be able to rid themselves of a token status and become integrated into the inner circles and more able to openly express themselves. Since the 1970s, however, Kanter's hypothesis has not been supported by research. Instead, when women make up about 15 percent of the occupational membership, they become less likely to be accepted into the inner circle.

A second social structural factor is the way occupations are segregated into "men's work" and "women's work." Most sociologists believe that gender segregation of jobs is the most important reason wages are so different for men and women. Men and women are in different jobs and men's jobs tend to pay better than women's jobs.

As you drive down the interstate and glance in the window of the semi traveling beside you, you see a woman at the wheel. Although you probably do not make any judgment about that, you notice it. When you go to a party and your friend introduces her husband, noting that he is a secretary, you might hear someone say "That's an unusual job for a man." The distribution of people into jobs by gender is part of our everyday life that often goes unnoticed unless we see someone who is an exception. This categorization of jobs as women's work or men's work is a part of our social scene that has remained remarkably stable despite the growing numbers of women entering nearly every occupation in the paid labor force.

An occupation is defined as gender segregated if 75 percent or more of the people who work in that field are of one gender. Because the paid labor force is almost 50 percent men and 50 percent women, a job would not be considered gender stratified if the people who held that job were also evenly divided. When a job reaches 75 percent it is considered to have tipped into dominance by women or men. Most people work in these kinds of

TABLE 6–6. Top Ten Jobs for Men, 2000

OCCUPATION	% OF WORKERS IN JOB WHO ARE MEN
Truck drivers	95
First-line supervisors of retail sales workers	58
Retail sales	48
Freight, stock, and material handlers	83
Carpenters	98
Janitor and cleaner	67
Managers other than first-line supervisors of retail sales and production workers	70
Construction laborers	96
Sales representative	72
First-line supervisors of production workers	79

SOURCE: Fronczak and Johnson 2003.

gender-dominated occupations. Nine of the ten most common jobs for women are in women-dominated positions (Bose and Whaley 2001).

Table 6–5 shows the top ten occupations for women in the United States. Secretarial work is the most common occupation for women and 97 percent of secretaries are women. Elementary and middle school teacher is the second most common job and 95 percent are women. Almost all of the jobs women are most likely to have are overwhelmingly dominated by women. Retail sales manager is the only occupation that is not segregated; women hold about half of those positions.

Men, too, are likely to work in gender-segregated jobs. Table 6-6 shows the top ten occupations for men and it also shows men are concentrated in "men's jobs." For example, 95 percent of truck drivers are men and 98 percent of carpenters are men. All of the top ten jobs are also occupations in which most of the workers are men, except retail sales, which is about half men.

The gender gap has declined somewhat in recent years, but remains high and the pace of change is slow. The occupational sex segregation index provides a measure of the gap and ranges from 0 to 100. The number refers to the proportion of women who would need to change occupations to create gender "desegregation" in the labor market. From 1900 to 1960 the occupational sex segregation index remained fairly constant at about sixty-five in the United States. This means that for the first sixty years of the twentieth century, about two-thirds of women would have had to change their jobs to reach this balance. In the 1970s the index dropped eight points. It has continued to drop since the 1980s but much more slowly (Bose and Whaley 2001).

Climbing the Ladder of Success. Another feature of the social structure of the labor market is that not only is it gender segregated, but women's jobs are structured differently than are men's jobs. Many businesses and agencies have systems for promoting employees within the organization. Sometimes these job ladders have many people at the bottom and very few at the top, so that the odds of moving up are low. For example, if you visit a hospital, you see many nurses on every floor doing many different kinds of jobs. Only a few nurses become heads of their division and only a handful become hospital administrators. On the other hand, some jobs have many rungs and only a few people on each step. The sales division of a company that provides auto parts for large manufacturers might have several jobs with only a few people feeding into the next level: a stock clerk, a sales trainee, a sales representative, an assistant sales manager, and a manager. The odds at each level are good that the person will move up into better paid, more prestigious positions (Reskin and Padavic 2001).

Women's jobs are more likely to be in positions that have short or no ladders. For example, teaching is a profession that is "feminine" and has no ladder. Teachers might sometimes move into administrative positions, but running a school is quite different from being a classroom teacher and the odds of becoming a principal are small as there are so many teachers per principal. There are no promotions from one teaching position to another. All the teachers in a school are relatively equal in their responsibilities and rewards (Tomaskovic-Devey 1993).

Women are also segregated into jobs within businesses that are more low profile than men's work. They are less visible to those who are choosing people to promote within the company (Reskin and Padavic 2001). For example, women lawyers are more likely to be assigned jobs in research and men are more likely to receive assignments in litigation. Both tasks are essential to the work, but courtroom appearances place litigators in the limelight, whereas research is done behind the scenes (Epstein 1993).

Bringing Politics into the Picture. Barbara Reskin and Irene Padavic (2001), however, contend that gender segregation of the labor market is not a sufficient explanation of why women's wages remain lower than men's. They suggest a fourth explanation arguing that while the social structural factor of gender segregation of jobs is a key factor, politics is even more important. They argue that underlying structural factors such as gender segregation of the labor market are issues of power. They assert, furthermore, that focusing on gender segregation will lead us to develop ineffective solutions because we are not tackling the deeper problems that underlie this inequity. Reskin and Padavic (2001) believe that the political character of gender is the underlying and more important cause of the wage gap. They explain "the basic cause of the income gap is not sex segregation but men's desire to preserve their advantaged position and their ability to do so by establishing rules to distribute valued resources in their favor" (Reskin and Padavic 2001,258). (Some) men have power to make the rules and they wish to maintain both their power to write the rules and their ability to benefit from them. According to Reskin and Padavic, the cause of low wages for women's work is power differences and the result is less access to resources for women.

Reskin and Padavic argue that a gender-segregated labor market is a useful tool for maintaining a wage gap. They continue, however, that even if the labor market became less segregated, men would be able to rewrite the rules in a way that would place them and their jobs in a more highly valued and more highly rewarded category.

By looking at causes of the gender gap in wages historically, Reskin and Padavic explain how changing the rules can re-create inequality in a new form. In the nineteenth and early twentieth century, men were paid higher wages and this inequity was defended by the argument that men's work should be more highly paid because they were heads of household and responsible for families and therefore entitled to a family wage. Women, in contrast, were seen as secondary earners working for "pin money" when their husbands' wages were the real source of their livelihood. During the twentieth century, women overcame this characterization of their work. Women now are recognized as contributing a large proportion of household income in dual-earner families and women are more likely than men to be single heads of households. Today women are indisputably primary breadwinners. The rules, however, have been changed.

The idea of a family wage could benefit women now because women are often heads of households and nearly always significant contributors to their families' economic status. However, these factors are no longer emphasized and occupation has become a "better" method of valuing work, and as we have seen, women and men do not have the same occupation.

Just making a distinction between two types of work, however, does not necessarily mean that one will be better paid than the other. Some value has to be placed on the work, making one job more important and therefore, justifiably better paid. Women have different jobs than do men and women's work is less valued than men's. Engineering work is more highly valued and highly paid than nursing. Truck driving is more valued than secretarial work. Teaching is low paid and child care workers are among the very lowest valued and lowest paid occupations. Are these women's jobs really less skilled or less important to society? If they are not, what political struggles will we encounter in trying to rewrite the rules in a way that recognizes the value of women's work?

How Can the Gender Gap in Promotion Be Closed?

Workplaces are resistant to change (Reskin and Padavic 2001). Nevertheless, there are some actions that can be taken to address the problem.

- Building bridges from one job ladder to another. In positions where there are few opportunities for advancement, workers could be offered chances to move into another field within a company without losing seniority. For example, clerical workers in dead-end jobs could move to sales divisions where the likelihood of promotion is greater.
- Creating formal processes. Instead of relying on informal methods of personnel decisions that could be biased by individual managers, formal rules and procedures could be established. Rather than management guessing which employees might be interested in promotions, written announcements should be displayed for all workers to respond to.
- Raising the cost of discrimination.

Beyond these specific policies, a broader set of changes may be required to address the wage gap because so many women and men are in gender-segregated occupations. One way of eliminating the pay gap between women and men is to distribute men and women in occupations more evenly and make sure that they receive the same pay for the same work. Given the segregation in the labor market, however, what can be done to provide women and men equitable pay even if they are in different occupations? Comparable worth policy is one answer that has been given to this question.

COMPARABLE WORTH. Comparable worth policy designs systematic ways to evaluate jobs to create pay scales that do not discriminate against occupations that are dominated by women. Four factors are typically used: skill, effort, responsibility, and working conditions. These factors may be a good start but they need to be revised to make sure that they are not used in a way that continues to discriminate against workers in occupations dominated by women. For example, when employers look at the factor of skill they do not look at skills associated with clerical work like knowledge of grammar, ability to write correspondence, and knowledge about organizational shortcuts. Clerical jobs are usually evaluated as "needing no specialized knowledge." Clerical jobs are usually held by women. In contrast, craft jobs, which are usually held by men, are rated as requiring "limited specialized knowledge."

Responsibility is another issue that should be rethought. Sometimes women and men are doing the same tasks in different settings but the tasks are defined differently and more favorably for the men's jobs than the women's. For example, managers, who are more often men, and secretaries, who are mostly women, often do the same work running an office. The manager is perceived as exercising authority and responsibility, whereas the secretary is doing similar tasks with a similar result but her work is not seen as managerial (Steinberg 2001).

Working conditions is another issue that needs to be revisited. When they look at working conditions, employers have paid attention to noisy machinery but not to the difficulty of working with incontinent or dying patients or exposure to disease. Men are more likely to work around machinery and women are more likely to be in caring professions.

Success Stories of African American Women and the Importance of Families. Although the focus of the discussion has been on the difficulties women have in moving into well-paid prestigious jobs, many women, of course, have succeeded. Elizabeth Higgenbotham and Lynn Weber (2000) looked at the experience of upward social mobility for white and black women. Besides looking at differences in race ethnicity, they also looked at the social class of the women's families. Some women were raised in families in which their parents were in blue collar jobs and some were raised in middle-class families where their parents had professional, managerial, or administrative jobs. The women, themselves, however, had all obtained a college education and taken a professional position. White women from working-class families had received the least support for their aspirations from their families. Middle-class white families expected their daughter to attend college and were better able to help them financially and emotionally achieve that goal.

White working class women also less often had parents who stressed the necessity of having an occupation to succeed in life. Nearly all of the black families, middle and working class (94 percent), stressed the importance of getting a good job. By comparison, 70 percent of white middle-class families stressed this with their daughters, but only 56 percent of the white working-class families stressed it. White women were more likely to feel that their parents emphasized the importance of marriage. One white woman from a working-class family explained her parents' ambivalence about her decision to become an attorney:

> My parents assumed that I would go to college and meet some nice man and finish, but not necessarily work after. I would be a good mother for my children. I don't think that they ever thought I would go to law school. Their attitude about

my interests in law school was, "you can do it if you want to, but we don't think it is a particularly practical thing for a woman to do." (Higgenbotham and Weber 2000, 349)

Black and white women also felt differently about the debt they owed to their family and community for the achievements they had accomplished in establishing their careers. Black women felt that they were obligated to their family for their support. They were especially likely to acknowledge the support their parents had provided helping them to raise their children. White women, in contrast, felt their accomplishments were because of their own work. When asked whether she felt she owed a lot to her family and relatives for their help, one white woman who was a judge said, "No, I feel I've gotten most places on my own" (Higgenbotham and Weber 2000, 351).

Success Stories in Engineering. Engineering is one of the most tenacious occupations in regard to gender segregation. Engineering is both a critical occupation and one where women have still made few inroads in employment. Technology in the twenty-first century is central to the global economy. Engineering is the gateway into advanced technology, but women still comprise only 8.4 percent of all the people in the labor force with engineering degrees (Commission on Professionals in Science and Technology 1997). The future for women in engineering, in addition, does not look good because only 5 percent of people with engineering PhDs are women. Their low numbers in the profession as practicing engineers and as teachers mean that women will have little affect on the shaping of technology and on the shaping of those who are designing that technology (Fox 2001).

Engineering has long been associated with men and masculinity because of its ties to the military (Fox 2001). The term *engineering* was first used when military men were developing devices for warfare in the fifteenth century. In the United States, the first engineer education was established at West Point Military Academy in 1802. Engineering continues to be associated with supposedly masculine characteristics of mathematical ability, rationality, and self-discipline (Cardwell 1957).

Moving women into a profession so long identified with men and masculinity is a difficult challenge. Mary Frank Fox (2000), however, has examined the characteristics of universities that have successfully increased the proportion of women in their engineering programs. She has found that institutions like universities can be structured for inequality but they can also be restructured in ways that promote equality by paying attention to their organization and creating ways that make better use of the talents of underrepresented groups, including women. Universities that have been successful at reducing inequality have the following traits (Fox 1991, 1995, 1996):

- A history of leadership on issues related to increasing participation of women
- Chairs and faculty members who had taken time to consider what constitutes a "good environment" for study
- Clear and standardized criteria for job evaluations
- Written guidelines for evaluating faculty performance and progress
- Open processes in hiring, promoting, and allocating rewards
- Increased opportunities for collaboration between junior and senior faculty, including placement of new people into ongoing projects

Retirement

Retirement marks the end of paid employment but our work histories have an important effect on our experience of retirement. Because our work lives are so marked by gender, it is not surprising that retirement is also a gendered episode. Box 6–4 reports a survey of working women about what worried them most. Retirement was reported as one of the top worries (AFL-CIO 2006).

A pension is a payment that is made to people who are no longer working. Sometimes it comes from a fund set up by an employer, or it could be a fund an individual sets up for himself or herself like a savings plan that will not be used until after retirement. Social Security is the public pension program maintained by the government in the United States. When working people decide to retire many of them rely on Social Security for at least part of their support. Working people and their employers pay into the social security fund and when Americans reach the age of sixty-five they can draw a monthly check from the fund.

Social Security is supposed to treat people equally. Its design, however, is based on work and social roles of white men. When white women and women and men of minority racial ethnic groups use the Social Security program they find that it does not treat them as well as it does most white men. Table 6–7 shows the benefits paid to different people by race ethnicity and gender. Table 6–7 shows that men in all categories are paid higher monthly averages for Social Security but race ethnicity also makes a significant difference. How exactly does Social Security discriminate?

Social Security benefits are tied to income. Because men on average earn more than women, they are more likely to be eligible for maximum benefits ($2,185 a month in 2008). Men are also more likely to be in the paid labor force more years because women often leave

---

Box 6–4 WHAT ARE WORKING WOMEN WORRIED ABOUT?

The AFL-CIO is a large union in the United States. It keeps track of the issues about which union members are concerned. The latest list in their polls of working women shows the top concerns. The percentage refers to the proportion of women who mentioned the issue as one that causes them to worry.

Health care costs	97%
Rising cost of living	96
No retirement	80
Higher education costs	79
Jobs overseas	83
Jobs with benefits	82

SOURCE: AFL-CIO 2006.

TABLE 6–7 Average Monthly Social Security Benefit by Race Ethnicity and Sex, 2004

Group	Benefit
White men	$ 1,101
White women	836
Black men	913
Black women	766
Other men	836
Other women	702

Source: Social Security Administration 2005.

the labor market for family obligations. In thirty-five years of employment, men average one year out, whereas women average twelve years out (Harrington-Meyer, Wolf, and Himes 2000). Social Security assumes recipients have had a long-term stable career in which they have experienced a constant increase in pay over the years (Calasanti and Slevin 2001).

Social Security was originally deliberately planned to treat women and men differently. The program assumed that women and men were married and that they lived in households where the man was the only breadwinner. Women were thought of as appendages to those men. When wives and widows were added to the program as beneficiaries in 1939, their benefits were not based on their contributions as paid employees but by their relationship— wife—to men in paid work. In 1935 when Social Security was introduced, 40 percent of black women were in the labor force, but their activity was ignored (Harrington-Meyer 1996).

Furthermore, women who obtained wife and widow benefits received only half of the amount their husbands did. Women who had divorced their husbands were not eligible for any amount. The laws have now changed so that women who were married more than ten years before their divorce are eligible as beneficiaries (Calasanti and Slevin 2001).

Compared to men, benefits for women are still much more tightly tied to their marital status. Discontinuous marriage because of divorce or widowhood has important effects on retirement income for women more often than for men. In 1995, women who had been continuously married to their husbands averaged only about $85 less than men. However, women who had interrupted marital histories received $356 less then men (DeViney and Solomon 1995). This is a particularly serious disadvantage for black women who are more likely to marry late or not at all. By age forty-two, 63 percent of white and Hispanic women have been married ten years, whereas only 44 percent of black women have been married that long (Harrington-Meyer et al. 2000).

About 56 percent of full-time workers are eligible for private pensions through their jobs. On retirement, they receive not only Social Security benefits but pensions as well. Employees with jobs that are covered by pensions are disproportionately white, well educated, and work for large companies (Johnson, Sambamoorthi, and Crystal 1999). They are also likely to be men (Stoller and Gibson 2000). The effect of these differences in Social Security and pension plans is greater economic insecurity for women, especially black, Hispanic, and Native American women (Calasanti and Slevin 2001).

When Work Disappears: Masculinity and Homeless Men

The history of Social Security reflects the ideology that unpaid work is part of the social construction of femininity. To be a woman is to be skilled at domestic tasks like taking care of children and cooking. Paid work is part of the social construction of masculinity. Men are supposed to be good at establishing a career and making money and a man who cannot hold a job is not considered fully adult nor fully masculine (Fuller 2001; Connell 2002).

Robert Connell (2005) describes four substructures of masculinity: division of labor, power relations, emotional relations, and symbolization. This chapter focuses on the first of these. Connell notes that paid work is closely associated with manliness in many cultures. Around the world, men are in fact more likely to be in the paid labor force in most countries. Ideologies define working (for wages) as men's realm and a man is not really a man unless he has a regular (paid) job. In a survey in Costa Rica, men were asked what most made them feel like real men. They answered getting a job, having sex, and drinking alcohol.

European scholars assert that the main basis of gender is the distinction in Europe between the household, which is based on gift exchange and is the women's world, and the commodity economy, which is based on the buying and selling of labor, which is men's work. This way of thinking about and experiencing gender has been exported to colonial and neo-colonial societies around the world (Holter 2003). In the next section we examine the household and the exchange of "gifts" of cleaning, cooking, and child care. Before moving to that issue, however, let's look at what happens when men do not succeed in their world of buying and selling of labor.

The discussion of poverty shows that many people in the world, men and women alike, are unable to find work that brings them a living wage. Because paid work is so closely tied to masculinity, what happens when men are unable to find a job and earn a living? Homeless men provide an answer to this question. They are stripped of their connection to the symbols of masculinity—a job, a car, a house. Some are able to find a way out of their poverty. Others give up and escape only through addiction and death. However, some men survive on the streets by reconstructing their ideas about what it is to be a man (Nonn 2001).

Timothy Nonn (2001) interviewed homeless men in the Tenderloin district in San Francisco. He found that men invented three types of countermasculinities: the urban hermit, the cool pose, and the perfect copy. All three of these allowed the men to cope with the difficulties of living on the street, providing them with feelings of self-worth, and allowing them to remain men, despite their break with the symbols and activities associated with dominant views of masculinity.

Urban hermits were mostly white heterosexuals. These men identified themselves as self-sufficient and many retreated into isolation, spending their time alone in hotel rooms. Despite their failure to succeed in the dominant society, they persisted in their belief in individual responsibility for everything that happens to them. They cannot remain men by having a good job and achieving material success, but they can remain men by taking responsibility for their own situation. One disabled man expressed this point of view: "It's a difficult struggle. But you can't blame anybody but yourself. Because it is you yourself. Like with me. It's me myself that has the illness. Not the people of the government. Not the people of the different businesses. And things like that. It's me" (Nonn 2001, 244).

Heterosexual black and Latino homeless men often take on a cool pose (Majors and Billson 1992). Respect is the central feature of this kind of countermasculinity. One man explained, "One of the techniques you use—and this is a prison technique—is getting big. You work out hard. You carry yourself in an intimidating manner. Your body language says, 'I'll kill you if you even think about approaching my space'" (Almaguer 1991, 80).

Homosexual homeless men frequently developed a countermasculinity called perfect copy. This consists of either hypermasculine or hyperfeminine roles. One man describes his experience performing the perfect copy role (hypermasculine) and the response of heterosexual men: "They feel like their manhood or sexuality has been threatened because I'm more butch than they are. I am more of a man than a straight man can be around here. They're threatened. Not only to me but to themselves" (Nonn 2001, 246). Another describes how others respond to his perfect copy (hyperfeminine): "I think [they] are very jealous of gay men because we're so open and free with our feelings. We speak what we have to say. We don't hide our feelings. We cry at sad movies. Heterosexual men think that men don't cry" (Nonn 2001, 246). In both cases the exaggeration of the roles juxtaposed with homosexuality destabilize stereotypes of manliness.

Feminization of Poverty

Poverty is of course not just a problem for men. Women are even more likely to be poor, although race ethnicity also plays an important role in determining one's chances of being poor. Table 6–8 shows that for every racial ethnic group in the United States poverty rates are higher for women than they are for men. The greater tendency for women to be poor is called the feminization of poverty. Table 6–8, however, also shows a large gap in poverty rates by race ethnicity and white women have lower rates than both women and men who are black or Hispanic. Gender is not the only problem and the feminization of poverty is more descriptive of the situation for whites than for other racial ethnic groups.

Unemployment is an important cause of poverty. Although working increases income, it does not guarantee that employees will rise above poverty. For example, a full-time, year-round federal minimum wage job ($6.55 an hour) would gross $13,100 annually, which is below the poverty level for a family of two ($14,237).

Poverty is a critical international problem. The United Nations estimates that nearly half of the world (44 percent)—about 3 billion people—live on less than $2 a day, and because of poverty millions lack access to even basic human needs like water, food, sanitation, and literacy (New Economic Foundation 2006). Table 6–9 shows the proportion of the population living on less than $2 a day in different regions.

The $2 figure does not refer just to the amount of money received by each individual. It is the value of all the goods, money, and services received. A British organization explains that if a woman in the United Kingdom were earning minimum wage (about $7.50 an hour in Britain), paid $2,400 in taxes and was unable to borrow, had no savings to draw on, and received no benefits or free goods from any source, she would have to be supporting eighteen dependents to experience life like those living at the below $2 line (New Economic Foundation 2006).

TABLE 6-8 Poverty Rates by Race Ethnicity and Gender, in the United States, 2004 (Percentage Poor in Category)

All people	**12.7**
Men	11.5
Women	13.9
Black	**24.7**
Men	22.6
Women	26.5
Hispanic	**21.9**
Men	19.4
Women	24.0
Asian	**9.8**
Men	9.3
Women	10.3
White	**8.6**
Men	7.7
Women	9.5

SOURCE: U.S. Bureau of the Census 2004.

TABLE 6-9 Percentage Living Below $2 a Day Poverty Line in the World by Region, 2001

Region	Population	Proportion Living Below Poverty Line
East Asia and Pacific	1,823 million	46.4
Eastern Europe and central Asia	474	19.1
Latin America and Caribbean	519	25.2
Middle Eastand north Africa	279	23.2
South Asia	1,378	77.7
Sub-Saharan Africa	674	76.2
High-income nations	982	0.0
World	6,128	44.3

SOURCE: New Economic Foundation 2006.

At the same time so many are poor, great wealth has accumulated among others. The assets of the 200 richest people in the world were greater than the combined income of the poorest 40 percent of the world. That gap continues to grow as the wealthiest 5 percent of people in the world receive 82 percent of the income (Munck 2005; Randerson 2006).

Poverty to some extent around the world is gender blind. Men and women and boys and girls live in dire situations and the gap is most dramatic between those people who live in the poorest nation compared to the wealthiest. Within each nation, however, gender does show

Box 6–5 WOMEN AGRICULTURAL WORKERS, HUNGER, AND GENDER

Hunger is a devastating problem for millions of people in the world. In 2004, 11 percent of Latin Americans, 22 percent of south Asians, and 32 percent of sub-Saharan Africans were undernourished. Women and girls are even more likely than men and boys to be undernourished in these areas (Ramachandran 2006). In poor households, in particular, the incidence of severe malnutrition is greater among girls. In fact, gender is the most statistically significant determinant of malnutrition among young children, and the most common cause of death among girls below the age of five years.

A study in India found that although boys and girls had roughly similar calorie intake, girls were given more cereals, whereas boys were given more milk and fats with their cereal (Bose 2003). Discrepancies exist among adults as well. For example, studies in India have shown a sharp difference in calorie intake among adult men and women, with women consuming approximately 1,000 fewer calories than men (Development Gateway 2004). Women in Bangladesh eat after men and the children, making do with what is left. A similar pattern prevails in most south Asian countries.

A common coping strategy adopted by households faced with seasonal food shortages involves reduced food consumption by women as a first step followed by skipping of meals to ensure that the men of the family and the children have larger portions of food from the meager store (Ramachandran 2006). Even pregnant women are caught up in the cycle of self-denial and food deprivation.

Nutritional deprivation has two major consequences for women: They never reach their full growth potential and they suffer from anemia. Both are risk factors in pregnancy. High levels of anemia complicate childbearing and result in maternal and infant deaths and low-birth-weight infants (Coonrod 1998).

up. The poorest of the poor are women and children who comprise 70 percent of poor people in the world and (UNESCO 2007; see Box 6–5).

UNPAID WORK THROUGH THE LIFE CYCLE

Paid work is only a part of the work that takes place in our society. Although a lot of work has moved from families into factories and offices, much still remains as unpaid housework. Since the 1960s, researchers in the United States have been studying how people spend their time. Thousands of people have filled out twenty-four-hour time diaries describing everything they did in the previous day. The research finds that:

1. Women in all categories do more housework than men do. Women do about 35.1 hours of unpaid housework each week compared to about 17.4 hours for men.

Ironically women are not only the most likely to suffer from food shortage; they are also highly likely to be engaged in food production. A large portion of the world's food output originates in the hands of women farmers. In most developing countries, women provide over half the agricultural workforce. However, they have little control over the land they work because laws favor inheritance by sons rather than daughters or widows.

Bhutan is the only south Asian nation that does not allow discrimination against women socially, economically, politically, or legally. Women are accorded a dominant role in the legal system, especially in family and inheritance law. The law of inheritance reserves equal rights for all children and in many parts of Bhutan, society is matrilineal.

Households where women have access to their own incomes and exercise decision-making powers tend to have an expenditure pattern different from those dominated by men. Research in Asia, Africa, and Latin America has found that improvements in household food security and nutrition are associated with women's greater access to income and greater power over household decisions on expenditure. Women in poor households spend most of the earnings under their control on basic household needs such as food, clothes, children's education, and health, whereas men tend to spend a significant part of theirs on personal goods such as alcohol, tobacco, and so on (Agarwal 2002; Kelkar, Nathan, and Jahan 2003; Ramachandran 2006).

For women farmers to use land more efficiently and thereby make a greater contribution to food security, they need access to land, management control of land-based resources, and the economic incentives that the security of tenure provides (Food and Agriculture Organization 1996).

2. Women who are not in the paid labor force do more housework than women who are in the paid labor force and men who are not in the paid labor force do more housework than men who are in the paid labor force.
3. Employed women do more housework than nonemployed men.

Besides these differences in the amount of time women and men spend on housework, men and women do different kinds of tasks. Women are more likely to do cooking, washing dishes, indoor cleanup, laundry, shopping, and child care. Men are more likely to do repairs and maintenance, gardening, and pet care.

The value of the unpaid work done by women is estimated to be worth about $138,095 for stay-at-home mothers for the hours put in as housekeeper, day care teacher, cook, computer operator, laundry machine operator, janitor, facilities manager, van driver, chief executive, and psychologist. For women who are also in the paid labor force, the value of unpaid domestic work is $85,876 annually (Wulfhorst 2006; DeFao 2007).

Box 6–6 MR. MOYO GOES TO THE DOCTOR

"What is your job?" asked the doctor.

"I am a farmer" replied Mr. Moyo.

"Have you any children?" the doctor asked.

"God has not been good to me. Of fifteen born, only nine alive," Mr. Moyo answered.

"Does your wife work?"

"No, she stays home."

"I see. How does she spend her day?"

"Well, she gets up at four in the morning. Fetches water and wood, makes the fire, cooks breakfast and cleans the homestead. Then she goes to the river and washes clothes. Once a week she walks to the grinding mill. After that she goes to the township with the two smallest children where she sells tomatoes by the roadside while she knits. She buys what she wants from the shops. Then she cooks the midday meal."

"You come home at midday?"

"No, no she brings the meal to me about three kilometres away."

"And after that?"

"She stays in the field to do the weeding, and then goes to the vegetable garden to water."

"What do you do?"

"I must go and discuss business and drink with the men in the village."

"And after that?"

"I go home for supper which my wife has prepared."

"Does she go to bed after supper?"

"No, I do. She has things to do around the house until nine or ten."

"But I thought you said you wife doesn't work"

"Of course she doesn't work. I told you she stays at home."

SOURCE: Oxfam 1994.

Despite the obvious importance of this unpaid work and the huge amount of human energy and talent it represents, it is often largely invisible. Box 6–6 describing Mr. Moyo's conversation with his doctor illustrates both the heavy load unpaid women bear as workers and the invisibility of their efforts.

Why Is Women's Work Invisible?

In the discussion of paid employment, we looked at one aspect that is invisible—emotion work. In the discussion of housework and especially in Box 6–6, we saw that housework is also an invisible form of work. One other kind of invisible work largely done by women is called sociability work, which is the work done by volunteers in the community to help support important activities and institutions (Daniels 1985). This might include raising funds for a museum or organizing a marathon to raise money and awareness for breast cancer.

Even though these events take a lot of energy and skill they appear to be effortless and the work behind them is usually unseen. The work behind them is also largely done by women (Blackstone 2004). In Amy Blackstone's research on sociability work of women organizing a run for breast cancer to raise money for more and better diagnostic equipment, research, and health education, she found sociability workers put in up to twenty hours a day motivating volunteers, convincing donors to help pay for tents, and encouraging the community to participate. Their work is essential to the community and the efforts they made are significant but their work is trivialized. The marathon and its mission are recognized but the work that enabled the event to occur is not.

Why is this kind of work along with housework and emotion work invisible? Arlene Kaplan Daniels (1985) writes that it is invisible because it is "women's work" and is seen as a "natural" part of women's nurturing and caretaking, something to be expected but not recognized. Daniels argues that we cannot seriously understand work if we turn a blind eye to so much work that is going on unnoticed.

Children and Housework

Gender differences also appear in the distribution of housework between boys and girls in families. Table 6–10 shows the kinds of housework boys and girls do and the amount

TABLE 6–10 Children and Chores

	% Who Do This Chore		Average Hours per Week	
Task	Girls	Boys	Girls	Boys
Cleaning my room	93%	85%	1.6	1.2
Cleaning house	87	74	2.2	1.4
Laundry	79	57	2.9	2.0
Doing the dishes	75	53	2.0	1.4
Cooking	68	62	2.6	1.8
Caring for pets	50	53	4.0	3.8
Grocery shopping	42	32	1.8	1.3
Setting the table	39	35	0.7	0.5
Taking out trash	37	70	0.6	0.6
Yard work	22	64	1.2	1.8
Caring for children	38	23	13.8	6.0
Caring for elderly	5	6	4.6	3.1
Other tasks	41	44	3.8	5.5
n 506 446				

SOURCE: Aronson, Mortimer, Zierman, and Hacker 1996.

of time they spend doing it. Table 6–10 shows that both boys and girls are likely to clean their room and clean their house and neither spend much time taking care of elderly relatives. Girls are much more likely to do the dishes and the laundry and boys are much more likely to do yard work and take out the trash. The biggest difference seems to be in the amount of time spent caring for younger children. About 38 percent of the girls and 23 percent of the boys say they spend some time during the week taking care of younger children. However, girls spend fourteen hours per week compared to only six hours spent by boys.

The burden of housework that teenage daughters carry, especially in low-income families, is significant. Girls are responsible not only for house chores and child care, but also do a lot of emotion work in helping their parents to handle troubles and instability they may face in trying to keep the household afloat (Dodson 1999).

Housework remains an important site of gender inequality and scholars have puzzled about how these differences can persist especially in light of the changes in the division of paid work. We saw that when it comes to working for wages, women and men are becoming increasingly similar, at least in terms of whether they are in the paid labor force or not. Women and men and boys and girls are also becoming more similar in the division of housework. But why is change so slow?

What's Behind the Way People Divide up Housework?

Doing housework is part of almost everyone's life and the gender differences we find in this activity have led to much speculation on the part of scholars about why the work is divided the way that it is. Three theories have been suggested to answer this question: socialization theory, rational choice theory, and feminist theory.

SOCIALIZATION. Socialization theorists emphasize the early experience of children especially in families. Socialization theory is a large school of thought with many different ideas about how and where socialization occurs and why it is important. Socialization theorists, however, would agree that we teach our boys and girls skills in certain kinds of housework and we train them to feel responsible and comfortable with some activities and not others. These scholars would point to the data on children in Table 6–10 and argue that they provide support for the argument that dividing housework between women and men is a product of the lessons learned by boys and girls about what men and women and boys and girls should feel and do when faced with a dirty kitchen. From a socialization theorist's point of view, the solution to inequity in the division of housework is to teach boys and girls all of the skills they will need to take care of themselves and others in households and to teach boys and girls to feel responsible for and comfortable doing all kinds of tasks.

RATIONAL CHOICE. A second framework is rational choice theory. These scholars would argue that as boys and girls we may learn to identify some housework tasks with girls and women and others with boys and men; these childhood experiences are important. The real question in understanding the way in which men and women divide housework, however, comes from their interactions with one another as adults in households. Rational choice theorists argue that women and men enter into negotiations about housework and make rational choices based on questions such as which partner knows how to do the work and which partner has other responsibilities in the paid labor force or brings home a larger paycheck that allows him or her to bargain out of doing housework. Rational choice theorists would solve the problem of injustice by suggesting that couples learn to communicate and negotiate in a fair manner and encourage them to create ways of dividing housework that rationally take into consideration individuals' skills and other responsibilities and activities.

FEMINIST THEORY. A third framework is feminist theory. Feminists argue that the way in which housework is divided cannot represent two equals negotiating an equitable and rational decision because gender inequality interferes with those rational choices. They would point out that who does the housework is both a reflection of gender inequality in families and in other social institutions as well as a way in which gender inequality is generated. Housework is both a cause and an effect of the political inequality between women and men. Women do more housework because they do not have as much power as men do. Furthermore when women do more housework and when women and men do different kinds of housework, gender is being reproduced.

Feminists maintain that housework is a "gender factory." Men can reaffirm their masculinity by not doing the dishes, whereas women reaffirm their femininity by doing them. The division also reaffirms the relationship between genders—women work for men, men dominate, and women are subordinate (Berk 1985).

To solve this dilemma, feminists argue that people must consciously overcome gender by doing "inappropriate" jobs. Behaving in new ways will create new ways of thinking and feeling that will further break down gender stereotypes. In addition, feminists would argue that we need to pay attention to the connection between paid work and unpaid work. As long as women are paid less than men, their ability to negotiate changes in the division of unpaid work will be hampered.

GLOBALIZATION AND GENDER

Both paid employment and the unpaid work in households are embedded in a global system. Globalization refers to the integration of the world's economies, political systems, informational networks, and ecology into one large system (Lenz 2004). This integration touches everyone's life in ways we might not often think about. Economic globalization affects all of the issues we have considered so far in this chapter. Think about what you ate for breakfast today. You may have had a glass of orange juice from Mexico, bread from wheat grown in Canada, prepared in a toaster made in China from steel from Russia on a stove fueled by energy from Venezuela. The integration of the production and distribution of goods from many different places in the world is a sure sign of globalization.

Globalization has some benefits because it means consumers have access to goods from every corner of the world. Globalization also often produces goods more cheaply and potentially allows more people access to those goods. Globalization has huge downsides as well, however, especially for those who live in nations that are referred to as "developing" nations (Berberoglu 2003).

The United Nations identifies 128 nations in Africa, Latin America, and Asia as "developing." The "least developed" of these include countries such as Afghanistan, Cambodia, Niger, Rwanda, Haiti, and Yemen, which face extreme poverty and most of whose citizens lead difficult lives. Because most of these nations are in the Southern Hemisphere and the richest nations are largely in the north, the terms Global South and Global North have come to indicate the gap between countries.

Women in the Global South like women in the Global North are often lower in status and power than are men. For example, women provide 80 percent of the agricultural labor in Uganda and most of the rest of Africa but they are much less likely to own land. Only 3 percent of the women in Uganda own land, and this is not unusual in the Global South. If women do not own land or other property like cattle, they cannot participate in development programs or receive loans and credit. Only about 1 percent of loans to develop the land are made to women in Uganda, for example (Wamboka 2002).

Women work hard but they are even more likely than men in poor countries to live in absolute poverty. Since the 1980s in Africa, the proportion of men living in absolute poverty has increased by 30 percent and the proportion of women in absolute poverty rose 50 percent (Emasu 2002).

These problems have been exacerbated by international economic pressures. One of the most important of these in the Global South is debt. Between 1970 and 2002, the continent of Africa received $540 billion in loans from wealthier nations and the World Bank. The debtor nations have paid back $550 billion of their debt but they still owe $295 billion. Yes these numbers are correct. The difference, of course, is a result of compound interest. When borrowers take a loan they agree to pay back the amount they borrowed plus the interest accrued. The relationship between debtor nations and wealthy nations or the institutions they control like the World Bank creates a situation in which more money is transferred from poor countries to rich countries than vice versa (*Cape Argus* 2004).

To continue to pay back the interest as well as original loans, nations are forced to create SAPs (Structural Adjustment Programs) and PRSPs (Poverty Reduction Strategy Papers). SAPs and PRSPs are policies that tighten the belts of government spending in poor nations, cutting programs in education, health care, transportation, and other government-funded projects to accumulate money to pay back the interest on loans. SAPs and PRSPs harm the debtor nations and their citizens, regardless of gender, but women are hardest hit because they are already the very poorest members of those countries. In addition, women's responsibilities for children mean they rely on government programs for food, schools, and medical aid for their children and when those programs are cut they have no place to turn (World Resources Institute 1994–1995; Blumberg 1995; Connelly et al. 2000).

Globalization also has important effects on work in wealthy nations like the United States. When work is globalized, jobs are transferred to those places where labor is cheapest. Because American workers are then competing with very low-wage workers around the globe for jobs, the pay scales for the jobs that remain in the United States are kept down. Saving labor costs is beneficial to stockholders and investors but it does not benefit employees from either poor or wealthy nations. In the United States, we have seen the reflection of these changes in an increasingly productive and profitable economy at the same time that the typical worker's real wages have declined since 2001 and problems like homelessness have continued to grow (Tonelson 2000; Berberoglu 2003; Mishel and Eisenbrev 2005; Bernstein 2006).

For example, since the North American Free Trade Agreement (NAFTA) was signed in 1993, 794,174 jobs were created but 1,673,453 were lost in the United States. The jobs that were lost paid on average 21 percent more than the ones that were gained. During this same period wages fell between 15 percent and 20 percent in Mexico. NAFTA was an agreement to open up trade among the United States, Canada, and Mexico, making it more profitable and efficient (Scott 2003).

These kinds of trends may create more gender equity in pay because men's wages are pushed down to the levels of women's wages. Researchers who have looked at the closing gap in women's and men's pay in the United States in recent years have noted that it may be largely due to sinking or at least stagnating wages among men rather than rising wages among women. In other words women are not catching up with men; men are "catching up" with women. Workers in wealthy nations are "catching up" with those in the poorer ones.

WID, WAD, and GAD

Feminist scholars have offered three models for understanding the global economy and creating policies to try to alleviate the economic difficulties of the world and to eliminate the gender gap (Moser 1993; Smith, March, and Mukhopadhyay 1998). The first of these is called women in development (WID). This approach maintains that poor nations should model themselves after wealthier ones and that women in all countries, but especially the Global South, should become more like men by moving into the paid labor force to work alongside men. International economic policies should facilitate these transitions by allowing multinationals to build factories and invest in agribusiness. Those corporations should be sure to include women in their workforce.

The second approach, women and development (WAD), is critical of WID, asserting that women already are active workers although they may not be receiving wages. They point out that like the wife in the story in Box 6–6, women work many hours a day hauling water and wood, raising children, selling goods in the market, and working in the fields, offices, and factories. When unpaid and paid work are both considered, 66 percent of the world's work hours are by women (UNESCO 2007).

WAD advocates also question whether the model of the Western developed nation is the only or best way to build effective economies. They believe that international economic policies should recognize the invisible work of women and design ways to support and compensate it. In addition, they argue that a range of possible paths to economic development should be created to avoid some of the pitfalls of Western capitalism, such as environmental degradation, huge gaps between the rich and poor, and the inequities between women and men.

The third approach is gender and development (GAD; Moser and Moser 2005). These scholars criticize WID and WAD for treating women as a homogenous group. They point to the enormous differences in women's experience by race ethnicity, social class, and nation and call for a conceptual model and policies that recognize the diversity among women. GAD advocates, for example, would point to the numbers of people living on less than $2 a day, the trafficking in women described in chapter 4 on sexuality, and the problems refugees who are mostly women and children face as issues that touch the majority of the world but are not part of the everyday experience of most women or men living in the Global North. GAD also argues that we cannot talk about women in isolation but rather must think of the relationships between women and men, gender relations. For example, we cannot address the problem of violence against women without considering the ways in which violence is part of the social construction of masculinity. GAD activists support policies that look at gender, rather than women in isolation. They also see gender equity as part of a larger exercise of human rights and a mission of transforming the global economy to one that is based on human needs and cooperation rather than profitability and competition.

REFERENCES

Ackman, Daniel. 2004. Walmart and sex discrimination by the numbers. *Forbes*, June 23. http://www.forbes.com/2004/06/23/cx_da_0623topnews.html.

AFL-CIO. 2006. *Ask a working woman survey report*. Washington, DC: AFL-CIO. www.aflcio.org/issues/politics/labor2006/upload/awwsurvey.pdf.

Agarwal, B. 2002. Are we not peasants too? Land rights and women's claims in India. *Seeds* 21:29. www.popcouncil.org/publications/seeds/seds21.pdf.

Almaguer, Tomas. 1991. Chicano men: A cartography of homosexual identity and behavior. *Differences* 3 (2)75–100.

Amott, Teresa. 1999. *Caught in the crisis: Women and the U.S. economy today*. New York: NYU Press.

Antal, Ariane, and Dafna Izraeli. 1993. A global comparison of women in management: Women managers in their homelands and as expatriates. In *Women in management: Trends, issues and challenges in managerial diversity*, ed. E. Ganeson, 52–96. Newbury Park, CA: Sage.

Aronson, Pamela, Jeylan Mortimer, Carol Zierman, and Michael Hacker. 1996. "Generational differences in early work experiences and evaluations" In *Adolescents, work and family: An intergenerational development analysis*, ed. J. Mortimer and M. Finch, 25–62. Beverly Hills, CA: Sage.

Belkin, Lisa. 2007. "The Feminine Critique" *New York Times* November 1.

Bellas, Marcia. 1999. Emotional labor in academia: The case of professors. *Annals of the American Academy of Political and Social Science* 561 (January): 96–110.

——— . 2001. The gendered nature of emotional labor in the workplace. In *Gender mosaics*, D. Vannoy, ed., (pp. 269–78). Los Angeles: Roxbury.

Benokraitis, Nijole. 1997. Sex discrimination in the 21st century. In *Subtle sexism: Current practice and prospects for change*, ed. N. Benokraitis, 5–33. Thousand Oaks, CA: Sage.

Benokraitis, Nijole, and Joe Feagin. 1986. *Modern sexism: Blatant, subtle and covert discrimination*. Englewood Cliffs, NJ: Prentice Hall.

Berberoglu, Berch. 2003. *Globalization of capital and the nation state*. New York: Rowman and Littlefield.

Bernstein, Jared. 2006. You know how to add, don't you? *Los Angeles Times*, May 7.

Berg, D. 1987. Cross-examination. *Litigation Journal of the Section of Litigation, American Bar Association* 14 (1): 25–30.

Berk, Sarah Fenstermacher. 1985. *Gender factory*. New York: Plenum.

Bianchi, Suzanne, and Jane Dye. 2001. The participation of women and men in the U.S. labor force: Trends and future prospects. *Gender mosaics*, ed. D. Vannoy, 460–72. Los Angeles: Roxbury.

Blackstone, Amy. 2004. Sociability work and gender. *Equal Opportunities International* 23 (3–5): 29–44.

Blumberg, Rhoda. 1995. Gender, microenterprise, performance and power. In *Women in the Latin American development process*, ed. C. Bose and E. Acosta-Belen, 194–226. Philadelphia: Temple University Press.

Bose, A. B. 2003. *The state of children in India: Promises to keep.* New Delhi: Manohar.

Bose, Christine, and Rachel Bridges-Whaley. 2001. Sex segregation in the US labor force. In *Gender mosaics*, ed. D. Vannoy, 228–39. Los Angeles: Roxbury.

Calasanti, Toni, and Kathleen Slevin. 2001. *Gender, social inequalities and aging.* Walnut Creek, CA: Altamira.

Cape Argus. 2004. Cancel Africa's debt, UN says. September 30.

Cardwell, Donald. 1957. *The organization of science in England.* London.

Catalyst. 2007. *The double bind dilemma for women in leadership.* New York: Catalyst.

Commission on Professionals in Science and Technology (CPST). 1997. *Professional women and minorities: A total human resource data compendium.* Washington, DC: CPST.

Connell, Robert. 2002. *Gender.* Cambridge, UK: Polity Press.

——— . 2005. Globalization, imperialism and masculinity. In *Handbook of studies on men and masculinities*, ed. R. Kimmel, J. Hearn, and R. Connell, 71–89. Thousand Oaks, CA: Sage.

Connelly, M. Patricia, Tani Murray Li, Martha MacDonald, and Jane Parpart. 2000. *Feminism and development:. Theoretical perspectives on development.* http://www.irdc.ca.

Conway, Margaret, David Ahern, and Gertrude Steuernagel. 1999. *Women and public policy: A revolution in progress.* 2nd ed. Washington, DC: Congressional Quarterly Press.

Coonrod, C. S. 1998. *Chronic hunger and the status of women in India.* New York: The Hunger Project. www.thp.org/reports/indiawom.htm.

Cornwell, Rupert. 2007. One million women could sue Wal-Mart in sex bias class action. *The Independent/UK*, February 8.

Daniels, Arlene Kaplan. 1985. Good times and good works. *Social Problems* 32 (4): 363–74.

DeFao, Janine. 2007. Mother's work, in dollars. *San Francisco Chronicle*, May 4.

Development Gateway. 2004. *News on food security, intra household gender disparities and access to food.* Washington, DC: Development Gateway. http: //www.topics.developmentgateway.org/gender.

DeViney, Stanley, and Jennifer Solomon. 1995. Gender differences in retirement income: A comparison of theoretical explanations. *Journal of Women and Aging* 7:83–100.

Dodson, Lisa. 1999. *Don't call us out of name.* Boston: Beacon.

Economist. 2005. The conundrum of the glass ceiling. July 21.

Emasu, Alice. 2002. Get the land, the rest will follow. *AfricaWoman*, August.

Epstein, Cynthia Fuchs. 1993. *Women in law.* 2nd ed. Chicago: University of Illinois Press.

Featherstone, Liza. 2005. Down and out in discount America. *The Nation*, January 3.

Food and Agriculture Organization (FAO). 1996. *FAO focus: Women and food security: Women hold the key to food security.* http://www.fao.org/FOCUS/E/Women/WoHm-e.htm.

Fox, Mary Frank. 1991. Gender environmental milieu and productivity in science. In *The outer circle*, ed. H. Zuckerman, J. Cole, and J. Bruer, 108–204. New York: Norton.

——— . 1995. Women and scientific careers. *Handbook of science and technology studies*, ed. S. Jananoff, G. Markle, J. Persen, and T. Pinch, 205–23. Thousand Oaks, CA: Sage.

——— . 1996. Women, academia and careers in science and engineering. In *The equity equation: Fostering the advancement of women in the sciences, mathematics and engineering*, ed. C. Davis, C. Hollenshead, B. Lazarus, and P. Rayman, 265–89. San Francisco: Jossey Bass.

——— . 2000. Organizational environments and doctoral degrees awarded to women in science and engineering departments. *Women's Studies Quarterly* 28:47–61.

Fox, Mary Frank. 2001. Women, men and engineering. In *Gender mosaics*, ed. D. Vannoy, 249–57. Los Angeles: Roxbury.

Fronczak, Peter, and Patricia Johnson. 2003. *Occupations 2000*. Washington, DC: U.S. Census Bureau.

Fuller, N. 2001. Social construction of gender identity among Peruvian men. *Men and Masculinities* 3 (3): 316–31.

Gutek, Barbara. 1985. *Sex and the workplace: The impact of sexual behavior and harassment in women, men and organization*. San Francisco: Jossey-Bass.

Harrington-Meyer, Madonna. 1996. Family status and poverty among older women: The gendered distribution of retirement income in the U.S. In *Aging for the twenty first century*, ed. J. Quadagno and D. Street, 464–79. New York: St. Martin's.

Harrington-Meyer, Madonna, Douglas Wolf, and Christine Himes. 2000. Linking benefits to marital status. *Feminist Economics* 11 (2): 145–62.

Higgenbotham, Elizabeth, and Lynn Weber. 2000. Moving up with kin and community: Upward social mobility for black and white women. In *Gender through the prism of difference*. 2nd edition, ed. M. Baca Zinn, P. Hondagneu-Sotelo, and M. Messner, 346–56. Boston: Allyn & Bacon.

Hochschild, Arlie. 1983. *The managed heart: Commercialization of human feeling*. Berkeley: University of California Press.

Holter, O. 2003. A theory of gender, patriarchy and capitalism. In *Among men*, ed. S. Ervo and T. Johansson, 29–43. Aldershot, UK: Ashgate.

Hospitality Industry Quarterly. 2005. Ninth Circuit says firing female employee for not wearing makeup is not discrimination. *Hospitality Industry Quarterly* 16 (1): 3.

International Labour Office. 2007. *Equality at work: Tackling the challenges*. Geneva: International Labour Office. http://www.ilo.org/global/What_we_do/Publications/Officialdocuments/lang—en/docName—WCMS_082607/PDF.

Johnson, Richard, Utha Sambamoorthi, and Stephen Crystal. 1999. Gender differences in pension wealth: Estimates using provider data. *The Gerontologist* 39:320–33.

Joyce, Amy. 2005. Wal-Mart appeal status of class-action bias suit. *Washington Post*, August 8.

Kanter, Rosabeth Moss. 1977. *Men and women of the corporation*. New York: Basic Books.

Kelkar, G., D. Nathan, and R. Jahan. 2003. We were in fire, now we are in water: Micro-credit and gender relations in rural bangladesh. Working Paper Series No. 19. New Delhi: Institute for Human Development.

Kierstead, D., P. D'Agostino, and H. Dill. 1988. Sex role stereotyping of college professors: Bias in students' ratings of instructors. *Journal of Educational Psychology* 80:342–44.

Kroll, Luisa, and Allison Fass. 2006. The world's billionaires. *Forbes*, March 9. http://www.forbes.com/billionaires/.

Lenz, Ilse. 2004. Globalization, gender and work In *Equity in the workplace*, ed. H. Gottfried and L. Reese, 29–52. New York: Lexington.

Lorber, Judith. 2000. Guarding the gates: The micropolitics of gender. In *The gendered society reader*, ed. M. Kimmel, 270–94. New York: Oxford.

MacKinnon, Catherine. 1979. *Sexual harassment of working women*. New Haven, CT: Yale University Press.

Majors, Richard, and Janet Mancini Billson. 1992. *Cool pose: The dilemmas of black manhood in America*. New York: Lexington Books.

Martin, Lynn. 1991. *A report on the glass ceiling initiative*. Washington, DC: U.S. Department of Labor.

Menkel-Meadow, C. 1985. Portia in a different voice: Speculations on a women's lawyering process. *Berkeley Women's Law Review* Fall:39–63.

Mishel, Lawrence, Jared Bernstein, and Sylvia Allegretto. 2005. *The state of working America, 2004–2005.* Washington, DC: EPI.

Mishel, Lawrence, and Ross Eisenbrev. 2005. What's wrong with the economy? EPI memoranda. Washington, DC: EPI.

Mitchell, Susan. 1996. Hard work or luck In *The official guide to American attitudes,* 222. Ithaca, NY: New Strategist Publications.

Moran, Stahl, & Boyer, Inc. 1988. *Status of American female expatriate employees: Survey results.* Boulder, CO: International Division, Moran, Stahl, & Boyer, Inc.

Moser, Caroline. 1993. *Gender planning and development theory: Practice and training.* London: Routledge.

Moser, Caroline, and Annalise Moser. 2005. Gender mainstreaming since Beijing. *Gender and Development* 13 (2): 11–23.

Munck, Ronald. 2005. *Globalization and social exclusion.* Bloomfield, CT: Kumerian.

New Economic Foundation (NEF). 2006. *Growth isn't working.* London: NEF. www.neweconomics. org/gen/uploads/hrfu5w55mzd3f55m2vqwty502022006112929.pdf.

Nonn, Timothy. 2001. Hitting bottom: Homelessness, poverty and masculinity. In *Men's lives.* 5th edition, ed. M. Kimmel and M. Messner, 242–51. Boston: Allyn & Bacon.

Oxfam. 1994. Mr. Moyo goes to the doctor. Presented at the Women's Regional Ecumenical Workshop, Harare, Zimbabwe.

Paludi, Michele. 1997. Sexual harassment in schools. In *Sexual harassment: Theory, research, and treatment,* ed. W. O'Donahue, 224–49. Boston: Allyn & Bacon.

Peterson, V. Spike, and Anne Runyan. 1999. *Global gender issues.* 2nd ed. Boulder, CO: Westview.

Pierce, Jennifer. 2001. Rambo litigators: Emotional labor in a male-dominated occupation. In *Men's lives.* 5th edition, ed. M. Kimmel and M. Messner, 225–41. Boston: Allyn & Bacon.

Ramachandran, Nira. 2006. *Women and food security in South Asia.* Helsinki: UNU World Institute for Development Economics Research (UNU-WIDER).

Randerson, James. 2006. World's richest 1% own 40% of all wealth, UN report discovers. *The Guardian,* December 6.

Regensburger, Linda. 2001. *The American family: Reflecting a changing nation.* Detroit: Gale Group.

Reskin, Barbara and Irene Padavic. 2001. "Sex Differences in Moving Up and Taking Charge." Pp. 253–262 in L. Richardson, V. Taylor, and N. Whittier (Eds.), *Feminist Frontiers,* Fifth Edition. New York: McGraw-Hill.

Rondblud, Georganne. 2001. Gender, power and sexual harassment. In *Gender mosaics,* ed. D. Vannoy, 353–62. Los Angeles: Roxbury.

Rose, Stephen, and Heidi Hartmann. 2004. *Still a man's labor market.* Washington, DC: IWPR.

Rothman, Robert. 2002. *Inequality and stratification: Race, class and gender.* 4th ed. Upper Saddle, NJ: Prentice Hall.

Roux, Angela. 2001. Rethinking official measures of poverty: Consideration of race, ethnicity, and gender. In *Gender mosaics,* ed. D. Vannoy, 290–99. Los Angeles: Roxbury.

Scott, Robert. 2003. *The high price of free trade.* Washington, DC: EPI. www.epinet.org.

Smith, Ines, Candida March, and Maitrayee Mukhopadhyay. 1998. *A guide to gender-analysis frameworks (Oxfam Skills & Practice).* London: Oxfam Publications.

Social Security Administration. 2005. *Annual statistical supplement.i* Washington, DC: U.S. Government Printing Office. www.ssa.gov/policy/docs/statcomps/supplement/2005/5a. html#table5.a1.1.

Statham, Ann, Laurel Richardson, and Judith Cook. 1991. *Gender and university teaching: A negotiated difference.* New York: SUNY Press.

Steinberg, Ronnie. 2001. How sex gets into your paycheck and how to get it out. In *Gender mosaics,* ed. D. Vannoy, 258–68. Los Angeles: Roxbury.

Steinberg, Ronnie, and Deborah Figart. 1999. "Emotional demands at work" a job content analysis. *Annals of the American Academy of Political and Social Science* 561 (1): 177–91.

Stoller, Eleanor Palo, and Rose Campbell Gibson. 2000. *Worlds of difference: Inequality in the aging experience.* Thousand Oaks, CA: Pine Forge Press.

Tomaskovic-Devey, Donald. 1993. *Gender and racial inequality at work.* Ithaca, NY: Cornell University Press.

Tonelson, Alan. 2000. *Race to the bottom.* New York: Union of Radical Political Economists.

UNESCO. 2007. *Quiz.* New York: United Nations.

U.S. Bureau of Labor Statistics. 2006a. Household data annual averages: Table 5. Employment status of the civilian noninstitutional population by sex, age, and race. Washington, DC: U.S. Bureau of Labor Statistics.http://www.bls.gov/cps/cpsaat5.pdf.

——. 2006b. Table 6: Employment status of the Hispanic or Latino population by sex, age, and detailed ethnic group. Washington, DC: U.S. Bureau of Labor Statistics. http://www.bls.gov/cps/cpsaat6.pdf.

U.S. Census Bureau. 1998. *Poverty in the United States, 1997.* Washington, DC: U.S. Bureau of the Census.

——. 2004. *Age and sex of all people, family members and unrelated individuals iterated by income-to-poverty ratio and race: Annual demographic survey.* March supplement POV01. http://pubdb3.census.gov/macro/032005/pov/new01_100.htm.

——. 2005. *Current population survey.* Washington, DC: U.S. Bureau of the Census.

U.S. Department of Labor, Bureau of Labor Statistics. 2004. *Annual averages.* Washington, DC: Bureau of Labor Statistics.

Wamboka, Nabusayi. 2002. Closest to the land, furthest from the cash: Poor women less likely to own land or have access to credit. *AfricaWoman special edition august:2.*

Wharton, Amy. 2005. *The sociology of gender.* Malden, MA: Blackwell.

Williams, Christine. 2000. The glass escalator: Hidden advantages for men in the "female" professions. In *The gendered society reader,* ed. M. Kimmel, 294–310. New York: Oxford University Press.

World Resources Institute. 1994–1995. *World resources: A guide to the global environment.* Oxford, UK: Oxford University Press.

Wulfhorst, Ellen. 2006. Study: U.S. mothers deserve $134,121 in salary. Reuters, May 6. www.mom.salary.com.

7

FAMILIES

CUSTOMARY MARRIAGE LAWS

Chikumbutso was born into a Malawian family that did not have a lot but lived comfortably in a small house with furnishings and a green Toyota pickup in the backyard. In 2000, Chikumbutso's father died of AIDS and his mother died the following year. The family home and all of their belongings, including the green Toyota, were taken by his father's nephew soon after their deaths, leaving him and his three sisters orphaned and homeless. Before she died, his mother pleaded with the nephew to at least leave the children the truck so that they could sell it and have some means to survive. Instead the uncle left behind only a battery-powered transistor radio. Chikumbutso, age eleven, says, "I feel very bitter about it. We don't really know why they did all this. We couldn't understand." The answer to his question is: customary marriage laws (LaFraniere 2005).

Customary marriage laws, which are practiced in many nations in southern Africa, provide for the retention of property in the man's family. In each generation, the oldest son inherits the property and the other brothers may be allowed to live and work there. When the sons marry, they must pay the woman's family. Historically this payment has been made in the form of cattle, but in more modern times it is made in cash. Wives move to the husband's farm and their only tie to the household is through their husband. If he dies, she and her children are asked to leave. Any property that is accumulated by the sons is absorbed into the husband's family. Because a price has been paid for the wife, she must prove herself worthy to her husband's family and enters the household at the very bottom rung of the ladder.

Customary marriage laws are hotly debated in southern Africa, where they are practiced in many communities. In the nation of South Africa, customary law has been ruled unconstitutional because the South African constitution, written after the abolition of Apartheid in 1994, explicitly protects equality by gender, race, ethnicity, religion, and sexuality. Although the laws have changed, opinions about customary law remain contentious. Even young people in South Africa often believe that customary marriage laws are good because they bind families together and protect cultural diversity (Bozalek 2004). Ideas and practices about families are not easily changed. Because families are so important to the maintenance and practice of gender, families can be barriers to reshaping gender.

Family is an institution in which gender plays a prominent role. The work we do, the relationships we have with other adults and children in families, and the experience of family change through marriage, divorce, and death are all experienced differently by women and men. In chapter 8 we explore violence in families and the ways that gender shapes those issues, and in chapter 6 we examined the division of labor in housework as a gendered experience. This chapter explores gender in four other important areas in families: marriage, parenting and caregiving, balancing work and family, and divorce.

MARRIAGE
Marriage as a Legal Contract and the Challenge of Gay Rights Activists

Marriage is a legal contract in the United States that is tightly controlled by the government. Only certain people can legally marry, and those who do marry enter into a contract that is largely determined by laws rather than by the parties who are marrying. Although we think of marriage as a personal choice, the marriage contract provides less freedom than other legal contracts. For example, if you wished to sell a car, you could set up nearly any contract to which you and the buyer agreed. The government would interfere with the contract by requiring that certain taxes are paid and that certain assurances of the mileage and ownership of the car were valid., But issues like who can buy and who can sell, when and where the exchange would take place, and the price and payment schedule would be up to you. The details of a marriage contract, in contrast, are specified, and when the contract is ended through divorce, the state makes the final decision over nearly all arrangements.

One important specification of the marriage contract in the contemporary United States is that the couple must be heterosexual. Gay men and lesbians do not have the legal right to marry except in the states of Massachusetts and California. Amendments are currently being considered that may curtail or abolish that right in Massachusetts (Johnson 2005). This restriction has been criticized because it prevents gay and lesbian couples from making choices about their lives and because it implies that homosexuality and lesbianism are bad or unnatural.

The restriction prohibiting marriage for gay people also creates practical problems. For example, a gay couple may live together for years, pooling their resources. They often are not allowed, however, to carry each other on policies for health insurance or life insurance when that benefit is provided by their employer for workers' heterosexual spouses. Even when a gay or lesbian couple chooses to live together and to take care of each other, they often do not have the legal right to make decisions about each other's health care as a heterosexual married couple does.

In a few places in the United States, some concessions have been won. In New York, a gay person may inherit an apartment lease if a partner dies. A number of employers provide partner benefits for unmarried partners of their employees, including gay and lesbian partners. Civil unions or domestic partnerships are legal in Vermont, Connecticut, New Jersey, and New Hampshire.

Civil unions are certified by a justice of the peace, a judge, or member of the clergy and grant the couple rights and responsibilities similar to those of marriage for heterosexuals. For example, civil partners can claim each other for tax and insurance benefits and they have the right to make decisions for one another in a crisis such as if one is incapacitated and needs decisions made about medical care. In addition, couples who become civil union partners and decide to separate must go through the family courts and obtain a formal dissolution, similar to a divorce for married couples (Ferdinand 2000). Gay marriage advocates, however, believe these reforms fall short of full legal equality with heterosexual marriage.

At the national level, gay rights to marriage have suffered setbacks in the past decade. Forty-two states now have specific legislation forbidding same-sex marriages. Federal laws prohibit gay couples from receiving federal marriage benefits such as time off under the Family and Medical Leave Act, veteran's benefits, and Social Security. In addition, the Defense of Marriage Act (DOMA) signed into federal law in 1997 defines marriage as only heterosexual unions and allows states to ignore marriages that have occurred between same-sex partners in other states.

The United States is behind many countries in the world on this issue. In 2005 South Africa joined Spain, Canada, the Netherlands, and Belgium as the fifth nation to allow same-sex marriage and several nations in Europe recognize same-sex partners (Krauss 2005). Ten nations in Europe, New Zealand, and Israel extend immigration rights to include same-sex partners. Many nations are currently considering extending marriage rights to gay and lesbian couples.

History of Marriage in the United States

Dorothy Stetson (1997) observes that there have been three major periods of marriage and family law in U.S. history. The first was the doctrine of couverture, which defined marriage as a unity in which husband and wife became one, and that one was the husband. Stetson quotes an early nineteenth-century document to explain what couverture meant: "By marriage, the husband and wife are one person in law: that is, the very being or existence of the woman is suspended during marriage, or at least is incorporated and consolidated into that of the husband" (Blackstone 1803, 442).

Under the doctrine of couverture, married women could not own property. They had to turn over their wages to their husbands. If someone wanted to sue a married woman, she or he had to sue the woman's husband.

The second period was marked by the passage of the Married Women's Property Laws, which allowed women the right to own property and to control their own earnings. These laws were first passed in Mississippi in 1839 and eventually were passed in all the states by the end of the nineteenth century. The case that opened the door for married women to own property in Mississippi was a dramatic example of class and racial ethnic inequality. The property about which the woman brought suit and was granted the right to own was a slave.

Marriage during this period was perceived as a union between two separate and different but equal individuals (Stetson 1997). Women and men had different responsibilities and rights in marriage, but neither was supposed to overshadow the other. The wife was expected to provide services for her husband. One court case, for example, specified that a wife was "to be his helpmate, to love and care for him in such a role, to afford him her society and her person, to protect and care for him in sickness, and to labor faithfully to advance his interests" (Weitzman 1981, 60). Sexual accessibility was also part of these laws and it was not until 1993 that marital rape became a crime in all states in the United States. The husband in turn was obligated to provide for the economic needs of his family. The laws that designated men as the "head and master" were overturned in 1979 (Coontz 2006a).

The third doctrine identified marriage as a shared partnership in which spouses would have equal and overlapping responsibilities for economic, household, and child care tasks. This doctrine has been developing for about forty years in the United States. The greater equality in the legal definition of marriage these changes have brought have been welcomed by many. We have seen, however, that legal equality has not necessarily meant social equality. The division of housework, market work, and child care are still all influenced by gender. Box 7–1 describes another way that equality in the eyes of the law may not create equality in real relationships if husbands and wives have very different choices about marriage, for example in marriages of mail-order brides.

In addition, the third doctrine has created problems in some cases when equality between women and men is upheld. For example, changes in laws that make women more equal to men in divorce proceedings are based on assumptions that women are equal to men in their responsibility for children and in their ability to earn an income. The laws assume equality between women and men, which is a valuable reform. Because women and men remain unequal in reality, however, problems have developed for divorcing women, especially when they are awarded the custody of children, as we shall see later in this chapter.

In each of these historical periods, the government has created a legal notion of what a man is and what a woman is and what constitutes a valid or real gender relationship. In the first period, gender was enforced as separate and unequal. The institution of marriage prescribed that women and men are very different from one another and that men were the superior beings. The second period opened up some measure of equality between women and men around economic issues, but it left in place definitions of womanhood and manhood and the different obligations husbands and wives have to one another in marriage.

The third period establishes the idea of gender equality in the eyes of the law. The current debate around gay marriage marks a fourth period in which another factor, sexuality, is most salient. Those who maintain that marriage should only be allowed between one man and one woman are reminding us again that men and women are not equal. They are different beings who can only unite with someone of the "opposite sex" in marriage. Furthermore, antigay marriage laws are telling us that to be properly gendered we need to be heterosexual.

The Colorado Family Action organization, a political group lobbying against gay rights and especially the right to marriage, for example, claims that the right for gay men and lesbians to establish domestic partnerships "harms children by sending confusing messages about gender" (Chernus 2006).

Thinking about intersexed people or transgendered people helps us to see how the narrow definition of marriage as only legal between one woman and man creates rules about gender. You should recall from chapter 2 that intersexed people do not fall into one of the two categories, male or female. Instead they have characteristics, genetically, structurally, and/or hormonally that put them into categories between male and female. Transgendered people are those who represent themselves as a gender that is "inconsistent" with their sex. For example, males who might fit clearly into that biological category may represent themselves as women. Whom should intersexed and transgendered people be allowed to marry? If they represent themselves as women should they only be allowed to marry someone who represents as a man?

Box 7–1 MAIL-ORDER BRIDES

Finding hard data on the number of men who find their wives through catalogs is difficult. Correspondence services like those commonly listed in newspapers advertise "Asian women desire romance" and "Attractive Oriental ladies seeking friendship, correspondence." Men who respond to these ads receive pictures and descriptions of women, along with addresses, for a small fee (Agbayani-Siewert and Reeilla 1995).

The Philippines is the major source of mail-order brides from Asia. The Philippines report that 19,000 mail-order brides leave that country every year to marry men in other countries (Tolentina 1996). Many of these women come to the United States, although we do not know the exact number. Many women also come from other areas of the world as mail-order brides for American husbands.

Some of these arrangements result in happy marriages, but there are some important problems that can occur. The first problem with this practice is the possibility that the women involved are not making their own choices to enter themselves into the service. Researchers have found that mail-order women who seek counseling in Seattle, for example, frequently do not speak English and come from isolated rural areas (Mochizuki 1987). One might suspect, therefore, that they did not make a free or informed choice to be listed in the magazines or to marry someone in the United States. Perhaps the choices they had were so limited that they could not really be considered a humane range of options.

Other researchers have found that the level of marital satisfaction among mail-order brides is similar to that of other intermarried Asian women who found their husbands through other means. Mail-order brides, however, report more physical and psychological abuse (Lin 1991).

The idea of a man from a wealthy nation finding a wife from a poor country who is advertised as a commodity illustrates the convergence of gender inequity and national inequality. Although many men and women may find happiness in these arrangements, they illustrate how marriage can represent and validate relationships between two kinds of people with starkly different resources and choices.

What if a partner chooses to become transgendered after he or she legally marries? Should the government tell people how we should represent ourselves and whom we should marry?

Marriage Promotion in the United States

In the 1990s, the U.S. Congress passed DOMA. This act defines marriage, narrowly, as a legal relationship between one man and one woman, but it also asserts that the institution of marriage is a fundamental piece of society and virtually everyone should be married. The law demands that women and men unite in marriage, especially women and men who are poor.

Box 7–2 describes the concern that other nations such as Japan and South Korea have about the drop in the proportion of people who are marrying. In those countries, the discussion about promoting marriage has not emphasized any particular social class, although it has targeted women, rather than men, as the focus. In the United States the concern and the governmental policies center around poor people. In the past decade, the U.S. government has decided to "promote marriage" as a way to address the problem of poverty. The goal "is to transform single-mother families into families headed by married biological fathers" (Mink 2006, 159).

In 1996, changes in welfare laws created a new program called Temporary Aid to Needy Families (TANF). The laws reward states that increase the marriage rate of the families receiving grants and states reward couples who are on welfare who marry. For example, in West Virginia unmarried families receive $100 less per month than married families (Solot and Miller 2002). In 2002, ten states received $10.2 million as family formation bonuses (Mink 2006). In 2006, the White House and Congress allotted $100 million a year for the next five years to programs that strengthen marriage (M. McManus 2006).

Box 7–2 PROMOTING MARRIAGE IN JAPAN AND KOREA

Marriage promotion is an issue in many places around the world where governments are concerned about the numbers of people who are choosing to marry much later than previously or not at all (Ganahl 2004). In Japan, a study from Japan Life Insurance shocked the nation when it reported that about half of Japan's single women from—thirty-five to fifty-four have no intention of ever marrying. In addition, nearly three-quarters of women in the same age group said they never want children. In South Korea, it is much the same picture. Around 40 percent of South Korean women are staying single into their thirties as they increasingly prioritize their education and careers. Twenty years ago, only 14 percent of women in South Korea were still single at thirty (Ganahl 2004). The number of single Japanese women may rise even more dramatically as a new divorce law is now in effect that awards up to half of a man's pension to his ex-wife (Hardin 2007).

When the Japanese women were asked why they want to remain single, they explained that they wished to maintain a wide spectrum of friends and pursue their careers. The Japanese report also found that employed women were concerned about the work environment, which they perceived as unfriendly to mothers (Retherford and Ogawa 2005).

The response from the government has been highly critical of women. The former prime minister of Japan gave a speech angrily suggesting that women who never became mothers were selfish and should not be entitled to government retirement pensions (Ganahl 2004).

Interestingly, the statistics are even more dramatic for men, although they have not received the same level of criticism. The proportion of men single at age fifty went from 2 percent to 25 percent between 1970 and 2000. The proportion of women single at age fifty went from 3 percent to 19 percent in those same years. The average age of marriage between 1975 increased from 27.6 to 30.8 years for men and from 24.5 to 28.8 years for women (Retherford and Ogawa 2005).

There are four flaws in the premise of this program. First, it assumes that failure to marry causes poverty. In fact, the reverse is probably true. Poverty seems to inhibit people's ability to marry. Poor people often would like to get married but feel they are not able to take on this responsibility until they are better off financially. Furthermore, to escape poverty, poor single people must marry well. They must find partners who are able to financially provide for them—a tall order in an impoverished neighborhood (Coontz and Folbre 2002).

Second, the program does not acknowledge the issue of quality. Happy, healthy, stable marriages might be a good goal, but not all marriages are healthy and happy. Furthermore, those marriages that are not healthy and happy are likely to become unstable (Coontz and Folbre 2002). Most people believe that one important feature of a healthy, stable marriage is that the partners love one another, which is discussed in the next section.

Third, marriage does not cure the money problem for many poor couples. Almost one-third (27 percent) of low-income children live in families with two parents. In addition, the majority of married low-income parents are employed. Low wages and lack of employee benefits leave married couples and their children with inadequate economic resources (National Center for Children in Poverty 2005).

Fourth, single parenthood does not necessarily lead to poverty. Only 1.2 percent of children whose single mothers have college degrees and year-round, full-time jobs are poor. In many other nations, single parents and their children are provided with safety nets that raise them above poverty (Coontz and Folbre 2002).

In addition to these flaws in the plans to get Congress into the marriage business, the program also is problematic because it marks a remarkable intrusion of the government into what most of us believe to be private relationships. We have many reasons for choosing to enter into marriage or not. Making government bonuses and government approval part of those reasons mark a significant and, for many, unwelcome change.

Because women are the majority of adults who receive welfare grants, the marriage program creates an especially questionable situation for women. These new rules mean that entitlement to government funds is to be based on the relationships women establish with men. They derive from the belief that good, deserving women get married. Bad, undeserving women do not. Those women who tie the knot are entitled to more support. Those women who choose to remain independent of men (at least as wives) are not.

Love and Marriage

Marriage has existed for many centuries but its meaning has changed significantly over time (Coontz 2006a). In earlier centuries, marriage was primarily an economic arrangement: Wealthy people entered into marriage to consolidate wealth, transfer property, and lay claim to political power, even to settle wars. Middle-class people married for similar reasons on a smaller scale. And even lower class people married to conjoin farms, to share tools, and to bring more labor into a household. Love was not a reason to get married, nor was the lack of love a reason for divorce, which was usually to improve one's economic circumstances or because of childlessness (Coontz 2004).

In the seventeenth century in Europe and North America, the ideal of a love match and lifelong intimacy as a basis of marriage began to take hold. Since then, love has grown to become the most important reason for marriage. The connection between love and marriage is now a powerful ideology. In a survey of college students in the 1960s, three-fourths of the women said they would marry men they did not love, if those men met other criteria such as being a reliable breadwinner, not drinking too much, and not being physically abusive. Only one-fourth of the men said they would marry women they did not love. Today both women and men say love is the top priority (Coontz 2004).

Ironically love is the basis of both the arguments to allow gay men and lesbians to marry and the arguments to allow heterosexuals to remain unmarried. Gay rights advocates who support marriage assert that loving couples should be allowed all of the responsibilities and privileges of legal marriage, regardless of sexuality or gender. Heterosexuals maintain that it is inhumane and uncivilized for the government to tell parents that to acquire access to support for themselves and their children in programs such as TANF, they must marry even if they do not love one another.

The debates over marriage for gay and lesbian couples and rules requiring marriage for poor people bring into opposition two key issues, gender and love. Those who are against gay marriage and in favor of the government promoting marriage for poor people believe that gender is key. Marriage is for one man and one woman and every man and every woman must be married regardless of love. Those who are in favor of allowing gay marriage and allowing heterosexuals (and others) to choose whether they will marry based on their feelings about their partner believe that love is more important than gender. Which do you think is more important? Love or gender?

Widowhood

One final way marriage is different for women is that men are more likely to live out their lives in a marriage, whereas women are more likely to be widowed. Because women tend to live longer than men, marry men who are older than they, and are less likely to remarry after the death of a spouse, women are much more likely to be widows than men are to be widowers. Table 7–1 shows the proportion of all women and men who were widowed in 2004. Table 7–1 shows that race ethnicity creates some differences but gender differences are striking for all groups.

About one-third of women over sixty-five are widows, and on the average widows live about fifteen years after their husband's death (Federal Interagency Forum on Aging-Related Statistics. 2004)). At every age, men are much more likely to be married and much less likely to be widowed. Seventy percent of men over sixty-five live with a wife, whereas 35 percent of women over sixty-five live with a husband. Of women who are widowed or otherwise single, 16 percent

TABLE 7–1 Proportion of Widows and Widowers in the United States, 2004

Race Ethnicity	Women	Men
White	9.8%	2.5%
Black	9.2	2.6
Hispanic	5.5	1.3

SOURCE: U.S. Bureau of the Census 2004.

live with other relatives, compared to 7 percent of men who live with other relatives. Almost half of women over sixty-five (42 percent) live alone compared to only 16 percent of men over sixty-five who live alone (Federal Interagency Forum on Aging-Related Statistics. 2004).

PARENTING AND CAREGIVING

Both the real experience of being a parent and our ideas about what parents should be like are shaped by gender. Mothers and fathers experience being parents differently and when we think about what makes a good mother or a good father, we think in gendered terms.

Research shows that mothers spend more time with their children than do fathers (Aldous, Mulligan, and Biarnason 1998). Race ethnicity, however, makes a big difference and African American fathers compared to white American fathers are much more likely to participate in child care (Orbuch and Eyster 1997). Gender, however, remains a strong distinction in parenting. On the average in American households with two heterosexual parents, mothers spend about eleven hours per week taking care of their children and fathers spend just over three hours per week. Mothers are also more likely to be single parents. Of all households in the United States, 12.4 percent are single women and their children, whereas 4.3 percent of households are single men with their children (U.S. Bureau of the Census 2005). These numbers reflect a strong belief about the close link between being a woman and being a mother.

Motherhood Mystique

Gender ideologies, ideas about what it means to be a woman or a man, are closely tied to our ideas about parenting. The idea of being a mother and being a particular kind of mother are strong expectations for women. Beliefs about what makes a good father are quite different and currently seem to be going through some important changes.

Much of contemporary belief about motherhood idealizes mothering and ignores the problems real mothers face in raising children. This is called the motherhood mystique. The motherhood mystique tells us that (Hoffnung 1989; Hays 1999):

1. Women achieve their ultimate fulfillment by becoming mothers. Mothering is supposed to replace all other interests. Fathers, in contrast, are also supposed to be delighted by their children, but men are expected to maintain other interests besides their children.
2. Mothers must be involved in every aspect of their children's lives.
3. Mothers are the best providers for all of the emotional, social, and intellectual needs of their children. Other people, such as fathers or paid caregivers, can provide for these as backup, but the ideal situation is for children to be primarily or solely in the care of their mothers.
4. Mothers should provide a buffer for their children from the worst of the outside world.
5. Intense exclusive devotion of women to their children is good for children.

Does the motherhood mystique affect all women in the same way? African American women's experience with mothering is different from the model for middle-class and upper class white women in the United States. White women have been constrained by the motherhood mystique, but African American women have often been excluded from that role. Historically slavery and Jim Crow and then poverty forced African American women into the labor market where they often had to care for white children (and their parents) while being prevented from spending time with their own children. Mothering has been central to the role of African American women, but it is more likely to be shared with men and other women, or "othermothers." African American women have organized woman-centered networks of blood mothers and othermothers, aunts, grandmothers, neighbors, and friends to take care of children, sometimes for long periods of time and even as informal adoption (Collins 2000).

WORK AND FAMILY IN LATINO AND AFRICAN AMERICAN FAMILIES. Mothering among African American women has also not been experienced as something that holds women back from other activities as it is among upper class and middle-class white women. African American mothers have been part of the paid labor force. Furthermore, they have used their status, connections, and responsibilities as mothers and othermothers as a motivation and facilitator of their community activism (Collins 2000).

Patricia Zavella (1987) found that Chicanas' experience with motherhood and paid labor were also somewhat different from that of white women. She interviewed Chicanas who worked in canneries in California about the tensions between work and family in their lives and how they made the decision to get a job. The women she interviewed had been encouraged and socialized as girls to become full-time housewives and mothers. A typical pattern was to work outside the home in the early days of their marriage and quit when their first child was born. When it became clear that their husbands' paychecks could not adequately support the household, the women returned to work in the cannery. Choosing to work in the cannery, however, was not perceived as an alternative to their responsibilities as wives and mothers but as an extension of that role (Aulette 2007).

Research on white women in the United States (Gerson 1987) presents the two roles, employee and wife and mother, as two opposing possibilities. The women in Zavella's (1987) research saw them as contiguous. The cannery workers fit into another category in which the women seek outside employment, not because they wish to move away from their domestic role, but because they wish to be better wives and mothers. The Chicanas argue that they chose to go to work because of their obligation to their families. When Zavella asked one woman why she had sought work in the cannery, for example, she said, "I did it for my family. We needed the money, why else?" (Zavella 1987, 88). Another woman who was asked this question responded by motioning to her child, who was carrying a large doll, and saying, "That's why I work, for my daughter, so I can give her those things" (Zavella 1987, 134).

Research on employed women often finds that white women choose to work for wages as an alternative to staying home. The Latina women in Zavella's interviews, in contrast, insist that work and family are not two alternatives, but that working for wages is a way of fulfilling their role in their family (Segura 1999).

WORKING MOTHERS AND THE MOMMY WARS. Even though our review of gender in the labor market in chapter 5 showed that nearly all women in the United States are in the paid labor force, the motherhood mystique remains strong among Americans today. However, these goals often do not fit well into real women's lives (Hays 1999). Women from all racial ethnic groups have increasingly entered the paid labor force and now make up nearly half of the employees in the United States. In 1993, the labor force participation of mothers aged twenty-five to fifty-four was 14 percent lower than that of childless women in the same age group. In 2000 it was 10 percent lower and by 2004 it was just 8 percent lower. When women do leave work to take care of their children, most of them return to work sooner than did mothers in generations past (Coontz 2006b).

What happens to those women who combine employment and motherhood? Michelle Budig and Paula England (2001) looked at the "motherhood penalty" on working women. They found that women's income declined by 7 percent for each child they had. At least four possible explanations exist for the association between lower wages and mothering. First, employers may discriminate against mothers. Laws to protect prospective employees from being asked about marital or family status are vague, nonexistent, and ignored. MomsRising. org has launched a program to expose this situation and to call for laws that can protect mothers from being discriminated against.

Even women who can overcome discrimination are forced to make difficult "choices" because of the organization of work. Mothers may choose to trade higher wages for mother-friendly jobs or they may interrupt their job history, making them less competitive in the labor market. Finally, mothers may be more distracted and exhausted at work and therefore less productive.

Budig and England (2001) found that that the lower productivity of mothers may be the most significant factor in the wage penalty. Budig and England argue that we should not, however, conclude that this is a problem of the mothers themselves and is not the responsibility of the businesses that employ them or the larger community. They assert instead that the rest of us are free riders on the employed mothers who are contributing doubly to the community by raising children and working in the paid labor force, even though they are given little support for their efforts.

Regardless of which route they take, women face problems: "What this creates is a no-win situation for a woman of childbearing years. If a woman voluntarily remains childless, some will say that she is cold, heartless and unfulfilled as a woman. If she is a mother who works too hard at her job or career, some will accuse her of neglecting the kids. If she does not work hard enough some will surely place her on the mommy track and her career advancement will be permanently slowed by the claim that her commitment to her children interferes with her workplace efficiency" (Schwartz 1989, 74). "And if she stays home with her children, some will call her unproductive and useless. A woman, in other words can never fully do it right" (Hays 1999, 434).

Hays (1999) calls the tension between the motherhood mystique and our expectations that adults earn their way in our society the "mommy wars." The mommy wars illustrate a dilemma for all women who are required to be good mothers according to the motherhood mystique and responsible citizens who work in the paid workforce. The mommy wars, however, show up most dramatically for low-income women in debates around welfare.

WELFARE MOTHERS. Welfare serves about 5 percent of the population at any given time and accounts for 1 percent of the federal budget and 3 percent of state budgets. Despite these small numbers, welfare is a constant issue of political debate. About two-thirds of the people who receive welfare grants are children under the age of eighteen. The majority of adults who receive welfare grants are single mothers. Over the past several decades, government officials have tried to alter welfare policy in ways that bring those mothers into the labor force (Albelda and Tilly 2000). Two important values exist side by side: the work ethic and the family ethic.

The work ethic says that everyone should contribute to society by participating in the paid labor force—by going to work for wages. Doing the job of mothering is not considered work because mothers do not earn wages. The family ethic and the motherhood mystique, however, say that families are the building block of the nation: Children should be cared for by their mothers, and children require a lot of attention from their mothers. Poor mothers increasingly are required to enter the paid labor force. They cannot live up to the expectations of good mothers when they are forced to spend time away from their children. Furthermore, because the motherhood mystique creates an assumption that children are cared for by mothers best, no alternatives like publicly funded high quality child care are developed. Children whose mothers are not "good" mothers are left without proper or sufficient adult attention. One welfare mother described her dilemma: "I know I can [go to the job search program and go to school], but who would my kids be eating dinner with? Who would put them to bed if I were to work nights and go to school during the day? Even AFDC [welfare] kids need their moms" (Abramowitz 1996, 41). The motherhood mystique has created an impossible dilemma for her and it has created a vacuum of care for her children.

The obvious solution to this problem is to acknowledge that the work women do to raise children is worthy of remuneration. The Sloane Foundation notes that TANF may in fact operate as a form of "paid pregnancy leave" because the United States is unique in the developed world in its lack of any publicly funded paid leave for new parents (Levin-Epstein 2006). Welfare, in fact, may be moving in the opposite direction, providing less and less support for parents. Welfare grants now require more hours of work outside of families from their participants.

TEMPORARY AID TO NEEDY FAMILIES. In 1996, the U.S. federal government replaced the sixty-year-old Aid to Families with Dependent Children (AFDC) program with a new program called TANF (Trattner 1999). TANF included major alterations in existing welfare programs:

1. Welfare is no longer an entitlement. Before TANF, AFDC was guaranteed to eligible Americans. The federal laws demanded that the state governments provide grants for needy families that qualified. The new law is a block grant, which means that the federal government provides a set amount of funds to each state. The states in turn must create their own systems of dispersing the funds. The federal money is now capped at $16.5 billion annually. When the funds run out, states are not legally obligated to provide services, even for families that would otherwise be eligible. Of eligible families, 45 percent to 50 percent are currently not receiving assistance. This proportion is up from 20 percent in 1996 (Fremstad 2004).

2. Time limits were placed on the number of years people are eligible for grants. TANF, a federal law, states that households are eligible for support for only two years at a time and for five years in the lifetime of any adult in the household, regardless of need. Nine states have opted for shorter limits (for example, Arkansas, two years; Florida, four years; and Utah, three years).

3. Legal immigrants are barred from receiving TANF and food stamps. Undocumented immigrants were already barred from receiving any assistance except for emergency medical care or education for their children.
4. Criteria for receiving disability payments are more stringent. About 135,000 disabled children lost welfare assistance with the new laws.
5. The food stamp program was cut by $27 billion. No legal immigrants are allowed to receive food stamps, and able-bodied adults under the age of fifty are restricted from receiving food stamps for more than three months in a three-year period.
6. States are allowed to place caps on the number of people within a household who are considered eligible for support. Twenty-one states, for example, refuse to pay larger sums to larger households or to parents who have children while they are on welfare. This restriction is based on the assumption that limiting welfare will reduce fertility among recipients. Ironically, lower birth rates are associated with more generous welfare programs in countries in western Europe, Scandinavia, and Canada.
7. Poor families can own larger amounts of assets and still be eligible for assistance. Previously, a family could have only a vehicle worth up to $1,500, a burial plot, and $1,000 in other assets. Now families are allowed to save some money for education or buying a home. Most states allow them to own a car valued at up to $5,000 and an additional $2,000 in assets.
8. States are required to assign all individuals in a welfare household to job-training and job-finding activities. People may be exempt because they are ill, incapacitated, aged, under sixteen or in school full time, already working at least thirty hours per week, more than six months pregnant, caring for an ill or incapacitated family member in their home, or caring for a young child. States have much flexibility defining these exemptions. For example, Massachusetts allows parents of children under six years old to be exempt to take care of their children. (Greenberg 1999). Eleven states require work of parents of babies over three months old and six states have no exemptions for parents no matter how young their children are (Rowe and Russell 2004).
9. Medicaid coverage continues for persons who leave welfare to go to work for one year after they leave welfare (N. Walker, Brooks, and Wrightsman 1999).
10. States are not required to provide child care for children of TANF recipients who participate in job support programs (N. Walker, Brooks, and Wrightsman 1999). These changes strengthen the idea that taking care of children is the individual responsibility of parents (who are mostly mothers). They ignore the work involved in raising children. The policy strongly promotes the work ethic and abandons the family ethic. However, poor women continue to be judged by the ideology of the motherhood mystique (Aulette 2007).

Parenting by Fathers

Changing ideas about gender and, therefore, about what mothering and fathering look like, influence men's and women's behavior and their relationships with children. Structural changes, such as the introduction of women into the paid labor force, have also shifted definitions of gender and the links between being a woman and man and being a parent. Changes in work and family are also altering gender for men. When men do the work of mothers, the feelings and experience of men are altered and new ways of being men and being fathers begin to emerge. Fathers who play the role of mother begin to behave and think in feminine ways in other areas of their lives.

Barbara Risman discovered in her research on single parents that doing can become being. Risman (1987) surveyed four kinds of parents: single mothers, single fathers, two-parent households where only the father was in the paid labor force, and two-paycheck families. She measured variation in parenting by looking at three factors: time spent in housework, parent–child intimacy, and overt affection. She found that single fathers, single mothers, and housewives spent more time than married fathers or married employed mothers on housework. Single fathers often did not hire others to do the work for them and therefore were forced to take responsibility for these household tasks.

The second factor, parent–child intimacy, was measured by how often children shared their emotions—sadness, loneliness, anger, happiness, pride—with their parents. Here she found that femininity was the most important predictor of parent–child intimacy. Parents who considered themselves more feminine on a range of issues were more likely to report higher rates of parent–child intimacy. This was true regardless of the sex of the parent. Fathers who were more feminine (according to personality scales) were more likely to report parent–child intimacy than mothers or fathers who were less feminine. Single fathers reported levels of femininity similar to those of employed mothers, suggesting that the activity of parenting may create different expressions of personality, which in turn helps fathers build parent–child intimacy.

The third factor was overt affection, which was measured by the amount of physical contact—hugging, cuddling, wrestling—children had with their parents and the kinds of interactions that took place when the parent and child were alone with each other. This factor was affected by the gender of the parent and the parental role. Mothers, regardless of household type, displayed more overt affection. But parents in two-paycheck families were more likely to express overt affection than single mothers, single fathers, and married fathers in one-paycheck families. In these cases, both single fathers and single mothers reported less overt affection than married mothers in two-paycheck families.

Risman (1987) concludes that the activities of parenting have an important effect on the behavior and personalities of people who do that parenting. Fathers who become the primary parents learn to be capable of caring for their children and they begin to behave similar to women parents; caring fathers become more feminine. Risman argues that changes in gender, especially in the ways men parent, cannot begin with ideas but with action that engages men in the activities of primary caregivers.

MEN BALANCING WORK AND FAMILY. The "mommy wars" may be slowly eroding the ideas that tie women to motherhood and simultaneously tie men to breadwinning and inhibit men's connections to their children. Ideas about a new kind of father are changing more rapidly, however, than the conduct of men. The culture of fatherhood, beliefs about what men should be doing with their children, changed significantly in the last few decades of the twentieth century (LaRossa 2000). A new style of fatherhood emerged: "A good father is an active participant in the details of day-to-day child care. He involves himself in a more expressive and intimate way with his children, and he plays a larger part in the socialization process that his male forebears had long since abandoned to their wives" (Rotundo 1985, 9). This model is more likely to be talked about than to show up in men's behavior. Today, men express a desire to spend more time with their children but their behavior often has not kept pace with their aspirations (Townsend 2002). Nevertheless, men from many walks of life are attempting to renegotiate the terrain of work, family, and gender (Aulette 2007).

When Judith Gerson (1993) interviewed men about this new no-man's land, she found they fell into three categories. One group represented a "stalled revolution" seeking to maintain their breadwinning role. The men in this group prioritized their responsibility to provide for their family. They also expected to have their economic contribution translate into authority in their homes. One man explained:

> There has to be a leader. And the responsibility of the leader is to be fair, not just to boss people, but to make decisions, right or wrong. I provide the money, so it's a success. There has to be a system, and that's ours. . . . My wife loves her lifestyle; she's got it made. She drives a new car, has great clothes, her friends, no responsibilities. What the hell does she need a job for? She's got her freedom. What more could you want? (Gerson 1993, 86)

Another group of men, "the rebels," chose another path, autonomy over parenthood. They, too, prioritized breadwinning but felt they needed to separate themselves from family rather than to translate their workplace activities into relationships of authority with a wife and children. Some of these men had children but had become estranged. Others had chosen not to have children. One man in this group said, "Nobody has a hold on me. I do as I wish, and if tomorrow I don't want to, I don't have to. It's very important that I never feel trapped, locked in. It leads me away from feeling angry, mad, hostile, all those sorts of things" (Gerson 1993, 109).

The third group tried to integrate paid work and family, especially raising children, and became "involved fathers." One man in this group described his experience:

> I thought I was going to be a wild and crazy guy for the rest of my life. I never thought about getting married. But the real me is what's been happening from being married on, not beforehand. Being responsible, getting married, having a child, bringing up a family, becoming responsible for our daughter. This is the real me. (Gerson 1993, 142)

All three of these paths are difficult. Men are faced with the decision of either protecting the privilege of not having to come home to do housework or child care, or accepting arrangements that ease their economic burden or emotional isolation. Men who choose the breadwinner or autonomy route resist family involvement and domestic participation to protect their benefits. However, they also face problems of having to work long hours in the paid labor force to single-handedly support their families, dealing with wives who may not approve of their choices, or being cut off from close relationships altogether (Gerson 1993).

Involved fathers face difficulties, too. First they face the predicament of both spending time making money and spending time with their children. Second, if they want to develop in their careers, they may be asked to travel or to take classes after work, resulting in additional time crunches. Third, even if they are able to balance work and family, they still face the problem of trade-offs of freedom or commitment and their ability to find time for their personal interests in leisure activities, community involvement, or just sleeping late once in a while (Gerson 1993).

Although Gerson found that few men had fully adopted complete equality with their wives, many men were moving in this direction. She cites a *Time* magazine survey that found that 56 percent of a random sample of men said they would give up one-fourth of their salary for more personal and family time. In the same survey, 45 percent said "they would probably refuse a promotion that involved sacrificing hours with their family" (Gerson 1993, 254). In 2007, Monster.com did another survey and found that these kinds of changes are continuing to develop. Of fathers in their study, 70 percent said they would consider being stay-at-home dads if money was not an issue and 71 percent had taken paternity leave when it was offered by their employer (Armour 2007).

THE FATHERHOOD RESPONSIBILITY MOVEMENT. Why is it so difficult to change ideas and practices of fathering? Two competing models for understanding and addressing this issue illustrate Robert Connell's (1995) idea of masculinity politics (Gavanas 2002). Connell writes that masculinity politics are mobilization and struggles where the meaning of masculinity and men's position in gender relations is at issue.

Fatherhood is currently one of the battlegrounds for masculinity politics with two competing wings: the pro-marriage group and the fragile families group. Both of these positions are part of the fatherhood responsibility movement. Both are concerned about what they see as the exclusion of men from the lives of their children. They both cite the growing numbers of children born to single mothers, the high rate of divorce, the large proportion of children awarded to the custody of their mothers, and the lesser role of many men in their children's lives as one of modern life's greatest social evils. Both groups are concerned about children, believe that fathers are essential to children's well-being, and maintain that "the family" is a foundation of society (Gavanas 2002).

The two wings, however, have very different ways of understanding what the roots of the problem are and what should be done to address it. The promarriage group represented by organizations such as the National Fatherhood Initiative. This group stresses the importance of gender differences and what they see as the natural difference between fathers and mothers. For them, marriage cements these two human types, men and women together. They argue, for example, that only men can provide masculine models of risk taking, independence, testing limits, self-regulation, hard but fair discipline, and self-sacrificing protection. Children, therefore, must be raised in heterosexual marriages to satisfy their need for both a mother and a father. They also advocate government intervention to ensure that nuclear families prevail and to promote the proper family values to maintain them (Gavanas 2002). As we saw earlier in this chapter, this group has had some success changing social policy, especially regarding welfare laws, in ways that reflect their promotion of heterosexual families as a key factor in improving fatherhood.

The second faction, the fragile families group, is represented by organizations such as Partners for Fragile Families. This group emphasizes the similarities between women and men and the need for fathers and mothers to work as a team to raise children. Although this group is not antimarriage, they also do not believe that marriage is essential to provide strong, effective platforms for raising children. Most important, they do not believe that marriage can guarantee children will be properly cared for. Their focus is on economic opportunities, especially for fathers (Gavanas 2002).

Fragile families advocates argue that fathers must have jobs with decent wages and benefits to fulfill their role as good fathers and good providers. They believe that women and men need to share in this task of breadwinner, but low-income men, especially low-income men of color, often have not had a chance to play this role because of high unemployment and declining wages. One fragile families advocate explains, "The stereotypical definition of man in this society is to be able to care for his family, to be a provider. And when a man can't be a provider, he does not engage in that process as a full player" (Gavanas 2002, 225). Fragile family advocates look to the government to develop job training, job opportunities, and protection of wages and benefits as the solution to the crisis in fatherhood.

Biology and Parenting

"A woman lawyer is exactly the same as a man lawyer. A woman cop is just the same as a man cop. A pregnant woman is just the same as" (Rothman 1989, 248). The discussion so far has emphasized the social character of parenting and the ways the social construction of gender intersects with our ideas, experience, and behavior regarding parenting. Mothers and fathers are the gendered models of parents and this review of the literature has pointed out how mothering and fathering are different. The underlying argument, however, is that mothers and fathers are not natural categories. Fathers can learn to become better "mothers." Parenting, however, usually also includes a biological component. In nearly every human activity, women and men are the same, or the differences between one woman and another woman are as great as or greater than they are between a woman and a man. Pregnancy and childbirth, however, make some females different from all males. Pregnancy and childbirth also have an especially important connection to parenting.

Both females and males contribute equal amounts of genetic material to a fetus, but it is only the female's body that contributes nine months of gestation and the labor of giving birth. Rothman (1989) argues that this difference is important and should play a role in legal battles, like that in the case of Baby M.

Bill Stern wanted a child who came from his sperm, but his wife Betsy had multiple sclerosis and had been told that bearing a child might worsen her condition. The Sterns decided to hire Mary Beth Whitehead as a surrogate mother to carry Bill's child. For a fee Whitehead allowed herself to be inseminated with Stern's sperm and agreed to give the baby to the Sterns. Whitehead, however, changed her mind after the child was born and hid herself and the baby for four months while the courts deliberated the case.

The court said that the contract between the Sterns and Whitehead was not binding. However, because the child was genetically related to Bill Stern, he had the right to sue for custody. According to the court, he and Whitehead were equally parents. The case was then decided on the basis of who would be a better parent: Stern, a wealthy professional, or Whitehead, a working-class wife and mother. In the proceedings, evidence was presented that Whitehead had been a go-go dancer, had dyed her hair, and had trouble with her husband (Rothman 1989, 24). The court decided in Stern's favor.

According to Rothman (1989) the mother's link to the child was incorrectly reduced to that of the father, thereby making them equal parents. Bill Stern and Mary Beth Whitehead had equal genetic links to Baby M. The baby was a product of equal parts of Stern's and Whitehead's genes. Rothman argues that the fact that Whitehead had the additional connection to the child of being a pregnant and birthing mother, however, should not have been dismissed as irrelevant. The court's decision was based on the assumption that men and women are equal. Even though males and females are not equal in their contribution to reproduction, the factors that make them unequal were ignored. The larger contribution (pregnancy and delivery) made by the mother was made invisible. The one way they are equal—their genetic contribution—was the only criterion acknowledged.

Rothman (1989) demands that a new framework be developed that can capture the need for women to be treated as equal to men while not dismissing the unique character of the relationship between biological mothers and their children. She proposes a policy in which the contribution biological mothers make in pregnancy and childbirth and the contribution fathers, mothers, and others make in caring for children after they are born is factored into equations leading to decisions about questions like custody. Specifically, Rothman suggests that policy should be based on the following rules:

1. Infants belong to their mothers at birth because of the unique nurturant relationship that has existed between them up to that moment; genetic ties will not give parental rights.
2. Adoption can only occur after birth, and the birth mother has six weeks to change her mind.
3. All custody cases after six months will be determined by the amount of care provided by the adult with joint custody if this role is fully shared.
4. There is no such thing as surrogacy under this system. Every woman who bears a child is the mother of the child she bears, with full parental rights regardless of the source of the egg or the sperm (Rothman 1989, 254–60).

Another Kind of Family Caregiving: Elder Care

Taking care of children is only one important place where gender shows up in caregiving in families. Care work refers to the unpaid job of taking care of parents, grandchildren, spouses, and other family members, as well as neighbors and other members of the community. Care work includes practical help like mowing the lawn and fixing meals as well as providing emotional support. Caring means the work is both providing for some need of another and feeling affection and responsibility for the person being provided the care (Calasanti and Slevin 2001). Increasingly, care for older family members, elder care, is a concern in American families.

Most care for older people with disabling and chronic conditions is provided by family members and is called informal care. About 65 percent of informal care is done exclusively by family and friends. Another 30 percent of care is done by family and friends with some paid help. Only 5 percent of care is provided by paid help alone (Blair and Northway 2001).

Care for a broader group of people than immediate family is more common among African Americans than among whites or Hispanics in the United States(Shirey and Summer

2000). In African American families, grandchildren provide for 10 percent of the care for older people (Shirey and Summer 2000). First Nation people are also engaged in broad networks of community members, kin, and extended family in the care of the elderly in First Nation communities (John 1999).

Several changes have occurred in recent decades causing elder care to take a more prominent role in our lives (Singleton 1998).

- Kin networks are becoming more top heavy, with more older family members than younger. For the first time in history, the average married couple has more parents than children.
- Longer life expectancy and lower birthrates are causing shifts to occur in time spent in various family roles. Middle-generation people in the future will spend more years with parents over sixty-five than with children under the age of eighteen.
- Declining birthrates also mean fewer siblings. More people are only children or have only one or two siblings to share the care of their elderly parents.
- Childbearing at later ages means that women are more likely to be simultaneously caring for young children and aging parents.
- High divorce rates eliminate care for elderly by their spouses, shifting the responsibility to children of those older people.
- Lack of attention by the government to the growing needs of families and reduced funding for existing social welfare programs is resulting in insufficient support for care activities (A. Walker 1996).

All of these changes mean more hours spent in caregiving. Caregivers average twenty hours per week devoted to elder care and when there is a health or personal crisis they spend even more time. Caregivers often report conflict with their caregiving and their work schedules. Many must take time off work, rearrange their work schedules, and take unpaid leave. Furthermore, at least some working people must keep their caregiving activities a "secret." University faculty, especially women, with family responsibilities hide their caregiving responsibility to prevent biased, negative career implications. They do not request flex time for fear it will look bad, and they make excuses for absences or missed meetings rather than admitting caregiver responsibilities (Drago and Colbeck 2006).

In addition to the hours, the tasks themselves are not easy. Care work includes bathing, dressing, feeding, toileting, providing transportation, helping with medication, and doing household tasks. In many sick people's homes, nonprofessional women also use high-tech equipment to deliver treatments for acute and chronic conditions and to treat systemic infection and cancer. They supervise exercise, give mechanical relief to patients with breathing disorders, feed by tubes those unable to take food orally or digest normally, give intramuscular injections and more tricky intravenous injections, and monitor patients after antibiotic and chemotherapy treatments (Glazer 1990). This kind of difficult work may be especially present in care for racial ethnic groups, such as Latinos who have higher health risks for certain diseases such as diabetes that require special kinds of care and cause people to develop disabilities at higher rates earlier in life (Aranda and Knight 1997).

Caregiving, like parenting, is marked by gender differences. Nearly all of the work that is done for ill or dependent elderly people in households is done by women. Only among

Asian Americans do we find men and women providing care at about the same rate (National Alliance for Caregiving and AARP 1997). According to the Bureau of the Census, 75 percent of the 7 million Americans who provide informal unpaid care are women. Women devote about thirty-five years of their lives to caring for children, grandchildren, and parents (Adams, Nawrocki, and Coleman 1999). People who provide care for these groups are called the "sandwich generation" because they are sandwiched between caring for older parents and raising their children (Blair and Northway 2001).

Many caregivers, however, are women who are older themselves. The average age of a care worker is forty-six, but 12 percent are over sixty-five and those in this older category provide the most care for those who are most in need (Calasanti and Slevin 2001). For example, 60 percent of those who care for older people are wives caring for older disabled husbands; 73 percent of these wives are over sixty-five (Cantor 1994).

A spouse is the most likely person to provide care for a husband or wife. Because men typically marry women who are younger than they and because women on average live longer than men, women are more likely to be giving care than receiving care. When a husband or wife is not available for taking care of a person, however, gender shows up in another form. Adult daughters are next in line and then daughters-in-law and sisters, rather than sons or brothers (Calasanti and Slevin 2001).

Abel (1986) argues that women take on this responsibility for a number of reasons. First, external sources push them into caring for their relatives. These include a dominant ideology that says that women are natural caregivers, and lower pay for women so that their economic contributions from paid work are more disposable. In addition, women caregivers themselves believe that sacrifices they make in caring for their parents are necessary and honorable (Aronson 1992).

The organization of society, especially of the government, however, also plays a role in answering the question of why women do so much care work. One woman care worker summed it up: "Who else is going to do it?" (Aronson 1992). The government assumes that individual families, and particularly women in individual families, will take care of the work and make little effort to help bring down the costs of providing paid care workers or providing care for those who need it (Calasanti and Slevin 2001). In fact, changes in health care have increased the amount of unpaid care work needed when patients are sent home early from hospitals (Glazer 1990). Today, unpaid care work would cost about $196 billion if caregivers were paid. This is much more than the present bill of $32 billion for home health care and $83 billion for nursing home care (Shirey and Summer 2000). The work is valuable but it is not publicly valued. Like housework as described in chapter 8, care work is invisible and it is highly gendered. It is women's work.

GENDERED STYLES OF CARE WORK. Despite the fact that care work is identified with femininity and it is done mostly by women, many men participate as well. How do women and men approach the work differently and what consequences do their activities have for the caregiver's well-being? When women and men care workers are asked about their experience, women are more likely than men to report anxiety, depression, physical strain, health problems, and lower life satisfaction (Shirey and Summer 2000).

Three explanations have been given for this discrepancy in the health effects on women and men caregivers. First, men may have a different style and approach to caregiving. Men's style of caregiving has been called more managerial because they separate caring for and caring about. They are able to separate themselves emotionally from the work, allowing them to provide care but also to take time off and maintain outside interests. Women caring for demented partners, in contrast, grieve the lost relationship between themselves and their husband. They do not seem to be comforted by their caring activities, as men are. The difference is not in the care they provide, but rather in the feelings they have about their caring work (Rose and Bruce 1995).

Second, men elicit more recognition for the care work they do because it is more "unusual." Family and friends see a man caring for his wife or parents as honorable because he is not only providing care, he is also stepping outside expectations about men and caregiving.

Third, men seem to have larger support networks. For example, sons giving care get more help from their spouses than daughters do. In addition, men, who are often financially better off, are more able to purchase support (Calasanti and Slevin 2001).

GRANDPARENTS AND CARE WORK. older people do not just receive care, they often provide care. Of all children in the United States, 5.5 percent (4 million households) live in households maintained by a grandparent, and these numbers are rapidly growing (Park 2005). Table 7–2 shows the distribution of grandparent-headed households. Table 7–2 provides information on three social factors: gender, race ethnicity, and poverty. It also provides information on whether the parents are also present in the household; that is, whether it is a three-generation household. Table 7–2 indicates that grandparents who are heads of households and are raising grandchildren are likely to be women, poor, and black (Bryson and Casper 1999).

The first line of numbers tells us that a household with both grandparents and at least one parent is most common (34 percent) and a household with a grandmother and a parent is second most common (29 percent). The second line of numbers tells us that the households

TABLE 7–2 Grandparent-Maintained Households, 2001

	No Parents Present		Some Parents Present (Skipped Generation)		
	Both Grandparents	Only Grandmothers	Both Grandparents	Only Grandmother	Only Grandfather
% of all grandparent-maintained households					
	17%	14%	34%	29%	6%
% poor					
	14%	57%	10%	27%	20%
Race ethnicity of grandmother					
White	63%	28%	57%	39%	64%
Black	19	54	16	45	20
Hispanic	15	16	21	13	15
Other	3	3	7	4	2

SOURCE: U.S. Census, Survey of Income and Program Participants 2001.

raising grandchildren that are most likely to be poor are those that have only a grandmother and her grandchildren (57 percent are poor). The households with the most adults—both grandparents and at least one parent—are least likely to be poor (10 percent).

The third set of numbers shows us the race ethnicity of the different types of households. White grandmothers are the majority in all but one of the types because white people are the majority of the total population in the United States. Black grandmothers are the majority (54 percent) of one household type—grandmother alone with grandchildren.

Little research has been done on the experience of grandfathers in households raising grandchildren. One qualitative study (Bullock 2005) found that grandfathers faced many difficulties in trying to care for their grandchildren. Although they are not as likely to be as poor as grandmothers are, many did have financial difficulties. Most important, though, the men were not prepared to take care of the children and, therefore, faced other problems. Some of the men spoke of feeling that the task of parenting was one about which they had little choice. One man said, "I don't feel I'm ready to take care of a small child this late in life, but we didn't have any choice. My wife said, we [were] all the child had left. What in the world would have happened to the child if we didn't do?" (Bullock 2005, 4).

The grandfathers also spoke about feeling that they had not learned the skills of child care and did not feel capable of many of the tasks. One man explained:

> I would want to do more as a parent, but I never had to cook, clean, and never had to pick up after the children. So, now I can't just go in the kitchen and make a meal if she is hungry. I don't wash clothes either. Sometimes, I feel like helping more, but I don't really know what to do. Nobody is trying to help me figure how I could do this better. I mean the grandparenting. (Bullock 2005, 5)

The gender histories of the men meant they had divided labor in their families in ways that did not prepare them for caregiving as grandparents.

Care work is highly stratified by gender across age groups. Care work is also stratified by social class and nationality. One option wealthier families from wealthier nations have chosen to help alleviate the care gap is to hire care workers from the Global South. However, this choice is not without problems, especially for the women who work as nannies in the United States and Europe. Box 7–3 discusses this issue.

BALANCING WORK AND FAMILY

What do young men and women want today? Research on young Americans finds they are keenly aware of the obstacles to integrating work and family life in an egalitarian way, but men and women alike wish to forge a lifelong partnership that combines committed work with devoted parenting. Amy describes her ideal work family situation: "I want a 50–50 relationship, where we both have the potential of doing everything—both of us working and dealing with kids. With regard to career, if neither has flexibility, then one of us will have to sacrifice for one period, and the other for another." Michael shares her view saying:

> I don't want the '50s type of marriage, where I come home and she's cooking. She doesn't have to cook; I like to cook. I want her to have a career of her own. I want to

Box 7–3 CARE WORK AND THE SERVANTS OF GLOBALIZATION:
GLOBAL NANNIES

Globalization has created a work world that crosses international boundaries. Companies and jobs move from wealthy nations to poorer ones to reduce the company payroll. Factories manufacture products in one country that are sold in another. Service workers provide information and assistance via phones and the Internet. However, some jobs cannot take place from far away. Care work must take place where the person who needs the care lives. This has created a huge migration of care workers from the Global South to the North (UNFPA 2006). As a result, for the first time in history, half of all migrants are women. In some places, such as the Philippines, Sri Lanka, and Thailand, women are the majority, and their average age is twenty-nine, which means that many of them are mothers (Bunting 2005). Rhacel Parrenas (2001) interviewed women who came from the Philippines to work as nannies for families in Rome.

Some of the Filipina women had been gone from home for as long as sixteen years and sent back as much as $400 a month. They are proud of the economic support they have provided, talking about how their pay allowed not only their children but their nieces and nephews to attend school. However, the price they pay is great. One woman explained, "What saddens me most about my situation is that during the formative years of their childhood, I was not there for them. That is the time when children really need their mother and I was not there for them" (Parrenas 2001, 87). Another's loss was felt even more deeply. She said, "The first two years I felt like I was going crazy. I would catch myself gazing at nothing, thinking about my baby. My youngest, you have to understand, I left when he was only two months old" (Parrenas 2001, 89).

One way the women coped with the difficulties of their jobs and the pain of missing their children was to transfer their love to the children they were caring for. One woman described her situation:

> Even though it paid well, you are swimming in the amount of your work. Even while you are ironing the clothes, they can still call you to do the kitchen to wash the plates. It was also very depressing. The only thing you can do is give all your love to the child. In my absence from my children, the most I could do with my situation is give all my love to that child. (Parrenas 2001, 86)

be able to set my goals, and she can do what she wants, too, because we both have this economic base and the attitude to do it. That's what marriage is about. (Gerson 2007, 3)

As the men and women in the interviews described their ideal work–family arrangements, they also were aware that their aspirations might quickly run into rigid, time-demanding jobs and a dearth of child-care or family-leave options. In response, they have developed fallback strategies as insurance in the all-too-likely event that their egalitarian ideals prove out of reach (Gerson 2007).

The second-best strategies are not only different for women and men; they are at odds with each other. Women say that if they cannot find a supportive, egalitarian partnership, they prefer individual autonomy over becoming dependent on a husband in a traditional marriage. Most men, in contrast, say that if they cannot have an equal balance between work and parenting, they will fall back on a neotraditional arrangement that allows them to get married and have children and to put their own work first, relying on their partner to take care of their family life (Gerson 2007).

Rachel illustrates women's backup plan with her fall-back strategy: "I'm not afraid of being alone, but I am afraid of being with somebody who's a jerk. I want to be under the right circumstances, with the right person. . . . I can spend the rest of my life on my own, as long as I have my sisters and my friends, I'm OK" (Gerson 2007, 5–6).

Josh, like many of the men, has a different backup plan. He says that if he and his partner are unable to share work and family, he will choose to divide it up along gendered lines, with his wife caring for the children while he provides financially for them. He says:

> All things being equal, it [caretaking] should be shared. It may sound sexist, but if somebody's going to be the breadwinner, it's going to be me. First of all, I make a better salary, and I feel the need to work, and I just think the child really needs the mother more than the father at a young age. (Gerson 2007, 6)

Josh's plan B may reveal gender ideas in the United States that are lagging behind other nations. A poll was conducted in several nations in 1983 or 1992 and then again in 2002 asking people if they agreed with the statement: "The father of the family must be the master in his own home." In Canada 42 percent agreed with the statement in 1983 but by 2002 only 17 percent did. The numbers also dropped dramatically in Europe. In the United States, however, the numbers rose from 42 percent in 1992 to 48 percent in 2002 (Pearson 2002).

International Comparisons on Family Support Programs

Finding solutions to the problem of balancing work and family would help both women and men in families. It would also reduce the gender gap between women and men. Alan Walker (1996) argues that teaching caregivers to better cope with the stresses they face is important but can only partly solve the problems of balancing work and family. More important, he argues, we need to create public solutions by altering social institutions.

Although this solution sounds monumental and even utopian, in some nations, just these kinds of structural reforms have been implemented. For example, the work week in the Netherlands was reduced to thirty-eight hours in the 1980s and thirty-six hours in some industries like health care in the 1990s. All full-time workers in Germany and Sweden (as well as some other nations) receive five to six weeks of paid vacation every year. Paid maternity leaves of at least fourteen weeks are available to all women in the European Union. Some countries, like Sweden, provide employed parents an additional paid leave for sixty days to care for care a sick child or other close relative (Applebaum et al. 2002).

Table 7–3 shows the leave policies of several nations. (Go to the website listed as the source for a complete list.) Out of 173 countries studied, 168 countries offer guaranteed leave with income to women in connection with childbirth; ninety-eight of these countries offer fourteen or more weeks of paid leave. The numbers illustrate the kinds of policies that are characteristic of the European Union. For example, Germany and France are the leaders in providing support for family care. It also shows that some nations that are relatively poor, such as Mexico, Cameroon, and Pakistan, provide paid leave for mothers at the same time that wealthy nations such as the United States provide no paid leave. Although in a number of countries, many women work in the informal sector, where these government guarantees do not always apply, the fact remains that the United States guarantees no paid leave for mothers in any segment of the workforce. This leaves the United States, the wealthiest nation in the world, in the company of only four other nations: Lesotho, Liberia, Papua New Guinea, and Swaziland (Heymann, Earle, and Hayes 2007).

Finally Table 7–3 indicates that many nations distinguish among maternity leave, paternity leave, and parental leave. Sixty-five countries ensure that fathers have a right to paid parental leave; thirty-one of these countries offer fourteen or more weeks of paid leave. Once again the United States fails fathers, guaranteeing men neither paid paternity nor paid parental leave (Coltrane 2007). Neglecting fathers has two effects. First, it hurts men who would like to spend more time with their children. In addition, it hurts women by defining them as solely responsible for taking time for paid work for family care.

Sweden is an example of a country that has consciously tried to encourage families to divide family care in a more gender-equitable manner through their parental, maternity, and paternity leave policies. Swedish families receive twelve months of paid parental leave. Only one parent can take the time off at one time. If the father takes at least one month of the time, the total time is extended to thirteen months of paid leave for the household. Parents can take the time off by the hour rather than by the day. For example, a parent could work six hours a day and then take the other two hours as paid leave (Applebaum et al. 2002).

Besides these kinds of alterations of the social institution of government, individual businesses have also changed in Sweden. The pay that parents receive while caring for children amounts to 80 percent of their regular pay, up to a cap. Because men make more money on average in Sweden (as they do all over the world) it is more advantageous to have the mother rather than the father stay home. However, some companies add to the government's check to equal 80 percent of all workers' pay, which erases this disadvantage and allows men to take parental leave (Applebaum et al. 2002).

Applebaum and her colleagues (2002) summarize what they believe to be six cornerstones to solving the work–care dilemma:

- Hours of work legislation: Shorter work week including caps on hours required of salaried workers
- Flex time at the discretion of the employee
- Equal pay for women and for part-time workers
- Shared cost of care for workers' families
- Access to health care and family leave for all workers regardless of workplace
- Reform of income security protections improving unemployment benefits, pensions, and supports for single parents

TABLE 7–3 Parental Leave Policies Around the World

Country	Type and Duration of Leave	% Wage Replaced
Afghanistan	3 months maternity	100%
Australia	1 year	Unpaid
Austria	16 weeks	100%
	+30 months	Child care allowance
Belgium	15 weeks maternity	75–80%
	+3 months parental	Flat rate
Cameroon	14 weeks maternity	100%
Canada	17 weeks	55%
	35 weeks for each parent	55%
China	3 months	100%
Chile	18 weeks	100%
Czech	28 weeks maternity	69%
	3 years parental leave	Unpaid
Denmark	18 weeks maternity	90%
	2 weeks paternity	100%
	10 weeks parental	60%
	52 weeks for child up to 8	60%
Finland	18 weeks maternity	65%
	18 days paternity	Flat rate
	26 weeks paternal	Flat rate
France	16 weeks maternity	100%

DIVORCE
The Gendered Economics of Divorce

Divorce laws vary from one nation to another and even within nations, such as the United States, where divorce laws are different in every state. Some forms dominate, however. This section reviews a few of the most common kinds of divorce laws: no-fault in the United States, no-fault in South Africa, covenant divorce laws in the United States, repudiation laws in conservative Muslim nations, and reformed repudiation laws in more liberal Muslim nations, such as Tanzania. All of these variations both reflect and shape gender arrangements.

Divorce is a common experience in the United States today. From the late 1950s to the early 1980s the divorce rate rose significantly and then fell a little and leveled off. Although the rate has been flat for more than two decades now, it remains high and it is estimated that about half of the most recent marriages will end in divorce (Cherlin 1992). Divorce is a key issue in the expression and reproduction of gender in family life. Divorce is experienced differently by women and men, and divorce causes further distinctions between women and men, particularly in terms of finances.

One way men and women experience divorce differently is that women are two to three times more likely to initiate divorce. Between two-thirds and three-quarters of divorces are initiated by wives.

A second way women and men experience divorce differently is in regard to social stigmatization. Although both women and men are still stigmatized for divorcing, the reasons for

Country	Type and Duration of Leave	% Wage Replaced
Germany	14 weeks maternity	100%
	2 years parental	Flat rate
	1 year parental	Unpaid
Greece	17 weeks maternity	50%
	3.5 months/parent	Unpaid
India	12 weeks	100%
Italy	5 months maternity	80%
	10 months parental	30%
Japan	14 weeks	60%
Mexico	12 weeks maternity	100%
Norway	52 weeks parental	80%
Pakistan	12 weeks	100%
Poland	16 weeks maternity	100%
Russia	28 weeks	100%
	1 year	Flat rate
	(minimum wage)	
South Africa	26 weeks	45%
Turkey	12 weeks maternity	66 2/3%
United Kingdom	6 weeks maternity	90%
	12 weeks maternity	Flat rate
United States	12 weeks parental	Unpaid

SOURCE: Kamerman 2004.

which they are stigmatized are different. Divorce has become more common and polls show that people are more tolerant of divorce and divorced people than they were years ago. For example in the 1960s, the majority of Americans believed that people with children should stay together rather than divorce "for the sake of the children." By the 1980s these opinions had changed and 80 percent no longer support this belief (Kosmin and Lachman, 1993), but stigmatizing still exists. The divorced are no longer thought to be sinners or criminals. Divorce, however, continues to set people apart and can represent a mark against them.

Whether those who divorce are stigmatized depends on the way people perceive the specific conditions of the divorce, and these specific conditions vary by gender. Men who have affairs before the divorce are stigmatized as "cavalier homewreckers" (Gerstel 1987, 186). For women, the key question is whether they have young children. Women with young children are "bad divorcees" when they do not sacrifice their own needs and feelings to try to keep the marriage together.

A third way divorce is experienced differently by men and women is in regard to resulting finances. Women face a 30 percent decline in their incomes after a divorce, whereas men on average see a 15 percent increase (Petersen 1996). Despite the economic difficulties, many women say they still feel more satisfied with their financial situation after the divorce because they feel more in charge, able to make their own decisions, and relieved they do not have to account to their husbands for their choices (Ahrons 1994). Nevertheless the decline is significant. Thirty–nine percent of single women with children live below the poverty level.

The picture for men and divorce is not quite as clear cut (P. McManus and DiPrete 2001). Some researchers have found that men generally seem to see their economic situation improve after divorce (Smock 1994; Petersen 1996; Bianchi, Subahya, and Kahn 1999). Some argue that although many men benefit, most men do not. For example, African American men do not benefit as much as white men. Men who lived in households where their wives contributed more to the household income or men who retain custody of their children after the divorce often see declines in their economic situation. Men as a group, however, never see their finances decline as sharply as women do. Divorced women are likely to be poorer than they were when they were married and they are likely to be poorer than their ex-husbands.

What underlies the different economic effect of divorce on women and men? Divorce law in itself in the United States is gender neutral. The laws tell the courts to treat women and men the same. Divorce, however, takes place in a gendered society. Marriage is gendered, divorce court decisions are gendered, and especially the labor market is gendered.

In many households, marriage has a different effect on women's and men's earning capacity. One of the most important investments people make is in their careers and in their ability to earn money. Married couples tend to make these decisions in a way that diminishes wives' earning capacity and enhances husbands' earning capacity (Buehler 1995; Maume 2006).

For example, a couple may decide that one spouse will work while the other obtains an education. Couples may spend money on a special license or membership in a professional organization. They may choose to relocate for one of them to accept a better job, or to stay in an area so that one person can build seniority, a professional practice, or a pension. If these kinds of decisions are made to improve the earning ability of one partner, they enhance the economic standing of the whole household as long as they stay together. After a divorce, however, this investment is usually not considered part of the property to be divided equally, but rather the property of the individual to take with him or her from the marriage. These kinds of decisions are frequently made in ways that favor the husband, partly, at least, because the "payoff" for the investment in a man is greater than it is for a woman. Education, on average, helps everyone to raise his or her wages, but men still make more money than women at all education levels. So as a couple a husband and wife's wisest economic decision is to get the husband educated and into the labor market quickly as possible and then see to the woman's education.

This strategy, however, does not work well for the woman if the couple parts ways. If wives invest less in their earning capacity, they may leave a marriage with less ability to support themselves. Some wives, of course, do not allow marriage to stand in the way of gaining an education or building a career., But even these wives leave marriage at a disadvantage compared to their husbands because education and labor market participation do not necessarily result in equal pay for women.

Look at Table 6–3 in chapter 6 and notice that women with various amounts of education earn less than men at those same levels. In fact, the table shows that women with a college degree earn only a little more than men with a high school diploma. Pay scales vary by race ethnicity and education but in all comparisons, women earn less than men do. Although divorce laws are gender neutral, gender inequality in the labor market means that women who divorce and stop pooling their income with a husband receive less than half of the household's income.

Alimony is money the court requires one spouse to pay to support another after a divorce. Historically, alimony was a payment a husband was required to make when separating from or divorcing a wife. Theoretically, alimony was a way to overcome the inequity between women and men in the labor market. Divorced women were assumed to be unable to earn as much money as their husbands, and alimony was a method of closing the gap between their incomes. In reality, however, alimony was always rare and the payments were small.

Alimony is now called spousal support. Many people still believe that most women receive spousal support when they divorce. As in the past, however, only about 14 percent are awarded this kind of support in the United States today (Stetson 1997). Black women are even less likely to receive spousal support (Shelton and Deen 2001).

Another feature of the gendered context in which divorce occurs is the division of property in the divorce proceedings. The gender neutrality of the divorce laws requires that property is divided equally between the two spouses. What is defined as property, however, may not include some of the most important assets a couple owns. For example, pensions and education are not usually considered assets to be divided and they go with the individual who has been granted the degree or obtained the pension through his or her work.

Probably the most significant factor in the division of households and property in divorces is the question of child custody. Mothers are much more likely to retain custody of minor children. The property is divided down the middle but it is awarded to two different-sized groups. One half goes to the husband and one half goes to the wife and children.

Child support was designed to help even out financial responsibility between the parents but the awards are not sufficient and support often goes unpaid. Sixty-one percent of divorced single mothers who live with minor children were awarded child support in 2000. Of that 61 percent, 22 percent had received none of the award and another 78 percent had received only partial payment (U.S. Bureau of the Census 2000). Noncustodial mothers are equally bad about keeping up with child support when fathers have custody of children, but 83 percent of children are placed in the custody of their mothers after divorce (Grall 2007).

The mean amount received per year was $3,660 for custodial mothers and $3,491 for custodial fathers (Grall 2007). This amounts to less than half the amount required for child care costs alone per year. Children, of course, also entail many other expenses besides child care: food, clothing, health care, education, and recreational expenses (Kurz 1995). In addition, child support usually ends at eighteen, although in many families, children are far from financially independent at that age.

Challenges of Divorce for Men

When parents divorce in the United States, nearly all children (83 percent) are placed in the custody of their mothers. We have seen how that creates economic difficulties for many women. However, men who are not custodial parents also face problems when they divorce. Divorce often elicits or exacerbates anger with their ex-wives, but many men want to maintain relationships with their children despite their feelings about their ex-wives. Terry Arendell (1995) found that men had three ways of trying to cope with the situation.

One group she called traditionalists. They had limited contact with their wives and continued to define them as the enemy. These men were especially distressed about their loss of control over their wives and children that resulted from the divorce. Their main way of responding was to disengage, avoiding contact or responsibility for their ex-wives or children. One traditionalist father explained how he had come to this response:

I finally decided that I was putting too much into this divorce war with my ex-wife. We've played this game for over four years. So I pulled out.... She didn't know when to quit. Someday if my son wants to get to know me he can find me. My daughter, she could care less. She's been totally brainwashed by [the former wife]. (Arendell 1995, 145)

Neotraditionalists, the second type, had some of the same animosity toward their wives but wanted to maintain contact with their children and felt that collaboration with their ex was possible. They wanted to stay close to their children while avoiding their wives. They were especially concerned about being the masculine role model for their children and about sustaining a meaningful relationship with their children, rather than being just a weekend visitor:

She [the former wife] complains about my teaching them to shoot and hunt; she says it's dangerous and unnecessary. "Too macho," she says. But what's really bugging her is that she can't stand it that I have something to offer them that she can't. They're boys. I understand that. She doesn't. They need this sort of input from me. She can't give them that. (Arendell 1995, 173)

Innovators, the third type, focused on their own parental responsibility for their children rather than their rights as fathers. They did not find it easy to develop cooperation with their wives, but they were willing to be very flexible, rearranging schedules, and finding options to create parenting partnerships with their ex-wives. They were more able to set aside their anger at their wives and to dismiss conventional views of masculinity than the other two types of divorced fathers. An innovative father said:

Our relationship is amicable, if that's the proper word. I would describe it that way, an amicable relationship. I don't particularly go out of my way to talk to her. I have my moments and sometimes I really want to talk to her. Other times I don't want to talk to her at all and I just leave. I don't want to be there. We're both concerned about the children. We went together to see the principal. We also went to see the school counselor. Or if my son has a soccer game, we'll be together. (Arendell 1995, 190)

Comparing Divorce Laws Among Nations

SOUTH AFRICAN DIVORCE LAWS. In 1994, South Africa successfully toppled Apartheid government and created a new constitution. A central feature of the constitution, laws, and policies of the new government was the commitment to equality. The opening scenario illustrates one set of family laws regarding customary marriage that were changed in South Africa. Changes in the divorce laws also reflect this commitment. South African divorce laws are similar to the American version of no-fault. Either party (and since South Africa allows gay marriage the parties might be a man and a woman or both women or men) can file for a divorce. The reasons given for divorce can be traditional ones of fault divorce, such as abuse or abandonment, but they can also include no-fault or irreconcilable differences.

South African law, however, differs in some important ways from the American model. Although the South African law, like the U.S. law, is gender-blind, it does not treat two spouses as necessarily equal. Divorce is granted in a gender-blind manner but property division is done with an eye to acknowledging inequality and coming up with a solution that is fair but not necessarily equal. For example, if one spouse walks away from the divorce with a better job and a better education, that person is granted a lesser share of the property. In addition, South African divorce courts consider child custody along with the divorce. In the United States these are two separate decisions. The South African court takes into consideration who has physical custody of the children and how that might affect household finances differently for the two divorcing parties.

Covenant divorce in the United States. In the 1990s, antidivorce rights activists in the United States won some legal ground in their promotion of the covenant marriage to replace no-fault divorce. Louisiana, Arizona, and Arkansas have enacted covenant marriage legislation. Fifteen states have considered the laws and rejected them and they are now being considered in about twenty other states (National Conference of State Legislatures 2005). Couples who choose a covenant marriage must receive premarital counseling and sign an affidavit that confirms their lifetime commitment to one another, as well as their understanding of the limited grounds under which they may receive a divorce. They cannot divorce except in extreme cases specified by the law. Regardless of the circumstances, covenant couples must also agree to go through counseling to work through problems before a divorce can be obtained.

The covenant laws state that those who marry under the covenant option can divorce only for the following reasons: adultery by the other spouse, commission of a felony that results in imprisonment or the death penalty, abandonment by the other spouse for one year or more, physical or sexual abuse of the spouse or child by either partner, living separately from the spouse for two or more years, habitual alcohol or drug abuse, and cruel treatment or severe ill treatment. Irreconcilable differences are not acceptable reasons for divorce in a covenant marriage.

Only a few hundred newlyweds have chosen covenant marriage so far, but several thousand couples who are already married signed covenant agreements. A number of churches have also declared their congregations to be "no-fault-free zones" and are refusing to marry people who do not choose the covenant option (Aulette 2007).

Repudiation in muslim nations. Like covenant divorce in conservative Christian cultures, repudiation in conservative Muslim communities is shaped by religious beliefs. Repudiation is the unilateral prerogative for a man to terminate a marriage at will without judicial intervention under Islamic law (*shari'a*). For example, a Muslim Egyptian man has a unilateral and unconditional right to divorce with little legal proceedings (*talaq*). He simply needs to repudiate his wife by saying "you are divorced" three times and register the divorce within thirty days with a religious notary to make it official. A repudiated woman has to observe a waiting period (*'idda*) not exceeding one year, during which she is not allowed to marry another man. An Egyptian woman who is repudiated by her husband is entitled to the deferred dowry, "maintenance" (*nafaqa*) during the waiting period, and compensation (*mut'a*) of at least two years maintenance (with consideration for the husband's means, the circumstances of the divorce, and the length of marriage) (Human Rights Watch 2004).

Egyptian law is a reformed version of repudiation. In other nations, under the most conservative repudiation law, a woman's rights to divorce are quite different. If she wishes to divorce, she must go to a religious judge and prove to him that her husband harmed her. The procedure takes years and judges usually rule against the wife. Even if she successfully divorces she receives no continued economic support. Under the new procedure in Egypt, the wife must wait six months if she has children or three months if she does not while the judge tries to reconcile the partners. Then the judge must grant the divorce, but the woman has to return all money, property, and gifts that she received during the marriage, and cannot receive alimony (*Off Our Backs* 2000).

In Egypt, recent changes have loosened these restrictions—a wife no longer has to prove she has been harmed—but Egyptian women still face difficulties obtaining a divorce. Egyptian women seeking divorce today often have to make a difficult "choice" of forfeiting their financial rights to avoid burdensome and uncertain court proceedings. If they ask their spouses to divorce them, the process is shortened but the women lose any right to property accumulated during the marriage or alimony after (Human Rights Watch 2004).

Repudiation is common in many Arab Muslim nations, although recently laws have changed to eliminate repudiation in several nations. Repudiation laws were changed, for example, in Tunisia after they were criticized and contested in court and eventually replaced by no-fault laws. The critics of repudiation laws cited four problems:

1. Repudiation laws do not require court procedure.
2. Only men have the right to divorce.
3. After repudiation, men have no financial responsibility for their wives.
4. The process is too easy for men.

In the 1980s, divorce law was changed in Tunisia and other Muslim nations have followed suit. The current divorce laws in Tunisia allow for either the man or woman to request a divorce. The person who requests the divorce must compensate the nonconsenting person. The law also has special protections for women. A nonconsenting woman must be provided with alimony for life by her divorcing husband. In addition, child custody laws have changed. Children used to be placed in the custody of their mothers until puberty and then transferred to their fathers. Today, child custody is decided on the basis of the best interest of the child. The new laws are better than the old ones were for women because women now can obtain a divorce on the same grounds and through the same process as men and they can be paid alimony. Some disadvantages remain, however, such as the stigma associated with divorce and the compensation women must pay if they initiate the divorce.

Making Comparisons

All of these variations of divorce both reflect and reinforce gender. Divorce law is an important vehicle by which the government shapes gender. In the review of the no-fault laws in the United States, we see that the laws attempt to ignore gender but because divorce takes place in a highly gendered social context, the end result of divorce exacerbates differences, especially economic differences between women and men.

Repudiation laws reflect a sharp gender distinction between women and men. The laws are explicitly gendered and the results exacerbate the inequality between women and men by keeping women in unhappy marriages and impoverishing women whose husbands choose to divorce them. The U.S. laws include more gender equality than do the repudiation laws, but neither provides for gender equity. In both cases, divorce leaves women in difficult economic and social situations after a divorce, no matter how much an improvement the end of the marriage may bring to their lives in other ways.

South Africa appears to attempt to use divorce law as a way to promote both gender equality and gender equity. The laws do not distinguish between women and men; that is, they reflect gender equality. Men and women, and spouses (regardless of gender) are equal before the law. However, the laws provide for protecting all of the parties by (1) incorporating child custody into the divorce proceedings, and (2) protecting the more vulnerable people in the divorcing household. This is an example of promoting gender equity.

These contrasts illustrate the distinction between two important ideas: gender equality and gender equity. What exactly are these terms? The World Health Organization (WHO 2001, 9) provides these two definitions:

> Gender equality means equal treatment of women and men in laws and policies, and equal access to resources and services within families, communities and society at large. Gender equity means fairness and justice in the distribution of benefits and responsibilities between women and men. It often requires women-specific programmes and policies to end existing inequalities.

REFERENCES

Abel, Emily. 1986. Adult daughters and care for the elderly. *Feminist Studies* 12(3): 479–93.

Abramowitz, Mimi. 1996. *Under attack and fighting back: Women and welfare in the U.S.* New York: Monthly Review Press.

Adams, Stephanie, Heather Nawrocki, and Barbara Coleman. 1999. *Women and long-term care.* Fact Sheet No. 77. Washington, DC: AARP Public Policy Institute.

Agbayani-Siewert, Pauline and Linda Revilla. 1995. Filipino Americans. In P. Min (ed.), Asian Amerians: Contemporary trends and issues (pp. 95–133). Thousand Okas, CA: Sage.

Ahrons, Constance. 1994. *The good divorce.* New York: HarperCollins.

Albelda, Randy, and Chris Tilly. 2000. It's a family affair: Women, poverty and welfare. In *Reconstructing gender: A multicultural anthology.* 2nd edition, ed. E. Disch, 363–69. Mountain View, CA: Mayfield.

Aldous, J., G. Mulligan, and T. Biarnason. 1998. Fathering over time: What makes the difference? *Journal of Marriage and the Family* 60:809–20.

Applebaum, Eileen, Thomas Bailey, Peter Berg, and Arne Kalleberg. 2002. *Share work, valued care: New norms for organizing market work and unpaid care work.* Washington, DC: Economic Policy Institute.

Aranda, Marie, and Bob Knight. 1997. The influence of ethnicity and culture on the caregiver stress and coping process: A sociocultural review and analysis. *The Gerontologist* 37 (3): 342–54.

Arendell, Terry. 1995. *Fathers and divorce.* Thousand Oaks, CA: Sage.

Armour, Stephanie. 2007. Workplace tensions rise as dads seek family time. *USA Today*, December 10.

Aronson, Jane. 1992. Women's sense of responsibility for the care of old people: "But who else is going to do it?" *Gender and Society* 6 (1): 8–29.

Aulette, Judy. 2007. *Changing American families.* 2nd ed. Boston: Allyn & Bacon.

Bianchi, Suzanne, Kekha Subahya, and Joan Kahn. 1999. The gender gap in the economic well-being of nonresident fathers and custodial mothers. *Demography* 36:173–84.

Blackstone, William. 1803. *Commentaries on the laws of England.* London: Strahan.

Blair, Cornelia, and Helene Northway. 2001. *Women: New roles in society.* Detroit, MI: Gale Group.

Bozalek, Vivian. 2004. Recognition, resources, responsibilities: Using students' stories of family to renew the South African social work curriculum. Doctoral dissertation, University of Ultrecht, Netherlands.

Bryson, Ken, and Lynne Casper. 1999. *Co-resident grandparents and grandchildren.* Washington, DC: U.S. Bureau of the Census.

Budig, Michelle, and Paula England. 2001. The wage penalty for motherhood. *American Sociological Review* 66:204–25.

Buehler, Cheryl. 1995. Divorce law in the United States. *Marriage and Family Review* 21:99–120.

Bullock, Karen. 2005. Grandfathers and the impact of raising grandchildren. *Journal of Sociology and Social Welfare.* 32(1): 43–59.

Bunting, Madeleine. 2005. Importing our carers adds up to emotional imperialism. *The Guardian,* October 24.

Calasanti, Toni, and Kathleen Slevin. 2001. *Gender, social inequalities and aging.* Walnut Creek, CA: AltaMira Press.

Cantor, Muriel. 1994. Family care-giving: Social care. In *Family care giving,* ed. M. Cantor, 1–9. San Francisco: American Society on Aging.

Cherlin, Andrew. 1992. *Marriage, divorce, remarriage.* Cambridge, MA: Harvard University Press.

Chernus, Ira. 2006. Why are they afraid to call it marriage? CommonDreams.org. http://www.commondreams.org/views06/1027–22.htm.

Collins, Patricia Hill. 2000. The meaning of motherhood in black culture and black mother–daughter relationships. In *Gender through the prism of difference.* 2nd edition, ed. M. Baca Zinn, P. Hondagneu-Sotelo, and M. Messner, 268–78. Boston: Allyn & Bacon.

Coltrane, Scott. 2007. Marriage, work and family in men's lives. *American Prospect,* March 5.

Connell, Robert. 1995. *Masculinities.* Cambridge, UK: Polity Press.

Coontz, Stephanie. 2004. The world historical transformation of marriage. *Journal of Marriage and Family* 66:974–79.

——— . 2006a. Just which "traditional" marriage should we defend? Press release from Council on Contemporary Families.

——— . 2006b. Myth of the opt-out mom: The number of US mothers who also work outside the home is actually on the rise. *Christian Science Monitor,* March 30.

Coontz, Stephanie, and Nancy Folbre. 2002. Marriage, poverty and public policy: A discussion paper from the Council on Contemporary Families. Presented at the fifth annual CCF Conference, New York.

Drago, Robert, and Carol Colbeck. 2006. Care givers hide actions to enhance careers. Paper presented at the Annual Meetings of the American Association for the Advancement of Science, St. Louis, MO.

Federal Interagency Forum on Aging-Related Statistics. 2004. *Older Americans 2004: Key Indicators of Well-Being.* Washington, DC: U.S. Government Printing Office

Ferdinand, Pamela. 2000. Gays achieve breakthrough in Vermont. *Washington Post,* March 17.

Fremstad, Shawn. 2004. *Recent welfare reform research findings.* Washington, DC: Center on Budget and Policy Priorities. www.centeronbudget.org/1–30–04wel.htm.

Ganahl, Jane. 2004. Single minded women in Asia are starting to say "I don't." *San Francisco Chronicle,* November 14.

Gavanas, A. 2002. The Fatherhood responsibility movement. In *Making men into fathers,* ed. B. Hobson, 213–44. New York: Cambridge University Press.

Gerson, Judith. 1987. How women choose between employment and family: A developmental perspective. In *Families and work*, ed. N. Gerstel and H. Gross, 270–88. Philadelphia: Temple University Press.

——. 1993. *No man's land: Men's changing commitment to family and work*. New York: Basic Books.

——. 2007. What do women and men want? Many of the same things. *American Prospect*, March 5.

Gerstel, Naomi. 1987. Divorce and stigma. *Social Problems* 34 (2): 172–86.

Glazer, Nona. 1990. The home as workshop: Women as amateur nurses and medical care providers. *Gender and Society* 4 (4): 479–99.

Grall, Timothy. 2007. *Custodial mothers and fathers and their child support:2005*. Washington, DC: U.S. Census Bureau.

Greenberg, Mark. 1999. Welfare restructuring and working poor family policy. In *Hard labor*, ed. J. Handler and L. White, 24–47. New York: Sharpe.

Hardin, Blaine. 2007. Learn to be nice to your wife, or pay the price. *Washington Post*, November 26.

Hays, Sharon. 1999. The mommy wars. In *Family in transition*. 10th edition, ed. A. Skolnick and J. Skolnick, 432–48. New York: Addison Wesley.

Heymann, Jody, Alison Earle, and Jeffrey Hayes. 2007. *The work, family, and equity index: How does the United States measure up?* Montreal, Canada: Project on Global Working Families.

Hoffnung, Michelle. 1989. Motherhood: Contemporary conflict for women. In *Women: A feminist perspective*, ed. J. Freeman, 147–75. Mountain View, CA: Mayfield.

Human Rights Watch. 2004. Divorced from justice. HRW Publications 16(8). New York: Human Rights Watch.

John, Robert. 1999. Aging among American Indians: Income security, health and social support networks. In *Full color aging: Facts, goals and recommendation for Americas' diverse elders*, ed. T. Miles, 65–91. Washington, DC: The Gerontological Society of America.

Johnson, Glen. 2005. Massachusetts sets gay marriage convention date. *Findlaw Legal News and Commentary*, August 25.

Kamerman, Sheila. 2004. *Table 1.11: Maternity and parental leaves, 1999–2002*. New York: Clearing House on International Developments in Child, Youth and Family Policies, Columbia University. http://www.childpolicyintl.org/maternity.html.

Kosmin, Barry, and Seymour Lachman. 1993. *One nation under god: Religion in contemporary American society*. New York: Crown.

Krauss, Clifford. 2005. Gay marriage is extended nationwide in Canada. *New York Times*, June 29.

Kurz, Demie. 1995. *For richer or poorer*. New York: Routledge.

LaFraniere, Sharon. 2005. AIDS and custom leave African families nothing. *New York Times*, February 18.

LaRossa, Ralph. 2000. Fatherhood and social change. In *Gender through the prism of difference*. 2nd edition, ed. M. Baca Zinn, P. Hondagneu-Sotelo, and M. Messner, 298–309. Boston: Allyn & Bacon.

Levin-Epstein, Jody. 2006. *Getting punched: The work and family clock*. Washington, DC: CLASP.

Lin, J. 1991. Satisfaction and conflict in Asian correspondence marriages. *Focus* 5:1–2.

Maume, David. 2006. Gender differences in restricting work efforts because of family responsibilities. *Journal of Marriage and Family* 68 (4: 859–869.

McManus, Michael. 2006. Millions a year for marriage. *Washington Times*, March 19. http://washingtontimes.com/commentary/20060318–102756–7627r.htm.

McManus, Patricia, and Thomas DiPrete. 2001. Losers and winners: The financial consequences of separation and divorce for men. *American Sociological Review* 66:246–68.

Mink, Gwendolyn. 2006. Ending single motherhood. In *The promise of welfare reform*, ed. K. Kilty and E. Segal, 155–215. New York: Haworth.

Mochizuki, K. 1987. I think Oreintal women are just great. *International Examiner*, 7, May 13.

National Alliance for Caregiving and AARP. 1997. *Caregiving in the U.S.* www.caregiving.org.

National Center for Children in Poverty (NCCP). 2005. Many children with married parents are low income. Fact sheets. http://nccp.org/fact.html.

National Conference of State Legislatures. 2005. *Covenant marriage.* http://www.ncsl.org/programs/cyf/marriage.htm#covmar.

Off Our Backs. 2000. Egypt divorce laws change. March.

Orbuch, Terri, and S. Eyster. 1997. The division of household labor among black couples and white couples. *Social Forces* 76:301–32.

Orbuch, Terri, and Susan Timmer. 2001. Differences in his marriage and her marriage. In *Gender mosaics,* ed. D. Vannoy, 155–64. Los Angeles: Roxbury.

Park, Hwa-Ok. 2005. Grandmothers raising grandchildren. *Focus* 24 (1): 19–27.

Parrenas, Rhacel. 2001. *Servants of globalization: Women, migration and domestic work.* Chicago: Stanford University Press.

Pearson, Patricia. 2002. "Father" means more than household master. *USA Today,* June 13.

Petersen, Richardson. 1996. A re-evaluation of the economic consequences of divorce. *American Sociological Review* 61:528–36.

Retherford, Robert, and Haohiro Ogawa. 2005. *Japan's baby bust: Causes, implications, and policy responses.* Population and Health Series No. 118. Honolulu, HI: East West Working Papers.

Risman, Barbara. 1987. Intimate relationships from a microstructural perspective: Men and women who mother. *Gender and Society* 1 (1): 6–32.

Rose, Hillary, and Errollyn Bruce. 1995. Mutual care but differential esteem: Caring between older couples. In *Connecting gender & aging: A sociological approach,* ed. S. Arber and J. Ginn, 114–28. Buckingham, UK: Open University Press.

Rothman, Barbara Katz. 1989. *Recreating motherhood.* New York: Norton.

Rotundo, E. 1985. American fatherhood: A historical perspective. *American Behavioral Scientist* 29:7–25.

Rowe, Gretchen, and Victoria Russell. 2004. *The welfare rules databook.* Washington, DC: Urban Institute.

Schwartz, Felice. 1989. Management, women and the new facts of life. *Harvard Business Review* 67:65–76.

Segura, Denise. 1999. Inside the worlds of Chicana and Mexican immigrant women. In *Feminist philosophies,* ed. J. Kourna et al, 180–88. Upper Saddle River, NJ: Prentice Hall.

Shelton, Beth Anne, and Rebecca Deen. 2001. Divorce trends and effects for women and men. In *Gender mosaics,* ed. D. Vannoy, 216–26. Los Angeles: Roxbury.

Shirey, Lee, and Laura Summer. 2000. Caregiving: Helping the elderly with activity limitations. *Challenges for the twenty-first century: Chronic and disabling conditions,* no. 7. Washington, DC: National Academy on an Aging Society.

Singleton, Judy. 1998. The impact of family caregiving to the elderly on the American workplace: Who is affected and what is being done? In *Challenges for work and family in the twenty first century,* ed. D. Vannoy and P. Dubeck, 201–16. New York: Aldine de Gruyter.

Smock, Pamela. 1994. Gender and short-run economic consequences of marital disruption. *Social Forces* 73:243–62.

Solot, Dorian, and Marshall Miller. 2002. *Let them eat wedding rings.* New York: Alternatives to Marriage Project.

Stetson, Dorothy. 1997. *Women's rights in the U.S: Policy debates and gender roles.* New York: Garland.

Tolentina, Roland. 1996. Bodies, letters, catalogs: Filipinas in transnational space. *Social Text* 48(fall): 49–76.

Townsend, Nicholas. 2002. *The package deal.* Philadelphia: Temple University Press.

Trattner, William. 1999. *From poor law to welfare state.* New York: Free Press.

UNFPA. 2006. *State of the world population, 2006.* New York: United Nations.

U.S. Bureau of the Census.2000. *Poverty in the U.S.* Washington, DC: U.S. Government Printing Office.

—— 2001. Survey of Income and Program Participants. *Washington, DC: Government Printing Office.*

—— . 2004. *Population division: Current population survey, 2004.* Washington, DC: U.S. Government Printing Office.

—— . 2005. Families and living arrangements. *Current Population Reports.* http://www.census.gov/ population/www/socdemo/hh-fam.html.

Walker, Alan. 1996. The relationship between the family and the state in the case of older people. In *Aging for the twenty-first century: Readings in social gerontology,* ed. J. Quadagno and D. Street, 269–85. New York: St. Martin's.Walker, Nancy, Catherine Brooks, and Lawrence Wrightsman. 1999. *Children's rights in the United States.* Thousand Oaks, CA: Sage.

Weitzman, Lenore. 1981. *The marriage contract.* New York: Free Press.

World Health Organization. 2001. *Transforming health systems: Gender and rights in reproductive health.* New York: World Health Organization.

Zavella, Patricia. 1987. *Women's work and Chicano families.* Ithaca, NY: Cornell University Press.

8

VIOLENCE

INHUMANITIES AND HUMAN RIGHTS

Violence against women is the greatest human rights scandal of our times.

(Amnesty International, http://web.amnesty.org/actforwomen/scandal-index-eng)

Three years ago, here in London, I was a guest at the local Quaker meeting house where a panel of eight women from Israel had been invited to speak. Having spent so much of my life covering "men's" activities in the Middle East—investment and trade, oil and politics as well as outright war—I thought it about time I took a look at what women were doing. The panel included four Palestinians and four Israelis, all from divergent backgrounds: a poet, sociologist, historian, social worker, Christian, Muslim and Jew.

There were some quite direct, pointed questions from the audience about where truth, justice and progress lay. Would Israelis be better off without the occupation of the West Bank and Gaza? Would Palestinians agree to end suicide bombings? The answers varied, both among the Palestinian and Jewish women, and amongst themselves, whatever their nationality.

But when the moderator put the final question, "What, in your opinion, do you think is the worst problem you face?" the answer was surprising. One would have expected the Palestinian women to say, "the occupation of the West Bank and Gaza by Israel since 1967." For the Israeli women, one would have thought the answer would be "security, a right to live in peace with Israel's neighbors and, above all, an end to suicide bombings."

Surprise, surprise. One by one, the eight women stood up, faced the 70 or so in the audience of mostly women and declared: "The militarization of our men." For the Palestinians, seeing their sons subjected to the cannon-fodder rhetoric of ignorant sheikhs, the test of manhood their teen sons were exposed to when it came to throwing stones, or the death and injury of their fathers, sons and brothers were the key points. For the Israeli women, the brutalization of the men they must live with, their sons, brothers and spouses in the Israeli Defense Forces, was the main point. And, unlike the Palestinians, Israelis are required to serve in the

Israeli Defense Forces unless they can prove they are conscientious objectors or members of certain Jewish religious denominations.   (P. A. Smith 2006)

These two quotes summarize much of our experience and thinking on violence and gender. The first from Amnesty International informs us that women experience violence most often as victims. Women's experience, although widespread and profound, is a human rights scandal because it is so pervasive, destructive, and especially because it exposes the treatment of so many women as less than human.

The second quote tells us about the links between masculinity and violence. The voices are women's, but the focus of their concern is men. The mothers, wives, sisters, witnesses, and victims of violent men tell us that social forces demand that men behave in violent ways to be counted as men. The men and women they hurt are victims of masculinity defined in this way. The men who are the perpetrators are also victims because their humanity is diminished when they behave in "manly" ways required by their leaders, their governments, and their societies.

THE GENDERED CONTINUUM OF VIOLENCE

Perhaps you know of the global epidemic of violence against women that extends from so-called private and personal violence between intimate partners, acquaintances, and strangers to sex trafficking, militarism, and wartime rape, whose main victims now are civilian women and children. The Palestinian and Israeli women quoted by P. A. Smith (2006) in the opening scenario see connections between the violence experienced by women in their private lives and these global horrors. In this chapter we examine the various points along the gendered continuum of violence and the threads that connect them. We explore how the force and violence required to sustain inequalities link the multiple sites of violence we visit here: street harassment and community-based violence, rape and domestic violence, state-sponsored violence in prisons, militarization and militarism, and sexual violence in conflict zones around the world.

Riane Eisler (1987, xix) argues that gender constitutes all human societies, affecting all our institutions, our values, and now, in the nuclear age, our survival. According to her "cultural transformation theory," a *dominator model* structures hierarchical societies, which depend on threat and violence to survive. Diverse societies, in her view, share this underlying commonality. Hitler's Germany, contemporary Iran, the Japan of the Samurai, and the Aztecs of Meso-America are all "rigidly male dominant...have a generally hierarchic and authoritarian social structure and a high degree of social violence, particularly warfare." On the other hand, a different social arrangement—a *partnership model*—organizes societies that are more sexually equalitarian, peaceful, less hierarchical, and less authoritarian. There have been such societies in human history. Today they include the marginalized preliterate !Kung of Botswana, Angola, and Namibia, and contemporary Scandinavian nations.

In this chapter, we survey the gender relations within and between dominator societies. We explore the epidemic of violence against women, connecting it to hierarchies of race, class, sexuality, nation, as well as gender. We also look at the visitations of violence on and by men to show that men, too, suffer from the systems of violence. For example, bullying and hazing are forms of gendered violence by boys and men against other boys and men, and violent sports are almost exclusively men's domain (see chapter 11). Feminist men's studies scholars argue that bullying and violent sports help to construct and maintain aggressive masculinity. Subordinated men, like women, have been targets of masculine aggression, showing that gender alone cannot explain violence. Gay men are victimized for their sexuality and men of color for their race ethnicity. Black women and Latinas are more at risk for violence than white women, and working-class women are less safe than women of the middle and upper classes. The intersecting relations of race ethnicity, class, and sexuality shape gendered power relations and the violence that supports these relations.

The first half of this chapter treats what is often seen as personal or private violence. It reviews studies of street harassment, rape and sexual assault, and domestic violence and introduces some of the work of scholars and activists engaged in challenging these forms of violence. The second half of the chapter explores violence perpetrated or allowed by the state against women and men, including gendered violence in men's prisons and violence against women in conflict zones around the world. A final section introduces readers to the work of international bodies involved in ending violence against women.

SOME STATISTICS ON VIOLENCE

Violence is everywhere, from private homes and city streets to sports arenas, prisons, and workplaces, on national borders, and within states locked in battle with insurgents. Intimate partner violence—rape and domestic violence—is widespread in the United States and around the world and women bear the brunt of it. The U.S. Department of Justice estimates that every ninety seconds a person over twelve is sexually assaulted. Almost 90 percent of the victims are girls and women and 99 percent of the perpetrators are men and boys. Table 8–1 shows that from 1993 to 2004 about 97 percent of women experiencing nonfatal intimate partner violence were victimized by a man and about 2 percent reported that the offender was another woman. By contrast, about 84 percent of men experiencing nonfatal intimate partner violence were victimized by a woman and about 12 percent of men reported that the offender was another man. The Department of Justice estimates that there are more than 5 million cases of domestic violence every year, most of them assaults by husbands, sons, boyfriends, acquaintances, and brothers against women (see Table 8–1). Despite the tenacious "myth of the Black rapist" (which we discussed in chapter 4), domestic violence and rape are primarily intraracial.

Violence between intimates crosses class and income levels, but violence is more likely to occur between poor rather than between more wealthy couples. Persons living in households with lower annual incomes have the highest rates of violence compared with persons in households with other income levels (see Figure 8–1). These statistics may reflect the greater ease of escape from violent situations enjoyed by women of some means. However, in every income category, women are at greater risk than are men.

In the United States approximately 1.5 million women are raped or physically assaulted by their boyfriends or husbands each year, and nearly 25 percent of all women have been raped or physically attacked at some point in their lives. Forty percent of women who are assaulted in this way are seriously injured. In contrast, 7.5 percent of the surveyed men said they were raped or physically assaulted by a wife or girlfriend at some time in their lives. Lesbian couples report less

TABLE 8–1 Average Annual Percentage of Nonfatal Intimate Partner Victimizations by Gender of Victim and Offender, 1993–2004

	Gender of Offender			
Gender of Victim	Total	Men	Women	Both
Woman	100%	96.9%	2.1%	0.9%
Man	100	12.0	83.9	4.1

SOURCE: U.S. Department of Justice. Office of Justice Programs. Bureau of Justice Statistics. Intimate Partner Violence in the U.S. Offender Characteristics.

FIGURE 8–1 Intimate partner violence by income level.

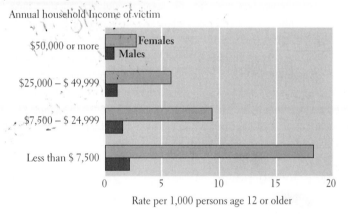

Average annual nonfatal intimate partner victimization rate by income and gender, 1993–2004

Annual household Income of victim

Rate per 1,000 persons age 12 or older

SOURCE : Bureau of Justice Statistics. Intimate Partner Violence in the U.S., Victim Characteristics. http://www.ojp. usdoj.gov/bjs/intimate/victims.htm.

partner violence (11 percent) than heterosexual (21 percent) or gay men couples (23 percent). The figures may be inexact, but it is clear that from birth to death, in times of peace as well as war, women face high levels of violence in their everyday lives and men are often engaged in violence against women and men (U.S. Department of Justice 2005).

Intimate partner violence against women is part of a systematic pattern of gender dominance and control, but the existence of lesbian and gay battering demonstrates that violence is related to power over others, and is not simply a matter of men's power over women. However, violence is overwhelmingly men's violence.

According to the Chicago Foundation for Women (2007), we are in the midst of a global epidemic of violence against women and girls that involves child abuse, street harassment, stalking, bullying, sexual assault, domestic violence, human trafficking, the sex trade, and

Read

Box 8–1 THE SCOPE OF GENDERED VIOLENCE: UNITED STATES AND CANADA

According to the Chicago Foundation for Women (www.whatwillittake.org), we are in the midst of a global epidemic of violence against women and girls that involves child abuse, street harassment, stalking, bullying, sexual assault, domestic violence, human trafficking, the sex trade, and elder abuse. The facts and statistics that follow are only the tip of the iceberg. Most violence is unreported. Gender and sexual violence should be seen for what it is, a form of global terrorism.

DOMESTIC VIOLENCE

- Domestic violence is primarily a crime against women. An estimated 5.3 million cases of domestic violence occur among U.S. women eighteen and older each year, resulting in nearly 2 million injuries.
- In Canada, spousal violence makes up one-fourth of all violent crimes and two-thirds of all family violence cases. The rate of spousal violence has been on the increase. Eighty-five percent of spousal violence victims are female. In Canada, two-thirds of domestic violence crimes are committed by a spouse or ex-spouse (YWCA Canada, 2004.) http://www.ywcacanada.ca/public_eng/advocacy/index.cfm?Heading1_link=focal_issues&Heading2_link=violence_against_women&Heading3_link=violence_against_women_statistics&Heading4_link=violence_against_women_statistics&Hlinks=3<cu:>).
- On the average, more than three women in the U.S. are killed each day by an intimate partner. In 2000, 1247 women were killed by a husband or boyfriend, while 440 men were killed by an intimate partner. (Bureau of Justice Statistics Crime Data Brief, 2003).
- Young women between sixteen and twenty-four are most vulnerable to domestic violence, with the highest per capita rates of nonfatal intimate partner violence (YWCA Fact Sheet). In Canada, women aged twenty-five to thirty-four accounted for the highest rates of spousal violence.
- Black women age twenty to twenty-four experience higher rates of domestic violence than white women of the same age, twenty-nine acts of domestic violence per 1,000 black women versus twenty per 1,000 white women. Both black and white women experience domestic violence at the same rate in every other age group (Tjaden, P. and N. Thoennes, 2000. Publication No. NCJ 181867).
- Similar to African American women, Hispanic/Latinas have higher rates of incarceration than European American women, increasing the likelihood that they will be victims of sexual violence. (Amnesty International USA. 1997).
- In a survey by the U.S. Conference of Mayors, 56 percent of cities surveyed cited domestic violence as a primary cause of homelessness. Barriers to locating safe and

affordable housing for domestic violence victims and their children include lack of available low-income housing in the United States and, often because of perpetrator's actions, poor landlord references, poor credit history, and lack of financial resources.

In heterosexual relationships, 95 percent of all victims are female and 95 percent of all perpetrators are male. In same-sex relationships, domestic violence happens with the same statistical frequency as in heterosexual relationships. According to the National Coalition of Anti-Violence Programs web site, the prevalence of domestic violence in LGBT ¨relationships was similar to that in heterosexual couples. Gay and bisexual men experience abuse in intimate partner relationships at a rate of 2 in 5, one comparable to that of domestic violence experienced by heterosexual women (Greenwood, 2002). Among lesbians, slightly more than half of 1,109 respondents had been abused by a woman partner in their lifetime (Gwat-Yong Lie and S. Gentlewarrier 1991, 15).

- As many as 324,000 women each year experience domestic violence during their pregnancy. Fifty to 70 percent of men who abuse women also abuse children.

RAPE

- Women of all races ethnicities experience rape. Thirty-four percent of Native American and Alaskan Native women, 24.4 percent of mixed race women, 18.8 percent of black women, 17.7 percent of white women, and 6.8 percent of Asian-Pacific Islander women report that they experienced a completed or attempted rape at some point during their lifetime (Department of Health and Human Services, 2006).
- Black women have the highest rates of sexual assault per 1,000 persons. Approximately 40 percent of Black women report coercive contact of a sexual nature by age eighteen. Most rapes and sexual assaults against women are not reported to police. Between 1992 and 2000, only 36 percent of rapes, 34 percent of attempted rapes, and 26 percent of sexual assaults were reported to police.
- About 44 percent of rape victims are under age eighteen, and 80 percent are under age thirty.
- Each year in the United States, college women are at risk of various forms of violence including rape, sexual assault, harassment, and stalking. It is estimated that 4.9 percent of college women experience a completed or attempted rape in each calendar year.
- Increasingly, teenage girls find themselves involved in violent relationships. Between 12 percent and 35 percent of teenagers have experienced some form

of violence in a dating relationship. According to the Youth Risk Behavior Surveillance Survey (YRBSS), a national survey of high school students, 7.7 percent of students had been forced to have sexual intercourse when they did not want to.

- Rates of rape have declined precipitously since the 1990s. However, the FBI estimates that only 37 percent of all rapes are reported to the police. U.S. Justice Department statistics are even lower, with estimates of only 26 percent of all rapes or attempted rapes being reported to law enforcement officials.

STALKING

- Stalking is the most prevalent form of violence against women and the strongest indicator of extreme violence. Women from all backgrounds, regardless of race, ethnicity, class background, sexual orientation, marital status, and age are stalked each year in the United States, and one out of every twelve are stalked during their lifetimes.

IMMIGRANT WOMEN

- Immigrant women are at higher risk of being victims of domestic violence due to their sex, race, and immigration status. Immigrant women face barriers in accessing social services and leaving their partners, who may threaten to report the woman's immigrant status to employers or the immigration authorities, leading to deportation and separation from their children.

WELFARE RECIPIENTS AND LOW-INCOME WOMEN

- Poverty leaves women at higher risk of being physically assaulted by an intimate partner than other women with higher socioeconomic status. As many as 60 percent of women receiving welfare have been subjected to domestic violence as adults, compared with 22 percent of women in the general population.

SOURCES: U.S. Department of Justice, Bureau of Justice Statistics (http://www.ojp.usdoj.gov/bjs/cvict .htm); Amnesty International (http://web.amnesty.org/actforwomen/domestic-index-eng); Chicago Foundation for Women (www.whatwillittake.org).

elder abuse. Violence is one of the leading causes of death worldwide for people aged fifteen to forty. The statistics in Box 8–1 are only the tip of the iceberg. Most violence goes unreported.

STREET HARASSMENT: A GEOGRAPHY OF FEAR

Safe public space is a precondition for democratic community and a platform for launching popular movements. Black churches in the South functioned as safe spaces that allowed activists to stage the civil rights movement. The student and antiwar movements of the 1960s found safe spaces in universities. Other movements have been connected to the public spaces within which they emerged and grew: Kent State, Tiananmen Square, Stonewall, Selma, and Seattle (Smithsimon 2000). Chapter 10 shows how claiming public space is a central feature of women's peace activism.

Democracy is nurtured not only by political mobilization in public space, but also by the everyday sociability that is the foundation of public interaction and trust. Fear of crime, of strangers, and of dangerous streets destroys trust and, in the view of many, divests citizens of their ability to assemble and to voice their political concerns. In post-9/11 America, fear of others is magnified by militarized policing and increasing surveillance in the public arena (Parenti 1999). Distrust, fear, and surveillance provide the context within which street harassment and street violence are situated.

When some people think about the threat of violence, they bring to mind menacing strangers in public spaces. Although statistics tell a different story—violence is much more likely to occur between people who know each other—we routinely encounter stories of random crime and violence in the news and by word of mouth. Women and girls are warned to take precautions while walking in certain parts of the city or riding on public transportation. Parents and friends, as well as police and city governments, offer safety tips to their constituencies and publics.

If you are a woman reading this book, you are probably familiar with these messages and are vigilant when you are out and about, especially after dark. If you are a man reading this, you may know that women are counseled to be careful in public, but perhaps have not felt particularly threatened yourself. Nonetheless, women's precautions echo a familiar narrative in contemporary American culture and in sociology: the decline of civic engagement and trust among Americans (Putnam 2000).

The fear of crime and of public violence is gendered. In North America and Europe, street harassment falls near the "merely annoying" pole of the continuum of gendered violence, an irritating but perhaps less threatening fact of public life for women. A study of street harassers in Berlin, Los Angeles, Rome, and Vienna turned up the interesting fact that men in those cities usually only harass women during the day. Why? Wouldn't harassment at night be more intimidating? The authors suggest that is precisely the reason why men refrain from nighttime catcalls and other annoying encounters with women in public. Such encounters would be "too effective. The woman, not merely annoyed or unnerved but genuinely alarmed, might well be driven to an 'extreme' response (such as calling for help) that the good citizen would not like to have to explain" (Benard and Schlaffer 1993). What do men say about this behavior? Apparently many harassers do not really think about it. Benard and Schlaffer's interviews with and observations of sixty street harassers revealed that the idea that women disliked this behavior never occurred to most of them. Instead, most saw their

Box 8–2 USHA B N: PATRIARCHY'S BRUTAL BACKLASH: ACID ATTACKS

Kerosene, poison and now, acid—the new weapon against women. Haseena, a 19-year-old girl from a middle-class family was attacked with acid in 1999 by her boss because she turned down his marriage proposal and refused to continue working in his office. Two liters of pure sulphuric acid were poured on her. In 2000, Noorjahan, a mother of two children who ran a tea cart in front of a factory, was attacked by the factory owner's son. In 2001, Dr. Mahalakshmi, a doctor in Mysore, was attacked with acid by her landlord; later in the same year, Shanthi, a teacher in Mysore, was attacked by her husband. The list goes on.

In the last seven years, sixty-two women in Karnataka have been victims of acid attacks. These are the cases that have been reported or registered according to a recent Campaign and Struggle Against Acid Attacks on Women (CSAAW) report. There could be many more in actuality. The list of sixty-two includes women of all ages, castes, and class backgrounds. All of them were independent women who asserted themselves against coercion, pressure, and violence. All were attacked by someone they knew—acquaintances aspiring to be lovers, husbands, bosses, landlords. It's clear that acid attacks are being used as weapons in the brutal backlash of patriarchy towards women who show any form of agency.

Acid attacks are extremely difficult to treat: The acid seeps into the layers of the skin to cause long-term infection and corrosion. Victims often need multiple complicated and expensive surgeries. Not everyone can afford such treatments. So far, most families have sold their houses and other property to meet the expenses. To make matters worse, only some super specialty hospitals in Bangalore are equipped to treat acid attack victims. Government hospitals (including the burns ward in Victoria Hospital in Bangalore)

harassment as an entertaining sport and believed women enjoyed the attention. One forty-five-year-old construction worker "portrayed himself as a kind of benefactor to womanhood and claimed to specialize in older and less attractive women to whom, he was sure, his display of sexual interest was certain to be a highlight in an otherwise drab and joyless existence." Twenty percent of the men only harassed women when they were with friends. The authors suggest that this fact shows that harassing women is a means for men to bond with each other, to show solidarity and "joint power" (Benard and Schlaffer 1993, 443).

Although some consider it trivial, street harassment of women is hostile and intimidating and tells women that the streets belong to men. Likewise, our public parks and recreation areas are not always welcoming to unescorted women. Three decades ago, the women's movement took up the ways women were discouraged from engaging in sports and outdoor recreation and lobbied for the passage of Title IX legislation guaranteeing funding for women's athletics. However, women's feelings of vulnerability in the outdoors and the fear of lurking have no facilities whatsoever to adequately handle such cases. Some doctors are not even aware of basic first aid measures such as flushing acid out of the body immediately after the attack. Many women do not survive because they're unable to access proper medical care after the attack. And one cannot begin to articulate the emotional trauma of the woman and her family.

There is no law in our country that recognizes acid attack as a crime. Cases are registered under IPC section 326 (causing grievous injury) or IPC section 307 (attempt to murder). There is no law that looks at these attacks as gendered crime. In many cases, the accused person gets out on bail despite these sections being non-bailable and continues to threaten the victim. Police investigations invariably begin with questions on the sexual history and purity of the woman. Most cases that have reached the courts have faced procedural delays. Survivors, who are already coping with so much, have to contend with legal harassment as well. Campaign and Struggle Against Acid Attacks on Women (CSAAW), a coalition of women's rights groups, media activists, and students and concerned citizens, was started in 2003. The group has been working to help victims reclaim their lives as well as demanding that the government respond to their needs. These are some of their broad demands:

- Control over availability of acid as acid is easily available.
- A specific law that recognizes acid attack as gendered crime against women.
- Proper medical facilities and medical aid for victims. All the government hospitals should be able to provide proper treatment to acid victims.
- Necessary rehabilitation for the survivors.

SOURCE: Ultra Violet: Patriarchy's Brutal Backlash: Acid Attacks. Posted on September 27, 2007 by Usha B N http://youngfeminists.wordpress.com/2007/09/27/patrarchys-brutal-backlash-acid-attacks

strangers still deny them free use of recreational sites. Wesely and Gaarder (2004) interviewed 128 women, mainly white and college educated, who used South Mountain Park in Phoenix, Arizona, the largest urban park in the United States. They found that women who used the park believed it prudent to develop strategies to keep themselves safe. They told friends where they were going, varied the times they visited the park, exercised in different locations within the park, and only visited the park when accompanied by companions or a dog. These precautions may not be sufficient, as one woman explained:

Last year, I was hiking on an off-trail…with a friend. As we were hiking, we heard male voices and saw a tent and saw some smoke. A little later we stopped to soak our feet in a creek bed and heard a shotgun sound real close. Then we heard hysterical laughter and a lot of obscenities. We quickly got moving and changed directions. We switched trails and went back another way. That's why I don't hike alone anymore.

I like to go with someone else. . . . I'd like to get up on Sunday morning and just go out hiking by myself, but I don't. (Wesely and Gaarder 2004, 656)

Women avoided the park at night and carried cell phones for safety. One commented that she feared that if she used the less traveled trails, she would be "raped, murdered, and left where no one will find me." The women said that catcalls and other forms of harassment ("when guys walk by and turn around and look at you") made them feel less safe.

Street harassment may be a worldwide phenomenon. Women in India face "Eve-teasing" when in public. After ten years abroad, Kavitha Rao (2006) returned to India and to its particular violations against women on the street. She wrote:

Being back in India brings back memories. I suddenly recall an overnight bus journey when I was 18. I spent the entire night shrinking in my seat to avoid the furtive groping of a man behind me. I remember the elderly man who sat next to me on another bus trip, moving his thigh ever nearer. Like most other victims, I have never complained. I ignore the comments, move out of range or change my seat. Why? Because I was—and am—afraid.

According to Rao, Indian men still harass women—and girls as young as nine—although most back down when confronted. However, there are enough exceptions to make women fearful. In 2005, a woman in the town of Lucknow was shot and killed for protesting the harassment of her daughter-in-law. Sometimes harassers stalk women or throw acid at them (see Box 8–2). There is widespread tacit approval of this practice. Shiv Sena, the political party that controls large sections of Mumbai, blames women for their troubles because they "wear revealing clothes" or "mingle with men."

Rao suggests that Indian men who harass women are threatened by changes in women's lives. In India, women have been leaving home to take jobs and go to college. Many wear Western clothes. Some Indian men feel threatened by these signs of women's independence. Sexual harassment is the easiest way to put a woman in her place and "to assert their traditionally unquestioned male rights."

A growing number of blogs encourage women to "holler back" at harassers and to post their stories of harassment on HollaBack websites, along with photos of harassers captured with cell phones and cameras. HollaBack started in New York, but has spread to fourteen cities in the United States and Canada. Stories about the sites have been printed in American, Canadian, Italian, and Swiss newspapers. Hits to HollaBack websites come from as far away as South Africa and South America. In India, Black Noise, a national movement modeled on HollaBack, places photos of harassers on the Internet and organizes "interventions" on the streets.

Literally thousands of stories have been posted on HollaBack websites (you can access these sites at http://hollabacknyc.blogspot.com/). Some of the stories are of men who do not understand how and why their comments are harassing, similar to the construction worker described earlier, who imagined he was bringing joy into the drab lives of middle-aged women. Many stories, however, tell of strangers groping women on public transportation, following them home, or threatening them with violence, such as this one, from December 2006:

Tonight around 10 PM, on a train back to her apartment in Williamsburg, a hooded man seated next to my best friend, a 22 year old woman, whispered in her ear "I am going to follow you when you get up." He did follow her, just a step behind, up the subway steps of her stop and out onto the street. With great clarity in a life-threatening moment, she stepped inside a bodega, while he stood outside, waiting for her, and was fortunate to find a couple who were willing to walk her the few steps from the market to her apartment door. When they exited the bodega, the hooded man was still there, waiting for his (potential) victim. Unfortunately, it took the help of two people—a woman to make her feel safe, and a man to protect her—to allow this woman to arrive home unharmed (Horton, 2008)

The HollaBack sites have brought to light an international problem that women confront in their daily lives and have started a public conversation about it. This conversation moves the problem from an individual matter that women face alone to a discussion that gives voice to the victims of harassment and allows them to discuss together the ways to grapple with it (see Box 8–3).

Most stories of harassment that are posted on the HollaBack sites end without physical harm to the mainly white and mainly middle-class young women who post them. Violence may be "merely" threatening to many young, white women on the city streets, but street violence is an even more common occurrence in poor and minority neighborhoods, where frequent robberies and shootings keep people on edge. The violence is a result of the lethal combination of gangs, drugs, guns, and police. Mothers in these neighborhoods worry about how aggressive policing, which they see as racist, will harm them and their children (Epstein 2003). Gangs and drug dealers also threaten the street life of these communities. One resident of a poor New York City neighborhood told a reporter, "I had to be worried all the time, you know. Are the children gonna get hit by a car? Is something gonna happen? We've lived in neighborhoods with a lot of drugs, a lot of people getting killed. You'd read about it in the paper the next day and think: Oh, God! That's only two blocks from here (Epstein 2003, 102)"

One outcome of the reign of terror in poor neighborhoods is that residents, especially children, get sick. Poor parents, terrified that their kids will be killed on the street, tend to keep them inside, with the windows shut and the TV on, where they are constantly exposed to contaminants in indoor air and have little opportunity to exercise. The epidemics of childhood asthma, obesity, and diabetes that trouble poor families are outcomes of the wars among gangs, drug

---

Box 8–3 CAREFUL! WOMEN ANSWER BACK

This text is taken from a German feminist poster. It was translated and posted on the blog Feministing, setting off a debate on whether women were justified in preaching violent retaliation for harassment. What do you think? See the comments at http://flickr.com/photos/yog/171269949/.

> If you stupidly stare at a woman, talk rubbish or touch her, you have to be aware that she might insult you loudly, a glass of beer is emptied over you or you might be hit in the face. We strongly advise you to refrain from this kind of harrassment.
>
> Women, migrants, homeless people, transgender people, gays and lesbians are often victims of assaults. Don't look away, interfere!

dealers, and police. A clinical psychologist quoted in the article noted the surprising impact of the reign of terror on neighborhood mothers and their children "The best parents—the people who are the most upright, the churchgoers, the most protective mothers—keep their kids inside, and they are at the intersection of the asthma and obesity epidemics (Epstein 2003, 98)."

Accounts of life in poor New York neighborhoods reveal several dimensions of gendered violence. There is the violence of gang members and criminals, mainly but not solely men, that threatens neighbors in the community. There is the masculinized and militarized violence of police, chiefly men, whose professional status entitles them to threaten and (literally) push the women and men bystanders around. There is the less visible violence of landlords and the public housing authorities, who fail to provide adequate dwellings for their tenants. This violence gives mothers little peace of mind. They suffer the anxiety that visits those with little control over the dangers they and their children face in the neighborhood. These women suffer the intersecting oppressions of race, poverty, and gender that structure their lives and their prospects.

MEN'S PERSONAL SAFETY AND GENDERED VIOLENCE

Men are supposed to know how to protect themselves from violence and in fact most report that they do not feel threatened by public violence or worry about their personal safety. Actually, men's dismissal of public violence does not reflect reality, because men's rates of victimization in public space are higher than those of women (Stanko 1990). Perhaps such fearlessness is an example of masculine bravado, a way of being masculine or, as discussed in chapter 3, of "doing masculinity."

Men first learn about gendered dangers as boys, in the context of other boys' violence and threats. Such dangers are masculinized and often sexualized as well. What do boys learn about violence in childhood? Rather than learning to avoid violence, as girls do, many boys must learn to take violence and to dish it out. James Messerschmidt sees violence as a resource for "doing masculinity." Many boys learn as they grow up that aggressiveness and the capacity for violence can affirm their masculinity in the contexts of home, school, and sports (Messerschmidt 2000, 13-14). Using violence against others is learned, among other sites, in school sports (Messner 1992, 64-81) and is supported by peer groups and teachers as they celebrate the dominant gender conventions surrounding boy athletes and girl cheerleaders. Sociologist Don Sabo (2002) recounts how his feelings of inadequacy as a boy shaped his school football career. Feeling "too fat, too short, [and] too weak," Sabo learned to take pain like a man. "Calisthenics until my arms ached. Hitting hard and fast and knocking the other guy down. Getting hit in the groin and not crying…By the time I reported for my first high-school practice…I already knew what was expected of me…The way to succeed was to be an animal…Being an animal meant being ruthlessly aggressive and competitive." (Sabo 1994, 12)

Aggression and threat are sexualized as well. High-status boys in grade school and high school maintain their position in the male peer group through heterosexist and misogynist banter or highly competitive "cut talk." Messner describes such a contest with Chris when he was a fifth grader (Messner 2002, 33):

> I thought I was doing pretty well until Chris hit me with one for which I had no answer: "Messner," he asserted, "blow me!" I didn't know what to say back, and so

of course I lost the cut fight. But behind my lack of response was confusion. In my eleven-year-old mind, I knew a few things about sex but was unclear about others One thing I had recently learned from friends was that there were some men who had sex with other men. They were called homosexuals, and I was told that they were sick and sinful individuals. So…if Chris was saying, "blow me" to me, he was in effect asking me to be involved in some homosexual act with him. If homosexuality is such bad and shameful thing, why then did *he* win the cut fight?…Now I can see that insults like "you suck," "blow me," or "fuck you" smuggle into children's and preadolescent groups a powerful pedagogy about sexuality, power, and domination. In short, though children obviously do not intend it, through this sort of banter they teach each other that sex, whether of the homosexual or heterosexual kind, is a relational act of domination and subordination. The "men" are the ones who are on top, in control, doing the penetrating and fucking. Women, or penetrated men, are subordinate, degraded, and dehumanized objects of sexual aggression.

RAPE AND DOMESTIC VIOLENCE

One of the most prevalent myths about rape is that "rapists are hiding in the bushes." In fact, most sexual assaults and rapes of women are committed by their husbands or boyfriends (28 percent), relatives (7 percent), or friends and acquaintances (38 percent). It is men who are more likely to be assaulted by strangers. Fifty-four percent of those who violently attacked men in 2005 were strangers, and only 3 percent were intimates (U.S. Department of Justice 2005). Figure 8–2 shows that the rate of sexual assault of women by men from 1993 to 2004 is 0.5 per 1,000, whereas the rate of sexual assault of men by women is virtually nonexistent. About 4.5 women per 1,000 are assaulted by the men they know, and assaults by women on men are less than 1 per 1000 (.07). On average between 1993 and 2004, women experienced higher rates of nonfatal intimate partner violence than men regardless of the type of crime.

The most likely victims of rape are young women and girls, and of these the most vulnerable to rape are young women of color and working-class women. About half of all rape victims are in the lowest third of income distribution (U.S. Department of Justice 2005). Estimates of the rates of sexual violence are difficult to make because more than half of all rapes are unreported, according to the National Crime Victimization Survey. Rape crisis counselors believe that underestimates are even more significant. They maintain that only one in fifty raped women report the crime to the police.

Men are estimated to be about 10 percent of all victims of rape. Shame, confusion, and fear of being seen as homosexual often make male victims reluctant to call the police. Some believe that most male rape occurs in prison, but research suggests prison is not the only place men and boys are raped. In Western countries, 5 to 10 percent of men report a history of childhood sexual abuse. A 1991 study of incarcerated and nonincarcerated male rape victims in Tennessee found that men and teenage boys (the more likely victims) are most often raped in remote areas outdoors or while hitchhiking. The assault usually involves penetration of the victim anally, orally, or both. Gang rape is more common in cases involving male victims than those involving female victims. Weapons and serious physical injury are

FIGURE 8–2 Average annual rate of nonfatal intimate partner victimization 1993–2004.

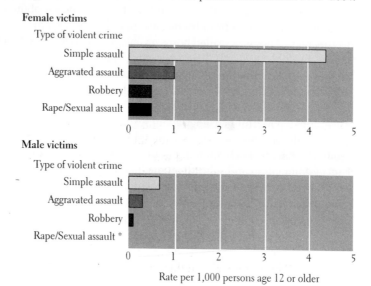

Rate per 1,000 persons age 12 or older

SOURCE: Bureau of Justice Statistics. Intimate Partner Violence in the U.S. http://www.ojp.usdoj.gov/bjs/intimate/circumstances.htm#type.

more likely to accompany male-on-male rape (Lipscomb, Muram, Speck, and Mercer 1992; National Center for Victims of Crime 1995).

Adolescent girls and college women are at risk of becoming victims of "acquaintance" or "date rape." A 1996 national study found that 25 percent of college women surveyed reported having had unwanted sexual intercourse. Of these women, 84 percent knew their assailant, 57 percent of the episodes occurred on dates, and 41 percent of the women stated that they were virgins at the time of the assault. These data probably underestimate the true incidence of date rape, because students often do not report attempted or completed rapes, nor do they define many such assaults as rapes (New York City Alliance Against Sexual Assault 1997). Date rape is more likely to occur in fraternities and is associated with alcohol and gender stereotyping of women (Martin and Hummer 1989). In the 1996 study, one out of every fifteen male college students admitted he had raped or tried to rape a female student during the preceding year. A 1998 survey asked young British men whether they would force a woman to have sex. One in eight said they might in a long-term relationship, and one in sixteen would if they had "'spent a lot of money on her' or if she had 'slept with loads of men'" (Martin and Hummer 1989, 284).

Recent Decline in Rape Statistics

There has been a significant decline in rape over the past several decades. Since the 1970s, the number of rapes in the United States has fallen by over 85 percent. In 2005, reported rape fell even as other violent crime increased.

Why has this decline occurred? Some argue that the statistics are flawed because so many rapes are unreported. The change may only mean we are getting a little better at gathering realistic statistics. Some advocates who work with rape victims also do not believe that rape has declined. Rather, they say, it has moved from the cities, from which the Justice Department's National Crime Victimization Survey draws its statistics, to the suburbs, which are not included in this survey. Other experts, however, believe the decline is real and they credit changes that have emerged in laws, policies, and ideas as a result of four decades of work by feminists.

Activists have established rape crisis hotlines and services, convinced police and the courts to show greater sensitivity toward rape victims, and convinced news organizations to respect victims' privacy. They have encouraged women to take charge of their own security by sponsoring self-defense classes and "Take Back the Night" demonstrations. College and high school students now learn about the rules of consent and that "no means no." However, as Table 8–2 shows, the greatest decline in gendered violence has not been men's violence against women, but homicides of men by wives, girlfriends, and other female intimates. This trend may also reflect that there is more material support for battered and abused women, who need not take the desperate measures they once did to escape a violent home or relationship. These changes and their implications are discussed further later in this chapter.

Accounting for Rape: Evolutionary Theory, Individual Psychology, and Inequality

Although rape may be declining in some places, it remains a major problem throughout the world. Scholars have tried to understand why it persists and why rape is so commonplace. Three kinds of theories have been advanced to explain the prevalence of rape: those that emphasize the understanding of Darwinian evolutionary theory; those that maintain that rape results from individual psychological deviance and pathology; and those that argue that rape is a political issue and an outcome of power inequalities in society.

DARWINIAN EVOLUTION. In the book *A Natural History of Rape: Biological Bases of Sexual Coercion*, Thornhill and Palmer (2000) maintain that sexual selection propels men to rape.

TABLE 8–2 Intimate Homicide Victims by Gender: 1976–2004

Year	Women	Men
1976	1,596	1,348
2004	1,159	385

SOURCE: Bureau of Justice Statistics. http://www.ojp. usdoj.gov/bjs/intimate/victims.htm.

According to their evolutionary theory of rape, men's proclivities to rape have evolved to enable men to procreate. The theory that men have drives that must be met at all costs is similar to popular notions of men's sexual needs. This theory superficially resembles the views of radical feminists such as Andrea Dworkin and Catherine MacKinnon, who contend that all men are predators against women. However, unlike these feminists, who focus on ways to end male violence, the proponents of evolutionary theory contend that men are compelled to rape because women, to the disadvantage of the species, tend to resist sex. This logic relieves men of responsibility for their violence ("it's only natural") and makes women complicit in their own victimization. To curb men's natural, hard-wired drives, Thornhill and Palmer (2000) recommend that women should neither flirt nor wear provocative clothing—advice similar to that given by the men of Shiv Sena in India! The evolutionary theory of rape assumes that the patterns of sexual violence in the United States are universal, but cross-cultural research shows that the incidence of rape varies greatly from culture to culture. If the biological imperative to rape is as powerful and as universal as Thornhill and Palmer (2000) insist, why does its frequency vary so much across cultures? Why don't all men commit rape?

Peggy Reeves Sanday reviewed ethnographic data from around the world to rank ninety-five preliterate societies on a continuum from rape-free to rape-prone. An example of a rape-prone society is that of the Brazilian Yanomamo. In this society, women are men's property. Groups raid each other for wives in an area where marriageable women are in short supply due to the practice of female infanticide. The number of marriageable women is also affected by the desire on the part of successful warriors to have several wives to mark their superior status as "fierce men" (Sanday 2007).

In rape-free societies, rape is infrequent or absent. In these societies, women have important productive roles and are respected. There is relative gender equality and recognition of women's contribution to the life the society. There is also general distaste for violence in all interactions. H. P. Philips (1966) describes one such society. Note the lack of a highly elaborated gender division of labor. Everyone, men and women alike, performs essentially the same tasks. This description fits the partnership model of social organization that Riane Eisler connects with equalitarian and peace-loving societies.

> Central Thai families were remarkable for the absence of any meaningful division of labor by sex: men were as likely as women to carry out household duties including child care, and women as likely as men to plow or manage the family business. Divorce was common, people preferring to separate rather than live with discord. Community norms disdained aggression; other nonviolent means of conflict resolution were plentiful and preferred. (424)

The central Thai community was the opposite of the Yanomamo, where there was concern over diminishing resources, where men had greater prestige, and where women were property to be controlled by their owners (men). In contrast in the Yanomamo community sexual violence was a strategy men used to assert their ownership.

Are these studies of hunter-gatherer societies relevant to our own postindustrial ones? Although it is bad science to compare large contemporary societies with smaller preliterate ones, there are suggestive parallels. America has one of the most rape-prone of all contemporary cultures. Despite great strides toward women's equality in the United States, men remain dominant economically, politically, and culturally, although in many ways their dominant status is precarious. For many men and their families, resources are diminishing as jobs are outsourced, unemployment grows, and wealth inequality reaches unprecedented levels. As more and more women enter the workforce to share breadwinning tasks with men, many men feel that they have lost their dominant economic position relative to women. They learn from the media and the wider culture that force is the prevalent and legitimate way to pursue national goals. No wonder some believe that violence can help them to resolve their own problems and worries. This cultural context of violence sets the stage for interpersonal violence.

In this context, what do declining rates of rape suggest? We suggested previously that we might credit the decades-long and increasingly international women's movements for publicizing the issues of violence against women and for making important changes in the laws, in educating women and men about gendered violence, and in some women's and men's willingness to work for fundamental changes. The background to these changes includes women's growing labor force participation, which allows many to leave violent and potentially violent situations and the growth of organizations devoted to challenging violence against women. Perhaps the current epidemic of gendered violence reflects what Riane Eisler suggests is a "dying system's violent efforts to maintain its hold" (Eisler 1987, 171) and suggests we are on the cusp of a new order.

INDIVIDUAL PSYCHOLOGY. Psychological explanations of rape focus on the disturbed and pathological personalities of individuals who have been identified as rapists. Some studies suggest that men who rape children were themselves sexually abused as children. The psychological damage caused by their experience as children results in their aberrant behavior as adults. Other studies focus on rapists' emotional need to dominate and feel power over their victims, their inabilities to relate to women, or their feelings of anger toward and hatred of women. These explanations may clarify why individuals choose violent strategies to resolve their troubles. However, there are two problems with exclusive reliance on individual psychology to explain violence as a collective phenomenon. First, by ripping individual acts from their social contexts and viewing sexual violence as the conduct of deviant or troubled individuals, we miss seeing the structured dimensions of violence. We are blind to the ways social institutions shape our behavior. Second, we are unable to explain why violence is predominantly men's violence. Boys and girls are both sexually abused. Men and women are both likely to feel anger and a desire to control others. Why are men so much more likely to respond by resorting to violence? The contexts within which individual violence erupts—institutions of social control based on violence and a climate condoning violence against women and violence in general—are certainly important parts of the puzzle. Ideas about what boys and men are supposed to be like and the tie between masculinity and violence are critical but often ignored factors by those who explain violence as a individual psychological problem.

Some examples of individualized psychological explanations of violence are the media descriptions of the school shootings that erupted occasionally in the past decade. These reports ignored the central feature of the shootings: Middle-class white boys were the shooters (see Box 8–4). Michael Kimmel (2000) asks his readers to "try a little thought experiment":

Box 8–4 JACKSON KATZ: COVERAGE OF "SCHOOL SHOOTINGS" AVOIDS THE CENTRAL ISSUE *OCTOBER 11, 2006* COMMONDREAMS.ORG

In the many hours devoted to analyzing the recent school shootings, once again we see that as a society we seem constitutionally unable, or unwilling, to acknowledge a simple but disturbing fact: these shootings are an extreme manifestation of one of contemporary American society's biggest problems— the ongoing crisis of men's violence against women.

October is Domestic Violence Awareness Month, so let's take a good hard look at these latest horrific cases of violence on the domestic front. On September 27, a heavily armed 53-year-old man walked into a Colorado high school classroom, forced male students to leave, and took a group of girls hostage. He then proceeded to terrorize the girls for several hours, killing one and allegedly sexually assaulting some or all of the others before killing himself.

Less than a week later, a heavily armed 32-year-old man walked into an Amish schoolhouse in Pennsylvania and ordered about 15 boys to leave the room, along with a pregnant woman and three women with infants. He forced the remaining girls, aged 6 to 13, to line up against a blackboard, where he tied their feet together. He then methodically executed five of the girls with shots to the head and critically wounded several others before taking his own life.

Just after the Amish schoolhouse massacre, Pennsylvania Police Commissioner Jeffrey B. Miller said in an emotional press conference, "It seems as though (the perpetrator) wanted to attack young, female victims."

How did mainstream media cover these unspeakable acts of gender violence? *The New York Times* ran an editorial that identified the "most important" cause as the easy access to guns in our society. NPR did a show which focused on problems in rural America. Forensic psychologists and criminal profilers filled the airwaves with talk about how difficult it is to predict when a "person" will snap. And countless exasperated commentators—from fundamentalist preachers to secular social critics—abandoned any pretense toward logic and reason in their rush to weigh in with metaphysical musings on the incomprehensibility of "evil."

Incredibly, few if any prominent voices in the broadcast or print media have called the incidents what they are: hate crimes perpetrated by angry white men against defenseless young girls, who—whatever the twisted motives of the shooters—were targeted for sexual assault and murder precisely because they are girls.

What is it going to take for our society to deal honestly with the extent and depth of this problem? How many more young girls have to die before decision-makers in media and other influential institutions stop averting their eyes from the lethal mix of deep misogyny and violent masculinity at work here? In response to the recent spate of shootings, the White House announced plans to bring together experts in education and law enforcement. The goal was to discuss "the nature of the problem" and federal action that can assist communities with violence prevention. This approach is misdirected. Instead of convening a group of experts on "school safety," the president should catalyze a long-overdue national conversation about sexism, masculinity, and men's violence against women.

For us to have any hope of truly preventing not only extreme acts of gender violence, but also the incidents of rape, sexual abuse and domestic violence that are a daily part of millions of women's and girls' lives, we need to have this conversation. And we need many more men to participate. Men from every level of society need to recognize that violence against women is a men's issue.

A similar incident to the Amish schoolhouse massacre took place in Canada in 1989. A heavily armed 25-year-old man walked into a classroom at the University of Montreal. He forced the men out of the classroom at gunpoint, and then opened fire on the women. He killed fourteen women and injured many more, before committing suicide.

In response to this atrocity, in 1991 a number of Canadian men created the White Ribbon Campaign. The idea was for men to wear a white ribbon as a way of making a visible and public pledge "never to commit, condone, nor remain silent about violence against women." The White Ribbon Campaign has since become a part of Canadian culture, and it has been adapted in dozens of countries.

After the horrors in this country over the past two weeks, the challenge for American men is clear: will we respond to these recent tragedies by averting our eyes and pretending that none of this happened? Or will we at long last break our complicit silence and work together with women to turn these tragedies into a transformative cultural moment?

Jackson Katz is the author of The Macho Paradox: Why Some Men Hurt Women and How All Men Can Help *(Sourcebooks, 2006).*

SOURCE: Jackson Katz: 2006.

Imagine that the killers in Littleton—and in Pearl, Mississippi, Paducah, Kentucky, Springfield, Oregon, and Jonesboro, Arkansas—were all black girls from poor families who lived in New Haven, Connecticut, Newark, New Jersey, or Providence, Rhode Island. I believe we'd now be having a national debate about inner-city poor black girls....Yet the obvious fact that these school killers were all middle class white boys seems to have escaped everyone's notice....Yet gender is the single most obvious and intractable difference when it comes to violence in America. Men and boys are responsible for 95% of all violent crimes in this country. (Kimmel 2000, 5)

A second problem with individual explanations is that they draw on biased samples of captured and convicted rapists to develop theories of rape. Such samples overrepresent poor men and men of color, who are most likely to be charged and prosecuted for these crimes and often wrongly convicted and imprisoned. White men, powerful men, and wealthy men who rape may be relatively immune from criminal charges, and therefore are rarely part of such studies (see Weitzman 2000).

RAPE AS AN OUTCOME OF GENDER INEQUALITY. Kimmel (2004) proposes an alternative to evolutionary and psychological explanations of male violence. He suggests that gender is the *outcome* of inequality, not its cause. In other words, power differences between men and women produce gender domination and subordination, leading to men's sexual entitlement and rape. Gender legitimizes these inequalities by naturalizing them. Women seem naturally submissive and men seem naturally dominant. However, gender is not natural. It is socially constructed along lines of differential power. Kimmel goes further to suggest that the social positions people occupy—for example, their class and racial ethnic locations—account for more differences among them than does gender alone. In this view, Kimmel invokes the theory of "intersectionality." You should recall from chapter 1 that intersectionality helps us to see the broad range of social factors that tie us together and the ways that systems of inequality and power by gender, race ethnicity, and social class intersect to create relationships, sometimes violent, that reflect and maintain those system of power.

However, the same power relationships that create and nourish inequality and violence also bring forth resistance. Power creates resistance. Gender inequalities, together with the power and violence that sustain them shift and change with time. Until the nineteenth century, physical punishment of slaves, children, and wives was legitimate. Indeed, "spare the rod and spoil the child" was a common sentiment that held sway among educators and parents long into the twentieth century. Husbands had the right to punish their wives physically under English common law, but mid-nineteenth-century feminists began to question that right. It was more than a century later, in the 1970s, that the feminist movement against violence had an impact. At that point, feminists successfully named several forms of intimate violence including date rape, sexual harassment, and domestic violence. They redefined rape to include forced sex in marriage. They argued that so-called "private" violence—individual men's use of force against women they knew—was as illegitimate and as criminal as raping or beating strangers. This history shows that what counts as rape or unacceptable violence changes with our changing circumstances and consciousness.

An assumption often underpinning evolutionary and psychological theories of rape is that it is universal, because men's bodies have the biological "equipment" to rape and women's bodies the equipment to be raped. These ideas sneak biology back into the discussions of sexual violence. Canadian feminist Susan Griffin (1979, 3) invoked nature when she wrote, "I have never been free of the fear of rape. From a very early age, I, like most women, have thought of rape as part of my natural environment—something to be feared and prayed against like fire and lightning. I never asked why men raped. *I simply thought it one of the mysteries of human nature*" (emphasis added).

Gordon and Reiger (1991, 3) called rape "the female fear," and maintained that "every women has it to a degree and all women are affected by it." Helliwell (2000) suggests that these assumptions falsely universalize Western women's experiences. We have seen that not all cultures masculinize men and feminize women as two opposite and unequal genders. Helliwell suggests that Western inequalities of wealth and power between women and men (Kimmel's argument) give meaning and impetus to the practice of rape, but there are other societies in which rape has no meaning. Her research supports Sanday's findings regarding rape-free societies.

A second implicit assumption in some rape studies and in the popular imagination as well is that rape is a feature of violent black or third-world cultures. As we saw in the discussion of rape and racism in chapter 4, images and laws regarding rape have a long history of tying together racist ideologies, rape, and relationships among women and men of different racial ethnic groups.

Ending Rape

Cross-cultural data on rape-free societies holds out the possibility of a world without sexual violence. Kimmel's idea that inequality produces gender differences and that gender difference legitimizes and naturalizes inequality suggests that ending inequalities of power, wealth, and status between men and women will help us to bring that world into being.

Breaking the silence and naming the experiences of rape has been the first step toward ending sexual violence. The terms date rape and marital rape identify actions that were once accepted and invisible as actionable criminal offenses. Antiviolence activists encouraged fighting back, overturning the conventional wisdom of an earlier day that women should submit to their attackers to avoid further violence. They renamed raped and battered women survivors, not victims. They built organizations and services to tackle these newly identified crimes: hotlines, support groups, and rape crisis centers. They offered training to women in martial arts and ways to reclaim public space. Take Back the Night marches became annual events on many college campuses. Men have been enlisted in the antirape movement and many have formed their own antiviolence projects (see Box 8–5). After all, isn't rape men's problem?

THE DISCOVERY OF DOMESTIC VIOLENCE

Like rape, domestic violence was invisible until it was named by feminists in the 1970s. Of course many people knew individual women who had been beaten by a husband or boyfriend, or perhaps they themselves had been battered. Each incident seemed no more than an unfortunate event, the outcome of an argument, a sign of individual pathology, the

Box 8–5 MEN CAN STOP RAPE CELEBRATES 10 MILESTONES DURING 10 YEARS OF PREVENTION

Men Can Stop Rape mobilizes male youth to prevent men's violence against women. We build young men's capacity to challenge harmful aspects of traditional masculinity, to value alternative visions of male strength, and to embrace their vital role as allies with women and girls in fostering healthy relationships and gender equity.

1. TRAVELING MEN

Only three days after launching a new website following the incorporation of the Men's Rape Prevention Project on January 13, 1997, the Co-Directors received an email from North Park College in Chicago, IL, requesting a workshop on its campus, heralding the organization's first out of town trip. During February 1997, Patrick and Jonathan traveled to Chicago where they facilitated an early version of what became one of Men Can Stop Rape's signature exercises, The Continuum of Harm, with 40 North Park College students.

2. FINDING AN OFFICE AWAY FROM HOME

Pat McGann, MCSR's Communication Director, initially started as Volunteer Coordinator in the summer of 1998. Jonathan, Patrick, and Pat worked from their homes and all were unpaid, until the organization hired Jonathan in April 1999 to write grants for four hours a week. By September 1999, enough funding had been secured to allow the three of them to take work out of their homes and move it into Men Can Stop Rape's first office, located in the Josephine Butler Center, a 40-room Renaissance-revival style mansion that formerly served as the Embassy of Hungary and Brazil. The Center was named after one of Washington, DC's most respected activists.

3. BUILDING MEN OF STRENGTH

By 1999, after conducting numerous presentations in DC high schools, the Co-Directors had become frustrated with the limitations of the one-workshop model. That same year, Charles Miles, Director of the Ballou Boys and Girls Club of Greater Washington, contacted the Men's Rape Prevention Project about presenting to the boys in the club. Jonathan and Patrick pitched the idea of five or more workshops. Mr. Miles enthusiastically responded, proposing meeting once-a-week for 10 weeks. After prompting by Mr. Miles to name the group, Jonathan brainstormed the Men of Strength (MOST) Club, and meetings began in January 2000. Under the guidance of Neil Irvin, hired in the spring of 2001 as Community Director, the Club has become the national model for mobilizing young men to prevent violence against women.

4. A CITY OF STRENGTH

In late 1999, John Stoltenberg, Board President of the Men's Rape Prevention Project, was asked by the co-directors to review the organization's information sheet, "What Men Can Do." Trying to come up with more inspirational language, he added to the end of the page, "My Strength Is Not for Hurting." Talk quickly turned to developing a media campaign using the phrase as the theme line. An advisory committee consisting of school administrators, faculty and staff was formed, funding was secured from Barbara Lovenheim and BIL Charitable Trust, and in February 2001, the groundbreaking Strength Media Campaign was launched in all seventeen Washington, DC public high schools. For the first time in the history of the city, bus shelter and bus side ads, REP Magazine, and posters in school hallways and classrooms declared that young men could be strong without using intimidation, force, or violence. And for the first time, all the PSA media materials had the name, Men Can Stop Rape, printed on them.

5. VIRGINIA'S STRENGTH IS NOT FOR HURTING

Immediately after the Strength Media Campaign ended in DC, Men Can Stop Rape began selling the Campaign's posters, which spread across the country like wildfire. Robert Franklin first learned of the posters while at the University of Maine, Orono, but moved to Virginia when he was hired by the state's Department of Health as Sexual Violence Male Outreach Coordinator. Both he and his supervisor, Rebecca Odor, wanted to use the posters' messages, although in a campaign that would specifically be identified with the Virginia Department of Health (VDH). As a result of this interest, VDH in 2003 was the first in a line of agencies, coalitions, and organizations to license what are now referred to as Strength Mediaworks materials.

6. EARNING SPECIAL DISTINCTION

Every year the Ms. Foundation for Women recognizes those men and women whose work is in line with the Foundation's past, as well as its vision for the future. Men Can Stop Rape was honored to be a part of this tradition as a recipient of the 15th Annual Gloria Awards on May 15, 2003 at the Waldorf-Astoria Hotel in New York City. The entire MCSR staff attended the evening's events, brushing shoulders with Ms. Foundation celebrity guests and supporters like Kathy Najimy, Gloria Steinem, Marlo Thomas, and Phil Donahue. Honored for its pioneering efforts in the men's movement to join with women as allies in ending sexual violence, MCSR earned special distinction as the first organization targeting its services toward men to receive a Gloria Award. Yoko Ono Lennon flew in from L.A. to present the Award to Co-Founders Patrick Lemmon and Jonathan Stillerman, as well as 17-year-old Men of Strength Club member, William Powell.

7. SCHOOLING IN EVALUATION

Lacking expertise in evaluation but recognizing its absolute necessity, Patrick Lemmon submitted a proposal to the Centers for Disease Control and Prevention for a technical assistance grant that would assess best practices for primary prevention programs aimed at preventing young men and boys from committing sexual assault. Neil Irvin, hired specifically to grow the Club as Community Educator, had made substantial inroads so that, in the short span of a year, the number of Clubs had jumped from one to four. This healthy growth and a strong commitment to evaluation prompted the CDC to select the Men of Strength Club as one of four nationwide participants in a two-year evaluation project starting in 2003. Initial results in 2005 led the CDC to declare the MOST Club a promising strategy and to support further evaluation.

8. BE BOLD, BE STRONG, TAKE ACTION

In February 2004, Pat McGann, then Director of Outreach, had a burst of insight: why not have MOST Club members take action in their schools during all of April, Sexual Assault Awareness Month and call it 30 Days of Strength? Neil Irvin, Community Director and now National Director of the Men of Strength Club, embraced the idea and its tagline—Be Bold, Be Strong, Take Action. Committees consisting of two to three Club members at School Without Walls DC Senior Public High School coordinated open meetings for their peers, passed out "Action Sheets" listing weekly awareness and prevention activities, put up 30 Days' messages on the school computers' screen savers, informed the student body about issues of teen dating violence during morning announcements, and hung "My Strength Is Not for Hurting" posters throughout the school.

outburst of an out-of-control husband, or a response to a nagging wife. Like the discontent of middle-class housewives identified a decade before by Betty Friedan, it was hard to see battering as a large-scale social issue. Domestic violence was another "problem that had no name," raising little public concern until the women's movement discovered and publicized it. Feminists rejected the sentimental notion that families were naturally supportive and loving units and the conviction that violence in families was a private matter. They reframed families as sites of political struggle and renamed battering as a criminal act. They drew attention to institutionalized male dominance and looked to police, prosecutors, and judges in the criminal courts to support women's safety by making it easier to bring batterers to justice.

Readers of this book are learning to identify the cultural, political, and social changes in the 1960s and 1970s that helped to move domestic violence into the public eye. People were

9. CALIFORNIA DREAMIN'

In late spring of 2005, the California Coalition Against Sexual Assault (CALCASA) initiated an exhaustive search for sexual assault primary prevention campaigns targeting high school age young men so they could decide how best to develop their own campaign. In the end CALCASA chose to license MCSR's Strength Campaign specifically because it offered a positive, integrated, comprehensive approach unlike any other. Starting in September 2005, the bolder, new look of the multimedia component of the My Strength Campaign blanketed the cities and towns of the 66 rape crisis centers across the state. Never before had such a vast array of "My Strength Is Not for Hurting" media materials highlighted positive masculinity. And in conjunction with the media campaign, six MOST Clubs were established in a wide variety of settings throughout California, from urban multicultural to rural white to rural Spanish-speaking. The launch of the Campaign received coverage in a remarkable 150+ news stories, a new precedent for rape prevention initiatives throughout the nation.

10. REACHING ACROSS THE GLOBE

Although Men Can Stop Rape had already licensed media materials outside the United States, Strength Mediaworks traveled farther from home than ever before in November 2005 when MCSR struck up a licensing agreement with EngenderHealth for South African Men as Partners Network and the Western Cape Office on the Status of Women. Twelve posters conveying messages in English, Afrikaans, and isiXhosa, peopled with South African models, and bathed in rich pastels and earth tones, gave Mediaworks a new vibrant look. The posters' positive prevention messages reached South African men across the country during "16 Days of Activism Against Gender Violence"—a worldwide campaign—that ran from International Day for the Elimination of Violence Against Women, November 25, through International Human Rights Day, December 10.

SOURCE: http://www.mencanstoprape.com.

marrying later or not at all and divorcing more often, thereby avoiding or cutting short many potentially abusive situations. A changing division of labor that brought women into the workforce allowed women to attain more education and compressed their childbearing years, so that many women were becoming less dependent on men for support. More directly, the growing movements for women's rights lent weight to the cause of terrorized and beaten women.

Early studies of domestic violence showed that many attacks on women by the men they lived with were prompted by their failures to be "good wives" or to "do family" properly. For example, women were assaulted for not cooking or cooking well, for failing to do housework, or failing to be adequately deferential to their men. Interviews with batterers found that men believed it was their right as men to beat wives who disobeyed them. Such violence was most likely to occur in households in which both wife and husband agreed that male dominance and control was legitimate.

Sexual jealousy and possessiveness also precipitated active violence. Batterers often treated other men, but also wives' friends and family, as competitors, and used marital rape as punishment for challenging their claim to women's presence and their bodies (Ptacek 1988).

Laws now criminalize battering in many nations, but even today where the laws are in place some police and some courts continue to treat violence between spouses as a personal problem that does not belong in the criminal justice system. In the 1970s, when women first attempted to use the criminal justice system to restrain violent men, they discovered that it was at best a crude instrument. Most police were reluctant to arrest men for domestic battery and many judges shied away from imposing sentences on the men who were brought before them. They were strongly opposed to ousting "good fathers" from their homes and suspected women of making "exaggerated claims" to win benefits from the courts (Radford 1987). Prosecutors and public defenders in Chicago's domestic violence court called some of the women who brought charges against abusers themselves "abusers" of the criminal justice system and blamed them for their false claims and vindictiveness toward men (Wittner 1998).

The laws themselves were difficult to apply to domestic violence cases (Eaton 1986). For example, a woman charged with battery or murder could claim self-defense only if she acted to defend herself from immediate attack. This "reasonable person" standard of the law assumed women should be able to call on their own physical strength to defend themselves in the face of a threat. However, most women's size, strength, socialization, and lack of training in hand-to-hand combat assured they would be no match for an assailant. If her assault on an abuser took place while he was asleep or was not immediately threatening her, it did not meet the legal standard of self-defense no matter how brutal, unrelenting, and abusive he might have been. The result was that women who retaliated against abusers often faced long prison sentences.

Juries often held stereotyped views of battered women as defendants in criminal cases. Such biases reflected the attitudes of an unsympathetic wider public. A survey conducted in upstate New York in the mid-1980s found that most respondents believed that women were at least partially responsible for the assaults they suffered and thought of them as masochistic or emotionally disturbed if they remained with their husbands (Ewing and Aubry 1987). An article addressed to attorneys for women who killed abusive mates in self-defense cautioned against constructing a defense around battering as a women's issue, because many jurors could not recognize abuse or would not rule in favor of the women to preserve families (Thompson 1986). In fact, the assumptions that guided criminal justice professionals and the wider public regarding domestic violence were close to the rationalizations employed by convicted batterers. For example, Ptacek (1988) found that police officers, court clerks, and judges agreed with batterers that wives often provoked the violence husbands visited on them.

In summary, as domestic violence was emerging as a social issue, women who looked for safety and protection from the criminal justice system were learning that institutional practices and practitioners implicated women in their own victimization and excused violent partners. Stereotypes of women informed professionals and the public. There was more interest in preserving families than in women's safety.

Studies of Domestic Violence

During the 1970s and 1980s, the battered women's movement gained strength and visibility, garnering sympathy for battered women, changing the laws and women's reception in the courts, and influencing national legislation for the protection of victims of domestic violence. Scholars participated in this national awakening to personal violence in families.

Studies conducted by sociologist Murray Straus and his associates stressed that women and men were equally responsible for violence in families. The individual violent acts reported in their national random sample study of family violence seemed to show that women were as violent as men. These data prompted one of the principal investigators, Suzanne Steinmetz, to coin the phrase, "the battered husband syndrome" and to argue that abuse of husbands was as common as wife battering (Steinmetz 1978; Straus, Gelles, and Steinmetz 1980). Lenore Walker (1979) attributed failure to leave an abusive relationship to "learned helplessness," a psychological explanation that drew on and amplified the stereotype of battered women as passive and helpless.

By the late 1970s, feminist scholars began to question these stereotypes. They argued that Straus's survey data did not take into account the contexts of violence. What if these data were reflecting women's attempts to defend themselves? Was a wife's slap the equivalent of a husband's punch? Was "learned helplessness" an accurate description of women's actions, or was getting away from violent men harder than it seemed? Certainly there was evidence that many abused women looked for help from families, neighbors, doctors, and others (Labell 1979). And why was "family violence" almost invariably men's violence against women and children?

Partially on the basis of such research, activists successfully pressured the courts to provide better legal services to women complainants and to change court procedures. There were dramatic changes in the responses of police and the courts to women's complaints. Increasingly the courts came to accept domestic violence as a crime rather than as a personal trouble. Throughout the 1980s, states passed laws giving police the power to arrest batterers for misdemeanor assaults and required police to provide battered women with information about their legal options and the services available to them. In some cases, police departments adopted a policy of mandatory arrest (Hanmer, Radford, and Stanko 1989, 157).

Kathleen Ferraro (1988) investigated the actual practices of police in domestic violence calls. Police statistics showed that there were 21,000 calls to police coded as family fights in 1984 in Phoenix. Of these, 1,250 resulted in arrests and 2,000 more in detective reports. What happened to the other cases? To answer this question, Ferraro accompanied police on domestic violence calls to observe firsthand the context of police decision making. She found that police attitudes about domestic violence informed their responses. For example, police believed that women could easily choose to leave an abusive household, and if they did not, it proved their complaints were frivolous. If the violence did not spill out into public space, but remained contained within the home, police saw it as a private fight, in which they had no right to intervene. They were even less likely to consider battering a serious crime when it occurred in minority and low-income households.

Disillusionment with criminal justice solutions to the problem of family violence soon emerged. Even with mandatory arrest policies in place, police often turned a deaf ear to women's complaints and failed to tell complainants about the services and alternatives available to them. Even more chilling, mandatory arrest policies sometimes resulted in women's arrests and, sometimes, the deportation of abused women who were undocumented. Women still could not count on police protection.

Failures of the police and justice system to protect American women from violence mirrored failures in other parts of the world, although the latter continue to have more

Box 8–6 HONOR KILLINGS IN EGYPT

The legal system in Egypt is contradictory in that it guarantees women's rights in the public arena, restricting them in the private sphere. The personal status law for example, permits not only male polygamy, but the right of the husband to divorce his wife for no good reason and the expulsion of a divorced woman from the marital residence if she has no children or her children are beyond custody age. It also requires the wife's obedience if she needs the husband to spend on her. Family law prioritizes the reproductive role of women, assuming that men alone are responsible for providing for the family. It places the protection of the family unit above individual rights within the family, giving men privileges to go with the role of sole provider. Likewise women are not treated as individuals, but rather as wives, mothers, and daughters expected to obey the patriarch; and the control of the sexuality of girls and women is observed and monitored by male members of the family...

Girls are socialized to consider marriage life's mission, because a woman does not have status unless she is married. As a result, women tend to accept and tolerate injustices that take place in the family. Many women, especially from low and middle income classes, tend to sacrifice their individual rights for the sake of preserving the marriage. Control of women's sexuality is a major obstacle to their practice of rights. Religious extremists place the blame for excessive libidinal drive on women alone, with the result that female genital mutilation is universally practiced and veiling is increasingly imposed and honour crimes practiced. Honour crimes refer to the murder of a woman by her male family members for a perceived violation of the social norms of sexuality, or a suspicion of women having transgressed the limits of social behaviour imposed by traditions. This includes seeing or meeting a man even if this is only a suspicion or a gossip. Honor crimes include also a husband kills his wife whom he or other family members suspected her of adultery. It is difficult to estimate the overall number of honour killings that take place yearly in Egypt. An Egyptian report based on 1995 statistics counted 52 honor killings (out of 819 murders) reported.

Neither Shariah nor modern laws have appropriately penalized the practice due to the strong influence of the tribal system and popular beliefs about women's sexuality. In addition, modern penal codes and also the practices reinforce the notion that men have a "right" to punish women for improper sexual behavior.... Egyptian films represent honour killing as part of highly valued and well respected tradition. Family honour is shown as dependent on the sexual conformity of its female family members. With the strong wave of conservatism in Egypt, strong criticism of the practice of honour killing by activists is rejected by many. They consider activists who condemn the practice as deviants from the religious principles and from good traditions and that they are only attempting to adopt a western agenda that does not respect family's honour and that permits females to practice premarital and extra marital relationships...

In the court case No. 831 of 1998 in Qena, a girl's father and brother killed her. She was mentally retarded and suffered from psychological disorders. She used to go out of the house without permission. She also used to spoil the food when cooking and ruin some of the household equipment. Her father and her brother could not tolerate her any longer. After her mother's death, they both pushed to far away place so that nobody could see them or hear her voice. They both strangled her with a red shawl she was wearing; they also hit her hard on her back and tummy with a stick and left her dead.

The court found out that there was no proof that the girl's chastity was in question. Both the father and the brother said that they killed her because of their deep concern and fear that she might get involved with a stranger due to her frequent trips outside the house. In spite of the fact that the court was sure that the two men had committed murder of first degree, the judge used article 17 of the Penal Code and gave the father a verdict of imprisonment for ten years only. Article 17 allows judges to decrease the sentences given in the case of murder when they decide that the condition of the murderer requires so. Such reductions reach as little as six months that could also be spent during the trial. Therefore the murderer can escape being imprisoned and walks free.

Source: Excerpted from Fatma Khafagy. 2005.

consistently gruesome results. For example men in Bangladesh, Great Britain, Brazil, Ecuador, Egypt, India, Israel, Italy, Jordan, Pakistan, Morocco, Sweden, Turkey, and Uganda have committed honor killings (see Box 8–6) and acid assaults with impunity on women who displeased husbands, fathers, and brothers or violated community standards of female conduct. Police often refuse to believe women who ask them for protection and turn a blind eye to these assaults and murders. In India, more than 5,000 brides die each year because their husbands and in-laws deem their dowries too small. Others are accused of "shameful behavior." This form of violence against women is often supported by mothers, mothers-in-law, sisters, and cousins, who fear the shame such women are said to bring on the family. If the killers are arrested, they may serve a few months in prison, if at all.

From Universality to Intersectionality

By the 1990s, the battered women's movement had successfully redefined domestic violence as a public problem by arguing that women of every class, racial and ethnic group, sexuality, and nationality were subjected to male domination and violence and that the criminal justice system should be the first line of defense for battered women. More than two decades of hard work on behalf of battered women had won the movement notable successes. Police were better informed about domestic violence and often mandated the arrest of abusers. Prosecutors and judges were more aware of the law and more willing to act on behalf of complainants. There was more public awareness of violence against women and more support for holding batterers accountable. Battering was no longer the "problem with no name." Activists had publicized and politicized it, adding terms such as battering and domestic violence to public discourse. Domestic violence shelters and services were available to many endangered women. The movement's influence on domestic violence policies went all the way to the national level. In 1994, Congress passed the Violence Against Women Act (VAWA), providing $1.6 billion to investigate and prosecute domestic violence crimes and to provide restitution and redress in cases that local prosecutors failed to bring forward. VAWA has been reauthorized several times, most recently in 2005.

Nevertheless, problems accompanied these successes. The "one size fits all" approach to remedies did not take into account the special situations of women of color, poor women, lesbians, and immigrants, who often suffered further abuses at the hands of police or in the legal system. The first generation of antiviolence activists did not dwell on the connections between violence and race or violence and poverty for fear of supporting racist stereotypes and class biases (Sen 1999). In other words, violence against women was treated as the same problem affecting all women. It was not until the 1990s that the problems of violence against women were reframed to recognize how race ethnicity, class, and immigrant status intersected with gender to shape the different fates of battered women and to call for different solutions.

Activists had assumed that battered women would make use of the services provided them by professionals. They could call the police, go to a safe shelter, or press charges against their abusive mates. For women without additional resources, these routes to safety were difficult, if not impossible solutions. Lacking alternatives, many battered women returned to their abusers. Criminal justice responses to domestic violence could not protect such women if they ignored the underlying structural conditions that made certain women vulnerable. For example, immigrant women needed bilingual and bicultural services to free themselves from their abusers; religious women needed special food and living arrangements; lesbians needed access to services that were not biased against them; and poor women needed affordable housing, accessible shelters, good, inexpensive child care, living wage jobs, and "humane welfare policy" (Dasgupta 2005; Sokoloff and Dupont 2005).

Researchers began to show how reliance on the criminal justice system for relief from violence had unintended negative consequences for women of color. First, reliance on the police heightened the dangers poor women faced. Women who called the police to intervene when they were threatened were sometimes also arrested. Arrest sometimes set in motion a chain of events that led women to lose their children to foster care. In some cases, after police removed a batterer from the premises, the angry abuser returned to seek retribution. Third, many immigrant women would not call the police, fearing that their immigrant status could be questioned. Fourth, in neighborhoods and communities where police brutality was an issue and where high proportions of the population faced incarceration, a woman calling the police might be labeled a snitch, or might fear contributing to stereotyping men of color as violent (Sen 1999).

Beyond Criminal Justice: Marginalized Battered Women at the Center

As it became evident that gendered violence had multiple, interconnected sources and consequences, scholars began to explore the ways that women's specific social locations of race ethnicity, class, and immigrant status shaped their experience of domestic violence and their responses to it (Josephson 2005). The idea that all women were equally at risk from all men missed the convergence of specific inequalities of class, race ethnicity, and nation in the lives of actual women and men. Moreover, listening to the experiences of domestic violence from the most marginalized and least privileged women showed that the criminal justice system also perpetuated violence against them. When white and middle-class women confronted personal violence, it was a terrifying tragedy, but many such women found the resources that allowed them to press for safety and justice. With access to health insurance, they could receive medical attention and psychological counseling. If they were employed in well-paying and secure jobs, they could obtain private legal assistance and find safe places to live. If they called the police, they need not worry that they might lose their children, their citizenship, or their freedom. On the other hand, when marginalized women of color used the criminal justice system, it was very likely to disempower and revictimize them. Aside from the immediate danger to them of calling the authorities, the system also created wider-ranging problems. First, it was disempowering to women if calling the police was the only way they could stop the violence. Second, tax income spent on policing and prisons was money that did not go to shelters, welfare, or affordable housing, leaving women less able to escape violent households. Third, the professional knowledge of workers in the criminal justice system—lawyers, social workers, and police—took precedence over the everyday knowledge of women living with violence.

If criminal justice was not the solution to violence, what was? The specifics of women's situations pointed in new directions: housing for poor battered women, bicultural and bilingual services for immigrants, shelters that accepted lesbians or homeless women, and special food and living arrangements for religious women. Placing women of color at the center of the analysis identified their specific needs. The analysis of the intersecting dimensions of risk among poor women and women of color also helped show the benefits to be gained from uniting personal struggles against gendered violence with community struggles against state violence such as police brutality, prisons, racism, and economic exploitation (Sokoloff and Dupont 2005).

An example is the coalition between the antiviolence organization, INCITE! Women of Color against Violence, and the organization, Critical Resistance, which works to eliminate the prison-industrial complex (see Box 8–7). INCITE! is a national activist organization of radical feminists of color who seek to "end violence against women of color and their communities through direct action, critical dialogue and grassroots organizing." Critical Resistance is an international movement to end the prison-industrial complex by challenging the belief that "caging and controlling people makes us safe." Security and safety will be won, they argue, when all people have their basic needs met for food, shelter, and freedom, exactly what the women's antiviolence movement also promotes (Sudbury 2005).

Andrea Smith, a longtime anti-violence and Native American activist, scholar, and cofounder of INCITE!, explains the importance of this coalition from the vantage point of the women's antiviolence movements:

> Any movement seeking to end violence will fail if its strategy supports and helps sustain the prison industrial complex. Prisons, policing, the death penalty, the war on terror, and the war on drugs, all increase rape, beating, isolation, oppression and death. As an anti-rape organization we cannot support the funneling of resources into the criminal justice system to punish rapists and batterers, as this does not help end violence. It only supports the same system that views incarcerations as a solution to complex social problems like rape and abuse. As survivors of rape and domestic violence we will not let the anti-violence movement be further co-opted to support the mass criminalization of young people, the disappearance of immigrants

---

Box 8–7 CRITICAL RESISTANCE/INCITE! JOINT STATEMENT: GENDER VIOLENCE AND THE PRISON INDUSTRIAL COMPLEX. 2001

We call on social justice movements to develop strategies and analysis that address both state AND interpersonal violence, particularly violence against women. Currently, activists/movements that address state violence (such as anti-prison, anti-police brutality groups) often work in isolation from activists/movements that address domestic and sexual violence. The result is that women of color, who suffer disproportionately from both state and interpersonal violence, have become marginalized within these movements. It is critical that we develop responses to gender violence that do not depend on a sexist, racist, classist, and homophobic criminal justice system. It is also important that we develop strategies that challenge the criminal justice system and that also provide safety for survivors of sexual and domestic violence. To live violence-free lives, we must develop holistic strategies for addressing violence that speak to the intersection of all forms of oppression http://www.incite-national.org/index.php?s=92.

and refugees, and the dehumanization of poor people, people of color, and people with disabilities. We support the anti-rape movement that builds sustainable communities on a foundation of safety, support, self-determination, and accountability. (A. Smith 2005, 426–27)

Antiviolence scholar-activists such as Smith believe that organizing against violence should be part of a comprehensive community empowerment agenda involving environmental, peace, human rights, and economic activism for living wages. Within this framework, members of the community would pursue alternatives to the criminalization of violent men while holding batterers accountable, and would work to eliminate structural violence, such as police brutality, street violence, and mass incarceration (West 2005). These suggestions for change may seem utopian, but they are based on a powerful analysis of gendered violence and its remedies. If nothing else, these visions can set a new direction for activists and scholars.

STATE VIOLENCE AGAINST MEN

As we have seen, private violence is linked in important ways to the criminal justice system. In this section, we look at another link, the gendered aspects of the mass imprisonment of men in the United States (see chapter 10 for a discussion of women's prisons). Since the 1980s, access to welfare, health care, shelter, and higher education—resources that could help poor and working-class women leave violent households and help poor and working-class men realize their potentials and restore their abilities to support and nurture families—has been severely curtailed. The retreat from public protections of vulnerable women and their families is actually a form of state-sponsored violence against women, who may find themselves without safe haven from abusers for lack of affordable alternative shelter or, if forced into homelessness, vulnerable to rape and violent crime on the streets (Fine 1999). The criminalization of poor men of color and their massive incarceration in federal and state prisons is a form of state violence against these men. Together these assaults add up to a major national offensive against poor communities. In many cases, then, the public violence of incarceration compounds and supports the harms of private violence.

At the end of 2005, more than two million people were in prison in the United States (22 percent of the world's prison population), and an additional five million were on probation or parole. The United States has the highest proportion of citizens in prison worldwide—726 prisoners for every 100,000 people as of 2004. The Cayman Islands with 664 prisoners per 100,000 population and Russia, with 638, rank second and third, respectively. Contrast these rates with those of Canada (116), Japan (48), Italy (95), and England (139). The prevalence of crime in the United States does not explain these figures. Twenty-one percent of the population in seventeen industrialized countries was victimized by crime in 1999, the same proportion as was victimized in the United States. In fact, the increase in prison construction and incarceration has taken place in the face of a 20 percent decrease in the rate of violent crime in the United States since 1991 (Sentencing Project 2004).

Prison construction and mass incarceration began in the era of the Reagan presidency and have become the "social" programs of our time. Public investment in prisons has flourished at the expense of investments in health, education, housing, and other forms of social expenditure. For example, from 1977 to 1995, average funding for prisons nationwide was twice the funding for public colleges (and six to one in Texas). The connection between loss of public funding for social programs and increase of public funding for prisons is often very direct. Between 1988 and 1998, the New York State legislature cut investment in public higher education in the same proportion as it increased funding for prisons. What happened in New York has also happened throughout the United States.

What accounts for the prison construction boom? The sharp rise in incarceration has pushed the demand for new prisons (although it is equally plausible that the building of new prisons increases the demand for prisoners). As prison construction proceeds, new interests are cultivated. Communities, needing jobs and tax dollars, lobby for prisons to be built nearby. Prison guards press for more prisons, looking to enhance their job security, raise their salaries, and increase their benefits. Private firms that contract with the prison authorities for assorted supplies and for cheap labor want to expand their profitability by tapping into the $35 billion a year spent on prisons. Angela Davis compares the institutionalization of private corporate interests in prisons to the "military industrial complex," the term for the permanent armaments industry allied with the United States military. Davis explains that:

> As the U.S. prison system expanded, so did corporate involvement in construction, provision of goods and services, and use of prison labor. Because of the extent to which prison building and operation began to attract vast amounts of capital—from the construction industry to food and health care provision—in a way that recalled the emergence of the military industrial complex, we began to refer to a "prison industrial complex." (Davis 2003, 28)

The vast majority of people caught up in the feverish expansion of prisons are Latino, First Nations and African American men and, increasingly, women of color.

Sexual Violence in Men's Prisons

It is unusual for men to admit to feeling afraid on the streets and in other public venues. However, men who go to prison do fear sexual assault, and they are right to do so. The Bureau of Justice Statistics special report, based on a survey of 1,856 adult correctional facilities in the United States, reported 6,241 allegations of sexual violence in prisons and jails in 2006, up from 5,386 in 2004. A report on male rape in U.S. prisons begins as follows:

> A Florida prisoner whom we will identify only as P.R., was beaten, suffered a serious eye injury, and assaulted by an inmate armed with a knife, all due to his refusal to submit to anal sex. After six months of repeated threats and endurance, he tried to commit suicide by slashing his wrists with a razor. In a letter to Human Rights Watch, he chronicled his unsuccessful efforts to induce prison authorities to protect him from abuse. Summing up these experiences, he wrote: "The opposite of compassion is not hatred, it's indifference" (Human Rights Watch 2001, 1)

There are no national data on prison rape, but surveys in men's prisons in several states show that between 20 and 33 percent of male inmates have been forced or pressured into sex or raped in prison. If these figures hold true around the country, at least 140,000 inmates have been raped while under state supervision. Inmates are targeted because of their looks, age, and size; because they are white, gay, or lack "street smarts"; and because they are, in some ways, tagged as "feminine." Prison rapists are usually younger, larger, and stronger than their victims, convicted of violent crimes, and often gang members (Human Rights Watch, No escape: Male rape in U.S. prisons, 2001).

As the preceding quotation from the prison report suggests, prison rape can be brutal and extremely violent. Gang assaults are common and victims may be viciously beaten and sometimes killed. Human Rights Watch describes the case of one prisoner who entered a Texas maximum security prison in August 1994, and was attacked within the week by twenty inmates demanding sex and money. When he refused he was beaten for almost two hours and left to die. Guards said they had not noticed that the beating was happening.

Prison rape is an example of "doing gender" backed up by the threat of overt violence. Victims are forced into sexually subordinate roles, marked as "turn outs" or "punks" who are sexual targets of other prisoners. Once labeled, their reputation follows them throughout the prison system. To escape their fate, such prisoners may agree to become the property of another prisoner who will protect them in exchange for sex and domestic labor. The prisoner may be forced to wash his protector's clothes, give massages, cook his food, and clean his cell. "Owners" of slaves often rent or sell them to other prisoners for sex. Like oppressed housewives, choices about how to dress and to whom to speak may be controlled by the person who "owns" them. Their name may be replaced by a female one. Prison staff regularly ignore these relationships, despite the attempt of victims to report assaults and to gain protection. In men's prisons, violence that creates such differences is as damaging to the victims as is the rape of women. Prisoners suffer nightmares, depression, shame, and self-hatred, just as raped women do. They often become suicidal. Victims are sometimes killed outright by their abusers, or killed indirectly, when rapists infect them with AIDS.

Another form of prison violence visited on prisoners is the masculinized sexual violence made familiar to Americans by the scandals of Abu Ghraib in Iraq and other secret American prisons overseas. There is evidence to suggest that the practices exposed in Iraqi prisons are routine in many U.S. prisons. Long-term isolation, mock executions of prisoners, the use of dogs to intimidate prisoners, restraint hoods, belts and beds, stun grenades, tethers, waist and leg chains, air tasers, and other forms of militarized control and sexual torture are forms of rule in our prisons at home and abroad (Magnani and Wray 2006). Such gendered treatment is a stunning violation of prisoners' human rights and it links domestic terror in prisons to the gendered terror of war in conflict zones.

GENDERED VIOLENCE IN CONFLICT ZONES

Gender and sexual violence are forms of global terrorism that take millions of lives each year. The violence that occurs in families or between intimates is largely invisible. It is also the case that most war victims—civilian women, children, and the elderly—are invisible too (see Box 8–8). The principal victims of violence in wars these days are civilians, often women and children (Marshall 2004b).

There are no longer hard and fast boundaries between war zones in which armies clash and the home front where civilians live in relative safety. Much of this violence grows from

Box 8–8 SOME CHARACTERISTICS OF GLOBAL
GENDERED VIOLENCE

"Violence against women persists in every country in the world as a pervasive violation of human rights and a major impediment to achieving gender equality," according to then-UN Secretary General Kofi Annan, as the UN launched the first-ever in-depth report on gender violence worldwide on October 9, 2006. A 113-page landmark UN study on gender violence says women continue to be victims of sexual harassment, human trafficking, and blatant discrimination worldwide (see http://www.un.org/womenwatch/daw/vaw/ngo-contributions.htm).

- At least 60 million girls who would otherwise be expected to be alive are "missing" from various populations, mostly in Asia, as a result of sex-selective abortions, infanticide, or neglect (UNFPA State of the World Population 2000, Ending Violence Against Women and Girls. http://www.unfpa.org/swp/2000/english/ch03.html).
- In Bangladesh, 47 percent of adult women report physical assault by a male partner (UNFPA State of the World Population 2000).
- Globally, at least one in three women and girls has been beaten or sexually abused in her lifetime. (The World Bank 2005. www.worldbank.org).
- The trafficking of women and children is a form of violence. Each year, an estimated 800,000 to 900,000 women and children are bought, sold, or forced across national borders. It is estimated that between 18,000 and 20,000 of those women and children are trafficked into the United States annually for sexual exploitation or forced labor, but some estimates are as high as 50,000. Only ninety-three UN member states have some legislative provision prohibiting human trafficking. "Where legislation exists, it is often inadequate in its scope and coverage and/or not effectively implemented," the report notes.

the determination of states and corporations to control the abundant natural resources in these regions. For instance, in Congo at least eighty-five multinational corporations, including some of the largest U.S. companies, covet Congo's minerals, such as coltan (used in cell phones and laptops), cobalt, copper, gold, diamonds, and uranium (Goodwin 2004). Resistance movements and government forces alike sometimes take women and children hostage. In northern Uganda, a years-long conflict is characterized by sexual and gender-based violence against women and girls by the Lord's Resistance Army (LRA) and government forces. UNICEF estimates that more than 32,000 children were abducted by the LRA between 1986 and 2002 and used as child combatants and sex slaves. Ugandan government forces also committed mass rapes. Likewise, in Sierra Leone, one-third of all women and girls were deliberately systematically targeted for rape, sexual slavery, and forced pregnancy during the conflict between 1991 and 2002. To date, there has been little effort to provide

- An estimated 1 million children, mostly girls, enter the sex trade each year (UNICEF). In a study of 475 people in prostitution from five countries (South Africa, Thailand, Turkey, United States, and Zambia), 62 percent reported having been raped, 73 percent reported having experienced physical assault, and 92 percent stated that they wanted to escape prostitution immediately. (Farley et al. 1998).

- So-called honor killings take the lives of thousands of young women every year, mainly in north Africa, western Asia, and parts of south Asia. According to official crime statistics in India, 6,822 women were killed in 2002 as a result of violence related to demands for dowry—the payment of cash or goods by the bride's family to the groom's family.

- Of the 1,322 marriages across six villages in Kyrgyzstan, nearly half were the result of kidnappings, and as many as two-thirds were nonconsensual.

- In South Africa, it is estimated that a woman is raped every eighty-three seconds. Only 20 percent of these cases are ever reported to the police (Vetten, Lisa. 2000. Rape statistics are not a closed subject. Johannesburg, S.A.: Centre for the Study of Violence and Reconciliation. Http://www.csvr.org.za/wits/articles/artrec1.htm)

- More than 90 million African women and girls are victims of female circumcision or other forms of genital mutilation. In some countries, most women are subjected to this practice. For example, according the British medical journal *The Lancet,* 92 percent of all women in Mali have undergone female genital surgery. Efua Dorkenoo (Cutting the Rose: Female Genital Mutilation : The Practice & Its Prevention 1996 Austin, TX: Harry Ransom Humanities Research Center) claims that 6,000 young girls around the world undergo genital cutting each day. Female genital mutilation has been reported in twenty-eight countries in Africa, several countries in the Middle East and Europe, Latin American, Malaysia, Indonesia, and the United States. Some activists in the West compare surgeries to "normalize" intersex infants to female genital mutilation.

justice, care, or reparations for these victims (Amnesty International 2006b, 2007). In the next section, we look more closely at one country in the throes of militarized violence.

Guatemala: A Case Study

Rape, torture, and murder is the fate of thousands of women caught in the globalized economic, social, and political transformations located in conflict zones in poor countries such as Mexico, Guatemala, Colombia, and Peru. In Central and South America, thousands of young women, students, housewives, and low-wage workers in *maquiladoras* (export assembly plants) where they assemble consumer goods such as clothing, shoes, toys, and electronic equipment at a fraction of the cost of production in the United States, have been abducted, tortured, and murdered, their

Box 8–9 THE JUAREZ PROJECT: NAFTA AND THE FEMICIDES

It is important to recognize that the femicide in Ciudad Juarez and Chihuahua does not exist in a vacuum. The problem has its roots in the economic disparity that ravages the US-Mexico border, and we are already seeing this problem spread to other cities facing the same problems.

These murders really accelerated in 1994–1995, which is significant because it was the first few years after the implementation of the North American Free Trade Agreement, or NAFTA. This was a time period when we began to see massive migration of people from the Mexican rural countryside to the cities. Most of these migrants were young men and women, coming alone or with little support structure, trying to earn money to send home to their families. This was because of an economic agricultural crisis created by NAFTA.

NAFTA, a trade agreement designed to eliminate barriers to trade, forced Mexico to reduce price supports for Mexican agricultural producers to "level the playing field" for US producers to sell their goods on the Mexican market. However, the US, through a major loophole in NAFTA, was allowed to raise already high tax-payer subsidies for our agricultural producers. We did this largely to compete with the European Union and Japan which also heavily subsidize their agricultural producers. However, these subsidies have allowed producers in powerful industrial countries to drastically undercut producers in the developing world. For example, in Mexico, US subsidized corn is being sold at about 33% below the actual cost of production. This means that Mexican farmers simply can't compete. Not because they don't produce corn efficiently, but because they don't receive the kind of tax payer subsidies that US producers receive. Now in the US, a very small percentage of the population still farms the land. Most farming is done by a handful of large-agribusiness companies. In fact, the few small farmers left in this country receive very little support. 70% of subsidies go to only 30% of the producers. In Mexico, on the other hand, about a quarter of the population still relies on farming as their primary source of income. This population has been devastated by the flooding of cheap-subsidized agricultural products on the Mexican market. About 1.5 million farmers have had to leave their land and look for work in other sectors. They are moving to the cities, especially along the US-Mexico border, looking for work in the maquiladoras (factories that produce for export), or they are attempting to immigrate to the US, often as undocumented workers, to look for work they desperately need to feed their families. This migration has created a class of desperately poor and unprotected people, especially women, along the US-Mexico border. In fact, many of the femicide victims were workers in US-owned companies. Most of the victims had not lived in the region for more than a few years. Some of the bodies are unidentified and it is thought that they may be migrants from southern Mexico or Central America who simply don't have family in the area who know they are missing. Wages in the factories have gone progressively down in the years since NAFTA was implemented as factories replace their workers regularly with new migrants to the area more desperate for work and willing to work for even lower wages. Women, like workers in the region, are treated as disposable commodities. Something to be used up and thrown away.

FEMICIDES OF JUAREZ AND CHIHUAHUA

For more than a decade, the cities of Chihuahua and Juarez, near the US-Mexico border, have been killing fields for young women, the site of over 400 unsolved femicides. Despite the horrific nature of these crimes, authorities at all levels exhibit indifference, and there is strong evidence that some officials may be involved. Impunity and corruption has permitted the criminals, whoever they are, to continue committing these acts, knowing there will be no consequences.

A significant number of victims work in the maquiladora sector—sweatshops that produce for export with 90% destined for the United States. The maquiladoras employ mainly young women at poverty level wages. In combination with lax environmental regulations and low tariffs under the North America Free Trade Agreement (NAFTA), the maquiladoras are amassing tremendous wealth. Yet despite the crime wave, they offer almost no protection for their workers. High profile government campaigns such as Ponte Vista (Be Aware), a self defense program, and supplying women with whistles have been ineffective and are carried out mainly for public relations purposes.

Small advances in the struggle for justice are due to the perseverance of victims' families who cannot be silenced despite the efforts of state and federal authorities to keep them quiet. Campaigns by local, national and international non-governmental organizations are also important. Often grassroots groups work in a climate of threats and defamation by government officials for making one simple demand—STOP THE FEMICIDE!

SOURCE: The Juarez Project (juarezproject@yahoo.com), Match 26, 2007.

bodies dumped on the outskirts of cities. Three hundred and seventy-three women were murdered in Bolivia in 2003 and 2004, 143 in Peru in 2003, and more than 2,200 in Guatemala.

These assaults were first identified and named "femicide" (Russell 1992) in the Mexican cities of Ciudad Juarez and Chihuahua, located on the U.S. border, where more than 500 women have been found raped, tortured, and murdered since 1993 and where dozens more remain missing (see Box 8–9). The crimes take place in a climate of hypermasculinity and acceptance of violence against women (Amnesty International USA 2006a).

Some of these attacks on women are directly and indirectly connected to wars that have plagued the region. The Colombian military, as well as right wing paramilitary forces, have been implicated in rapes and killings of women. Peru's Truth and Reconciliation Commission identified rape as a form of torture during that country's civil wars between 1980 and 2000 (Paterson 2006). The connection of women's murders with militarism is particularly apparent in Guatemala, which suffered a thirty-year civil war. Rape and sexual violence were among the tactics used by the armed forces in that country to intimidate and silence opponents.

The overthrow by the U.S. Marines of the democratically elected government of Guatemala in the 1950s inaugurated the decades-long period of state-initiated gendered violence. There were genocidal attacks on the indigenous peasant majority. Between 1960 and 1996, the military threatened, tortured, and killed with impunity. Entire villages were massacred. Women were attacked as "mothers of guerillas," pregnant women had their wombs slit open, and women and girls were gang raped. Young men from these communities who were suspected of supporting the resistance or avoiding conscription were brutally tortured and murdered. U.S.-backed government troops and their paramilitary allies routinely raped, tortured, and murdered women to destroy targeted villages. Captured women were taken as sex slaves and forced to wash and cook for the troops as well (just as the perpetrators of male prison rape did), strengthening assumptions men may already have about women as providers of sex, food, and clean clothes.

The war has ended, but similar tortures and murders of women continue. Killings of women in Guatemala rose between 2001 and 2006, according to Amnesty International USA. Up to 665 cases were registered in 2005, 527 in 2004, 383 in 2003, and 163 in 2002. In 2006, 299 cases were reported between January and May—a faster pace than in 2005. Female murder victims in Guatemala often suffer exceptional brutality before being killed, including rape, mutilation, and dismemberment.

What explains this level of violence against women? What has created killers who show such contempt for and hatred of women? In Guatemala, some men consider women their servants and property. Neither domestic violence nor sexual harassment is a criminal offense in that country. This continuing violence echoes the violence of Guatemala's past. Some suspect that former soldiers, trained in sadistic methods of combat and demobilized after the war without any plans for readapting them to civilian life or providing them with jobs, are involved in the killing. Some former government soldiers have turned to gangs and organized crime; others work for private security agencies or the police. Militarization of this society damns both women and men. Women live in fear on a daily basis; men shore up their militarized masculinity through violence and intimidation.

As the case of Guatemala shows, militarism and conflict intensify the epidemics of violence against women around the world. Rape and sexual assault are part of war. As the "property" of the enemy, women are seen as a way to "get" at men. In addition, military training belittles women. Pornography and prostitution are officially sanctioned as entertainment for soldiers (Enloe 2000). Sexual harassment and rape of women in the military are ongoing problems that are not confined to conflict zones. Domestic abuse on American military bases is widespread, as men (and some women) returning from active duty feel entitled to use violence at home (Marshall 2004a).

WHAT IS TO BE DONE? CEDAW, THE INTERNATIONAL CRIMINAL COURT, AND SECURITY COUNCIL RESOLUTION 1325

Women are not only victims of state terror and war. Women and men have also contributed to the global human rights movement to establish women's most basic right to physical safety. Largely because of grassroots pressure from women's groups around the world, the United Nations has created three promising mechanisms for eradicating gender violence: the Convention on the Elimination of All Forms of Discrimination Against Women (CEDAW), the International Criminal Court, and Resolution 1325 of the UN Security Council.

CEDAW, adopted by the UN General Assembly in 1979, is often called a bill of human rights for women. It calls on governments that signed the treaty to remove all forms of discrimination against women; to ensure women's equal access to political and public life, education, health, and employment; and to protect their reproductive rights. The United States is one of a handful of nations that has not ratified CEDAW.

The existence of this treaty requires countries to examine the conditions of life for women and girls, to report on structures and customs that discriminate against them, and to take action against the barriers to equality. The treaty has been important in stopping violence against women (Amnesty International USA 2006b). In Colombia, the courts ruled in 1992 that the absence of legal recourse then available to a female victim of domestic violence violated her human rights to life and personal security. The state now ensures protection for all such women. Ugandans have created programs and policies to campaign against domestic violence, using state funds for the purpose. In Costa Rica, the courts are authorized to order an abusive spouse to leave home and to continue providing economic support. Training and programs to combat sex crimes are being established, and women officials must handle rape investigations and prosecutions.

In 2001, for the first time, the military was held accountable for sexual violence in a time of conflict. Justice Florence Mumba of Zambia sentenced three Bosnian Serb soldiers standing trial on charges of rape and torture to twenty-eight years, twenty years, and twelve years imprisonment, respectively, the first case of wartime sexual enslavement to come before the International War Crimes Tribunal in The Hague. At the Hague trial, women testified about how paramilitary soldiers entered the "rape camps," and selected women and girls as young as twelve for nightly gang rapes and sexual torture. These sentences were a victory for the international women's movement, which lobbied the United Nations to include wartime rape in the jurisdiction of the International Criminal Court. Rape has also been prosecuted in Rwanda. In 1998, the Rwanda tribunal found former mayor Jean-Paul Akayesu guilty of nine counts of genocide, crimes against humanity, and war crimes. Women now are demanding that they be fully involved in all international efforts to hold armies and security forces accountable for sexual terrorism, as well as in all efforts to maintain and promote peace and security.

Also in 2001, the UN Security Council passed the landmark Resolution 1325, giving women the right to participate in conflict resolution and peace-building efforts. The resolution mandated that participants in peace-making operations take a gender perspective on conflict and pay special attention to the needs of women and girls in reconstruction efforts. Although Resolution 1325 has not yet been implemented, it frames attempts to bring women's political energies into the work of the UN Security Council and it has inspired grassroots activists in conflict zones. Women in Melanesia have established women's community media to spread information about the resolution and to inform women about what others are doing to make it a reality at the community level. Women from the Democratic Republic of Congo lobbied for a gender office within the UN peacekeeping mission to that country and have worked closely with that office to spread information about Resolution 1325 and to insert a gender perspective into all levels of government. Women in Kosovo have sponsored television shows explaining the resolution and have built a network of women around the resolution. Iraqi women have used Resolution 1325 to support their call for women's equal rights and responsibilities. Cohn believes that these grassroots efforts "broaden the gaze" beyond the traditional political and military aspects of peace and security.

> It affirms women's rights to protection and participation; and should it be widely implemented, women's experience of conflict and their ability to prevent or end it could be substantially transformed. What could also be transformed by this "broadening of the gaze" is the mainstream belief in the adequacy of restricting one's vision to the traditional political and military aspects of peace and security. Resolution 1325, as it moves from rhetoric to reality, could potentially transform our ideas about the prevention of war, the bases for sustainable peace, and the pathways to achieve them. (Cohn 2004, 9)

In 2004, the NGO Working Group on Women, Peace and Security was invited to submit a paper, "No Women No Peace," to the UN High-Level Panel on Threats, Challenges, and Change (NGO Working Group 2004). The paper urged a framework for collective action based on prevention, the participation of women in peace and security, and the protection of civilians. The paper recommended that the UN and the international community embrace the full and equal participation of women in peace processes; that they collaborate with women's local peace groups; that they encompass economic development, social justice, and environmental protection in security efforts; that they build a culture of peace growing from equality between women and men; and that they engage men and boys, including young men who have been trained to brutalize and kill, in the struggle for gender equality.

Box 8–10 AMERICANS' SPECIAL RESPONSIBILITY

Explore the website PeaceWomen (www.peacewomen.org), which shares information from activists around the world, and the website of the United Nations Development Fund for Women (UNIFEM; www.womenwarpeace.org), which is designed to inform activists about women in conflict situations, gender issues, and peace-building activities. Learn about the issues. Then think about the ways your new knowledge can help you to challenge American insularity.

These suggestions are a recipe for fundamentally transforming our gender-divided and violence-generating world by placing women and gender at the center of antiviolence and peace-building activities. They are a formula for promoting the partnership model of society described by Riane Eisler.

The fact that the United States has not signed UN Security Council Resolution 1325 or CEDAW gives U.S. women and men a special responsibility for challenging and changing our country's insularity and its role in perpetuating violent conflict around the world (see Box 8–10).

This chapter has traced the continuum of gendered violence from the most intimate corners of our private lives to spaces as large and diverse as universities and prisons, police forces, armies, and the widest global arenas. Space limitations mean that this chapter only scratches the surface. We could fill many volumes documenting the forms of gendered violence in the world today, and more that trace the violent past. Nor has this chapter begun to explore the work of the peace makers, those men and women who are laboring to end local and global gendered violence.

What explanations for the epidemic of gendered violence have emerged from this review? First, force is necessary to maintain the inequalities of power and wealth that accrue to the masculinist strata of ruling elites. Naturalizing such inequalities as biologically, evolutionarily, or psychologically necessary has served the status quo, but that unjust order has become harder and harder to maintain. As women and men come to see gender inequalities and gender injustice as part of the world we have made and can alter, they take steps toward ending gender inequality and promoting gender justice (see Box 8–11). Second, feminist

---

Box 8–11   STATEMENT OF CONSCIENCE: A FEMINIST VISION FOR PEACE

As citizens of Planet Earth we affirm our freedom.

We declare our right to live free from aggression and violence, and we encourage every person who reads this statement to add their own experience of terrorism in all its forms and proclaim the freedom of peace again and again.

We declare the rhetoric of "good" versus "evil" invalid. Every battle pretends to be for "good." But victory is too often celebrated by further loss of life, the rape of mothers and children, and the forced sexual servitude of daughters. Those who create and nurture life are both the first and last casualties of violent conflict. Those who wield violence are declared heroes.

When efforts to quiet violent conflict are made, women, whose stake in the resolution of conflict is at least as high as men's, must be involved as full members of peace negotiation teams. Any "peace" that does not address the worldwide pandemic of violence against women and girls is not peace.

As women and men of conscience, we call for an end to the terrorism that forces upon women and children the obscene choice between prostitution and starvation, a choice that degrades us all. Warfare and its chaotic aftermath intensify the environment and opportunities for abduction and trafficking. The period following violent conflict exacerbates domestic violence. Usurping the healthy social role of men in neighborhoods under attack must also be addressed. Violent destruction, especially when followed by an apathetic and delayed restoration, effectively demoralizes families and destroys the well-being of communities. War strips men of their livelihood and dignity, and fosters hateful attitudes toward women, even their own wives, mothers, and daughters. The systematic use of rape as a weapon of war increases the alienation between men and their assaulted families. The detention, rape and torture of women and children as a strategy of warfare against their male relatives is evil in its most vile form.

As women and men of conscience, we demand that the use of rape as a weapon of war be stopped. As the linkages between gender, conflict, and a more rapid spread of the deadly HIV/AIDS plague are better understood, so too must be the devastating consequences for the women violated and the babies born of this hellish form of warfare. Special programs must be fielded on an emergency basis in former war zones to prevent, and to address, the widespread suffering faced by victims of rape and forced sexual servitude.

As women and men of conscience, we call for the education of women and girls in every nation, especially in war-damaged societies. We demand immediate response to the pleas of women in these societies for immediate assistance with literacy programs to ensure their full participation in brokering peace, in decision-making, and in post-conflict reconstruction.

We defy those who would limit our experience of life to the maintenance of a caste system that supports the pursuit of profit and personal aggrandizement at the expense of meeting basic human needs. We challenge world leaders to put an end to the terrorism of hunger, thirst, sexual servitude, racism, patriarchy, nationalism, joblessness, homelessness, able-ism, homophobia, ignorance, child molestation and elder neglect that many of the Earth's citizens face daily. When every child of this world is adequately nourished, clothed, educated and healthy; when every adult who wishes to work has life-sustaining employment; when women and children are free from abuse then human life on earth will have become so highly valued that terroristic activity will lose its attraction.

and race-sensitive research has broadened and complicated the picture of violence against women. Older ideas that all women were victimized by all men have been jettisoned. We now see that inequalities of race and class place some women in greater jeopardy from sexual and gendered violence than others. We also see that inequalities of race ethnicity, class, gender, and nation shape men's fate as well. We are also learning how these forms of violence are

In the meantime, we will defend the lives of our children with our own lives, as necessary, but we refuse to endorse pre-emptive strikes that result in the massacre of thousands of innocents as a response to crimes against humanity.

We oppose terrorism in all its forms, whether sponsored by non-governmental groups or the state. We grieve deeply at the loss of life at the World Trade Center and the Pentagon on September 11, 2001. We also grieve the untold thousands of non-combatants slaughtered in the rain of bombs in Afghanistan in the aftermath of the September 11 attacks. Our hearts ache with sorrow as the slaughter of Iraqi citizens is justified to the world with the marketing of lies and fear. We are thankful that we have not yet become immune to grief.

We oppose terrorism in all its forms, but we steadfastly support the right to a fair trial, in an international court, and based on clear evidence, of all those accused of terrorism. We steadfastly oppose any prejudgment of the guilt of any individual accused of terrorism based on the color of their skin or the mother-blessing of their name. We demand a lifting of the cloak of secrecy, that prevents disclosure of evidence, in the investigations of the mass murder of thousands of our brothers and sisters in New York and Washington on September 11, 2001. We demand accountability for the lack of indictments and statements of progress.

We repudiate payment for a war machine that compromises our capability to feed and educate our children and care for our parents in their old age. We demand a full accounting of expenditures for war during the past year.

We resent and resist the gratuitous encouragement of fear. We become more cynical toward the source and motives of each new rumor of imminent terrorist attack. But our children do not have our insight, and their childhoods are being destroyed by nightmares about powerlessness and destruction.

We lift our heads proudly and boldly, and join our sisters and brothers throughout the world in a call for peace and justice, in full knowledge that our plea will be labeled treasonous by those world leaders who would defend peace by generating war.

We repudiate warlords and praise peacemakers. We are brave enough to step back from the brink of global warfare, and we demand leaders who are strong enough to endure peace.

SOURCE: Feminist Peace Network, September 2002. http://www.petitiononline.com/FemPeace/

connected, how gendered personal violence can feed off of gendered state violence, as when remedies for personal violence against women shore up a system of criminal justice that visits violence on batterers and battered alike, or when war leaves the mark of sexual terrorism on the postwar society. These new understandings of the ways gendered violence affects individuals, communities, and states suggest pioneering remedies and courses of action.

Does gender matter? In terms of violence and its termination, it is central.

REFERENCES

Ahn, Christine, and Gwyn Kirk. 2005. Why war is all the rage. *San Francisco Chronicle*, May 29.

Amnesty International USA. 1997. Women's human rights: Women in prison. http://www.amnestyUSA.org/women/womeninprison.html.

———. 2006a. Killings of women in Guatemala continue unchallenged, says Amnesty International. http://www.amnestyusa.org/countries/guatemala/document.

———. 2006b. Stop violence against women. http://www.amnestyusa.org/women/cedaw/index.html.

———. 2007. Sierra Leone: Getting reparations right for survivors of sexual violence. http://www.amnesty.org/en/report/info/AFR51/005/2007.

Benard, Cheryl, and Edith Schlaffer. 1993. "The man in the street": Why he harasses. In *Feminist frontiers III*, ed. Laurel Richardson and Verta Taylor, 388–391. New York: McGraw-Hill.

Bureau of Justice Crime Data Brief. 2003. Intimate Partner Violence, 1993–2001. February 2003.

Chicago Foundation for Women. 2007. What will it take? http://www.whatwillittake.org.

Cohn, Carol. 2004. Feminist peacemaking. *Women's Review of Books* 21 (5), 8-9.

Dasgupta, Shamita Das. 2005. Women's realities: Defining violence against women by immigration, race, and class. In *Domestic violence at the margins: Readings on race, class, gender, and culture*, ed. Natalie Sokoloff with Christina Pratt, 56–70. New Brunswick, NJ: Rutgers University Press.

Davis, Angela. 2003. *Are prisons obsolete?* New York: Seven Stories Press.

D.C. Rape Crisis Center. 2008. Male survivors of sexual assault. http://www.dcrcc.org/male-survivors.htm. Accessed June 25, 2008.

Department of Health and Human Services. 2006. Women of Color Health Data Book: Factors Affecting the health of women of color. Office of Research on Women's Health NIH publication number 06–4247.

Eaton, Mary. 1986. *Justice for women? Family, court, and social control*. London: Open University Press.

Eisler, Riane. 1987. *The chalice and the blade: Our history, our future*. San Francisco: Harper & Row.

Enloe, Cynthia. 2000. *Maneuvers: The international politics of militarizing women's lives*. Berkeley: University of California Press.

Epstein, Helen. 2003. Ghetto miasma: Enough to make you sick? *New York Times Magazine*, October 12, 81–105.

Ewing, Charles, and Moss Aubrey. 1987. Battered women and public opinion: Some realities about the myths. *Journal of Family Violence* 2 (3): 257–64.

Farley, Melissa, Isin Baral, Merab Kiremire, and Ufuk Sezgin. 1998. Prostitution in five countries: Violence and posttraumatic stress disorder. *Feminism & Psychology* 8 (4): 405–26.

Ferraro, Kathleen. 1988. An existential approach to battering. In *Family abuse and its consequences*, ed. Gerald Hotaling, David Finkelhor, John Kirkpatrick, and Murray Straus. Newbury Park, CA: Sage, 126–138.

Fine, Michelle. 1999. *The unknown city: The lives of poor and working-class young adults*. Boston: Beacon Press.

Goodwin, Jan. 2004. Silence = rape: While the world looks the other way, sexual violence spreads in the Congo. *The Nation*, March 8, 18–22.

Gordon, Margaret T. and Riger, Stephanie. 1989. *The female fear*. New York: Free Press.

Greenwood, Gregory L, 2002. "Battering victimization among a probability-based sample of men who have sex with men," American Journal of Public Health, 92, No. 12, December.

Griffin, Susan. 1979. *Rape: The politics of consciousness*. San Francisco: Harper & Row.

Hanmer, Jalna, Jill Radford, and Elizabeth A. Stanko. 1989. *Women, policing, and male violence: International perspectives*. London: Routledge.

Helliwell, Christine. 2000. "It's only a penis": Rape, feminism, and difference. *Signs* 25 (3): 789–816.

Horton, Teresa, 2008. Hollaback web site. http://www.hollabacknyc.blogspot.com/ Accessed May 28.

Human Rights Watch. 2001. No escape: Male rape in U.S. prisons. http://www.hre.org/reports/2001/prison/report1.html. Accessed June 22, 2008.

Josephson, Jyl. 2005. The intersectionality of domestic violence and welfare in the lives of poor women. In *Domestic violence at the margins: Readings on race, class, gender, and culture,* ed. Natalie Sokoloff with Christina Pratt, 83–101. New Brunswick, NJ: Rutgers University Press.

Katz, Vackson. 2006. Coverage of "School Shootings" words the central issue. CommonDreams.org, October 11.

Kimmel, Michael. 2004. The Gendered Society, Second Edition. New York: Oxford.

——. 2000. Manhood and Violence: The Deadliest Equation. *Brother.* Louisville, CO: National Organization for Men against Sexism.

Labell, L. S. 1979. Wife abuse: A sociological study of battered women and their mates. *Victimology* 4:258–67.

Lie, Gwat-Yong and S. Gentlewarrier. 1991. Intimate violence in lesbian relationships: Discussion of survey findings and practice implications. *Journal of Social Service Research* 46: 15.

Lipscomb, G.H., D. Muram, P.M. Speck, and B.M. Mercer. 1992. Male victims of sexual assault. *Journal of the American Medical Association.* June. 3064–3066.

Magnani, Laura and Harmon L. Wray. 2006. Beyond prisons: A new interfaith paradigm for our failed prison system. Minneapolis: Augsberg Fortress.

Marshall, Lucinda. 2004a. The connection between militarism and violence against women. *ZNet,* February 21. http://www.zmag.org/ZNET.tm.

——. 2004b. Unacceptable: The impact of war on women and children. *CommonDreams.org,* December 18. http://www.commondreams.org/views04/1219–26.htm.

Martin, Patricia Yancy, and Robert A. Hummer. 1989. Fraternities and rape on campus. *Gender and Society* 3:457–73.

Messerschmidt, James W. 2000. *Nine lives: Adolescent masculinities, the body, and violence.* Boulder, CO: Westview Press.

Messner, Michael. 2002. *Taking the field: Women, men and sports.* Minneapolis: University of Minnesota Press.

——. 1992. *Power at play: Sports and the problem of masculinity.* Boston: Beacon Press.

National Center for the Victims of Crime. 1995. Sexual Assault Legislation. *Get Help Series.* Washington, D.C..

NGO Working Group for Women, Peace and Security. 2004. Making Peace Work for Women. April. http://www.womenpeacesecurity.org/news-analysis/analysis/2004/nowomen-nopeace.html Accessed June 22, 2008.

Parenti, Christian. 1999. *Lockdown America: Police and prisons in the age of crisis.* London: Verso Books.

Paterson, Kent. 2006. Femicide on the rise in Latin America. International Relations Center Americas Program Report. http://americas.irconline.org/am/3142.

Philips, H. P. 1966. *Thai peasant personality: The patterning of interpersonal behavior in the village of Bang Chan.* Berkeley: University of California Press.

Ptacek, James. 1988. Why do men batter their wives? In *Feminist perspectives on wife abuse,* ed. K. Yllo and M. Bograd. Newbury Park, CA: Sage.

Putnam, Robert. 2000. *Bowling alone: The collapse and revival Of American community.* New York: Simon and Schuster.

Radford, Lorraine. 1987. Legalizing woman abuse. In *Women, violence, and social control,* ed. J. Hanmer and M. Maynard. Atlantic Highlands, NJ: Humanities Press International, 135-151.

Rao, Kavitha. 2006. 'Eve-Teasing' Makes India's Streets Mean for Women. *Women's E-News* December 11. http://www.womensenews.org/article.cfm/dyn/aid/2991/context/ourdailylives Accessed June 22, 2008.

Russell, Diana. 1992. *Femicide: The politics of woman killing.* New York: Twayne.

Sabo, Don. 1994. *Sex, violence, and power in sports: Rethinking masculinity*. Freedom, CA: The Crossing Press.

Sanday, Peggy Reeves. 2007. *Fraternity gang rape : sex, brotherhood, and privilege on campus:* 2nd ed. New York: New York University Press.

Sen, Rinku. 1999. Between a rock and a hard place: Domestic violence in communities of color. *Color Lines* 2 (1), 1–4.

Sentencing Project. 2004. New incarceration figures: Growth in population continues. http://www. sentencingproject.org/pdfs/1044.pdf.

Smith, Andrea. 2005. Looking to the future: Domestic violence, women of color, the state, and social change. In *Domestic violence at the margins: Readings on race, class, gender, and culture*, ed. Natalie Sokoloff with Christina Pratt, 416–34. New Brunswick, NJ: Rutgers University Press.

Smith, Pamela Ann. 2006. Mideast events vivify women's "worst problem." *Women's E-News*, April 20.

Smithsimon, Greg. 2000. People in the streets: The promise of democracy in everyday public space. http://www.columbia.edu/ gs228/writing/importanceps.ht.

Sokoloff, Natalie, and Ida Dupont. 2005. Domestic violence: Examining the intersections of race, class, and gender—An introduction. In *Domestic violence at the margins: Readings on race, class, gender, and culture*, ed. Natalie Sokoloff with Christina Pratt. New Brunswick, NJ: Rutgers University Press, 1-14.

Stanko, Elizabeth. 1990. Everyday violence: How women and men experience sexual and physical danger. London: Pandora.

Steinmetz, Suzanne. 1978. The battered husband syndrome. *Victimology* 2 (3–4): 499–509.

Straus, Murray, Richard Gelles, and Suzanne Steinmetz. 1980. *Behind closed doors: Violence in the American family*. New York: Doubleday/Anchor.

Sudbury, Julia. 2005. Gender violence and the prison industrial complex: Interpersonal and state violence against women of color. In *Domestic violence at the margins: Readings on race, class, gender, and culture*, ed. Natalie Sokoloff with Christina Pratt, 102–14. New Brunswick, NJ: Rutgers University Press.

Thompson, B. Carter. 1986. Defending the battered wife: A challenge for defense attorneys. *Trial* 22: 74–80.

Thornhill, Randy. and Craig Palmer. 2000: A *Natural History of Rape: Biological Bases of Sexual Coercion*. Cambridge, MA: MIT Press.

Tjaden, P. and N. Thoennes, 2000. Extent, Nature, + Consequences of Intimate Partner Violence: Findings from the National Violence Against Women Survey. Washington, D.C.: Department of justice publication No. NCJ 181867.

U.S. Department of Justice, Bureau of Justice Statistics. 2005. *National Crime Victimization Survey: Rape in America. A report to the nation*. http://www.ojp.usdoj.gov/bjs/cvict.htm accessed June 23, 2008.

Walker, Lenore E. 1979. *The battered woman*. New York: Harper & Row.

Weitzman, Susan. 2000. *"Not to people like us": Hidden abuse in upscale marriages*. New York: Basic Books.

Wesely, Jennifer, and Emily Gaarder. 2004. The gendered "nature" of the urban outdoors: Women negotiating fear of violence. *Gender & Society* 18 (5): 645–63.

West, Carolyn. 2005. Domestic violence in ethnically and racially diverse families: The "political gag order" has been lifted. In *Domestic violence at the margins: Readings on race, class, gender, and culture*, ed. Natalie Sokoloff with Christina Pratt, 157–73. New Brunswick, NJ: Rutgers University Press.

Wittner, Judith. 1998. Reconceptualizing agency in domestic violence court. In *Community activism and feminist politics*, ed. Nancy Naples, 81–106. New York: Routledge.

YWCA Canada. 2004, A turning point for women, Violence against women statistics. http://www. ywcacanada.ca.

9

HEALTH AND ILLNESS

When it comes to health, do sex differences make a difference? Yes, says the Society for Women's Health Research in its 2001 report, "Exploring the Biological Contribution to Human Health: Does Sex Matter?"

- After consuming the same amount of alcohol, women have a higher blood alcohol content than men, even when allowing for size differences.
- Women who smoke are 20 to 70 percent more likely to develop lung cancer than men who smoke the same amount of cigarettes.
- Women tend to wake up from anesthesia more quickly than men—an average of seven minutes for women and eleven minutes for men.
- Some pain medications are far more effective in relieving pain in women than in men.
- Women are more likely than men to suffer a second heart attack within one year of their first heart attack.
- The same drug can cause different reactions and different side effects in women and men—even common drugs like antihistamines and antibiotics.
- Women have stronger immune systems to protect them from disease, but they are more likely to get autoimmune diseases (diseases where the body attacks its own tissues) such as rheumatoid arthritis, lupus, scleroderma, and multiple sclerosis.
- During unprotected intercourse with an infected partner, women are twice as likely as men to contract a sexually transmitted disease and ten times more likely to contract HIV.
- Depression is two to three times more common in women than in men, in part because women's brains make less of the hormone serotonin.
- After menopause women lose more bone than men, which is why 80 percent of people with osteoporosis are women.

The Society for Women's Health Research focuses on the biological differences between women and men, but as you are now aware, social factors relating to gender are a powerful influence in our lives. This chapter provides one more example by exploring how these social issues may be of equal or greater importance in producing illness or health. Women may get drunk more quickly than men, but it is getting drunk at a fraternity party that can put them in danger of being raped. Women are more at risk for a second heart attack than men. Perhaps this risk reflects women's greater average hours of work (paid and unpaid) in comparison with men, their greater responsibility for child care, or the stresses due to lack of control over their work. Women are more liable to contract a sexually transmitted disease, particularly AIDS, than men. However, an important social issue in the transmission of HIV/AIDS is women's ability to protect themselves from risky sex.

HEALTH AND ILLNESS AS SOCIAL ISSUES

Health is not simply the absence of disease. The WHO considers health a "state of complete physical, mental, and **social** well-being" (Ruzek, Olesen, and Clarke 1997). A narrow focus on illness itself leaves out the social contexts and forces that shape women's and men's health, such as the fundamental differences of class, race, sexuality, and nation. For sociologists, sickness and health are not simply biological matters. The causes of disease and injury, the experience of illness, its treatment, and its resolution take shape in a social context.

Undoubtedly, women have come a long way economically, politically, and socially in the past few decades, but they have not achieved complete equality with men. Economically, women's earnings average less than men's and women control fewer resources compared with men. Worldwide, women put in more hours of work than men, but average 30 percent to 40 percent less pay, and often no pay at all for domestic and caring work. Politically, women hold fewer positions of power. In every nation they are less likely to be decision makers, policymakers, or politicians. Socially, women have lower status than men, as shown in rates of female infanticide and honors awarded. How does such pervasive inequality contribute to the diseases that affect women? How does men's social, political, and economic dominance contribute to men's diseases? What about the health and illness of men of color, working-class men, and poor men? How do race ethnicity and class complicate the health differences between women and men? Does the health status of poor men resemble that of elites or does it resemble the health status of women of their communities? How does race ethnicity intersect with gender and class (poverty) to produce different health statuses? How shall we envision health? If health and illness exist within a social context, and not simply in individual men's and women's bodies, how are health and illness embedded in communities, nations, and the globalized world (Ruzek, Olesen, and Clarke 1997)?

NATION AND LIFE EXPECTANCY

Epidemiology has been called "the basic science of public health." Epidemiologists study life expectancy rates, the distribution and causes of disease, and rates of maternal and infant mortality in different populations (Jackson 2003, 11). These rates suggest that where a person is born has a powerful impact on life and death. For example, look at the differences in life expectancy for a range of selected countries, from the richest to the poorest, shown in Table 9–1.

The rates show that babies born in wealthy nations of Europe and North America can expect, on the average, to live many years longer than people born in the poor countries of the Global South. A Swedish, Australian, or Canadian baby born in 2004 could live eighty or more years, but a baby from Nigeria, Kenya, Rwanda, or Namibia will be lucky to reach the age of fifty. In Lesotho, with one of the world's highest rates of HIV/AIDS and where 40 percent of the population lives on less than one dollar a day, life expectancy is thirty-five years, less than half as long as it is in the rich West.

An interesting exception to the rich country–poor country difference is Cuba, a poor country noted for its first-class public health system. With few resources, but with a commitment to preventive health care for everyone, Cuba is a third-world country whose citizens enjoy first-world health status. In Box 9–1 you can read what students from the Harvard School of Public Health thought about the Cuban health system after a visit to that country. Their report suggests that a broad system of public health care and preventive medicine can create a successful national health policy. Cuba is an exception among poor and not-so-poor nations in providing its citizens high-quality, accessible health care.

TABLE 9–1 Life Expectancy by Sex in Selected Countries

	LIFE EXPECTANCY AT BIRTH		
Selected countries	*Total*	*Male*	*Female*
Sweden	81	78	83
Canada	80	77	82
United Kingdom	78	76	81
United States	78	75	80
Cuba	77	75	79
China	72	70	74
Indonesia	68	66	70
Russia	66	59	72
India	62	61	63
Philippines	60	57	63
Iraq	59	57	60
Sudan	57	56	59
South Africa	52	50	53
Kenya	47	48	46
Rwanda	44	42	45
Nigeria	44	43	44
Lesotho	35	36	35

SOURCE: 2005 World Population Data Sheet

Box 9–1 THE CUBAN PARADOX

Perhaps best known for vintage cars, cigars, and communists, Cuba is also distinguished by something far more enticing to the students and staff of the Harvard School of Public Health—its health care system. The Cuban government assumes full fiscal and administrative responsibility for the health care needs of all its citizens, providing free preventive, curative, and rehabilitation services. This National Health System, as it's called, is an international success story and, for the last three years, a small group from the School has made its way down to this sunny island nation to learn more about what makes it tick. "It's good for people to see another system," says Richard Cash, senior lecturer in the School's Department of Population and International Health. "Seeing for yourself is far more important and to see what Cuba does with limited resources and to contrast it with our system and other systems is valuable. Everyone that has gone to Cuba has come away clearly educated by the process."

This March, Cash was joined in this educational experience by 12 MPH students. Roberta Gianfortoni, director for professional education at the School, has organized the trip since its inception and coordinated this year's excursion with Medical Education in Cooperation with Cuba (MEDICC), a non-profit organization that specializes in offering elective experiences in Cuba to US and Canadian students in the health and medical sciences. The School's contingent traveled under a special license granted to the MEDICC. Over an eight-day stay in the Cuban capital of Havana, the group visited institutions such as the Ministry of Public Health, maternity hospitals, schools of medicine and public health, AIDS sanatoria, and community health clinics. "The objective is to look at an alternative system," says Gianfortoni. "It's an interesting model to study. Our students are going to go to both developed and underdeveloped countries so it's interesting to consider how Cuba's concepts and methods can translate to other parts of the world."

Socio-economic development is typically measured by health indicators such as infant mortality and life expectancy at birth. However, in Cuba, a nation beset by severely limited resources and political tensions both internal and external, these health markers are essentially the same as those in the United States and other parts of the industrialized world. Cuba also boasts the highest rate of public health service in Latin America and has one of the highest physician-to-population ratios in the world. Alone remarkable for a developing country, these feats are even more extraordinary considering the context of a US embargo that's been in effect since 1961. Because its access to traditional sources of financing is seriously hindered by the sanctions, which until recently included all food and medicine, Cuba has received little foreign and humanitarian aid to maintain the vitality of its national programs. And herein lies the paradox of Cuba's health care system: because Cuba has so few resources, prevention has become the only affordable means of keeping its population healthy.

"I find Cuba's system to be very inspiring because it is so public health focused," says Tracy Rabin, who has made the Cuba trip twice. She traveled the first time as a student in the Department of Immunology and Infectious Diseases; this year she participated as a research associate and program manager for the Program on Ethical Issues in International Health Research in the Department of Population and International Health. Her impressions are not an illusion: despite the economic difficulties of recent years, spending on public health in Cuba has increased steadily, which reflects the political will to maintain successes achieved in this area. An August 1960 law established the Ministry of Public Health as the highest authority responsible for health care. The same year, the Rural Social Medical Service was created, allowing Cuba to place doctors and nurses in the country's remotest areas to bring medical attention to inhabitants there.

Economic constraints have also forced the Cuban health system to get creative when it comes to solving health problems. Cuba does a lot of work with alternative and herbal medicines, which can be more accessible and affordable to a broader population. A testament to their resourcefulness: they recycle magnets from ballistic missiles for their electromagnetic therapy. Cuba is also internationally recognized for its innovative National Immunization Program, begun in the '60s, through which vaccination is integrated into primary care services and depends on active community participation. And the health care system is aggressive in terms of intervention. Since doctors live in the community, if patients skip appointments it's only a matter of hours before the doctor is knocking at their door. "There is a certain kind of caring there that we lose out on in the United States," observes Ella Oong, who just finished up her MPH.

"For me the Cuban system reinforces a commitment to community health," notes Rabin. "It's nice to see that a lot of these public health theories can work in a medical context—there isn't necessarily a division between medicine and public health; there's an effective way for the two to come together. The more that health professionals are educated about different systems the better the US system will be." Rabin, who plans to go to medical school and study emergency medicine, also hopes to integrate the two. "The emergency room is often the first place that people go for treatment for a wide range·of health problems—everything from mental health to domestic violence to infectious diseases," she says. "I think that Cuba would be a prime place to visit for someone with a strong commitment to public health and to viewing patients as both individuals and members of a community and other groups."

A functional blend of public health and medicine, Cuba's commendable health care system is nevertheless a product of a socialist revolution—so whether its methods can be feasibly applied to the United States remains an open question. What does the School's contingent bring back to their homeland from its weeklong visit? "Well, the students salsa more," quips Cash, popping a Latin-music CD into his computer. "But seriously, it hits people differently. Some students are impressed by the use of traditional medicine; others are impressed with the immunization programs. And many are conflicted about the AIDS programs." One of the most controversial of Cuban health programs has been the sanatorium-based care for AIDS, which originally obligated all HIV-positive patients to live out the rest of their lives in these small clinic-based communities. Today, an outpatient option is offered to those who qualify, but many patients don't take advantage of it because they are often ensured better care in the sanatoria. "Really, what we have is a conflict of ideology—the conflict between personal freedom and public health," notes Cash. "What works for Cuba may not work for us."

But everyone on the trip wished that they had a little more time to find out. Ella Oong and Todd Reid, who is studying for his master's in epidemiology, said they wanted to stay a bit longer to conduct case studies and evaluate how the integration of various practices work. For example, the recent dengue outbreak and eradication campaign would have been perfect models to study Cuba's comprehensive health care system. Oong, who just graduated this year, won't return to Cuba with the School. Reid, however, will revisit next year. He is already learning Spanish in preparation for the trip, which will be extended to a three-week excursion. "There's nothing that replaces the actual experience of being in the midst of the population," says Reid. "You can read all you want, but I readily understood the importance of being immersed in a different culture. You get so much more just talking to people. You connect with them. You find out what you share."

Source: Merz, 2002.

GENDER AND LIFE EXPECTANCY

Table 9–1 shows that women's life expectancy is greater than men's in almost every country and region of the world. In the Global North, girl babies born in 2004 can expect to live five years longer than boy babies born in the same year. In poor countries, where HIV is spreading more rapidly among women and where many women have little, if any, access to prenatal care, men have a slightly higher life expectancy. In the impoverished country of Lesotho, for example, boys born in 2005 can expect to live to the age of thirty-six, one year longer than girls born in that country that year.

Less than a century ago in the United States, women's life expectancy was shorter than men's, a difference reflecting frequent childbearing and chronic malnutrition. In developing countries, women's life expectancy is still subject to the risks incurred by frequent, unattended childbearing, sexually transmitted diseases, malnutrition (as family caretakers, wives and mothers often go without food to feed their families), domestic violence, and, increasingly, HIV. Some differences in life expectancy may be differences of biological sex, not social gender. In the United States today, a woman's life expectancy at birth is seventy-nine, whereas a man's is seventy-two. Human male fetuses die more often than female fetuses and each year after birth more males than females die, so that by the age of 100 there are only eleven men to every hundred women. Biologists believe that, among other things, women have a genetic advantage over men because they have two copies of the X chromosome, which protects them from X-linked diseases such as hemophilia and muscular dystrophy.

The line between biology and society is blurring as the longevity gap between women and men narrows. For example, there has been an increase in "male" diseases among women. Heart disease and stroke are now the leading causes of death of women in the United States (39 percent of all women's deaths) and in most Western countries. Tobacco is another contributor to women's lower life expectancy. Since women began to smoke more, women's risk of lung cancer has climbed. Currently, more women die each year from lung cancer than breast cancer, uterine cancer, and ovarian cancers combined.

Not all men are equally at risk for poor health. African American men, disabled men, gay men, poor men, and rural men are responsible for men's higher mortality rates. Nonetheless, women with the same kinds of social disadvantages have lower rates of mortality, disability, chronic illness, and injury.

The unexplained difference between men's and women's health may reflect the costs to men of maintaining masculinity (Schofield et al. 2000, 248–49). In that respect, some men's recent lifestyle choices—healthier diets, more physical activity, less time spent at work, more involvement with their children—may also be lengthening their lives. With changes in lifestyle and advances in knowledge about nutrition, exercise, and stress reduction, and in the face of increasingly similar expectations and obligations in families and at work between men and women, the longevity gap may continue to narrow.

In the United States, the impact of racism on life expectancy is startling. Table 9–2 shows that white female babies born in the United States in 2002 can expect to live eleven and a half years longer than African American male babies born in the same year. White male infants can expect to outlive black males by almost six years and white female infants can expect nearly an additional five years of life when compared with black female infants. The difference in life expectancy between white boy and girl infants narrowed slightly between 1950 and 2002, from 5.5 years to 5.2 years. However, the differences between black infants grew, from an advantage to girls of 3.8 years in 1950 to an advantage of 6.8 years in 2002, showing the significance of race ethnicity to the life expectancies of African Americans, male and female.

The Eight Americas study, conducted in 2006 on mortality data from 1987 to 2001, found that life expectancy in the United States varies enormously on the basis of race ethnicity and gender. Researchers found a greater than twenty-year gap in life expectancy between high-risk urban black men and Asian women and almost thirteen years between Asian women and low-income, rural, Southern black women. In sum, although the more favored groups in the U.S. population enjoy high levels of health, tens of millions of poor, black, and Native American men and women have levels of health more typical of middle-income and developing countries (Murray et al. 2006).

WOMEN'S HEALTH
The Gendered Division of Labor

Schofield and her colleagues (2000) suggest that the key to understanding sex differences in health lies in studying the relations between women and men in the gendered division of labor. Men have often worked long hours in the paid labor force while women did unpaid household work. Men have also often taken jobs in occupations that are most dangerous, such as mining, manufacturing, and the military. In addition, paid work is often done in the context of stressful hierarchies where employees have little control over their work, resulting in high blood pressure, heart disease, and stroke. Higher mortality rates for men may be associated with all of these workplace factors. In addition, gender expectations of men require that they refrain from talking about their emotions or disclosing their feelings of depression. Men who are unhappy with their work lives have few outlets for expressing their unhappiness, which then may be expressed in their higher rates of alcoholism and drug use.

Women, in this gendered division of labor, have been made responsible for unpaid housework and care work. Housewives and other domestic workers in the West face health

TABLE 9-2 Estimated life expectancy at birth by race and sex in the U.S., 1930–2002

	WHITE		BLACK	
	Men	Women	Men	Women
2002	75.1	80.3	68.8	75.6
1970	68.0	75.6	60.0	68.3
1950	66.5	72.2	59.1	62.9
1930	59.7	63.5	47.3	49.2

SOURCE: National Vital Statistics Reports, 53 (6), November 10, 2004: 33.

and safety hazards from cleaning products, insecticides, pesticides, pollutants, and a variety of toxic chemicals flooding into households. Wage workers may be alert to the physical and chemical hazards they face on the job, but housewives and domestic workers often use toxic cleaning compounds without adequately understanding the potential of these chemicals to cause cancer and respiratory diseases.

Most important, however, is the housework itself. Women who are full-time housewives have higher rates of anxiety, depression, and discontent. Women with full-time jobs who share housework and child care with husbands have lower rates of depression and anxiety. However, as we learned in chapter 6, women still do more housework than men. And in chapter 7 we noted that care work in families is most likely done by women. Especially when women are in the paid labor force and also in charge of caring for children and elders, and housekeeping, domestic work that is physically taxing, never done, and often invisible, their physical and mental health may be jeopardized.

The Health Risks and Benefits of Women's Employment in the West

Studies in the United States since the 1970s show employed women enjoy better mental health than those who are not employed. Nevertheless, most jobs add significant new health-related stresses to women's days. An indicator of the social origins of many "men's" diseases is the fact that rates of affliction for such maladies as lung cancer, heart disease, and stroke are rising among women along with their rates of labor force participation. When women go to work for pay, they also remain responsible for more than an equal share of the necessary child care and domestic work. Men have not made the reverse trip by substantially increasing their share of this work. Hochschild (1989) called men's failure to take up their fair share of domestic labor as their wives entered the labor force the "stalled revolution." This additional work time for women creates stresses that can translate into high blood pressure, anxiety, lack of sleep, and other sources of ill health.

Some of the most pressed for time are women professionals, academics, and managers. These women have transformed the masculine professions of medicine, law, university teaching, and business in profound ways. What they have not changed is the culture of work that demands sixty- and seventy-hour work weeks. The expectation that professionals will give so many hours each week to employers arose in an era when professional men had wives at home who saw to family needs. The work model has remained the same even though households now almost always have all adults in the labor force. As a result, women professionals (and their willing husbands) must figure out how to reconcile long hours at work with child care and housework.

Poor and working-class women are also pressed for time. Increasingly responsible for sharing in the economic support of their families or, as single parents, their families' sole support, they may work at two or more part-time jobs while continuing to be responsible for housework and family needs. The majority of women are employed in service and clerical jobs; the women's "professions" of nursing, teaching, and social work; and in the lower strata of various industries and institutions. Among the health consequences of stereotypically female jobs is burnout resulting from lack of control. Woman-dominated service-oriented jobs and jobs caring for others often evoke feelings of anger and frustration that workers must struggle to handle. Care workers and service workers with the least control over their work and earning the lowest pay are most at risk of experiencing exhaustion, digestive problems, high blood pressure, heart disease, and depression (see Box 9–2).

Poor women in the United States experience stress with significantly fewer social, financial, and educational resources than professional women. For poor single mothers who are heads of households solely responsible for providing for their families, daily life is a constant struggle. Such mothers may be unemployed or relegated to low-paying jobs, poorly educated, and victims of racism and sexism. They may have to rely on public transportation to shuttle their children back and forth from home to day care. If they work for hourly wages at service jobs, they may not be free to make or receive calls while on the job, to leave the job in an emergency, or to stay away from work on days when their children are out of school or sick. If they have older children, they may worry about their safety if no one is at home when they return from school. This is especially the case when children return to neighborhoods where gangs rule and where there are few adults around who are able or willing to provide protection. As you learned in chapter 7, our welfare system has mandated that everyone must be employed to qualify for assistance. As a result, the mothers and sisters who once might have looked out for the children of their extended families must now leave home for work that enriches corporations and leave behind work that enriches human beings.

Box 9–2 FEELING STRESSED AT WORK MAY BE MAKING YOU SICKER THAN YOU EVER IMAGINED.

When women have jobs that are high in stress but low in levels of control, their health can be thrown into a state of decline, according to a study published in the *British Medical Journal* claims that job-induced stress can take a serious toll on a woman's physical and mental health. The study, which spanned the course of many years, focused on more than 21,000 women nurses in relatively good health. Researchers discovered that when women work in a high-pressure environment where they have little control over their work and no social support system, their health-related quality of life can be drastically impaired. On the other hand, women with lower-demand jobs and higher levels of control over their duties were shown to have better health. The researchers also discovered that having someone to talk to about problems at work is beneficial, and that the health of all women in the study was improved by having a social support network in the workplace.

Being overloaded with tasks or having minimal control over the amount of work you perform and the time frame in which it must be completed, may cause you to experience feelings of frustration or unhappiness. The result? Your body produces stress hormones. Stress hormones are typically released when an individual experiences psychological distress, and they negatively affect the body and its organs. Stress increases your susceptibility to heart disease, high blood pressure, depression and bodily pain, and strikes a blow to the overall health of women everywhere.

SOURCE: (i-Village.co.uk: The website for Women) http://www.ivillage.co.uk/workcareer/survive/stress/articles/0,,156473_156840,00.html

Poor Women's Health Risks on the Job in Developing Countries

Overwhelmingly, it is the poor in developing areas of the world and in the pockets of poverty in industrial nations whose lives are shortened by poverty and disease (Farmer 2003). The poor and powerless live at great risk of life-changing and life-threatening violence, infectious diseases, workplace accidents, lack of medical attention, and the stresses and struggles of trying to survive under difficult conditions. As the global economy reorganizes the sites and forms of production, women and men in poorer countries take jobs in transnational corporations manufacturing products and services that were once produced in the West. They manufacture textiles or electronics components in Southeast Asia and eastern Europe. They take phone orders in India and the Philippines for American catalog and computer markets. They grow food for export on large commercial farms in India, Asia, and Latin America. As in the West, paid work reduces women's economic and social dependency, relieves them of their isolation at home, and offers them friends and networks of support. On the other hand, long hours of work may keep them from tending family plots that feed their families. For example, Zimbabwean women work on farms growing food for export, even as they and their children experience high rates of malnutrition (Doyal 1995, 159).

In some rural regions of poor countries, housework is especially onerous. In these areas, "housework" involves the arduous labor of carrying water over long distances, tending crops, foraging for wood, and more. It is likely that this heavy labor is a factor in third world women's poor health and shortened life span. In the West, the introduction of running water, gas, and electricity in the first third of the twentieth century eased some of the hard physical labor of housework (Luxton 1980), but this transformation has eluded many rural societies in Africa, Asia, and Latin America. One example of activity that may contribute to the discrepancy in infant mortality is the fact that women in these communities cannot afford to rest or to avoid heavy lifting during pregnancy, hard labor that often threatens their babies' and their own survival.

Additionally they may be exposed to agricultural chemicals, wood smoke from cooking fires, and other domestic fuels. If they do paid piecework at home, they may suffer eye strain, backache, fire hazards, and exposure to toxic materials (Doyal 1995). Farm workers in poorer parts of the world (and the United States) are also exposed to agrochemicals that are wrongly used or badly labeled. The WHO estimates that 3 million farm workers are hospitalized yearly from pesticide poisoning. Chronic and long-term effects of such exposure include cancers; birth defects; sterility; asthma; eye problems; and damage to lungs, heart, kidney, liver, and the central nervous system. Employers often assign these lowest paid and least valued workers to dangerous and unpopular tasks. For example, on Malaysian plantations, women are 80 percent of the workers spreading herbicides. They work with no protective clothing or equipment for safety. Women who cultivate the cut flowers in the factory greenhouses of Colombia (see Box 9–3) tend the plants during spraying. Fertility problems, stillbirths, and deformed infants are not unusual among such women, along with headaches, impaired vision, nausea, conjunctivitis, rashes, and asthma-like problems. Although both men and women suffer from lack of protection in these factory greenhouses, women's jobs put them at greater risk for damage to their reproductive systems and to the children they may birth.

Box 9–3 EVIN WATKINS, DEADLY BLOOMS: COLOMBIA'S FLOWER INDUSTRY IS BASED ON THE EXPLOITATION OF ITS WOMEN WORKERS (THE GUARDIAN, 2001)

"Flowers," wrote Goethe, "are the beautiful words and hieroglyphs of nature, with which she shows us how much she loves us." Then again, he never had to make a living by picking them.

Up on the high plains of the Savanna region around the Colombian capital of Bogota, you get a different view. Here flowers are hieroglyphs not of nature, but of exploitation. "For me flowers mean hard work, bad conditions and bad health," says Elida Duarte, a 29-year-old flower picker working for the Dole corporation, which now controls one fifth of Colombia's exports.

The Savanna is flower country. Today, Colombia is the second largest source of flower exports to the world market after Holland. The giant greenhouses dotted across the landscape generate $600m a year in export revenue. Only coffee and coca earn more. One of every two flowers sold in the US now originates on the Savanna; and the chances are that the last bunch of roses you got—or gave—on Valentine's Day included a Colombian bloom.

The flower boom has generated huge environmental costs. The water table on the Savanna has been shrinking almost as quickly as export earnings have been rising. Around the town of Madrid the aquifer has fallen from 20 meters to 200 meters, and water is now imported from Bogota. Highly toxic residues of pesticides banned in Europe, such as lindano, have been found in dangerously high levels in groundwater.

But the flower trade has created jobs. Around 80,000 women now work in the greenhouses, many of them seeking an escape from rural poverty. Wages are low. On an average day, one woman will pick over 400 top grade carnations. Four of them will cost you £2 in your local florist, which is more than a flower worker earns in a day. But in an area with 40% unemployment, a job in the flower industry offers hope.

It also generates risk. Flowers leave the Savanna with their blooms in an immaculate state to meet American and European inspection standards. They are grown in sterilized soil in greenhouses that are fumigated every day with fungicides, insecticides and nemoticides. One-fifth of the chemicals used in the greenhouses of the Savanna are carcinogens or toxins that have been restricted for health reasons in the US. Women workers testify to spraying dichlorpropene, categorized by the World Health Organization as carcinogenic, without protective clothing and with only handkerchiefs to cover their mouths. Medical surveys carried out by Cactus, a Bogota-based non-government organization, show that nearly two-thirds of Colombia's flower workers suffer from maladies associated with pesticide exposure, ranging from nausea, to conjunctivitis, muscle pains, and miscarriages.

Workers in the industry face more than immediate health risks. While Colombian law provides wide-ranging maternity rights and social welfare rights, these count for nothing in the greenhouse economy. In theory, pregnant women have the right to 80 days' paid maternity leave. In practice, many companies simply sack women who become pregnant. Membership of a trade union is a one-way ticket to instant dismissal.

In the small town of Tocancipa on the northern Savanna, Cactus lawyers provide a legal advice service for flower workers who have been unfairly dismissed. "We deal with around 60 new cases every month, and well over half of them concern dismissal linked to pregnancy," says Cactus director Laura Rangel. Mother's Day may generate windfall profits, but the Colombian flower industry views pregnancy and motherhood as a "crime" meriting instant dismissal.

Efforts have been made to clean up the flower industry. The Colombian Association of Flower Exporters has been pressing its members to adopt a voluntary code of conduct on employment rights and pesticides. The problem is that voluntary codes of conduct provide scant protection in countries like Colombia where governments fail to enforce basic labour rights. "In the absence of effective monitoring and enforcement through the labor movement and government environmental agencies they are little more than unenforceable wish-lists," says Barbara Dinham of the Pesticides Action Network.

In many ways Colombia is a microcosm of globalization applied to flowers. Competition among poor countries to sell flowers to rich ones is pushing supply up, and prices down. In a $4bn world market, corporate producers like Dole can still make huge profits on slim margins. For the high-priests of globalisation in the World Bank and the G8, Colombian flowers are an outstanding success story. For anti-globalisers they are a metaphor for all that is wrong with international trade—and prime candidates for sanctions.

Both sides have got it wrong. The women flower workers on the Savanna want their jobs, but they also want employers to respect their rights. They want solidarity, not consumer boycotts. As consumers, we have a responsibility to listen, and to press for better standards. Think about it next time you buy flowers.

SOURCE: http://society.guardian.co.uk/societyguardian/story/0,,543351,00.html

The neoliberal free trade system that eliminates trade barriers and allows corporations to travel the world in search of the cheapest labor with minimal regulation has disrupted local economies, forced massive migrations of people in search of jobs, and accelerated the immiseration of workers around the world. In "The Return of the Sweatshop," sociologists Edna Bonacich and Richard Applebaum (2007) describe the growth of sweatshops—small factories or homework operations—that are central to the garment industry in the United States and around the world. Typically these businesses violate whatever wage and hours regulations that exist in their host countries (workers are not paid overtime, they are not paid minimum wage, and sometimes they are not paid at all). Even if a workplace adheres to the letter of the law, however, the low standards of pay and long hours of work mean that workers are battered by health problems and poverty. Women working in the textile industry are exposed to cotton dust, which contributes to disabling brown lung disease. Women who sew garments may be sickened by dyes and other chemicals in the cloth they use, they may be injured by sewing machine accidents resulting from speedups, and they can suffer from fatigue resulting from long hours of work. Without regulation, these enterprises get away without restricting the onerous conditions of work or providing health care to their employees.

Other global factories rely on the work of women and subject them to health hazards on the job. Women microelectronics workers in east and Southeast Asia (where they comprise more than a quarter of the manufacturing labor force) and in California are increasingly exposed to hazardous chemicals, fumes, toxic substances, and heavy labor. They have three times the rate of headaches, dizziness, nausea, and blurred vision compared with workers in general manufacturing. The strict discipline imposed on this factory labor force, the extremely low pay, and speedups in the work all contribute to high stress levels among workers in this industry. Doyal (1995, 158) suggests that the occasional mass outbreaks of illness in these factories are forms of "covert industrial conflict." In these cases, illness is understood as a form of women's collective resistance to labor discipline, and not a result of germs and viruses (see also Ong 1987).

Sexual and Reproductive Health

Women's sexual health depends in large part on the health of their partners and on their ability to control the conditions and frequency of sex. If women do not have control over the terms of their sexual encounters with men, they are at risk. For example, using condoms during intercourse can protect women from STDs, but condoms work to protect health only if women have the ability to negotiate their use with their partner and the right to refuse intercourse altogether. Unfortunately, women do not have this level of social power in many communities. The consequences are evident around the world, as women, increasingly, fall victim to HIV and other STDs.

In some communities, women often cede the power to determine sexual behavior to men who are their partners. They may believe that men's "need for sex" takes precedence over their own personal health concerns and agree that men have the right to demand sex from wives and girlfriends, even by force. Often, women's attempts to convince partners to use condoms can provoke rape and battery. Poverty and desperation also coerce sex. Prostitution or taking a sexual partner in exchange for a place to live or food to eat may be the only way some women can support themselves and their children.

When health care is not available, women's risk—and their suffering—increases. Where women have access to public health screening and medical services—Canada, Iceland, Norway, Finland, Sweden, Denmark and Scotland—deaths from cervical cancer have declined. Where they do not have access to medical care, their risk of dying from cervical cancer is heightened. Lack of medical care explains the high proportion of reproductive tract infections in many parts of the world. A 1989 study of two rural villages in the Indian state of Maharashtra found that 92 percent of women there had gynecological or STDs, averaging 3.6 diseases each (Doyal 1995, 76). STDs are more socially damaging to women than to men. If the disease makes a woman infertile, she may lose her partner and thus her means of support. Additionally, STDs increase women's risk of HIV transmission.

In developing countries, women suffer from chronic ailments such as reproductive tract infections, poor nutrition, and communicable diseases. All of these diseases and troubles are connected to poverty. For example, reproductive tract infections in women are connected to the absence of toilets, the lack of sanitary pads, and the absence of privacy. When clean water becomes too expensive, which is the case when international banks force poor countries to privatize water in exchange for loans, poor women must make do with polluted and unsafe water, which affects their reproductive and general health, as well as the health of their children and family members.

Persistent hunger accounts for the fact that in poor countries of the Global South, at least 44 percent of all women are anemic (and 88 percent of Indian women) compared with 12 percent in the West. The rising number of malnourished women adds to the proportion of high-risk pregnancies women experience. The quintessential disease of poverty—tuberculosis—is reemerging among women and men around the world (Farmer 2003).

In the West, women have more chronic health problems than men, and women of color are most affected. This is particularly true of poor women in the United States, who are also likely to be without health insurance. In 1999, 5.9 million mothers caring for young children were without health insurance and one out of every three of these mothers (4.3 million) was ineligible for Medicaid. In half the states, mothers earning over $9,780 a year (nearly $5,000 below the poverty line of $14,630) were too "well-paid" to qualify for Medicaid. In Louisiana, a mother with two children is ineligible for Medicaid if her earnings exceeded $3,048 a year! These mothers cannot afford preventive care, such as Pap smears and mammograms. As a result, uninsured women are more likely to be diagnosed with breast cancer at a later stage of the disease, and are therefore at greater risk of dying from it (Guyer and Dude 2002). Poor African American women have a higher risk of giving birth to babies who die as infants than do women who are either poor or African American (Kreiger 1990).

MEN'S HEALTH

Men are more likely than women to die of heart disease, although heart disease is now the major cause of death for women in the United States as well. Men also die more readily from homicide, suicide, HIV (although women are catching up fast), and drug and alcohol abuse. Research has linked men's mortality from these and other causes of sickness and death with masculine identity, masculine roles, and men's socialization. For example, men's breadwinner role required them to take on life-threatening jobs in greater numbers than women. As a result, men's deaths from occupational causes have historically been higher than deaths of women workers. That pattern continues today.

Ideologies of masculinity continue to encourage men to take up risky pursuits to be regarded as "real" men. Men must drive fast, use drugs and alcohol, engage in riskier sexual behavior, and generally take chances or face being thought of as unmasculine (Waldron 1995).

Masculinity as a Health Risk

A national sample of boys ages fifteen to nineteen interviewed in 1980 and 1988 shows the health effects on men and boys of pressures to "be a man" (Sabo and Gordon 1995). The survey associated traditional attitudes toward masculinity with risky behaviors such as drinking, drug use, and having several heterosexual partners. These behaviors raise the risks of HIV transmission and other STDs, accidents, and homicide. For example, compared with young women, young men who drive have substantially higher rates of minor crashes, crashes resulting in injuries, and fatal crashes. Many studies show that young men are more likely to be aggressive drivers. What is it about being young and male that promotes risky driving? Such aggression has been linked to young men's greater involvement (compared with women and older men) in physical fighting and violent crime. A related influence is "sensation seeking," which leads boys to seek out risks, including risks on the road. Finally, some observers suggest that popular culture equates masculinity with reckless driving. The car chase and the game of chicken have long been featured in action movies directed toward teenage boys and young men (Arnett 2002).

Steroid use among bodybuilders is another example of activity that seems to draw on an ideology of masculinity. Steroid use is associated with serious illnesses such as liver cysts, elevated blood pressure, and heart disease. The drug can cause wide and erratic mood swings, irrational behavior, increased aggressiveness ("steroid rage"), irritability, and depression. In the United States, the reported rate of anabolic steroid use is 6 percent to 11 percent among high-school-aged boys, including an unexpected number of nonathletes, and about 2.5 percent among high-school-aged girls. In a national survey, the most common reason given for anabolic steroid use was improvement of athletic performance; second was improvement of appearance. A typical user is a male (95 percent) athlete (65 percent), usually a football player, heavyweight wrestler, or weight lifter (Beers, Porter, Jones, Kaplan, and Berkwits 2006).

Anthropologist Alan Klein (1993, 1995) studied the use of steroids among bodybuilders. He found widespread insecurity among these powerful-looking men. Klein's informants explained why they were willing to risk their health by ingesting steroids: "I was small and weak," "my brother got into it…cuz his friend used to beat him up all the time," "My parents never gave me credit for anything," or "I was thin." Klein suggests that "the more insignificant" a bodybuilder feels inside, the more he obsesses about "appearing large." Steroids make it possible for bodybuilders to look like powerful men and that, for them, is worth the risk. Klein extends this analysis to men who are not bodybuilders. In an article comparing female anorexics to male bodybuilders, Martha McCaughey (1999) disputes Klein's interpretation of bodybuilders' motives, claiming that these men, like women who starve themselves, are not trying to become more masculine, nor women more feminine, but both seek to be less vulnerable in a threatening world. However, one could argue that invulnerability is an aspect of dominant masculinity in Western culture. Whatever the interpretation, one unanticipated consequence of steroid use may be gynecomastia, or enlarged male breasts, according to many surgeons who are increasingly enlisted to surgically remove the enlarged breasts of teen boys. A Florida plastic surgeon quoted in the *Thursday Styles section* of the *New York Times* (Kuczynski 2007, 1) explains, "They have hopped up their testosterone levels, and so when they get off the stuff, there is a change in the hormonal milieu. It can reset itself, but many times if they have abused steroids, you have to send them to an endocrinologist to address the problem, or if that doesn't work they come back here for surgery."

Although most men would probably stop short of steroid use and plastic surgery (although presently, their numbers are growing), watered-down versions of this complex affect significant numbers of men in our society. Consider the lengths to which men go to appear manly to others: suppressing emotion in public, displaying denial or bravado in the face of physical or mental health problems, reckless driving, binge drinking, or exhibiting aggression in their work and private lives. Steroid use may be understood as a more extreme version of proving one's masculinity, but it is still a part of a cultural legacy that is dangerous to men's well-being as well as to the well-being of those who are the targets of their aggressiveness (Klein 1993, 119).

In chapter 11 you will learn more about the ways that violence, pain, and risk of injury are an accepted, perhaps desired, price of participation in male sports. Some observers suggest that the male sports world gives preference to "hypermasculine competitive sport" in which physical force and violence are valued over skill and gamesmanship (White, Young, and McTeer 1995). In the sports world, pain is normal, even welcomed, but succumbing to injury is a sign of weakness. White, Young, and McTeer (1995) note the paradox: that "the systematic destruction of the male body in sport is framed as empowering for masculinity" (177). They conclude that "For male athletes, body mass, physical endurance, risk taking, and forms of body discipline, including pain denial, are integral features of culturally prescribed versions of masculinity" (179–80).

Masculinity and Heart Disease

Some observers suggest that men's greater risk for heart disease is connected to cultural notions of masculinity. Helgeson (1993) reports that studies measuring masculinity-related traits such as competitiveness, self-control, inexpressiveness, impatience, and achievement orientation found three ways that "extreme" masculinity is linked to heart disease: type A behavior, impoverished social networks, and poor health care.

- *Type "A" behavior* is behavior that is ambitious, competitive, impatient, hurried, angry, and hostile, traits related to masculinity as defined by personality theorists and social psychologists. A type A individual is a "person who is aggressively involved in a chronic, incessant struggle to achieve more and more in less and less time, and if required to do so, against the opposing efforts of other things or other persons" (Sharma 1996). This person is a man (or woman) who hides weaknesses, inhibits emotions other than anger, has little empathy with others, fears homosexuality, and lacks self-knowledge (Helgeson 1995, 76). Research with men has shown a relation between the Type A pattern and coronary heart disease.

- *Lack of a social support network* is a second dimension of risk for men. The existence of social support is correlated with qualities associated with femininity, but not with masculinity, such as caring, comfort, empathy, and emotional expressiveness. The masculine ideal encourages men to experience and display less emotion than women. Toughness, detachment, and control—"sucking it up"—are standards of manly behavior. Men—and boys—don't cry. Those classic figures of popular culture—the loner, the remote and distant man, the cowboy—need no network of support. Nevertheless, studies show that the extreme individualism that sets the "manly" man apart from others increases his vulnerability to illness and early death when the props of his masculine identity—job, status, sexual potency—disappear (Helgeson 1995, 80).
- The third dimension of social risk is men's unwillingness or inability to seek help for health problems and symptoms. Manly men solve their own problems, do not admit they are vulnerable, and endure pain, lest they show weakness.

These factors make a strong case for naming stereotypic or "hegemonic" masculinity as hazardous to men's health. Nevertheless, we need to note the class- and race-bound character of the analysis. The competitiveness attributed to all men is really an occupational hazard of men (and women) in specific occupations, in which one's own advancement and tenure depends on winning scarce positions. However, those elites who have "arrived" do not face the dangerous and punishing physical labor allotted to many men of color, or the health-damaging consequences of poverty and homelessness. It makes no sense to place homeless men, athletes, working-class men, underclass men, gay men, men with HIV, prison inmates, and men of color in the same health pool as middle- and upper class white men.

THE HEALTH CARE SYSTEM IN THE UNITED STATES IS STRUCTURED ALONG GENDER, RACE, AND CLASS LINES

The statistics showing the racial inequalities in life expectancy that began this chapter are indicators of the severe stratification of access to health on a world scale. For example, until recent inroads by women and people of color into the medical profession, doctors were likely to be white men. They still are, but less so. There has been a slow increase in the proportion of women physicians and physicians of color. In 1980, women were 11.6 percent of all doctors, but by 2003, they accounted for 25.8 percent of the physician population in the United States. By the year 2000, women were 40 percent of the medical students in the United States, Mexico, and Hong Kong, and one-third of the medical students in Egypt. Racial ethnic minorities are also increasing their proportions as medical professionals. In 1980–1981, 85 percent of the medical school students in the United States were white. African Americans were an additional 5.7 percent of all students, Hispanics 4.2 percent, Asians 3 percent, and First Nation peoples 0.9 percent. By 2002–2003, the proportion of white students dropped to 64 percent and the proportions of students of color rose (see Table 9–3). Black students were 7.4 percent of all medical students, Hispanics 6.4 percent, Asians 20.5 percent, and Native Americans 0.9 percent. Such slow change has not yet disturbed the basic racialized (and the gender and class) structure of the health care system.

Below physicians and administrators in the health care hierarchy are nurses, once a pre-dominantly white women's profession (Reverby 1987). Reporting to nurses are nurses' aides, who are mostly immigrant women of color. These women do the daily work of cleaning, toileting, and feeding patients in nursing homes and hospitals. Black and Latino men make up the janitorial labor force in these settings. Private patients are usually white. We should not forget the many unpaid care workers assisting disabled and elderly family members and friends who provide services vital to the system and to those in need.

In the United States, health care is a commodity, provided to those who can afford it, rather than a human right of everyone who needs it. A 2003 study concluded that almost 100,000 people die in the United States each year because of lack of needed care—three times the number of people who die of AIDS (Navarro 2003). Uninsured adults have a 25 percent greater mortality risk than do insured adults, and others suffer a lifetime of ill health as a result. Without routine health care, uninsured children may develop chronic diseases and impairments. The problem is not a lack of resources. The United States ranks highest in health care spending compared with other industrial countries as a percentage of its gross domestic product (GDP). In 2004, spending on health care was 16 percent of the GDP and rising. Yet Americans' health status ranks lower than all but one developed nation. The United States is twelfth of thirteen industrialized nations and twenty-fifth of twenty-nine developed countries in male life expectancy, nineteenth in female life expectancy, and has the highest infant mortality rates.

This health care system is currently in profound crisis. Health care has become too expensive for millions of Americans. It is incredible that as of 2008, almost 50 million Americans had no health insurance, and the situation is getting worse. Millions more Americans, at least 10 million of whom are children, are underinsured and must go without necessary health services and medications. The United States is now the only developed nation in the world without a national health program that guarantees affordable access to health care for all people.

CARE WORK: THE PAID OR UNPAID, BUT OFTEN INVISIBLE, FOUNDATION OF HEALTH CARE

In terms of pay, prestige, power, and social status, physicians—until recently predominantly well-to-do, white men—are at the top of the health care hierarchy. Caregivers, those

TABLE 9–3 Racial Ethnic Distribution of Medical Students, 1980–81 and 2002–2003.

Race/ethnicity of medical students	1980–1981	2002–2003
White	85%	64%
African American	5.7	7.4
Hispanic	4.2	6.4
Asian	3.0	20.5
First Nation	0.9	0.9

predominantly poor, racial ethnic, and female workers who daily maintain, comfort, and sometimes even heal the sick and dying, are its invisible foundation. Whether unpaid or simply relegated to the lowest pay and status in the health labor force, care workers are essential to the health care system in the United States (Schiller 1993).

Traditionally, women have done the work of care without pay for family and friends. However, women's entry into the labor force, the rise of single parenting, and the increase in people living alone explain why a growing proportion of children, the elderly, and the disabled are being cared for by paid care workers. Like unpaid care work, paid caring is devalued and the skills required are unrecognized. Employers—hospitals and home care agencies—cut costs on the backs of these workers (Cancian and Oliker 2000).

The structure and location of the work of caring has shifted since the 1980s, when health insurance supported hospitalization over home care. Since that time, a cost-cutting agenda has propelled the shift to home-based care, where policymakers assumed that the free labor of women, supplemented by the low-wage female labor force of care workers, would take on the extra work of having sicker family members at home. In fact, unpaid as well as underpaid labor is essential to the U.S. health care system. Invisible, its costs hidden, women's caring labor completes and often even supplants the work of paid providers, nurses, aides, and others that hospital administrators have eliminated to cut costs. The work does not go away. It disappears into private homes and families where its real costs are borne by caretakers.

When the paid labor of medical workers is redistributed to unpaid women family members, a "work transfer" has taken place (Glazer 1993). In this case, the work of caring is privatized, moved from the public sphere of hospitals and clinics to the private sphere of homes and families. Think of the enormous changes that follow this shift. Services once provided for a fee now become additional work for household members. Most studies confirm that in this situation, women, whether paid or not, increase the hours and intensity of the work they do. For family caregivers, this increase in family labor comes at a time when women's labor force participation is almost equal to men's, and in some cases exceeds that of men. Yet private, household-based care of sick and elderly family members may require as much or more time and attention as the care of young children. Invisible, or seen as something women are best fit to undertake, free and low-cost care work makes profits for the health care industry, as costs continue to rise precipitously.

Despite the growing need for home care, fewer women are at home to do that work, opening the door for private agencies to take up the slack. This work is associated with higher levels of job stress and lower levels of job satisfaction (Denton et al. 2002). This comes as no surprise. Home care workers now do what nurses used to do in hospitals, even as they juggle heavy workloads and unpaid overtime. The companionship, compassion, and attention that care workers give their clients is devalued, hardly noticed, and sometimes actively opposed by employers whose focus is on the efficient completion of instrumental (and measurable) tasks (Diamond 1995). Cost-cutting policies and increased control by management mean that care workers have less time for the caring part of their work. Instead they face limited control over their tasks and schedules, difficult clients, and low wages, as well as "pressures, tensions, anxiety, demoralization, dissatisfaction, frustration, feelings of guilt, and reduced support and supervision" (Aronson and Neysmith 1996).

Of course this work is stressful for unpaid caretakers of close relatives and friends as well. At least when the work is done for a wage, patients and workers frame the caring relationship as a case of client–worker relations, a frame that may help to limit the expectations of both parties. When relatives do similar work in the home for free, expectations and emotions differ. We may expect to care for our elderly parents, and we may welcome the opportunity when it arrives. However, a little-discussed emotion surrounding caretaking, especially (but not exclusively) unpaid caring by close relatives—a wife, a daughter or son, a cousin, or a mother—is rage. Isolated in their homes with little support, sometimes forced to leave jobs or careers, caretakers may profoundly resent their lot. The feeling often goes both ways with, perhaps, the invalid locked into a dependent relationship with her or his caregiver. However, feelings of rage and resentment are difficult to express in the face of romanticized notions of selfless caregiving to relatives. The parties to the relationship may try to keep the rage inside, "silenced and repressed" (Schiller 1993, 503).

Rage is more than an individual feeling. It is one of several emotional costs of care work that are socially produced by a society unwilling to guarantee health care to all and borne individually and in isolation. Clearly, a movement of paid and unpaid care workers and their patients is necessary to give voice to the concerns of those who must survive in the everyday world of health care with little individual power to change its institutionalized structures of inequality.

WOMEN'S HEALTH MOVEMENTS

Women and men occupying the lowest stratum of the paid health care labor force—janitors and aides—have been relatively voiceless, but recently aides and janitors have participated in some successful union organizing drives that may ultimately lead to increased pay and better working conditions. They are the most recent expression of activism that has been important to the shape of health care since the 1960s.

The women's health movement emerged in the United States in the late 1960s, as women began to take stock of the gendered, class-based, and racialized system of medicine that had controlled their health care. What was the social context of this rising activism by women?

- First, the social movements of the 1960s—civil rights, Black Power, La Raza, the American Indian movement and, of course, women's liberation—promoted a critical awareness of the ways that existing institutions disadvantaged women and a growing conviction that ordinary people could make change.
- Second, legislation stimulated by the civil rights movement—the Equal Pay Act (1963), the Civil Rights Act (1964), and Affirmative Action (1965)—contributed to a growing public discourse about the parallel problem of women's rights.
- Third, the contraceptive pill contributed to an increase in premarital sex among white women, often called a "sexual revolution."
- Fourth, women were flooding into the labor force and, as a consequence, were marrying later, having fewer children, and divorcing more than their mothers and older sisters.

These cultural and political shifts help to explain the multiple local beginnings of the women's health movement. Meeting in women's "rap groups" and conferences, young

Box 9–4 "OUR BODIES, OURSELVES": GOING, GOING, GONE GLOBAL

(WOMENSENEWS)—In Asia, it teaches Buddhist nuns how to ease muscle cramps caused by hours of sitting meditation. In Africa, it cautions women not to overeat; a health risk in a region where being overweight is the standard of feminine beauty.

In Latin America, it urges women to rethink the anti-choice stance of the region's Roman Catholic Church. Across the globe, "Our Bodies, Ourselves," the pioneering text that became an underground sensation in the United States after it was first published here in 1970, is adapting itself to the regional variations of women's global reality.

After coming out in its first foreign-language edition in 1976 in Spanish, the text is now available in 17 languages and Braille. It has been published in 15 nations and will soon be released in India, South Korea and Poland. It has sold millions of U.S. copies and—with global distribution—garnered 20 million readers worldwide. In addition, it recently inspired the creation of a similar African health text, "Notre Corps, Notre Sante," which features original content in French and is being distributed to women in 21 African countries.

AN INNOVATIVE APPROACH TO WOMEN'S HEALTH

Created by a group of Boston health activists 35 years ago, "OBOS," as it is widely known, takes health information that was once exclusively in the hands of medical experts and places it in the hands of ordinary women. In all its translations, the book maintains its trademark approach of presenting medical information in the form of communal feminine narrative. Testimonials from ordinary women—about everything from menstruation through menopause and beyond—are interspersed with articles, charts, graphs and diagrams. Speaking to readers like a mother or a friend, "OBOS" covers reproduction, contraception, exercise and nutrition.

As it spreads into other languages and other cultures, the text is sparking a variety of consumer health movements. The Armenia version of OBOS has inspired women's activists there to open a storefront health center where they distribute pamphlets about family planning and sexually-transmitted diseases. In Japan, the book spurred its translators to survey 200 clinics and hospitals about their policies regarding women's health. In Latin America, the text provided material for an anti-smoking campaign specifically geared toward women. "Education is the most powerful tool for lifting the plight of women worldwide," says Sally Deane, chair of the board for the Our Bodies, Ourselves collective, the Boston-based non-profit that oversees "OBOS" publications. "We hope to reach a global audience while maintaining our core of personal stories and accurate information about health topics that all women must know."

The creators of OBOS also hope to eradicate health threats that are of specific concern to women. "We're concerned by the rise of religious fundamentalism, which impinges on women's ability to control their reproductive lives," says Judy Norsigian, the executive director of the Our Bodies, Ourselves collective. "We're alarmed by government cutbacks in developing countries that are preventing women from getting basic health care. We're also concerned that the pharmaceutical industry is blocking the production of generic drugs so developing countries must pay high prices to import them from abroad."

EACH EDITION IS UNIQUE

Back in 1976, when they realized their message could benefit women of all cultures, the creators of "OBOS" translated their original text into Spanish. That success led to more foreign-language texts and the OBOS Global Translation/Adaptation Program, which helps health advocates across the globe amend the book to suit their needs. With a $75,000 annual budget (garnered mostly from foundations), OBOS administrators transfer the publication rights for the token sum of one dollar, then provide technical assistance with fundraising, negotiating publishing contracts, promoting books and distributing them. Sometimes, health advocates write their own testimonials and use photographs of women from their own countries. Sometimes, they use ready-made wording and graphics provided by the OBOS head office.

With each new publication of "OBOS," women's health advocates work to tell their own stories in their own voices. In their testimonials, they talk about issues that are universal among women: breastfeeding, having an abortion, living with a sexually transmitted disease and going through menopause. They also talk about topics that are unique to their own cultures, such as struggling to gain access to health care in a developing country and struggling to recover from a rape perpetrated by soldiers as an act of war.

The unique set of health needs of each group of readers has led to some surprising spin-offs. In Bulgaria, the shift from Communism to democracy is taking a somewhat anti-Western form. One aspect of that is a widespread antipathy toward feminism, which is seen as Western, anti-male and anti-family. As a result, the Bulgarian translation emphasizes women's rights as consumers, patients and citizens. It refrains, however, from discussing the idea that women are an oppressed or marginalized group. Much of the Serbian adaptation was produced during the prolonged war in the Balkan region in the 1990s, so the privation of readers there was a major consideration. "The authors dropped the nutrition chapter," says Judy Norsigian. "It just seemed terrible to speak of food when people in the region were starving." In Armenia, where a declining birthrate and economic hardship are causing massive emigration from the country, many people are wary of contraception and are pro-natalist. Out of cultural deference, the version published here emphasizes childbirth and gives somewhat shorter shrift to birth control.

Differences like these are reflected in "Our Bodies, Ourselves Transformed Worldwide," a collection of selected English translations of prefaces from international adaptations, which is available on the collective's Web site.

FUTURE PROJECTS

In addition to publishing texts in foreign languages, the Our Bodies, Ourselves collective also has its hands in health projects worldwide. It has distributed 300,000 free books—most of them in English or Spanish—to international groups. It contributes to small-scale projects such as helping Nigerian activists adapt the OBOS text to radio public service announcements and to large-scale programs run by leading health organizations such as the Contraceptive Research and Development Program, Family Health International, the National Women's Health Network, and the World Health Organization.

By the end of this year, women's health advocates hope to launch three new international editions of OBOS. For the Tibetan version (to be published

movement activists began to discuss their own experiences with the medical system, medical experts, and standard medical procedures. Was the pill safe? What were the reasons for the high rates of Caesarean sections in the United States? Were the routine radical mastectomies and hysterectomies performed on women actually necessary? Why did doctors control access to abortion? Did treating women's depression as a medical problem deny the very real causes of female unhappiness with their lives (Plechner 2000; Rosen 2001)?

After gathering steam in the 1960s, the movement took off in 1969 (Morgen 2002). In that year, a workshop on women and their bodies led to the founding of the Boston Women's Health Book collective and to the publication of *Our Bodies Ourselves* (OBOS), now in its eighth edition. Participants came to the 1969 workshop because they believed that women needed to take back knowledge about and control over their bodies from medical professionals (Ehrenreich and English 1972). The workshop participants decided to gather information about women's anatomy and physiology, birth control, sexuality, abortion, pregnancy, childbirth, medical institutions, and the organization of health care in India, home to a vast community of Tibetan exiles), they are writing about personal hygiene, which is crucial for women living in monasteries that house more than 500 people. For the Korean version, they are addressing parts of the text to Russian sex workers and other foreign women who are flooding into the country in search of employment. For the Polish version, they are expanding the section on reproductive care since basic sex education is not available in the country's predominantly Catholic schools.

In the United States, the collective is about to publish its eighth revision of the English-language text. In the Middle East, the advocates are working to translate and distribute the chapter on childbearing to women in five Arab countries. In China, Nepal, Vietnam, Turkey, Kenya and Brazil, activists are meeting with private funders to drum up financing for new translations. As OBOS international publishing continues to grow, its supporters hope it will continue to reach thousands of new readers; women who likely have nowhere else to turn for accurate health information. "Most books about women's health are not woman-positive or designed to be used by women," says Mavi Kalem, a health advocate working to publish "OBOS" in Turkey. "Of all the books we have looked at, 'OBOS' is the one volume that provides a model that fills these needs. We want women to say, 'I read this book, and it changed my life!'"

SOURCE: Molly M. Ginty. "Our Bodies, Ourselves Turns 35 Today" Women's eNews http://www. womensenews.org/article.cfm/dyn/aid/1820

in the United States and to publish their findings. In 1970, the first edition of *Our Bodies Ourselves* circulated in a newsprint version as a course on women and their bodies. Since the publication of the first edition of *OBOS*, much about women's health care has changed, but much remains the same, as the introduction to the 2005 edition shows (Boston Women's Health Book Collective 2005; see Box 9–4). Another 1969 publication, *The Doctor's Case Against the Pill* (Seaman 1969), raised serious questions about the safety of the contraceptive pill.

Local activists around the country began developing their own alternatives to the established medical system. They organized feminist clinics and health centers, supported midwifery and birthing centers over hospital births, encouraged women to enter medical school, and criticized reproductive technologies, medicated childbirth, and cosmetic surgeries. They encouraged women to learn about their bodies and to become active medical consumers. They introduced and promoted alternatives to scientific medicine, including midwifery, acupuncture, and herbalism.

Abortion in the United States

Abortion was legal in the United States, practiced by midwives, until about 1880, when restrictions were imposed in the backlash to that century's women's suffrage and birth control movements and in response to the panic over what was then called "race suicide," the declining birth rate among whites. (Ironically, in the 1970s, Black Power activists also called black women's attempts to control their own fertility "race suicide.") These restrictions prevented midwives from providing abortions, and they gave medical doctors greater control over the decision to abort pregnancies.

Making abortion illegal merely drove abortion underground and increased its dangers to women. Women who could afford to do so traveled to Cuba and England where they had access to hospital abortions. Poor and middle-class women faced the dangers of back-alley abortions or tried to abort themselves with knitting needles and coat hangers, or by swallowing or douching with dangerous chemicals. Some physicians tried to help women. In the 1960s, the Clergy Consultation Network operated as a referral service to help women find safe abortions. In 1969, students and housewives active in the Chicago Women's Liberation Union (CWLU) acted on their belief in reproductive rights for all women by organizing to offer low-cost and no-cost illegal abortions, which they learned to perform themselves (see Box 9–5). By 1973, when the U.S. Supreme Court, in *Roe v. Wade (1973)*, struck down all criminal abortion laws on the basis of women's "right to privacy," the women of the Abortion Counseling Service or "Jane" had provided more than 10,000 safe abortions.

Roe v. Wade ended the thousands of deaths and the tens of thousands of health complications that occurred yearly as a result of illegal and self-abortions. Immediately anti-abortion activists, naming themselves "pro-life" began a campaign to restrict and ultimately end legal abortions. They blockaded abortion clinics, threatening and intimidating abortion providers and the women who used their services. By 2004, seven abortion providers had been murdered, clinics had been

---

Box 9–5 STATEMENT OF THE ABORTION COUNSELING SERVICE OF THE CHICAGO WOMEN'S LIBERATION UNION. 1971

This statement is from the informational brochure passed out by the Abortion Counseling Service of CWLU to the women they served. It remains the basic tenet of pro-choice feminism:

> "Women should have the right to control their own bodies and lives. Only a woman who is pregnant can determine whether she has enough resources— economic, physical and emotional—at a given time to bear and rear a child. Yet at present the decision to bear the child or have an abortion is taken out of her hands by governmental bodies which can have only the slightest notion of the problems involved."

SOURCE: http://www.cwluherstory.com/CWLUFeature/Janebroch.html).

bombed or set on fire, and clinic personnel were subjected to anthrax threats and acid attacks. The homes of doctors who provided abortions were picketed and their names and photos appeared on wanted posters circulating on the Internet. These tactics created a climate that contributed to the decline in abortion services, growing state restrictions on publicly funded abortions, and the continuing threat that *Roe v. Wade* could be overturned by the Supreme Court.

Beyond *Roe v. Wade:* The Struggle Continues

In 1973, the U.S. Supreme Court overturned all state laws outlawing or restricting abortion on the grounds that they violated the constitutional right to privacy. The debate over this decision is now in its fourth decade. Although surveys show that fully 70 percent of Americans support abortion rights, pro-life activists have had notable success in restricting access to abortions, despite the fact that they are now legal. President Ronald Reagan spurred opposition to *Roe* by making it his "litmus test" for federal judicial appointees. In 2005, President George W. Bush appointed two anti-*Roe* justices to the Court, fueling speculation that the law might soon be overturned. Between the presidencies of Reagan (1980–1988) and G. W. Bush (2000–2008), several Supreme Court decisions upheld the law in the face of challenges. In *Planned Parenthood v. Casey* (1992) the court reaffirmed women's constitutional right to abortion. *Stenberg v. Carhart* (2000) struck down state attempts to ban late-term abortions. In the face of the Court's decisions to uphold *Roe*, Congress and the states acted to restrict abortion rights. For example, the Hyde Amendment (1977) imposed waiting periods on women seeking abortions, as well as parental consent laws. In 1986, the state of Missouri enacted legislation that placed a number of restrictions on abortions: Public employees could not perform or assist abortions except to save the mother's life, abortion counseling was prohibited, and doctors were required to perform viability tests on women in their twentieth (or later) week of pregnancy. In *Webster v. Reproductive Health Services* (1989), the Supreme Court upheld Missouri's abortion restrictions. In 2003, Congress passed and President G. W. Bush signed a bill banning so-called partial birth abortions and in April 2007 the Supreme Court in a narrow five-to-four decision, upheld the ban. The majority said its ruling reflects the government's "legitimate, substantial interest in preserving and promoting fetal life." The procedure involves removing an intact fetus, then destroying the skull to complete the abortion. Doctors and pro-choice advocates maintained the procedure minimizes the risk to mothers' health. Justice Ruth Bader Ginsburg called the majority decision "alarming." She wrote "It tolerates, indeed applauds, federal intervention to ban nationwide a procedure found necessary and proper in certain cases by the American College of Obstetricians and Gynecologists." The ruling does not bode well for the fate of *Roe v. Wade*.

Women of Color and Sterilization Abuse

Most of the women who participated in the abortion counseling service were white, college-educated, and middle class. They believed that abortion rights were the key to women's control over their bodies. However, they also were aware that women of color faced genocidal challenges to their reproductive rights.

Although the women of the service and other abortion rights activists recognized that sterilization abuse also denied women control over their reproductive lives, it was poor and minority women activists who brought a broader focus to the movement by spotlighting this practice.

The United States has a long history of coercive sterilization practiced on poor women and women of color. In both the South and the North, black and poor women and girls had been sterilized by doctors without their consent. An infamous case is the experiment performed in the 1950s on Puerto Rican women who were used as experimental subjects in the testing of the birth control pill. Physicians touted the pill as the "solution" to the problem of unemployment on the island. Sterilization had been the medical solution prior to the pill, and it was so far-reaching that by 1958, one-third of all women of childbearing age in Puerto Rico had been sterilized.

In 1973, the Southern Poverty Law Center filed a lawsuit to end federal funding of sterilizations after finding that 100,000 to 150,000 poor women, nearly half of them black, had been sterilized annually under government programs. Women on welfare had been pressured into consenting to sterilization after giving birth. Native American women were also targeted. By the 1970s, one-quarter of all Native American women had been sterilized. In the 1960s and 1970s, Mexican American women in California who gave birth to children in public hospitals were sterilized without their informed consent. Activist Ana Nieto Gomez recalled that doctors "saw themselves as agents of the public, saving taxpayers money by preventing women on welfare from having more children" (Ruiz 1998, 113). The racist aspect of these policies is evident. Whereas women of color were pressured to consent to be sterilized or, in fact, sterilized without their knowledge or consent, white, middle-class women had difficulty finding doctors willing to perform the operation on them. For these women, most hospitals used the "120 formula"—a woman's age multiplied by the number of children she had should equal 120—for a woman to qualify for sterilization (see Roberts 1997).

By mounting resistance to sterilization abuse as well as to restrictive abortion laws, activists demonstrated that there were many consequential differences among women of different races, ethnicities, and classes. Sterilization and birth control represented freedom and autonomy for white, middle-class women, but they were tools used by governments to control the reproductive lives of poor and minority women. Black and Latina feminists influenced the reproductive rights movement by raising awareness of these differences, and in so doing they transformed the abortion rights movement into a movement for reproductive freedom (Nelson 2003). By fighting for the rights of the most vulnerable women to be free of forced sterilization and to bear as many children as they chose, women of color broadened the women's rights agenda by bringing "other than white" and "other than middle-class" views of reproductive harms and rights to the center of the burgeoning women's health movements (Eisenstein 2004). They demonstrated that reproductive rights must include the freedom to choose to bear children, as well as the freedom to choose not to bear children. Beyond promoting reforms to legalize abortion and regulate sterilization, they posed new questions for women and families. Realizing the goal of making a woman free to have exactly as many children as she wants, when she wants, if she wants required that she have the economic means to support her children and equality in her home and community. Otherwise, in what sense is she free to choose? By bringing the reproductive issues of women of color and poor women to the center of the debate, these activists demonstrated how women's rights to health and care mean nothing in the absence of their rights to adequate housing, income, education, and democratic inclusion in policymaking processes that affect their lives (Silliman, Fried, Ross, and Gutierrez 2004).

Box 9–6 DEPO PROVERA, RACE, AND CONTRACEPTION.

With much joy, we had our first child, Adriancito in November of 1993. After him, we decided that although the Catholic Church did not allow the use of contraceptives, because of our economic situation we had to plan our family to fit our reality. With that in mind, we went to Kaiser so that we could get information on all the contraceptives available. We thought that since Kaiser was a prestigious hospital, (we thought!!) we would receive the necessary information we needed to pick a method appropriate for my health and my family as a whole. What they gave us was a list of contraceptives from which they highly recommended Depo-Provera. From there, we decided that Depo would be our method of contraception since it was convenient (1 injection every 3 months) and because from what we knew there were not going to be any complications.

The first injection came after our first child. I never thought we were going to go through a horrible nightmare! I began to feel horrible. Emotionally, I could not tolerate anything, everything bothered me and I cried a lot. I would get so depressed that at one time I was feeling worthless and believed that I was a terrible wife. Physically, I gained 40 pounds, which of course contributed more to my depression. The only great thing during that time was that my husband was very supportive and would always console me. I really do not know what I would have done without him.

One day, I mentioned that I was using Depo to my sister-in-law, she in turn was extremely surprised and upset. Consequently, she told me of all the horrible side effects and sent us detailed information from the NLHO about Depo. When my husband and I read all the information we got really scared but more than anything upset with Kaiser. They had never given us this information. Thank God, now we know that what I was going through was related to Depo-Provera and that I was not actually crazy.

This May, I was due to take the next injection. Fortunately, because of all the information we received, we decided not to go through with it. Today, I still don't get my period regularly (At one time, I didn't get it for more than five months), my ovaries still hurt, and I am losing lots of hair. Imagine! The good thing is that I have lost more than 20 pounds, and I know that little by little my body is getting back to normal.

I recommend to all women—before you start anything, demand that all the information is given to you to be able to make good decisions. What is the point of taking care of yourself by being cautious with pregnancy, if you are going to be unhappy?

SOURCE: Lorena Sahagun, Depo-Provera: The Nightmare of One Women and Her Family. *National Latina Health Organization Newsletter*, Winter 1995. http://clnet.ucla.edu/women/nlho/news/win1995.html

Globalizing Sterilization

Forced sterilization has been a worldwide problem (along with forced pregnancies, lack of reproductive health care, and a host of other medically based violations of women's and men's human rights). For many years, beginning in the nineteenth century and continuing long into the twentieth century, the United States had a eugenics program that sterilized thousands of poor people of color in the name of ending "feeble-mindedness," crime, and mental illness. The poor, the illiterate, minorities, epileptics, manic-depressives, prostitutes, alcoholics,

---

Box 9–7 A SHAMEFUL LITTLE SECRET: NORTH CAROLINA CONFRONTS ITS HISTORY OF FORCED STERILIZATION.

March 28 issue—Elaine Riddick dreamed of motherhood. She and her husband tried to conceive for months without luck, so they consulted a doctor. The diagnosis was shocking: she had been sterilized four years earlier without her knowledge. She soon learned that the operation had been performed by state order in North Carolina in 1968, when she was just 14, and had given birth to a baby after being raped. At the time, she'd assumed doctors were just performing a routine post-birth procedure. The sterilization-consent form had been signed by her neglectful father and her illiterate grandmother, who had marked her assent with an X. Today, three decades later, she's still reeling from the revelation she blames for the death of her marriage and her eventual hysterectomy. "I felt like I was nothing," says Riddick, her fists clenched in anger. "It's like, the people that did this, they took my spirit away from me."

Now North Carolina is pondering ways to make amends to Riddick and thousands of others sterilized as part of the eugenics (or "good breeding") movement that began nationally in the early 20th century and continued into the 1970s. The state offered a public apology two years ago. Now lawmakers are debating ways to make reparations to those robbed of the chance to be parents. More than 30 other states had eugenics programs during the last century; they were ruled constitutional in Buck v. Bell, a 1924 Supreme Court decision that is still the law of the land. Roughly 70,000 Americans in all were sterilized before the notion fell out of favor, becoming linked in the public's mind to Hitler's Germany after World War II. But North Carolina is the first to appoint a panel to study what to do now for its victims, from health care and counseling to financial reparations. The state is also considering addressing the shameful practice—finally halted in 1974—in its classrooms. "Some people have tried to pretend it never happened," says North Carolina State Rep. Larry Womble, a reparations activist. "It's painful to remember."

homeless, and criminals were usually the targets. Since the turn of the twentieth century, 60,000 Americans—men, women, and children, whose only problem appeared to be their racial identity or their poverty—have been sterilized without their consent (see Box 9–7).

Americans may know more about forced sterilization in Nazi Germany, where 400,000 Jews and others were forcibly sterilized, than about their own country's history of forced sterilizations. In fact, some of Hitler's sterilization program was borrowed from the American eugenics movement of the early twentieth century. More recently, several countries struggling with poverty have used forced sterilization as part of a poverty reduction program. For example, Peru's poverty reduction program offers women food and clothing for their children

North Carolina's sterilization program zeroed in on welfare recipients. Over the last 15 years of its operation, 99 percent of the victims were women; more than 60 percent were black. The truth began to emerge after Johanna Schoen, author of "Choice and Coercion," a new book dealing with the subject, was given access to sealed records by a state employee. In some cases, the reasons for sterilization were as flimsy as being considered lazy or promiscuous. Nial Ramirez says she was sterilized at 18 after social workers threatened to cut off her mother's welfare benefits. "We had no way to fight back," says Ramirez, now 58.

Jacob Koomen served on the board that voted to sterilize Riddick. Decades later, he told Schoen that he was "uncomfortable" making such irrevocable decisions: "We did it because the law obligated us to. It isn't something we would have volunteered to do." North Carolina Gov. Mike Easley issued an apology to the victims in 2003, and ordered a commission to find concrete ways to make amends. But the state's budget is already a billion dollars in the red, and nothing has happened yet. To date, no one who underwent forced sterilization in this country has received assistance for it. Some critics say North Carolina is stalling. But others say this state, at least, is trying to own up to its history, and that others should follow suit. (In December, the National Black Caucus of State Legislators passed a resolution calling for federal and state programs to identify victims nationwide and get them health care and counseling.) "We're in uncharted territory here," says Carmen Hooker Odom, the head of the North Carolina Department of Health and Human Services. "We want to create a model other states can follow." Riddick isn't holding her breath. "They're waiting for all of us to die out," she says. "Then the problem disappears." It's little surprise she has scant faith in a state that has done her, and so many others, so wrong. But at least now the ugly secret is out.

SOURCE: By Rebecca Sinderbrand, Newsweek. © 2005 Newsweek, Inc. http://www.msnbc.msn.com/id/7243352/site/newsweek/

to bribe them into consenting to be sterilized. Under such conditions, these women can hardly be said to be giving their consent freely. In some cases, women who give birth are sterilized without their knowledge. In Japan, where sterilization was practiced until the 1990s, doctors told women that the procedure could be reversed. Not only do forced sterilizations deny people their right to bear children, they are also medically risky. The procedures are often done in poor sanitary conditions and there is lack of follow-up treatment or medication. Women may die from complications (Woolf 2000).

The work of women of color activist groups such as CARASA, the National Black Women's Health Project, the National Latina Health Organization, and the Reproductive Rights National Network helped to raise opposition to coercive sterilization programs and to write restrictions such as informed consent, waiting periods, and other protections into U.S. law. However, sterilization programs have returned in less coercive guises, such as those that promote the drugs Norplant and Depo-Provera to poor women. Moreover, the United States has helped to introduce sterilization into third-world family planning programs. The U.S. Agency for International Development (USAID) has funded programs to bring foreign medical practitioners to the United States to learn sterilization techniques. It also funds the Association for Voluntary Surgical Contraception (AVSC), an organization once linked with the eugenics movement, which works in over sixty countries around the globe.

Sterilization programs are only one prong of U.S. policy regarding programs in developing countries that target women's reproductive status. Since the 1970s the United States has refused to fund programs that provide assistance to women seeking abortions. This policy was further codified by Ronald Reagan in the Mexico City policy and reestablished by George W. Bush in 2001.

GENDER AND THE GLOBAL AIDS PANDEMIC

Like the Black Death that swept over Europe in the fourteenth century, killing one-third of the population, and the flu pandemic of 1918 and 1919, which killed between 20 million and 40 million people, including an estimated 675,000 Americans, HIV/AIDS is another global epidemic that is killing and disabling millions around the world. Between 1981 and 2005 more than 25 million people died of AIDS and an estimated 40.3 million people worldwide were living with HIV (the virus that eventually causes AIDS) or AIDS itself (Department of Health and Human Services Centers for Disease Control and Prevention 2005).

There is some good news. In Addis Ababa, HIV prevalence fell to 11 percent by 2003, down from a peak of 24 percent in the mid-1990s. In Kenya, HIV prevalence fell from 13.6 percent in 1997 to 9.4 percent in 2002. Nonetheless, the epidemic is far from being reversed. In fact it is growing among women and among heterosexuals, people who at first believed they were beyond the reach of the disease.

What does AIDS have to do with gender? Everything. At first, HIV/AIDS was seen as a disease principally affecting men who had sex with other men or men who injected drugs. More recently, it has become clear that an increasing number of people are becoming infected through unprotected heterosexual sex. Nearly half of all people worldwide now living with HIV are women. However, not all women are equally at risk. It is poor women of color, women with the least control over their lives and health, who are most vulnerable

(Farmer 2003). In the United States, AIDS disproportionately affects African American, Native American, and Hispanic women: AIDS ranks among the top three causes of death for African American women aged thirty-five to forty-four years and is the third leading cause of death for Latinas. In the eastern Caribbean, women make up close to 60 percent of all AIDS cases (Joint UN Programme on HIV/AIDS and the WHO 2004). In sub-Saharan Africa, there are now more new infections among women than among men (Farmer, Connors, and Simmons 1996).

The world community, through the United Nations, is searching for a way to control and contain the virus. Many AIDS programs focus on individual behavior and education. For example, supporters of the popular ABC approach to preventing the spread of AIDS claim that the program has cut the rates of HIV/AIDS in several countries. The ABC program advises three behaviors to avoid infection: abstain, be faithful, and use condoms. This advice may work for women who have the power to control the situations they encounter in their daily lives, but it is far from reliable for women who are dependent on or subordinated to others.

- Abstinence assumes that women do not engage in sex except when they choose, but women frequently do not have the choice to say no to sex. All over the world, including the United States, poor and powerless women are forced to exchange sex for material support. Sex work may be the only work some women can find to feed and house themselves and their children. The use of rape and sexual violence, especially in times of war, puts women at great risk. Women and children are abducted or tricked by sex traffickers who take them to parts of the world where they may not speak the language or know how and where to get help. All such women have limited, if any, control over their sex lives and are unable to choose abstinence. In addition, women who wish to become pregnant cannot use condoms and in many places women who do not bear children are highly stigmatized. Some may be injection drug users with no help or treatment available. Women's risks are not simply a matter of economic survival or force and violence, however. Male cultural domination of sexual encounters also creates risky situations for women, who may feel that a male partner's desires are paramount, and that they cannot assert their right to safe sex or no sex (Doyal 1995, 78).
- Being faithful can prevent infection, but being faithful to a partner who is engaged in risky sexual behavior or is HIV positive will not protect a woman from exposure to HIV. Indeed, husbands who have risky sex with multiple partners are responsible for the explosion of HIV/AIDS among married women around the globe.
- Using condoms or having nonpenetrative sex requires men's cooperation. Many men refuse to use condoms. In some cases, if a woman demands that a sex partner use condoms, she puts herself at risk of being beaten and raped by him. Beatings and violent rape, by the way, increase the risk of HIV transmission through cuts and abrasions to the skin.

Explaining the Women's Epidemic: Structural Violence

The AIDS epidemic feeds on both poverty and inequality. It travels along lines of gender, race, class, and region, "vectors that converge in the bodies and lives of individuals" (Connors

2003, 93). The ABC approach to dealing with the epidemic around the world—and most agency responses—works on the assumption that AIDS is caused by individual behaviors and is changed by changing those behaviors. Physician and anthropologist Paul Farmer criticizes this view:

> To continue to pretend that a two-hour session with an AIDS educator, for example can measurably increase "self-esteem" in a person who has lived an entire lifetime in a context of violence, discrimination, and abject poverty, or that the problem of "empowerment" lies solely in convincing the subject that he or she has power, regardless of whether this is the case, is to completely miss the mark about why people engage in risk behaviour. (Farmer 2003, 202)

If Farmer is correct, the ABC prevention approach based on educating individuals and exhorting them to take responsibility for their sexual behavior will not work unless there are major changes in women's access to power and resources. Without property rights, basic education, and access to a decent job, many women and girls do not have the social power they need to enable them to claim sexual and social autonomy. Tell a young girl raped by a member of her family, a family friend, or a stranger, to abstain. Tell a wife whose husband has girlfriends or visits prostitutes to rely on faithfulness. Tell women to withhold sex from violent men unless they agree to sex with condoms. Each of these situations is beyond the control of individual women.

In other words, risk is not determined by lack of education about risks, nor is it reliably diminished by more education. These solutions assume the epidemic can be brought under control when individuals decide to change their behavior (abstain, be faithful, use condoms). But risk is the result of a basic lack of economic equality and social rights that set the stage for what Farmer calls *structural violence*—forms of extreme suffering such as hunger, rape, torture, and AIDS that are visited on the poor and the powerless of the world (Farmer 2003, xiv).

The concept of structural violence focuses attention on the broader social determinants of risk, such as changing patterns of work, family, and sexual relations. For example, some Southeast Asian countries promote sex tourism to increase foreign exchange by recruiting rural women and girls who migrate to cities to help their impoverished families. Their impoverished families are the victims of state policies supporting export over subsistence agriculture and free trade.

Also, war puts women at greater risk of rape by pillaging soldiers. Indeed the spike in AIDS in Rwanda is directly attributable to the mass rapes of Tutsi women during that country's genocide in the 1990s.

Growing landlessness creates economic insecurity that encourages women to engage in "transactional sex" with older men in exchange for goods, services, money, or basic necessities. Even in wealthy nations, inner-city blight, the growth of long-term unemployment, and racism structure risk for poor women and women of color.

FIGHTING BACK: WOMEN'S HEALTH MOVEMENTS AROUND THE WORLD

Farmer's concept of structural violence suggests that poor women must achieve economic security, political power, and cultural respect to defeat the HIV/AIDS epidemic and other threats to women's reproductive and general health. If they are successful, then universal, comprehensive health services will take precedence over market forces. If they are successful, men and children will benefit as well.

The struggles over women's health in third-world or debtor countries are responses to conditions that have made it increasingly difficult for women to get access to good health care. For example, in many such nations, free or subsidized health care was cut back or eliminated as required by international lenders such as the World Bank and the International Monetary Fund. These structural adjustment schemes, which were imposed on the debtor nations by the wealthy lenders, put debt repayment ahead of human health. The restructuring affected the availability of food as well, because lenders demanded that local farmers engage in commercial agriculture for export to help raise funds to repay their country's debts. In these ways, third-world debt led to harsh and deteriorating health conditions affecting ordinary citizens, particularly women and children, in the Global South.

Conflicts over family planning policies have also restricted access to health services in developing countries. As one of his first acts in office, President George W. Bush reinstated the Mexico City policy first established by Ronald Reagan in 1983. Known by its opponents as the "global gag rule," the policy denies U.S. funding to any family planning NGO in developing countries that provides abortions or abortion counseling and information to its clients, even if these services are legal in the country in question and are funded with NGO money. The rule prevents NGOs from even participating in public debates or speaking out on issues concerning abortion. Box 9–8 contains two statements, one from the National Conference of Catholic Bishops that supports the Mexico City policy and the other from an article published in *MS. Magazine* opposing it.

The global health movement has responded to deteriorating conditions of women's health by bringing together activists from widely differing circumstances. The Latin American movements for women's health have emerged in the context of democracy movements in that part of the world. The South Asian movements arose in the context of sterilization promotion and rising trafficking of young rural women whose families lost the ability to support themselves through subsistence farming. In Africa, extreme poverty and the HIV/AIDS pandemic are the context within which women's health movements must struggle. In the face of this diversity, a series of UN conferences made dialogue among women on a global scale possible. These conferences helped feminist activists build transnational networks and develop their vision of reproductive health beyond control over fertility.

Since the 1980s and 1990s, transnational women's organizations—NGOs and transnational coalitions—led by women from the poor nations of the Global South—have reshaped the former international consensus that saw control of women's fertility as a means to population control and economic development. These new women's organizations rejected these attempts to use women's reproductive lives as the means to other ends. Instead they embraced and enlarged the concept of reproductive rights by placing it in a human rights framework.

What does it mean to put reproduction into a human rights framework? If reproductive health, and health in general, is a human right then it follows that governments must provide the conditions within which such rights are guaranteed. How can a woman exercise her human right to reproductive choice

if she lacks the financial resources to pay for reproductive health services or the transport to get to them; if she is illiterate or given no information in a language she

Box 9–8 WHY DO WOMEN'S GROUPS CALL THE MEXICO CITY POLICY THE GLOBAL GAG RULE?

SUPPORT FOR THE MEXICO CITY POLICY. NATIONAL CONFERENCE OF CATHOLIC BISHOPS APRIL V18, 2002

Dear Member of Congress:

"The poor cry out for justice and equality and we respond with legalized abortion." Thus wrote dissenting commissioner Grace Olivarez, when the Rockefeller Commission on Population and the American Future proposed almost two decades ago that abortion be used to control population and reduce poverty in the United States.

That the mindset of the Rockefeller Commission majority still lives among us is apparent from some reactions to the reinstatement of the "Mexico City Policy" governing U.S. population assistance. Abortion advocacy groups have reacted with outrage, claiming to speak for the women of developing nations who allegedly want help in aborting their children more than any other form of foreign aid.

Because President Bush does not believe the U.S. government should subsidize organizations that promote and perform abortions in the Third World, he is accused of seeking to "hurt the women of the world" [Congressional Record, Feb. 15, 2001, page S1506]. This charge is made by the sponsors of S. 367, a bill designed to rescind the Mexico City policy and give free rein to U.S.-funded organizations to promote abortion abroad.

Under S. 367 and its companion bill, H.R. 755, non-governmental organizations could attack human life and human dignity and continue to receive U.S. funds, so long as their practices could not be shown to violate the host country's law or U.S. federal law. Population control groups could again distribute abortion kits in nations where abortion is illegal, evading local laws by calling them "menstrual regulation" kits and neglecting to perform pregnancy tests before performing abortions. They could even perform abortions and other "health or medical services" that endanger women, since such abuses may not be adequately addressed by host countries' laws and are seldom addressed by federal law in the U.S. In recent cases in this country involving women's injury or death at the hands of those performing supposedly legal abortions, redress has been entirely through state law. It is tragically ironic that legislation ostensibly designed to prevent "unsafe" abortion may give U.S.-funded organizations new leeway to practice exactly that.

In our view, the Mexico City policy respects the dignity of poor women in developing nations, as well as the laws and cultures of the vast majority of nations, far better than such gravely misguided legislation does. The President has rightly removed the United States from the business of exporting a culture of death.

As the U.S. bishops' Committee for Pro-Life Activities testified in 1989, the Mexico City policy is needed because the agenda of many organizations receiving U.S. population aid has been to "promote abortion as an integral part of family planning—even in developing nations where abortion is against the law...Far from being perceived as an imposition on developing nations, the United States policy against funding abortion activity has been greeted by those nations as a welcome reform. The vast majority of these countries have legal policies against abortion, and virtually all forbid the use of abortion as merely another birth control method."

When President Bush reinstated the Mexico City Policy this year, some complained that the policy amounts to "powerful" politicians forcing their policies on powerless women. But as we have learned from our experience in international conferences on population, the promotion of permissive abortion attitudes is much more likely to cause resentment, especially when it is perceived as a means by which the West is attempting to impose population control policies on developing nations as conditions for development assistance.

Poor women in developing nations are not calling for help to abort their children. They are calling for education, food, housing, and medicine for themselves and their children so that they can lead lives of full human dignity. The United States can best respond to their pleas by holding firm to the Mexico City Policy, while increasing true development aid from its scandalous level of one-tenth of one percent of GNP, the lowest percentage of all major donor countries. I urge you to reject S. 367 and H.R. 755, and to uphold the Mexico City policy.

Sincerely,

Gail Quinn, Executive Director

Secretariat for Pro-Life Activities

National Conference of Catholic Bishops Are U.S.

CRITIQUE OF THE MEXICO CITY POLICY: MICHELE KORT, 2008.
ARE U.S. POLICIES KILLING WOMEN?

Even as we commemorate the landmark 35th anniversary of *Roe v. Wade* this year, U.S. reproductive-health policies are having an inordinately negative effect *outside* of our borders. They're causing women to die or be maimed. Harsh words, but true. For the past 24 years, except during the Clinton presidency, U.S. administrations have maintained a global gag rule against providing counseling or referrals for abortions at U.S.-

funded clinics in developing nations. It's a rule that only thwarts *safe* abortions, while reducing the already limited availability of other family-planning services. The global gag rule has also led to a pullback in overseas delivery of contraceptives, according to recent testimony by Rep. Nita M. Lowey (D-N.Y.) before the House Foreign Affairs Committee: "U.S. shipments of contraceptives have ceased to 20 developing nations in Africa, Asia and the Middle East. In some areas, the largest distribution centers for contraceptives have experienced decreased access for over 50 percent of the women they serve."

Women's health and rights activists in the U.S. have spent the past two decades fighting against such actions, and advocating on behalf of global reproductive health issues. But progress has come slowly. While maternal mortality has been declining at 1 percent annually, it needs to decline by 5.5 percent a year in order to be three-quarters reduced by 2015 (one of the United Nation's Millenium Development Goals). Sounds like a lot—but it would require just about $6.1 billion more in annual funding—the price of three weeks of the Iraq war—to achieve that goal. Without that commitment, more than 500,000 women will still die annually from childbirth and its complications, with an estimated 70,000 of those deaths due to unsafe abortions.

Take, for example, the situation of women in Kenya, where abortion remains illegal unless the pregnant woman's life is in danger (a loophole some compassionate doctors interpret liberally, as they know that desperate women will risk their lives to abort anyway). An estimated 250,000 to 320,000 abortions are carried out in the country each year, with unsafe procedures causing a shocking toll: Globally, 13 percent of maternal deaths result from abortion-related complications, but in Kenya it's as high as 40 percent.

In public hospitals such as Kenyatta National in Nairobi, about 20,000 Kenyan women are treated each year for abortion-related complications. Nearly two-thirds of the beds in the notorious gynecological section—Ward 1D—are occupied by those patients, who suffer everything from excessive bleeding to

understands, if her workplace is contaminated with pollutants that have an adverse effect on pregnancy; or if she is harassed by parents, a husband or in-laws who will abuse or beat her if they find out she uses birth control? (Petchesky 2004, 19)

How can health be assured if a woman and her family have no home, no money for food, and no health care? These, too, are fundamental human rights. If reproductive tract infections in third-world countries are linked to the absence of toilets, sanitary pads, and privacy, then adequate sanitation is a women's right. If high infant and maternal mortality are brought on by the lack of potable water, then that also is a woman's right.

injured organs to sepsis. Those sufferers include women such as Wangui (not her real name), who drank a boiled concoction made from trees and took several doses of an anti-malaria drug in order to abort because her impoverished household couldn't support a fifth child. She ended up in Ward 1D because she required an urgent blood transfusion to save her life...

Maternity care in general is problematic in Kenya's public hospitals. The 2007 report "Failure to Deliver," produced by the Federation of Women Lawyers-Kenya (FIDA Kenya) and the Center for Reproductive Rights in New York, pointed out that public health facilities often suffer from lack of supplies and congestion. Claris Ogangah-Onyango, legal counsel for FIDA Kenya, points out the obvious: When the majority of beds in maternity hospitals are occupied by women with post-abortion complications, there is not enough space and care for other women.

"The government is mostly concerned with post-abortion care," she says, "and most of the funding goes to that. But they're not doing anything to stop [unsafe] abortions."

"What has really affected our work in Kenya is that we have very few women in our parliament [just 18 of 222 members]," says Ogandah-Onyango. "When we take our issues to the government, they are blocked. FIDA and other women's organizations have approached the candidates for the next parliament to sign a document that they will support gender-friendly bills. Putting more women in government would make a big difference."

And what can women in the U.S. do to help their Kenyan sisters? "Lobby for change in the policies that govern reproductive health," she says. U.S. women can also support the efforts of groups such as FIDA Kenya, which is now part of the Reproductive Health and Rights Alliance in Kenya.

Sisterhood is a global mission. Economics and politics and even social conscience aside, we know that only by empowering all women can we ensure the future of the world.

Women from the Global South have pioneered in developing this revolutionary framework linking reproductive and sexual health to a wide range of conditions: housing, education, employment, property rights, legal equality, and freedom from abuse, genital mutilation, and gender violence. Petchesky (2004, 48) calls this new direction "a major historical achievement and a mark of the power of transnational women's NGOs and feminist ideas" (see Box 9–9).

In this chapter we have explored the many ways that illness and health are gendered around the globe. We have seen how men's and women's social locations, their paid and

Box 9–9 VICTORY FOR WOMEN'S RIGHTS IN AFRICA

Nairobi, Kenya—Solidarity for African Women's Rights (SOAWR), a coalition of groups across Africa campaigning for the popularization, ratification and domestication of the Protocol to the African Charter on Human and Peoples' Rights on the Rights of Women in Africa, welcomes the 15th ratification by Togo of the Protocol on 26 October.

The Protocol will now come into force within 30 days, marking a milestone in the protection and promotion of women's rights in Africa and creating new rights for women in terms of international standards.

The other countries that have ratified the Protocol are Cape Verde, The Comoros, Djibouti, The Gambia, Lesotho, Libya, Malawi, Mali, Namibia, Nigeria, Rwanda, Senegal, South Africa and Benin.

For the first time in international law, this groundbreaking Protocol explicitly sets forth the reproductive right of women to medical abortion when pregnancy results from rape or incest or when the continuation of pregnancy endangers the health or life of the mother. In another first, the Protocol explicitly calls for the legal prohibition of female genital mutilation, and prohibits the abuse of women in advertising and pornography. The Protocol sets forth a broad range of economic and social welfare rights for women. The rights of particularly vulnerable groups of women, including widows, elderly women, disabled women and "women in distress," which includes poor women, women from marginalized populations groups, and pregnant or nursing women in detention are specifically recognized.

"The 19 national, regional and international organizations of SOAWR have been working tirelessly since July 2003 when the Protocol was adopted for ratification," said Muthoni Wanyeki of FEMNET, a coalition member. "This moment is a testament to their work and the work of other civil society groups working across Africa for ratification." The coalition delivered to heads of state a petition for which signatures were collected from across Africa by pen, email, online and by text messaging (SMS) from people encouraging their governments to ratify the Protocol. "To our knowledge, this is the first time that SMS technologies were used on a mass scale on the African continent in support of human rights," said Firoze Manji of Fahamu, the SOAWR member that developed the technique.

"The protocol should not be viewed in isolation," added Hannah Forster of the African Center for Democracy and Human Rights Studies. "It would be prudent to approach its domestication and implementation in consonance with other relevant international instruments." Added Gladys Mutukwa of coalition-member WiLDAF, "There are 38 member states of the African Union that have not yet ratified the Protocol. Our work will not end until they too show their commitment to women's rights in Africa and become party to the Protocol."

"The coming into effect of the Protocol is just the first step in securing the protection of the human rights of African women," explained Faiza Jama Mohamed of Equality Now, another coalition member. "However our task remains incomplete until state parties exercise the political will to protect, promote and respect these rights."

Source: Equality Now ˙ SOAWR Secretariat: www.equalitynow.org

unpaid labor, their race and class positions, and the political and economic position of the nations in which they live structure their opportunities to enjoy good health or the likelihood they will fall victim to disease and other bodily harm. Although some risks are apparent to individuals and even avoidable by them, others are not. The hazards of some jobs, the chemical dangers surrounding household work, the inadequacies of health care, or the lack of access to care cannot be offset by individual precautions or undertakings. Health is a collective good, which only action at the level of communities and societies can ensure.

In this chapter we have also seen how women and men have organized to change health systems and health priorities. The language and politics of reproductive rights originated in the women's movements of the 1970s and 1980s as women sought the right to control their bodies. By the 1980s, women of color groups, such as the National Black Women's Health Project and the National Latina Health Organization, were linking reproductive rights to issues of racism and poverty. In the 1980s and 1990s, a series of UN conferences internationalized the politics of women's health. Participants in these conferences created transnational organizations "to secure women's reproductive and sexual health and rights within a broad context of social development and gender equality" (Petchesky 2004, 35). Although fundamentalists and anti-choice activists seem to have structured the public discussions of reproductive rights and freedoms in struggles such as the one over the global gag rule, and although the Supreme Court appears poised to overturn *Roe v. Wade*, women's transnational movements are making progress in linking reproductive health to a wide range of rights: housing, education, employment, freedom from violence, and health services that take priority over market forces. The struggle continues. We have yet to see who will win the day.

REFERENCES

Arnett, J. J. 2002. Developmental sources of crash risk in young drivers. *Injury Prevention* 8: 17–23.

Aronson, Jane, and Sheila M. Neysmith. 1996. "You're not just in there to do the work": Depersonalizing policies and the exploitation of home care workers' labor. *Gender & Society* 10 (1): 59–77.

Beers, Mark H., Robert S. Porter, Thomas V. Jones, Justin L. Kaplan and Michael Berkwits. 2006. Anabolic Steroids. *The Merck manual of diagnosis and therapy*, 1690–1692. Whitehouse Stations, N.J.: Merck Research Laboratories.

Bonacich, Edna, and Richard Applebaum. 2007. The return of the sweatshop. In *Intersections of gender, race, and class: Readings for a changing landscape*, ed. Marcia Texler Segal and Theresa Martinez. Los Angeles: Roxbury, 289–299.

Boston Women's Health Book Collective. 2005. *Our bodies ourselves*. New York: Touchstone.

Cancian, Francesca and Stacey Oliker. 2000. *Caring and gender*. Thousand Oaks, CA: Pine Forge Press.

Centers for Disease Control, National Center for Health Statistics. 2005. Total enrollment of minorities in schools for selected health occupations. In *United States, 2005*, 364. Atlanta, GA: CDC. http://www.cdc.gov/nchs/hus.htm.

Connors, Margaret. 1996. XXX In *Women, poverty, and AIDS: Sex, drugs, and structural violence*. Eds. Farmer, Paul, Margaret Connors, and Janie Simmons. Monroe, ME: Common Courage Press.

Denton, Margaret, Isik Urla Zeytinoglu, Sharon Davies, and Jason Lian. 2002. Job stress and job dissatisfaction of home care workers in the context of health care restructuring. *International Journal of Health Services* 32 (2): 327–57.

Diamond, Timothy. 1995. *Making grey gold: Narratives of nursing home care*. Chicago: University of Chicago Press.

Department of Health and Human Services Centers for Disease Control and Prevention (CDC). 2005. *United States HIV & AIDS statistics by age.* http://www.avert.org/usastata.htm.nb.

Doyal, Lesley. 1995. *What makes women sick: Gender and the political economy of health.* New Brunswick, NJ: Rutgers University Press.

Ehrenreich, Barbara and Deirdre English. 1972. *Witches, midwives and healers: A history of women healers.* New York: The Feminist Press at CUNY.

Eisenstein, Zillah. 2004. *Against empire: Feminisms, racism, and 'the' west.* London: Zed Books.

Farmer, Paul. 2003. *Pathologies of power: Health, human rights, and the new war on the poor.* Berkeley: University of California Press.

Farmer, Paul, Margaret Connors, and Janie Simmons, eds. 1996. *Women, poverty, and AIDS: Sex, drugs, and structural violence.* Monroe, ME: Common Courage Press.

Glazer, Nona. 1993. *Women's paid and unpaid labor: The work transfer in health care.* Philadelphia: Temple University Press.

Guyer, Matthew Broaddus, and Annie Dude. 2002. Millions of mothers lack health insurance coverage in the United States: Most uninsured mothers lack access both to employer-based coverage and to publicly subsidized health insurance. *International Journal of Health Sciences* 32 (1): 89–106.

Helgeson, V.S. 1995. Masculinity, men's roles, and coronary heart disease. In *Men's health and illness: Gender, power, and the body.* Eds. D. Sabo and D. F. Gordon, 66–104. Thousand Oaks, CA: Sage.

Hochschild, Arlie 1989. *The second shift.* New York: Viking.

Institute of Medicine. 2002. Joint UN Programme on HIV/AIDS and the World Health Organization. 2004. *AIDS epidemic update 2004.* http://www.unaids.org/wad2004/EPIupdate2004_html_en/epi04_00_en.htm.

Klein, Alan. 1993. *Little big men: Bodybuilding subculture and gender construction.* Albany: State University of New York Press.

——. 1995. Life's too short to die small: Steroid use among male bodybuilders. In *Men's health and illness: Gender, power, and the body,* ed. D. Sabo and D. F. Gordon, 105–20. Thousand Oaks, CA: Sage.

Kreiger, N. 1990. Racial and gender discrimination: Risk factors for high blood pressure. *Social Science and Medicine* 30:1273–81.

Kuczynski, Alex. 2007. A sense of anxiety a shirt won't cover. *The New York Times,* June 14, Thursday Styles, 1.

Luxton, Meg. 1980. *More than a labour of love: Three generations of women's work in the home.* Toronto: Women's Educational Press.

McCaughey, Martha. 1999. *Fleshing out the discomforts of femininity: The parallel cases of female anorexia and male compulsive body-building.* New York: Aldine De Gruyter.

Merz, Chelsea, 2002. The Cuban paradox. Harward Public Health Review. Summer.

Morgen, Sandra. 2002. *Into our own hands: The women's health movement in the United States, 1969–1990.* New Brunswick, NJ: Rutgers University Press.

Murray, C. J. L., S. C. Kulkarni, C. Michaud, N. Tomijima, M. T. Bulzacchelli, Terrell J. Iandiorio, and Majid Ezzati. 2006. Eight Americas: Investigating mortality disparities across races, counties, and race-counties in the United States. *PLoS Med* 3(9): e260.

Navarro, Vicente. 2003. The inhuman state of U.S. health care. *Monthly Review* 55 (4), 56–62.

Nelson, Jennifer. 2003. *Women of color and the reproductive rights movement.* New York: NYU Press.

Ong, Aihwa. 1987. *Spirits of resistance and capitalist discipline: Factory women in Malaysia.* Albany: State University of New York Press.

Petchesky, Rosalind Pollack. 2004. *Global prescriptions: Gendering health and human rights.* London: Zed Books.

Planned Parenthood v. Casey, 505 U.S. 833 (1992).

Plechner, Deborah. 2000. Women, medicine, and sociology: Thoughts on the need for a critical feminist perspective *Social Factors* 18:69–94.

Reverby, Susan. 1987. *Ordered to Care: The Dilemma of American Nursing: 1850–1945.* Cambridge: Cambridge University Press.

Roberts, Dorothy. 1997. *Killing the black body: Race, reproduction, and the meaning of liberty.* New York: Vintage.

Roe v. Wade, 410 U.S. 113 (1973).

Rosen, Ruth. 2001. *The world split open: How the modern women's movement changed America.* New York: Penguin.

Ruiz, Vicki L. 1998. *From out of the shadows: Mexican women in twentieth-century America.* New York: Oxford University Press.

Ruzek, Sheryl, Virginia Olesen, and Adele Clarke, eds. 1997. *Women's health: Complexities and differences.* Columbus: Ohio State University Press.

Sabo, Donald, and David Frederick Gordon. 1995. Rethinking men's health and illness: The relevance of gender studies. In *Men's health and illness: Gender, power, and the body,* eds. Donald Sabo and David Frederick Gordon, 1–21. Thousand Oaks, CA: Sage.

Sahagun, Lorena. 1995. Depo-Provera: The nightmare of one woman and her family. *National Latina Health Organization Newsletter, Winter 1995.* http://clnet.ucla.edu/women/nlho/news/win1995. html.accessed June 23, 2008.

Schiller, Nina Glick. 1993. The invisible women: Caregiving and the construction of AIDS health services. *Culture, Medicine, and Psychiatry* 17:487–512.

Schofield, Toni, R. W. Connell, Linley Walker, Julian Wood, and Dianne Butland. 2000. Understanding men's health and illness: A gender-relations approach to policy, research, and practice. *Journal of American College Health* 48:247–56.

Seaman, Barbara. 1969. *The doctor's case against the pill.* NY: Peter Wyden, Inc.

Silliman, Jael, Marlene Gerber Fried, and Loretta Ross. 2004. *Undivided rights: Women of color organizing for reproductive justice.* Cambridge, MA: South End Press.

Society for Women's Health Research. 2001. Women and men: Ten differences that make a difference. http://www.womenshealthresearch.org/site/PageServer?pagename=hs_sbb_10diff. Accessed June 23, 2008.

Stenberg v. Carhart, 120 S. Ct. 2597 (2000)

Waldron, Ingrid. 1995. Contributions of changing gender differences in behavior and social roles to changing gender differences in mortality. In *Men's health and illness: Gender, power, and the body,* eds. Donald Sabo and David Frederick Gordon, 22–45. Thousand Oaks, CA: Sage.

Watkins, Kevin. 2001. Deadly blooms. *The Guardian Unlimited,* August 29. http://society.guardian. co.uk/societyguardian/story/0,,543351,00.html

Webster v. Reproductive Health Services 492 US 490 (1989).

Weisman, Carol S. 1998. *Women's health care: Activist traditions and institutional change.* Baltimore: Johns Hopkins University Press.

White, Philip, Kevin Young, and William McTeer. 1995. Sport, masculinity, and the injured body. In *Men's health and illness: Gender, power, and the body,* eds. Donald Sabo and David Frederick Gordon, 158–82. Thousand Oaks, CA: Sage.

Woolf, Linda. 2000. Forced sterilization. http://www.webster.edu/ woolflm/forcedsterilization.html. Accessed June 23, 2008.

10

POLITICS AND LAW

AFFIRMATIVE ACTION IN SPANISH POLITICS

When Jose Luis Rodriguez Zapatero was elected prime minister of Spain in 2004 he fulfilled his promise to make the government more responsive to women. During his first week in office, the new Spanish government made history twice. First, at the inauguration ceremony, half of the sixteen ministers sworn in as members of Zapatero's cabinet were women. Then, he appointed Teresa Fernandez de la Vega the first ever woman vice premier. Besides these high-level appointments, Zapatero, a Socialist Worker's Party member who calls himself a radical feminist, also tapped women to head several ministries, including those of culture, education, environment, and agriculture. Voters in Spain have played their part as well in this gender revolution, electing 126 women (27 percent) to the 350 seats in the Spanish Congress in the 2000 elections. These milestones show how far Spain has come in the twenty-nine years since the end of the arch-conservative dictatorship of General Francisco Franco, when a man had a legal right to "discipline" his wife by beating her.

The new Spanish government is not only bringing more women into high offices, it also has made the government more supportive of women's rights by changing laws and public policy to streamline divorce proceedings, legalize gay and lesbian marriage, and legalize abortion, which had been illegal in Spain except in cases of rape and severe birth defects. Spain is also increasing police support for battered women and expanding public education on the problem of violence against women. In addition, the Spanish government passed controversial laws banning overly thin models from high-fashion runways. The political leaders declared that girls and young women were adversely affected by these images of emaciated women who were supposed to represent feminine beauty. Spanish legislators have even passed legislation that obliges men (and women) to "share domestic responsibilities and the care and attention" of children and elderly family members. The new marriage law requires that couples live together, remain faithful, help one another, and now share with housework and care for family members as part of their spousal obligations (Tremlett 2005).

The news coming out of Spain shows great strides made in the direction of greater gender equality in politics. These changes are based on an affirmative action approach, setting goals for increasing the numbers of women at the top of the government and promoting policies that will improve gender equity.

What do you think of this kind of affirmative action approach to increasing the numbers of women in high-level political positions?

The strategy in Spain implies that more women in office will mean more attention to women's issues and a more liberal approach to programs and policies that serve women. Does it make any difference if more women are in office? If more women are in office, will the approach to social issues change? Will the government become more liberal or more conservative? If more women become government leaders, will women's issues gain greater attention?

Political office is only one part of the government. How do women and men compare in other branches of the government such as the criminal justice system and the military?

This chapter is organized around the broad issue of gender and politics. We begin by looking at the general topic of politics and power and the state. We then examine three important political arenas within the state: electoral politics, the military, and the criminal justice system. In the last section, we explore the theoretical question of how we define political and how our ideas about what is political are influenced by gender.

POLITICS AND GOVERNMENT

Politics is the expression and organization of power. In the 1970s feminists declared that "the personal is political." By this they meant that power differences and political relationships exist between individuals even in the most personal areas of their lives with their families, friends, partners, and children.

Politics is more commonly understood, however, as a public issue. When most of us use the word *political* we think about activities like voting or waging wars. In this chapter we look at politics in the public arena by examining electoral politics, the military, and the criminal justice system. In doing this we examine pieces of a large social institution we call the state.

A state is broad political organization that organizes and wields power in a society. In the United States, the word *state* is used to describe the fifty political and geographic units that make up the country. For example, we talk about the states of California, Kansas, and Virginia. When social scientists use the term *state* they mean something different. Sociologists refer to the state to indicate a social institution that can operate at several levels within a country. In the United States, the state includes the Supreme Court, the president, the Armed Forces, the Internal Revenue Service, the Bureau of the Census and Congress at the federal level, as well as governors, legislatures, and more local bodies like city councils, school systems, welfare offices, and local police departments. States can be defined as "organizations that extract resources through taxation and attempt to extend coercive control and political authority over particular territories and the people residing in them" (Skocpol and Amenta 1986, 131).

A state then, is the social institution that makes laws and uses force (when necessary) to protect itself and enforce its laws. Elected officials, the military, and the criminal justice system are all part of the state. Men and women have different roles and experiences in all of these arenas. Gender is illustrated by who is elected to office, how individuals participate in military operations, and how people are treated by the criminal justice system. This chapter explores each of these three areas—electoral politics, the military, and the criminal justice system—to see how gender and politics interact.

Voting Rights

Elections in the United States are deeply gendered in several ways. Most obviously, the electoral playing field is dominated by men. Candidates and most behind-the-scenes campaign strategists and consultants—the pollsters, media experts, fundraising advisors, and those who develop campaign messages—are also men. Furthermore, the network news reporters and anchors charged with telling the story of elections are often men. Gendered language permeates our political landscape as elections are described in analogies and metaphors drawn from the traditionally masculine domains of war and sports. Our expectations about the qualities, appearance, and behavior of candidates also are highly gendered. We want our leaders to be tough, dominant, and assertive, masculine stereotypes in American culture (Carroll and Fox 2005). This section explores the gendered character of electoral politics in the United States and around the world.

The right to vote in a democratic nation is an essential aspect of political activity. The American Constitution withheld this right for a long time from most Americans. Only property-owning white men were allowed to vote for at least a century after the American Revolution. Gender was one of the key criteria for determining whether a person could exercise the right to suffrage. The long, bitter battle for women's suffrage lasted many decades and although it sounds strange to us today, allowing women to vote was feared by many. One senator spoke against the amendment in the early twentieth century, claiming it would "convert all the new harmonious elements of society into a state of war, and make every home a hell on earth" (Flexner 1975, 151). In 1920, Congress finally passed the Nineteenth Amendment giving [white] women in the United States the right to vote.

In 1893, New Zealand became the first nation to allow women to vote and Australia (except Aboriginal women), Canada (except First Nations women), and several European nations passed women's suffrage laws before 1920. Many, however, such as France, Italy, and Japan, did not pass women's suffrage until the 1940s. Kuwait in 2005 was the most recent to add women to the voting ranks. Today Saudi Arabia is the only nation where men can vote but women cannot. Saudi men were granted the vote in 2005. Before that their parliament was appointed (BBC 2004).

By the end of the twentieth century, women in the United States had begun to dominate in regard to numbers at the voting booth. Women now make up the majority (51.8 percent) of Americans eligible to vote. Women (63.5 percent) are also more likely to register to vote than are men (60.6 percent). Since 1980, women (61 percent in 2004) have been more likely than men (58 percent in 2004) to exercise their right by going to the ballot box. In 2004 8.8 million more women voted than men in national elections in the United States (Center for the American Woman in Politics [CAWP] 2006).

Besides voting, how do women and men differ in their political activities? Since 1952, the National Election Studies (NES) has kept track of political behavior. They (Nagy and Rich 2001) found that:

- Women are now more likely to show up to vote.
- Women are about as likely as men to work for a candidate or party, attend a political meeting, or wear a button or display a sticker or sign.
- Men are still more likely than women to discuss politics, talk to others to try to convince them to support a candidate, and donate money. The differences are small, however, and the difference in donating money may be a result of who is asked to donate to political campaigns. Men report donating money more often than women. They also report being asked in person, by phone, and by mail more often to make a donation. Perhaps men are not more likely to contribute money to a candidate; they are just more likely to be given the opportunity to make a donation (Conway, Steuernagel, and Ahern 1997).

The Gender Gap in Voting

Men have historically controlled the ballot box and have been more likely to run for office. What difference does it make when women make their presence known in the electoral arena as voters and as candidates? The gender gap refers to the difference between women and men in whom they vote for and in their opinions on political issues. This term came into use during the 1980s (Bourque 2001).

The gap between women and men grew during the 1990s. Men's voting behavior created the change, as women's voting behavior remained fairly stable through the 1980s and 1990s. But men shifted their loyalties away from the Democrats and toward the Republicans during those decades (Seltzer, Newman, and Leighton 1997). By the 2000 election, the gap in voting between women and men was 11 percent. In the 2000 presidential election, men favored George Bush by 53 percent to 42 percent, and women favored Al Gore by 54 percent to 43 percent (Connelly 2000). In 2004, the gap narrowed but women were still more likely to vote for John Kerry than George W. Bush. Race ethnicity also made an important difference, as 55 percent of white women voted for Bush and 62 percent of white men did. Among nonwhite voters, 24 percent of women voted for Bush and 30 percent of the men did (CAWP 2006).

The gender gap indicates a split between women and men voters and sometimes the gap makes a difference in who gets into office. Some observers believe that electing women could result in different decisions by the executive and legislative branches of government because women and men seem to have different points of view on political matters. These differences are not just ideological, but relate to the different responsibilities and problems women and men have in their everyday lives. Polls on opinions as well as for whom they vote show that compared to men, women are:

- More likely to favor a more activist role for government.
- More often opposed to U.S. military intervention in other countries.
- More supportive of programs to guarantee quality health care and meet basic human needs.

- More supportive of restrictions on firearms.
- More supportive of affirmative action and efforts to achieve racial equality.
- More critical of business.
- More pessimistic about the performance of the economy.
- Less likely to say they have little confidence in Congress.
- Less likely to believe the government wastes many of our tax dollars (Seltzer, Newman, and Leighton 1997; CAWP 1998; Kaufmann and Petrocik 1999).

The positions favored more by women voters are more consistent with goals of the Democratic Party. The Republican Party has become identified with opposing programs that benefit women more than men and those that are favored by women voters such as Medicaid, Social Security, parental leave, and nutritional programs for women and children. The Democratic Party has been more likely to endorse policies that women are more likely than men to approve of, like gun control, environmental protection, health issues, education, and job training (Rothman 2002).

The relationship between political party and gender runs both ways. Women seem to identify more strongly with Democrats, whereas men are more likely to identify with Republican candidates and ideas. The Democratic Party has also been more supportive of women candidates running for and being elected to office. In the 1990s, Democrats nominated nearly twice as many women for seats in the House as Republicans did (Fox 2000).

Republican voters seem to be more hesitant to support women candidates. A poll in 2004 conducted by the Republican Party asked voters whether they would support a candidate who was a successful business person who had never run for office and whose top priority was reducing government spending and waste. Half were told the candidate was a woman and half were told he was a man. Among Republican men, 57 percent said they would support the man but only 43 percent would support the woman. Among Republican women, 53 percent of Republican women said they would support the man and only 42 percent would support the woman. Democrats had the reverse reaction. Both women and men Democrats were more likely to say they would vote for a woman (Morin 2004).

Gender, however, does not exist in isolation and seems to interact with other factors like knowledge and race ethnicity. When men and women have little knowledge of political issues, their opinions are similar. As political knowledge increases, the gap widens. Better informed men tend to become more conservative, whereas better informed women tend to become more liberal in their political opinions (Carpini and Keeter 2000). The gender gap is also affected by labor force participation. Employed women overwhelmingly supported Gore (58 percent) to Bush (39 percent) in the 2000 elections (CAWP 2000).

Race ethnicity is another factor that alters the gender gap. As a group, Latinas, like other women, are likely to identify with the Democratic Party, but Latinas with different national origins have a wide range of opinions on party affiliation. Puerto Rican American women are strongly Democratic, but Cuban Americans are likely to be Republicans. African American women are overwhelmingly Democratic but so are African American men (Rothman 2002).

The gender gap is important but it is not the only divide and, in fact, it is not the widest one. In 1994, there was a voting gap of 12 percent between married and single people, 19 percent between rich and poor, 29 percent between urban and rural voters, and

50 percent between blacks and whites (Seltzer, Newman, and Leighton 1997). These kinds of differences persist (CAWP 2006).

Women Elected Officials

The largest difference between women and men is the proportion of women who are elected by voters and appointed to office by elected officials. The exercise of political leadership by being elected or appointed to office is also probably the most critical political role Marger 2002). Voting as an individual citizen may be important, but creating policy and voting within elected bodies like the Senate is vastly more significant.

The numbers of women in public office have slowly increased in the United States since the first woman, Jeanette Rankin, was elected to Congress from the state of Montana in 1917. By the beginning of the twenty-first century, 11,500 men had been elected to the House but fewer than 200 women had taken their seat in the House (CAWP 1998). Only thirty-five women have served in the Senate. In 2006, Congress had the greatest proportion of women in history: Sixteen women senators and seventy-four women representatives were members of the 110th Congress, making up 16 percent of the Senate and 17 percent of the House of Representatives (Women's Policy Institute 2008). A full 215 years after Congress was established, Nancy Pelosi was the first woman elected Speaker of the House, the highest rank of a woman in Congress ever achieved. Because the Speaker of the House is second in line to the presidency just behind the Vice President, Pelosi has also come closest to the presidency of any woman in American history.

The start of the twenty-first century was also record setting for women at the state level. Women were elected governors in nine states in 2006 (CAWP 2006), and women held 29 percent of the 324 other state executive positions in jobs like lieutenant governor, attorney general, and secretary of state (CAWP 2000). State legislatures and local governments made more room for women than Congress. By 2006, 23 percent of state legislators were women and 20 percent of the mayors of cities larger than 100,000 were women (Blair and Northway 2001; CAWP 2006). Table 10–1 shows the percentage of women in state legislatures in those states with the ten highest levels of representations of women.

At the executive level of the federal government in the United States, women have not fared as well. No woman has served as president or vice president and only eight presidents

TABLE 10–1 Ten States with the Highest Percentages of Women State Legislators, 2006   2009 111th Congress

State	% Women	State	% Women
Vermont	38	Arizona	33
Colorado	36	Hawaii	33
Washington	35	Oregon	32
New Hampshire	35	Maryland	31
Minnesota	35	Maine	31

Source: CAWP (2006).

have appointed a total of thirty women to their cabinets since George Washington took office. It was 1997 before the first woman, Madeleine Albright, occupied the position of secretary of state, the top seat in foreign policy (Borelli 2000). The UN reports that the United States ranked ninety-third in political empowerment of women, placing it in among countries such as Chad and Morocco (Drexler 2006).

Around the world, progress for women has been uneven, although the 1990s seemed to indicate a breakthrough at least in some places. Table 10–2 shows that women were heads of state in twenty-two nations in 2008. The most woman-dominated government is Finland, which has a woman president, and where 42 percent of the parliament and 60 percent of the cabinet are women (Bowen 2007).

Table 10–3 shows the proportion of women in national legislatures or parliaments. In 2006, women comprised 17 percent of the members of parliaments. Moreover, of 181 countries with national parliaments, over 94 percent have at least one woman in parliament. These achievements are tempered, to some degree, by the fact that only nineteen countries have so far managed

TABLE 10–2 Women Heads of State, 2008

DATE ENTERED OFFICE

1952—*H.M.* Elizabeth II of United Kingdom of Great Britain and Northern Ireland and Her Other Realms and Territories *Queen, Defender of the Faith, Head of the Commonwealth*

1972—*H.M.* Margrethe II, *by the Grace of God,* Denmark's Queen

1980—*H.M.* Beatrix, *By the Grace of God,* Queen of the Netherlands

1997—President Mary McAleese, Ireland

1997—Governor-General Hon. Dr. *Dame* C. Pearlette Louisy, St. Lucia

1999—*Prime Minister* Hon. Helen Clark, New Zealand

2000—*President* Tarja Halonen, Finland

2001—*Executive President* Gloria Macapagal-Arroyo, The Philippines

2004—*Prime Minister* Luísa Días Diogo, Moçambique

2004—*President* of the General Council Nassimah Magnolia Dindar, Réunion (French Overseas Territory)

2005—*Governor-General* Michaëlle Jean, Canada

2005—*Federal Chancellor* Angela Merkel, Germany

2006—*Executive President* Ellen Johnson-Sirleaf, Liberia

2006—*Executive President* Michelle Bachelet Jeria, Chile

2006—*Minister-President* Emily de Jongh-Elhage, Nederlandse Antillen (Self-governing part of the kingdom of the Netherlands)

2007—*President* Pratibha Patil, India

2007—*Acting President* President Nino Burjanadze, Georgia

2007—*Executive President* Cristina E. Fernández de Kirchner, Argentina

2007—*Governor General* Louise Lake-Tack, Antigua and Barbuda

2007—*President* Borjana Kristo, The Federation of Bosnia (Bosnia-Hercegovina)

2007—*Prime Minister* Yuliya Tymoshenko, Ukraine

2007—*Premier* Viveca Eriksson, Åland (Finish External Territory)

SOURCE: Christensen (2008).

to reach the 30 percent threshold of women in national parliaments, a figure widely considered to signify the point at which women can make a meaningful impact on the work of the parliament. Table 10–3 also lists the nine nations that still have no women in their national legislatures.

Rwanda currently has the largest proportion of women in parliament with about 49 percent of the seats. Part of this is probably because the genocide in Rwanda that killed at least 800,000 people in 1994 left the sex ratio at 7:3 in favor of women. Rwanda, however, has also implemented important affirmative action policies that have resulted in many women entering public life as political leaders at the national and local levels of government. For example:

- 30 percent of decision-making-related positions were assigned to women.
- Local funds and microcredits were provided for production projects led by women.
- In 2003, Article 187 of the new Rwandan Constitution formalized equity promotion structures such as the National Council of Women.
- A Gender Issues Monitoring Office was created to facilitate the participation of women in public life and to ensure that development initiatives are egalitarian in generating benefits for both women and men (Social Watch 2008).

After Rwanda, Costa Rica, along with several European nations, has the largest proportion of women in government. Sweden, Denmark, and the Netherlands have women in more than one-third of the seats. Sweden tops the list in Europe with women making up more than 47 percent of their parliament (Rothman 2002). Sweden, Norway, and France also have more than one-third of their cabinet positions filled by women (Henig and Henig 2001).

In some places, however, women have lost ground. In Eastern Europe, women's participation in parliament dropped from 22 percent in 1987 to 6.5 percent in 1993 (UN, Department of Public Information 1995). In the Netherlands in the 1990s, the right-wing Protestant party SGP banned women altogether from membership because they believe the Bible forbids women to be politically active (Riley 2003). The Netherlands, nevertheless, has a high proportion (37 percent) of women in its parliament.

As a way of seeing how many people live in countries that have few women representatives in government, Table 10–3 lists the most populous nations in the world in order of their size and shows the proportion of women in their national legislatures. None of them has reached the magic 30 percent mark, with China (20 percent) and Pakistan (22 percent) coming closest, and seven of the ten countries lower than the international average of 17 percent.

What Difference Does It Make?

Women appear to still be outsiders in electoral politics, at least as elected officials. Would it make any difference if women became a larger proportion of political leaders? Three benefits have been attributed to increasing the numbers of elected women officials:

- Increased democratic justice and equity.
- More possibility of addressing the interests of women.
- Better use of all available resources (Henig and Henig 2001).

Most people would argue that seeing women in a proportionate number of positions is necessary to the ideals of a democracy. Even if women in public office do not behave in ways

TABLE 10–3 Women in National Legislatures (Lower or Single House), 2007

TOP TWENTY NATIONS WITH HIGHEST PERCENTAGE OF WOMEN

Country	% Women
Rwanda	49%
Sweden	47
Finland	42
Costa Rica	39
Norway	38
Denmark	37
Netherlands	37
Cuba	36
Spain	36
Argentina	35
Mozambique	35
Belgium	35
South Africa	33
Austria	32
New Zealand	32
Germany	32
Burundi	31
United Republic of Tanzania	30
Uganda	30
Peru	29

that are different from men, their presence is necessary to maintain legitimacy and public confidence in institutions (Henig and Henig 2001).

A second reason to bring more women into office comes from those who believe that women will behave differently from men in office. They assert that women have at least some different interests from men and those interests are not as likely to be addressed if decision-making institutions are dominated by men (Henig and Henig 2001). If women are more concerned about issues like health care, sexual harassment, and family leave, as their numbers increase we would expect to see these problems and policies to address them given wider coverage by governmental bodies (Kahn and Gordon 1997).

Research shows that women compared to men are more likely to campaign on issues rather than personal traits like their own integrity, honesty, and intelligence. Women are also more likely than men to campaign on "feminine" issues like education, health care, and child care. These gender contrasts are true for both Republican and Democratic candidates in the United States. Women candidates are also more liberal within each of the parties compared to their male counterparts. These differences suggest that more women in elected positions will change the agendas and the debates (Kahn and Gordon 1997), but it is difficult to say how far those differences would go. Research on decisions by women judges, for example,

NATIONS WITH NO WOMEN IN NATIONAL LEGISLATURE OR PARLIAMENT

Micronesia (Federated States of)
Nauru
Palau
Qatar
Saint Kitts and Nevis
Saudi Arabia
Solomon Islands
Tuvalu
United Arab Emirates

% OF WOMEN IN PARLIAMENT OR NATIONAL LEGISLATURE IN TEN MOST POPULOUS NATIONS

Country	% Women
(In Order of Population Size)	
China	21
India	8
United States	16
Indonesia	11
Brazil	15
Pakistan	22
Bangladesh	15
Russia	10
Nigeria	6
Japan	9

SOURCE: Inter-Parliamentary Union (2007).

shows that gender does not seem to make much difference. Women judges do not make more feminist decisions in cases, nor are they more liberal (Mezey 2000).

Using all available talent is the third argument given for promoting policies that increase women's participation in elected positions. Women constitute half the population and therefore half the skills and ideas necessary to address social issues. When women are absent, their talents are wasted (Henig and Henig 2001). As we saw in chapter 5 on education, women are increasingly entering institutions of higher education and are obtaining advanced training and degrees. Their ability to use the skills they develop is hindered by their inability to take a leadership role in the government.

Why So Few Women?

There appear to be many good reasons to build an electoral system that is gender equal. Why do women lag behind men in political representation? Scholars have come up with several answers to this question. In the United States perhaps the most important reason so few women have been elected to office is because they do not often run. In 1994, for example, women ran for only 14 percent of the seats in the House. The proportion of women holding office at every level of the government is similar to the percentage that entered the race (Seltzer, Newman, and Leighton 1997).

When women do decide to run, incumbency is a barrier for women. Incumbents are the people who currently are in office; they have an advantage in an election because they are a known quantity. They have name recognition and their time in office gives them media coverage. In addition, incumbents often establish themselves as people who can do the job. Incumbents are reelected 95 percent of the time. The problem of running against incumbents is an issue for both women and men who are not currently in office. Because women as a group, however, have been in the political arena for less time, they must either wait for the person who is in office to retire, resign, or die or they must run elections challenging incumbents.

A third factor that prevents women from gaining office is gender ideologies. Some people still believe that women belong at home, not in the House and Senate. Even when these people do think it is acceptable for women to run for office, they associate the characteristics of good leadership with masculine stereotypes. You should recall from chapters 1 and 2 that a major component of dominant ideas about masculinity identifies men with public activities and conflates masculinity with characteristics such as leadership. Man is the default leader. Polls show, for example, that 90 percent of the American public says they would support a woman for president (Seltzer, Newman, and Leighton 1997). When they are asked what a good president is like, however, they answer that a good president is one who has the conventional traits of masculinity: strength, self-confidence, determination, and decisiveness. Stereotyped feminine traits like warmth, gentleness, and compassion are more likely to be associated with lower level nonexecutive governmental positions, such as judges (Rothman 2002).

Women who have succeeded in holding a high office are often perceived as exceptional women who "act like men" (Peterson and Runyan 1999; Marger 2002). When women "act like men", however, they often face criticism for being unfeminine and unlikeable. Women leaders in business and politics are perceived as competent or likeable, but rarely both. Furthermore, being unlikeable implies fewer social skills and less ability to influence others (i.e., not a good leader.

This kind of gender bias in assessing the leadership skills of women varies cross-culturally. The characteristics of a good leader are defined differently in different nations, but in all cases women come up short, no matter what the criteria. For example, people in the United States and United Kingdom say inspiring others is the most important leadership quality. Nordic nations, in contrast, assert that the ability to delegate authority is most significant. In the United States and the United Kingdom, men are perceived as best able to inspire others, whereas those in Nordic nations believe that the men are best at delegating tasks (Belkin 2007).

A fourth factor holding women back from elected office is the link between having a paid job and participating in electoral politics. Women are still more likely than are men to be outside the paid labor force. Being employed in general seems to affect political participation. Women and men who are not in the paid labor force are less likely to participate in electoral politics. Among people who are employed, 42 percent of women and 55 percent of men said they had participated in a campaign. Among people who were not in the paid labor force, 32 percent of the women and 45 percent of the men said they had been involved in a campaign (Conway, Steuernagel, and Ahern 1997).

Among women and men who are in the paid labor force, only some kinds of jobs "track" them into political office. Most political candidates in the United States are drawn from a narrow group of elite occupations. In 2001, 26 percent of the members of Congress were lawyers, 23 percent were executives from business and banking, 19 percent were drawn from public service occupations, and 13.5 percent were educators (Hirschfield 2001). Women are less likely to be in the first two kinds of positions and as we saw in the chapters on work and education, women in education or public service have less prestigious positions in those fields.

Women's success in running for office in the judicial system shows how certain jobs are more likely to track people into political office. It also shows how getting into the right jobs demands getting onto the right educational path. Women have made significant inroads in winning judgeships. Nine women are chief justices of state supreme courts and seventy out of 357 state supreme court members are women. Their numbers are now three times what they were in the mid-1980s (Marger 2002). The most important factor in the increase of women in judgeships is access to legal education. The numbers of women in law school increased by ten times since the 1970s (Conway, Steuernagel, and Ahern 1997). By the end of the twentieth century, 43 percent of law school students were women (Conway, Ahern, and Steuernagel 1999). Earning a law degree sets people on the necessary pathway to becoming a judge and women are increasingly getting on the right track.

A fifth factor that may inhibit women's political activity is family obligations and lack of time. Working on a political campaign, running for office, and even voting take time. Voter turnout among men is not affected by the number of children a man has. For women it is directly related, as 80 percent of women with no children go to the polls, whereas 57 percent of those women with four or more children say they vote (Conway, Steuernagel, and Ahern 1997). Perhaps these same kinds of time constraints also affect women's participation in running for office. Even if these time constraints are not real barriers to women being effective political leaders, voters may believe that family obligations will interfere with women's work if they are elected to office.

A final factor that may hold some women back from winning office is treatment by the media. In senate races, women candidates receive less coverage (Kahn 1993). Furthermore, when journalists do cover women candidates they often focus on the gender of women candidates and question the ability of a woman candidate to win (Rothman 2002). Some journalists also treat women candidates differently. One woman described her experience with the press while running for office: "[The media covering the race] concentrate[d] on stupid, little things such as clothes, hair, etc., which never comes up with a man. They also use loaded adjectives to describe us, such as feisty, perky, small and lively" (Poole 1993, quoted in Fox 2000, 244).

GENDER AND CAMPAIGNS. Whether a person runs for office and wins an election is affected by gender. Men are more likely to run for office and they more often win. Men are also more likely to be running against another man in political campaigns (Fox 1997). Does gender also affect the process of elections? What happens when a woman enters the race against a man? Men change their campaign strategy in two ways. First, they are more hesitant to engage in negative campaigning. Fearing the public might think them ungentlemanly, men who campaign against women sometimes avoid aggressive confrontations. One man candidate told a researcher:

> I don't think it is proper to attack a woman. I was completely constrained in how I went about campaigning. It was a constant struggle to show the proper politeness towards my opponent. Women cannot handle criticism or high stress so I had to watch what I said closely so that I would not appear to be causing my opponent any grief. (Fox 2000, 248)

The second way in which running against a woman changes men candidates is that they go to greater lengths to show they are in touch with women's issues. The men who were running for office in Fox's (2000) research believed that women candidates have an edge with women voters and therefore the men felt they must reach out more to the women voters. A campaign aide for a man running for office explained, "The congressman decided that this year we would have a separate group of women supporters. This way, if his woman opponent ran around claiming she was the candidate for women, we could combat this by demonstrating our support from women" (Fox 2000, 251).

Three Models for Reform

Three models have been proposed for evening up the representation of women and men in elected political bodies: meritocratic, affirmative action, and radical (Norris and Lovenduski 1995). The meritocratic model sees women as deficient and seeks to remedy those shortcomings. The affirmative action model emphasizes the need for policies that can give women "a leg up" to overcome historical discrimination. The radical model asserts that the system may need major overhauling rather than just better integration of women into the existing model of politics.

MERITOCRATIC REMEDIES. The meritocratic model assumes that those who merit a reward will gain it. In the case of election results, someone from this standpoint would argue that women need to be more competitive to successfully run for office. They seek ways to narrow the gap by encouraging and training women to run for and fill more political offices, and especially to provide funds for their campaigns. EMILY's list is a good example of this approach. EMILY stands for Early Money is Like Yeast (www.emilyslist.org). Founded in the United States in 1985 by Ellen Malcolm, EMILY is a fund-raising and political training organization that has helped fund successful campaigns for fifty-three members of Congress, four governors, and eleven senators (Bourque 2001).

The EMILY's list model was replicated in Japan where a network of housewives' cooperatives initiated a movement to bring more women into political office. Their cause was taken up by WINWIN, the Japanese version of EMILY's list, which raised money for women candidates in Japan who supported issues like child care, health care, and environmental protection. Three-quarters of the candidates they supported won and Japanese women prevailed in more than 1,000 elections in 1999 giving them 10 percent of the total races (Freedman 2002). Since the 1990s, WINWIN and other similar organizations such as Shinano have succeeded in increasing women's elected representation by as much as tenfold in some of the areas (Funabashi 2003).

AFFIRMATIVE ACTION REMEDIES. The second model, affirmative action, advocates setting target numbers and quotas for women in political office. This strategy has been especially successful in Europe, but the practice is widespread. Half of the nations in Latin America (eleven) have quotas for women's candidates and about sixty countries throughout the world have now adopted quota laws (Ross 2007).

The structure of party politics has been identified as the key reason that women do not run for office. To win an election, a candidate needs the support of a political party. If the party does not develop an affirmative action policy, women and other underrepresented people are not likely to win elections. In the 1970s, European women tried to gain power outside of political parties by forming their own organizations or caucuses within political parties. In the 1980s they began to move inside the parties when they decided that their outsider status was not getting them into positions of power. Their efforts to gain a foothold in the parties, however, were hampered by those who did not want them to take on leadership positions and by the women's lack of experience in the organizations.

Advocates of gender equity developed a quota system as the solution. Party activists sought to break into the structures by demanding that women fill a minimum number of places on committees within the party so that the number of women in the party leadership would match the number of women in the party. Norway led the way here when their Socialist Party set a quota declaring 40 percent of their candidates were to be women. Left parties in Denmark, The Netherlands, Spain, and France have now established woman quotas. The Green Party, active across Europe, has the highest quota (50 percent), and Green Party delegations in Germany, the Netherlands, and Sweden now have a majority of women (Henig and Henig 2001).

Affirmative action programs have not remained only at the party level, however. In France, affirmative action became the law of the land in 2000. Because the government funds elections in France, the National Assembly was able to pass a law called *parite* reducing funds to parties that fail to field equal numbers of women and men candidates. One year after the law was passed, women won 47.5 percent of municipal elections, twice the number they had won in previous years. In India, the numbers are even more astounding. Since the passage in 1993 of a constitutional amendment reserving one-third of all village council seats for women and those from the lowest castes, 1 million women took office on village councils or as village heads. Their efforts have resulted in better water, sewer, and transportation systems and more girls in school (Freedman 2002).

The story about the Zapata election in Spain at the beginning of the chapter was an example of the affirmative action approach. Zapata declared during his campaign that he would appoint equal numbers of women and men and when he was elected he kept his promise, appointing eight women and eight men to his cabinet. His approach is common in Europe, but nations all over the world have also created affirmative action programs. In 2000 at the Beijing+5 Summit, a 50/50 Program was championed and sixty nations in the world now have some kind of gender equity quota system (Gouws 2004). The Sudan, United Republic of Tanzania, Jordan, Antigua, Argentina, South Africa, and Bangladesh provide examples from across the globe of nations that have created quotas for women in office (Women's eNews 2007).

Some nations like Hungary, however, have taken the opposite tack. After employing affirmative action for forty years, Hungarians abolished the practice in the 1990s as part of their transition from a socialist to a capitalist system. The number of women occupying seats in government plummeted from 30 percent to 7 percent (Inter-Parliamentary Union 1997). Because after affirmative action ended Hungary so quickly went back to low proportions of women in elected office, it's experience suggests that affirmative action alone will not solve the problem in the long run. Some scholars have suggested more radical reforms.

RADICAL REMEDIES. The third model for improving the representation of women in government is a radical one (Lister 1997). This model calls for restructuring political institutions in a number of ways (Norris and Lovenduski 1995). Those who advocate radical change point to factors in the social organization of elections and representative government that need change. For example, many people have suggested that American elections with only two parties, an electoral college, gerrymandered districts, and a winner-take-all approach to voting may lock many people out of true political representation. These factors may create especially difficult barriers for women and people in racial ethnic groups who have only relatively recently been allowed to participate.

One strategy is to increase the numbers of representatives. When larger numbers of seats are available for candidates, parties may feel they can "risk" supporting women for those slots. Changing legislative bodies by increasing the number of people in the group can improve the chances of women and other underrepresented people to win a seat.

Another structural change that might open up women's chances is to limit terms, which would give more nonincumbents an opportunity to win elections. Because incumbents are more likely to win and men have dominated legislative bodies, men are more likely to be incumbents. Limiting the number of terms a Congress member could stay in office would allow more new people, many of whom would be women, to run for and win seats.

Increasing the number of political parties is another way to bring a broader range of voices into government. In the two-party system of the United States, for example, women have a huge challenge in being accepted and supported in their bid for seats. If there were more parties, some of which would be newer and less established with power less entrenched in the hands of those who have traditionally been in power, perhaps women could rise more quickly.

The radical model also supports making political institutions more woman-friendly by, for example, providing day care and keeping family-friendly hours. For example, as part of their quest for gender equity, when the new South African government took power in 1994 one of its first actions was to create a day care center for the children of parents working in parliament.

Finally, the radical model asserts that the culture of political bodies needs to be changed from confrontational, competitive arenas to ones that are more cooperative and compassionate (Jones 1993). Remember that one of the barriers to women becoming president in the United States is the kind of characteristics voters believe are necessary for being a good president. Perhaps their assessment that a good president is one who is strong, self-confident, determined, and decisive is because the context in which an American president leads demands these traits.

POLITICAL INSTITUTIONS: THE COURTS AND PRISONS

Who are criminals? The second major political institution within the state we explore here is the criminal justice system, especially the courts and prisons. Although men constitute about 50 percent of the population, they make up 80 percent of those who are arrested. Since the 1960s the proportion of people who are arrested for serious crimes who are women has risen from 10 percent to 26 percent (Small 2000). This is a large increase, but crime (at least reported crime) is still generally a man's activity. Prostitution is the only crime for which more women than men are arrested; between 30 percent and 50 percent of the arrests of women are for prostitution.

As we read in chapter 8, men are also more likely than women to serve time, at least at the state and federal level. They make up about 95 percent of the prison population and the conditions of prison life are more difficult in some ways for men. Women prisoners often have rooms rather than cells, can sometimes wear their own clothes, can decorate their rooms with personal items, and are less likely to be surrounded by barbed wire or walls.

Women prisoners face other difficulties, however. Because there are few women's prisons, women may be incarcerated a long way from their homes, making family visits more difficult. Women's prisons also have fewer training or recreational facilities, libraries, or medical care (Conway, Ahern, and Steuernagel 1999). Women prisoners spend about seventeen hours a day in their cell and are allowed outside one hour a day, whereas men are allowed outside an hour and a half.

Women also have special health needs that are not addressed in prison. Congress has banned the use of federal funds for abortions for women in prison. If a woman wishes to have an abortion and she can pay for it, she must convince prison officials to take her to a clinic. If she continues with a pregnancy she is unlikely to receive prenatal care, her prison diet will not meet minimum standards for pregnant women, and she may be forced to go through labor and delivery while shackled (Siegel 1997).

In 1997–1998, more than 2,200 pregnant women were imprisoned and more than 1,300 babies were born to women in prison. Many of these women are shackled while giving birth, a violation of responsible medical practice and a form of torture (Ehrlich and Paltrow 2006). Psychological pain is also inflicted on these women when their babies are taken from them almost immediately after birth or at the time the mother is discharged from the hospital, a practice in forty states. One woman who endured this practice described how she gave birth while an inmate of Cook County Jail in Chicago:

> The doctor came and said that "yes, this baby is coming right now," and started to prepare the bed for delivery. Because I was shackled to the bed, they couldn't remove the lower part of the bed for the delivery, and they couldn't put my feet in the stirrups. My feet were still shackled together, and I couldn't get my legs apart. The doctor called for the officer, but the officer had gone down the hall. No one else could unlock the shackles, and my baby was coming but I couldn't open my legs.... Finally the officer came and unlocked the shackles from my ankles. My baby was born then. I stayed in the delivery room with my baby for a little while, but then the officer put the leg shackles and handcuffs back on me and I was taken out of the delivery room. (Rebecca Project for Human Rights 2007)

Amnesty International also reports that sexual violence against women prisoners in the United States is widespread. Men show up much more often in Amnesty's reports of torture and abuse of prisoners in the United States, but women are more likely to be raped and victims of other forms of sexual abuse at the hands of the male staff (Crossett 1998; Davis 2003).

Young People in the Criminal Justice System

The rates of arrest among juveniles vary by gender. Like adults, boys are arrested much more often than girls. Arrests of girls, however, have increased dramatically in recent years, rising 74 percent for white girls during the 1990s and 106 percent for black girls (Gullo 2001).

The reasons for arrest are also different for boys and girls. If a girl is arrested it is likely to be for status offenses, which are activities such as being out after curfew, running away, or drinking alcohol. These activities are considered crimes only when young people participate in them; they are not considered crimes for adults (Belknap 2001). Of children arrested for running away, 58 percent are girls (U.S. Bureau of the Census 2001).

Boys and girls who are arrested for running away are an indication of the injustice in the system for youngsters who are sexually abused. Girls and boys who are sexually abused often run away from home as a survival response. This injustice is especially important for girls because sexual abuse is more common among girls. Ironically, girls who run away are more harshly treated by the criminal justice system than are boys. Girls are more likely to be arrested and to be detained (Belknap 2001).

GIRLS, GANGS, AND GENDER. Like many other examples of crime and punishment, young men join gangs more than young women do. But young women are increasingly showing up around gangs and forming their own gangs. The experience of women compared to men is different in gangs and is affected by gender. Jody Miller (2001) talked to gang girls in Columbus and St. Louis and found that gender appeared in gang life in three ways. First, sexual assault and other kinds of abuse of girls, especially by people close to them, was a common experience among girls in gangs. Fifty-two percent of young women in gangs have been sexually assaulted. However, girls in gangs claim that this is less of a problem than assault when they are not in a gang. Even though girls are victims of violence when they participate in gangs, they say the violence within a gang is more tolerable and manageable and therefore worth the risk.

Second, gender allows women to restrict their participation in some highly dangerous gang activity, for example, using guns. This protection, however, also works to relegate the women to inferior status within gangs because taking on the most dangerous activities provides the member with status and power. The hierarchy of high status and low status is also used as a basis for violence against subordinate members. In addition, girls do use weapons, although they tend to avoid guns. One young woman explained why she used her fists and knives but no guns, "We ladies, we not dudes for real. We don't be rowdy, all we do is fight. A dude, he quick to go get a gun or something, a girl she quick to pull out a knife" (J. Miller 2001, 140).

Third, gender makes women play particular roles within gangs. The perception that women are less suspicious for criminal activity makes them useful for disguising the criminal activities of the men. One young woman in a gang explained,

Like when we in a car, if a girl and a dude in a car, the police tend not to trip off of it. When they look to see if a car been stolen, police just don't trip off of it. But if they see three or four n****** in that car, the police stop you automatically, boom....When my brother was gonna be locked up, the police was looking at my cousin Janeeta, she [was in the car with him]. She got a nice little body and face. He let my brother go....He was trying to make on her, you know what I'm saying. Little ways that we got to get them out of stuff sometimes, we can get them out of stuff that dudes couldn't do, you know what I'm saying. So they need us girls. They need us. (J. Miller 2001, 157–58).

The War on Drugs

Although drug use began to decline in the early 1980s, in the late 1980s the U.S. government expanded its efforts to stop drug abuse by increasing arrests and incarceration of drug offenders. The new law and order policies of the "war on drugs" include mandatory sentencing, longer sentences and "three strikes and you're out" legislation. In 2001, the U.S. Patriot Act further stepped up measures to investigate, detain, and arrest.

Much of this get tough on crime, and especially the war on drugs, is directed toward African Americans, although rates of drug use among whites and African Americans are similar. Research on drug use, not arrest for drug use, shows that rates are similar for different racial ethic groups, although the type of illegal drug used varies. In addition to racial ethnic discrimination by police, several other law enforcement techniques result in higher arrest rates among African Americans: the priority placed on outdoor drug venues, the geographic concentration of police resources in racially heterogeneous areas, and especially law enforcement's focus on crack offenders (Beckett, Nyrop, and Pfingst 2006). African Americans are more likely to use crack cocaine, whereas wealthy whites use powdered cocaine. Until 2007, crack had a mandatory sentence of five years for possession or trafficking. Powdered cocaine carried no mandatory sentence. In addition, for trafficking in the drug, it takes 100 times more powder cocaine than crack to trigger the same mandatory minimum penalty (the so-called 100 to 1 quantity ratio) (Sabet 2005). On November 1, 2007, reduced federal sentencing guidelines for crack cocaine went into effect.

The African American population constitutes about 12 percent of the total population in the United States but black women comprise a little more than half (51 percent) of the women's prison population and black men make up half of the men's population (50 percent; Bush-Baskette 1998). The racial ethnic gap in drug arrests increased dramatically for black people during the war on drugs. In 1976, 22 percent of those arrested for drugs were black. In 1990, 41 percent of those arrested were black. This increase was even more significant for black women than for black men (Bush-Baskette 1998).

The war on drugs has also been a war on women. The change in arrests and imprisonment for drugs increased the prison population for both men and women. The increase has begun to level off, but 50 percent more people are in prison in the United States today compared to the numbers in the 1980s. The number of arrests for women, however, increased twice as fast. Imprisonment of women has skyrocketed even more rapidly than the overall arrest rate. The arrest rate of women climbed 31.4 percent between 1987 and 1996 but the number of women in prison increased by 159 percent during this same period (Chesney-Lind 1997). Drug offenses

Box 10–1 MINOR CRIMES, MAJOR SENTENCES: THE CASE OF SERENA NUNN

After spending 11 years behind bars, Serena Nunn, now 36 years old, is the proud recipient of a law degree from the University of Michigan Law School. Although her journey to accomplishing this feat has been one filled with determination and persistence, it has also been fraught with injustice and tragedy.

Because of financial difficulties at Morris Brown College in Atlanta, Serena returned home to Minnesota in 1988. There she met and fell in love with Ralph Nunn (no relation), the son of a drug dealer. Her involvement in his drug activities included driving him to meetings with other dealers and taking his messages.

In 1989, only 19 years old at the time, Serena was convicted of conspiracy to possess and distribute cocaine. At the time of her sentencing, she refused to testify against Ralph and because of stringent federal mandatory minimum sentencing policies, Serena, with no prior criminal record and a minor role in her boyfriend's drug ring, was sentenced to 15 years and 8 months in prison. "I never try to come across as some naïve innocent," said Serena in a interview with the *Detroit News*, "I just think the punishment should fit the crime. I deserved punishment. But to lock me away for my entire 20s." The drug ring leader, who had prior drug, rape, and manslaughter convictions, was sentenced to seven years because he assisted the prosecution.

Serena's story mirrors those of many other women who, because of their minor involvement in drug rings, have little information to trade and are left with little bargaining power with prosecutors. They end up facing excessive time in prison; meanwhile, their men counterparts receive reduced sentences in return for their testimony.

Serena was luckier than most. Federal, state and local officials lobbied for her clemency and U.S. District Court Judge David S. Doty, who sentenced Serena, wrote to President Clinton in support of her. He argued: "If mandatory minimum rules did not exist, no judge in America, including me, would have ever sentenced Ms. Nunn to 15 years in prison based on her role in the conspiracy, her age and the fact that she had no prior criminal convictions." Finally, on July 7, 2000, 11 years into her sentence, Serena was released with a commutation from President Clinton.

SOURCE: Sentencing Project (2006.)

were the main reason for this increase. In the mid-1980s, 26 percent of the women in federal prisons were there for drug offenses. By the 1990s, 72 percent of them were. In women's state facilities the increase in drug offenders went from 10 percent in 1979 to 33 percent in 1991 (Greenfeld & Snell 1999). Many of the women have been swept into prison through mandatory sentencing laws despite the relatively minor roles the women have played in the drug trade. Box 10–1 describes one woman's experience. Her story explains that because women are only peripherally involved they have less leverage in prosecution and sentencing than men who are much more central to the drug-dealing activities (Women in Prison Project 2002).

The imprisonment of women has increased in many nations. For example imprisonment rates for women tripled in Canada in the 1990s. The United States remains at the top, though, with ten times as many women in prison as nations in western Europe (Kirk and Okazaw-Rey 2004). Sentences also increased during this time period. In 1982, the average sentence for a drug offender was fifty-five months, whereas it was 133 months for a violent offender. In 1991, drug offenders averaged eighty-six-month sentences and violent offenders received mean sentences of ninety-one months.

Besides sending more women to jail for longer periods of time, the war on drugs has exacerbated gender inequality because stricter drug enforcement has caused ripple effects that result in a decline in the economic status of women (Danner 1998). Increased spending on prisons required cuts in other government services of 40 percent over eight years in the 1990s. Because women are more likely to rely on services like welfare, they suffered the consequences of the cuts disproportionately. In addition, women are more likely to be employed in social services and therefore see their jobs disappear when the government shifts spending from social services to prisons. The war on drugs sends more men than women to prison but women bear a heavier burden of the unintended consequences (Owen 1999).

Why Are Men So Much More Likely to Be in Prison?

The differences between women and men in the rates of criminal activities and imprisonment are remarkable. Four kinds of theoretical explanations have been offered to try to explain both the difference and the recent closing of the gap: masculinity theory, opportunity theory, economic marginalization theory, and chivalry theory (Small 2000).

Masculinity theory asserts that criminal activity is associated with characteristics of masculinity, such as being aggressive, pushy, hard-headed, and violent. These behaviors are part of being a man in our society and as a result they make men more prone to committing crimes. Theorists from this point of view argue that as expectations about women and the behavior of women become more masculinized, we should expect that women will become more similar to men and will commit more crimes and become a larger proportion of the prison population (Adler and Adler 1975).

Opportunity theory asserts that property crimes are a result of being in the right place at the right time and that to commit a crime, a person must have certain skills. This theory argues that as women enter the workplace, they gain skills, social connections, and opportunities to commit acts like theft, embezzlement, and forgery (Simon 1975). On the other hand, opportunity theorists note that as women gain greater economic independence they also improve their ability to leave abusive relationships before they escalate to committing assault or murder of a husband or boyfriend. Opportunity theorists predict that as women continue to take on paid jobs, we will see women committing more property crimes but fewer violent crimes.

A third theory is economic marginalization theory (Chesney-Lind 1997). These theorists are not as optimistic about seeing women's economic fortunes improve just because they are in the labor force. They argue that women are working outside the home but they remain poor, and crime is an avenue for supplementing their income. They predict that women's criminal involvement will increase as women are more economically independent but still less able to provide sufficiently for themselves and their families (Small 2000).

The National Resource Center on Domestic Violence provides evidence to support this point of view by describing another way women are vulnerable in addition to economic marginalization. They note that today, women's incarceration is often directly related to the combined impact of rape, battering, and a variety of state violence that fall heavily on their shoulders. According to the National Resource Center on Domestic Violence, "the overwhelming majority of women defendants in the criminal justice system have extensive histories of childhood and adult abuse that may result in homelessness, substance abuse, and economic marginality that force them into survival by illegal means" (S. Miller 2005). Recent changes in welfare, housing, immigration policies, drug enforcement, mandatory arrest, prosecutions, and sentencing policies further criminalize women's efforts to survive, escape, and cope with abuse. Low-income women of color are most at risk (Gilfus 1992).

The fourth theory is chivalry theory (Steffensmeier and Allan 1996). This perspective maintains that women's behavior has not changed as much as the criminal justice system's treatment of women. According to this point of view, women have been similar to men in their criminal behavior in the past but that similarity was obscured by leniency in the system, making women appear to be less criminal. They predict that as chivalry falls away, women's true criminal activity will become more visible and will appear to be greater than in previous decades.

POLITICAL INSTITUTIONS: THE MILITARY

The military is a third social institution within government that shows how important gender is. Women have served in the armed services throughout history, but the military is clearly recognized as a masculine institution. It remains one of a few social institutions left in the United States that legally restricts participation by gender.

Women, however, increasingly are participating in the military. What seems to push women into the military or at least allow them to enter? Three sets of factors are important (Bourg and Segal 2001):

- Demand for personnel. When a nation or a social movement needs more members such as in times of war, women are a large resource that can be tapped.
- Demographic or economic changes that alter the supply of potential recruits. If unemployment is low or in a generation that was born during a low birth rate, fewer men are available and women are drawn in.
- Cultural values. In societies with more egalitarian ideas about gender or during historical periods when gender equality is emphasized, women are more likely to increase their numbers in the military.

All three of these appear to be significant features of the current social context. We would expect that women will continue to increase their numbers in the military.

Up until 1967 the U.S. military maintained a 2 percent ceiling on women. The quota was lifted in the late 1960s and in the 1990s significant additional changes took place in military policy. In 1991, Congress repealed laws prohibiting women from flying on aircraft in combat missions. In 1994, women began to be allowed to serve on Navy combat ships, although women are still not allowed on submarines or in the special warfare units, SEALS. There are 1.7 million women now who are military veterans and another 211,900 currently serving in the armed forces (U.S. Bureau of the Census 2006).

Overall 15 percent of active-duty troops and 17 percent of National Guard and Reserve forces are women. Table 10–4 shows the breakdown in the proportion of women in various branches of the military and the proportion of women among officers. The numbers vary but women are certainly a minority in all categories.

About 20 percent of all military jobs are still off-limits for women in the United States (Bourg and Segal 2001). In addition, a 1997 study on women in the military by RAND's National Defense Research Institute found that only 815 of the 47,544 military jobs opened to women in 1994 were now occupied by women (Jacinto 2004).

Women Marines are barred from the highest number of jobs and are still segregated from the men in training, eating, and barracks, although their training is becoming much more similar to men's. All Marines, women and men, must rappel forty-seven-foot towers, crawl under barbed wire, learn martial arts, swim in camouflage fatigues, march, run, and survive a fifty-four-hour hike. At the rifle range the requirements for passing are exactly the same for women and men (St. George 2002).

In the world, the proportion of women in the military remains small. Ninety percent of the world's armed forces are men, and women are still barred from serving in many countries.

Women in Combat

Combat remains a restricted activity for women around the world. Only seven countries allow women in all combat roles (Australia, Canada, Belgium, the Netherlands, Denmark, Norway, and Spain). Seven others allow women in many combat roles (France, Finland, Ghana, Israel, Japan, United Kingdom, and United States; Peterson and Runyan 1999). These policies, however, describe only the official position of women in combat. The UN reports that women are much more likely to be unofficially involved in combat than the

TABLE 10-4 Women in Different Branches of U.S. Armed Services, 2006

	% of Positions Open to Women	Women as % of Enlisted	Women as % of Officers
Air Force	99%	20%	18%
Navy	94	15	15
Army	70	15	15
Marine Corps	62	6	6

SOURCE: Bourg and Segal (2001, 337); U.S. Bureau of the Census (2006, Table 501).

Box 10–2 SHOULD WOMEN GO TO WAR?

Women are officially barred from military combat in the United States and most other nations, but the recent wars in Iraq and Afghanistan are marked by unclear boundaries, suicide bombers, attacks on supply convoys, and a shortage of American troops. This means that regardless of official assignments, women are in the line of fire and are using weapons to defend themselves and others in direct confrontation with the enemy, including flying combat missions. And they have died in battle (eighty-two women have died in combat and 470 have returned from the Iraq War wounded) (Ginty 2007).

The laws appear to be lagging behind the on-the-ground reality of the battlefield. Although Congress has considered changing the rules to formally allow women in combat, they have so far continued to defend the ban on women in combat. The American public is about evenly split on whether women should be assigned to ground combat.

Retired Lt. Gen. Claudia J. Kennedy, the highest ranking woman to ever serve in the Army, predicts that as the Iraq war continues, more women soldiers will be called up for active duty. She notes that military recruiting is down by 27 percent, and estimates that 30,000 to 50,000 more soldiers may be needed in Iraq. She asserts that women "are vital to this mission and should not be segregated. Women soldiers deserve to be treated just as all soldiers should be treated—properly trained, properly equipped and given the proper respect" (Ginty 2005).

Does this gap between the rules and reality mean that women are less well trained and less well armed because they are not officially in combat roles? Is it endangering them or their comrades? Is it disrespectful of women who have died in battle to ignore their combat heroism and sacrifice?

laws suggest. Since 1990, for example, girl soldiers have been in fighting forces in sixty-four countries (Brett 2002).

In the United States, the official rules have been changing in the past few decades. Congress lifted the ban on women in the cockpit in 1993, and Lieutenant Colonel McSally was the first woman to log combat time. She has flown 100 sorties over Iraq and directed combat rescue missions in Afghanistan (Bergquist 2006).

Currently, 11 percent of the troops in Iraq and Afghanistan are women. Officials assert that women military personnel in Iraq and Afghanistan are as much on the front line as they can be (Kelley 2004). Box 10–2 discusses some of the controversies surrounding this increased participation in informal and formal combat positions.

Women and Men in the Military Today

The laws changed in the 1990s in the American armed services to allow women into more positions. In 1996, women won their cases at the Citadel as well as the Virginia Military Institute to enter these formerly all- men schools. Expectations for military women appear to have been changing dramatically in the past few decades. Until 1980, for example, women in the Marines did not learn to fire arms. Most of their training resembled charm school. They were issued elaborate cosmetic kits and taught how to apply lipstick and how to properly stamp out a cigarette. They were required to learn how to iron a crisp shirt and sit on a bar stool. At the end of their training they were tested in their social graces as they sipped punch, strolled around in high heels, and made small talk with the officers (St. George 2002).

Although policy has changed, some problems remain. Some men in the military resist the idea of women in the military. Table 10–5 shows the opinions of men and women currently in the armed services in different ranks about whether women should continue to increase their numbers. Table 10–5 shows large differences of opinion between women and men. Women are, not surprisingly, more supportive of more women in the military. Rank also influences opinions. Men in the highest ranks are most likely to believe there are too many women in the armed services (L. Miller 2000).

Gender and rank also affect opinions about what women should be doing in the military. Among men, 44 percent of men believe combat roles should be open to women. Among women, 64 percent of enlisted women and 68 percent of officers believe women should be allowed into combat roles. Race ethnicity also affects the opinion of women in combat. Among black, Hispanic, and those of racial ethnic groups other than white, 68 percent believe women who want to volunteer for combat services should be allowed to do so. Only 18 percent of white officers and 39 percent of white enlisted members share this opinion (L. Miller 2000).

Gender Harassment in the Military

In chapter 6 on work, we examined the problem of sexual harassment. You should recall that sexual harassment was defined as a range of activities from "gender harassment which is inappropriately calling attention to women or men's bodies, sexuality or marital status, to sexual harassment which is turning a professional, work or student–teacher relationship into a sexual relationship that is not wanted by one of the people involved and that is coercive because the initiator has some power over the other person" (Lorber 2000, 291).

TABLE 10–5 Soldiers' Opinions About Numbers of Women in the Military

	ENLISTED		NONCOMMISSIONED		OFFICERS OFFICERS	
	Men	*Women*	*Men*	*Women*	*Men*	*Women*
Too many women in the military	11%	2%	16%	1%	24%	0%
About the right amount	36	31	38	48	9	44
Too few women in the military	33	50	22	38	7	49
Not sure	20	17	24	13	10	7

SOURCE: L. Miller (2000, 417)

Laura Miller (2000) investigated gender harassment in the military. She defines gender harassment as behavior that is not sexual and is used to enforce traditional gender roles or in response to violation of those roles. Gender harassment tends to target women who are supposedly not feminine enough but can also be used against men who fail to live up to "masculine ideals." L. Miller (2000) argues that women may see their numbers increase and their opportunities expand in the military but they might not find themselves working in a more supportive or even tolerant environment. Gender discrimination in policy that restricts women in the military may be eliminated but it might be replaced by more subtle but equally problematic gender harassment.

Gender harassment can take the following forms:

- Resistance to authority. A man soldier refuses to follow directions from a superior who is a woman.
- Constant scrutiny. Women in the services report that they feel they must work harder and live up to higher standards because they are under surveillance by men who are waiting for them to make a mistake.
- Gossip and rumors. An example is a "popular" untrue rumor that some women soldiers in the Gulf Wars made a fortune by setting up a tent and working as prostitutes for the men there.
- Sabotage. Equipment and tools being used by women in nontraditional jobs has been reportedly purposely damaged.
- Indirect threats. Comments have been alleged about the inevitability of women being raped if they were present in deployments or in infantry or armor units. These comments are often given as concerned warnings, but the end result is to communicate to women that they will be in danger if they challenge the gender lines in combat.

Why the Hostility Against Women in the Military?

Why do some men in the military see women in the military as the enemy? L. Miller (2000) interviewed men about their hostility toward women and found it was based on their belief that men are discriminated against in the armed forces. One reason for this is different and easier physical training standards for women. One noncommissioned officer (NCO) explained, "I can't be adamant enough. There is no place for women in the infantry. Women do not belong in combat units. If you haven't been there, then you wouldn't understand. As far as equal rights, some women say they are as physically strong as a man. Then why are [physical training] standards different?" (L. Miller 2000, 421).

Others asserted that women are unfairly advantaged and take advantage of pregnancy for limiting their physical training or labor. Some of the men also said restrictions on women's roles end up advantaging women because they then have better educational opportunities or better assignments, while men are relegated to the combat jobs. They also believe that women get away with more than men do and quotas exist that result in undeserved promotions for women. White men were especially distressed because they thought that all of these advantages accrued to racial ethnic minorities relative to white soldiers as well (L. Miller 2000).

Remember that these beliefs are not necessarily valid. However, the men who expressed them also felt there was no opportunity for them to talk about their anger. They had been silenced but their feelings sometimes were expressed in gender harassment. Allowing women into the services and allowing them to participate more fully can be altered by changing policy, but these changes need to be accompanied by uncovering some of these more hidden ideas and the accompanying behaviors.

Masculinity and Heterosexuality in the Military

As we saw in chapter 4, sexuality is a key component in the social construction of gender. The armed forces are an important source of the rules that define proper behavior for women and men as heterosexual. Heterosexuality is a requirement, from the point of view of the military, for a truly masculine man or feminine woman (Bourg and Segal 2001).

In the 1950s, the U.S. military explicitly barred gay men and lesbians from military service. For more than forty years, rules about sexuality became increasingly restrictive. In the early 1990s, however, polls showed that 65 percent of Americans opposed the exclusionary policy. In addition, the General Accounting Office announced in 1992 that the practice of hunting for gay men and lesbians in the military, prosecuting them, and dismissing them from the service was costing $27 million a year (McFeeley 2000). In 1993 these rules were revised to drop the statement that homosexuality is incompatible with military service. The armed services are no longer allowed to ask potential recruits or members about their sexual orientation. This new policy is commonly known as "don't ask, don't tell." Gay men and lesbians can still be dismissed from service for engaging in a homosexual act or openly discussing their sexuality, and they cannot live with a life partner or seek to marry (Bourg and Segal 2001).

Why Are Differences in the Treatment of Women in the Military Important?

The military plays a significant role in creating and perpetuating gender inequality in three ways. First, gender inequality in the activities of women and men in the military contributes to the continuation of cultural images of masculinity and femininity among military personnel and in the general population who observe members of the armed forces. The military trains its members to identify with and express gender in a stereotyped manner. Men in the military are under constant pressure to prove their manhood by being tough, adversarial, and aggressive. Words like little girl, woman, and lady have been used as derogatory terms for men who fail to live up to military standards. To fail is to be female (Stiehm 1981). The practice of referring to trainees as "girls" in the service is now officially prohibited (Bourg and Segal 2001).

Second, barring women from some activities in the military limits their access to power and resources such as jobs, job training, or educational benefits. The military, for example, arms its members. Because women are less likely to be in the military and are barred from particular activities like combat they have less legitimate access to weapons, weapons training, and the use of weapons than do men (Bourg and Segal 2001).

Third, the association of military service and citizenship means that discrimination in the military can help perpetuate gender inequality in the legal rights of citizens. For example, as we saw in the discussion of elections, getting into a track that leads to political leadership is a key to electing more women to office. The military is a powerful arm of the state. It commands a large proportion of government spending and employs more people than any other single organization in the United States. Those at the top of the organization, not surprisingly, have much influence over public officials. In addition, those who are in public office use their military service as a way of selling themselves to the public. Men with military experience, such as Dwight Eisenhower, Colin Powell, and John McCain, have used that credential as a basis for garnering votes or being appointed to important positions. Although public opinion appears to be changing, 45 percent of the American public still believe that women in public office are not capable of effectively handling issues such as the military, war, homeland security, and foreign policy. If women do not have access to high-level, high-profile military positions, including those in combat, they do not have access to this track to political leadership.

Be Careful What You Wish For

Breaking down barriers to gender inequality is a laudable goal. In the case of electoral politics, making women more equal to men would benefit women, men, and the community. Making women more like men in the military and in the criminal justice system is less justifiable. In the case of the criminal justice system, the forces that seem to be associated with greater criminal activity of women such as greater public participation by women, especially in economic activities, are good and perhaps criminal activity is just part of the package.

In the case of the military, we can see that bringing women into the armed forces on an equal footing with men has some benefits because the military is an important source of jobs and because it is a powerful institution from which women do not want to be excluded. However, some have grappled with the problem of promoting the practice of more women in the military, particularly when the country is at war. Should our goal be to encourage women to be warriors as skilled as men? Or should our goal be to make men better at the ideas and behaviors associated with women like cooperation, compromise, reconciliation, and pacifism?

Women and Peace

The discussion of the military has emphasized the exclusion of women from military work, especially combat. The focus has been on the problems associated with leaving women out and the changes that have been fought for to bring more women into the military and into war making. Internationally, though, women are recognized as instrumental in preventing and stopping armed conflict and building peace. Both during and after conflict, women have been integrally involved in peace-building processes, seeking solutions to problems such as resource degradation; demobilization and reintegration of former child soldiers; violence against women and children; effects of militarization; and sustainable economic, environmental, and political development (McKay and de la Rey 2001). Women have also been shown to be more likely to support peace-making efforts; for example, in the Gulf Wars, American women are less hawkish than men. A recent Gallup Poll reported that 62 percent of American women believed the troops should come home from Iraq by the end of the year compared to 53 percent of men who took this position.

Like formal combat, however, women are seldom included in formal peace processes. Women are rarely represented among decision makers and military leaders, the usual participants in these processes. Nevertheless, women have a long history of peace making. Even in the most difficult areas of conflict such as the Middle East, women have maintained a high profile in trying to build coalitions across national borders to work for peace (Naraghi 2007). Women in Black, an international women's peace organization, for example, works in a highly contentious and politically difficult area, the Middle East (Powers 2003). Women in Black is comprised of Israeli and Palestinian women who have marched through the streets carrying banners reading "We will not be enemies." They have also engaged in a broad range of educational and relief activities (Cockburn 2004a, 2004b).

Women in Black began by claiming a public space for women to be heard, standing at public intersections with their signs day after day. This tactic of claiming a public space had been part of the work of the women's group called the Black Sash, which organized against Apartheid in South Africa, and the Madres de la Plaza de Mayo, which sought information and justice about the "disappeared" in the years of political repression in Argentina. These organizations were rooted in the work of earlier groups of women who explicitly refused violence, militarism, and war, such as the Women's International League for Peace and Freedom, the oldest women's peace organization formed during World War I in 1918, the Greenham Common Women's Peace Camp in the United Kingdom, and related groups around the world that opposed the deployment of U.S. missiles in the 1980s. Israeli and Palestinian Women in Black stand in public places with high volumes of traffic to call for peace and justice (Women in Black 2008).

Elise Boulding (2000) writes about this technique of "claiming public space for the practice" of peace culture. She notes that because that public space has not been traditionally available to women, they have had to be inventive about claiming it. She argues that women have been "marginal to public decision making in the existing social order" and "have fewer vested interests to protect" (Powers 2003). From these "weaknesses" in women's role in the public world, however, Boulding maintains that women have created strengths in the peace-making arena because they are more flexible and freer to reach across boundaries between social groups who are at war (Cockburn 2007).

In research on Women in Black, for example, participants spoke of what they believed was one of the most significant strengths of the organization: Any question could be put on the table. Unlike formal peace talks that spend so much time delineating which topics will be discussed, Women in Black discusses all issues, no matter how difficult (Cockburn 1998).

Assumptions about the role of women in society and especially in families have also created opportunities for women and girls in peace processes. For example, women from the Democratic Republic of the Congo, Kenya, Liberia, Rwanda, Somalia, South Africa, Sri Lanka, and the Sudan have drawn on their moral authority as mothers, wives, or daughters to call for an end to armed conflict. Women have organized as mothers, either to learn the fate of their children who have disappeared or to prevent their children from being conscripted or deployed to particular conflicts. Such groups include the Mothers and Grandmothers of the Plaza de Mayo in Argentina, the Mutual Support Group in Guatemala, the Group of Relatives of the Detained and Disappeared in Chile, the Association of Women of Srebrenica, the Committee of Russian Soldiers' Mothers in Chechnya, and Code Pink in the United

States. The concerns these groups have about their children give them a social legitimacy and a linkage with women from different sides of the conflict (UN 2002). The social role of women as mothers would seem to separate them from war and make them less connected to the politics of peace and less authoritative about the issues of war and peace. These organizations of women, however, have used this "disadvantage" to reveal their particular concern for peace and to give them greater authority in calling for peace and justice.

Boulding is careful to assert that the active role women have played in the peace movement is not because of any "natural" proclivity for peace making. She argues that it is the social position of women, as outsiders, parents, and citizens with weaker ties to political and economic interests that often makes them suited to this work. In addition, the social construction of femininity includes nurturance, cooperation, and aversion to conflict, which may make women more interested in and better at working for peace. All of these, however, are part of the social construction of femininity, not a natural inborn tendency of females. This means, of course, that we could reconstruct masculinity to include these traits as well and thereby build a more peaceful world where gender did not push men (and women) in the direction of war.

WHAT IS POLITICAL?

At the beginning of the chapter we looked at definitions of politics and the connections between the state and political activities. What exactly is political? Does it just mean running for office, holding elected or appointed positions, governing and advocating issues in the established institutions of government, or wielding the instruments of force in the military and the criminal justice system to enforce the decisions made by political leaders? Or should the concept be broader than this and include all of the activities in which people engage to link public and private concerns and develop power to bring about change in people's daily lives (Fowlkes 1997)? The first of these is the definition traditionally used by political scientists. Scholars who have paid attention to gender, however, have suggested that the second definition also needs to be considered. They assert that politics is a broader set of relationships and activities that defy, shift, or maintain power relationships in the community. Their questioning has challenged our understanding of what is political (Flammang 1997; McEwan 2005).

Scholars who have paid attention to gender puzzled over the activities of women around issues of power in their community and the invisibility of women in what is more commonly thought of as politics proper. They began to uncover a problem with the definition of political itself. "The invisibility of women's political activism is, in part, a reflection of the tendency to define politics within the narrow terms of the masculine sphere of formal politics. Once such a restrictive definition is abandoned, it has become almost an alternative conventional wisdom that informal politics represents a more feminized political sphere" (Lister 1997, 147).

As we have seen, men are much more likely than women to be politically active in formal positions as elected officials. Both women and men are active in more informal NGOs. Especially in those concerned with peace, human rights, economic justice, and environmental protection, women are likely to be very active (Peterson and Runyan 1999; Pardo 2000). Within these groups women are often a driving force (Chanan 1992). When formal leadership and formal management positions develop or a local protest campaign shifts to the national level, men begin to take over (West & Blumberg 1990; Lister 1997). But in the grassroots activities, women and men share participation or women are even more active than men.

Mary Pardo (2000) has examined the political activities of working-class Mexican American women in Los Angeles. The Mothers of East Los Angeles (MELA) provide an example of activism found in many places around the world. MELA is an organization of low-income Latinas that has focused on environmental issues in their community, such as stopping the construction of a toxic waste incinerator, but they represent a group that is not engaged in formal politics. The women come from social categories that are not perceived as power sources. They are not well-paid lobbyists or elected officials. They use networks and tactics that are not associated with politics, such as the contacts they have made working in the parents' club at their children's schools and the Catholic Church. They also use their role as mothers, not usually thought of a political one, as the basis of their work. One woman explained how the role of mother intrinsically calls on women to be politically active:

> You know if one of your children's safety is jeopardized, the mother turns into a lioness. That's why Father John got the mothers. We have to have a well-organized, strong group of mothers to protect the community and oppose things that are detrimental to us. You know the governor is in the wrong and the mothers are in the right. After all, the mothers have to be right. Mothers are for the children's interest, not for self interests; the governor is for his own political interests. (quoted in Pardo 2000, 464)

They identify themselves as not part of the world of elected formal politics but the impact they have on formal political institutions is significant. Their work, therefore, challenges our ideas about what is political and who is political.

If we think only about formal politics and elected officials, women's political activities become invisible. If we begin with gender asking what do women and men do and how might it be interpreted as political we are forced to look at the range of ways that women and men experience and express their politics. We have to look at both formal politics and informal politics and in doing so both women's actions and the activities of "outsider" politics become visible (Lister 1997).

More inclusive formal politics is necessary for the three reasons outlined earlier: increased democratic justice and equity, more possibility of addressing the interests of women, and better use of all available resources (Henig and Henig 2001). In addition, however, we need to redefine political action and civic virtue in a way that acknowledges informal political activities and organizations that are often the ways that women express their political citizenship. To do both of these things, we need to create ways to connect these two. We need to create grassroots global democracy (Lister 1997).

REFERENCES

Adler, F., and H. M. Adler. 1975. *Sisters in crime: The rise of the new female criminal.* New York: McGraw-Hill. BBC. 2005. "Islamists win in Saudi poll" BBC News http://news.bbc.co.uk/2/hi/middle_east/4252079.stm

Beckett, Katherine, Kris Nyrop, and Lori Pfingst. 2006. Race, drugs, and policing: Understanding disparities in drug delivery arrests. *Criminology* 44 (1): 105–37.

Belkin, Lisa. 2007. The feminine critique. *New York Times*, November 11.

Belknap, Joanne. 2001. The criminal-processing system: Girls and women as victims and offenders. In *Gender mosaics*, ed. D. Vannoy, 374–84. Los Angeles: Roxbury.

Bergquist, Carl. 2006. "First female pilot in combat reflects on career" December 6 Washington, D. C: United States Department of Defense http://www.defenselink.mil/home/faceofdefense/fod/2006-12/f20061207a.html

Blair, Cornelia, and Helene Northway. 2001. *Women: New roles in society*. Detroit, MI: Gale Group.

Borelli, MaryAnne. 2000. Gender, politics and change in the United States Cabinet: The Madeleine Korbel Albright and Janet Reno appointments. In *Gender and American politics*, ed. S. Tolleson-Rinehart and J. Josephson, 185–204. Armonk, NY: Sharpe.

Boulding, Elise. 2000. *Cultures of peace: The hidden side of history*. Syracuse, NY: Syracuse University Press.

Bourg, Chris, and Mady Wechsler Segal. 2001. Gender, sexuality and the military. In *Gender mosaics*, ed. D. Vannoy, 332–42. Los Angeles: Roxbury.

Bourque, Susan. 2001. Political leadership for women: Redefining power and reassessing political. In *Woman on power: Leadership redefined*, ed. S. Freeman, S. Bourque, and C. Shelton, 84–113. Boston: Northeastern University Press.

Bowen, Alison. 2007. Finnish women rule. *WeNews*, April 21.

Brett, Rachel. 2002. *Girl soldiers*. New York: Quaker UN Office. http://www.peacewomen.org/resources/DDR/GirlSoldiersQUNO.pdf

Bush-Baskette, Stephanie. 1998. The war on drugs as a war against black women. In *Crime control and women: Feminist implications of criminal justice policy*, ed. S. Miller, 113–29. Thousand Oaks, CA: Sage.

Carpini, Michael, and Scott Keeter. 2000. Gender and political knowledge. In *Gender and American politics*, ed. S. Tolleson-Rinehart and J. Josephson, 21–52. Armonk, NY: Sharpe.

Carroll, Susan, and Richard Fox. 2005. Introduction: Gender and electoral politics in the twenty-first century. In *Gender and elections: Shaping the future of American politics*, ed. S. Carroll and R. Fox, 1–9. New York: Cambridge University Press.

Center for the American Woman and Politics (CAWP). 1998. *Women in elected office*. New Brunswick, NJ: Center for the American Woman and Politics.

——. 2000. *Gender gap in the 2000 election*. New Brunswick, NJ: Center for the American Woman and Politics.

——. 2004. Sex differences in voter turnout. Fact sheet. New Brunswick, NJ: Center for the American Woman and Politics. http://www.cawp.rutgers.edu/Facts/sexdiff.pdf.

——. 2006. Women officeholders fact sheets and summaries. New Brunswick, NJ: Center for the American Woman and Politics. http://www.cawp.rutgers.edu/Facts.html.

Chanan, Gabriel. 1992. *Out of the shadows: Local community action and the European Community*. Luxembourg: Office for Official Publications of the European Communities, European Foundation for the Improvement of Living and Working Conditions.

Chesney-Lind, Meda. 1997. *The female offender: Girls, women and crime*. Thousand Oaks, CA: Sage.

Christensen, Martin. 2008. *Worldwide guide to women in leadership.Copenhagen, Denmark: Martin K.I. Christensen*. http://www.guide2womenleaders.com/index.html.

Cockburn, Cynthia. 1998. *The space between us: Negotiating gender and national identities in conflict*. London: Zed Books.

——. 2004a. The continuum of iolence. A Gender Perspective on War and Peace," in *Sites of Violence*, (eds.) J. Hyndman and W. Giles (eds.) University of California Press: Berkeley pp. 24–44.

——. 2004b. *The line*. London: Zed Books.

——. 2007. *From where we stand*. London: Zed Books.

Connelly, Marjorie. 2000. Who voted: A portrait of American politics, 1976–2000. *New York Times*, November 12.

Conway, M. Margaret, David Ahern, and Gertrude Steuernagel. 1999. *Women and public policy: A revolution in progress*. 2nd ed. Washington, DC: Congressional Quarterly Press.

Conway, M. Margaret, Gertrude Steuernagel, and David Ahern. 1997. *Women and political participation: Cultural change in the political arena*. Washington, DC: Congressional Quarterly Press.

Crossett, B. 1998. Amnesty finds widespread patterns of U.S. rights violations. *New York Times*, May 10.

Danner, Mona. 1998. Three strikes and its women who are out. In *Crime control and women*, ed. S. Miller, 1–11. Thousand Oaks, CA: Sage.

Davis, Angela. 2003. *Are prisons obsolete?* St. Paul, MN: Seven Stories Press.

Drexler, Peggy. 2006. Thanksgiving tastes sweet and sour to U.S. women. *WomensEnews*, November 22.

Ehrlich, Julie, and Lynn Paltrow. 2006. Jailing pregnant women raises health risks. *WomensENews*, September 20.

Flammang, Janet. 1997. *Women's political voice: How women are transforming the practice and study of politics*. Philadelphia: Temple University Press.

Flexner, Eleanor. 1975. *Century of struggle: The women's rights movement in the United States*. Cambridge, MA: Harvard University Press.

Fox, Richard. 1997. *Gender dynamics in congressional elections*. Thousand Oaks, CA: Sage.

——. 2000. Gender and Congressional elections. In *Gender and American politics*, ed. S. Tolleson-Rinehart and J. Josephson, 227–56. Armonk, NY: Sharpe.

Fowlkes, Diana. 1997. Moving from feminist identity politics to coalition politics through a feminist materialist standpoint of intersubjectivity in Gloria Anzaldúa's *Borderlands/La frontera: The new mestiza. Hypatia* 12 (2): 105–24.

Freedman, Estelle. 2002. *No turning back*. New York: Ballantine.

Funabashi, Kuniko. 2003. Women's participation in politics and the women's movement. In *Gender and development*, ed. M. Murayam, 119–151. New York: Palgrave Macmillan.

Gilfus, Mary. 1992. "From victim, to survivors to offenders: Women's routes of entry and immersion into street crime" *Women and Criminal Justice* 4 (1)63-90.

Ginty, Molly. 2005. Record number of female soldiers fall. *WomensENews*, March 22.

——. 2007. With more women at war, military rethinks vet care. *WomensENews*, March 20.

Gouws, Amanda. 2004. The quota made the difference. *Network News* July:3–4.

Greenfeld, Lawrence, and Tracy Snell. 1999. *Women offenders*. Washington, DC: U.S. Department of Justice.

Gullo, Karen. 2001. More girls go to jail. Associated Press, April 30.

Henig, Ruth, and Simon Henig. 2001. *Women and political power: Europe since 1945*. New York: Routledge.

Hirschfield, Julie. 2001. Congress of relative newcomers poses challenge to Bush leadership. *CQ Weekly* (January 20): 178–82.

Inter-Parliamentary Union. 1997. *Men and women in politics: Democracy still in the making—A comparative study*. Geneva: Inter-Parliamentary Union.

——. 2007. *Women in national parliaments (as of November 2006)*. Geneva: Inter-Parliamentary Union. www.ipu.org/wmn-e/classif.htm

Jacinto, Leela. 2004. Girl power. ABC News, May 20.

Jones, K. 1993. *Compassionate authority: Democracy and the representation of women*. New York: Routledge.

Kahn, Kim. 1993. Gender differences in campaign messages: The political advertisements of men and women candidates for U.S. Senate. *Political Research Quarterly* 46 (2): 418–502.

Kahn, Kim, and Ann Gordon. 1997. How women campaign for the U.S. Senate. *Women, media and politics,* ed. P. Norris, 59–76. Oxford, UK: Oxford University Press.

Kaufmann, Karen, and John Petrocik. 1999. The changing politics of American men: Understanding the sources of the gender gap. *American Journal of Political Science* 43:43–56.

Kelley, Matt. 2004. Women's role in Iraq revives debate. *Salt Lake Tribune,* January 3.

Kirk, Gwen, and Margo Okazaw-Rey. 2004. *Women's lives.* New York: McGraw-Hill.

Lister, Ruth. 1997. *Citizenship: Feminist perspectives.* New York: NYU Press.

Lorber, Judith. 2000. Guarding the gates: The micropolitics of gender. In *The gendered society reader,* ed. M. Kimmel, 270–94. New York: Oxford University Press.

Marger, Martin. 2002. *Social inequality.* 2nd ed. Belmont, CA: Wadsworth.

McEwan, Cheryl. 2005. Gender citizenship in South Africa. In *(Un)thinking citizenship,* ed A. Gouws, 177–98. London: Ashgate.

McFeeley, Tim. 2000. Getting it straight: A review of the "gays in the military" debate. In *Creating change: Sexuality, public policy, and civil rights,* ed. J. D'Emilio, W. Turner, and U. Vaid, 236–50. New York: St. Martin's.

McKay, Susan, and Cheryl de la Rey. 2001. Women's meanings of peacebuilding in post-apartheid South Africa. *Peace and Conflict: Journal of Peace Psychology* 7 (3): 227–42.

Mezey, Susan. 2000. Gender and the federal judiciary. In *Gender and American politics,* ed. S. Tolleson and J. Josephson, 205–226. Armonk, NY: Sharpe.

Miller, Jody. 2001. *One of the guys: Girls, gangs, and gender.* Oxford, UK: Oxford University Press.

Miller, Laura. 2000. Not just weapons of the weak: Gender harassment as a form of protest for army men. *Gender through the prism of difference.* 2nd ed., ed. M. Baca Zinn, P. Hondagneu-Sotelo, and M. Messner, 409–30. Boston: Allyn & Bacon.

Miller, Susan. 2005. *Victims as offenders: The paradox of women's violence in relationships.* New Brunswick, NJ: Rutgers University Press.

Morin, Richard. 2004. The GOP problem with women. *Washington Post,* January 11.

Nagy, Donna, and Aviva Rich. 2001. Constitutional law and public policy: Gender equity. In *Gender mosaics,* ed. D. Vannoy, 312–31. Los Angeles: Roxbury.

Naraghi, Sanam. 2007. *Women building peace.* Boulder, CO: Lynne Reinner.

Norris, P., and J. Lovenduski. 1995. *Political recruitment: Gender, race and class in the British Parliament.* Cambridge, UK: Cambridge University Press.

Owen, Barbara. 1999. Women and imprisonment in the United States: The gendered consequences of the U.S. imprisonment binge. In *Harsh punishment: International experiences of women's imprisonment,* ed. S. Cook and S. Davies, 81–98. Boston: Northeastern University Press.

Pardo, Mary. 2000. Mexican American women, grassroots community activists: "Mothers of East Los Angeles" In *Gender through the prism of difference.* 2nd ed., ed. M. Baca Zinn, P. Hondagneu-Sotelo, and M. Messner, 461–77. Boston: Allyn & Bacon.

Peterson, V. Spike, and Anne Runyan. 1999. *Global gender issues.* 2nd ed. Boulder, CO: Westview.

Poole, Barbara. 1993. Should women identify themselves as feminists when running for political office? Paper presented at the annual meeting of the American Political Science Association, Washington, DC.

Powers, Janet M. 2003. Women and peace dialogue in the Middle East. *Peace Review* 15 (1): 25–31.

Rebecca Project for Human Rights. 2007. *Women in prison.* http://www.rebeccaproject.org.

Riley, Niahm. 2003. *Civil and political rights.* WHRNET. http://www.whrnet.org/docs/issue-civilpolitical.html.

Ross, Jen. 2007. Chile kick-starts debate on gender quotas. *Women'sENews,* February 20.

Rothman, Robert. 2002. *Inequality and stratification: Race, class and gender.* Upper Saddle River, NJ: Prentice Hall.

Sabet, Kevin. 2005. Making it happen: The case for compromise in the federal cocaine law debate. *Social Policy and Administration* 39 (2): 181–91.

St. George, Donna. 2002. Finally in, facing new fight. *Washington Post*, April 28.

Seltzer, Richard, Jody Newman, and Melissa Leighton. 1997. *Sex as a political variable*. Boulder, CO: Lynne Reinner.

The Sentencing Project. 2006. "Serena Nunn" www.sentencingproject.org. http://www.sentencingproject.org/FeatureDetails.aspx?FeatureID=15 accessed June 2008.

Siegel, L. 1997. The pregnancy problem in the war on drugs. In *Crack in America*, **ed.** C. Reinarman and H. Levine, 249–59. Berkeley: University of California Press.

Simon, Rita. 1975. *Women and crime*. Lexington, MA: Lexington Books.

Skocpol, Theda, and Edwin Amenta. 1986. States and social policies. *Annual Review of Sociology* 12:131–57.

Small, Kevonne. 2000. Female crime in the United States, 1963–1998: An update. *Gender Issues* 18 (3): 75–104.

Social Watch. 2008. *Gender Equity Index. Montevideo, Uruguay: Social Watch*.

Steffensmeier, D., and E. Allan. 1996. Gender and crime. *Annual Review of Sociology* 22:459–87.

Stevens, Allison. 2006. Female vets put military mettle in House races. *WomensENews*, August 3.

Stiehm, Judith. 1981. *Bring me men and women: Mandated change in the U.S. Air Force Academy*. Berkeley: University of California Press.

Swers, Michele. 2004. Research on women in legislatures. In *Women's lives*. 3rd ed., ed. G. Kirk and M. Okazawa-Rey, 563–73. Boston: McGraw-Hill.

Tremlett, Giles. 2005. Blow to machismo as Spain forces men to do housework. *The Guardian*, April 8. http://www.guardian.co.uk/spain/article/0,2763,1454802,00.html.

United Nations. 2002. *Women, peace and security*. New York: United Nations. www.un.org/womenwatch/daw/public/eWPS.pdf.

United Nations, Department of Public Information. 1995. *Women and power: Where women stand today*. The advancement of women, Notes for speakers. New York: United Nations.

U.S. Bureau of the Census. 2001. Table 345. In *Statistical abstract of the U.S.* Washington, DC: U.S. Government Printing Office.

——. 2006. Table 501 and Table 509. In *Statistical abstract of the U.S.* Washington, DC: U.S. Government Printing Office.

West, Guida, and Rhoda Blumberg, eds. 1990. *Women and social protest*. New York: Oxford University Press.

Women in Black. 2008. http://www.womeninblack.org/history.html.

Women in Prison Project. 2002. *Fact sheet*. New York: Correctional Association of New York. http://www.correctionalassociation.org/WIPP/publications/Women%20in%20Prison%20Fact%20Sheet%202007.pdf.

Women's eNews. 2007. Jordanian MP celebrates her post-quota victory. November 29.

Women's Policy Institute. 2008. Women in the House of Representatives. http://www.womenspolicy.org/caucus/house110.html.

11

MEDIA AND SPORTS

FEMINIST ADS FROM NIKE

If you let me play
If you let me play sports
I will like myself more.
I will have more self-confidence.
If you let me play sports
If you let me play
If you let me play
I will be 60 percent less likely to get breast cancer.
I will suffer less depression.
If you let me play sports
I will be more likely to leave a man who beats me.
If you let me play
I will be less likely to get pregnant before I want to.
I will learn
I will learn what it means to be strong.
If you let me play
Play sports
If you let me play sports.

These are the words to a Nike commercial that shows close-ups of girls playing on swings, monkey bars, and a merry-go-round (Wharton 2005). The creators of the advertisement, Janet Champ, Rachel Nelson, Jennifer Smieja, and Angelina Vieira say their goal in making the ad was to help end discrimination against women and girls in sports and to tell parents, teachers, family, and friends, as well as girls themselves, how amazingly beneficial sports are for girls (Goldman and Papson 2004).

A survey of college students who watched the ad, however, showed mixed reactions. Some questioned Nike's altruism, asking "Does Nike really have a social conscience, or are they just trying to sell shoes?" (Goldman and Papson 2004). Other students, however, especially those from working-class families or small towns, were more likely to see it favorably; those women who were athletes were most likely to embrace the ad.

How do you feel about this ad? Is it just a promotion for shoes or can it have a bigger effect?

What about media in general? Do the media provide an omnipresent guidebook in our everyday lives about how we should think, feel, and behave in specific gendered ways? How do the media construct masculinities? Femininities? Do the images vary cross-culturally or within a society by race ethnicity and social class or other social factors?

Do you think advertisements, movies, television programs, and other media images help to maintain the status quo or can they challenge ideologies? Or do the media just reflect reality?

The ad is also about athletics. What is the connection between sports and advertising? Where do sports fit into our thinking about masculinities and femininities? Our experience as women and men? Where should athletics fit?

This chapter explores these questions. The chapter is divided into two major sections. The first is about media and gender. We review gender and its intersection with other forms of inequality in media and explore theoretical concepts such as legitimation, hegemony, and symbolic annihilation. In the second half we examine the world of sports as a form of entertainment intrinsically bound to advertising and media presentations.

MASS MEDIA

For a society, especially one with high levels of inequality, to maintain its stability and popularity, it needs to develop ways to legitimate itself. Legitimation involves creating an ideology, a set of beliefs and ideas that explain and justify the existing social organization. Legitimation also requires creating ways to transmit this ideology to its citizens. Mass media include the Internet, television, radio, newspapers, magazines, books, CDs, and films. They play an important role in both aspects of legitimation, creating ideas about how our society is the best of all possible worlds, and communicating that message to the common person (Marger 2002).

It is difficult to estimate how important the mass media are but nearly all of us say we receive most of our news about current events from television (Thomas and Vitica 1998). We spend more time watching television than in any other activity, besides sleep and work. The average American child grows up in a home with two television sets, two VCR/DVDs, three audiotape players, two CD players, and one computer. One-quarter of preschoolers have a TV in their room and three-fifths of teenagers do. Children spend about four and a half hours a day in front of some screen. This is equivalent to spending ten weeks a year, twenty-four hours a day doing nothing but watching television. On an average school day, if children come home from school about 4:00 and go to bed about 9:00, they have approximately one-half hour of screen-free time per day (Dunnewind 2002). If we add to this other kinds of media such as newspapers, radio, magazines, books, music, the Internet, and films, we can see that our lives are drenched in media images and sounds that tell us how to view, experience, and act on the world. Gender is one of the critical messages we receive.

In this book we explore the many ways that gender inequality permeates our lives. Media often legitimates this inequality by creating images and telling us which are valid or not.

Is Gender on Television Changing?

Television is a primary source of images of gender. Gender can be portrayed in a range of ways but two kinds of images are dominant: hegemonic masculinity and emphasized femininity. You should recall from chapter 1 that hegemonic masculinity includes the subordination of women, authority, aggression, and technical competence. Emphasized femininity includes dependence, sexual receptivity, motherhood, and subordination by men (Connell 1993).

In the 1970s, feminists in the Women's Liberation Movement in the United States were concerned about the media as a source of stereotypes of gender and a number of studies were done on the images the media presented of men and especially women. The National Organization for Women (NOW) was one of the first to conduct research in this area (NOW 1972). NOW, along with others, came to two general conclusions: First, men were numerically better represented on TV; second, the roles men played on TV were more diverse by factors such as age, appearance, occupation, and character. The roles played by women were more limited and more stereotyped.

But haven't television images of gender changed since the previous generation? Surprisingly, subsequent studies in the 1980s, 1990s, and as recently as 2004 do not find much change on these two factors (Browne 1998; Furnham and Mak 1999; Coltrane and Messineo 2000; Larson 2001, Stern and Mastro 2004).

Visibility of women has consistently remained lower on television over the decades. In all programming, except soap operas, men still outnumber women two to one, and most women are concentrated in situation comedies (Lont 2001). Even when women appear in shows, they are less likely to be the focus of the program compared to men. In a study of domestic comedies with a wife and husband and their children, for example, six times more jokes were by or about the men compared to those by or about the women.

Women are also missing in the production of media. A study of fifty-seven Fortune 500 corporations revealed that of 1,247 executives (senior vice presidents to CEOs), only sixty-eight were women in 2004 (Gibbons 2004). The missing woman in network news is another area of concern, although there has been some improvement in the past few decades. From 1977 to 1997, the proportion of women correspondents in network news grew from 16 percent to 24 percent (Lont 2001). In 2006, 57 percent of local anchors were women. However, women news anchors are still not equal to men. Women anchors' primary value rests on their appearance, whereas men anchors are valued because of their authority and expertise. Men are allowed to shows signs of maturity such as wrinkles and gray hair. Furthermore, as men have left anchor seats, the pay has declined and the median annual pay is now only about $31,320 (Blanchette 2006).

Another measure of inequality in the newsroom is the sources reporters use for their stories. Women are much less likely to be part of the news being covered. Currently about 17 percent of those interviewed on the news are women. In stories about politics and the government, women are least likely to appear (7 percent of those interviewed). In business and economics stories they are slightly more likely to be interviewed (9 percent). Health and social issues (33 percent) and arts and entertainment (32 percent) are at the high ends of visibility for women (Gallagher 1995). Women who do appear in news stories are also of lesser status than the men in the news. In a study in Europe, 47 percent of the ordinary citizens interviewed by the news media and 37 percent of the victims were women, whereas 72 percent of political leaders and 80 percent of experts were men (Gallagher 1995).

Some progress has been made. Women are now less likely to appear as domestics or dependent as they were in previous decades, but men still dominate in terms of numbers and some stereotypes are remarkably impervious to change: Women are young and men are knowledgeable authorities. In the most recent rating by NOW, we still find some of the same clichés of the 1970s.

In 2000, NOW rated 165 shows on four networks (NBC, ABC, CBS, and FOX). Their goal was to see how TV was presenting women and girls. They used four criteria.

1. The number and severity of acts of violence. The programs that ranked worse on this criterion showed a killing or had the camera linger over a dead body of a woman or girl.
2. The proportion of women in the cast. In addition to the absolute numbers of women, shows were given bonus points for diversity among the women shown and for positive role models. Points were deducted for stereotypes.
3. Sexual exploitation was rated on a scale from very respectful with no exploitation to substantial exploitation with no positive values.
4. Social responsibility was evaluated from strong social content with relevance to people's lives to irresponsible content with no redeeming values.

The top five shows rated as best according to these criteria were *Family Law, Chicago Hope, Once & Again, ER,* and *Sabrina the Teenage Witch.* The worst five shows were *Perfect Murder, Perfect Town; Who Wants to Marry a Millionaire; Independence Day (film); Getting Away with Murder;* and *Norm* (NOW 2000).

Overall they found that violence against women is still a popular topic and men still dominate the casts. Women who are not white, young, and thin are underrepresented and lesbians and people with disabilities are nearly nonexistent. Situation comedies were especially bad in regard to sexual exploitation. Much of the humor focused on men's advances on and humiliation of women.

In 2005, researchers looked at gender in situation comedies and dramas in prime-time television and found gender was a critical factor in the kinds of roles played by television characters. They also found that age combined with gender in interesting ways. The researchers looked at the proportion of television characters of different ages and genders compared to their proportion in the real American population. Men in their teens and twenties were underrepresented, as were men over sixty. Men in their thirties, forties, and fifties were overrepresented. Women in their teens and twenties and those in their forties were slightly overrepresented, women in their thirties were dramatically overrepresented, and women in their fifties and sixties were underrepresented (Lauzen and Dozier 2005).

The research also looked at the kinds of roles women and men played in the shows. They were especially interested in whether there were differences in depicting women and men as leaders providing guidance or direction to the other characters in the shows. Women and men in their teens, twenties, and thirties were about equally likely to play a leadership role. Older men, however, were much more likely than young men or any women to play a leadership role. In regard to authority, for men, aging was a positive factor.

Age benefited both women and men positively when it came to their occupational status. As women and men aged on the shows, they tended to have more prestigious jobs, moving from low-status jobs like unemployed and job applicants to high-status jobs like CEOs. However, in comparisons of men and women over sixty, men characters had higher status jobs than did women.

The researchers also looked at goals—whether the character was working toward something as the story line unfolded. On this issue there were important age and gender differences. Men characters, regardless of their age, had goals. Women characters, until they reached about the age of forty, also had goals. Women over forty, however, were much less likely to have goals than any men or younger women.

SYMBOLIC ANNIHILATION. Two key findings in the research on media illustrated in the discussion of television images are the greater number of men compared to women and the different images of women and men that are presented, for example, in the roles played in television shows. Men in all media presentations far outnumber women. This issue is part of all aspects of television programming, advertising, and films, as well as other parts of the media such as newspapers.

Gaye Tuchman and her colleagues (Tuchman, Kaplan Daniels, and Benet 1978) named this invisibility *symbolic annihilation.* They argue that when a group and their experience do not appear in the media, it sends a message that they do not matter and their views are unimportant. Because the numbers of women and girls in the media are smaller than those of men and boys, Tuchman and her colleagues argue that the women and girls have been symbolically annihilated. The message of the nonexistent images is that women and girls must not be as important. Their experiences and ideas are not as interesting or as significant as those of men and boys.

GENDER STEREOTYPES. A second finding of the review of media since the 1970s is that women and men are depicted in different and stereotyped ways. In the 1970s, men played a broader range of roles than did women. Physical appearance was also more limited for women, with women being mostly young and pretty. Women characters were also less competent than men (Lont 2001). These differences have remained remarkably similar in recent years. For example, in a study of top-rated programs in the twenty-first century, 42 percent of the men were shown at work, whereas only 28 percent of women were shown in paid labor roles. Even though women are almost as likely to be in the paid labor force in the real world, television still persists in presenting these old stereotypes.

In movies, the statistics are even more striking, with 60 percent of the men and 35 percent of the women shown earning a living. In addition, women, especially married women, are likely to be in women-dominated occupations. Single women are more likely to be depicted in gender-neutral jobs or even "men's jobs" (Sapiro 2002).

Women on television who are shown in professional jobs are also still stereotyped in their appearance. Lawyers, physicians, and business women are young, pretty, and thin and attired in tight, short clothes with low necklines and flirty hairdos hanging over their eyes that are not usually part of real-life professional women's wardrobes (Sapiro 2002).

Men on television still have a wider range of occupations, although television is highly overpopulated with men police officers, criminals, and doctors. However, when men are shown away from work, they are stereotyped, too. Television comedy programs portray men in stereotyped ways in family contexts where they frequently show men in the tired old situation of awkwardly and ineptly trying to run a household when the woman is away (Sapiro 2002).

In a review of men's roles on television programs, Harris (1995) found that images of men fit into four categories:

- Standard bearers: Men are supposed to do their best and achieve as much as they can.
- Workers: Men should earn a lot of money and develop a strong work ethic.
- Lovers: Men are to be romantic husbands and partners or playboy swingers.
- Rugged individualists: Men should engage in dangerous and adventurous acts and athletics.

Gender in Advertising

Like mass media, commercial media give us images of what real men and women are supposed to be like. Although the audience does not necessarily "buy" the images with which they are presented, advertisements provide confirmation of existing social arrangements and provide a source of stereotypes that become resources for understanding and interacting in the real world. Furthermore, because advertisements provide these stereotypes with flawless people in "magical encounters—the happy family, fun loving youth, and the ubiquitous romantic encounter," they are indeed powerful (Coltrane and Messineo 2000, 367).

What do advertisements tell us about masculine ideals? A historical review of masculine images in advertisements from 1930 to 1980 shows that two stereotypes were remarkably persistent: The sturdy oak (hard-working good providers) and the big wheel (socially and economically successful) (Frith and Mueller 2003). Two differences in the two historical periods were an increase in the 1980s in younger men and more sexualized images of men.

In the late 1990s another emphasis became prominent: independence and isolation (Patterson and Elliott 2004). This image is the essence of the earlier ads for the Marlboro man, a cowboy shown enjoying his cigarette alone with his horse in a vast expanse of range with no sign of other humans. In the 1990s this image of masculinity became increasingly popular.

An additional aspect of the masculine stereotype in advertising in recent years is a growing focus on physicality and especially body size and muscle development. The growth (literally) of the strong muscular model in the past four decades is illustrated by G.I. Joe dolls. If G.I. Joe were a real human, the size of his biceps would have grown from 12.2 inches in 1964 to 15.3 inches in 1974 to 16.4 inches in 1994 to a whopping 26.8 inches in 1998. In comparison, Mark McGwire, an athlete known for his strong muscular, perhaps steroid-produced, home-run-hitting arms, has biceps that are 20 inches (*New York Times* 1999).

Along with physical size and bulky muscles, the images tell men they should work hard, acquire wealth, and use violence. Violence appears as an important element of the stereotypes of men in advertisements. Commercials use heroes from history, such as cowboys, conquerors, military men, and crusaders, who were often violent to signify masculinity. They also use sports heroes in wrestling and martial arts whose muscles and techniques are associated with power and violence (Katz 1995).

MEN AND BEER. Advertisements tell men not only what men are supposed to be like, but how to become a man. Beer commercials, like all advertisements, are designed to sell a product. Along with the product, however, images of masculinity and femininity are also being sold. Beer commercials outline how men can accomplish masculinity. Drinking beer is the way to manliness and the commercials provide a blueprint for how to become a man by explaining when, why, and with whom men should drink beer. When should men drink beer? Beer signifies the end of the workday and the end of a job well done. In the world of beer, men work hard and they play hard. They must take on challenges of power boating, sailing, and playing sports. Then they reminisce on their triumphs in these challenges while they drink a beer (Strate 2001). "Miller Time" marks the period after work when it is time to drink beer.

Why should men drink beer? According to the ads, beer helps boys grow up. Beer commercials provide a transition in gender from boys to men. The ads show a young outsider who must prove himself to others; then he is rewarded by drinking beer with the older men (Strate 2001). As we will see in the next section on sports, the initiation of younger (or at least less experienced men) by older men is part of many cultures. In American culture, beer is part of this process and beer commercials provide the model. Beer commercials also tell men with whom they should drink beer. Part of being a real man is drinking beer with the other guys. Unlike the image of masculinity in the cigarette commercials, there are no loners like the Marlboro man. Beer-drinking men travel in groups (Strate 2001).

Finally, beer commercials tell men how to relate to women. Men comprise the largest proportion of figures in the ads and they are the central characters in beer commercials, but women sometimes appear. Beer-drinking men should be attractive but detached, cool, and confident when met with the challenge of a woman (Strate 2001).

ADVERTISING FEMININITY IN THREE NATIONS. The promotion of stereotypes of women is of concern in many nations in the world. Scholars in Turkey (Uray and Burnaz 2003), Japan (Arima 2003), and the United States (Coltrane and Messineo 2000) recently investigated images of women in commercials to see what progress has been made. Are women still being portrayed in limited and stereotyped ways?

Gender in Turkish Television. Since the 1980s important changes have occurred in Turkey, including a significant increase in the number of well-educated working women, an increasing income level, a shift from traditional large families toward small nuclear-type families, and the penetration of Western consumer values. Gender ideologies about women and men in families in particular and in society in general are changing. Turkey has also begun to transform from an agrarian society into a postmodern consumer society. One of the major driving forces behind this transformation has been the rapidly growing media, which promote Western lifestyles, values, and consumption. There are now four state-owned and twenty-two private television channels in Turkey. The number of total radio channels grew from one in

Box 11–1 GOFFMAN AND THE GAZE

Erving Goffman (1979) was one of the first scholars to look at gender in advertising. He explored the ways women models were placed and the poses they struck. He argued that these provided powerful, although somewhat hidden, messages about women, turning them into objects and emphasizing their sexuality and vulnerability. His work in the 1970s identified symbolic themes in images of women in advertising that still can be seen today:

- Body cant or bashful knee bends. Model curves her body, cocks her head, points her toes, and bends her knee in awkward contorted pose, making herself into a decorative object.
- Recumbent figure. Model reclines or semireclines on floor, bed, or sofa expressing passivity combined with sexual availability and vulnerability.
- Psychological or licensed withdrawal. Daydream or blank stare implying mental incompetence, air-headedness, and passive relationship with surroundings.
- Engaging gaze. Sexually seductive expression aimed at camera suggests sexual availability and role of women as sex objects rather than subjects of their own sexuality.
- Touching self. Model touches her face making her look girlish, shy, and submissive (Frith and Mueller 2003).

Goffman maintained that advertisements tell us to consume and when women are depicted as nonthinking, decorative objects they become part of the "things" to be devoured. Women's eroticized body parts depersonalize the actual human whose body is being shown. The whole person disappears and the body parts do not appear to belong to any one (human). She is no longer a living person but an object to be used by the viewer, buyer, or consumer (Roy 2005).

1992 to 1,200 today. Advertising is increasingly prevalent, although not nearly as pervasive as in the West. In 1996, for example, advertisers spent $14 per person in Turkey and $197 per person in Europe. But between 1996 and 1997 expenditures on advertising grew by 49 percent in Turkey and only 4 percent in Europe. Messages about gender are an important part of this expanding aspect of Turkish life (Uray and Burnaz 2003).

What images are Turkish television viewers seeing these days? Like those images in the West, gender in Turkish ads shows different and stereotyped roles for women and men. Media images of Turkish women are similar to those of Western women in their limited age range. Almost all women are young, whereas men span a broader age range. In addition, women are more frequently shown as married and less likely than men to be portrayed as employed (Uray and Burnaz 2003).

Unlike the West, women outnumber men in Turkish ads. The gender of the primary character, however, varies with the product advertised and follows gender stereotypes. Men are most likely to be primary characters in automobile and accessories, services (mainly financial), and food and drink advertisements. Women, on the other hand, are tied to families and home. Women are more likely than men to be primary characters in body products and home products advertisements, suggesting that their main tasks are to improve themselves and their homes. The main setting in which women appear is the home, whereas men are portrayed mostly out of the home. The connection to home may be the explanation for why women outnumber men because body and home products, which are mainly purchased and consumed by Turkish women, are the most popular items advertised on television (Uray and Burnaz 2003).

Women in Turkish advertisements also reflect a stereotyped expectation of women's demeanor. Turkish advertisements portray women as more relaxed than men, a behavior traditionally expected of women in Turkish families (Uray and Burnaz 2003).

Gender in Japanese Television. The presentation of gender in advertisements in Japan has also been studied (Arima 2003). Researchers have found that unlike American advertising, and similar to the Turkish ads, Japanese women (56.7 percent) outnumbered men (43.3 percent). However, stereotypes in the products they advertise and the roles they play in the ads are similar. Women appear as housewives and product demonstrators in ads for products associated with housework, cosmetics, and services, whereas men are shown as office workers and are linked to electronic products. Like the ads in Turkey and the United States, in Japan, men of many ages are shown but women are nearly always young (Arima 2003).

Arima (2003) explored further the gender "packages" presented in Japanese television commercials. Five types of characters were found:

- "Beautiful and wise housewives" (9.4 percent of the characters). They appeared in an apron or kimono, and advertised food, beauty products, or services to a woman audience.
- "Young ladies attracting people's attention" (20.7 percent of the characters). Most of these were young Japanese women dressed in swimsuits, underwear, or *yukata* (cotton summer sundresses). They appeared at home, leisure, or outside, advertising beauty products and tools used for housework aimed at women. Their appearance and the angles of the shots were designed to attract the attention of the viewer.
- "Young celebrities" (25.6 percent of the total characters). Most were famous young Japanese celebrities, including athletes. They often wore uniforms and acted as providers of the services being advertised and users of products in the role of office workers or salespersons with men colleagues. Men and women in these ads differed in that women were constantly smiling, whereas men appeared serious.
- "Middle-aged and old people enjoying private time" (20.7 percent of the total number of characters). Most were Japanese entertainers in the thirties to sixties age range and men (sixty-nine) outnumbered women (forty-one). They wore casual clothes and appeared at home or in stores with other adults or adults and children, usually playing parents' roles. They advertised alcohol and tobacco more often than did people in other clusters.

- "Middle-aged worker bee" (23.5 percent of the total). Most were men (118 people) and compared to the other clusters, there was more variety in ethnic background (twenty-three whites, five blacks, and fifteen east Asians in addition to Japanese). They appeared in offices, outside, or in the studio wearing suits with other men, characters, animals, or cartoon characters. They announced the names of medicine, electrical appliances, or automobiles, or explained the utility or efficiency of the products to a male audience (Arima 2003).

Gender in U.S. Television. Similar research on gender "packages" has been conducted in the United States. Box 11–2 summarizes what researchers have found most recently about gender in advertising in the United States. Much of the exploration of gender in advertising, however, has focused on gender to the exclusion of other significant social variables and it has revealed contradictions in the images of masculinity and femininity. Coltrane and Messineo (2000) argue that race ethnicity needs to be sorted out from gender as a separate powerful factor. When it is separated out, it helps to explain some of the contradictions in gender images in advertising.

They found four images emerge from a content analysis of television advertising in the United States:

- Powerful white men. White men are twice as likely to be giving orders or exercising authority, for example, as a tank commander barking orders or an authoritative physician in a white coat offering medical advice.
- White women sex objects. Twenty-five percent of white women are depicted as sex objects. This is twice the proportion of black women shown this way and three times the proportion of men, black or white. White women are shown as flirting, being checked out by a man, or trying to look pretty in ads like that for a low-calorie cereal with the woman looking at her slim body in a mirror and running her hands over her tight-fitting dress.
- Aggressive black men. Black men are three times as likely as white men to be shown behaving in a physically aggressive manner, for example playing rough on a basketball court. Black men are also less likely than any of the other categories to be shown at home: 40 percent of white women, 30 percent of black women, 26 percent of white men, and only 13 percent of black men are shown at home. Whites are shown two to three times more often as married.
- Inconsequential black women. Black women are less authoritative than white men, less aggressive than black men, and less engaged in family roles and sexual encounters than white women. They are more likely than white women to be shown in paid employment, but in general black women are just less visible or less significant to the interactions in the ads than the other categories. Similarly, men and women who are Latino, Asian Americans, and First Nations people are nearly nonexistent in the ads.

Although these studies from Turkey, Japan, and the United States are not entirely comparable because they use different methodologies, they do suggest similarities and differences among the three societies. In all of the nations, gender is expressed in television advertising. Some stereotypes are also common across the borders, such as the limited age range for

Box 11–2 SUMMARY OF RECENT RESEARCH ON GENDER IMAGES IN TELEVISION ADVERTISING IN THE UNITED STATES

In 2004, researchers reviewed all of the recent studies of television to see what images of masculinities and femininities were being presented by advertisers in the United States today (Stern and Mastro 2004). The studies showed that:

- Television ads underrepresent women compared to men. Men are twice as likely to appear in commercials, and voiceovers are largely men. Men do the voiceovers in 64 percent of the advertisements for domestic products and 89 percent of the advertisements for nondomestic products. In advertisements for children, boys outnumber girls two to one (Sapiro 2002).
- Among women, age makes a difference. Young adult women (compared to girls, middle-aged women, and older women) are better represented. Older women and men are equally less visible.
- Roles for men are more diverse. Young women, compared to other age groups of women, did seem to be catching up with men by appearing in more diverse roles as competent, authoritative, and outside the home. Young men and middle-aged men, however, still far outnumber young women in these kinds of roles.
- Women are associated with domestic cleaning products and cosmetics, men with nondomestic items such as cars, cameras, and electronics.
- Women are likely to be shown inside in a domestic residence; men are shown outside in a broad range of settings.
- Women are more physically attractive. For example, 75 percent of women in ads are physically fit compared to 25 percent of the men (Signorielli, McLeod, and Healy 1994).
- Women are shown in skimpy or sexy clothing and are three times as likely to be sex objects (Coltrane and Adams 1997). See also Box 11-1.
- Men are shown in more prominent and dominant positions in the workforce. For example, men are more frequently shown as professionals, whereas women are frequently shown doing housework or without a paid occupation and men are shown in positions of authority giving orders.
- Men are shown in more active roles.
- Similar differences exist in comparisons of children. Boys are active in the ads and girls are passive support figures. Colors, settings, and behavior further emphasize stereotypes. Boys wear dark-colored clothes and are filmed against bright dark green, gray, and blue. Girls wear light-colored clothes against pastel backgrounds. Boys are shown outside, whereas girls are filmed inside in bedrooms and playrooms (Frith and Mueller 2003).

women and the association of women with domestic products and family and home settings and activities. However, in each nation gender intersects with different variables. In Turkey the tension between East and West and the newness of commercial media are significant. In Japan, age stands out as an important issue and the association of men with a serious business image is notable. In the United States, race ethnicity takes center stage along with gender.

Films

Hollywood generates gender images for filmgoers all over the world. The greater screen time of men and boys on television is duplicated in movies. A review of American films from 1940 to 1980 found that men and boy characters outnumbered women and girl characters about two to one (Bazzini et al. 1997). Box 11–3 lists the top twenty grossing films worldwide as of 2006. The list shows that this proportion still holds true. The films that have been seen most widely at the box office around the world are nearly all ones that have a man or boy as a main character and some of them, such as *Independence Day*, the *Lord of the Rings* films, and the *Star Wars* series have almost no women or girls in them. Those women who do appear are in largely insignificant roles.

Some films, of course, do have women in key roles, but their parts tend to come from a narrow range of characters. In the film *The First Wives Club*, Goldie Hawn's character says, "There are only three ages for women in Hollywood: babe, district attorney, and Driving Miss Daisy" (quoted in Lauzen and Dozier 2005). This quote turns out to be true for popular films today.

Research (Lauzen and Dozier 2005) on the top 100 domestic grossing films in the United States in 2002 concluded that major masculine characters outnumbered feminine characters 73 percent to 27 percent. The researchers also found that most of the men characters were in their thirties and forties, whereas most of the women were in their twenties and thirties. Men had longer and more vital screen lives. The women in films seemed to "remain forever frozen in their 20s and 30s" (Lauzen and Dozier 2005, 437).

Those women characters that did remain in films beyond their thirties saw their mental, physical, and social capacities decline. The older the women were in the films, the less likely they were to lead purposeful lives and to have goals. Men characters, in contrast, saw their leadership and occupational power increase with age. Moviegoers see men in roles as religious, political, and military leaders, setting goals and attempting to reach them. These images reinforce the idea that men are "natural" leaders and that women are not (Lauzen and Dozier 2005).

Both men and women characters, however, are mostly young and all older people were dramatically underrepresented compared to their real numbers in American society. But the proportion of moviegoers who are fifty or older is increasing and this age group currently accounts for one-quarter of all the tickets purchased. This buying power may eventually alter the ages of characters on the screen, although judging from the top box office films, it has not influenced films so far (Lauzen and Dozier 2005). At the other end of the age spectrum are the youngest viewers. These kinds of issues have been studied in G-rated films directed at children moviegoers.

> **Box 11–3 TOP 20 GROSSING FILMS WORLDWIDE**
> **BY 2006, IN MILLIONS OF DOLLARS**
>
> 1. *Titanic* 1997 $1,835
> 2. *Lord of the Rings: The Return of the King* 2003 $1,129.2
> 3. *Harry Potter and the Sorcerer's Stone* 2001 $968.7
> 4. *Star Wars: Episode I: The Phantom Menace* 1999 $925.5
> 5. *Pirates of the Caribbean: Dead Man's Chest* 2006 $923.9
> 6. *The Lord of the Rings: The Two Towers* 2002 $920.5
> 7. *Jurassic Park* 1993 $920.0
> 8. *Shrek 2* 2004 $912.0
> 9. *Harry Potter and the Goblet of Fire* 2005 $892.2
> 10. *Harry Potter and the Chamber of Secrets* 2002 $866.4
> 11. *Lord of the Rings: The Fellowship of the Ring* 2001 $860.7
> 12. *Finding Nemo* 2003 $853.2
> 13. *Star Wars: Episode III* 2005 $850.0
> 14. *Independence Day* 1996 $813.1
> 15. *Spider-Man* 2002 $806.7
> 16. *Star Wars* 1977 $797.9
> 17. *Harry Potter and the Prisoner of Azkaban* 2004 $789.8
> 18. *Spider-Man 2* 2004 $784.0
> 19. *The Lion King* 1994 $771.9
> 20. *E.T.* 1982 $757.0
>
> SOURCE: http://www.the-movie-times.com/thrsdir/alltime.mv?domestic+ByDG

G MOVIES. Violence in films has been of special concern for researchers and policymakers and it is of particular interest to scholars interested in gender because of the links among gender, power, and masculinity that we explored in chapter 8. In the film world, "Violence is key to the rule of power. It is the cheapest and quickest dramatic representation of who can and who cannot get away with what and against whom" (Gerbner et al. 1980, 708).

In studies of G-rated movies, researchers have found that men and boy characters are dominant, disconnected, and dangerous. Men and boy characters are more prevalent and more important to the story than are girls and women. In a review of 4,000 characters in G movies, men and boys were the majority in every measurement used: 75 percent of all characters live or animated, 83 percent of the characters in crowds, 83 percent of the narrators, and 72 percent of the speaking characters. In addition, little change occurred in these proportions from 1990 to 2004. Women and girls were strongly outnumbered and the stories of men and boys prevailed. Race ethnicity also figures into these numbers. Among the U.S.

population, 36 percent are people of color, but only 15 percent of the characters in the movies are (Escholtz and Bufkin 2001; Kelly and Morrell 2006).

In addition to being more prevalent on the screen, boys and men are depicted differently from girls and women, especially in regard to family relationships. Men are only about half as likely (35 percent) as women (61 percent) to be parents. They are also much less often (32 percent of men) in a committed relationship or marriage compared to women (61 percent; Kelly and Morrell 2006).

The contrasts in family roles also depict racial ethnic differences as well as gender differences. Of nonwhites, 35 percent are parents, whereas 53 percent of whites are portrayed as mothers and fathers. Only 22 percent of nonwhites are in committed relationships compared to 53 percent of whites (Kelly and Morrell 2006).

Danger is the third factor observed by researchers of G-rated movies. Forty-four percent of the men and boy characters, 31 percent of white women and girls, and 38 percent of the nonwhite women and girls are depicted as physically aggressive or violent. The gender gap is relatively small but coupled with the fact that masculine characters also take three times as much screen time, the image of masculine violence is powerful (Kelly and Morrell 2006).

Sexualization of Girls and Women in Media

The connection between violence and masculinity in media is a matter of concern. Sexualization of women and girls in media is another controversial issue. In chapter 4, we examined the debate around pornography and the exploitation of women and girls. Here we look at more subtle kinds of sexualization. SEICUS (2004) distinguishes between healthy sexuality and sexualization:

> Healthy sexuality is an important component of both physical and mental health, fosters intimacy, bonding and shared pleasure, and involves mutual respect between consenting partner... In contrast, sexualization occurs when:

- A person's value comes only from his or her sexual appeal or behavior to the exclusion of other characteristiscs;
- A person is held to a standard that equates physical attractiveness (narrowly defined) with being sexy;
- A person is sexually objectified—that is, made into a thing for other's sexual use, rather than seen as a person with the capacity for independent action and decision making; and/or
- Sexuality is inappropriately imposed upon a person. (APA 2007)

The American Psychological Association (APA 2007, 3) offers the following examples to clarify their definition of sexualization:

- Imagine a five-year-old girl walking through a mall wearing a short T-shirt that says "Flirt."
- Consider the instructions given in magazines to preadolescent girls on how to look sexy and get a boyfriend by losing ten pounds and straightening their hair.
- Envision a soccer team of adolescent girls whose sex appeal is emphasized by their coach or a local journalist to attract fans.

- Think of print advertisements that portray women as little girls, with pigtails and ruffles, in adult sexual poses.

Sexualization, especially of women and girls, is prevalent on television. In one study, 84 percent of the episodes analyzed contained at least one incident of sexual harassment, averaging 3.4 per program. The most frequent acts were sexist comments describing women, for example, as broad, bimbo, and dumbass chick. The next most common occurrence insulted women's bodies, especially breasts, using words such as jugs, boobs, knockers, and hooters (Graueurholz 1997). Music videos are also a well-known source of sexualization of women and men. Of music videos shown on BET, 84 percent have been found to display sexual imagery, including sexual objectification and women dancing sexually (Ward and Rivadeneyra 2002). Lyrics in popular music often sexualize women and/or refer to them in degrading ways (APA 2007).

- So blow me bitch I don't rock for cancer/I rock for the cash and the topless dancers. (Kid Rock 1998)
- Don'tcha wish your girlfriend was hot like me? (Pussycat Dolls 2005)
- That's the way you like to f^{UCN} ... rough sex make it hurt, in the garden all in the dirt. (Ludacris 2000)
- I tell the hos all the time, Bitch get in my car. (50 Cent 2005)
- Ho shake your ass. (Ying Yang Twins 2003)
- Bitch, please—you must have a mental disease. Assume the position and get back down on your knees—c'mon. (Eminem 2001)

Magazines are another source of sexualization and are an increasingly popular form of media. The number of magazines targeted at teens rose from five in 1990 to nineteen in 2000. Almost half of eight- to eighteen-year-olds report having read a magazine the previous day (Roberts, Roehr, and Rideout 2005). The magazines typically encourage girls and young women to gain the attention of men by presenting themselves as sexually desirable by looking and dressing, "costuming for seduction," in a particular way and using certain products (Duffy and Gotcher 1996). Even articles on exercise emphasize increasing sexual desirability rather than its health effects.

Advertisements in magazines also sexualize women. One study of magazines such as *Time* and *Vogue* from 1955 to 2002 found that 40 percent of the ads featured women as decorative sexual objects (Lindner 2004). In magazines specifically targeted at men, 53 percent (targeted at white men) to 68 percent (targeted at black men) of the images of women depict them as decorative sexual objects (Baker 2005). (See Box 11-1).

The sexualization of women and girls may have important negative consequences for the women and girls who see the images and messages. Studies show they are linked to dissatisfaction with personal appearance, eating disorders, depression, and greater likelihood of seeking surgical alterations to make themselves appear more like the sexualized images. Trying to imitate the sexualized images in the media, ironically, may create problems in the workplace, as women who are applying for management positions and appear more sexual are judged to be less intelligent and less competent than those who are more conservative in appearance (Glick et al. 2005).

The self-objectification of girls that comes with their sexualization has negative consequences in terms of girls' ability to develop healthy sexuality. Self-objectification occurs when
women and girls "buy" the images and start to behave in ways consistent with them. Self-
objectification is linked directly with diminished sexual health among adolescent girls, as
measured by decreased condom use and diminished sexual assertiveness (Impett, Schooler,
and Tolman 2006). Self-objectification also detracts from the ability to concentrate and focus
one's attention, which leads to impaired performance on mental activities such as mathematical computations or logical reasoning (Fredrickson et al. 1998; Gapinski, Brownell, and
LaFrance 2003; Hebl, King, and Lin 2004).

Internet and Gender

The Internet is a recent addition to the media with which we interact. About 55 percent of
American households have Internet access and many other people have access through work,
school, and libraries (Day, Janus, and Davis 2005). Despite the fact that the Internet seems
a pervasive part of our lives, research on images of gender on the Internet is only beginning
(Beasley and Standley 2002). The research that has been done indicates that women and
girls are largely invisible (14 percent of all characters in video games, for example, are girls
or women). When women and girl characters do appear they are sexualized through their
clothing, behavior, and body shape.

More investigation has been done on gender and the use of the Internet (Ono and
Zavodny 2005). In the 1990s, scholars found a cybergap between women and men in the
United States with men much more likely to be using computers and surfing the Internet.
By the turn of the century, however, the gap had disappeared and even reversed. American
women (47.4 percent) now are more likely than men (39.2 percent) to use computers at work
and they have better typing skills, allowing them to get around more efficiently (Ono and
Zavodny 2005; Day, Janus, and Davis 2005).

Similar trends are found in children's use of the Internet. Very young girls and boys use
the Internet in equal numbers, but girls lead boys in Internet use by middle school (Lenhart,
Rainie, and Lewis 2001; Roberts, Roehr, and Rideout 2005). Overall among school-age children, girls (66.9 percent) are slightly more likely to use the Internet than are boys (65.8 percent) at school or at home (Day, Janus, and Davis 2005).

Factors other than gender, such as race ethnicity, income, and education, are more
important distinctions between groups in the United States who use the Internet and those
who do not (Calvert et al. 2005). For example, 79 percent of white children, 74 percent of
Asian children, and 42 percent of Latino and black children have access to the Internet at
home (Day, Janus, and Davis 2005).

This change toward greater gender equality, however, has not occurred in all nations. In
Japan, for example, women still seem to lag behind men in their use of the Internet. Japanese
women have less experience with computers and they have weaker typing skills compared to
Japanese men.

This contrast between Japanese women and men appears to be related to job experience and perhaps education. Japanese women are less likely to be in the paid labor force
compared to American women and they are more likely to be in part-time and temporary

positions. They are also less likely to be in college than are Japanese men, whereas American women are more likely than American men to go to college.

There are also still some differences for women and men on issues related to the Internet in the United States. Men dominate decisions about purchasing computers (Ono and Zavodny 2005). In addition, men and women differ in their perceptions of their skills in using the Internet (Hargittai and Shafer 2006).

Women and men have similar skills in locating information online. They are equally able to find sites for people, data, and organizations and maneuver through the websites quickly and effectively. Other factors such as age, education, and experience with computers are important predictors of skill but gender is not.

When women and men, however, are asked to rate their Internet skills, women give themselves lower scores. One study asked men and women, who tested equal on skills, to rate themselves on a five-point scale, and men's averages were higher. Not one man gave himself the lowest score-novice—and not one woman rated herself with the highest score—expert. When the participants in the study ran into trouble on the Internet, they also had different responses. Men tended to blame the technology, whereas women blamed themselves (Hargittai and Shafer 2006).

Media Theory

What is the relationship between media and society? Do media determine how we think about gender? Or do viewers play a role, interacting, responding, resisting, and even reconstructing those images in ways that can help create social change rather than maintain the existing systems of inequality? There are two opposing views on the role played by the media and especially television (McKinley 1997). Hegemony theorists (Marger 2002) argue that media play a conservative role in society, manipulating and persuading viewers that the status quo is the best of all possible worlds, or even the only possibility. This position was expressed in the beginning of the chapter when we discussed legitimation.

Some theorists, however, would disagree with the assertion that media always legitimate the status quo by persuading people that we live in the best of all possible worlds. They claim that television can elicit responses from viewers that challenge the status quo. Theorists in this second category assert that television can give voice to an otherwise silent point of view or programming can generate discussion that promotes resistance to hegemonic ideas including ideas about gender. Stuart Hall is one of the most well-known theorists who takes this point of view, which is called *reception theory* (Hall 1973). He argues that viewers, listeners, and readers are not just passive receivers, but engage in thinking about and giving meaning to what they take in. Each person, based on his or her social position and background reinterprets what the media deliver. Our ideas about issues such as gender are a combination of what the media sends and what we make of it, both accepting and resisting different messages.

RESISTING MEDIA. Resistance can take two forms. First, viewers can criticize the characters, images, and values in the presentation. When viewers watch TV programs and enjoy them, for example, they may not be persuaded that the characters or the stories are valid or honorable. Second, resistance can also occur when viewers transform the images into something that is more consistent with their own values or activities, and especially their own interests.

Research on the television program Beverly Hills 90210 illustrates the first kind of resistance. Viewers were influenced by stereotyped images of young women in the program, but the viewers also reacted and defied the images by criticizing the characters.

90210 was a television show popular in the 1990s about a group of high school students and their families who all lived in the zip code 90210 in Beverly Hills, California, an affluent suburb of Los Angeles. The program presented an image of women as passive, pretty, and nice and therefore, attractive to cute boyfriends. The message was that women should be allowed speak up and argue with other women, but when it comes to men, women should not say what they think nor do what they want if it contradicts men's view of the world. Women should not want sex but they should want marriage, as marriage is the only solid proof of a woman's worth. Girlfriends must not fight with their boyfriends and they must be faithful (McKinley 1997).

Although women viewers of 90210 claimed they were not influenced by the program, they admitted to learning about how to dress and behave from the characters on the show. They described the ways they memorized the treatment of social issues like rape, abortion, and drug use so that they could incorporate the ideas and arguments in discussions and decisions about these topics in their real lives (McKinley 1997).

The program also literally influenced their behavior when they altered their schedules so that they would not miss the show. One woman explains her devotion to 90210:

> I want to be able to hear every word they say. Sometimes I tape it as I'm watching in case anybody does walk in, um, I can rewind it again later and replay that part. I turn my ringer off. I won't answer the phone, I mean—and people know. Sometimes I'll leave a message, I go "You know what I'm doing. Why are you calling?" (McKinley 1997, 209)

The influence of the program on viewers' behavior suggests that hegemony theory is correct in its assertion that television is a powerful force shaping our ideas about gender. On the other hand, the women in this study also spent a lot of time reacting to the program as they watched it and discussing it later with their friends, who were also fans. They did not accept all of the views presented in the program and were critical of the behavior of many of the characters, which illustrates a more active role for viewers than is asserted by hegemony theorists.

Box 11–4 suggests another example of resistance to media images. In this case women in the Global South sift through the messages sent to them from media sources in the Global North. They express consciousness of the problems with the dominance of Northern media images and with the images themselves, but they also use pieces of the messages to wage their own struggles for greater gender equity (Gosovic 2000).

MUSIC VIDEOS. Research on music videos provides another example of the debate between a hegemonic view of the media and the perspective that acknowledges the possibility of resistance against hegemony. Music video fans can protest and challenge the images in an attempt to remove them from the public eye or they can reconstruct the images in ways that challenge stereotyped views of women.

Box 11–4 NORTH, SOUTH, HEGEMONY, AND RESISTANCE

Where do images of social roles come from? And where do they fit into the global picture of media? Many observers have noted the cultural flow from the North (wealthy powerful nations, especially the United States) to the South (poorer, less powerful nations in Latin America, Africa and Asia—the Southern portion of the globe). If you have traveled or lived in the Global South, you have probably noticed the familiar icons of American culture such as Nike, McDonald's, and Coke. And you have probably heard Britney Spears and seen Hollywood movies playing in those countries.

Some scholars and political activists worry that the dominance of Northern cultures will damage the Southern cultures. This is called global intellectual hegemony (GIH) and it appears to be a major feature of globalization (Gosovic 2000). GIH can promote negative features of Northern culture such as consumerism, cut-throat individualism, unhealthy products, or just bad music, and therefore is certainly a valid concern. However, media images that come from the Global North can also play a role in improving people's lives. In research in India, women described the ways that their exposure to global media allowed them to develop alternative ways of thinking and talking about gender relations in their communities. Those alternatives were important to challenging the dominance of men.

For example, one woman described her view of the importance of women entering the paid labor force and earning a living, an idea she developed at least in part from her exposure to media images of assertive "new women." Others spoke of feeling heartened by seeing strong women characters in advertisements, television, or films or in news stories about leadership by women politicians. Although the women expressed concern about the ways the Northern-produced media promotes a consumerist ideology and often portrays women in derogatory ways, media images of women driving and shopping unchaperoned by men and working in "unacceptable" professional occupations also provided new alternative ideas about womanhood (Ganguly-Scrase 2003).

Much has been written about the importance of music videos in young people's lives, particularly, the impact they have on African Americans trying to make sense of their lives, social relations, and the world around them (Emerson 2004). Hip hop artist Chuck D says that hip hop is the CNN of today's youth (Jackson 2007).

Hip hop is also a controversial medium. The discussion earlier in the chapter about sexualization of women and girls in media used some quotes from lyrics of popular songs. The lyrics stand out because they are so blatantly misogynist and racist. The debate over the music has been especially central in hip hop music.

Hip hop emerged in the Bronx in the late 1970s and has been strongly criticized by mainstream media as well as by hip hop insiders. Almost ten years ago, artists such as C. Delores Tucker, Dionne Warwick, and the National Political Congress of Black Women spoke out against degrading portrayals of women in hip hop lyrics and music videos (Kitwana

2002). More recently, Beverly Guy-Sheftall (Jackson 2005), a women's studies professor from Spelman College addressing a hip hop convention, said the nearly naked women in music videos remind her of America's racist past when women were paraded naked at slave auctions. These depictions are, "'reminiscent of old and obscene racial stereotypes that deprive (black women) of humanity,' she said, adding that the rising influence of hip hop means these images are circulating around the globe. Guy-Sheftall also noted, however, 'it's not the whip, it's the dollar bill' that keeps women oppressed" (Jackson 2005).

The hip hop movement itself is split over the antiwoman and antiblack messages, with many arguing that racist and sexist lyrics and images contradict the essence of hip hop, which is a movement to confront and expose a racist and sexist society in order to change it. Rapper turned activist Chuck D joins Guy-Sheftall in his call to bring hip hop back to its roots as a social change vehicle. He challenges especially black men to change the industry by confronting the music industry's sexual exploitation of black women with rap music. In a panel discussion on music videos, Chuck D said: "BET is the cancer of black manhood in the world, because they have one-dimensionalized and commodified us into being a one-trick image. We're [shown] throwing money at the camera and flashing jewelry at the camera that could give a town in Africa water for a year" (Zurawik 2007). He concluded, "The only thing that can turn the tide is black men" (Fullwood 2007).

Both Guy-Sheftall and Chuck D are arguing that the CEOs in the industry have distorted hip hop and that the music needs to be transformed so that it respects and honors women and African Americans and promotes images of masculinity that challenge violent, misogynist ideas about what it is to be a man. So far this discussion has portrayed the debate as one that has two sides: those who promote racist, sexist images and lyrics and those who oppose them and wish to eliminate them from the music. The promoters and the resisters both approach the issue from a hegemonic point of view, arguing that the medium is harmful and needs to be altered.

Another response to the music was explored by Emerson (2004). She argues that the music does not necessarily need to be changed. It is our response to the music that must change, from one of acceptance to one that accepts some of it and rejects other aspects. Furthermore, Emerson asserts that viewers already "censor" out the images and lyrics with which they disagree and accept the ones that they believe are positive for women today. She reviews a number of videos that show both hegemonic (and objectifying and exploitative images of women) as well as counterhegemonic images and ideas. Her study explores the ways listeners accept the counterhegemonic images and ideas at the same time they reject the hegemonic ones.

Emerson's (2004) review of music videos of black women musicians shows three types of stereotypical images. First they emphasize black women's bodies. Like the images in general of women in the media, body types are pretty much limited to thin, young, and pretty.

Second, they present black women as one-dimensional. Not only is their physical appearance limited, but many kinds of women like pregnant women, women over thirty, mothers, and lesbians are never shown. The roles of women are further limited to being objects of men's desire, and focused on romance and conspicuous consumption (Emerson 2004).

Third, the videos show men as "sponsors," always in the background calling the shots. Women's role is primarily as sex object and someone not to be taken seriously. Men appear as the expert, creative geniuses who are guiding the woman musician (Emerson 2004).

According to Emerson, however, that is not the only story being told in the videos. At the same time these negative stereotypes of women are present, women's resistance to the stereotypes is also part of the songs and images. First, the women in the videos embrace their race ethnicity and they project a sense of pride about being black women. Black is portrayed in a positive manner and the black women artists, actresses, models, and dancers in the videos who have darker complexions are emphasized in particular (Emerson 2004).

A second example of challenging negative stereotypes in the videos is in the behavior of the women. At the same time they are presented in subordinate roles, they are simultaneously depicted as active, vocal, and independent. They assertively express their discontent and challenge especially interpersonal relationships they find unsatisfactory. The women are shown defining their own identity and determining their own lives. "Speaking out and speaking one's mind are constant themes" (Emerson 2004, 263).

Sisterhood is the third factor providing evidence of music videos as a forum for black women's resistance to oppressive stereotypes. Women in the videos look to each other for partnership and support. Collaboration musically and in the stories in the videos is a recurring theme.

A fourth, and perhaps most important issue in these videos, is sexuality. The sexually explicit and objectifying character of music videos is well known. Emerson (2004) argues that there is also evidence of alternative models of women and sexuality. Women and men are frequently shown as coworkers and collaborators, suggesting that women can have relationships with men that are not sexual and are productive and creative for both women and men.

Women's sexuality is also combined with themes of independence, strength, street smarts, toughness, and the ability to act in one's own defense. The women are sexy and they are objects to be admired and observed, but they are simultaneously glamorous, savvy, and autonomous on their own terms. In addition, women's sexuality is portrayed as active with men's bodies the object of women's pleasure; men are something to be pursued as well as something to be looked at. In sum, the videos show contradictory images of women, sometimes subordinate, restricted, and designed for men's consumption. Simultaneously, though, the women are shown resisting those roles and creating a more independent and active image (Emerson 2004). The videos show both the ways media can legitimate the status quo and the ways it can be a vehicle for challenge and the ways that consumers can choose which messages to take from them.

THE SPECTACLE OF SPORT

Television, films, the Internet, and music videos are important and pervasive forms of media, but sports have been identified as an especially critical piece of our media lives. Athletic activities exist outside of media presentation but the sports we now are most likely to be exposed to are those that come to us through the media. Sports are also tightly tied to commercial products like the Nike ad mentioned at the beginning of the chapter. In addition, professional athletic teams and even many amateur events and activities are themselves commercial ventures that use the media to advertise themselves. Athletics is increasingly both a mass media and commercial media spectacle (Kellner 2003).

Sport is also a major aspect of gender and gender ideologies. Athletic events and activities represent and promote images of masculinity and femininity and have been identified as one of the central sites in the social production of masculinity in particular. For women, athletics have been a place of exclusion, expressing the idea that femininity does not include athletic ability and experience. Men and masculinity are closely tied to sports, and women have been outsiders.

Children, especially boys, are the spectators of media sports spectacles. The events boys are most likely to watch on television are, in order, professional football, men's professional basketball, professional baseball, professional wrestling, men's college basketball, college football, and extreme sports (Messner, Dunbar, and Hunt 2000).

Research on these popular sports programs reveals ten recurrent themes regarding gender that make up the television sports manhood formula: white males are voices of authority; sports is a man's world—women athletes are nearly invisible; men are foreground in commercials; women are sexy props or prizes for men's successful sport performances or consumption choices; whites are foreground in commercials; aggressive players get the prize—nice guys finish last; violence is natural and manly—boys will be (violent) boys; give up your body for the team; sports is war; and show some guts—reckless bravery in the face of danger is what it takes to be a winner and a man (Messner, Dunbar, and Hunt 2000).

The television sports manhood formula answers the question of what a real man is:

> A Real Man is strong, tough, aggressive, and above all, a winner in what is still a Man's World. To be a winner he has to do what needs to be done. He must be willing to compromise his own long term health by showing guts in the face of danger, by fighting other men when necessary, and by "playing hurt" when he is injured. He must avoid being soft; he must be the aggressor, both on the "Battlefields" of sports and in his consumption choices. Whether he is playing sports or making choices about which snack food or auto products to purchase, his aggressiveness will net him the ultimate prize: the adoring attention of conventionally beautiful women. He will know if and when he has arrived as a Real Man when the Voices of Authority—White Males—say he is a Real Man. But even when he has finally managed to win the big one, has the good car, the right beer and is surrounded by beautiful women, he will be reminded by these very same voices of authority just how fragile the Real Manhood really is: After all, he has to come out and prove himself over and over again tomorrow. You're only as good as your last game (or your last purchase). (Messner, Dunbar, and Hunt 2000, 390)

Sports and Masculinity

Sports is not just a spectacle, however; it is also something many of us experience directly. Becoming a man includes demonstrating physical competence (Whitson 1990). Boys begin to display and practice the connection between masculinity and physical interests and skills early on. In the United States, athleticism and prestige and power for boys crosses race and class lines among even very young elementary school boys. Although all boys may not like sports and many are not particularly skilled in athletics, all boys to some extent are judged by their ability (or lack of it) in competitive sports (Messner 2001). Physical aggression is associated with status and popular boys are likely to be those who most skillfully use physical aggression like pushing, shoving, and hitting. One researcher watching first graders found that not even a half-hour went by without boys wrestling around with each other (Hasbrook and Harris 2000).

Michael Messner (2001) interviewed men about the importance of sports in their childhood. He asked them what they remembered about their experience with athletic activities, especially the ways sports helped them to develop masculinity. The men experienced sports as so much a part of their life they felt it seemed like something natural. One man explained, "It was just what you did. It's kind of like, you went to school, you played athletics, and if you didn't there was something wrong with you. It was just like brushing your teeth; it's just what you did. It's part of your existence" (Messner 2001, 89–90).

Even though the activities seemed natural, the men also recalled the importance of older men in their lives, especially fathers, and the key role they played in initiating—exposing them and sometimes pushing them—into the male world of sports. One man described his introduction to sports by his father:

> I still remember like it was yesterday—dad and I driving up in his truck, and I had my glove and my hat all that—and I said, "Dad, I don't want to do it." He says, "What?" I says, "I don't want to do it." I was nervous that I might fail. And he says, "Don't be silly. Lookit: There's Joey and Petey and all your friends out there." And so Dad says, "You're gonna do it, come on." And in my memory he's never said that about anything else; he just knew I needed a little kick in the pants and I'd do it. And once you're out there and you see all the other kids making errors and stuff, and you know you're better than those guys, you know: Maybe I do belong out here. As it turned out, Little League was a good experience. (quoted in Messner 2001, 91)

Boys learn to be athletes and through those experiences they learn to be masculine. They also learn a particular way of thinking about themselves and relating to others. Messner (2001) calls this "conditional self worth." By this he means that boys learn that they must compete and they must win to be worthy of other people's concern. It is not enough to just be out there with others playing a game. They must win to be accepted. One man described the importance of being best: "It was expected of me to do well in all my contests—I mean by my coaches, my peers, and my family. So I in turn expected to do well and if I didn't do well, then I'd be very disappointed" (Messner 2001, 94). Being better than the other guy is the key to acceptance. When men learn this way of viewing themselves and the social world around them, it can cause problems in their ability to make intimate connections and express themselves in emotional ways (Messner 2001).

The attraction of sports for boys that comes from the ways in which it brought them closer to other men in their lives, like their fathers and brothers, and also the kinds of enjoyment they got from the recognition and success in sports crosses social class and race ethnicity lines. These social differences among men, however, affected their experience with athletics. First, boys from more privileged backgrounds experienced sports almost exclusively in terms of their immediate families. Black and poorer boys were brought into sports because of pressures, often negative, within the community. For example, one black man from a low-income neighborhood described his participation in sports as a survival strategy: "Sports protected me from having to compete in gang stuff or having to be good with your fists. If you were an athlete and got into the fist world, that was your business, and that was okay—but you didn't have to if you didn't want to. People would generally defer to you, give you your space away from trouble" (quoted in Messner 2001, 95).

Second, black and white middle-class boys practiced sports as one activity among many. They saw that the status of the adults around them was linked to their success in fields other than sports, such as school and jobs. Low-income boys, in contrast, saw much more limited opportunities for themselves and the adults in their lives. Sports offered immediate rewards of fun and attention and the potential, although small, of adult professional success. The opportunities for becoming a professional athlete are twice as good for white men compared to black men, but the numbers are miniscule in all groups. The chances of going professional are 4:100,000 for white men, 2:100,000 for black men, and 3:1 million for Hispanic men (Messner 2001).

HISTORY OF SPORT AND MANLINESS. The identification of manliness with sport appeared as a strong theme in the nineteenth century in the United States and Britain (see Box 11–5). The British Empire had spread its influence throughout the world and the United States had spread across the North American continent. Masculinity was threatened, however, at the close of the nineteenth century by political challenges to British imperialism and economic change in the United States that pushed men out of the rugged independent model of the small businessman and farmer. White men found competition from African American labor with the end of slavery and the waves of immigrants coming into the United States as well as the developing women's movement. The old Davy Crockett and Daniel Boone models of masculinity were washed away and a crisis in masculinity developed. In Britain a new kind of man was required to ensure that the sun continued to never set on the British Empire (Beynon 2002). Athletic images of masculinity were a central feature of these "new men" (Kimmel 1990).

Sports in a variety of forms took the place of the frontier and offered a way to reconstruct American manhood. In the last few decades of the nineteenth century, the first tennis court opened in Boston, the first basketball court was built, the American Bowling Congress was established, and the Amateur Athletic Union was founded (Kimmel 1990). The images of sport and masculinity were tied together, establishing enduring myths of masculinity consisting of unstoppable physical power and authority. These continue to influence our thinking about what real men should be like (Beynon 2002).

One feature of the image of the new athletic man of the nineteenth and early twentieth century has fallen away in recent years. In early years, sport and sex were seen as opposite poles in men's lives and athletic activities were believed to be regenerative for men. Athletic ability and activity meant that men were not depleting their stores of sperm and energy and were properly fit to take on all the pursuits required of men. Boys who did not engage in sports were likely to become womanlike, degenerate, and delicate. Men who did not persist in sports would lose control of their sexual desires and eventually succumb to sexual exhaustion. Today athleticism and sexual prowess are both important features of masculinity (Crosset 1990).

> ## Box 11–5 IDEAL TYPES OF HISTORICAL MASCULINITY
>
> - **Hero:** From ancient Greece, man of action and warrior, strong and courageous in battle. Women are here to serve men's needs
> - **Spiritual man:** Nonviolent, celibate, self-renunciating, focused on spiritual goals and forsaking earthly pursuits. Women are a seductive and dangerous threat.
> - **Chivalrous knight:** From medieval Europe, honorable, generous, and courteous. Women are to be idealized and loved from a distance.
> - **Renaissance man:** From seventeeth-century Europe, free thinking, scientific, and artistic.
> - **Hedonist:** From bourgeois society of the eighteenth century, wealthy, in a hurry to succeed, enjoying the fruits of his labors.
> - **He-man:** Hard bodies and outdoor work and play (Doyle 1989; Beynon 2002).

INITIATION RITES AND FOOTBALL. In the United States, American football has been identified as a place where boys become men. In fact, football fits the model of a male initiation rite in male-dominated societies that have been observed in many other cultures. An initiation rite marks a transition from one social role to another, especially the move from childhood to adulthood. These rites share a number of characteristics cross-culturally (Sabo and Panepinto 1990):

- Man–boy relationships. Two key groups are older men initiators and younger initiates.
- Conformity and control. Initiates must learn the rules and abide by them to successfully complete the initiation.
- Social isolation. Initiates are socially isolated from others in the community, especially women and girls who may be characterized as dangerous and polluting to the initiation and its goal of full manhood.
- Deference to men's authority. Initiates are shown the ladder of success, the way to climb the ladder, and the necessity of deferring to those above them.
- Pain. Initiates must show courage and the ability to endure pain to succeed in their initiation.

Football has each of these elements. First, it takes place in a nearly exclusive male theater with only boys and men interacting. When men recall their football years, they describe their coaches as everything from "almost a god" to "a mean son of a bitch," but they always agree that their coaches played an important role in their "growing up" (Sabo and Panepinto 1990, 119).

Second, officials and coaches exert much control of the players on and off the field with exercise regimes, dietary and dating restrictions, clothing regulations, and study programs, as well as training in athletic skills of the game. Third, training, playing, showering, traveling, and even sometimes eating takes place away from nonteam members. One former college football player described his in-season life:

We were figuring it out one night before an away-game at Boston College. During the season, we went to classes 5 days a week. We had 3 hour practices 5 days a week followed by team meals. Friday night was psych-up time and Saturday was game day. Sunday we reviewed game films for 3 hours and had a team meeting, not to mention that we were sore as hell and couldn't move worth a damn. The only time we could chase girls was Saturday night after home games, and, even then, the coaches said they'd prowl the bars to catch somebody drinking or breaking curfew. The only things we had time for was going to class, playing ball and jerking off. (Sabo and Panepinto 1990, 120–21)

Fourth, a variety of ranks exist in football from owners, coaches, and referees to first string, second string, and star players, each deferring to the next higher rank. Fifth, injury and pain are obvious components of every game and practice. In addition to hits on the field, players are sometimes inflicted with emotional pain when coaches yell at them or restrict their time on the field or even physically reprimand them. All the while players are told to "take their knocks" and "toughen up" (Sabo and Panepinto 1990). Football represents an important model of masculine initiation in contemporary American society. Football also strikingly represents the downside of sports, its danger to boys and men.

DANGERS OF MASCULINITY. Sports are an effective way of creating masculine men, but the kind of masculinity that is promoted in sports is a problem because of the damage it frequently can do to men's bodies (Messner 1992). The physical destructiveness of football epitomizes this problem. Among high school athletes, football is the most common source of serious injury, injury resulting in disability, and direct fatality.

Other sports are dangerous as well, particularly those in which men engage. Men and boys are much more likely than women and girls to be hurt and especially to be hurt seriously while participating in sports. Of those injured in sports accidents with long-term disability or death, 85 percent are men (Young and White 2000). In research on sports injury and fatality in Canada, water sports (boating, diving, fishing, water skiing, etc.) were the most dangerous and 87 percent of those injured were men and boys. Motor sports (ATV riding, snowmobiling, etc.) were the second most dangerous and 90 percent of those injured were men and boys.

TIME FOR A CHANGE? The connection between masculinity and violence in sports has detrimental physical effects on men, causing them injury and even death. In addition, the link between athletics and endless competition, a winner-take-all mentality, and disrespect for human bodies result in damage to men psychologically. If men achieve success in these goals they may hurt themselves on the field and they may restrict alternative values and beliefs. If they do not achieve success they may feel they are failures or others may judge them as inadequate.

The boys engaged in high school athletics are more likely to have "stunted identity development." Researchers conclude that the "high status afforded to male athletes was detrimental to their overall psychological development" (Stone and McKee 2002, 98). The celebrity status of boys who were high school athletes apparently prevented them from developing other aspects of themselves and from experiencing high school as a period of "growing up." In addition to damaging individual men, sports can also damage society. Athletics and athletes are an important source of values, especially for young people who look up to athletes. If sports and individual athletes serve as models for promoting values like excessive competition and disregard of human bodies on the fields that then permeate the rest of society, they do a disservice to society (Burstyn 1999).

MEXICAN BASEBALL PLAYERS CHALLENGE HEGEMONIC MASCULINITY IN SPORTS. Research on historical changes in masculinity from the nineteenth century and cross-cultural contrasts among baseball players show that masculinity is dynamic and although the dominant form is often accepted, it also sometimes challenged. Kimmel (1992, 166) writes:

> Definitions of masculinity are constantly changing. Masculinity does not bubble up into behavioral codes from our genetic makeup, nor does it float in a current of the collective consciousness, waiting to be actualized by any particular man and simultaneously all men. Masculinity is socially constructed, changing 1) from one culture to another, 2) within any culture over time, 3) over the course of any individual man's life and 4) between and among different groups of men depending on class, race ethnicity and sexuality.

Research on Mexican baseball players illustrates Kimmel's assertion. The term *macho* is a Spanish word. A macho man is one who displays hypermasculine bravado and posturing, is likely to respond physically to any slight, attempts to dominate women and other men verbally and physically, drinks too much, has many women lovers, and fathers many children. Latino men and men from Spanish-speaking nations have been stereotyped as macho. Researchers, however, have found that these stereotypes are not valid in the family life of the Latino community (Baca Zinn 1992; Hondagneu-Sotelo 1992). Recent research on Mexican baseball players also refutes the macho image of Latinos.

A two-year study of the Mexican baseball team, the Tecos, found that Mexican ballplayers were less macho than Anglos on the team and displayed clear contrasts to conventional ideas about machismo in three areas: attitudes about children, ability to express vulnerability, and touching between men (Klein 2000).

Mexican baseball players are sensitive and caring of children (Gutmann 1996). In his field notes on the Mexican team, Klein (2000) describes the following scene to illustrate the relationship between the ballplayers and their kids:

> On the field following batting practice and 30 minutes to game time, Romero with his three-day growth of beard looks like central casting's choice for a Mexican bandito. He laughs like a three-pack-a-day convict, but when he holds his little baby girl and zooms her around like a little pink dirigible (she's wearing a pink headband), he's the warmest, most comforting man imaginable. (Klein 2000, 78)

The Mexican ballplayers also displayed vulnerability, discussing their challenges and failures at home and on the field, sometimes weeping without embarrassment and seeking emotional support from others. Their physical interactions included not only masculine mock boxing but also touching, leaning against, and hugging their teammates. In all of these areas, the Mexican men challenge dominant ideas about masculinity and provide contrasts with the Anglo men on the team (Klein 2000).

Sportswomen

With all of problems associated with sports and masculinity, we might expect that women would want to avoid athletics. Why are women around the world concerned about bringing more women into athletics? Michael Messner writes, "Increasing women's athleticism represents a genuine quest by women for equality, control of their own bodies and self-definition, and as such represents a challenge to the ideological basis of male domination" (Messner 1992, 197). When women athletes use their bodies to challenge the notions that women are clumsy and weak they are creating new images and new ways of being for women. They are also creating a new kind of woman who is equal to men on the playing field and off it. In studies of the benefits of sports for girls, researchers (Stone and McKee 2002) have found that girls who are involved in athletics have more positive attitudes about school, higher academic achievement (especially in the sciences), and are less likely to drop out of school. Girl athletes also have stronger self-esteem, lower rates of depression, and greater leadership capacity. Their physical health is also enhanced and they are less likely to smoke or to become pregnant in high school.

Women all over the globe are working to bring women into athletics, but women in the world of sport have historically been outsiders. In the nineteenth century, women were not even allowed to be spectators at football games (Watterson 2000). Women athletes are still largely invisible in media surrounding athletics and when they are paid attention to they are looked at differently. Research on top newspapers and television shows that 92 percent of sports coverage is about men (Messner, Duncan, and Jensen 1993). Reviews of television sports news programs show women's athletics are mentioned 6.3 percent of the airtime. Furthermore, after increasing slightly since 1989 (5.3 percent of airtime), coverage of women's sports declined from 8.7 percent in 1999 to 6.3 percent of airtime in 2004. In addition, all sports news in one recent study led with men's sports and 94 percent of the anchors were men. The only good news is that women athletes are now less likely to be trivialized and humorous or sexualized images are more unusual than in earlier years (Duncan and Messner 2005).

When women and men athletes are shown, the depictions are gendered. Judith Lorber (2001) has argued that in the media the term *sportswoman* appears to be an oxymoron. Media images of men athletes emphasize strength, power, and violence. Media images of women athletes are more ironic. Images of sportswomen emphasize feminine beauty and grace like those of figure skaters (so that they are not really athletes) or their thin, small, androgynous bodies, like those of gymnasts (so they are not really women but still prepubescent girls) (Lorber 2001).

Although women are still perceived as outsiders in sport, the participation of women in sports skyrocketed in the last quarter of the twentieth century. In the United States in 1971 one of every twenty-seven girls were in high school sports; by 1994 that number was one in three. At the college level, in 1972 31,000 women participated in sports. At the end of the century, 120,000 women did (Oglesby 2001). Donna DeVarona won two gold medals in swimming at the 1964 Olympics but could not get an athletic scholarship to college because there were none available for women swimmers.

TITLE IX. Bringing women into sports has been part of the feminist agenda around the world. At the UN decade convenings of women around the world, sport is cited in the documents as one of the key issues to be addressed. In the United States, sports for women were given a significant push by passage of Title IX. In chapter 5 we explored Title IX and its importance in developing equity for girls and women in academic institutions. Title IX became law in 1971, prohibiting discrimination in education, including discrimination in athletic programs like scholarships and access to sports resources (see Box 11–6). Title IX has had an enormous impact on bringing women into sports in the United States, but problems remain. Spending is still much greater on men compared to women in athletic programs, as 32 percent of recruitment dollars, 36 percent of operating budget, and 43 percent of total athletic scholarship dollars go to women students. Men receive about $133 million more in athletic scholarships than do women (Shakib, Scalir, and Shakib 2003).

In addition, the law remains controversial because some people argue that the demand to level the playing field may have forced some universities to eliminate men's programs when they could not fund women's at an equal level. Since its passage, more than 170 wrestling programs, eighty men's tennis teams, seventy men's gymnastics teams, and forty-five men's track teams have been eliminated. Some maintain that these cuts are the fault of trying to create gender equality in sports on campus.

Others, however, assert that the problem is inequality among different sports rather than attempts to create gender equity. They argue that football and basketball take so much of the sports budget that other men's sports (as well as women's sports) cannot be supported. Many people believe that college football and basketball teams are revenue-generating and self-supporting programs, but two-thirds of college basketball and football programs, in fact, cost more than they generate. If colleges did not spend so much money on these two sports (which are also men's sports), they would have enough money to create gender equity and they could also support a broader range of sports for men as well as women.

Title IX advocates further note that 80 percent of colleges are out of compliance and that recent changes in the law has weakened it. Colleges and universities can now demonstrate whether they have met the interests of the underrepresented minority, women, by conducting an e-mail survey. If women do not respond or if they have already chosen to go to another school because the school did not offer an athletic program in which they were interested, the college can claim that it has met its obligation. This makes Title IX a unique civil rights law because it demands that the underserved minority prove their interest in attaining gender equity. The law does not defend the principle of equality. Rather than the government protecting the principle of equality, the underserved minority must protect its own interest; if it does not, for whatever reason, equality is set aside.

Despite these difficulties with legislation to support women athletes in schools, women have flooded into sports in the past few decades and most people credit Title IX with playing a positive role in these changes. Since 1970, the number of women in intercollegiate sports went from 30,000 to 157,000. The numbers of men have remained almost static from 197,446 in 1984 to 206,573 today (Pennington 2002).

Box 11–6 WHAT DOES YOUR SCHOOL NEED TO DO TO PROVIDE EQUITY ACCORDING TO THE TITLE IX GUIDELINES?

Here are some of the areas that need to be evaluated to make sure that gender equity is being achieved:

1. Select sports and levels of competition that effectively accommodate the interest and abilities of both genders.
2. Provide equipment and supplies.
3. Schedule games and practice time.
4. Provide travel and per diem allowances.
5. Provide opportunities to receive coaching and academic tutoring.
6. Assign and compensate coaches and tutors.
7. Provide locker rooms, practice and competitive facilities.
8. Provide medical and training facilities and services.
9. Provide housing and dining facilities and services.
10. Publicize sports events.

SOURCE: Shulman and Bowen (2001, 315).

College teams now field on average 8.34 women's sports at the college level. At the professional level, women's leagues in basketball, volleyball, and soccer have sprung up. As women have entered sports previously thought of as for men only, the images of women athletes as "skirted skaters" and "tiny tumblers" has been expanded to include "rough muscular women in their 20s and 30s who grunt, grimace and heave each other aside with their hips" (Eitzen and Baca Zinn 2004, 338).

Title IX has had one ironic effect on gender equity. As women's sports have gained support and numbers of participants, coaching and administration positions, which were previously nearly exclusively women, are now being taken by men. As a result, women who aspire to coaching and administration have fewer job opportunities (Acosta and Carpenter 2004). In addition, young women have fewer role models in these positions and gender hierarchies are created with men in dominant positions and women subordinate to them (Eitzen and Baca Zinn 2004).

INTERNATIONAL EFFORTS TO BRING WOMEN INTO SPORTS. At the international level, women in sports have gained attention from people concerned about equality on all fronts. In its recommendations to the nations of the world at the UN Fourth World Conference on Women in Beijing, delegates supported three items that related to sports (Shelton 2001):

- Pay attention to the importance of physical activity and sport in the lives of girls and women.
- Increase the need for increased opportunities for participation for girls and women in sport.
- Ensure that there are more women in leadership positions in sport.

TABLE 11–1 Women in the Olympics, 1900–2000

	Women Participants	Women as % of All Athletes	Nations with No Women Athletes
1900	19	1.6%	
1920	77	2.9	
1936	328	8.1	
1960	610	11.4	
1980	1,125	21.5	
2000	3,947	38.0	12
2004	4,884	44.0	5

SOURCE: Oglesby (2001, 297); Feminist Majority (2004).

In 1995, the International Olympic Committee committed itself to implementing these kinds of goals in its documents and activities. Table 11–1 shows that the Olympics increasingly appears to be meeting its goals of greater equity and participation by women athletes, as we see more women athletes competing from more nations. Table 11–1 shows a rise in women's participation in the Olympics from less than 2 percent of the athletes in the 1900 Olympics to 44 percent in 2004, when women competed in twenty-six of the twenty-eight sports.

BARRIERS TO BRINGING WOMEN INTO SPORTS. Four problems remain in ensuring that women succeed in sports (Shelton 2001). The first problem is sexual harassment. Most girls and women find athletics a source of personal fulfillment, fitness, and fun. However, some are subjected to sexual harassment and even sexual abuse by coaches and managers. This kind of abuse hurts the girls and women who are directly victimized. Sexual abuse and harassment also affects other women and girls who hesitate to participate or whose parents will not allow them to participate for fear of abuse (Shelton 2001).

The second problem is related to the pressure to maintain a low body weight. This sometimes leads to what is called the woman athlete triad: disordered eating, amenorrhea, and osteoporosis (Shelton 2001). Eating disorders are an important health issue for women.

The third problem is the continuing barring of women from sports because of cultural and religious constraints. There are 500 million women in the world who live in nations where they are not allowed to participate in public sporting events and where their Olympic teams have no women athletes (International Olympic Committee 1996). In the 2004 Olympics, four nations still had no women athletes. Atlanta Sydney Athens Plus (ATAP) is an organization that was founded to bring attention to this problem. They have called for excluding nations that do not allow women athletes to participate on their teams. The fourth problem is homophobia and heterosexism.

WOMEN ATHLETES AND HETEROSEXISM. Athletic skills are supposedly part of being masculine. Women athletes, therefore, challenge ideas about femininity. Women who participate in sports, especially sports that are the most masculine, are confronted with assumptions about their sexuality and their gender. Are they women or are they men? Are they heterosexuals or are they lesbians? Women athletes must prove themselves heterosexual and feminine in response to these challenges caused by their competence in a "masculine" realm. Instead of being congratulated on their skills, they are discredited for being "unnatural" women.

You should recall from chapter 4 that *homophobia* is the word commonly used to describe negative and prejudiced ideas about homosexuality and about gay men, bisexuals, and lesbians. Heterosexism is another related term that refers to the institutionalization of hatred and discriminated against gay men and lesbians. Homophobia and heterosexism are powerful controlling mechanisms and people who are labeled gay or lesbian are devalued, stigmatized, discriminated against, and even assaulted or murdered (Pharr 1988; Lenskyj 1991). Both homophobia and heterosexism are found in women's experience in athletics.

Women athletes are often assumed to be lesbians and therefore unacceptable as real women. Research reveals two themes in women athletes' response to this labeling: a silence surrounding the issue of lesbianism and an internalization of the stereotypes concerning lesbianism and women's sport. Both of these disempower women athletes by reducing their ability to form bonds that would enhance their social well-being as well as enhance the strength of their teams' performance. The internalization of the stereotypes—making the ideas their own—diminishes their feelings about themselves and it makes them critical of their teammates for either being lesbians or for not doing enough to prove they are "properly feminine and heterosexual" women (Schur 1984).

Women athletes speak of distancing themselves from teammates who are lesbians or who are not feminine enough. They also often seem to buy into negative stereotypes about lesbians and women athletes as frequently not heterosexual and not feminine (Blinde and Taub 1992). To counteract the stereotypes, athletic women talk about taking to wearing frilly underwear and makeup (Theberge 2000).

The policing of women athlete's gender and sexuality is not only done by themselves, however. Coaches, fundraisers, and others associated with promoting the team and the sports also contribute. Professional women hockey players, for example, on a championship team in Ontario were told by the coach that he would be unable to raise funds for the team if they wore jeans and work boots (Theberge 2000). Women who are involved in coaching children's teams or teaching sports education are especially likely to be policed.

Homophobia and heterosexism make all women athletes constantly prove themselves "real women," which undoubtedly causes them anxiety. Lesbian athletes face even greater pressures because proving themselves real (heterosexual) women means they must deny a part of their humanity. Homophobia and heterosexism may also interfere with the ability of teammates to form strong bonds that would enhance their sense of camaraderie and their teams' athletic strength. Finally, if women athletes do not "toe the line," they face social exclusion by teammates and coaches, as well as loss of economic and career rewards of positions on teams, as coaches and as teachers (Lenskyj 1991).

Venus and Mars Play Sports

This review of gender and athletics has exposed many problems with the connection between masculinity and athletics. The conflation of athletics and masculinity causes problems for men who are forced into participating as proof they are real men. This can have especially negative effects because of the character of sports as violent, aggressive, and competitive. In addition, the tie between masculinity and sports has excluded women. Both of these issues need to be addressed. Both women and men should be allowed to participate in athletics but sports also need to be transformed into more humane activities. Alternative versions of sports already exist and interestingly they are more characteristics of women's sports. Perhaps rather than trying to include women into men's sports our focus should be on integrating men into "feminine" athletics.

Sports can be divided into two types: power and performance sports, which are highly organized and competitive, and participation sports, which are comprised of more loosely defined and organized activities. Research on magazine images and articles shows that men's magazines emphasize performance sports, whereas women's magazines stress participation sports (Curry, Arriagada, and Cornwell 2002).

Performance sports:

1. Use physical strength, power, speed, and stamina to dominate opponents and win.
2. Include ideas that dedication, hard work, risk, and pain are necessary for excellence.
3. Emphasize breaking records.
4. Treat the body as a machine that needs to be monitored and controlled through technology.
5. Define opponents as enemies that must be defeated.
6. Select participants through competition.
7. Organize hierarchies of authorities from owners to coaches to athletes.

Participation sports, on the other hand:

1. Emphasize connections between people, between mind and body, and between physical activity and the environment.
2. Include an ethic of enjoyment, growth, well-being, and expression.
3. Express concern for teammates and opponents.
4. Experience the body as a source of pleasure and well-being.
5. Include participants of many levels of skills, rather than excluding by competition.
6. Facilitate cooperation between athletes and coaches.
7. Accept competition with, rather than against, others (Coakley 2001; Curry, Arriagada, and Cornwell 2002).

REFERENCES

Acosta, Linda Jean, and Vivian Carpenter. 2004. *Title IX*. Champaign, IL: Human Kinetics.

American Psychological Association, Task Force on the Sexualization of Girls. 2007. *Report of the APA Task Force on the Sexualization of Girls*. Washington, DC: American Psychological Association. www.apa.org/pi/wpo/sexualization.html.

Arima, Akie. 2003. Gender stereotypes in Japanese television advertisements. *Sex Roles: A Journal of Research* 49:81–91.

Baca Zinn, Maxine. 1992. Chicano men and masculinity. *Journal of Ethnic Studies* 10 (2): 29–44.

Baker, C. 2005. Images of women's sexuality in advertisements. *Sex Roles* 52:13–27.

Bazzini, D. G., W. D. McIntosh, S. M. Smith, S. Cook, and C. Harris. 1997. The aging woman in popular film: Underrepresented, unattractive, unfriendly, and unintelligent. *Sex Roles* 36:531–43.

Beasley, B., and T. Collins Standley. 2002. Shirts vs. skins: Clothing as an indicator of gender role stereotyping in video games. *Mass Communication and Society* 5 (3): 279–93.

Beynon, John. 2002. *Masculinities and culture*. Philadelphia: Open University.

Blanchette, Aimee. 2006. Disappearing male TV anchors. *St. Paul Minneapolis Star*, September 18.

Blinde, Elaine, and Diane Taub. 1992. Homophobia and women sports. *Sociological Focus* 25 (2): 151–66.

Browne, B. 1998. Gender stereotyping in advertising in children's television in the 1990s. *Journal of Advertising* 27 (1): 83–96.

Burstyn, Varda. 1999. *The rites of men: Manhood, politics, and the culture of sport*. Toronto: University of Toronto Press.

Calvert, Sandra, Victoria Rideout, Jennifer Woolard, Rachel Barr, and Gabrielle Strouse. 2005. Age, ethnicity, and socioeconomic patterns in early computer use: A national survey. *American Behavioral Scientist* 48 (5): 590–607.

Coakley, Jay. 2001. *Sport in society*. 7th ed. New York: McGraw-Hill.

Coltrane, Scott, and Michele Adams. 1997. Work family imagery and gender stereotypes. *Journal of Vocational Behavior* 50:323–47.

Coltrane, Scott, and Melinda Messineo. 2000. The perpetuation of subtle prejudice: Race and gender imagery in 1990s television advertising. *Sex Roles* 42:363–95.

Connell, Robert. 1993. *Rethinking sex: Social theory and sexuality research*. Philadelphia: Temple University Press.

Crosset, Todd. 1990. Masculinity, sexuality and the development of early modern sport. In *Sport, men and the gender order: Critical feminist perspectives*, ed. M. Messner and D. Sabo, 45–54. Champaign, IL: Human Kinetics.

Curry, Timothy, Paula Arriagada, and Benjamin Cornwell. 2002. Images of sport in popular nonsport magazines. *Sociological Perspectives* 45 (4): 397–413.

Day, Jennifer, Alex Janus, and Jessica Davis. 2005. *Computer and Internet use in the United States: 2003*. Washington, DC: U.S. Bureau of the Census.

Doyle, J. 1989. *The male experience*. Dubuque, IL: William C. Brown.

Duffy, M., and J. Gotcher. 1996. Crucial advice on how to get the guy. *Journal of Communication Inquiry* 20:32–48.

Duncan, Margaret, and Michael Messner. 2005. *Gender in televised sport 1989–2004*. Los Angeles, CA: Amateur Athletic Foundation of Los Angeles.

Dunnewind, Stephanie. 2002. TV or not TV, that's the question. *Seattle Times*, June 25.

Eitzen, D. Stanley, and Maxine Baca Zinn. 2004. *In conflict and order: Understanding society*. 10th ed. Boston: Allyn & Bacon.

Emerson, Rana. 2004. Where my girls at? In *The kaleidoscope of gender*, ed. J. Spade and C. Valentine, 259–269. Belmont, CA: Wadsworth.

Escholtz, Sarah and Jana Bufkin. 2001. Violence depicts power and masculinity. *Sociological Forum* 16 (4): 654–71.

Feminist Majority. 2004. *Gender equity in athletics and sport*. http://www.feminist.org/sports/.

Fredrickson, B. L., T. Roberts, S. Noll, D. Quinn, and J. Twenge. 1998. That swimsuit becomes you: Sex differences in self-objectification, restrained eating, and math performance. *Journal of Personality and Social Psychology* 75: 269–84.

Frith, Katherine, and Barbara Mueller. 2003. *Advertising and societies*. New York: Peter Lang.

Fullwood, Sam, III. 2007. Blacks also are longtime critics of rap, hip-hop, forum shows. *Cleveland Plain Dealer*, April 19.

Furnham, A., and T. Mak. 1999. Sex role stereotyping in television commercials. *Sex Roles* 41:413–37.

Gallagher, Margaret. 1995. *Women and the media*. New York: United Nations.

Ganguly-Scrase, Ruchira. 2003. Paradoxes of globalization, liberalization, and gender equality. *Gender & Society* 17 (4): 544–66.

Gapinski, K., K. Brownell, and M. LaFrance, 2003. Body objectification and "fat talk": Effects on emotion, motivation, and cognitive performance. *Sex Roles* 48:377–88.

Gibbons, Sheila. 2004. Inequities persist for women in the media. *WomenENews*, January 21.

Glick, P., S. Larsen, C. Johnson, and H. Branstiter. 2005. Evaluations of sexy women in low- and high-status jobs. *Psychology of Women Quarterly* 29:389–95.

Goffman, Erving. 1979. *Gender advertisements*. Boston: Harvard University Press.

Goldman, Robert, and Stephen Papson. 2004."'If you let me play:' Nike ads and gender". Pp. 71–74. In Sociology of Gender A. Wharton (ed.) Boston:Blackwell

Gosovic, Branislav. 2000. Global intellectual hegemony and the international development agenda. *International Social Science Journal* 15 (4): 447–56.

Graueurholz, E., and A. King. 1997. Primetown sexual harassment. *Violence Against Women* 3:129–48.

Gutmann, Matthew. 1996. *The meanings of macho*. Berkeley: University of California Press.

Hall, Stuart. 1973. *Encoding and decoding in the television discourse unknown binding*.

Hargittai, Eszter, and Steven Shafer. 2006. Differences in actual and perceived online skills: The role of gender. *Social Science Quarterly* 87 (2): 432–48.

Harris, Ian. 1995. *Messages men hear*. New York: Taylor & Francis.

Hasbrook, Cynthia, and Othello Harris. 2000. Wrestling with gender: Physicality and masculinities among inner-city first and second graders. In *Masculinities, gender relations, and sports*, ed. J. McKay, M. Messner, and D. Sabo, 13–30. Thousand Oaks, CA: Sage.

Hebl, M., E. King, and J. Lin. 2004. The swimsuit becomes us all: Ethnicity, gender, and vulnerability to self objectification. *Personality and Social Psychology Bulletin* 30:1322–31.

Hondagneu-Sotelo, Pierrette. 1992. Overcoming patriarchal constraints: The reconstruction of gender relations among Mexican immigrant women and men. *Gender & Society* 6:398–415.

Impett, E., D. Schooler, and D. Tolman. 2006. To be seen and not heard: Femininity ideology and adolescent girls' sexual health. *Archives of Sexual Behavior* 2:628–46.

International Olympic Committee. 1996. *Preliminary report*. International Olympic Committee's First World Conference on Women and Sport, Lausanne, Switzerland.

Jackson, Camile. 2005. Misogyny and rap: "Chickenhead" means you. April 11. Montgomery, AL: Southern Poverty Law Center http://www.tolerance.org/news/article_tol.jsp?id=1196.

——. 2007. The ABCs of hip hop. March. Montgomery, AL: Southern Poverty Law Center http://www.tolerance.org/teach/printar.jsp?p=0&ar=815&pi=apg

Katz, Jackson. 1995. Reconstructing masculinity in the locker room: The mentors in a violence prevention project. *Harvard Educational Review* 65 (2): 163–74.

Kellner, David. 2003. *Media spectacle*. New York: Routledge.

Kelly, Joe, and Stacey Smith. 2006. Where the girls aren't. Los Angeles: seejane.org.

Kimmel, Michael. 1990. Baseball and the reconstitution of American masculinity, 1880–1920. In *Sport, men and the gender order: Critical feminist perspectives*, ed. M. Messner and D. Sabo, 55–66. Champaign, IL: Human Kinetics.

——. 1992. Reading men: Men, masculinity and publishing. *Contemporary Sociology* 21:162–71.

Kitwana, Bakari. 2002. It's time for a renewed attack on hip-hop's women-hating. *Cleveland Plain Dealer*, December 2.

Klein, Alan. 2000. Dueling machos: Masculinity and sport in Mexican baseball. In *Masculinities, gender relations, and sports*, ed. J. McKay, M. Messner, and D. Sabo, 67–86. Thousand Oaks, CA: Sage.

Larson, M. 2001. Interactions, activities and gender in children's television commercials. *Journal of Broadcasting and Electronic Media* 45:41–65.

Lauzen, Martha, and David Dozier. 2005. Recognition and respect revisited. *Mass Communication and Society* 8 (3): 241–56.

Lenhart, A., L. Rainie, and O. Lewis. 2001. Teenage life online: The rise of the instant-message generation and the Internet's impact on friendships and family relationships. Washington, DC: Pew Internet & American Life Project www.pewinternet.org/pdfs/PIP_Teens_Report.pdf.

Lenskyj, Helen. 1991. Combating homophobia in sports and physical education. *Sport Journal* 8 (1): 61–69.

Lindner, K. 2004. Images of women in general interests and fashion advertisements from 1955 to 2002. *Sex Roles* 51:409–21.

Lont, Cynthia. 2001. The influence of the media on gender images. In *Gender mosaics*, ed. D. Vannoy, 114–22. Los Angeles: Roxbury.

Lorber, Judith. 2001. The social construction of gender. In *Race, class and gender in the United States*, ed. P. Rothenberg, 47–57. New York: Worth.

Lorde, Audre. 1984. *Sister outsider*. Trumansburg, NY: Crossing Press.

Marger, Martin. 2002. *Social inequality*. 2nd ed. Boston: McGraw-Hill.

McKinley, Graham. 1997. *Beverly Hills 90210*. Philadelphia: University of Pennsylvania Press.

Messner, Michael. 1992. *Power at play: Sports and the problem of masculinity*. Boston: Beacon.

——. 2001. Boyhood, organized sports and the construction of masculinities. In *Men's lives*. 5th ed., ed. M. Kimmel and M. Messner, 88–99. Boston: Allyn & Bacon.

Messner, Michael, M. Dunbar, and D. Hunt, D. 2000. The televised sports manhood formula. *Journal of Sport & Social Issues* 24 (4): 380–94.

Messner, Michael, Margaret Duncan, and Kerry Jensen. 1993. Separating the men from the girls: The gendered language of televised sport. *Gender & Society* 7:121–37.

Moraga, Cherie. 1983. *Loving in the war years*. Boston: Southend Press.

National Organization for Women (NOW). 1972. *Women in the wasteland fight back*. Washington, DC: NOW, National Capital Area Chapter.

——. 2000. *Watch out, listen up!* Media Activist Campaign, Feminist Primetime Report. Washington, DC: NOW. www.now.org/issues/medical/watchout/report.

New York Times. 1999. As G.I. Joe bulks up, concern for the 98 pound weakling. May 30.

Oglesby, Cynthia. 2001. Intersections: Women's sport leadership and feminist praxis. In *Women on power: Leadership redefined*, ed. S. Freeman, S. Bourque, and C. Shelton, 290–312. Boston: Northeastern University Press.

Ono, Hiroshi, and Madeline Zavodny. 2005. Gender differences in IT usage. *Sociological Perspectives* 48 (1): 105–33.

Patterson, Maurice, and Richard Elliott. 2004. Negotiating masculinities. *Consumption, Markets and Culture* 5 (3): 231–46.

Pennington, Bill. 2002. Men's teams benched as colleges level the field. *New York Times*, May 9.

Pharr, Suzanne. 1988. *Homophobia*. Inverness, CA: Chardon Press.

Roberts, D., U. Roehr, and V. Rideout. 2005. *Generation M: Media in the lives of 8–18 year olds*. Menlo Park, CA: Kaiser Family Foundation.

Roy, Abnik. 2005. The male gaze in Indian TV commercials. In *Women in the media*, ed. T. Carilli and J. Campbell, 3–18. New York: University Press of America.

Sabo, Donald, and Joe Panepinto. 1990. Football ritual and the social reproduction of masculinity. In *Sport, men and the gender order: Critical feminist perspectives*, ed. M. Messner and D. Sabo, 115–26. Champaign, IL: Human Kinetics.

Sapiro, Virginia. 2002. *Women in American society: An introduction to women's studies*. New York: McGraw-Hill.

Schur, Edwin. 1984. *Labeling women deviant*. New York: McGraw-Hill.

SEICUS. 2004. *Guidelines for comprehensive sexuality education*. 3rd ed. New York: SEICUS. www.iecus.org/pubs/guidelines/guidelines.pdf.

Shakib, Sohaila, Kevin Scalir, and Kuros A. Shakib. 2003. Title IX: Facts, figures, myths and reality. *Network News Sociologists for Women in Society* 20(1):18-22.

Shelton, Christine. 2001. From Beijing to Atlanta and beyond: The international challenges for women in sport. Pp. 171–198 In *Women on power: Leadership redefined*, ed. S. Freeman, S. Bourque, and C. Shelton. Boston: Northeastern University Press.

Shulman, James, and William Bowen. 2001. *The game of life*. Princeton, NJ: Princeton University Press.

Signorielli, Nancy. 1990. Television's mean and dangerous world. In *Cultivation analysis: New directions in media effects research*, ed. N. Signorielli and M. Morgan, 85–106. Newbury Park, CA: Sage.

Stern, Susannah, and Dana Mastro. 2004. Gender portrayals across the life span: A content analytic look at broadcast commercials. *Mass Communication and Society* 7 (2): 215–36.

Stone, Linda, and Nancy McKee. 2002. *Gender and culture in America*. Upper Saddle River, NJ: Prentice Hall.

Strate, Lance. 2001. Beer commercials: A manual on masculinity. In *Men's lives*. 5th ed., ed. M. Kimmel and M. Messner, 505–14. Boston: Allyn & Bacon.

Theberge, Nancy. 2000. *Higher goals: Women's ice hockey and the politics of gender*. Albany: State University New York Press.

Thomas, Evan, and Gregory Vitica. 1998. Fallout from media fiasco. *Newsweek* July 20:24–26.

Tuchman, Gaye, Arlene Kaplan Daniels, and James Benet. 1978. *Hearth and home: Images of women in the mass media*. New York: Oxford University Press.

Uray, Nimet, and Sebnam Burnaz. 2003. An analysis of the portrayal of gender roles in Turkish television advertisements. *Sex Roles* 48:77–88.

Ward, L., and R. Rivadeneyra. 2002. Dancing, strutting and bouncing in cars. Paper presented at the annual meeting of the American Psychological Association, Chicago.

Watterson, John. 2000. *College football history, spectacle and controversy*. Baltimore: Johns Hopkins University Press.

Wharton, Amy. 2005. *The sociology of gender*. Malden, MA: Blackwell.

Whitson, David. 1990. Sport in the social construction of masculinity. In *Sport, men and the gender order: Critical feminist perspectives*, ed. M. Messner and D. Sabo, 19–30. Champaign, IL: Human Kinetics.

Young, Kevin, and Philip White. 2000. Researching sports injury: Reconstructing dangerous masculinities. In *Masculinities, gender relations and sport*, ed. J. McKay, M. Messner, and D. Sabo, 108–26. Thousand Oaks, CA: Sage.

Zurawik, David. 2007. A daring look at hip hop. *Baltimore Sun*, February 20. http://www.baltimoresun .com/entertainment/tv/bal-to.hiphop20feb20,0,768281.story.

12

—

RELIGION

THE PROMISE KEEPERS

Established in 1990 by Bill McCartney, a former football coach for the University of Colorado, the Promise Keepers are dedicated to introducing a new man to America and reestablishing men as the leaders of their families. Based on their religious beliefs, the Promise Keepers support distinct and separate roles for women and men in families and in their communities. Men must stand up and be responsible, strong leaders to whom their wives and children can look up.

A book outlining their objectives, *Seven Promises of the Promise Keeper*, tells men:

> I can hear you saying "I want to be a spiritually pure man. Where do I start?" The first thing you do is sit down with your wife and say something like this: "Honey, I've made a terrible mistake. I've given you my role. I gave up leading this family and forced you to take my place. Now I must reclaim that role." Don't misunderstand what I'm saying here. I'm not suggesting that you ask for your role back. I'm urging you to take it back.... There can be no compromise here. If you're going to lead, you must lead. Be sensitive. Listen. Treat the lady gently and lovingly. But lead! (Phillips 1994, 79–80)

The Promise Keepers know that their ideas go against the grain in the contemporary United States, but they insist they must keep on. At one of their mass rallies, Gregg, a new Promise Keeper, stated:

> I've always felt that I should be assuming the leadership role in my family. But for a variety of reasons I have believed that I would be considered an egotistical dictator if I tried to operate in my family that way nowadays. Promise Keepers not only give men permission to do what I have felt to be right but encourages me and shows me practical ways to do it without offending my wife. (quoted in Abraham 1994, 21)

The Promise Keepers believe that women currently dominate American society and this unnatural situation is destroying our nation. Tony Evans, a spokesperson for the group, says, "The demise of our community and culture is the fault of sissified men who have been overly influenced by women. PK [Promise Keepers] is a version of a new kind of "'Muscular Christianity'" (Abraham 1994). Bill McCartney explains, "You do know, don't you, that we are raising our children at a time when it's an effeminate society. It's not the proper climate. We need young boys that are launched to be men, and that has to be imitated for them by Godly men."

A multimillion-dollar enterprise, the Promise Keepers have met many of their goals in the last decade within their families, spending more time with their wives and children and taking back the reins of the family and their place at the head of the table. Now the Promise Keepers are looking to spread their ideas beyond their families. They have marched on Washington to bring the word of their God on gender to the politically powerful. They plan to reach across America and even to other nations, shifting from their inward concentration on families to focus outward to political leaders whom they hope to influence on questions of gender and families like sex education, abortion, and gay marriage.

The Promise Keepers are an example of a growing religious movement around the world to a more fundamentalist practice of religion with precise views on how to live by the word of God and especially how women and men should behave and interact with each other. The Promise Keepers are a Christian group based in the United States, but they are part of a larger international movement among many religions in many nations.

What do you think about the message about gender given by the Promise Keepers? Are the Promise Keepers fundamentalists? What exactly is fundamentalism? Can only Christians be fundamentalists? What religions are most prevalent in the world today and what do they have to say about what it is to be a man or woman of god? How do women and men participate in religion?

This chapter addresses these questions by reviewing the dominant religions and the images, rituals, and activities of men and women that are part of their beliefs. The chapter begins by discussing what religion is and how important it is in people's lives. Included in this is a discussion of the fundamentalist branches of some religions. We then move to talking about less dominant spiritual communities and their view of gender and religion. The chapter concludes with a review of classical sociological theorists' ideas about the connection between religion and society.

WHAT IS A RELIGION?

Religion is an important social institution that fulfills many roles. Religions provide humans with answers to the questions we find most serious: Why are we on earth? Is there life after death? What do we need to do to live a good life? Religions also offer practical support, such as providing rituals to mark crucial events like birth, death, and marriage. They bring us emotional comfort or solace when we face difficulties in our lives. In addition, religions can enhance social solidarity and make us feel part of our community (Reineke 1995). In all of these aspects of religion, gender is reflected. Men and women are often required to behave differently to be considered godly. Men and women participate in religious institutions in different ways as leaders and as followers. Men and women play different roles in religious rituals and texts.

Religious institutions like other social institutions play a dual contradictory role in society as both vehicles of social control and of social change. The Promise Keepers in the opening scenario, for example, are part of a religion that seeks to control behavior and to maintain inequality between women and men. Religions, however, have also served as key resources in justifying, inspiring, and offering material comfort and support, places to meet, and forums from which to challenge inequality.

Religion is somewhat different from other social institutions because of its connection to something greater than humans or even the earth. Religions call on superhuman ideas and beings. Participating in religious institutions and especially challenging religious institutions takes on great significance because for many people going against the institution not only unbalances human relationships, it rocks the cosmos (Reineke 1995; Gerami 1996).

Importance of Religion in the World and in the United States

Religion is of great consequence in many societies, but it is especially significant in contemporary American society (Saad 1996). Among Americans, 88 percent say religion is very important or fairly important to them; 96 percent say they believe in God or a universal spirit; 85 percent believe the Bible is the word of God; 74 percent believe in life after death; and 59 percent say they believe that the apocalyptic prophecies in the Book of Revelation will come true (Sapiro 2003). Nearly half (47 percent) of Americans say that it is necessary to believe in God in order to be moral and have good values (Kohut and Rogers 2002).

Not many societies are as religious as people are in the United States. In a global survey, the United States ranks as the fifth most religious nation in the world behind Nigeria, Poland, India, and Turkey and ahead of thirty-seven other nations from Ireland to Brazil and Japan. The United States is also relatively narrow in its range of religious beliefs. Among Americans, 92 percent claim a specific religion and 70 percent say they belong to a particular church or other religious organization. Table 12–1 shows the distribution among religions for people in the United States who are overwhelmingly Christians (82 percent). The fact that such a large proportion of Americans identify themselves as Christians means that the United States is more Christian than Israel is Jewish, Egypt is Muslim, or India is Hindu.

TABLE 12–1 What Religion Are Americans?

%	Religion
82%	Christian
1%	Jewish
<1%	Muslim
3%	Other
8%	Atheist and agnostic
10%	No preference or no answer

SOURCE: Kohut and Rogers (2002).

Five Big Religions

Americans mostly belong to the world's biggest religious group, Christianity. Four other religions in addition to Christianity are currently the most important five religions in the world, with 73 percent of the world's population identifying with one of five major world religions. Table 12–2 shows the worldwide distribution of religions. Table 12–2 also tells a little about the religions. Christianity is the largest religion. Judaism has a small number internationally but is the third largest religion in the United States. Islam, Christianity, and Judaism are all part of the Abrahamic tradition because of the importance of the prophet Abraham in all three religions. Jews and Christians share the same sacred text in the Talmud or Old Testament of the Bible. Jews and Muslims view Jesus as an important prophet but they do not believe he was the son of God as Christians do. The gods and prophets of these religions are all men or at least masculine beings.

Founded approximately 6,000 years ago, Hinduism is the oldest religion among the five and it is polytheist, which means Hindus worship many deities, some masculine, some feminine, and some transgendered. A handful of Hindu deities are especially important, but no one god or goddess is most important. Buddhists do not believe in a deity. Instead they believe that godliness is possible for all humans, regardless of gender, who work to achieve that status. More than one-quarter of the world's people (26 percent) profess religions other

TABLE 12–2 Big Five Religions in the World

Religion	Number of Members	% of Population	Major Deity	Text
Christianity	2 billion	33%	God/Jesus Jesus son of God Born 04 BC	Bible
Islam	1.2 billion (7 million in U.S.)	20%	God Muhammad messenger from God Born 570 AD	Qu'ran
Judaism	15 million (6 million in U.S.)		God	Talmud
Hinduism	800 million (1.4 million in U.S.)	14%	Many Gods and Goddesses	
Buddhism	350 million	6%	non-theist all humans have potential for godliness Siddhartha Guatama became the "Buddha" Born 563 AD	
Other (or no) religions		26%		

SOURCE: Eitzen and Baca Zinn (2004).

than the big five or they have no religion at all. Gender is a part of the ideas, rituals, activities, and organization of all of these religions.

RELIGIOUS IDEAS ABOUT GENDER: SEPARATE AND UNEQUAL

Gender is expressed in religious ideas in two ways. First, religions teach that women and men are separate kinds of people. They proclaim and explain that women and men have different missions and standards of behavior. Second, religions often maintain that women and men are not only different, but that women are lesser than men. Although women and men may be equal in relation to the deity, women are subordinate to men (Sapiro 2003). Box 12–1 shows a set of quotations from sacred texts that illustrate gender inequity in five religions.

One example of this kind of separate and unequal perception of women and men shows up in religious explanations about the emergence of human life. Eighty percent of societies that have developed supernatural theories about the emergence of humans assert that their god, gods, or other spiritual force beyond human reason, ordain that men should rule over women, and that a male divine force is the origin of life. In the creation story in the sacred texts of Jews, Christians, and Muslims, this is illustrated in the Genesis story. God creates Adam to rule over the earth and animal kingdom. Eve, a physical outgrowth of Adam, is created to serve Adam. The story tells us that men and women have different roles and in their relationship to each other, women are subordinate to men (Daly 1968; Sanday 1981; Freedman 2002). In addition to the story of the original relationships between god and man and god and woman, all three dominant religions in United States worship a masculine god and recognize only men as prophets.

Buddhism, another of the big five internationally, is a little different from the three already mentioned because it was not originally associated with the subordination of women. However, Buddhism among many Buddhists today has come to incorporate gender inequality. Buddhists do not worship a masculine deity and they believe that women and men are equally able to achieve the highest spiritual level of Buddhism. Buddhism began as a gender-neutral story of enlightenment and retains that philosophical belief. As it has developed, however, the religion has come to emphasize masculine qualities of the Buddha and now mandates that women must obey men (Freedman 2002). Buddha himself asserted that men and women had equal potential for enlightenment but some Buddhist writings argue that women are impure and should submit to their husbands, honoring their demands. In addition, the organization of the religion gives men monks higher status than women monks and women monks must adhere to eight regulations spelling out their lower status. The regulations require that the women treat all men monks as their superiors and seek out men monks for instruction. Women, in contrast, cannot instruct or admonish men monks (Burn 2000).

These beliefs about the origins of humanity and the different connection between god and men and god and women are important not only as a set of ideas, but they have become important as bases for organizing religious institutions. Catholicism, for example, asserts that men are superior to women because men are more like god and, therefore, do not

> ### Box 12–1 QUOTES FROM THE WORLD'S RELIGIONS
> ### ON THE STATUS OF WOMEN AND MEN
>
> - **Confuscianism:** One hundred women are not worth a single testicle (Confucius 551–479 BC).
> - **Hinduism:** In childhood a woman must be subject to her father; in youth to her husband; when her husband is dead to her sons. A woman must never be free of subjugation (the Hindu Code of Manu (circa 100 AD).
> - **Judaism and Christianity:** If . . . the tokens of virginity are not found in the young women, then they shall bring out the young women to the door of her father/s house, and the men of the city shall stone her to death with stones because has wrought folly . . . so you shall purge the evil from the midst of you (Deuteronomy 22:20–21 Hebrew Bible/Old Testament).
> - **Christianity:** Let a woman learn in silence with all submissiveness, I permit no woman to teach or to have authority over men; she is to keep silent (I Timothy 2:11–15 New Testament).
> - **Islam:** Men are superior to women (The Qu'ran circa 650).
> - **Protestantism:** Women should remain at home, sit still, keep house, and bear and bring up children (Martin Luther, 1438–1546).
> - **Protestantism:** Woman in her greatest perfection was made to serve and obey man, not rule and command him (John Knox, 1505–1572).
>
> SOURCE: Bowman (1983, 28–29).

allow women to become priests. Furthermore, because women cannot be priests they cannot become bishops, archbishops, or popes.

Catholic leaders like John Paul II, who was pope from 1978 to 2005, argued that the ban on women priests is "founded on the word of God and that it is to be held always, everywhere and by all" (Steinfels 1995, 1). The Pope maintained that when the priest serves communion, he is *in persona Christi*. That is, the priest is thought to function "in the person of Christ" and it is essential, therefore, for him to share the same sex as Jesus. Sixty percent of American Catholics disagree and think the ordination of women would be a good thing (Steinfels 1995).

ISLAM

All the major religions today have treated women in unjust ways. Islam is sometimes held up as especially antiwomen. But are these images of Islam reasonable (Armstrong 2002)? When Islam was first founded by Mohammed, Muslims granted women a number of rights that were not available to women in pre-Islam societies. Islam actually acted as an impetus for greater equality for women in an area of the world and a moment in history when women, globally, were highly restricted. Islam emerged around the year 600, giving women legal rights of inheritance and divorce that Western women would not receive until the nineteenth century.

Muslims use two major sources of religious information. The first is the Qur'an, which many Muslims believe is the word of god as it was recorded by Mohammed during the early seventh century. The second source for moral and spiritual guidance are the hadiths, which are secondhand reports of Mohammed's personal traditions and lifestyles, which were collected soon after his death to help Muslims apply the dictates of the Qur'an. Together the Qur'an and the hadiths constitute the source of Muslim law (Read and Bartkowski 2000). In some areas, these documents definitely impose inferior status on women:

- A woman's testimony is only worth half that of men in a Muslim court.
- A daughter can only inherit half the share of a son.
- A Muslim man may marry a non-Muslim woman, but a Muslim woman may only marry a Muslim man.
- A man may marry up to four wives.
- Only men have been Muslim clergy, although very recently a few women have become Imams in South Africa, China, and other places.

These religious beliefs affect governmental policy in countries where Islam is the dominant religion. Egypt, for example, ratified the United Nations Convention on the Elimination of All Forms of Discrimination Against Women statement (CEDAW). All nations (185) in the world have ratified CEDAW except the United States, Somalia, Sudan, Tonga, Palau, Nauru, Iran, Qatar, and Brunei. The Egyptians, however, added an exception in their signing: "out of respect for the sanctity deriving from firm religious beliefs which govern marital relations in Egypt and which may not be called into question." This exception makes a husband responsible to provide financial support for his wife in a divorce. Wives do not have this obligation and as a result, "the sharia therefore restricts the wife's rights to divorce by making it contingent on the judge's ruling, where as no such restriction is laid down in the case of the husband." As we noted in chapter 7 on families, in many Muslim societies, husbands can seek a divorce without a judge's approval, although women can only seek a divorce if a judge declares it valid. Women, however, can receive financial support from their ex-husbands after a divorce but men cannot seek such support from their former wives (Deif 2004).

Some of the restrictions on women that are identified as part of Islam, however, are not part of Muslim sacred texts. There is nothing in the Qur'an that says anything about seclusion, education, or paid work for women. Islam does not demand that women be secluded. Seeking knowledge is mandatory for all Muslims and education is no less important for women. Islam does not oppose women's entry into paid employment (Sanad and Tessler 1990).

Hijab

Non-Muslim people often mention veils as evidence of the oppression of women in Islam. Muslims use the term *hijab* for the many variations of this practice today. Some women wear a hijab scarf to cover their heads as part of a contemporary stylish dress. Some wear a niqab across the lower part of their face, and others dress in long thick black robes called a burqa that covers their entire bodies, with only a small slit through which to see. How do these practices fit with the religion of Islam? Where did they come from?

The Qur'an does not make wearing a hijab obligatory and many Muslim women do not wear any special head covering. Not until about three centuries after Mohammad died did wearing a hijab or seclusion of Muslim women in harems emerge. It began at this time because Islam was developing among the Greeks of Christian Byzantium where women had long been secluded and wearing head and body coverings. Muslim women began to copy the veiling of the upper class Christian women in their community (Armstrong 2002).

In the nineteenth century, colonial armies, accompanied by government personnel and Christian missionaries, came from Europe to places like Egypt as conquerors and occupiers. They claimed that the clothing that covered the head and body of Muslim women who lived in Muslim countries was a barbarous practice. Christian missionaries in this same time period were trying to convince people in Africa and Polynesia that they should cover themselves with Western clothes because their method of dress was sinful. Remember this was the same time period when women in the West wore long, cumbersome, multilayered gowns with unhealthy cinches to show off their waists. Nevertheless, Western military, political, and religious leaders argued that unless the Muslim clothing styles were abandoned and Middle Eastern women became more like the women of the West, the countries would never advance in the modern world (Armstrong 2002).

Lord Cromer, the Consul General of Egypt, was especially outspoken about the need to "liberate" Middle Eastern women by causing them to shed their head coverings. Cromer, ironically, was also an outspoken critic of the suffrage movements in the Western world, where women were being beaten and force-fed in prisons because they wanted to vote. Cromer was a founding member of the London Men's League for Opposing Women's Suffrage at the same time he was an outspoken critic of the hijab of women in Egypt. Although he professed to be acting in defense of women's rights in Egypt, his commitment to equality is questionable. Middle-Eastern women wearing the hijab were not convinced that shedding it would open the door to freedom. In addition, the history of the association of colonial occupiers with the call to remove the head coverings from women in the Middle East resulted in the hijab becoming an important symbol of Islam and a sign of cultural integrity among the people in the occupied nations. Wearing a hijab was one way that women could stand up for their culture and resist the efforts of oppressive forces from other nations (Armstrong 2002).

The belief that a hijab does not represent oppression and in fact may mean quite the opposite to those who wear them is still an important aspect of the hijab for many Muslims today. In the 1950s in South Africa, Muslim women wore short skirts and did not cover their heads. When the Iranian people challenged the rule of the Shah of Iran who was put in place by Western forces, especially the United States, the Muslim women of South Africa began wearing long shirts and scarves on their heads as a sign of solidarity with the Iranian people against oppression and neo-colonial rule. For these women, wearing certain types of clothing and covering their hair did not represent oppression. Rather, it signified the women's assertion of their political beliefs. The hijab, however, is not a settled issue in Muslim communities and much debate continues to center on the importance of clothing.

How do Muslim women in the United States today feel about the hijab? In a study of Muslim women in Texas, the women gave two reasons for wearing a hijab (Read and Bartkowski 2000; see Box 12–2). First, they maintained that wearing one was a way of

Box 12–2 MUSLIM WOMEN VOICE THEIR OPINIONS OF GENDER AND ISLAM

When American women were asked in a Gallup poll (2005) "What do you admire least about the Muslim or Islamic world?" the top response was "gender inequality." Face-to-face surveys of 1,000 women were conducted in each of eight predominantly Muslim countries—Egypt, Iran, Jordan, Lebanon, Morocco, Pakistan, Saudi Arabia, and Turkey—to find out their opinions. When asked about their own societies, the majority of women in several predominantly Muslim countries disagreed. Muslim women do not think they are conditioned to accept second-class status or view themselves as oppressed (Andrews 2006).

They believe they should have the right to vote without influence, work outside the home, and serve in the highest levels of government. They did not see gender issues as a priority in their community because they believe that other issues are more pressing.

When asked what they resented most about their own societies, they answered that a lack of unity among Muslim nations, violent extremism, and political and economic corruption were their main concerns. Veils, which some Westerners claim are tools of oppression, were never mentioned in the women's answers. Only a handful (Saudi Arabia had the most, at 5 percent) mentioned gender issues at all.

Concerning women's rights in general, most Muslim women polled admired the political equality they associated with the West. Seventy-eight percent of Moroccan women, 71 percent of Lebanese women, and 48 percent of Saudi women polled linked legal equality with the West. A majority of the respondents, however, were concerned about the problems of promiscuity, pornography, and public indecency, which they also associate with the West.

One of the most pronounced themes to emerge from the study was the great importance Muslims attach to their faith. An overwhelming majority of the Muslim women polled in each country cited "attachment to moral and spiritual values" as the best aspect of their own societies. In Pakistan, 53 percent of the women polled said attachment to their religious beliefs was their country's most admirable trait. Similarly, in Egypt, 59 percent of the women surveyed cited love of their religion as the best aspect.

They also agree that Islamic principles should guide public policy. Majorities of women in all countries (Morocco 98 percent, Jordan 92 percent, Egypt 90 percent, Iran 82 percent, Lebanon 69 percent, Pakistan 68 percent) surveyed except Turkey (30 percent), which has a secular government said, "Sharia should be one source or the only source of legislation" (Mogahed 2006).

critiquing Western colonialism in the Middle East. Second, they argued it was an important aspect of their religious beliefs regarding gender differences and the need for women to protect their own modesty as well as control the behavior of men. However, covering their hair was not associated with believing that women were inferior to men or should be subordinated to them. Both Muslim women who wore a hijab and those who did not in Texas had similar strong opinions in favor of marital equality and especially women's rights in public life.

Religious advocates of the hijab assert that veils and modest clothing are useful because men often have difficulty controlling their sexual activity when they are around women. They argue, furthermore, that women are not as driven by their sexual urges and are responsible for controlling men's sexuality and protecting themselves. The hijab provides an effective means of protection. One Muslim woman from Texas who advocates women covering their hair and head said, "If the veil did not exist, many evil things would happen. Boys would mix with girls, which will result in evil things" (Read and Bartkowski 2000, 404).

Her argument has been criticized by those who claim that it makes women responsible for men's sexual issues and hides women from the outside world in a way that prevents them from fully participating. Covering their hair and heads demonstrates women's obedience to the tenets of Islam and is a sign of how Muslim women disdain profane, immodest, and consumerist cultural customs of the West. However, it also marks a clear distinction between women and men and symbolizes the place of women in the home rather than in more public spaces (Read and Bartkowski 2000).

Covering one's hair and head, however, has an additional twist in contemporary society. Some women argue that veiling is a vehicle for greater participation of women in society and more equal treatment by men. Muslim women in the Texas study assert that wearing a hijab allows them greater access to public life rather than preventing them from participating fully. One woman said, "Women who wear the hijab are not excluded from society. They are freer to move around in society because of it" (Read and Bartkowski 2000, 405). Another stated, "If you're in hijab then someone sees you and treats you accordingly. I feel more free. Especially men, they don't look at your appearance—they appreciate your intellectual abilities. They respect you" (405).

Muslim women who oppose covering their hair and head argue that the hijab represents oppressive social hierarchies and male domination. They also argue that covering their hair and head is a cultural practice, not a religious necessity. They emphasize the fact that the hijab originated outside of Muslim circles because it was practiced in non-Muslim communities in the Middle East long before the arrival of Islam. It is not a Muslim invention and, therefore, they believe it should not be used today as a standard of Muslim religiosity. Muslim women in Texas who did not wear a hijab maintained that other religious practices are more important. One said, "Being a good Muslim means believing in one God, no idolatry, following the five pillars of Islam and believing in Mohammed." Another explained, "Muslim society doesn't exist on the veil. Without the veil you would still be Muslim" (Read and Bartkowski 2000, 409). In addition, critics of the hijab point out that it originated and persists because of men's difficulties in managing their sexuality. One Texas woman argued, "Women are made to believe that the veil is religious. In reality, it's all political" (Read and Bartkowski 2000, 408). They also question the scriptural arguments made by some pro-hijab Muslims. The unveiled Muslim women counter that the Qur'an calls for both men and women to guard their modesty.

The women in this study who did not wear a hijab, however, were careful not to criticize women who did. The unveiled Muslim women said they "construe hijab as a product of patriarchal oppression and assorted masculine hang-ups (e.g., struggles with sexuality, a preoccupation with domination and control) and veiled women cannot legitimately be impugned for wearing hijab" (Read and Bartkowski 2000, 410).

FUNDAMENTALISMS

Other religions have equally complex and sometimes confusing views of gender. Christianity is the dominant religion in the United States and includes a broad range of sects with a variety of beliefs and practices. In some Christian churches women are fully participant and important leaders at the highest level, whereas in others women are not allowed to serve Eucharist, lead the congregation, hear confessions, baptize, enter the holy of holies, and preach to or teach men (Shaw and Lee 2004).

In the first decades of the practice of Christianity among European immigrants in the United States, both Puritans of the northern colonies and Anglicans of the south based their ideas about gender on their reading of the Old Testament. They asserted that women are supposed to be helpmates for their husbands, be fruitful and multiply, and submit to their husbands. Men were supposed to be the religious authority and the leader of their families (Sapiro 2003).

Among many Christians these ideas persist. In 2000, the Southern Baptist Convention declared:

> The husband and wife are of equal worth before God, since both are created in God's image. The marriage relationship models the way God relates to his people. A husband is to love his wife as Christ loved the church. He has the God-given responsibility to provide for, to protect and to lead his family. A wife is to submit herself graciously to the servant leadership of her husband even as the church willingly submits to the headship of Christ. She, being in the image of God as is her husband and thus equal to him, has the God-given responsibility to respect her husband and to serve as helper in managing the household and nurturing the next generation. (Southern Baptist Convention 2000)

The most conservative views of gender come from religions that are fundamentalist. The term *fundamentalism* was first used to describe Christians in the early twentieth century who professed a belief in the literal word of the Bible as a document without error (Ingersoll 2003). The term fundamentalism is the word now used to identify many religions that emphasize a conservative view of religion and of gender. We speak of Christian fundamentalists, Jewish fundamentalists, Muslim fundamentalists, and Hindu fundamentalists, for example. Fundamentalist movements are far from monolithic. They tend to converge, however, in their opposition to women's autonomy (Helie-Lucas 1994; Basu 2004).

Gerami (1996) studied three forms of fundamentalism—Christians in the United States, Muslims in Egypt, and Hindus in India—and found they were similar in a number of ways. First they all maintain that the ideal woman is submissive, asexual, and selfless. Motherhood must be the core of women's identity and family the center of women's lives. Families are a key feature of controlling and protecting female sexuality, which they believe is dangerous and destructive. Families must, therefore, conform to certain standards and women need to conform to those families.

Gerami (1996) argues that fundamentalism has been a conservative and discriminatory force in many people's lives, but ironically, has also sometimes been a force for progressive change in reducing gender inequity. Fundamentalism has inadvertently created potential for feminist change because it has made women the center of attention in political debates, especially in the Middle East. What women wear, whether they appear in public alone, and whether they should be employed or vote have all been given center stage in political controversies regarding the relationship between religion and government.

This debate has furthermore encouraged women to examine the sacred texts as part of being good women. As they have done so, some are beginning to interpret them from a more feminine or feminist point of view. Those women who have interpreted the texts in conservative ways have become an important political force in the struggle to make governments less secular. Those women who have interpreted them in more progressive ways are helping to shape the governments in ways that are both more religious in their interpretation as well as more gender equitable (Zoepf 2006).

Muslim Fundamentalism

Although fundamentalism originated among Christians and is currently a strong factor in Christianity, today we hear much about fundamentalist Muslims. The Muslim Brotherhood (Sanad and Tessler 1990), a Muslim fundamentalist group, sounds much like fundamentalist Christians in their beliefs that women should be confined to roles of wife and mother and not be permitted to work outside the home, especially married women. One leader in this group states, "A woman's mission is to be a good wife and a compassionate mother...an ignorant rural woman is better for the nation than one thousand female lawyers" (quoted in Haddad 1980, 80). What do women in countries dominated and controlled by leaders of a fundamentalist religion think about those ideas and the practices that reflect those beliefs? A survey (Sanad and Tessler 1990) of women in Kuwait about their opinion of fundamentalism found they support many of the religious beliefs of the Muslim fundamentalists who run the country. The women said they:

- Approve of raising Kuwait children according to the teachings of Islam (93 percent).
- Pray regularly (84 percent).
- Approve of the Muslim resurgence taking place in contemporary society (68 percent).
- Prefer religious teachings when making important decisions concerning their lives (51 percent).

Many of the women, however, also had liberal views on women's rights in the workforce and family law. They said that:

- Women should be equal to men in jobs, wages, and promotions (63 percent).
- Laws should be passed that punish men who take more than one wife or that give women the right of separation in such cases (59 percent).

- They approve of women and men working together in the same job setting (57 percent).
- Women should have the right to vote in national elections (48 percent).
- They approve of coeducation in high school and university (47 percent).
- Women should not be required to cease working after marriage to devote full time to their family (47 percent).
- Work in commercial, industrial, and specialized technical positions should be available to women (46 percent).
- Women should have the same rights as men with respect to being able to obtain a divorce (39 percent).
- The hijab is not mandatory (26 percent).

The responses to this questionnaire show that Muslim women in Kuwait are highly religious, but a large proportion of them also support equality in many aspects of social life. The fundamentalism among these women is strong in regard to religion and it is fairly strong in regard to social issues, but a large plurality of women and in some cases a majority support gender equality that runs counter to the ideologies and practices of their fundamentalist political system. A significant section of the Kuwaiti women in this study sound much like the evangelical feminists in the American Christian fundamentalist community, as we discuss later in this chapter.

Christian Fundamentalism

In the 1960s, religious experience and identity began to change in the United States. Mainstream churches began to lose membership but participation in smaller fundamentalist Christian churches began to rise. Christian fundamentalists are the most conservative wing of evangelicals. Evangelicals claim that the Bible is literally true and that it can and should serve as a practical guide to everyday living (Stacey 1998). Christian fundamentalism is marked by three tenets (Ammerman 1995):

1. A deep personal relationship with Jesus.
2. An emphasis on evangelism, a commitment to spreading the word by sharing their faith with others.
3. Belief that every word in the Bible is literally true.

This last tenet is especially important in regard to the stance fundamentalists have on gender. Their position on the proper behavior of men and women and appropriate relationships between women and men is drawn from their view of the literal words of the Bible. They believe that the Bible has given people a plan and it must be followed if we are to avoid the collapse of civilization:

At creation, God designed the family as the foundation of civilization. And for those who followed His directions. He provided a guarantee against structural damage and collapse. God's guidelines are that: Each family member must worship God only, trusting in Him for guidance and protection; A husband and wife must be monogamous, loving each other unconditionally; Children must be treasured, protected, and taught to live by God's laws. (Bush 1996, 4–5)

This description does not mention gender, but like the Promise Keepers in the opening scenario of the chapter, fundamentalists believe that the Bible tells them that in godly families, women and men have distinct roles. Fundamentalists are careful to simultaneously assert that women and men are equal and that men's leadership should be administered compassionately. Women, however, must submit to their husbands as leaders of their families and husbands must accept their authority as head of the home (Diamond 1998).

Christian fundamentalists pride themselves on offering such a clear unchanging blueprint for gender distinctions:

- Wives should submit to their husbands.
- Husbands should lovingly lead their families.
- Pastoral authority and church leadership roles are for men only.
- As much as possible women should find their calling at home caring for their families.

This blueprint focuses on roles and relationships of women and men in families or in the church. Some fundamentalists, however, extend these familial and church roles to the rest of society, arguing that women should never take leadership roles in any setting.

One fundamentalist Christian pastor, for example, explained that he would never hire a woman to be principal of his school

> because there would be male teachers who would then be required to submit to female leadership which we believe would be outside the standard of God....In the microcosm of the family you have two options. If you are a single woman, then you need always to be in the context of submitting yourself to men in general. If you're a married woman, then you need to submit yourself to the authority of your husband. (Ingersoll 2003, p.18)

Table 12–3 shows the connection between Christian religious beliefs and opinions about gender. Table 12–3 distinguishes among three categories: those who do not think religion is very important, those who think religion is important but do not consider themselves fundamentalists, and those who think religion is very important and identify themselves as fundamentalists. Fundamentalists are most likely among these three groups to believe that men should have more power and influence in government, politics, business, industry, as well as inand the family. Those who do not think religion is very important are least likely to

TABLE 12–3 Should Men have more power and influence than women?

	Importance of religion		
	1. Religion has little or moderate importance	2. Religion has great importance Not fundamentalist	Fundamentalist
In government and politics	8%	21%	41%
In business and industry	11%	25%	34%
In the family	3%	11%	28%

Source: Sapiro (2003).

believe men should have more power and authority in these arenas. Religion in general and especially fundamentalist religion seems to be associated with more conservative ideas about what women and men should do outside families as well as inside them.

FUNDAMENTALIST VIEWS OF MASCULINITY. Most of the attention to the connections between fundamentalism and gender issues has focused on women, but fundamentalists also have strong opinions about men. Their view of masculinity has been referred to as "religious machismo" (Hawley 1994). Fundamentalists from across a range of religions call on men to reassert themselves in families but also to take on family and community challenges as soldiers in a war against the decline in godliness in the world. Among fundamentalist Christians, the image of "Onward Christian Soldiers" is promoted as the hard line men should take against communism and other enemies they perceive are against the United States.

This sort of macho, militaristic view of men is not just part of Christian fundamentalism. For example, the men in Gush Emunim, a highly conservative Jewish sect, wear commando boots and flight jackets with their skullcaps and speak of the perfect match of the book of Talmud (Holy Jewish text) with an AK-47 (Hawley 1994).

American Christian fundamentalists believe that the breakdown in families and the subsequent breakdown in civilization is a result of the "feminization of the American male." One pastor writing about the Promise Keepers' view of men explained, "When I say feminization, I am not talking about sexual preference. I'm trying to describe a misunderstanding that has produced a nation of 'sissified men who abdicate their roles as spiritually pure leaders, thus forcing women to fill the vacuum'" (New Man 1994 20).

Control of sexuality is another key aspect of fundamentalist views of gender. Men are to control their naturally strong sex drive and women are to help men to keep themselves in check. Fundamentalist magazines like New Man, for example, warn men against reading or viewing pornography, indulging in fantasies about women other than their wives, and masturbating (Diamond 1998). Although men are presented as leaders of their communities, their church, and their family, in one area of family life women are supposed to control men: sex. Like Muslim fundamentalists, Christian fundamentalists assume that women are less easily or quickly aroused sexually and, therefore, must take responsibility for stopping inappropriate sexual encounters between, for example, unmarried people. They assume that strong sexuality is a natural part of being a man but it must be restrained to live a Godly life. Women are assumed to be naturally less interested in sex; if women are sexual they are regarded as unnatural and dangerous. One evangelist writes, "[s]ex before marriage... develops sensual drives that can never be satisfied and may cause a man to behave like an animal... [s]ome girls become that way, too... but most of them don't. When they do, it's the most awful thing that can happen to humanity" (quoted in Rose 2003, p.289).

FUNDAMENTALIST FATHERS. What effect have fundamentalist ideas had on family life in households where fathers are attempting to live up to their ideals? Researchers (Bartkowski and Xu 2000) interviewed fundamentalist fathers about their relationships with their children. They measured one factor, paternal supervision, by asking about control over TV viewing. Men who identified themselves as conservative Protestants who frequently attended church turned out to be considerably more likely than other groups—Catholics, modern and liberal Protestants, and those with no religion—to supervise their children's television viewing. However, age and race ethnicity were also significant as younger and African American fathers were also more likely to supervise TV, regardless of their religious affiliation.

The study measured another factor, affective fathering, by asking about hugs and praise. Conservative Protestants and frequent church attendees were considerably more likely to hug their children and praise them when they were good.

The third indicator of fathering the study examined was father–child interaction, which was measured by having meals together, spending leisure time together, helping children with homework, and having private talks. On this measurement, there were no differences among the different groups. Fundamentalist fathers were not more likely to spend time in these interactions than other fathers.

On two of the three dimensions, fundamentalist fathers scored higher than other religious groups. One possible result of this is that greater participation of men in parenting will create greater equality between mothers and fathers. The researchers, however, caution that stronger relationships between fathers and children could also result in greater gender inequality if men gain greater power and authority within their families and women are left on the sidelines in the supervision of their children (Bartkowski and Xu 2000).

EVANGELICAL FEMINISTS. Christian fundamentalists assert that god does not think that women are lesser than men, but rather that women and men are called to different tasks. The task of leader should fall to men, and the task of helper should be taken by women:

> Seven Affirmations of a Perfect Helper:
> I am the perfect helper for my husband, for God chose me out of all the women in the world especially for him.
> I am the perfect helper for my husband, for I share his hopes and dreams and bear his hurts and frustrations along with him.
> I am the perfect helper for my husband, for I bring him before God's throne in prayer every day.
> I am the perfect helper for my husband, for I encourage and comfort him in strategic moments.
> I am the perfect helper for my husband, for I put his sexual and emotional needs ahead of my own.
> I am the perfect helper for my husband, for I love him unconditionally.
> I am the perfect helper for my husband, for I enable him to become all God wants him to be and I assist him in accomplishing God's purposes. (Wilkinson 1998, 139)

These rules would be difficult for any woman to follow, but they present a special challenge for conservative Christian women. The division of labor between leaders and helpers assumes that both husband and wife share a common view of religion, but women are more religious than men, as shown in Table 12–4. Women pray more, they depend on religious texts to guide them, and they attend more religious services. In addition, more women than men are fundamentalists and women are at least the most enthusiastic or first in their household to convert. This creates a perplexing situation in which the woman is in fact the spiritual leader in her family—the first or only person to agree with the ideas—but the correct role for women is not leader but helper (Ammerman 1995).

TABLE 12-4 Women Are More Religious Than Men in the United States

	Men	Women
I attend religious services weekly or almost weekly	32%	42%
Religion is an important part of my life	70%	81%
I believe there is a heaven	86%	93%
I believe religion can answer today's important questions	56%	65%
Religion provides a great deal of guidance in my day-to-day life	38%	50%
I pray at least once a day	42%	62%
I never read the Bible	42%	32%
I believe the Bible is the actual word of God and is to be taken literally	31%	38%
I favor scheduled time for children to pray in school	26%	36%

SOURCE: Princeton Religion Research Center (1996); Sapiro (2003, 218).

A second problem has to do with the range of ideas about what the Bible says about the proper relationship between husbands and wives. Those who believe in the literal truth of the Bible can identify different texts to serve as guides. These different texts can have very different messages. Some fundamentalists agree with the kinds of passages cited in the discussion of groups like the Promise Keepers but another voice in the evangelical community is that of evangelical feminists, who also call themselves Biblical feminists or Christian feminists. They share many beliefs with fundamentalists about the importance of living directly by the word of the Bible, cultivating a close personal relationship with Jesus Christ, and bringing the "good news" to others. Evangelical feminists, however, have some important differences as well.

First, they claim the right of women to be leaders within the Christian community. They also assert that the Bible uses inclusive language, for example, by speaking of god as a being without sex rather than as a male. Third, they challenge the scriptural basis for the subordination of women, noting that passages cited for this purpose are taken out of context or misrepresented. When it comes to relationships between women and men, evangelical feminists argue that the Bible teaches that husbands and wives must be mutually submissive to each other and that an unequal marriage is an un-Christian one (Stacey 1998).

Hindu Fundamentalism

The third largest religion in the world is Hinduism, which originated in the ancient land that is now India. Hindus believe in a cosmic spirit that is everywhere and they worship many gods and goddesses and do not believe that women have a lesser standing in relationship to these deities. A woman's role in life among the most conservative Hindus, however, is to be a good wife, bear sons, treat her husband as a god, and facilitate his spiritual journey. Children take their caste from their mother, so a woman who has sexual relations with a lower caste man pollutes herself, endangers her future children, and subjects the whole community to danger. The chastity of unmarried women, therefore, is of great concern (Reineke 1995).

Conservative Hindu fundamentalists like Ram Janambhumi in India advocate highly restrictive codes of conduct for women (Ramsukhdas 1992). They assert:

- Women should not choose their own husbands.
- Women should not demand inheritance from their fathers.
- Women should accept harsh treatment by mothers-in law.
- Women should "pay attention to the comfort of her husband even at the cost of her comfort," treating their husband as a god and rising early to clean the house.
- If her husband beats her, a woman should accept it as punishment for sins she committed in a previous life.
- If a man's wife has an abortion, he should abandon her and the only acceptable form of birth control is celibacy.

One of the most egregious practices of some fundamentalist Hindus is *Suti*, which is portrayed by them as a high form of religious commitment. Suti is when a wife throws herself on the burning pyre of her dead husband. The practice has been illegal for a century, but has occurred as recently as the 1980s, when Roop Kanwar jumped on her husband's pyre and became an honored person among some fundamentalist Hindus. A religious cult has since then formed around Roop Kanwar, which reveres her as a devout Hindu (Shaw and Lee 2004).

Hindu men also have specific obligations. They must marry a good woman to sire sons and grandsons and advance toward *Moksha*, liberation or salvation from *samsara*. Samsara is what many Americans call reincarnation and refers to a long cycle of moving to different levels of spirituality to the bliss of Moksha (Reineke 1995).

WOMEN IN THE PULPIT

So far, we have been observing the gender inequality in religion. Women have been struggling successfully in many religions, however, to take their place alongside men in leadership. The first woman ordained a minister in the United States was Antoinette Brown of the Congregation Church in 1853. By the end of the nineteenth century, 3,400 women had been ordained in a dozen Christian denominations including Church of Christ, American Baptists, and the Disciples of Christ. A backlash in the early twentieth century, however, caused the numbers to plummet. By 1950, only 2.1 percent of ordained religious leaders were women. In the 1960s and 1970s in the wake of the women's liberation movement, women clergy's numbers again began to grow as women became ministers in nearly all Protestant denominations and rabbis in all the branches of Judaism. In 1980, the first woman, Marjorie Matthews, was elected a bishop of an American church, the United Methodists.

By the end of the twentieth century, 62 percent of religious workers, both clergy and lower level positions, were occupied by women. In the United States, women now make up more than half of the students preparing for the ministry and about one-quarter of students studying for advanced theological degrees. In addition, 21 percent of teachers of theology are women (Bonavoglia 2006). In the United Kingdom, for the first time, more women than men were ordained by the Church of England in 2006 (*Seltzer and Soguel 2008*).

Public opinion has also changed. Seventy-one percent of Americans polled say they favor opening up the clergy to women. These beliefs have not been fully put into action, however. Only 14 percent of official church and synagogue leadership are women (Nesbitt, Baust, and Bailey 2000). Half of the Christian denominations in the United States still do not ordain women.

The three biggest denominations that oppose the ordination of women are the Roman Catholic Church (the largest religious body in the United States), the Southern Baptists (the largest Protestant denomination in the country), and the Lutheran Church, Missouri Synod (Christiano, Swatos, and Kivisto 2002). Despite their conservative positions on many social issues related to gender, Holiness and Pentecostal denominations have the largest proportion of women in the clergy. This may be at least partly because not many men are available to take the positions because their congregations are 90 percent women (Gilkes 2000).

Very recently, reversals in the admission of women to church leadership have occurred in the Southern Baptist Church. Hundreds of women had been ordained since 1964, when the church opened up leadership to women, but in 2000, the Southern Baptist Convention declared, "while both men and women are gifted for service in the church, the office of pastor is limited to men as qualified by Scripture" (Sapiro 2003, 237).

This absolute barring of women from the priesthood is also the position of the Roman Catholic Church. The Pope feels so strongly about this that he forbade a Benedictine sister to even discuss the issue when she attended the first Women's Ordination Worldwide Conference in Dublin in 2000. The Vatican, however, may have to alter its view to preserve the church. The sharp drop in the numbers of men entering the Catholic priesthood has opened a window for women to take over many of the tasks of parish priests.

The number of priests in the United States has plummeted to about half their levels in the 1960s, when each priest administered to about 700 parishioners. By the end of the twentieth century, each priest was responsible to more than 1,400 members. In addition, more Catholic priests are now over ninety than under thirty (Christiano, Swatos, and Kivisto 2002; Bonavoglia 2006). The situation is even worse in other nations, where, for example, the ratio of priest to parishioners is 1:7,000 in South America and 1:4,700 in Africa. In the United States, 16 percent of parishes are without a resident priest, and worldwide, more than one-quarter of Catholic parishes do not have a priest in residence.

The response has been for laypeople to take over paid positions in the parish ministry. Today, approximately 30,000 lay ministers are filling empty positions where priests are not available in the Catholic Church, and 82 percent of these lay ministers are women (Bonavoglia 2006). The women who hold these positions, however, are restricted from performing many important rituals. For example, they cannot administer last rites. Even though they may be the religious representative closest to a family who has a member nearing death, an unknown priest must be called to say the prayers of last rites.

Many religions, of course, do allow women to complete training as priests and ministers, to take on leadership positions, and to perform all the most important rites. The women, however, may face additional barriers as they attempt to take leadership of congregations. These barriers have been called the stained glass ceiling. Like women in many occupations, women in the ministry tend to have difficulty getting hired and often remain in lower level and midlevel jobs despite interests and qualifications similar to men who rise more quickly through the ranks.

Women clergy with the same training as men are still less likely to be senior pastors and earn about $5,000 less in annual salary and benefits (Gushee 1997; Nesbitt, Baust, and Bailey 2000; Christiano, Swatos, and Kivisto 2002). In the mainline Protestant denominations, women make up 20 percent of lead or solo pastors, but women account for only 3 percent of the pastors at the top of the pay scale, largely those who lead big congregations (Carroll 2006).

Men and women clergy also have different career trajectories. Men move from smaller to larger and wealthier congregations, and from supervised to solo roles. Women get tracked into positions like assistant minister for children's education. The women remain in smaller, less wealthy churches and they are kept in assistant-level positions (Christiano, Swatos, and Kivisto 2002). In their second decade in ordained ministry, 70 percent of men have moved on to medium-sized and large congregations, whereas only 37 percent of women led medium and larger congregations (Carroll 2006).

Although women have been held back from official participation in the highest ranks of their religions, they continue to be the backbone of the church. Regardless of whether the church allows women to be priests, women dominate the congregation in their numbers and participation. Sundays may be run by men clergy, but the rest of the week, a local church is the domain of the women (Christiano, Swatos, and Kivisto 2002). Women have long been responsible for many tasks, such as caring for the altar, teaching Sunday School, serving food, fund raising, providing outreach to the poor and ill, and directing the choir.

THE DaVINCI CODE AND ANCIENT RELIGIOUS VIEWS OF WOMEN

A recent popular film and book, *The DaVinci Code* by Dan Brown (2003), illustrates another way women have been excluded from official positions within the Christian church. In this case, women are invisible in the sacred texts. Brown's book speculates that Jesus was married to Mary Magdalene and had children who have continued the line to the present. The novel and film are fiction, but the issues have been debated for a long time among religious scholars.

Some scholars point out, for example, that during the Easter season, one important story is excluded from the services and programs. According to the Christian Bible, Mary Magdalene was the primary witness to the most important moment in Christian mythology, the resurrection of Christ. She was the only one to see him after he had died and ascended to heaven. The Easter Sunday gospel, however, focuses on the men in the story, who never even see Jesus after his death (Bonavoglia 2006).

The role of Mary Magdalene in the early Christian church is only part of the debate around goddess worship, however. Most anthropologists believe that artifacts suggest that ancient pre-Christian Europeans worshipped goddesses because of women's ability to reproduce human life. The connection of males to reproduction may not have been known thousands of years ago and females were, therefore, seen as the only source of human life. Figurines as old as 25,000 years have been found that appear to exaggerate the bellies and breasts of pregnant women (Miles 2001). Most ancient art shows images of female bodies and mothers holding babies. The very earliest creation stories known describe a goddess mother as the source of all being (Eisler 1988).

In more recent ancient societies, such as the Greek and Roman, religions were polytheist and female gods were prevalent. Some of them were major deities, such as Isis, an Egyptian goddess whose temples appear in places such as Pompeii, Italy. Isis was believed to have introduced agriculture to her people. The goddess Ninlil, in the religion of the people in Mesopotamia, was said to have taught the people in her region to farm. The idea of a single masculine god is fairly recent in human history, first appearing about 6,000 years ago with the emergence of Judaism.

Riane Eisler (1988) writes that this evidence suggests that two major forms of spirituality and social organization have marked human history. Today our religions and our societies are centered on men. Women are subordinated in both the spiritual and material worlds. She refers to this as the dominator model (see chapter 8). Looking back at the archaeological evidence, however, Eisler observes that another form predated the dominator model and it lasted for a longer time, as most of the time humans have been on earth was before the emergence of men's dominance. Eisler calls this other model the partnership model. It was not matriarchal, nor was it patriarchal. Rather these ancient societies were ones of equality between women and men and a reverence for the special life-giving abilities of women's bodies through reproduction, birth, and breastfeeding. Eisler argues that we must reach back to these partnership roots if we are to transform our world into a more humane and sustainable one.

Today, some people are reaching back to these ancient polytheist roots to find a religion that is more gender equitable and more consistent with their beliefs in the sanctity of the natural world. Wicca is one example that arose in Britain the middle of the twentieth century. Wiccans focus on the connection among humans, spirits, and the natural world and many base their rites and rituals on what they believe was characteristic of ancient Celtic religions that created stone circles all over the British Isles. A mother goddess is a key character in the Wiccan religion.

Ecofeminism is another recent spirituality movement that appeared in the twentieth century that celebrates female biology and claims that humans must use the skills of women to pull back from the environmentally destructive features of contemporary societies. Many ecofeminists believe that women are closer to the earth and closer to life because of their reproductive and nurturing roles and are therefore better suited to provide spiritual and practical guidance. Other ecofeminists maintain that these skills are part of women's makeup, but they are not natural. Rather the capacity for caring is part of women's social experience because of our ideas about femininity and the kinds of activities women are encouraged or required to engage in. In any event, ecofeminism represents an alternative to mainstream religious ideas and leadership.

RELIGION AS A FREE SPACE IN OPPRESSIVE CULTURES

Is religion always oppressive for women? Although this chapter has shown how religion often shapes gender in ways that devalue women and restrict them, this is not always the case. Many women are involved in their religious communities and find them places of support and expression (Neitz 1998). Women in Pakistan, for example, live in a society that restricts women, and religion sometimes provides a place for them to express themselves and seek respite from the oppression of their everyday lives.

In demonstrations for equality, Pakistani women chant "Had I been a boy, I could have, I would have, I may have," expressing deep feelings of repression of their gender (Shaheed 1998). Controlled by a conservative religion, women's families and their government bar them from moving around freely, participating in work, and interacting with others, especially men who are not close relatives. Women are identified by their relationships with the men in their families rather than as individuals in their own right. Women have few choices about whom they will marry or whether they will stay married, even to an unsatisfactory husband. One woman in Pakistan summed it up: "A woman is considered inferior to men and she has to do everything with their permission" (Shaheed 1998, 151).

Pakistan is a highly religious society that is dominated by Muslim fundamentalists. The women in Shaheed's (1998) study, however, did not see religion as the root of their oppression. Quite the opposite, they viewed religion as an arena in which they could find freedom in an otherwise restricted world. Prayer time provided a respite from daily work. Women could take a break from their chores and create a physical and spiritual space for themselves to worship.

The women also welcomed religious events like *dars* (lectures) and *Khatms* (collective reading of the Qur'an or Sharif or celebrations marking an individual's first complete recitation) as a place of social interactions that are otherwise unattainable for most women. Women, unlike men, are not often allowed into the streets, markets, tea shops, and workplaces to socialize. Religious events provide them with a chance to socialize and support one another and to feel a sense of public participation and belonging (Shaheed 1998).

RELIGION AS A BASE OF RESISTANCE

The Hindu community in Sri Lanka is another place where women's lives are highly restricted. The women in the community, however, have used religious rituals that are for women only as a form of resistance. In the late 1980s and early 1990s, 60,000 young people who had protested the government's violations of human rights disappeared in Sri Lanka. "Bodies rotting on beaches, smoldering in grotesque heaps by the roadsides, and floating down rivers were a daily sight during the height of state repression" (Alwis 1998, 185). An organization of women, calling themselves the Mother's Front, emerged to challenge the murders and the conditions that led to the protests.

The women used religious activities to make their case. They grieved the deaths of their children and husbands at temples, breaking coconuts and beseeching the deities to return their family members and cursing those who were responsible. Weeping and wailing they chanted, "Premadas [the president], see this coconut all smashed into bits. May your head too be splintered into a hundred bits, so heinous are the crimes you have perpetrated on my child" (Alwis 1998, 191). In any other context, these actions would not have been tolerated, but the government found it difficult to restrain the religious grieving of the Mother's Front. It could not deny them the right to weep and curse because that is what is expected of women in the religious ritual of funerals. The action of the women received widespread media coverage and alerted the public of the crimes of the state.

Religion in the American Civil Rights Movement

One of the most important social movements of the twentieth century was the Civil Rights Movement directed at abolishing the apartheid of Jim Crow in the United States and at social and legal rights for African Americans. This movement was tightly embedded within the Christian church and provides another example of the progressive role religion can play in political struggles and in particular the ways religion can be used to challenge gender inequality by facilitating women's effective political participation. The civil rights leaders whose names are most familiar to us, such as Reverend Martin Luther King, Jr., were religious leaders. The songs we think of when we picture the Civil Rights Movement came from the gospels sung by the church choir. The church served as a critical forum for resistance and provided material and spiritual support for those who fought against racism.

Research on the role of women in the black church and in the Civil Rights Movement and on the role of religion in those women's lives shows that gender, social action, and religion are tightly tied together (Du Bois 1924). Women did not hold visibly dominant or formal positions of power in the church or the Civil Rights Movement. Black women, however, were the backbone of both of these (Gilkes 2000).

As far back as the era of slavery, researchers have documented powerful black women prophets who served as spiritual leaders and teachers in the slave community (Collier-Thomas 1998). Men slaves described their early socialization in both religion and politics as beginning with hearing their mothers and aunts, biological and fictive, praying for freedom. Famous black women abolitionists such as Sojourner Truth and Harriet Tubman were active religious leaders (Painter 1996; Clinton 2004). Truth served as a minister in the Adventist church and Tubman used the scriptures and music from the AME Zion church in her work as a conductor on the Underground Railroad (Gilkes 2000).

More recently, in the middle of the twentieth century, the church was an important resource for the black women who participated in the Civil Rights Movement. The church operated as a training ground for learning the essential skills of leadership, "running meetings, managing treasuries, keeping minutes, electing officers" (Gilkes 2000, 187). Churches also created a ready-made set of social connections among individuals and between communities.

Religion also provided a powerful spiritual set of tools, giving women strength and courage to confront bosses, police, public officials, and racist organizations. One woman explained that Jesus was her role model. Because he was "able to keep his commitments and make sacrifices, she was able to keep hers" (Gilkes 2000, 188).

The black church was gendered in a manner that disempowered women, excluding them from formal leadership positions. Nevertheless, the church provided women with resources that they then used to push forward the Civil Rights Movement, where although they were not identified as formal leaders, they in fact they played an effective and essential role.

The work of women in religious organizations that address issues of inequality continue today to press for change in organizations such as NTOSAKE, Women's Leadership Training Program, the Georgia Citizens' Coalition on Hunger, and Interfaith Worker Justice (Gamaliel Foundation 2007; Georgia Citizens' Coalition on Hunger 2007; Interfaith Worker

Justice 2007). In all of these organizations, religion serves to facilitate and support the work and to empower the women who work within them (Caiazza 2006).

CHALLENGING RELIGION FROM WITHIN

These examples among Muslims, Hindus, and Christians illustrate ways in which the existing church and its gender hierarchies have been used by women to support their political work and thereby challenge gender inequity that disempowers women. Wiccans and eco-feminists represent a challenge to religions from the outside. They have set up an alternative set of rituals and beliefs that challenge those of mainstream religions, especially the centrality of men in those religions. However, many people have also challenged the religious institutions themselves, demanding that they alter gender hierarchies and allow women greater equity.

Catholics for a Free Choice have organized to try to change the church's position on abortion and despite the ban on ordaining women priests, at least eight women have been ordained as Catholic priests since 2002 (Bonavoglia 2006). Corpus is an organization of Catholics who support married priests and Dignity is an organization championing the rights of gay and lesbian church members. Led by lay members (nuns are considered laity, not clergy, according to the church), these and other feminist Catholic groups have been created to challenge the church from within. Because they have invested their lives living by the gospel as they understand it, Catholic members of these organizations do not want to leave the church, although they disagree with many of rules established by the Vatican (Farrell 1996).

Conservative Muslim women in Syria have formed groups called *Qubaisiate*, which educate girls and women about religious texts. Girls memorize the Qur'an and are taught the principles of Qur'anic reasoning. In the past, the older girls were told, "This is Islam, and so you should do this." The women were made to feel that they could not really ask questions. In these new schools, however, the women say that when the occasion arises, they are able to reason from the Qur'an on an equal footing with men. "People mistake tradition for religion," Ms. Kaldi said. "Men are always saying, 'Women can't do that because of religion,' when in fact it is only tradition. It's important for us to study so that we will know the difference" (Zoepf 2006). Recent findings by a scholar at the Oxford Center for Islamic Studies in Britain suggest that these "new" schools, however, may be part of an ancient history. Mohammad Akram Nadwi, a Sunni *alim* or religious scholar, has rediscovered a long-lost tradition of Muslim women teaching the Qur'an, transmitting hadith, and even making Muslim law as jurists. In 1998, Akram began to search for women who were hadith scholars, expecting to find a few dozen examples. His research has already uncovered 8,000 women over the past 1400 years (Power 2007).

The recent history of Judaism presents another example of a successful challenge within a mainstream religion (Pinsky 2005). The twentieth century was a period of remarkable change in Judaism. Before the 1900s, it had been a long-standing practice that only men could become rabbis. In 1972 Reform Judaism and in 1983 Conservative Judaism began to allow women to be rabbis. The Shalom Hartman Institute in Jerusalem will ordain women as orthodox rabbis for the first time in 2009.

In 1922, the first public celebration of a Bat Mitzvah occurred, which allowed a girl to participate in the ceremony of coming of age and joining the community as a responsible adult. Before that, only boys could celebrate Bar Mitzvah. Reform and Conservative Jewish women can now participate in important rites, such as publicly reading the Torah, serving as a Cantor, and being counted as part of the *minyan* (a quorum required for public worship).

Conservative Judaism still retains some distinctions between women and men, but reform Judaism has accepted women and men as equals. Whereas other Jews believe that children can only claim Jewish descent through their mother's line, reform Judaism now maintains that if one parent is Jewish, father or mother, then the child is automatically Jewish as long as the child is raised as a Jew. Feminist rituals and feminist interpretations of theology are being practiced in the Reform synagogue.

What Difference Would More Gender-Equal Religions Make?

Making women and men more equal in the ideologies and practices of religions is an important goal of many feminists, but what difference would these changes make? One area that scholars have considered in relation to this question is the gendered use of language by religions.

The words that dominant religions use to describe god are gendered. Christians, for example, speak of God the Father, the Lord, and the Son. Some people argue that this is just a matter of words and that they have a gender-neutral meaning, but it would be difficult to substitute the feminine versions of these words, like goddess for god, lady for lord, queen for king, or even mother for father (Sapiro 2003). If women remain in marginalized support roles in religious institutions, they have less influence on decisions and practices regarding doctrine, programming, curriculum, and language (Nesbitt, Baust, and Bailey 2000). Could increasing the numbers of women clergy alter our view of what is god like? If more women were in the leadership of religions, representing god, would the congregation begin to think about god and religion differently?

Table 12–5 shows the results of a survey by the National Opinion Research Center (NORC) that asked people what words they identify with the images of god. NORC is a large research organization that conducts random polls of Americans. Table 12–5 shows the ranking of the different words mentioned. Most of the words are masculine and a few are gender neutral, but the feminine words rank last in the poll with only 3.2 of the respondents mentioning "mother." You might have noticed that the question itself uses a masculine word for deity, God.

However, other feminine words could be associated with god such as healer, friend, lover, and spouse. If we shifted to a more "feminine" view of god, might our view of religion and religious behavior change? Thinking about god as like a man, father, or lord makes us think of women as not god-like and feminine attributes as not godly (Shaw and Lee 2004). It also means that our image of god does not include some of the most highly valued components of maternal care, love, and friendship.

Language is not the only area scholars have thought about in their consideration of the effect of bringing women into more leadership roles in the church. Besides changing our ideas about god and godliness, the increased numbers of women in church leadership can also change the churches themselves. One study of women who took over clergy activities in

TABLE 12-5 Is God in the Image of Man?

What Images do You Associate with God?	
Masculine	
Master	48.3%
Father	46.8%
Judge	36.5%
King	20.6%
Gender-neutral	
Redeemer	36.2%
Creator	29.5%
Friend	26.6%
Healer	8.3%
Lover	7.3%
Liberator	5.5%
Spouse	2.6%
Feminine	
Mother	3.2%

Note: Participants could choose more than one image.
SOURCE: National Opinion Research Center (1989, 156–59).

Catholic parishes that lacked a priest showed that women's less authoritarian style in addition to their lay status caused the churches to become more democratically administered in contrast to the traditional model (Christiano, Swatos, and Kivisto 2002).

FEMINIST THEORETICAL MODELS FOR UNDERSTANDING THE COMPLEX RELATIONSHIPS BETWEEN RELIGION AND GENDER

This chapter has reviewed several religions, each with many connections to gender. Feminists who have explored religious beliefs and practices have taken a broad range of positions about how to assess them and what to propose to change them to make religion more a part of the movement for gender equity. Johanna Stucky (1998) has revised a framework originally proposed by Carol Christ (1983) to try to categorize the different feminist approaches. Stucky argues that feminists fall into one of four categories.

The first is called Revisionist. Revisionist feminists take the least extreme position. They argue that contemporary religions are not inherently discriminating and may in fact be an important tool in creating progressive social change. The task of feminists is to identify the "liberating message at the core of a tradition" (Stucky 1998, 17). They would look to the example of the way Christianity was used by the Civil Rights Movement or how Hindu funeral rituals were used by the Mother's Front in Sri Lanka as illustrations of how a religion could be a strong force to challenge the status quo.

The second framework is called Renovationist. Feminists with this point of view argue that the religion needs to be used as more than a progressive tool. Current religious beliefs, images, and rituals themselves must be altered. They might point to the creation of the Bat

Mitzvah by Jewish feminists as an example where one of the most significant rituals of the faith was altered to allow girls along with boys to come of age and enter the community as adults through a religious ceremony (Stucky 1998).

The third framework is called Revolutionary. Revolutionary feminists take one step further by bringing in the images and traditions of other religions, in particular those from goddess spirituality of ancient societies but also from First Nation, Celtic, and African traditions. The discussions over the role of Mary Magdalene in the Christian church popularized in *The Da Vinci Code* provide an example of a potentially revolutionary framing of Christianity. Those feminists who write about the important role Mary Magdalene may have played in early Christian history and argue for bringing her into contemporary Christian theology are reaching back to pre-Christian ideas about women in religious belief and adding those ideas to the conventional contemporary views of Christianity (Stucky 1998).

The fourth framework is called Rejectionist. Feminists who hold this point of view have left the traditional religions to construct spiritual traditions of their own. Wicca is an example of this last framework (Stucky 1998).

CLASSICAL THEORY ON RELIGION: DURKHEIM, MARX, AND WEBER

Sociologists have been interested in religion since the emergence of the discipline. The three classical theorists associated with sociology, Emile Durkheim, Karl Marx, and Max Weber, all wrote extensively about religion. Durkheim argued that religion was a core social institution existing in all societies. He believed that its role was to serve as a glue holding people together. Religion provided a set of ideas that members of a society shared and made them feel committed to the group and their participation in it. According to Durkheim, religion provided an answer to the questions of what is right and wrong and therefore helped each generation be socialized into the society, helping to strengthen the group and ensuring its survival.

Karl Marx agreed that religion provided a uniform set of ideas that helped maintain the status quo. He believed, however, that this worked against the interest of most people who were being exploited by dominant individuals and groups who used religion as a way to keep people from seeking social change. Marx was concerned with the fact that so many people were ruled by so few and that the political and economic structures of contemporary societies use the majority of people to provide an abundant life for a few who are at the top. He argued that religion was one important way that this unfair situation was maintained. Religious rituals and ideas led people to believe that the current system was the only possible moral way to organize society and that challenging it not only goes against the ruling class, it also confronts the sacred powers that created our society. According to Marx, religion is a result of the political and economic organization of a society and it is used as a tool to preserve the status quo.

Max Weber had a different opinion. Whereas Durkheim and Marx agreed that religion provided a mechanism for maintaining stability and hindering change, Weber thought that religion worked as a source of change. He argued that religion caused its adherents to create change in their societies and used the rise of capitalism as an example to support his argument. He asserted that Calvinists (Christians who followed the religious beliefs of John Calvin in the 1500s) were spurred on by their religious beliefs to develop industrial capitalism in Europe and North America. Calvinists believed that economic success was an indicator of their standing in the eyes of God. They, therefore, were driven to invent, invest, buy, and sell in ways that increased their wealth to prove their piety and provide a sign of their future in heaven. Weber wrote that their religious beliefs caused the transition from an agriculturally based feudal society to an industrial capitalist one.

How would these three theorists see the connections between religion and gender today? Durkheim would argue that the rituals and organization of religions do indeed provide a blueprint for gender. They give us rules about what it is to be a good man or a good woman and how women and men should relate to one another. Durkheim would assert that these rules are good because they provide stability and comfort. The rituals, holidays, and texts help us to know our place and what expect of others.

Marx would assert that knowing our place and what to expect of others hinders any progress toward greater gender equity. Religion in a gender-biased society (as all societies are) only helps to support inequality and reproduce it with every new generation. Marx would point to the rise of fundamentalisms around the world as an indication of the powerful force of religion in maintaining political relationships within and between nations. He would suggest that although religion may bring us comfort in a difficult world, those who are interested in progressive social change will need to confront religious ideologies and institutions that operate as roadblocks to justice and equity.

Weber would argue that religion can operate as a force for change. To alter the existing power relations, he would suggest that political activists need to harness religion to work toward great equality. Weber would point to the positive role religious organizations have played in the past in the antislavery movement and the Civil Rights Movement and assert that they can serve a similar purpose in the road to gender equity.

In this chapter we have seen that gender permeates religion. Although there are debates within religions and criticisms from without, religious institutions are fairly transparent in their expression of gender. They establish clear rules about gender and those rules are expressed in rituals, texts, ideologies, and leadership hierarchies. However, classical theorists remind us that the interplay between gender and religions does not take place in a vacuum. Powerful political forces may use religion to maintain stability or inequality.

REFERENCES

Abraham, Ken. 1994. *Who are the Promise Keepers?* New York: Doubleday.

Alwis, Malathi. 1998. Motherhood as space of protest: Women's political participation in contemporary Sir Lanka. In *Appropriating gender*, ed. P. Jefferey and A. Basu, 185–99. New York: Routledge.

Ammerman, Nancy. 1995. North American Protestant fundamentalism. In *Sociology and religion*, ed. A. Greeley, 416–25. New York: HarperCollins.

Andrews, Helena. 2006. Muslim women don't see themselves as oppressed, survey finds. *New York Times*, June 8.

Armstrong, Karen. 2002. The curse of the Infidel. *The Guardian*, June 20.

Bartkowski, John, and Xiaohe Xu. 2000. Distant patriarchs or expressive dads? *Sociological Quarterly* 41 (3): 465–86.

Basu, Amaritu. 2004. Hindu women's activism in India and the questions it raises. In *Feminist frontiers*. 6th ed., ed. L. Richardson, V. Taylor, and N. Whittier, 458–67. Boston: McGraw-Hill.

Bonavoglia, Angela. 2006. *Good Catholic girls*. New York: HarperCollins.

Bowman, Meg. 1983. Why we burn: Sexism exorcised. *The Humanist* 43: 28–29.

Brown, Dan. *The DaVinci code*. New York: Doubleday.

Burn, Shawn. 2000. *Women across cultures*. Mountain View, CA: Mayfield.

Bush, Rosaline. 1996. The end of innocence. *Family Voice* February: 4–5.

Caiazza, Amy. 2006. *Called to speak*. Washington, DC: IWPR.

Carroll, Jackson. 2006. *God's potters: Pastoral leadership and the shaping of congregations*. Grand Rapids, MI: Eerdmans.

Christ, Carol. 1983. Symbols of gods and goddesses in feminist theology. In *The book of the goddess, past and present*, ed. C. Olson, 231–51. New York: Crossroads Press.

Christiano, Kevin, William Swatos, and Peter Kivisto, eds. 2002. *Sociology of religion: Contemporary developments*. New York: Rowman and Littlefield.

Clinton, Catherine. 2004. *Harriet Tubman*. New York: Little Brown.

Collier-Thomas, Bettye. 1998. *Daughters of thunder*. San Francisco: Jossey-Bass.

Daly, Mary. 1968. *The church and the second sex*. Boston: Beacon Press.

Deif, Farida. 2004. *Divorced from justice: Women's unequal access to divorce in Egypt*. New York: Human Rights Watch. Dickinson University Press.

Diamond, Sara. 1998. *Not by politics alone*. New York: Guilford.

Du Bois, W. E. B. 1924. *The gift of black folk*. New York: Washington Square Press.

Eisler, Riane. 1988. *The chalice and blade*. New York: Harper & Row.

Eitzen, E. Stanley, and Maxine Baca Zinn. 2004 *In conflict and order*. 10th ed. Boston: Allyn & Bacon.

Farrell, Susan. 1996. Women, church and egalitarianism. In *The power of gender in religion*, ed. S. Farrell and G. Weatherby, 39–50. New York: McGraw-Hill.

Freedman, Jo. 2002. *No turning back*. New York: Ballantine Books.

Gamaliel Foundation. 2007. http://www.gamaliel.org/Ntosake/NtosakeIndex.htm.

Georgia Citizens' Coalition on Hunger. 2007. http://www.gahungercoalition.org/.

Gerami, Shahin. 1996. *Women and fundamentalism*. New York: Garland.

Gilkes, Cheryl. 2000. Exploring the religious connection. In *Women and religion in the African diaspora*, ed. R. Marie Griffith and B. Savage, 179–98. Baltimore: Johns Hopkins University Press.

Gushee, Steve. 1997. Female ministers gradually finding acceptance. *Denver Post*, September 27.

Haddad, Yvonne. 1980. Traditional affirmations concerning the role of women as found in contemporary Arab-Islamic literature. pp. 61–86. In *Women in contemporary Muslim societies*, ed. J. Smith. Cranbury, NJ: Associated University Presses.

Hawley, John. 1994. *Fundamentalism and gender*. New York: Oxford University Press.

Helie-Lucas, Mari-Aimee. 1994. The preferential symbol for Islamic identity. In *Identity politics and women*, ed. V. Moghadam, 391–407. Boulder, CO: Westview Press.

Ingersoll, Julie. 2003. *Evangelical Christian women*. New York: NYU Press.

Interfaith Worker Justice. 2007. http://www.iwj.org/.

Kohut, Andrew, and Melissa Rogers. 2002. *Americans struggle with religion's role at home and abroad*. Washington, DC: Pew Forum on Religion and Public Life.

Miles, Rosalind. 2001. *Who cooked the Last Supper?* New York: Random House.

Mogahed, Dalia. 2006. *Perspectives of women in the Muslim world*. Gallup Muslim ThinkForum, June 6.

National Opinion Research Center. 1989. *General social survey*, 156–59 Chicago: NORC.

Neitz, Mary Jo. 1998. Feminist research and theory. In *Encyclopedia of religion and society*, ed. W. Swatos, 184–86). Walnut Creek, CA: Altamira.

Nesbitt, Paula, Jeanette Baust, and Emma Bailey. 2000. Women's status in the Christian church. In *Gender mosaics*, ed. D. Vannoy, 386–97. New York: Oxford University Press.

New Man. 1994. How to be a new man. July/August:20.

Painter, Nell. 1996. *Sojourner Truth*. New York: Norton.

Phillips, Randy. 1994. Spiritual purity. In *Seven promises of a promise keeper*, ed. A. Hanssen, 73–80. Colorado Springs, CO: Focus on the Family.

Pinsky, Dana. 2005. You (don't) gotta have faith. In *Still believing*, ed. V. Erickson and S. Farrell, 102–12. Mary Knoll, NY: Orbis.

Power, Carla. 2007. Reconsideration: A secret history. *New York Times*, February 25.

Princeton Religion Research Center. 1996. *Emerging trends*. Princeton, NJ: Princeton Religious Research Center.

Ramsukhdas, Swami. 1992. *How to lead a householders life*. Gorakhpur, India: Gita Press.

Read, Jen'nan Ghazal, and John Bartkowski. 2000. To veil or not to veil? *Gender & Society* 14 (3): 395–417.

Reineke, Martha. 1995. Out of order: A critical perspective on women in religion. In *Women: A feminist perspective*, ed. J. Freeman, 430–47. Mountain View, CA: Mayfield.

Rose, Susan. 2003. Christian fundamentalism. In *Women: Images and realities*, ed. A. Kesselman, L. McNair, and N. Schniedewind, 286–92. New York: McGraw-Hill.

Saad, Lydia. 1996. American's religious commitment affirmed. *Gallup Poll Monthly* (January): 21–23.

Sanad, Jamal, and Mark Tessler. 1990. Women and religion in a modern Islamic society. In *Religious resurgence and politics in the contemporary world*, ed. E. Sahliyeh, 195–218. Albany: State University of New York Press.

Sanday, Peggy. 1981. *Female power and male dominance: On the origins of sexual inequality*. New York: Cambridge University Press.

Sapiro, Virginia. 2003. *Women in American society: An introduction to women's studies*. 5th ed. New York: McGraw-Hill.

Seltzer, Sarah and Dominque Soguel. 2008. "More news to cheer" Women's enews November 17.

Shaheed, Farida. 1998. The other side of the discourse: Women's experience of identity, religion, and activism in Pakistan. In *Appropriating gender*, ed. P. Jefferey and A. Basu, 143–64. New York: Routledge.

Shaw, Susan, and Janet Lee. 2004. *Women's voices, feminist visions*. New York: McGraw-Hill.

Southern Baptist Convention. 2000. The Baptist faith and message. http://www.sbc.net/bfm/bfm2000.asp.

Stacey, Judith. 1998Brave new families. Berkeley: University of California Press.

Steinfels, Peter. 1995. Vatican says the ban on women as priests is "infallible" doctrine. *New York Times* November 19.

Stucky, Johanna. 1998. *Feminist spirituality*. Toronto: York Center for Feminist Research.

Wilkinson, Darlene. 1998. A wife's role. In *Issues in feminism*. 4th ed., ed. S. Ruth, 136–48. Mountain View, CA: Mayfield.

Zoepf, Katherine. 2006. Islamic revival led by women tests Syria's secularism. *New York Times*, August 29.

INDEX

ABC (abstain, be faithful, and use condoms), AIDS prevention program, 289, 290

Abel, Emily, 190

abortion: African women's rights and, 9, 296; Catholics for a Free Choice, 394; clinic bombings, 282–283; counseling services, 282, 283; Mexico City policy or "gag rule," 288, 291, 292–295; parental consent laws, 283; partial birth abortion ban, 283; *Roe v. Wade* controversy, 282–283; sex-selective in Asia, 244; Supreme Court cases, 283; U.S. leadership role declining, 9; U.S. policy, 76, 282–283, 288; women in prison ban on federal funds for, 315. *See also* reproductive rights

Abortion Counseling Service, 282

Acker, Joan, 64–66

ADHD (Attention Deficit/Hyperactivity Disorder), 110–111

advertising: feminist ads from Nike, 334–335, 354; gender in Japanese television, 342–343; gender in Turkish television, 340–342; gender in TV advertising, 339–345; gender in U.S. television, 343–345; masculine stereotypes (Marlboro man), 339–340; media stereotypes, 13–14; men and beer ("Miller Time" slogan), 340; sexual content, 95; sexualization of women, 348

AFDC (Aid to Families with Dependent Children (AFDC), 182

affirmative action, 124, 277, 300–301, 307, 313–314

AFL-CIO, issues of concern to women, 153

Africa: customary marriage laws, 171–172; feminist activism, 8–9; honor killings, 245; women's rights, 9, 296

African American women: government workers, 139; lives and work of, 51–52; motherhood networks, 180; in prisons, 317; self-esteem of girls, 109; work and mothering, 180; workplace success stories, 151–152

African Americans: caring for the elderly, 189; family life, 52; police stops and searches of, 94; war on drugs and, 317

African Union (AU), women's rights and, 9

agency, term used by sociologists, 6

Aid to Families with Dependent Children (AFDC), 182

AIDS. *See* HIV/AIDS

Albright, Madeleine, 306

American Academy of Pediatrics, intersex birth guidelines, 36

American Psychological Association (APA), 347

Amnesty International, 209, 248, 316

androcentrism (or male-centeredness), 49

androgen insensitivity syndrome (AIS), 20, 20t, 35

Annan, Kofi, 244

APA (American Psychological Association), 347

Applebaum, Eileen, 195

Applebaum, Richard, 270

Arima, Akie, 342

Aristotle, 22

asexuality, 19

Asia: honor killings, 245; hunger issue, 158–159; sex tourism, 84, 290; sex-selective abortions, 244; sexual stereotypes of women, 83–84; women as mail-order brides, 84

Association for Voluntary Surgical Contraception (AVSC), 288

athletes. *See* sports; women in sports

Attention Deficit/Hyperactivity Disorder (ADHD), 110–111